GLOBAL ENVIRONMENTAL COMMONS

Global Environmental Commons

Analytical and Political Challenges in Building Governance Mechanisms

Edited by

ERIC BROUSSEAU, TOM DEDEURWAERDERE,
PIERRE-ANDRÉ JOUVET, MARC WILLINGER

OXFORD

UNIVERSITY PRESS

OXFORD
UNIVERSITY PRESS

Great Clarendon Street, Oxford, OX2 6DP,
United Kingdom

Oxford University Press is a department of the University of Oxford.
It furthers the University's objective of excellence in research, scholarship,
and education by publishing worldwide. Oxford is a registered trade mark of
Oxford University Press in the UK and in certain other countries

First Edition published in 2012

Impression: 2

British Library Cataloguing in Publication Data

Data available

Library of Congress Cataloging in Publication Data

Data available

ISBN 978-0-19-965620-2

Printed in Great Britain by
MPG Books Group, Bodmin and King's Lynn

To Elinor Ostrom whose contributions to the analysis of environmental governance inspire major advances.

Acknowledgments

This book is the result of a process of interaction among contributors from various disciplines, which has resulted in a set of chapters that have all been written interactively. The book is therefore really a collective endeavor, and the editors would like to warmly thank all the authors who agreed to take part in this process.

The collaboration was initiated during a week-long workshop which was organized in 2008 at the Scientific Institute from Cargèse (IESC, a conference center operated by the French CNRS, the University of Nice, and the University of Corte). This workshop was organized using the methodology of the Dahlem workshop in Germany, which is especially appropriate for the interdisciplinary approach to the governance of the global environmental commons that has been adopted in this book, based on contributions from political science, environmental sciences, and economics. The goal of the workshop was to produce a state-of-the-art document on the theme of analysis. Original review papers by eminent scholars in the mornings were alternated with writing sessions in working groups in the afternoons. The aim of the working group sessions was to produce a synthesis document, by organizing a collaboration amongst various scholars, including doctoral students, young scholars, and well-established academics.

The introduction and the conclusion to the book summarize the documents that were produced by this common writing process. The various chapters that are included were mostly inspired by the presentations made at the workshop, the discussions during the week, and subsequent interaction between the authors of the chapters.

It is difficult to thank all the scholars who have contributed to the research that is presented here, as it involved not only the workshop participants, the speakers, and discussants, but also the reviewers of the chapters and of the book—who all made a great job—and the contributions made by the doctoral students and young scholars to the synthesis documents. In particular, we would like to thank the authors who contributed to the three working-group synthesis documents. They are: Lee Alston, Tom Dedeurwaerdere, Timo Goeschl, Hiroe Ishihara, Eric Lambin, Natalia Lyarskaya, Unai Pascual, Charles Perrings, Jerome Sgard, Per Stromberg, and Oran Young (working group on "What is the optimal level of governance for each type of goods?"); Thierry Bréchet, Julien Chevallier, Denny Ellerman, Charles Figuières, Massimiliano Gambardella, Pascal Gastineau, Mélanie Heugues, Sebastian Hikisch, Hiroe Ishihara, Pierre-André Jouvet, Ann Kinzig, Garry Libecap, Gilles

Rotillon, and Timothy Swanson (working group on "What modes of governance produce what results in the provision of environmental goods?"); Mohamed Ali Bchir, Eric Brousseau, Graciela Chichilnisky, Simon Gächter, Gaston Giordana, Elinor Ostrom, Ingmar Schumacher, Daan van Soest, Arild Vatn, and Marc Willinger (working group on "What are the processes of building and revealing collective preferences?"). A big thank you also goes to the doctoral students and young scholars who provided transcripts of the working group discussions and notes on the presentations and the discussion sessions: Mohamed Ali Bchir, Julien Chevallier, Pascal Gastineau, Gaston Giordana, Mélanie Heugues, Sebastian Hikisch, Hiroe Ishihara, Natalia Lyarskaya, Ingmar Schumacher, and Per Stromberg. These allowed us to capitalize on the scientific exchanges that took place during the workshop week. Daan van Soest also acknowledges the financial support by the "Knowledge for Climate" research program.

Finally, the editors are grateful to everyone who helped us with the organization of this event, and in particular to Pascal Gastineau, for his tireless organizational support, his contribution to the elaboration of the synthesis reports, and his role in the completion of a first version of this book. We would like to thank Amandine Faurré, Valérie Hilson and Anne Thobois for their help with the final editing of the manuscript; Alison Kelly and Matt Darnel for their English language revision skills which greatly improved the manuscript, and Pierre Courtois, whose contribution to the index was essential. We are also grateful to the various sponsors of the workshop: the Cargèse Institute of Scientific Studies (CNRS), Economix (Université Paris Ouest/CNRS) and the Sixth European Framework Programme in research and development project "Reflexive Governance in the Public Interest" (REFGOV) funded by the DG Research of the European Commission. Elisabeth Dubois-Violette, who was the director of the IESC until the end of 2008, was at the origin of this initiative and she is warmly thanked for the support she provided. Many thanks to the staff of the IESC as well.

Contents

List of Figures

List of Tables

List of Abbreviations

AAUs	Annual Assigned Units
ACIA	Arctic Climate Impact Assessment
AMIS	agency-managed irrigation systems
BOD	biological oxygen demand
BSA	Burden-sharing Agreement
CBD	Convention on Biological Diversity
CDC	Center for Disease Control
CDM	clean development mechanism
CFCs	chlorofluorocarbons
CFP	Common Fisheries Policy
CITES	Convention on International Trade in Endangered Species
CMS	Convention on Migratory Species
CPR	common-pool resource
CSR	corporate social responsibility
CV	contingent valuation
CWS	CLIMNEG World Simulation
DAPs	designated access privileges
EBM	ecosystem-based management
EEZ	exclusive economic zone
EMAS	environmental management systems
EPA	Environmental Protection Agency (USA)
ERC	Emission Reduction Credits
ETS	Emissions Trading Scheme
EU	European Union
EUA	European Union Allowance
FAO	Food and Agriculture Organization (UN)
FCCC	Framework Convention on Climate Change
FIRST	Financing Initiative for Renewable and Solar Technology
FMIS	farmer-managed irrigation systems
FOCJ	functional, overlapping, and competing jurisdictions
GATT	General Agreement on Tariffs and Trade
GDP	gross domestic product

GEF	Global Environment Facility
GHG	greenhouse gas
GPGs	global public goods
IATA	the International Air Transport Association
IBES	International Bank for Environmental Settlements
ICAO	International Civil Aviation Organization
ICCAT	International Commission for the Conservation of Atlantic Tuna
IGO	Intergovernmental Organization
IHR	International Health Regulations
IMO	International Maritime Organization
IPCC	Intergovernmental Panel on Climate Change
IPO	Initial Public Offering
IPPC	International Plant Protection Convention
ITQs	individual transferable quotas
IVQs	individual vessel quotas
IUU	illegal, unreported, and unregulated
LMEs	large marine ecosystems
LMMC	Like Minded Mega-Diverse Countries
MB	marginal benefit
MCA	marginal cost of abatement
MEA	Millennium Ecosystem Assessment
MPA	Marine Protected Area
MSC	marginal social cost
MSY	maximum sustainable yields
NAAQS	National Ambient Air Quality Standards (USA)
NAP	National Allocation Plan
NCBG	Nash Cooperative Bargaining Game
NG	network governance
NGO	non-governmental organization
NIIS	Nepal Irrigation Institutions and Systems
NSPS	New Source Performance Standard (USA)
OIE	Office international des épizooties (World Organization for Animal Health)
OTC	Ozone Transport Commission (USA)
PANE	Partial Agreement Nash Equilibrium
PES	payments for environmental services
PG	public goods

PIS	potentially internally stable
PSSA	Particularly Sensitive Sea Area
R&D	research and development
RA	Recreational Area
RCCEs	rapid climate change events
RECLAIM	Regional Clean Air Incentives Market (California)
REDD	Reduced Emissions from Deforestation and forest Degradation
REPS	rural environmental protection scheme
RFMO	Regional Fishery Management Organisation
SCAQMD	South Coast Air Quality Management District (California)
SOM	supporting online material
SPS	Sanitary and Phytosanitary (Agreement)
TBT	Technical Barriers to Trade (Agreement)
TRIPS	Trade Related aspects on Intellectual Property Rights
UN	United Nations
UNCLOS	United Nations Convention on the Law of the Sea
UNEP	United Nations Environment Program
UNFCCC	United Nations Framework Convention on Climate Change
UNFCCD	United Nations Convention to Combat Desertification
USEPAUS	Environmental Protection Agency
WA	Wilderness Area
WHO	World Health Organization
WTO	World Trade Organization
WTP	willingness to pay

List of Contributors

Thierry Bréchet is Lhoist Berghmans Professor of Environmental Economics at the Université catholique de Louvain, Belgium. He is also a member of the Center for Operations Research & Econometrics (CORE) and of the Louvain School of Management. Before joining the UCL in 2002 he worked for the European Commission, the Belgian Federal Planning Office and then as a consultant in applied modeling. His research programme is devoted to the climate issue (integrated assessement modeling), the properties of policy instruments, intergenerational issues with overlapping generations models, and the evaluation of firms' environmental performance. In 2011–2012 he was visiting research fellow at the Grantham Institute for Climate Change at Imperial College London, and visiting professor at the European University at St Petersburg, Russia.

Eric Brousseau is Professor of Economics and Management at Paris-Dauphine University and at the European University Institute (Florence, Italy). He is a member of Dauphine Research in Management (DRM), a Joint Research Center between the CNRS and Paris-Dauphine. He is the founder and the director of the European School for New-Institutional Economics (ESNIE), and Vice-President of the International Society for New-Institutional Economics (ISNIE). His research agenda focuses on the economics of governance, with three main applied fields: innovation and intellectual property, Internet and digital economics, and environment. In the area of institutional economics, Eric Brousseau has been working extensively on the economics of contracts, multilevel governance, public vs self-regulation, and on the dynamics of institutions. He has published more than 80 papers in various academic journals and books, authored one book, and edited more than 15 books or journal issues. He has been involved in research funded by the French Government, the European Commission, the US National Science Foundation, the UN, and the OECD.

Graciela Chichilnisky has worked extensively in the Kyoto Protocol process, creating and designing the concept of the carbon market that became international law in 2005. Working closely for several years with negotiators of the United Nations Framework Convention on Climate Change, the organization in charge of deciding world policy with respect to global warming, Professor Chichilnisky acted as a lead author of the Intergovernmental Panel on Climate Change. The IPCC received the 2007 Nobel Prize for its work in this area. In 1997, when the Kyoto Protocol was signed by 163 nations, Dr Chichilnisky authored the Protocol language that led to the creation of the carbon market. She was the creator of the formal theory of Sustainable Development and of the concept of Basic Needs that was voted by 150 nations at the Rio Earth Summit of 1992, and created "catastrophe bundles," a widely used financial instrument in the reinsurance industry. A frequent keynote speaker, special adviser to several UN organizations and heads of state, her pioneering work uses innovative market mechanisms to reduce carbon emissions, conserve biodiversity and ecosystem services, and improve the lot of the poor. Graciela Chichilnisky is a Professor of Economics and Mathematical Statistics at Columbia University in New York, the Director of Columbia Consortium for Risk Management, the Sir Lewis Mathewson Distinguished Professor at Monash University, Australia, and a Distinguished Professor at Beijing Normal University and at the University of Nankai, China. She has taught at Stanford, Harvard, and Essex Universities, studied at MIT and UC Berkeley, where she earned two PhDs in Mathematics and in Economics. An editor of several scientific journals, and the author of some 300 scientific articles published in the preeminent academic journals covering economics, finance, and mathematics, she is the author of 14 books, the two most recent, *Saving Kyoto* and *The Economics of Climate Change* appearing in the UK in 2009 and 2010, respectively. She is a frequent guest and commentator on the BBC, CNN, and other TV networks. Graciela Chichilnisky was born in Buenos Aires, Argentina and is a US citizen. She has two children and lives in New York City.

Tom Dedeurwaerdere is Research Director at the Biodiversity Governance Unit of the Centre for the Philosophy of Law and Professor at the Faculty of Philosophy, Université catholique de Louvain. He is a graduate in polytechnical sciences and philosophy, with a PhD in philosophy. He is in charge of the direction of research sub-networks of European FTP project LOWINPUT BREET, BIOMOT, and MICRB3. He has also been awarded a starting grant from the European Research Council (GENCOMNONS). Representative publications include "From bioprospection to reflexive governance" in *Ecological Economics* and a special issue on the Microbiological Commons in *The International Social Science Journal* (fall 2006, vol. 188).

Denny Ellerman is an internationally recognized expert on energy and environmental economics with a particular focus on climate policy, emissions trading, and interactions with energy markets. He is part-time Professor at the Robert Schumann Centre for Advanced Studies at the European University Institute in Florence, Italy, and has retired from MIT, where he was for many years a senior lecturer and executive director of the Center for Energy and Environmental Policy Research and of the Joint Program on the Science and Policy of Global Change. Denny is co-editor of the *Review of Environmental Economics and Policy* and a co-author of the leading books on the US SO_2 and the EU CO_2 Allowance Trading Programs, *Markets for Clean Air: The US Acid Rain Program* and *Pricing Carbon: The European Emissions Trading Scheme.* He has a PhD in political economy and government from Harvard University and an undergraduate degree from Princeton University.

Johan Eyckmans obtained a PhD from the Katholieke Universiteit Leuven on the incentives of nations to form international environmental agreements. Since January 2004, he has worked as associated professor at the Hogeschool-Universiteit Brussel (HUB), where he is Research Director of the Centre for Research on Economic Markets and their Environments (CREME). Johan Eyckmans is associated professor at the Katholieke Universiteit Leuven, Center for Economic Studies. His research interests include the economics of climate change, emissions trading, applications of game theory to the formation of international environmental agreements, cost–benefit analysis, general equilibrium and integrated assessment modeling, evaluation of environmental policies, industrial organization, and normative economic theory.

Michael Faure received his Graduate Law Studies diploma from the University of Antwerpen in 1982 and thereafter completed his Graduate Studies in Criminology at the University of Ghent in 1983. In 1982 he also joined the Antwerp Bar as an attorney. In 1985 he earned a Masters in Law from the University of Chicago Law School, where he had studied on a Fellowship of the Belgium American Education Foundation. Thereafter, in 1989 he received the doctor iuris from the Albert Ludwigs Universitaet, Freiburg im Breisgau for his research on "Die Strafrechtliche Durchsetzung des Umweltrechts in Belgien". After employment as lecturer in environmental law at the School for Criminology of the Belgium Ministry of Justice and as senior lecturer at the University of Leiden, in 1991 Professor Faure was appointed Professor in Comparative and International Environmental Law at Maastricht University. He also became academic director of the Maastricht European Institute for Transnational Legal Research (METRO). In February 2008, as the pinnacle of his career for the time being, he joined the Erasmus School of Law. But not only does Professor Faure continue his work at Maastricht University on a part-time basis, but in addition to this, he is also academic director of the Ius Commune Research School and of the European Centre of Tort and Insurance Law. Finally, he is program director of the prestigious European Doctorate in Law and Economics Programme (EDLE).

J. Rupert Gatti is a lecturer and Director of Studies in Economics at Trinity College, University of Cambridge. His research interests and publications are in the areas of game theory, microeconomic theory, and the economics of the Internet.

Timo Goeschl holds the University Chair in Environmental Economics at the Department of Economics, University of Heidelberg. Previously, he was on the faculty at the University of Wisconsin-Madison and the University of Cambridge. His research interests are in environmental and resource economics, law and economics, and the economics of innovation. Timo's work has been published in the *Journal of Environmental Economics and Management*, *Environmental and Resource Economics*, the *Journal of the European Economic Association*, and other outlets.

Ben Groom is a Senior Lecturer in Economics at the School of Oriental and African Studies at the University of London, having obtained his PhD from University College London. He is an environmental and resource economist focusing on environment and poverty linkages in developing countries and social discounting in relation to climate change. He has advised the governments of China, Namibia, Pakistan, the United States, and the United Kingdom, inter alia, on environmental policy.

Hiroe Ishihara is currently a PhD candidate at Department of Land Economy, University of Cambridge. She has a strong baetground in sociology from her previous studies in Japan and in environmental policy from her work experience as a programme officer at UNDP. Her current research interest is in understanding the motivation behind the human behaviour to conserve nature or biodiversity and in applying these theories to environmental policy.

Pierre-André Jouvet holds a doctorate in economics and was dean of the faculty of Economics, Management, Mathemathics and Computer Science of the University of Paris Ouest-Nanterre, La Défense. He heads the Economics of Sustainable Development Masters (EDDEE) and the Environment and Territory Development Masters. Pierre-André Jouvet is the Scientifc Director of the Climate Economics Chair. He is an economist specializing in environmental economics and especially the economics of public and political regulation (taxes, pollution permits, voluntary contributions,...). His research is theoretical and covers the issues dealing with EU–ETS analysis, risk, the relation between environment and longevity, and endogeneous discounting.

Gary D. Libecap is Distinguished Professor of Corporate Environmental Management, Bren School of Environmental Science and Management and Department of Economics, University of California, Santa Barbara. He is also a Research Associate, National Bureau of Economic Research, Cambridge, Massachusetts and the Sherm and Marge Telleen Research Fellow, Hoover Institution. His PhD is from the University of Pennsylvania. He has authored, co-authored, or edited twleve books; edits the series Advances in the Study of Entrepreneurship, Innovation, and Economic Growth; and has written more than 150 journal articles and book chapters on property rights, natural resources, environmental, and other issues; and he serves on various National Science Foundation Panels. His research is on common-pool resources and property rights institutions—how they emerge, when they emerge, their structure, and how they affect resource use. His research focuses on fisheries, water, and land use. His latest books are *Environmental Markets: A Property Rights Approach* with Terry L. Anderson, Cambridge University Press, forthcoming and *Climate Change Past and Present: Uncertainty and Adaptation,* edited with Richard Steckel, University of Chicago Press and NBER, 2011.

Paulo A. L. D. Nunes graduated from the Katholieke Universiteit Leuven with a Master of Science in Economics and was awarded his PhD from the same institution. Nunes is currently Coordinator of the Research Program on Marine Economics at the Mediterranean Science Commission (CIESM), Head of the Policy Technical and Expert Committee for WAVES (at the World Bank), and visiting Professor at the Department of Agriculture and Natural Resource Economics, University of Padua. Nunes is author/co-author of more than 50 scientific publications in a variety of international journals in the areas of consumer behaviour, climate change, econometrics of ecosystem services, valuation of marine biodiversity, environmental policy, and cost–benefit analysis.

Laura Onofri holds a Master's Degree in Economic Science from the Catholic University of Leuven and a PhD in Economics from the University of Maastricht. She is currently Adjunct Professor of Industrial Economics and Microeconomics at the Economic Department of the University of Venice, Cà Foscari. She also holds a joint appointment with the Mediterranean Science Commission (CIESM) and the World Trade Organization as a policy expert. Onofri has authored/co-authored a variety of scientific publications in the field of industrial economics, with a focus on an econometric analysis of electricity and cultural markets. Particular emphasis is devoted to the study of consumer behaviour and firms' governance structures.

The Late **Elinor Ostrom** was Arthur F. Bentley Professor of Political Science; Senior Research Director of the Workshop in Political Theory and Policy Analysis, Indiana University, Bloomington; and Founding Director, Center for the Study of Institutional Diversity, Arizona State University. She was a member of the National Academy of Sciences and the American Academy of Arts and Sciences. She was awarded the 2009 Nobel Memorial Prize in Economic Sciences, and was a recipient of the Frank E. Seidman Prize in Political Economy and the Johan Skytte Prize in Political Science. Her books include *Governing the Commons; Rules, Games, and Common-Pool Resources* (with Roy Gardner and James Walker); *Local Commons and Global Interdependence* (with Robert Keohane); *The Commons in the New Millennium* (with Nives Dolšak); *The Samaritan's Dilemma: The Political Economy of Development Aid* (with Clark Gibson, Krister Andersson, and Sujai Shivakumar); *Understanding Institutional*

Diversity; and *Working Together: Collective Action, the Commons, and Multiple Methods in Practice* (with Amy Poteete and Marco Janssen).

Unai Pascual is Senior Lecturer in environmental economics and policy at the University of Cambridge, UK, and Ikerbasque Research Professor at the Basque Centre for Climate Change (Bilbao). His research mostly focuses on the economics of natural resource management and the design of biodiversity conservation policies, including advancing the design and implementation of Payments for Ecosystem Services. His research aims at bridging science and policy to advance the connection between development and the environmental conservation in socially fair ways. He has published more than 70 research papers and various books on biodiversity economics and he has recently been involved in international initiatives such as TEEB and various sub-global MEA (e.g. UK and Japan). He also actively participates in international policy fora such as the European Commission, UNEP, and FAO.

Charles Perrings is Professor of Environmental Economics at Arizona State University. Previous appointments include appointments at the University of York; University of California, Riverside, and the University of Auckland. He was the founding editor of the Cambridge University Press journal, *Environment and Development Economics*, and remains on the editorial board of this and several other journals in the field. He is Past President of the International Society for Ecological Economics and 2008 winner of the society's Kenneth Boulding Memorial Award. At ASU he directs the ecoSERVICES Group <http://www.ecoservices.asu.edu/>, which studies the causes and consequences of change in ecosystem services. His publications include 12 monographs or edited volumes and more than 100 scientific papers.

Andries Richter is a postdoctoral researcher at the Universsity of Oslo, Norway, where he is working on social complexity in resource management. He holds a PhD from Wageningen University, the Netherlands, on the multiple feedbacks between natural renewable resources and institutions governing these resources. His main field of scientific interest includes the evolution of scocial norms and cooperation, but also the governance of marine ecosystems. In 2007, he participated in the Young Scientists Summer Program of the International Institute for Applied Systems Analysis in Laxenburg, where he received the Mikhalevich award for his work on the evolution of social norms for renewable resource exploitation. He holds an MSc in Economics from the University of Groningen.

Timothy Swanson holds UCL's Chair in Law and Economics, and is a member of both the departments of law and economics. From autumn 2010, he has held the Andre Hoffman Chair of Environmental Economics at the Graduate Institute of International Studies, Geneva, Switzerland. He has published work that exists at the boundaries of both law and economics, especially in the field of environmental and international affairs. Previously he was the research director for the UK's Centre on Social and Economic Research on the Global Environment and a member of the faculty of economics at the University of Cambridge. He has undertaken research projects for both domestic governments, usually developing countries, and for international agencies. He has advised many international agencies (OECD, UNEP, World Bank) on issues dealing with burden sharing and institution building under international environmental agreements such as the Montreal Protocol and the Convention on Biological Diversity.

Daan van Soest holds a PhD in Economics (on the economics of tropical deforestation) from Groningen University. Since obtaining his PhD, Daan has worked for more than 10 years on issues in environmental and energy economics as Assistant and Associate Professor at Tilburg University. Currently he is Professor of Environmental Economics at the Department of Spatial Economics/IVM. His research is both theoretical and empirical in nature, and topics Daan has worked on include social norms and common-pool resource use, investments in energy-saving technologies, instrument choice in environmental policy making, etc. He has published in a wide variety of scientific journals, and is currently associate editor of *Environment and Resource Economics*.

Arild Vatn is Thor Heyerdahl Professor at the Norwegian University of Life Sciences (UMB), Department of International Environment and Development Studies. His main competences are in institutional and ecological economics. He has specifically concentrated on institutional questions, focusing on the theory of human action and environmental governance—for example, as in his latest book *Institutions and the Environment* (2005). For this book he was awarded the Veblen 150 years prize in 2007. He has served as president of the European Society for Ecological Economics (ESEE) (2006–09). He was also responsible for the European PhD summer school series "Theories and Methods for Sustainability Research (Themes)" running from 2006 to 2009. He has recently started a new international series named "The Thor Heyerdahl Summer School in Environmental Governance".

Marc Willinger is Professor of Economics at the University of Montpellier I and Institut Universitaire de France. His background is risk and decision analysis. His current research combines environmental economics and experimental economics, with a special focus on the design of policies and incentive schemes applied to social dilemmas (contributions to public goods and common-pool resources dilemmas). Recent papers deal with taxation schemes, binding agreements, and contract design under asymmetric information.

Oran R. Young is Research Professor of Environmental Policy and Co-director of the program on Governance for Sustainable Development at the Bren School of Environmental Science and Management at the University of California (Santa Barbara). The author of many books, Professor Young has longstanding interests in the role of bargaining in arriving at social choices and in the role of social institutions in governing human–environment relations. He also has a longstanding program of applied work dealing with issues of governance in the Circumpolar Arctic. His most recent book is entitled *On Environmental Governance: Sustainability, Efficiency, and Equity* has been published in 2012.

1

Introduction: Global Environmental Commons: Analytical and Political Challenges in Building Governance Mechanisms[1]

Eric Brousseau, Tom Dedeurwaerdere, Pierre-André Jouvet, and Marc Willinger

The increased interdependency of *socio-ecological systems* and the increased reach of human activity on the Earth have led to major political and scientific challenges in the governance of environmental resources. Indeed, the dimension of these biophysical challenges and the pace of changes—which are characterized by discontinuity and irreversibilities—makes action urgent to avoid potentially catastrophic evolution in terms of climate change, depletion of resources, reduction in biodiversity, increases in pollution and sanitary crises, and so forth. However, the current political and socio-economic governance mechanisms are poorly equipped to handle these issues: they often do not include the relevant stakeholders; they lack the knowledge to address effectively the problems they face; and they are insufficiently agile. Together these factors indicate that the existing environmental challenges are not well met institutionally, so new governance principles and architectures are needed. The proper management of environmental challenges may well require a reshaping of how the human community, with all its established subgroups and diverse motivations and coalitions, can (1) devise better mechanisms for making collective decisions to manage its shared environment; and (2) implement mechanisms

---

[1] This introduction offers an overview of the field and of this book. For readers who are not familiar with particular economic concepts and the governance debate, the Glossary (at the end of the book) explains the relevant notions and gives the main references. Glossary terms are *italicized* in this introduction.

aimed at channeling individual behavior so that these collective goals are reached.

The common characteristic of the environmental issues at stake is the management of resources that are relied upon by wide communities for all kinds of activities. However, these *commons* call for levels of governance depending on the extent of the affected population. Some (such as climate) have an entirely global aspect; others (such as clean air) cross boundaries but remain fairly localized; and still others (such as biodiversity) are multilevel in character. This variety clearly challenges existing *governance regimes*, which are built on nation states and international conventions. Morever, many "rights" regarding access to and use of these resources are only loosely defined, and many *externalities* (i.e. unmanaged interdependencies) result in the mismanagement of natural resources. Such mismanagement leads to depletion of resources and to the underproduction of collective services. These issues are exacerbated by scientific uncertainties and questions about the design of efficient policies, which creates a challenge for both natural and social sciences.

Since the publication of pathbreaking contributions on these issues in the early 1990s (Young 1989; E. Ostrom 1990; Carraro and Siniscalco 1993), a number of political initiatives have been taken, many governance experiments have been run, and a large and multidisciplinary field of research has arisen. The aim of this interdisciplinary book is to address new challenges in the provision of environmental goods by taking stock of the relevant but dispersed knowledge accumulated over the years. Our goal is to help construct a common knowledge base about the appropriate governance regimes for different types of global environmental goods.

Throughout this book, we show that three essential dimensions must be taken into account with respect to governance and the management of institutional change. First, we consider the issue of designing governance solutions: systems of rules, distribution of authority, levels of organization (from local to global), etc. These are the classical ways of tackling governance and institutional issues. The second crucial dimension of governance issues concerns implementability. Because there is no legally empowered global authority, possible instruments should not be considered merely from a design perspective: the negotiation process among stakeholders plays a critical role in reaching an agreement and in allowing *collective action*. In other words, implementability matters in a context where governance is shaped not only by games among nation states but also by the strategies of such nonstate actors as self-governed alliances, activists' movements, and nongovernmental organizations (NGOs). Third, compliance must also be taken into consideration because there is no last-resort enforcer. By "compliance" we mean actual changes in behavior that are generated by adoption of institutional arrangements. Compliance depends on a combination of formal rules (enforced by recognized authorities) and informal obligations, such as social and individual *norms*, whose violation is typically punished by private actors.

We begin in Section 1.1 by discussing the specificity and nature of global environmental challenges. Then we review the "state of the art" with respect to three main issues. First, in Section 1.2 we address the question of the optimal level of governance given that, in practice, environmental goods have wide variation in scope and can be produced according to various *aggregation technologies*. This leads us to the problem of multilevel governance and the efficient organization of federal systems. In an international context, it is also worth discussing the economics of treaties and coalition building, in addition to the interplay between *formal and informal* instruments and *norms*. Second, in Section 1.3 we argue that the design of governance instruments and regulation should be based on a relevant conception of human *motivation* and rationality. Too naïve a vision may, for instance, lead to *incentive mechanisms* that actually deter contributions to providing *public goods* (the *crowding-out* effect). More fundamentally, the exploration of human motivation, and especially of social preferences, raises important questions about how targets should be established when providing global environmental goods. The need to manage the constraints of participation, the consequences of inequalities, and the required intergenerational transfers makes it difficult to design policies that would be both effective and fair. Third, in Section 1.4 we revisit the governance toolbox and consider different modes of governing. In particular, we identify the costs and benefits of alternative tools—namely, property rights and incentives—by considering not only their characteristics (once established) but also the economics of their design and implementation. We conclude in Section 1.5 by briefly discussing the potential of polycentric and networked governance, as well as the need for more integration at the global level.

1.1 GLOBAL ENVIRONMENTAL AND GOVERNANCE CHALLENGES

Not all environmental goods raise the same challenges with respect to governance. According to this book's contributors, three factors must be taken into account: scale, time, and uncertainty. The many possible combinations of these dimensions affect how crucial are the environmental issues at hand and also the difficulty of their governance.

Let us consider each of these dimensions in turn. Scale (Section 1.1.1) determines whether a given environmental issue can be treated most effectively as a set of (linearly) cumulative local problems or rather as a global issue of linked problems requiring an approach in terms of systems (i.e. taking relationships among components into consideration). Timing (Section 1.1.2) contrasts processes of rapid systemic and possibly irreversible changes with the slow, partly reversible processes of evolution. Finally, uncertainty (Section 1.1.3) enters the picture as follows. Some environmental issues are characterized by risk; several (but not necessarily all) possible future scenarios can be imagined, and we do not know for certain which will transpire. In contrast, there are situations of (radical) uncertainty in which future scenarios are beyond the capability of human cognition—either because our understanding of the current situation is incomplete or because future developments are too complex to be predictable.

Each of these dimensions, taken in isolation, has an impact on the choice of the mode of governance, and in combination they severely complicate the task of choosing the best way to govern the global _commons_.

1.1.1 Scale effects, polycentrism, and coordination

The standard economics of federalism states that governance issues must be dealt with by the jurisdiction that covers all stakeholders affected by the potential externalities (for surveys, see Oates 1999, 2005). In the case of issues that have a transnational or even global dimension, the principal issue is how governance solutions are implementable at the appropriate level. After all, there is no actor to create an integrated order or to serve as guarantor in agreements among sovereign states. These conditions lead us to focus on the effectiveness and stability of decentralized solutions. _Environmental federalism_ maintains that the provision of many environmental goods can be performed on a decentralized basis, especially since many natural resources are localized in particular regions. Solutions based on Frey and Eichenberger's (1999, 2001) concept of functional, overlapping, and competing jurisdictions (FOCJ)—where each _public good_ is managed by a specific jurisdiction established at the right scale—tend, however, to be too costly in terms of _transaction costs_ (owing to the number of jurisdictions and consequent multiplication of governance efforts and structures), as well as being quite unrealistic from a political standpoint, since existing governments are generally reluctant to delegate sovereignty to new levels of government.

Hence there is a theory (and a practice) of optimal devolution of the provision of _public goods_ to the proper level of governance, a level that depends on natural characteristics (watersheds, forests, etc.) as well as societal ones (in particular, political organization, a shared culture, and integration of the economy). In fact, well-established _institutions_ for the traditional governance of natural resources have demonstrated the possibility of sustainably managing common resources at the local level. As pointed out in particular by the Nobel laureate Elinor Ostrom, efficient alignment of individual motivations and the use of specific knowledge have allowed self-organized communities to outperform public agencies consistently. The question is thus whether and how the features characterizing these successful, decentralized, resource management schemes can be scaled up to address problems at the global level. The biggest challenge seems to be establishing larger units that do not supersede the medium- and smaller-size units that facilitate citizen access to neighborhood-level public goods and common-pool resources. One approach is to encourage experimental efforts at multiple levels. When decision making is structured in this way, the level of public goods provision can be tailored to the specific circumstances—the tastes of residents, the costs of production, and other unique local characteristics—of each jurisdiction.

Difficulties in governing the provision of public goods generally arise either when one ecosystem supplies services that benefit people at different scales or when ecological and jurisdictional boundaries do not coincide. Coordination mechanisms at higher levels and new, regional, collective entities may be needed to create the best fit between governance mechanisms and the problems being considered.

An understanding of *aggregation technology* is required to determine where the balance lies in optimal integration of governance at the global level. This notion captures how individual contributions to the *collective good* determine the quality of the good available for consumption (Hirschleifer 1983; Cornes and Sandler 1984). With so-called summation goods, each unit contributed to the public good adds an identical and cumulative amount to the overall level of the good available for consumption. For example, any reduction in the emission of greenhouse gases corresponds to the aggregate (summed) cutbacks of the polluter countries. Other important types of aggregation technologies are: weakest-link public goods (e.g. pest eradication), where the smallest contribution fixes the quantity of the public good for the entire group; best-shot public goods (e.g. a cure for some disease), where the overall level of the public good equals the largest single individual provision level; and weighted-sum public goods (e.g. the cleanup of polluted sites), where different contributions can have different impacts. However, it is widely recognized that many global environmental issues involve opposing logics—for example, separability and systemic scaling effects—that call for hybrid solutions in the matter of governance.

If an environmental issue is characterized by summation in terms of *aggregation technology*, then local decision making and decentralized management are preferable within a framework of global coordination. Experience shows that informal rules and community pressure play a strong role in ensuring compliance at the local level, which explains why a decentralized context is favored for cost-efficient provision of public goods. Moreover, locally emerging rules reach the better fit with the nature of the problem and with the collective preferences. Thus, from a design perspective, the main governance implication of local and disjointed environmental problems (such as biodiversity or fisheries) is the significant efficiency gains that are possible in a decentralized governance framework. Yet these are trumped by cognitive and informational issues, since governance that is insufficiently connected may deprive a community of the information or knowledge needed to address an issue it faces. This highlights the need for cooperation and information sharing among independent governance devices.

On the one hand, stable agreements should follow from bargaining in small groups on local issues combined with coordination at a global scale. Externalities would not always be avoided, since there are often discrepancies between the scope of an environmental issue and that of a political jurisdiction. In this case, the issue becomes one of discovering and designing appropriate coordination among (decentralized) governance regimes.

On the other hand, systemic interdependencies at the global level may require multilevel governance arrangements, including an independent global entity of last resort. Affected here are environmental goods whose production exhibits a "weakest link" or "threshold" structure in terms of *aggregation technologies*, which means that the contribution of some stakeholders is useless when not combined with others' contributions. The issue here is the effectiveness of (generally hard-to-reach) international agreements. In many cases, the global entities and intergovernmental organizations that result from these negotiations lack their own financial resources and powers of implementation. A second-best solution in such cases is to delegate financing and enforcement to the nation states within the framework of a negotiated multilateral convention. However, global agreements—whether leading to framework conventions or to a global organization (e.g. the International Treaty on Plant Genetic Resources for Food and Agriculture)—raise the issue of stability (see Section 1.2.1.). Given the greater heterogeneity and size of the communities, compliance with the adopted agreements can be expected to increase in the presence of formal rules that strengthen the calculated or instrumental motivation for compliance. Hence, a dilemma pointing out the necessity to better understand the dynamic of international negotiation (which will be explored further in Section 1.2 below).

1.1.2 Abrupt changes and long-term monitoring needs

Political processes leading to the formation of an environmental regime are slow, and they have difficulty dealing with nonlinearities and strong uncertainty. This stands in sharp contrast to the reality of interactions between ecological and socio-economic systems, which evolve at a rapid pace and are difficult to predict. In fact, biophysical systems are characterized by processes of evolution that tend to be nonlinear, subject to abrupt changes, and irreversible. A case in point is species extinction, which occurs when a population reaches a critical threshold or tipping point and then crashes. This dynamic also characterizes regime changes, sanitary crises, depletion of resources, ecological disequilibrium, and so forth.

Systems that are subject to abrupt and radical changes need an early-warning mechanism in addition to a balance between mitigation and adaptation measures for dealing with change. Building such management and monitoring capacities in polycentric and decentralized systems is expected not only to increase the fit with local circumstances but also to increase the speed and diversity of available solutions. A global governance arrangement might increase the effectiveness of coordination, but reaching a global agreement is more difficult in situations of rapid change. Under such circumstances, appropriate methods of reaching stable agreements include well-designed contractual regimes (with ex ante agreements on negotiation procedures) and strong leadership. Thus we can reasonably expect the effectiveness of governance systems to be increased by the involvement of a leading political actor (typically the European Union (EU)) or a formal global collective organization with clear delegation of authority.

For environmental problems that extend over a long time horizon, a global governance arrangement is feasible and should increase efficiency; meanwhile, a certain level of network governance should improve compliance. Issues such as nuclear waste require investments in governance systems with long-term monitoring capacities. Also, bargaining should be organized to tackle the distributional issues that are unlikely to be addressed spontaneously through decentralized mechanisms—even when there is a strong *norm* of altruism.

Managing long-term issues requires that questions about the viability of long-term formal agreements be clarified. Indeed, over time there might be strong calls for renegotiation to reflect the evolving distributional consequences of compliance with the rules. To ensure compliance, it may therefore make sense to invest in establishing *social norms* (see Section 1.3 below).

1.1.3 Risk, uncertainty, and incomplete knowledge

The management of well-defined risks (i.e. situations of limited uncertainty) can be tackled by global governance arrangements, within a multi-actor network, to achieve efficient risk sharing. For specific goods that are characterized by well-defined risks (e.g. toxic waste), stringent limitations are required on a transnational scale. Such regulations call for the creation of international epistemic communities, with a clear institutional mandate, that can provide consensual knowledge on the state of the art to policy makers.

Combining regulation, legal liability, and *social norms* is crucial to ensuring high levels of compliance.

For goods characterized by strong uncertainty or controversy over the level of risk (e.g. nuclear energy, climate change, genetically modified organisms), there are advantages to taking a precautionary approach within a centralized framework. Strong uncertainty opens the door to value judgments, which therefore play a key role in the bargaining and decision-making processes. In order to reach stable arrangements, scientific knowledge must be balanced against value judgments. The need for extended peer review processes thus implies recourse to polycentric and decentralized arrangements for social learning about values in different local and regional settings. At the same time, effective governance of these risks requires coordination of (scientific and social) expertise, of risk assessment, of the setting of outcome targets, and of rule making. Compliance with precautionary measures will increase more in response to formally specified outcome targets than in response to liability (given the difficulty of attributing responsibilities) or *social norms* (which lead to ambivalent results). Substantial efficiency gains should result from a decentralized regime of licenses and permits aimed at reaching the outcome targets.

The biophysical properties of various environmental issues, their spatial and temporal scales, the available knowledge to consider them, and their supply technology together create challenges for existing governance regimes that seek to provide environmental goods. All the named factors must be better understood and matched with more precise knowledge about the effectiveness of alternative governance solutions. From a political standpoint, this conclusion suggests that policy making be (1) highly responsive when exploring how socio-economic systems can deal with the environment; and (2) highly flexible when adapting our governance solutions to the progress of knowledge and evolution of the challenges. The fundamental purpose of the rest of this introduction (and the book) is to explore key analytical points that guide the building of effective governance arrangements.

1.2 ADDRESSING GLOBAL ISSUES BY ARTICULATING GOVERNANCE FRAMEWORKS

For public goods that must be provided at the global level, the problem is that no global government exists. There is not even an established legitimacy of global politics. It is essential, then, to understand how international agreements can be reached and enforced (Section 1.2.1), to identify the main obstacles to their stability (Section 1.2.2), and to discuss potential improvements (Section 1.2.3) in the process.

1.2.1 International agreements among sovereign nations

Federalism reveals its limitations when it comes to the international level. In international relations, there is no last-resort enforcer and seldom any actor overseeing the players or promoting agreements. The ability to establish common rules and common (compatible) principles to deal with providing public goods at the global level eventually comes up against the harsh logic of interplay among self-interested actors.

In early contributions to the analysis of bargaining about the global *commons*, interaction among countries is characterized as a prisoner's/*social dilemma*, inevitably leading to a call for the establishment of a globally recognized sanctioning authority (Hampton 1987) or its equivalent, a set of global formal contracts (Snidal 1985). Yet even though the prisoner's dilemma does characterize some global commons issues, it does not describe all of them; in practice, there are many different game structures and related institutional solutions to consider (see Section 1.1). It is also important to recognize that, in most cases unanimity is not possible. The greater the heterogeneity among the players, the more difficult it is to reach a consensus. At the same time, a consensus is not a necessary condition for action: the actions of specific players (e.g. the EU) can have a substantial "demonstration" effect. Today this is true, for instance, of product safety regulation worldwide.

In fact, many large-scale environmental agreements have been signed and have remained relatively stable over time. Two important differences distinguish these arrangements from the prisoner's dilemma. First, it is possible to modify the conditions of the game through policy measures (and thus to enlarge the stable coalition) by implementing transfers or side payments, linking issues, and/or designing negotiation rules (e.g. establishing a minimum number of participants) (Carraro 2003: xvi–xviii). The second difference is that most real-life games in this context are actually "mixed" games that combine features of *social dilemmas* (a conflict over the use of the common resources, which means that the cooperation is not stable without external intervention) and those of *coordination dilemmas* (as when cooperation is stable but is not a dominant strategy absent an appropriate distribution of information).

A convenient way to assess the impact of global scale on the bargaining process is to consider the differing impact of scale on cooperation and coordination games (Snidal 1985). The impact of scale on the prisoner's/*social dilemma* has been studied extensively. The effect is negative, since cooperation is much easier in small coalitions. Cooperation in large groups seems to require asymmetry between players (so that leadership and minimal coalitions can play a role) and most frequently occurs when a benign hegemon imposes it on the other players. In the absence of such a hegemon, increasing the number of players makes cooperation more difficult in most circumstances. Thus, it seems that reaching an agreement through voluntary cooperation leads to stable coalitions only if they are small ones (see, e.g., Carraro and Siniscalco 1993; Bloch 1997; Ray and Vohra 1999).

In contrast, a greater number of players enhances regime stability in coordination dilemmas. The reason is that stability involves adherence to a convention—that is, a convergence of mutually reinforcing strategies (see Schotter 1981; Greif 2006). Although some environmental goods should be provided on a local scale, increasing the number of players that bargain over standards or other coordination issues enhances the intrinsic stability of the regime.

1.2.2 Why it is difficult to reach an international agreement

In negotiations, the parties reach an agreement when uncertainty is low, when differences in expected costs and benefits across constituencies are small, and when the aggregate benefits of collective efforts exceed the costs. Yet there are strong *free-riding* incentives, since it is difficult to convince others that they should give up part of their current wealth for the sake of uncertain gains in the future. In short, there are only weak political and economic drivers for entering an agreement and for attaining and maintaining its goals.

1.2.2.1 Heterogeneity and the difficulty of sharing a common burden

Reaching an agreement is especially difficult when there is considerable heterogeneity in costs and benefits among countries with respect to a global externality. Stronger inducement mechanisms may be required—for example, large transfers or incentives that involve punitive aspects. The underlying problem is always that of agreeing on an appropriate standard for sharing the common burden. For example, it is hardly surprising that developing countries do not regard 1990-level emissions as an appropriate basis for allocating rights to the global atmospheric sink; nor that they prefer population-based standards, which industrialized nations are unlikely to accept in a pure form.

That being said, some aspects of heterogeneity can be helpful. In particular, trading thrives on heterogeneity. When low-cost abatement resources are located outside the system, there is a common interest in making these resources part of the system. This principle is the basis of the Clean Development Mechanism (CDM) credits employed in the EU's Emissions Trading System (ETS). In this instance, heterogeneity is useful in setting up the conditions for participation, although it is still important to find an equitable basis for participation so that large differences can be bridged.

Inequalities tend, however, to make it more difficult to reach an agreement. In the relationship between the most developed and the less developed nations, in particular, cooperation is of more benefit to the former than the latter because the developed economies are more capable of exploiting the surplus generated by cooperation and the public good itself. Compensation payments fail to address this fundamental distributional problem of dividing up the cooperative surplus because such payments do not affect the distribution of assets. Not only is the world trapped in an inefficient equilibrium, but this equilibrium typically worsens in response to the game the poorest nations might play to enhance their bargaining positions. It is indeed rational for them to threaten destruction of their resources that are needed by developed countries. Yet suicidal strategies leading to the mass destruction of environmental goods, including some nonrenewable resources, threatens the dynamic of international cooperation on their provision. The failures of the Cancun and Copenhagen summits certainly resulted partly from such (negotiation) strategies.

This is why long-term stable regimes should be based on a better recognition of the actual inequalities of asset distribution between the North and the South. Inequalities in the ability to negotiate and to benefit should be taken into consideration—say, by overcompensating the South in the short run and, in the long run, having the North contribute to developing the South's stock of human capital. Thus, compensation for inequalities generated throughout history is not only a moral imperative but is also essential for any long-run guarantee of providing global public goods (GPGs). The governance of GPGs is thus far from a simple issue of *mechanism design*. The agenda must include distribution challenges, inequalities among nations, and the consequences of past wars and colonialism.

1.2.2.2 *The negative impact of uncertainty on consensus building*

The costs that individuals, firms, and governments have to bear in adjusting their behavior to protect GPGs are very uncertain. This uncertainty about the potential results of *collective action* is genenerated by incomplete and imprecise information on the effects of international action, the costs involved, and compliance. The volatility of all estimates depends greatly on variables—such as population, productivity growth, technological improvement, and patterns of consumption—that are difficult to predict in the long run. Uncertainty in calculating aggregate net gains and their distribution, when combined with asymmetric information, results in divergent views of the best overall solutions for addressing the externality and sharing the costs.

Uncertainty thus complicates the design of compensation schemes and encourages conflicts over the size, nature, and direction of compensation. In that context politicians may doubt their constituents' support for bargaining over an externality.

1.2.2.3 Dynamic effects

Abrupt change—for example, in conflicts over the use of resources—generally makes cooperation more difficult (Snidal 1985). Indeed, the structure of the game changes, and bargaining over the new regime's exact nature is usually intense. Only well-established governance regimes can orchestrate a successful transition without disrupting any ongoing cooperation. Well-designed contracts (including agreements on the negotiation procedures for dealing with adaptation) and strong leadership can address these challenges.

For extremely long time frames, the set of possible game forms to deal with resource conflicts or coordination problems is dramatically reduced. For instance, alleviating *collective acti*on dilemmas via face-to-face communication or bilateral contracting is impossible in intergenerational conflicts over the use of resources. Researchers have shown that altruistic norms in favor of future generations are an important motivational factor for the adoption of efficient behavior in that matter (see Fischer et al. 2004). However, altruistic norms per se can have counterproductive results. If the strategies of the different players are substitutes, then the optimistic belief that most people care about future generations diminishes each individual's perceived need to contribute. This question will be discussed further in Section 1.3.

1.2.2.4 The limits of enforcement among peers

There are good reasons for skepticism regarding the effectiveness of agreements, since many international organizations charged with overseeing such agreements are weak (Haas et al. 1993). Where monitoring or verification is difficult or impossible, compliance will be harder to achieve. For this reason, most agreements establish obligations that are easily monitored. This is one advantage of treaties that focus on actions (policies and measures) rather than outcomes (emission-level targets) (Barrett 2001). However, that emphasis is also a major reason why such treaties might not be effective.

Again, the limits of the formal mechanisms aimed at curving *extrinsic motivations* call for an exploration of other logics—in particular, grounded in "moral" beliefs and care about others—that might lead to agreements and compliance. The discussion on these issues is introduced in Section 1.3 below.

1.2.3 . . . and why some international agreements are successful

A few factors explain why, despite many obstacles, some treaties seem more stable and effective than others. In each case, the role of "third parties" seems central to channeling the behavior of decision makers.

1.2.3.1 The role of independent watchdogs

Although evidence from game theory suggests that international cooperation is difficult, there are instances of cooperation even in crisis situations. One recent example is the financial crisis, which—like several environmental problems—is globally systemic. It is important to recognize the conditions underlying cooperation in this specific context, which rely in particular on central bankers. Most of central banks are independent of (or at least insulated from) the executive and legislative branches of their country's administrations; most individual bankers share a similar view of how the monetary system works; they have previously interacted with each other, although they have not necessarily coordinated their activities directly; the players frequently meet behind closed doors, which facilitates consensus; they care about their reputations within the group as well as outside; and many are interested in their reputation for the history books (since they need not worry about being re-elected). These conditions characterize the role of watchdogs and thus also the institutional requirements for establishing analogous environmental agencies with the proper incentives and capabilities.

1.2.3.2 Public opinion

Another player to consider in coordination games is the public at large. Received wisdom suggests that the presence of special interest groups reduces the public's influence over the provision of public goods. However, competition among politicians will cater to the public interest and, in so doing, will cause politicians to reach out and learn about the public's values (Denzau and Munger 1986). Governments may, for instance, sign and adhere to an environmental convention—even when, in purely economic terms, the payoff from *free-riding* is higher—because they fear being labeled as opportunistic or uncooperative (Hoel and Schneider 1997).

Given this, and since citizens' value structures may not be stable, especially under conditions of uncertainty, the media and some leaders might have the opportunity to shape public opinion so as to press governments to address more effectively global environmental issues (while, as pointed out in Alston et al. 2010, it might be the reverse). In addition, psychosocial interventions are essential to effecting widespread changes in *social norms*, which will be needed to initiate the changes in lifestyle and the economy that are essential to addressing these issues

1.2.3.3 *Mechanisms for reaching consensus: scientific and multistakeholder forums*

Many researchers have addressed the problem of uncertainty's role in decisions made about environmental issues. Two general but important lessons emerge from this literature. First, in order to be effective, scientific assessments should produce knowledge that is legitimate, salient, and credible (Clark et al. 2002). Second, an assessment's effectiveness is enhanced if the assessment body (1) has a clear institutional mandate for knowledge production, and (2) has a certain independence from the policy arena (Haas 2004).

Thus, despite the many factors hindering cooperation at the international level, some levers are available to modify the logic of the "game" played. That, said, as suggested here and there in this section, the actual structure of the problem of environmental good provisions needs to be explored more deeply by getting a better understanding of the motivations of stakeholders in front of environmental, and more generally, collective and societal issues.

1.3 SOCIAL PREFERENCES, INTRINSIC MOTIVATIONS, AND THE DESIGN OF *INSTITUTIONS*

The debates about sustainable development and the construction of norms and policies for providing environmental public goods are usually set up according to Hardin's (now) standard economic approach to the so-called *tragedy of the commons* (Hardin 1968). The desirable "natural" or "physical" characteristics of a certain good explain its underprovision because individual selfishness collides with the nonexcludability of such goods. This argument draws on a rather erroneous vision of how individual and collective preferences are built.

While the traditional approach to public goods provision relies on simplifying assumptions, it should not be "thrown out with the bathwater" because its "baby" can drive useful results—for example, political recommendations that would enable better alignment between individual incentives and collective needs (see Section 1.4). However, implementing exclusion mechanisms that are grounded in property rights, or incentives based on relative price manipulations may prove to be counterproductive. The *crowding-out effect* is the best-known example: implementing incentives to contribute may deter voluntary contributions, leading to an overall reduction in the good's provision.

Identifying these problems suggests that our models (of the human mental processes underlying most economic reasoning) may be too crude to yield a relevant analysis of the issues related to the provision of public goods—and in particular to the provision of environmental goods, which are likely to be impure public goods. More precisely, two sets of issues have been highlighted. First, organizing *collective action* to ensure the provision of public goods requires some definition of collective objectives; this raises the question of how social preferences are formed. Second, after goals have been established, collective action may require the implementation of tools that seek to influence individual behaviors. Aligning individual preferences requires an understanding of them. Therefore, both sets of issues underscore the necessity of understanding individual and collective preferences when advocating and establishing environmental policies. This link between preferences and policies is the subject of important research and discussions on their relationship. These debates are introduced in the balance of this section. The notion of *social preferences* is developed in Section 1.3.1, and its role in the formation of collective preferences is discussed in Section 1.3.2. Then, in Section 1.3.3, we tease out the consequences for the design of governance mechanisms.

1.3.1 Reciprocity and future-oriented social preferences

Over the past two decades, experimentalists from various social sciences have accumulated a large body of evidence supporting the universality of social (other-regarding) preferences. Clearly, we must reconsider the standard behavioral hypothesis of *homo œconomicus:* selfish rational agents. In contrast to that model's assumptions, most people care not only about their own material resources but also about other people's resources. This view has been advocated by leading economists since Adam Smith (1759), including Becker (1974), Arrow (1981), Samuelson (1993), and many others. In particular, most people express a preference for preserving resources for future generations. Parental altruism is a popular illustration of this preference type. Other, more general social preferences include desire for reciprocity, aversion to inequality, and preference for fairness. After taking such preferences into account, the predictions (and policy recommendations) of economic models can change radically. For example, estimates indicate that most effects of global warming will be felt *after* the death of the current generation. This means that actions taken now to deal with global warming will mainly benefit future generations—although their cost is sunk for the present generation, which actually may not profit (even partially) from these actions. This imbalance raises substantial problems. When deciding about collective actions, for example, what weight should a society attach to the welfare of future generations?

Social preferences are based on the assumption that individuals' satisfaction are interrelated. For instance, large differences between own and others' material resources may induce guilt or envy, respectively (for a general overview of social preferences models, see Fehr and Fischbacher 2005). At this point, two questions arise. First: how can we understand social preferences, such as *altruism*, and how do they relate to the selfish dimension of preferences? Second: what link (if any) is here between *institutions* and social preferences? In other words, do social processes play a role in forming individuals' preferences?

There are several ways in which social preferences can be understood. One way is to view them as a ranking of others' different states of welfare that individuals compare with their own welfare. Hence altruism and care for others is commensurable with individual preferences, which implies that both own and others' material payoffs carry value for the individual. This understanding is compatible with the standard economic model of choice. An alternative to this interpretation originates in sociology and classical institutional economics. From this perspective, social and individual preferences pertain to different orderings. On the one hand, social preferences are learned norms and so acting socially is to follow the relevant norm (i.e. acting appropriately). On the other hand, private preferences stem from the individual's own welfare and so utility maximization applies.

These two interpretations lead to different analytical models, and they also correspond to different visions of the interplay between individual and collective preferences. In the former view, individual and collective preferences are independent. In the "different orderings" view, these preferences conflict for much of the population—which is an impetus for changing the norm.

The second issue is whether social preferences are individual characteristics or rather social constructs (i.e. learned and hence endogenous). Societies educate each member by emphasizing values and *norms* that are central to them. These values and norms are embodied in commonly accepted rules about how to treat other people. Hence, they are social constructs that individuals internalize in the process of becoming socialized. But what is the very origin of such collective norms? According to the "individual" interpretation of preferences, we are imprinted with motivations to support other people because the human kind endogenizes the interdependencies among its members.[2] In contrast, the "different orderings" interpretation argues that we learn certain ways of acting applicable to certain situations and that following this prescription is, in fact, what gives meaning to the situation.[3]

---

[2] Note that there are controversies on how this process of endogenization occurs: by a process of selection or of learning.

[3] It may be that institutions (such as norms) exert influence in ways other than establishing social preferences. For example, they may also help us distinguish between different situations—

1.3.2 Establishing norms for sustainable development

Social preferences raise a major challenge for *preference aggregation* and for defining a collective objective function. The central issue is whether people's preferences regarding others' satisfaction should be taken into account in the planner's objective function, or whether only the selfish part of their preferences should be counted. The standard view is that each generation should be treated equally (leaving the discounting issue aside). But if the current generation cares about the next generation's well-being, then the latter's well-being will be double-counted in the social planner's objective function. Thus, whether (or not) the altruistic component of individuals' preferences is taken into account will affect the ranking of options in matters of collective choice.

The traditional view is that the altruistic component should not be counted, since altruists could simply make cash transfers to those toward whom they feel altruistic. In this view, the other-regarding component of preferences should be excluded because it is inconsistent with utilitarianism. The main argument here is that each person should count for one and only one. More recent critiques of double-counting (e.g. Bergstrom et al. 1986; Milgrom 1993; Yew-Kwang 1999; Bernheim 2002) have also adopted this point of view. For example, Milgrom (1993) argues against incorporating altruism into cost–benefit analyses on grounds of allocative efficiency. Others argue that altruism violates impartiality. Similarly, Yew-Kwang (1999) suggests that informed preferences should be used instead of actual preferences or "happiness." This approach, he argues, would lead to the exclusion of external preferences. But are altruistic preferences not fully informed?

One could well argue that there is no good reason to exclude altruistic preferences from cost–benefit analyses. The Kaldor–Hicks principle simply states that a given change is desirable whenever its benefits for the winners can (potentially) balance out the losers' losses. This principle can easily account for both altruistic and selfish benefits and losses. On this basis, other-regarding preferences could be taken into account.

Another issue raised by other-regarding preferences is the existence of evil preferences. If one argues in favor of including the preferences of all others, then on what grounds can evil preferences—or, more generally, the "dark side" of social preferences—be excluded? Can we legitimately consider only positively oriented social preferences while ignoring negatively oriented ones? If

---

as when some contexts are defined as individual while others are seen as social. Thus the market, the firm, the community, and the family are characterized by different expectations concerning the balance between individual and social interests. Shifting between such institutional contexts can be viewed as shifting between different preference orderings, which in turn implies changes in the utility function's parameters.

we take an impartial view of aggregation then we should, of course, be fair to everyone: all preferences should count, even the selfish ones. Yet one objection to that view is based on the freedom of choice. Consider the case of envy, which is a negative response to others' well-being. Envious people derive positive utility from reductions in the endowments of those whom they envy; for example, envious people feel better when the freedom of others is *reduced*. Altruists respond differently: they feel better when the freedom of others is *increased*. If we can agree on some moral principles—for example, that the freedom of others should never be reduced—then evil preferences will be filtered out in the aggregation. The question is thus transformed from "which preference types should be counted" to "which principles should be adopted in carrying out the aggregation."

Choosing an aggregation technique for individual preferences helps us to disentangle selfish and altruistic preferences as well as to discount altruistic preferences (and thereby preclude the "dictatorship of the future"). Some techniques overweight the well-being of future generations with respect to that of the present generation. In contrast, other techniques allow the interests of the various generations to be properly balanced. Aggregation, however, raises another important issue: on what ground does the social planner have the legitimacy to decide which generation/social group (if any) should be sacrificed? Research on these issues is still in its infancy, and it raises important philosophical issues, beyond the development of discounting and aggregation techniques.

1.3.3 Individual motivations and institutional design

Social preferences constitute a major challenge to the design of environmental policy. Current policy instruments and targets are based on the standard behavioral assumptions (i.e. selfish preferences) of welfare economics. If other-regarding preferences are widespread and if the socially oriented component of individual preferences is nonnegligible, then standard policy instruments will seldom reach their objectives because private costs and benefits will be misrepresented. Furthermore, if people have other-regarding preferences then "economic incentives may be counterproductive when they signal that selfishness is an appropriate response" (Bowles 2008). If standard *incentives* are implemented in such a context then people will, over time, come to adopt a more self-interested viewpoint at the expense of their *intrinsic* social *motivations*.[4] For example, agents with a strong altruistic orientation will bear costs

---

[4] Even worse, standard incentives may generate irreversible effects on individuals' preferences—in other words, effects that persist even after the incentives have been withdrawn (see, e.g., Gneezy and Rustichini 2000b). Thus, incentives designed for selfish rational agents may

and enjoy benefits in excess of those deriving from the selfish dimension of their preferences—provided their motivation is not undermined by economic incentives. But if social preferences are misrepresented or contradicted by antagonist signals, then the outcomes of standard policies may be counterproductive (as when *lower* contributions to the provision of a public good result from "incentives" designed to increase them; see Section 1.3.3.1). However, this crowding-out effect is often attenuated because individuals' motivations for contributing to environmental public goods, and the systems that influence individual behavior, are far more complex than those considered in the theory or the laboratory (Section 1.3.3.2).

1.3.3.1 *The threat of* crowding-out

The idea behind *crowding-out* is that government spending on public goods provision may, partially or totally, squeeze out private contributions. A standard result on the voluntary provision of public goods (Warr 1983) states that, for any arbitrary exogenous income, any redistribution among contributors is neutral with respect to the aggregate supply of public goods. This neutrality theorem has been extended by Bergstrom et al. (1986) and by Iritani and Yamamoto (2004). Bergstrom and colleagues show that redistribution from the rich to the poor might even reduce the total amount of public goods provided. Another neutrality result—public debt neutrality, also known as the Ricardian equivalence theorem—applies to intertemporal resource allocation. The idea, developed by Becker (1974) and Barro (1974), is that any attempt by the government to reallocate resources across generations is offset by a compensatory reshuffling by households via their altruistic bequests.

How do other-regarding preferences affect private contributions? Do altruistic agents provide more public goods because they care about the impact of public goods provision on the well-being of others? The tentative answer is "yes." If agents have altruistic preferences, then their marginal utility from providing the public good is greater and so they will make a larger contribution to the public good. Nonetheless, crowding-out still occurs since the contribution of agents is influenced not only by their own utility but also by others' altruistic utility. In short, it remains unclear just how social preferences affect voluntary contributions to public goods.

Suppose crowding-out is complete. Then policies designed to increase provision of a global public good will fail to achieve that objective if they are based on income transfers between agents. Hence the question becomes: "When can we neglect crowding-out?" There are at least two conditions

---

crowd out the intrinsic motivations of socially oriented agents, who consequently amend their preferences to more nearly match those of the selfish rational agent.

under which crowding-out will be limited: when impure altruism (or "warm glow") is a factor and when nonlinearities are present in production of the public good. The first case has been extensively investigated in the theoretical and experimental literature (see Andreoni 1989, 1990, 1993; Bolton and Zwick 1998; Eckel et al. 2005). Impure altruism means that agents derive utility from the act of giving itself: they care less about others' utility than about their own utility gain from giving (which thus can be interpreted as a private good). So even if they have a lower income and others have more, these agents still contribute to the public good because they derive utility from doing so. Such impure altruism leads to partial crowding-out, an outcome that is compatible with most empirical findings from the field and from various types of experiments. Also, if the governement's production technology differs from that of private individuals, then crowding-out still occurs, but only at the margins (Hattori 2003). Empirical evidence of insignificant nonlinear crowding-out is reported in Gibson et al. (2006).

To conclude, crowding-out exists, but its magnitude and therefore its actual impact on policy tools needs to be explored further.

1.3.3.2 Altruism, long-term thinking, and compliance

More generally, taking the complex motivations of individuals into account leads to a better understanding of how actual policies should utilize various imperfect tools to manage the processes of institutional design. For instance, the presence of a strong altruistic norm in favor of future generations might be used to establish constitutional rights for those generations. Survey data indicate that voters or members of a collectivity who are unwilling to exhibit restraint when their income is immediately affected might nevertheless vote for a general rule. In other words, the norm of altruism makes it possible to change a situation of conflict into a coordination problem.

Also, other's regarding preference might impact on compliance. Promoting altruistic norms will have a positive effect on the stability of any coordination equilibrium that arises. As suggested earlier, then, compliance with principles derived from the logic of sustainable development can be achieved only by combining the enforcement of formal rules with adherence to informal norms of behavior. For this reason, the adoption of new institutional arrangements frequently requires an actual change in behavior. Yet characterizing compliance as pure obedience would miss the broader point that agents commonly share and accept the rules, thus making these rules their own. This internalization of the norm encourages actors to accept the common good's primacy over their individual objectives (Tyler 1998: 271).

There is an important distinction to be made between calculated and normative motivations for compliance (Burby and Paterson 1993; Winter and May 2001). In the former case, an agent's willingness to comply is determined by calculating the expected positive or negative outcomes from following or disobeying a rule. The main factors in this calculation are the likelihood of being detected while breaking the rule, the size of the punishment or reward, and the credibility of the threats of punishment. There is overwhelming empirical evidence (see Nadeau 1997) that strengthening enforcement produces higher compliance in such calculating agents. Also, increasing the formality of rules leads to greater compliance because it increases both transparency and the probability of being convicted (Almer and Goeschl 2010). In the latter case of normative motivations, concern about gaining respect or incurring opprobrium from other group members also plays a role in encouraging compliance. We should also mention the impact of self-esteem when complying (or not) with the socially imprinted rules that establish, for most individuals, what is right and what is wrong.

In sum, managing environmental policies more efficiently will require a much deeper understanding of factors that explain the co-evolution of *norms* and *institutions*. More generally, the nature of our environmental *commons* makes it worthwhile for the social sciences to explore further the nature of individual preferences—and especially the processes by which they can be articulated to build the social preferences required for viable decisions about the commons.

1.4 DESIGNING *INCENTIVE MECHANISMS* WHEN CONSTRAINED BY A SOCIO-POLITICAL GAME

In the presence of externalities, letting agents decide how to use a resource leads to the impacts on others being ignored. Two solutions to this problem have been envisioned: implementing *property rights* (Section 1.4.1) and designing mechanisms to correct incentives (Section 1.4.2). However, with either approach the possible choices are constrained by the role of complex motivations and the logic of socio-political games. We insist here, and in this book, on the impact of the later on the implementability of these solutions.

1.4.1 The difficulties and dilemmas of creating a property rights system

Because they internalize or eliminate externalities, *property rights* can be a viable way of solving some problems of the global commons. Of course, the privatization of resources can generate a welfare loss because some parties are thereby deprived of access to the public good. But if perfectly defined and enforced, property rights allow decision makers to balance the social benefits and costs so that excessive extraction, pollution, or harvesting does not occur. Property rights can evolve bottom-up under international law; but where *transaction costs* preclude this process, property rights can be created top-down. Property rights involve issues of allocation, measurement, boundaries, and enforcement.

1.4.1.1 *The political economy of property rights design and distribution*

The assignment of property rights to address open access enables the most direct and transparent assignment of benefits and costs, yet it requires costly policies to implement them. Any meaningful property right involves exclusion, which has the potential to produce distributional conflicts. Furthermore, a property right may increase in value (for any number of reasons), in which case new wealth, status, and political influence is conferred on those who secure that right. Such changes alter existing social and political positions, inciting controversy that may be costly to politicians. Finally, constituencies that benefited from the previous regulatory arrangements are likely to be disadvantaged by any new rights system. Even inefficiencies can generate constituencies for maintaining the status quo. Demsetz (1967) suggests that property rights could emerge gradually with the rise in resource values, thus offsetting the costs of definition and enforcement. However, experience has indicated that the process of institutional change is more complex than Demsetz envisioned. Allocation is contentious because of the assignment of political influence and distribution of wealth associated with exclusive property rights. Political conflicts and negotiations determine the arrangements that ultimately emerge as well as their timing and effectiveness. For this reason, the political creation of property rights attracts rent-seeking efforts to influence their distribution—efforts that are costly in themselves.

1.4.1.2 *Three* allocation mechanisms

As emphasized by Coase (1960), allocation rules are always important for distribution and will affect efficiency in the presence of *transaction costs*. Worldwide, "prior use" is the dominant method used to establish property rights: it assigns ownership to the entities that implicitly and freely exercised the right prior to the scarcity created by the introduction of the new policy. Prior-use rules are attractive because they recognize incumbent parties, who will be important constituents in any distribution of property rights (given in particular their concern about past investment in specific assets); incumbents are typically the highest-valuing users once a new policy is initiated. Moreover, prior-use rules do not undermine efficiency. Instead they create opportunity costs, which will lead recipients to treat these rights as a valuable asset and to use them judiciously—including experimentation with ways to increase the efficiency of resource use in response to the new cost. Another advantage of prior-use arrangements is that the pre-policy market determines the optimal claim size. In contrast, assignments under other allocation systems are determined by bureaucratic or political considerations. If the results are not compatible with optimal production size then further trade is required, and if *transaction costs* are high then such exchange may be limited.

Rules based on equal sharing bypass distributional procedures based on prior use and better reflect egalitarian goals. If there are no restrictions on the subsequent exchange of property rights and if *transaction costs* are low, then equal sharing has few efficiency implications because the resource still migrates to high-value users. In addition, a uniform allocation avoids the costs associated with verifying claims about past production or use and can also avoid the inefficiencies—in particular, overinvestment in the race to capture property rights—that result when a forthcoming allocation rule is known to be based on prior use. A lottery is one example of a uniform allocation.

A third allocation mechanism is the auction. Auctions put assets directly into the hands of those who place the highest value on them, thereby avoiding the *transaction costs* of reallocation. Auctions also generate resources for the state and avoid "windfall" profits, which could be divisive if viewed as being unearned. Auction returns can be used to cover the costs of defining and enforcing property rights and other costs of resource management, as well as to fund a wide range of other social policies, including the reduction of distortionary taxes on factors of production. As with lotteries, auctions work best for new, unallocated resources for which there are no incumbent claimants. Incumbents naturally resist auctions for the allocation of rights: they do not wish to pay for something to which they consider themselves already entitled by virtue of their prior use. Auctions can be employed in conjunction with other allocation arrangements to provide an "adjustment margin," as may be needed when some parties are not allocated enough property rights for efficient production yet the *transaction costs* of increasing them are high.

1.4.1.3 The timing dilemma

Our discussion of allocation mechanisms suggests that there is an underlying *collective action* problem associated with the definition and assignment of property rights. The main issue is that establishing property rights involves high resource and political costs relative to their expected gains, at least in the short term. The issues become even more problematic when multiple parties claim a stake in the resource. Then an open-access equilibrium is often self-sustainable from a political standpoint despite entailing inefficiencies and resource depletion.

Even if collective action has previously been impossible, it can become more likely when a crisis occurs. New information emerges about the severity of the problem, which decreases uncertainty and measurement costs while reducing information asymmetries. The resource becomes more valuable (perhaps owing to its greater depletion), and this increases the benefits of action. New techniques or technologies are developed to lower the costs of closing the externality. Finally, the number of involved parties declines to reflect the decline in private returns to exploitation.

It should be clear that, just as in the national political arena, politicians have incentives to delay action until there is a crisis. The open-access problem is serious enough to generate the information needed to clarify the distribution of costs and benefits across and within countries and constituencies. Only then will politicians be able to mobilize political support for action that requires costly production adjustments as well as transfers, both internal and external, to mobilize collective efforts.

The point is that establishing property rights may result in serious short-comings. There is often a war of attrition between the various stakeholders, each of which wants the others to pay for the privatization process. This is why property rights might not be established until *after* the resource has already been overexploited and mismanaged. Note also that, to shore up their support, politicians influence the assignment of property rights so as to weaken the regime's ability to manage the considered resource more efficiently.

1.4.2 *Mechanism design*: playing off the cushion

1.4.2.1 *Incentive mechanisms*

The property rights approach rests on the possibility of excluding agents from the benefits of a good unless they have a specific right to enjoy it. But excludability is often not possible because it is too costly or difficult to implement. In such cases, outside intervention is necessary. An externality can be viewed as an unpriced commodity, so another option is to create a market for the externality. This approach is known as the "mechanism design" solution.

This idea has led to a broad literature on the use of economic *incentives* to reach environmental goals. The term "economic" is usually reserved for incentives that specify a particular goal but leave it for market participants to decide (via financial incentives) how that outcome is reached. Thus, environmental taxes and emission trading are normally considered to be examples of market- or incentive-based instruments. Yet if this notion is taken literally then the more traditional legal policy instruments (such as liability rules and regulation) are also incentive-based because they incentivize market participants to reach a particular policy goal (such as reducing specific emissions). The main differences between the two instrument types are the amount of flexibility allowed and the sanctions applied if a particular goal is not reached.

We should, however, consider still another perspective. It is based on the idea that most environmental goods are jointly produced in that they draw from ecological systems, which from a production perspective are multiproduct and multiprocess by definition. The provision of clean, drinkable water to an increasing urban population can employ natural filtration techniques, which require natural spaces and especially forested areas. Forests are carbon sinks as well as reservoirs of biodiversity. Therefore, revenues generated by the provision of water to cities (and to agriculture) can and should be "socialized" to fund reforestation and support populations living in forested areas. In the spirit of the Rio convention on biodiversity, the provision of many (public) goods could be cross-subsidized by marketing jointly provided goods for which exclusion is manageable. Of course, this in turn would raise the issue of monitoring cross-subsidies to avoid mismanagement of resources and could also cause other socio-political distortions.

1.4.2.2 *The issue of compatibility*

When considering multilayered governance, we must not overlook a key issue: the possibility of interplay between policy instruments that are implemented at different levels. These instruments may even be in conflict and destroy each other's effectiveness. The solution to this problem is multilevel coordination; the issue has been partially addressed in the literature, and there are three main strands. The first concerns policies that have a harmful impact on the environment, usually because their effect on pollution has been completely ignored (OECD 2007). The second strand is devoted to fiscal policy and explores how implementing a carbon tax may be suboptimal unless pre-existing taxes are taken into account (Wendner and Goulder 2008). Third, some studies have examined the interplay between supranational regulations (e.g. markets for tradable permits) and national fiscal policies. It has been shown that such interactions are sources of inefficiencies and that promoting higher-level regulation *without* lower-level harmonization may not be optimal. See, for example, Santore et al. (2001) on the US sulfur dioxide market and Bréchet et al. (2007) on the EU's Emissions Trading System.

Important elements of continued compatibility include regular assessment of the contributions of each implementation mechanism as well as democratic debate about these evaluations. Also critical are forms of reflexive governance that involve communities and social networks in the implementation frameworks.

1.5 CONCLUSION: THE CHALLENGES OF POLYCENTRIC AND NETWORKED GOVERNANCE

Taken together, the distinctive features of the governance of environmental issues call for innovation in systems of governance. We will explore in particular two promising trends—decentralized networked governance in federal systems and global environmental governance—that developed in response to the shifting demands on governance. We also ask a series of questions about the capacity of these governance forms to handle a range of issues involving scale, time, and uncertainty.

Decentralized (or polycentric) networked governance has been extensively studied (Reinicke and Deng 2000; E. Ostrom 2001; Hajer and Wagenaar 2003; Haas 2004; Slaughter 2004). It can be characterized as an attempt to take into account the increasing importance of NGOs, the private sector, scientific networks, and international organizations in performing various governance functions. The aim of networked governance is to foster synergy between different types and sources of knowledge in order to deal with complex and interlinked problems. From this perspective, governance is best accomplished through decentralized networks of private and public actors associated with international, national, and regional organizations.

However, we have seen that such a mode of governance is insufficient in cases of systemic change. Here, interdependencies may dictate that individual networks act in ways that run counter to the actions of others. Under the Montreal protocol, for example, China could start producing CFCs even as other countries were cooperating to reduce their production. Global environmental governance is the answer to problems raised by functional interdependencies on a global scale.

These trends are illustrated by an especially interesting example of global governance: the Earth System Science Partnership (Biermann 2007). In 2001, four global change programs—DIVERSITAS, the International Geosphere–Biosphere Programme, the World Climate Research Programme, and the International Human Dimensions Programme on Global Environmental Change—joined forces to intensify their cooperation through the establishment of an overarching Earth System Science Partnership. The research communities represented in this partnership contend that the earth system now operates "well outside the normal state exhibited over the past 500,000 years" and that "human activity is generating change that extends well beyond natural variability—in some cases, alarmingly so—and at rates that continue to accelerate" (Biermann 2007). To cope with this challenge, the four global change research programs have called urgently for "an ethical framework for global stewardship and strategies for Earth System management" (Steffen et al. 2004).

Both global environmental governance and decentralized or polycentric networked governance are emerging as responses to the *collective action* problems raised by environmental goods and the need to address them. These governance modes share two important features: (1) recognition of the role played by hybrid networks composed of state actors and nonstate actors (civil society, community organizations, nonprofit organizations, industry associations) in providing different types of collective goods; and (2) assignment of new roles to government (Delmas and Young, 2009).

In the case of decentralized or polycentric networked governance, the new role of governments is to facilitate network dynamics. Previously, the government's role in regulating networks was restricted to managing negative externalities—as generated, for example, by the capture of rents in network industries. The rents and the externalities remain, but network activities are increasingly situated in a complex web of interdependencies that entail both positive and negative effects. In this new context, governments must not only manage negative externalities but also facilitate the generation of positive network effects, such as the provision of collective goods. Governments have consequently become more involved in such activities as stimulation of social learning, building of adaptive capacities, support for research into standardization, and other issues of common concern.

In the case of Earth system governance, global arrangements are created that place new constraints on member states. These constraints can take the form of new independent authorities of last resort (e.g. independent dispute resolution authorities), global funding schemes, or a set of instruments designed to relay information and improve coordination. In this context, states become intermediary players between the demands and constraints of lower-level constituencies on the one hand and, on the other hand, the global order consisting of different state and nonstate actors.

Part I

Global Issues: Environmental and Governance Challenges

Part I is dedicated to the presentation of global issues, the challenges they raise for societies and their environment and the need for new governance architectures. As such Part I does not tackle directly the three main questions addressed in this book, but rather delineates the framework within which the answers to these will be provided in the three following parts. This framework is set up by three complementary contributions by Arild Vatn, Charles Perrings, and Oran Peyton Young.

The chapter by Arild Vatn points out the crucial need for an understanding of natural interdependences for designing new instruments that will help to address the environmental challenges. He makes a strong claim about the weakness of existing institutions for governing contemporary environmental challenges: the currently predominating regime of private markets combined with ex post regulation is flawed to govern "generalized interdependencies." As potential "solutions" to the coordination problem, Vatn suggests ex ante regulation, stronger involvement of the state as a property-owning actor, and the increased use of common property regimes. Vatn advocates the need for a coupled development of institutional structures across the boundaries that often separate the state, markets, and community-based means of coordination.

The chapter by Charles Perrings extends Arild Vatn's intra-state analysis to a broader perspective and into an international setup. The author demonstrates how aspects such as the bio-physical properties, spatial and temporal scales, the supply technology, and existing governance regimes impact on the strategic incentives for governing public goods. Understanding the implications of these aspects, Perrings states, is a necessary condition for the implementation of effective governance mechanisms. A key issue is that a single problem of environmental governance can involve multiple goods, each of which might operate at a different scale and lead to a different kind of strategic game. Careful analysis of the public goods at stake and of the structure of the payoffs of alternative strategies is therefore needed to design systems of governance which overcome the non-cooperative status quo. The global integration of essential issues through webs of dynamic processes calls for alternative ways to institutionally connect actions that normally have no direct relationship to or impact on each other.

The chapter by Oran Young adds another dimension to the analysis of why environmental governance is challenging and why it needs innovative institutional approaches. The author points out that our usual policy instruments presume that changes occur in a linear, gradual, and reversible fashion. However, many biophysical and socio-economic processes are non-linear, discontinuous, abrupt, and often irreversible. Matching institutional governance regimes to these systemically inherent features constitutes a major challenge and calls for new institutional arrangements which reflect these aspects. According to Young, reflexivity, enhanced adaptive capacity which most prominently includes continuous monitoring, and better ways to cope with uncertainty are essential criteria that need to be taken up in the new institutional arrangements. It is compelling in this view to be able to combine formal and informal arrangements, in order to meet the challenges of nonlinear, abrupt, and irreversible changes, at least in the short run. This would provide policy makers with tools that not only capture the systemic features of socio-ecological systems, but also offer sufficient degrees of flexibility to adjust policy trajectories to abrupt and discontinuous changes.

2

Environmental Governance: The Aspect of Coordination*

Arild Vatn

2.1 INTRODUCTION

The main challenge facing environmental governance is to institutionally connect actions that are physically connected by necessity. Human action is interconnected through changes we make in the various biogeochemical cycles of the earth's system—for example, the carbon and nitrogen cycles. More generally, the common-pool characteristics of environmental resources like space, water, and air make the act of one influence the opportunities for others. The increased scale of economic activity has augmented the magnitude of these interconnections vastly, and the perspective taken here is that we seriously lag behind regarding the process of institutionally reconnecting choices made by various separated decision units.

In its basic form, the problem is rather simple. A set of decision units exists using resources with consequences going beyond the borders of each unit. The problem is to ensure that these consequences are taken into account when decisions are made. In reality, however, the problem is very challenging as the number of units is large, the effects are geographically often very widely spread, and the environmental systems with which human activities interact are incredibly complex, involving time lags and non-linear responses.

Solutions to these challenges often take the form of incremental adjustments to existing institutional structures. While there are certainly merits to such a procedure, one risks "painting oneself into a corner." In the medium to long run, the effects of this ad hoc or piecemeal strategy could be very problematic indeed. My reasoning is based on the fact that present institutional structures for economic activity are to a large extent developed as if environmental interconnections were insignificant. At a time when we realize

* The author would like to thank Malte Faber and Valborg Kvakkestad for comments to an earlier draft.

that this is not the case any longer, we should take stock and allow ourselves to think more fundamentally about the roads ahead.

The aim of this chapter is therefore to give an assessment of a set of alternatives that could strengthen coordination. While institutional reform in practice will have to be contextual, I have here chosen to focus on a set of generic solutions to coordination problems. This is motivated by a need to strengthen the debate over the more fundamental choices we are facing. This demands an analysis of type solutions, being complementary to the equally important contextualized studies. In doing this, I have chosen to delimit the analysis in this paper to the state and intra-state level. This is a vast simplification as environmental problems to a large extent are international. It is, however, also so that very many of the principal questions concerning environmental governance can be treated when looking at the coordination problems appearing at the state/intra-state level.

The paper is divided into four sections. First, I will specify what I mean by the concept of a coordination problem. Next, I move to the issue of governance. Here I will first offer a description of a set of generic resource regimes and next characterize the presently dominating governance system and discuss the way we currently try to handle environmental coordination. A set of serious shortcomings and principal contradictions is observed. Section 2.4 is hence devoted to sketch alternative ways to the contemporary solution, giving also a brief assessment of these. Certainly, no new system can forget the past. No ideal system exists. We will have to choose among various shortcomings. Therefore, the chapter closes with a discussion of the realism of various solutions against present trends. It also offers a set of cautions as to how the assessments made in this chapter should be taken forward.

2.2 THE COORDINATION PROBLEM

Coordination is about facilitating interactions between agents that can produce wanted or better outcomes according to some standard. Coordination is involved when producing and trading goods. It is also about handling external effects of various actions. In the context of this paper, it will be useful to distinguish between coordination problems where action is *independent* and where it is *interdependent*. Coordination concerning independent acts will here be termed *simple coordination* problems. Coordination concerning acts that are interdependent will be termed *complex coordination* problems.[1]

---

[1] For those familiar with the language of game theory, it should be noted that the concept of a coordination problem as defined here goes beyond that of a coordination game. First, it includes coordination when there are no games—when choices are independent as in (competitive)

Human coordination involves institutions—a set of conventions, norms, or formal rules that define outcomes (Scott 1995; Vatn 2005). There are three issues of importance when studying coordination. First, we have the rights governing distribution of resources or endowments—the basis from where any activity can take place. Rights concern also rights to potential cost shifting between decision units. Certainly, this brings elements of conflict into the issue of coordination as understood here—that is, rights is about whose interests get protection. Hence, protecting access to a resource for some implies the exclusion of others. Cost shifting may be a wanted outcome as seen by those causing it.

Second, we have the costs of coordination—that is, transaction costs. Note that if coordination is cost free, there is no way to distinguish between different institutional structures concerning coordination. Competitive markets, oligopolistic structures, firms, state organizations, etc. are equally efficient (Williamson 1985).

Finally, we have the issue of motivation and how institutional structures influence these. This is an issue that is rarely covered in the literature on coordination. Agents are mostly taken to behave according to the same logic independent of under which institutional structure they operate. If choices are interdependent they are typically assumed to act strategically. This assumption will be challenged in this chapter. Certainly, coordination problems may often have solutions that somebody disapproves of. At the same time, norms about good conduct or responsibilities for future generations may over-ride the more narrow personal interest.

While we often encounter the idea that it is theoretically permissible to assume a world of no transaction costs—for example, standard welfare theory—I find that discarding transaction costs from the analysis of coordination is erroneous not least at the level of theoretical analysis. Note that the cost of coordination depends on the institutional structure—for example, the number and type of transactions necessary to handle a coordination problem, and the capacity of the individuals included. Hence, a comparative study of institutional structures—be it empirical or theoretical—must include the costs of coordination. I will have more to say about this issue later. For now it is sufficient to emphasize the restricted cognitive capacity of individuals.

Given this, a *simple coordination problem* involves choices with only trivial information problems and no external effects. The former can be illustrated by

---

market coordination. Second, coordination games are typically seen as symmetric and cover situations where both (all) parties gain from making mutually consistent decisions—e.g. agree on a set of technology standards, agree on which side of the road to drive, etc. While some of the situations named complex coordination problems above will be of this kind, some will be asymmetric or involve what in game theory are characterized as cooperation problems—i.e. where there is no stable cooperative solution to the game given standard assumptions about strategic behavior.

a situation where all agents involved have a set of endowments—while being of different kinds, the elements of each kind are homogeneous.[2] Using or transforming these assets results, moreover, in homogeneous goods. The coordination problem concerns how the various assets can be combined to produce the goods wanted and next distributed or exchanged. This is the standard case of pure exchange as described in neoclassical welfare theory where markets are able to coordinate action in the sense of producing Pareto optimal outcomes. The findings of welfare theory, however, demands the assumption of zero transaction costs to universally hold. As emphasized above, under this assumption it is impossible to distinguish between different institutional structures on standard efficiency grounds. They may work differently concerning distribution and motivational structures, though.

In the case of complex coordination problems, I will distinguish between two types relying on the kind of interdependency involved. In the case of a *complex coordination problem* with *specific interdependency* there is interdependency between parties that engage directly with each other—typically a two- or few-party relation. It may be the result of characteristics of the involved good. A case much emphasized in the literature concerns contracts over specific as opposed to homogeneous assets—for example, Williamson (1985, 2005). Asset specificity creates interdependency as the parties to a deal face problems with defining the various characteristics of what is to be produced/delivered. Given positive transaction costs/limited cognitive capacity, this is a situation which leads to incomplete contracts. In the literature, hierarchical solutions like firms are then favored over markets.

In the case of a *complex coordination problem* with *generalized interdependency* there is indirect interdependency. Agents' choices are interdependent because they take place in a common environment where choices have implications beyond the one/those directly acting. This is typically due to the interlinkages in that environment. Generally, endowments are not separable items. They are relational goods as they are integrated in webs of dynamic processes—for example, biological/ecosystem processes.

Given the kind of world we live in, it is actually hard to imagine any coordination problem that does not involve some generalized interdependencies. All production activities demand inputs of natural resources which next change their characteristics. Moreover, all production and consumption results in waste. There is no "free disposal." So at both the "input" and "output" side of economic activities some consequences with implications for others not directly involved will appear. If these are minor, building institutional structures that disregard them may be acceptable. If they are more substantial, this may not be the case.

---

[2] I.e., no variation in quality across assets of the same kind.

2.3 GOVERNANCE

In relation to the above I will define governance as the establishment, maintenance, and change of institutions to foster coordination and resolving conflicts. The subset of environmental governance is then governance related to coordination and resolving conflict over the use and maintenance of environmental resources—cf. also Paavola (2007).

Governance is, however, not only about institutions. It certainly also includes the actors that form and are formed by these institutions. It includes the state/the government, communities, businesses, and nongovernmental organizations (NGOs). The institutions form the positions of and relationships between these actors. In relation to this, the concept of resource regimes is core.

2.3.1 Resource regimes

A resource regime is here understood as the institutional structures governing the use of resources in the production of goods and services. Two issues are central: the rules governing *access* to productive resources and the rules concerning the *interactions* between actors having such access. The first element covers property rights and use rights as defined by formal or customary law. It distributes resources between actors and defines rules concerning the transfer of the resource itself. The second element—the interaction rules—consists of rules for the transfer of the outputs from production between the actors. Note that what is output could be both goods/services and "side-effects" like pollution. Hence, the rules regulating the "transfer" of the side-effects of production—what is protected or forbidden cost-shifting—are also included under the concept of interaction rules.

Concerning access, we may simplify and look only at property rights. It is standard to distinguish between four broad types of such rights: private property, public/state property, common property, and open access (Bromley 2006). They are legal rules implying that a third party—normally the state—guarantees the access of the property owner to certain benefit streams. In this sense a property right is a social relation between the rights holder and the rights regarders as defined and supported by a specific authority structure.

Moving to the interactions between actors, we may also divide into four classes. First, we have *exchange*. This is interaction between parties that are formally equal—horizontal interaction. It is what takes place in markets when goods and services are transacted. As a type form, exchange is thought of as non-relational—as impersonal. Second, we have *command*. This type of interaction is based on hierarchical power, typically resting with the state.[3] It is this power that is used to guarantee legally defined property rights. It is also used to set up programs of redistribution. It is this type of interaction that is used when public standards are set concerning product quality and when rights and responsibility concerning pollution are defined. The third category of interaction is *community-based interaction rules*, of which *reciprocity* is a typical form. These interactions are also operating horizontally. They differ from exchanges in being relational and personal. Note that community rules "regulate" many pollution activities. They are typically including norms concerning how we are allowed to intrude into each other's "everyday" lives. Finally, we have *no rules* as a fourth option. This implies that actors are free to do whatever they wish despite the consequences for others. Side-effects like pollution often originate in this category giving an implicit "right" to the emitters.

Together the four property rights structures and four interaction rules create 16 possible type combinations—see Table 2.1.

The distinction between the types of property rights is not very clearcut (Vatn 2001). Public or state property could, as an example, be viewed as a special form of common property (cf. also Paavola 2007). Likewise, there are similarities between some types of private and common property.[4] Finally, all three forms of property except open access include some kind of internal hierarchical or command structures. Even in the case of common property—the type with the strongest horizontal coordination—there is a hierarchy related to the internal coordination rules where some common decision procedures are made to facilitate cooperation. Hence, there are both operational

Table 2.1. Resource regimes

Type of property right Type of interaction	Private property	Public Property	Common property	Open access
Market exchange				
Command—state/public-based interaction rules				
Reciprocity—community-based interaction rules				
No distribution rules				

[3] Note that the firm is also a command structure (Williamson 1985). While important to observe, command here concerns only internal relationships. It is an aspect of the type of property right. Hence, it is not relevant to include it when studying rules governing interaction between actors. In the case of the state, it has command power both over other actors and internally. It is the former power that is emphasized here.

[4] For a more elaborate presentation of the way I see this, see Vatn (2001; 2005). See also Bromley (1991; 2006).

and collective-choice rules (Ostrom E. 2005b). The aim here is still not to delve into the "grey" areas, but to emphasize the type characteristics of the four categories.

While property rights are important as they take sides in resource conflicts, they also function as coordination devices. The same concerns the interaction rules. As emphasized in the literature on business organization, one important issue is which rule is the best to use. The dominant literature on this—for example, Coase (1937, 1992); Williamson (1975, 1985, 1999, 2005) concerns the choice between hierarchies (firms) and markets and relate to the economizing of transaction or coordination costs. Hence, there are substitution opportunities between the two types of coordination—the within and between entities coordination.

One might typically link private property and market exchange, state property with command-/state-based interaction rules and common property with reciprocity-/community-based interaction rules. There is, however, no reason why products from, for example, a state-owned entity, could not be distributed in markets. Similarly, products from a private property could be distributed using public distribution rules. Examples are abundant—for example, publicly owned electricity plants selling energy in markets; private health businesses distributing their services according to a set of publicly defined rules.

Concerning interaction, we have emphasized outputs—both goods/services and side-effects or waste. The latter creates complex coordination problems of the generalized type, and demand ownership and distribution rules. Actually, as all production in the end becomes waste, these rules may be seen as at least as important as the rules for handling the goods and services. The fact that we do not seem to have realized this yet will be treated in the next section.

The fundamental question related to the above is how well different regimes facilitate coordination over both products and waste. So far institutional development over the former issue has dominated—that concerning simple coordination and complex coordination problems of specific interdependence. As the amount of generalized interdependencies increases, the regime question is shifted towards evaluating the trade-off between the capacity to coordinate the production of goods and how easy it becomes to coordinate waste handling and side-effects. In relation to this, it should be noted that regimes (e.g., legal regulation, taxes) influence both which side-effects appear and how they can be treated.

2.3.2 Resource management: the character of present governance systems

All the sixteen resource regimes illustrated by Table 2.1 can be found in practice. Nevertheless, if we look at production—measured both in economic terms and in tons of material throughput—the dominant resource regime at present is that of private properties/firms operating in markets. This is, however, only half the story since for waste output the dominant situation is open access and no distribution rules. Historically, the treatment of waste was very much handled by community norms. The tremendous growth of these flows over the past century has vastly transcended the community as a unit for coordination. It has been gradually regulated mainly by increasing the role of state/public distribution rules (e.g., legal regulations, taxes). Presently, though, we are witnessing an increased interest in market solutions also in this area— for example, payments for environmental services (Wunder 2005).

In relation to the above, we should first note that the state as third party has played a fundamental role in the deliberate construction of the private property–market regime. The history of this regime is long and consists of many turns both concerning the establishment and expansion of private property—types of firms and the rules governing these—and the format of markets (e.g. Veblen 1904; Commons 1934; Polanyi 1944; Bakan 2004). Finally, states have played a decisive role also in constructing rules for the interactions of private properties/firms across state borders, such as the Bretton Woods institutions, the GATT/WTO, etc. One of the basic aims behind establishing private property has been to ascertain security for investments through establishing a direct link between activity and individual returns from that activity. Not least through the creation of the stock holding company, the dynamism was substantially expanded as individual capitals could be easily pooled. Together with various trade liberalization efforts, this has created a very forceful system resulting in a level of economic growth that is historically unprecedented.[5] A core element in this has been to foster *separation of decisions* and hence *separation of responsibilities*. From the above, this system works best, however, for simple coordination problems. It may function reasonably well also in the case of a complex coordination problem with specific interdependency—for example, high asset specificity. Under these conditions, formulating market contracts is demanding, resulting in high transaction costs, and we observe the tendency to move from market coordination to hierarchical structures such as vertically integrated firms (Williamson 1985, 2005). While this shifts the power from the market to

---

[5] Certainly, the level of growth experienced in China during the last couple of decennia with a combination of state property/command and "free" enterprise indicates that this "hybrid" may outcompete the more pure firm–market regime. Moreover, the introduction of the welfare state—taken to its farthest development in Scandinavia—indicates that economic growth may not be hampered by a large public sector. The opposite may rather be the case. Whether privatization always is a success in growth terms is also an issue with certain qualifications— e.g., Rozell and Swinnen (2004) comparing the transition of agriculture in China and the former Soviet Union.

inside the firm, it is nevertheless a development within the market–private property or market–firm resource regime.

2.3.2.1 *The market–firm regime and generalized interdependencies*

The main problem with the market–firm regime in connection to the issues discussed here is its inability to handle generalized interdependencies. One type is the kind illustrated by the present financial crisis, where there are interdependencies in expectations' formation following from tremendous information problems/restricted cognitive capacities in a system with many independent decision units. The more important effect of separation is, in our case, nonetheless related to the effects on natural resource qualities and management. In a system where natural resource use is divided into separate entities and all interaction happens through markets, the only way that coordination of the utilization of natural resources can happen is through the price mechanism. This demands next that all resources are owned and that the price mechanism works properly. Let me start with the latter.

According to Hayek (1931, 1948) the price mechanism is superior as it is able to solve the vast information problem that humans face when coordinating their activities. He emphasizes that knowledge is local and specific. The strength of the market is that it does not depend on anyone possessing all this localized knowledge. The price mechanism distributes the information necessary "to coordinate the separate action of different people" (Hayek 1948: 85).

There are two problems related to this reasoning (see also O'Neill 1998). The first concerns the problem of making decisions into the future, as commodity prices only convey information about the present and not about future plans. Firms have motives not to offer such information. The second problem—the one of most interest to us—concerns whether the price conveys the most relevant type of information processing for capturing the status of ecosystems/environmental resources. These are complex entities with a multiplicity of dimensions as they are also involved in a multitude of processes. As emphasized by Martinez-Alier et al. (1998) and Vatn and Bromley (1994), there is a tremendous reduction of information involved when condensing this information into one price. Certainly, for coordination to be possible, some loss of detail is necessary. The question is whether the price mechanism offers the relevant loss of detail for environmental governance to work well.[6]

---

[6] In his discussion of control hierarchies in natural systems, Patte (1973) studies their structure–function duality—the interface between the detail of structure and the abstraction of function. Here he emphasizes that a function or control can only arise through some selective loss of detail. The question of importance in our case is what functions should be defined and supported and hence which loss of detail is preferable.

There are strong arguments for this not being the case. The market price is a measure of relative scarcity based on aggregate demand. Even when we simplify the issue to focus only on the demands for securing the functionalities of a resource at hand—for example, sidestepping the various ethical issues involved[7]—we observe large problems. As environmental resources are integrated in webs of relations, it is their role in the functioning of these wholes that is the important question. These relations are first of all situated locally. Hence, their importance varies across space and time demanding local prices. Second, while each of the multiple functions that a resource expresses represents a simplification of information, collapsing all of these functions into one measure demands substitutability between them. While some natural resources can be substituted for each other in functional terms—consider the fact that different species can deliver the same function(s)—this does not imply that it is a generalizable feature. Rather, natural resource systems are characterized by complementarities, hence restricted substitution possibilities.

So even if we assume that Hayek is right in his claim that the price of *a commodity* is the only message that is needed for agents to make their decisions whether or not to buy that commodity in their local contexts, the argument must be turned on its head when looking at the making of the commodity or the disposing of the commodity after it is reduced to waste. Concerning production, the commodity itself carries scant information about the changes in the functioning of the systems from which the resources necessary to make that commodity were taken. If these consequences or costs are shifted beyond the firm making it, no information is captured. If they are within these bounds, they are reduced to one dimension—that of exchange value.

Finally, natural living systems are characterized by discontinuities—that is, they embody thresholds with rather abrupt changes when these thresholds are exceeded (Perrings 1997). This implies that up to a certain level, changing a living system may not change its fundamental functioning. This is the obvious result from the observation that living systems have evolved so that different processes (species) deliver the same function(s). This makes the system resilient and has been important for it to handle changes in its environment. Nevertheless, beyond a certain level of change, the fundamental dynamics of a system may be changed—an attractor shift has occurred. A price, as a measure of marginal values, is specifically unable to capture this.

The other side of the above "coin" is that attaching private property to all environmental resources is for practical purposes impossible. As environmental resources are foremost interlinked processes, dividing them into separate

---

[7] As emphasized in the philosophical literature, ethical issues like those concerning the rights of species are of another kind than issues concerning the utility of consumers—they belong to two incommensurable value dimensions (e.g. O'Neill 1993; Holland 2002).

units would either destroy their functional capacities or just be a formality, implying that the processes would *de facto* transcend the different units of decision making. To the extent that these processes are changed, we will observe *specific and/or generalized cost shifting*.

Certainly, if a meaningful set of local prices could be attached to each of these "costs"—actually making markets for all processes with their specific and generalized effects—the regime could still do well. The problem is that by splitting up the protected access to the resources into individual pieces, the number of processes that are interrupted and the number of borders across which this interruption happens is vast. So as Bromley (1990) has emphasized, what makes the internal system work well—the maximization of competing units in markets—also maximizes the transaction costs related to the bargaining over side-effects or cost shifting.

2.3.2.2 The capacities of ex post state regulation

Certainly, the above problem has resulted in increased "state intervention" in the form of legal regulations—for example, the prohibition of certain cost shifting activities—or by installing economic instruments like taxes or tradable quotas. Hence, as economic activity has increased—driven by the internal dynamism of the resource regime—the enlarged amount of cost shifting created has been countered by expanding the role of the state as a third party.

The main effect of this is the establishment of a hierarchical control resulting in reduced transaction costs, making it possible to handle many "externalities" or cost-shifting activities which would escape the market. Following the ideas of Simon (1973), the hierarchy represents a simplification of the information flow. First, each economic agent needs to confront only one other agent—the state—and not the web of interrelations established through the flows of matter across the borders of myriads of other entities—generalized interdependence. Second, the hierarchy offers the option to classify—to group units at the lower level and treat them as similar under one authority structure. Combined, these two mechanisms reduce necessary transactions and information flows vastly, making it possible to treat a series of interrelationships that would evade any horizontal treatment. Certainly, establishing, for example, taxes reflecting the cost of emissions at the margin is not a simple task, and even the state needs to balance the cost of setting up precise regulations against the gain of being precise (Vatn 1998).

While state regulations have made it possible to make a lot of progress in the field of environmental governance, there are plenty of challenges ahead. I would like to emphasize two, which were both implicit in the above. The first concerns the two-stage character of the instituted processes. The second concerns the trade-off between simplification and specificity of knowledge that this system also faces.

Concerning the first issue—the two-stage character of the instituted processes—the challenge relates to the sequencing of decision making and information flows. While the economic units at level 1 of the system—firms—are controlled by a level 2 set of institutional structures—as formulated by the state—this control is based on the assumption that ex post correction is sufficient. By ex post I mean that state regulation is instituted after harm is observed and the cause of the harm is proven. The historical development of the system was—as emphasized above—based on separating decision units and fostering horizontal interaction in markets. The system really established an unbounded type of positive feedback where the growth of one unit supported the growth of others.[8] As already emphasized, doing so must have been based on the belief that physical interdependencies across separated units would cause only minor problems that could be forgotten or efficiently corrected ex post.

At the present stage it becomes more and more problematic that the economic system is based on allowing agents to develop through various positive feedback as if there were no (or just minor) unnoticed influences across the borders of these agents—that is, no specific or generalized interdependency. When the problem grows large enough so that the second level agent—the state—observes that there is a problem, it must prove what causes it, and finally institute a reaction if the gain of doing so is found to be sufficiently large. There is a problem of time lag in this. Past harm will not be treated. Time spans from the problem first being caused till action is taken may cover several decennia or even centuries—for example, European Environment Agency (2001). Moreover, as resources cannot be reallocated without costs, we observe path dependency or lock in. This implies that the costs of correcting a problem ex post depends on previous investment decisions made under the assumption that there would be no problem. In addition, those involved in producing under this assumption will be interested in protecting the status quo rules. Hence, the two-stage model produces interests that will oppose regulations, as that will imply a shift of costs back on them. Path dependency is not only technical or economic. It also becomes political.

One could certainly argue that the system is in its making and that over the longer run this problem will disappear as rules will gradually change the path and hence also the interests involved. This conclusion seems to underestimate the combined effect of creativity and path dependency. The level 1 agents—the firms—face institutional structures that motivate them to construct new products and new production processes. This is the way they can establish an edge towards other competing units. So new types of potential cost shifting will steadily be produced. The level 2 agent—the regulator/the state—is hence

---

[8] cf. Says law.

facing a quickly moving target which can only be influenced by historically proven cost shifting, not by the new or emerging types. Taken together the two-stage model—the ex post regulation model—will produce a path that is very different from what could be envisioned by other institutional structures. Specifically, the path we are now on implies a steadily increased level of economic activity measured in gross domestic product (GDP) terms at about a factor of 8–10 per century (Vatn 2008a). The present financial crisis indicates quite strongly that the working of the system moreover depends on such growth. While growth in GDP does not demand a similar increase in material throughput and energy use, the aggregated implications of 2–2.5 percent growth over time demonstrates a need for thinking creatively about other forms of regulation.

Concerning the second problem—the trade-off between needed simplification in information flows and the specificity of knowledges necessary for local management—the state–firm hierarchy faces several challenges, too. These concern both the specificities of natural resource dynamics, and that of human motivation. Certainly, Hayek is right in emphasizing that local knowledge is specific and that the state cannot collect and handle all this information. Rather, for the functioning of the state regulation, loss of detail is necessary. On the other hand, knowledge of some detail is important when carrying out actions at the lower level. Hence, state action depends on its necessarily coarse messages being transformed into lower-level action that is more informed and specific. This demands that it must become in the interest of the lower-level units not just to follow the coarse message to the minimum—that is, exploit the fact that the state has restricted capacity in evaluating and controlling lower-level action—it also demands that lower-level units internalize the goals formulated at the higher level and take local action that is well adapted to their circumstances.

There are certainly huge variations in what is demanded, as the information problems vary substantially across topics. Hence, in the case of homogeneous emissions from economic activity—by which I mean that an input into the economy results in the same environmental consequence independent of how it is used and where emissions take place[9]—information problems at the interface between the controlling and the operative level are relatively small. As in the case of CO_2 emissions from fossil fuels, a tax or tradable quota on inputs is in principle all that is needed if we look at it in pure informational terms. The amount of CO_2 emissions is proportional to the input and where the emissions happen it has no impact on the climate change effect. Since fossil fuel is a marketed good, it is technically quite easy to regulate this way.[10]

---

[9] See Vatn (1998) for further clarification and proofs.

[10] Certainly, it may still be very demanding to put such regulations in place as they will have great negative implications for many economic agents and these will be interested in questioning

In the case of ecosystem management, including adaptation to climate change, effects are localized and/or dependent on the specific technology used. In such situations regulation is technically much more demanding. To get good results, the lower-level agents have to take the aim of the policy—not only the specific signal or incentive directed at their behavior—into account to ensure a necessary transformation of the regulatory message to the local context.[11]

2.4 ALTERNATIVE DIRECTIONS TO TAKE

The above characterization of the problems we face is meant as a basis for starting to think about alternative ways to organize ourselves to better handle generalized interdependencies. This is both a huge intellectual and political problem. While my area is the former, I certainly acknowledge that we are far away from having solutions even at the conceptual level. I will nevertheless try to take some steps further to indicate the kind of issues we are up against. As already emphasized, I will restrict myself to the problem at the level of a single state.

I will briefly indicate three different paths to follow. First, I will look at a change in the present regime based on private property/firms and markets moving from ex post to ex ante state regulations of externalities. Next, I will look at a movement towards increasing the role of the state as property owner, and finally I will look at an increased role of common property and civil society engagement. In comparing these three alternatives, both information/ transaction cost issues and the kind of motivational structures that are fostered through the various institutional arrangements will be underlined.

Emphasizing these alternatives, we are far from exhausting all opportunities. One alternative to ex ante regulation could be to institute full liability for future consequences of agents' economic choices. Another could be to institute a broadening of the motivational structures of firms beyond the economic bottom line, including also social and environmental responsibility

---

proofs concerning the negative impacts of rising climate gas levels. That issue is, however, more related to the question of "path dependency" as raised above. Here the issue is not on the decision whether to regulate, but the complexities involved in regulation. Certainly, in the case of some carbon mitigating options—e.g. carbon sequestration in forests—it is shown that the total capacity is dependent not only on the total area of forests, but also on the type and structure. Hence, many small forest patches have lower capacity to sequester carbon than more continuous forest cover (Goldman et al. 2007). This implies the need for involving local knowledge to succeed.

[11] The above conclusion is supported by Tietenberg (2002) and Rose (2002), while their perspective is a bit different from the one presented here.

(Vatn 2008a). I have chosen not to evaluate these options here. This is partly due to space considerations. It should, however, be mentioned that there is also some clear overlap between the challenges of ex ante regulation and that of full liability. There is similarly some overlap between changing the system of motivations directing firms and shifting to a common property regime.

2.4.1 Ex ante regulations

Private property is linked to establishing freedom of choice, facilitating both a certain type of creativity and decisions made on localized knowledge.[12] Generalized interdependency makes this, however, a less convincing solution, as argued above. Instead of the dominating ex post regulations of these interdependencies, regulation could be strengthened by more systematical use of ex ante state measures. This would, in our situation, imply that firms have to get an ex ante acceptance from the society that a certain activity could be started, including also specified conditions for it to continue as a going concern. In practice, such a right would have to be granted by the state and represent a strengthening of hierarchical power.

Compared to ex post regulation, this would imply turning the burden of proof around and demanding ex ante proof of safe or acceptable levels of harm. It would represent a substantial change compared to the present situation concerning how private property is generally viewed and institutionalized. It could even be argued to be against the very idea of private property with its role in granting freedom of choice. Nevertheless, Honoré (1961), in discussing what characterizes full ownership, emphasizes the prohibition of harmful use as one of 11 points. Hence, according to this understanding, ownership does not include a right to harm others. Following from the above situations with generalized interdependencies, avoiding harmful use would, however, be impossible. Therefore one could argue that it is not against, rather it is in line with, the idea of private property to institute comprehensive ex ante regulations securing avoidance of unwanted harm in the case of generalized interdependencies.

Since society depends on the production of goods and services, the rules established would nevertheless have to balance the need for avoiding harm with the need for a well-functioning production sector. This is the challenge for ex ante regulation not least because it will be very demanding, as most production activities will include some generalized interdependencies and the assessment must be based on uncertain information about future consequences of various levels of regulation. Taken to its limit, ex ante regulation

---

[12] Certainly, in the case of large corporations, the latter condition will often not hold.

could be understood as demanding a documentation showing that harm beyond certain predefined limits will not happen. Offering such proof would in a strict sense not be possible in most cases, implying that either many potential producers would be unable to prove their products to be socially acceptable or the ex ante regulation would have to include quite a significant level of flexibility around the limits set.

One way of establishing flexibility is to institutionalize a learning procedure beyond the initial evaluation, hence combine weaker ex ante regulation with a continuous evaluation of consequences facilitating learning. This solution could be seen as analogous to the idea of adaptive management as advocated among scholars in the field of ecosystem management (e.g., Folke et al. 2005). The challenge for instituting this in a private property–market setting relates not least to the fact that private property holders would need some security for their investments in order to be willing to invest. Instituted "adaptive learning" in such a setting faces the risk that the will to invest could collapse and that unnecessarily low production/high unemployment rates would prevail.

Despite this, one should observe that there are already examples of this kind of regulation in place. They concern, however, mainly products where human health is involved—for example, rules demanding the pre-testing of drugs against potential negative health effects. The European regime for regulating the production and use of genetically modified organisms (Kvakkestad and Vatn 2008) is another example where ecosystem issues are involved. The latter case illustrates the problem with proving harm with respect to safety. As, for example, EU rules are formulated, only short-run consequences are assessed, while the issues raised from, for example, some ecologists concern consequences over a much longer time horizon (Kvakkestad et al. 2007).

2.4.2 Expanding state property

In a case of generalized interdependencies, one way would be to opt for a solution where all interdependencies are made internal to a single decision unit. As in the case of the firm (Coase 1937) including the vertically integrated business (Williamson 1985) one would then bring the involved interdependencies—the type of dynamics that markets are weak at handling—under the same information and authority structure. As the side-effects of production are generalized—that is, influencing everybody in some sense—the only logical "business" with the capacity to directly include all relationships would be a single firm or the state. Circumventing here the question about what would be the difference between the two, I will sketch some questions concerning what a solution with moving to state property would imply.

Bringing the decision under "one roof" would, *in principle*, make it possible to assemble all the necessary information to evaluate where to strike the balance between protection and expansion, between commodity production and the level of acceptable environmental harm. It should, in principle, remove the type of strategic information games characterizing the state regulation of private businesses. One could also avoid the specific uncertainty around investments discussed above and facilitate learning without potentially endangering the will of investment in future production. The above conclusion is even strengthened by the findings of Lange and Taylor (1938) that a planned economy could solve the allocation problems at least as well as the market,[13] recognizing that this conclusion was made in a situation where issues concerning generalized interdependency were not even involved. So the case for overall state ownership should seem much stronger in the context of this chapter.[14]

While the breakdown of the Soviet Union was not only the result of problems related to centralized planning, the experience it offers certainly makes us reluctant to go down that alley. The problem can be split in two—that of information overload and that of agents' motivation.

2.4.2.1 *The information problem in state planning*

While the logic of generalized interdependencies points towards establishing a regime where these could be treated simultaneously under one decision structure—that is, removing transaction costs—this does not eliminate the information problems in themselves. What is done is to establish a structure where the information is treated under one common authority. This makes it possible to treat uncertainties in a different way compared to both ex ante and ex post regulations of firms. The system should in principle also allow for greater flexibility concerning changing strategies when new information is available. It will not depend on renegotiating terms with involved firms. Moreover, this system should not be hampered by strategic conflicts over harm/safety proofs as is the case with external regulations.

These are all important potentials that should be seriously considered. The problems relate not least to information overload and the following need to split or specialize information flows and decision arenas. Concerning overload, some of these problems could obviously be avoided by letting state properties operate in markets for goods and services, off-loading the system with having to separately produce information about commodity demand. Compared to the above discussion, one could still escape some of the problems with a strategic use of information asymmetries and investment reluctance, as in the case of ex ante regulations of private firms.

---

[13] See also Lavoie (1985) on the issue of "who won the socialist calculation debate."

[14] Certainly, environmental externalities evade the state border. In a principal discussion of state property, this question can be sidelined. I will, however, return to this specific problem later.

Concerning specializing information flows and decision arenas, the challenge would be that while formally part of the same hierarchy, this division would tend to create epistemic subcultures. This could easily result in internal rivalry between branches of the state as is observed even today. Specifically, in the case of market-oriented state firms, conflicts between state firms operating in markets and the "regulatory" branch of the state would most probably occur. So while the authority structure would be different to that of state–private, the problems would far from vanish.

As emphasized earlier, there is also an issue of local information related not only to commodity demand, but to ecosystem functioning as well. Hence, we face the issue of "optimal" loss of detail, or of balancing which decisions should be taken high up in the state hierarchy and what could be decentralized. The function of the higher levels would be to coordinate, while that of the lower would be to offer sensitivity to changes, to capture necessary information detail, and to learn about ecosystem dynamics. Maintaining a necessary degree of freedom at the lower levels is very important, but will also create a tension in the system as it is a potential source for internal conflict with higher-level decisions.

2.4.2.2 The motivational aspects of state planning

This takes us to the aspect of motivation. On the basis of the standard public choice literature (Niskanen 1971; Dearlove 1989)—one would argue that state power would rather have to imply an abuse of power and no capacity to solve common problems. Public authorities would support what is best for themselves, not for society. Moreover, each official would follow what is individually best for him/her. In a certain sense this argument is quite logical. It follows from the idea that humans are motivated only by individual interests—that is, they maximize individual utility. Given this, it would be necessary to construct a private reward structure for public officials that systematically reflects their provisioning of common goods. This is not only very demanding in informational terms, it is also impossible, as it demands agents involved that do not depend on such motivation—that is, those constructing the motivation structures for the subordinates. The logic of all-encompassing individual interests ends in an infinite regress concerning any capacity to solve common problems.

While logical from the perspective of strict individualism, this reasoning would imply that no society could really exist. This is counter to observation. So while the problem of bureaucratic control is a serious one, it is most probably so that the model of the agent used in public choice theory is far too restrictive. Based on a century of observations from both anthropological and sociological studies, and from recent experiments in economics and social psychology, there are strong arguments in favor of the hypothesis that motivations are plural (Barth 1967; Etzioni 1988; Bowles 1998; Fehr and Gächter 2000; Gintis 2000; Gneezy and Rustichini 2000b; Gintis et al. 2005). While some situations are quite well described by the standard model of individual utility maximization, these are first of all typically characterized being quite simple (Davis and Holt 1993). When complexity is increased, problems appear, cf. issues like framing effects and preference reversal (Tversky and Kahneman 1986). What is the more interesting observation here is that people in many contexts act in ways that take the interests of others into account. They show willingness to share. They follow up on contracts with no control. Finally, including individual incentives may reduce efforts in certain settings (Frey 1997; Gneezy and Rustichini 2000b). There are certainly different ways of interpreting these findings. Some favor expanding the utility function by including elements of selfish altruism (Andreoni 1990). Others explain the observations by emphasizing variations in individual types (E. Ostrom 1998a; Gintis 2000). The latter literature includes, however, the mechanism of socializing and the effect of norms on human behavior (E. Ostrom and Walker, eds 2003; Fehr and Gintis 2007).

Based on the ideas of Etzioni (1988), the latter thinking could be generalized to an idea viewing institutions as rationality contexts (e.g. Vatn 2005, 2008b, 2009). This implies that different socially defined arenas like the market, the public office, the family, the local community, are defined by different rationalities pertaining to the activities under each of these domains. Hence, there is both individual and social rationality, the latter implying that people take the interests of the group or "the other" into account when making choices. The idea here is that different institutional structures facilitate different rationalities through defining different norms and roles for those involved.

From this perspective, it becomes possible to understand "taking public office" as something very different from "taking private office." Certainly, securing that norms and rules for public officials are in place and followed is no simple task. Plurality of motivations and seeing institutions as rationality contexts opens up opportunities to facilitate public representation as something specific and available for social construction and reconstruction. Following March and Olsen (1995) governance takes place not least by the creation of the identities of the officials.

The state itself cannot have this power. It must flow from its constituencies. This moves the perspective to civil society and how the relationships between the state and civil society are constructed. Certainly, it is quite evident that one of the problems experienced in the structures of the Soviet Union was the lack of a flourishing civil society. As I see it, this follows from a fundamental lack of acknowledging the importance of this level, as it also demands an understanding of the vital role of pluralism. This implies emphasizing democracy beyond that of free elections. It points towards an increasing role for deliberative democracy (Dryzek 2002)—a solution that does not make the coordination simpler, but is necessary both for democratic control, and maintaining *and* developing the vitality of the system. It would also demand a systematic circulation of office, again increasing coordination costs. It would, however, be necessary to avoid the danger of power concentration and emphasize that the coordination lies in the "offices"—the institutions—and not the "office holders."

2.4.3 Expanding the role of common property

Given the above observation, one may ask if common property could be a better way to facilitate coordination than state property-based coordination. It has been shown to be a success in many cases of natural resource management (E. Ostrom 1990, 2005b), while not a panacea either (E. Ostrom 2007). The reason to look into this option is partly because of the possibility of including a wider set of considerations compared to that of the "single-minded" firm, and a stronger link to the civil society as compared with the state.

Common property, in the perspective established here, could be seen as a certain segment of a continuum from private to state property. It is defined as private property of a group of co-owners (Bromley 1991). If co-owners are firms, a common property regime first of all expands the domain of power for these co-owners. As such it could be viewed as an integrated firm. However, as in the case of a farmers' cooperative, it is based on a set of rules quite distinct from that of, for example, a stock-holding company. This concerns the way investments are made and the various community elements included in decision making, such as the rule of "one member one vote." If the co-owners are all inhabitants of an area—for example, a common school—the common property borders that of public property and it expands even further the opportunity to make decisions on other bases than revenue maximization. Similarly, if a forest is owned in common by nearby villagers, we would again see the strong public dimension of ownership.

So as a "middle" solution, could common property capture the beneficial capacities from both of the other worlds and avoid their deficiencies? The strength would be its bottom-up basis. That is, however, also its weakness. Certainly, it has the (potential) capacity to coordinate local—that is, within its bounds—interdependencies. That is exactly what Ostrom shows. While this is a gain, it is just one step in solving the kind of interconnection problems emphasized in this paper. We are talking about coordination on much larger geographical scales. Common property dominantly concerns the management of natural resources where mainly direct interdependencies are involved. Instead of vertical, there is mainly horizontal integration. As the economy has grown, challenges are more related to indirect interdependencies, and this feature would demand that the common properties were themselves regulated by the state, as in the case of the firm–market regime, or we would have to establish one common property for all environmental resources.

It should be emphasized that state regulations of common properties could be quite different from state regulations of private firms. As the common properties would be owned by communities of people, there would be society dimensions to both the first and second level. This would imply a potential to create communicative systems of different formats compared to those between the state and firms.

In the second case—that of a common property for all resources—the solution will be more like that of state property. The framework of common properties points, however, towards a stronger emphasis on the bottom-up processes. One could envision it more like a hierarchy of common properties. While this may look like something very similar to a state with decentralized decision power, it is different in one important way. Coordination is about coordinating local common property units, and not about issuing decentralized power from a state—that is, from the top.

The above accentuates the importance of local community and civil society engagement. This is a very strong potential feature of common property organization, emphasizing that community-based management brings in a wider set of motivations for action than, for example, traditional firm structures, as also emphasized by the many positive experiences with community-based management (Lemos and Agrawal 2006).

2.5 DISCUSSION AND CONCLUSION

In the above analysis I have emphasized generic solutions without being concerned about what is realistic given the present state of institutional development. There are already certain changes to be observed concerning ways to better handle interdependence. They seem, however, to be based mainly on strengthening horizontal coordination. First of all we should acknowledge the concept of corporate social responsibility (CSR), where the idea has been to expand the responsibility of firms beyond that of producing shareholder value including environmental and social issues. While there could be a potential here to include an element of social rationality into the governing principles of firms, this solution has also some strong limitations attached to it (Sjåfjell 2007; Uttig and Clapp, eds 2008). From the perspective developed in this chapter, this should come as no surprise. Nevertheless, this development shows that the business sector is engaged in building relationships with civil society, not least through interaction with NGOs. Given the strong power of large corporations, it may be argued that a development along this line combined with increasing ex ante state regulations is the only politically realistic solution.

Next we have the increased interest for the idea of payments for environmental services (PES). Like CSR, this is an institutional reform much built on the idea of making agents more sensitive to environmental issues, in this case by creating markets for environmental goods—compare the definition of PES in Wunder (2005). A lot of experience with the working of PES projects is now building up (Corbera et al. 2007; Kosoy et al. 2007; Engel et al. 2008). These studies show, however, that the dominant buyers are public bodies, in particular, states. NGOs also play a significant role as intermediaries. So while the idea with PES has been to establish an alternative to state regulations, the state or local public bodies are found to be dominant actors not least because of free-rider problems and the high level of transaction costs in managing markets for environmental services (Vatn 2010). So while the name for state or public transfer is changed from the politically less acceptable "subsidy" to the now more accepted concept of a "payment," there is less real change observed in the format of the interaction. It is more hierarchical than horizontal.

Finally, I would emphasize the developments observed under the umbrella of network governance (NG). This is again a development accentuating horizontal interaction. As Sørensen and Torfing (eds) (2007) argue, neo-liberalism did not produce less state. More markets resulted instead in more state. Again, from the emphasis of this chapter on the increased amount of generalized interconnections following economic development, this is not surprising. In the literature on NG (Kooiman, ed. 1993; Mayntz 1993; Sørensen and Torfing, eds 2007), NG is seen as a development towards negotiated relations between fairly stable sets of interdependent organizations.

I find that this development strengthens some of the arguments developed in this chapter. NG is, however, a solution only for specific interdependencies. As such it is parallel to vertical integration between firms and the establishment of common property, while not formalized in the same sense. It is more of a "loose coupling" based on negotiated agreements and the establishment of a normative community among agents. It is a proactive type of governance. It facilitates distribution and aggregation of information across agents as it seems to have the potential to assist consensus building and reduce the risk of implementation resistance (Sørensen and Torfing, eds 2007).

There are, however, also many NG failures. Due to conflicting interests, the potential for consensus is often weak. NG participants may also be caught in strategic games of various kinds. This has resulted in an emphasis on a need for hierarchical "facilitation" of horizontal interaction. So even in the case of specific interdependencies, the restrictions of relying on pure horizontal coordination are evident.

I think the above offers some important lessons. It shows that we have a very long way to go before we have structures in place that are able to handle the issue of generalized interdependency more fundamentally. It shows also that one should most probably not aim for the "ideal generic" solution. There are several arguments for the latter. First of all, it is not realistic to build new structures independent of what has already been in existence. Hence, it is unrealistic to search for "the" ideal solution. Second, the solution would have to be a compromise between emphasizing hierarchical control vs local-level autonomy, information specificity vs the need for simplification, and balancing individual vs social rationality. Finally, while coordination is a strong demand, any system must carry with it elements that can challenge the dominant structures to ensure its vitality. This is the fundamental contradiction of any enduring system.

In relation to this, I find the recent increase in civil society engagement and the development of network governance interesting, as it may form a necessary basis from which to start integrating and strengthening a *coupled development* of institutional structures along both the horizontal and vertical axes. What is now needed is a special focus on strengthening the vertical dimension of integration. I also think it demands a development of institutional structures at both the horizontal and vertical levels in forms not yet seen to make this possible. Making new institutional structures is, however, not a new thing. It is what has constituted all larger shifts in the history of humanity.

3

The Governance of International Environmental Public Goods

Charles Perrings

3.1 THE CHALLENGE

Global environmental change poses a number of challenges for governance, amongst which the least tractable is the development of institutions of governance that map well both to the scale of the problem and to the characteristics of the environmental public goods involved. Part of the difficulty in identifying the right scale and form of institutions of governance is that the same problem can involve multiple public goods, each of which has a different natural scale. The mitigation of climate change is a pure global public good. The effects of mitigation in any one location benefit people everywhere. None can be excluded from accessing those benefits, and access by one party does not reduce the benefits available to other parties. Adaptation to climate change, on the other hand, may be either a private good or a public good—at many different scales. While the installation of air conditioning is almost always a private good, for example, the installation of water reservoirs, protective bunds or dykes, the establishment of transboundary protected areas and biocorridors are almost always "local" or "regional" public goods that offer benefits to constituencies of varying size.

This chapter considers the challenges for governance posed by the array of environmental public goods at risk under biosphere change. More particularly, it considers the challenges for the governance of environmental public goods affected by changes in biodiversity. The Millennium Ecosystem Assessment (MEA, 2005) described the benefits that people get from the environment in terms of two broad categories of services directly consumed by people—the provisioning and cultural services—together with the services that both regulate and support their supply. Many regulating and supporting services have the characteristics of public goods. The supporting services are the basic ecosystem processes that underpin the production of all the things that people value in nature. They include photosynthetic energy production, nutrient cycling, and the array of biogeochemical cycles that drive the atmosphere, the hydrosphere, and the biosphere. Some, like the carbon cycle, operate at the global scale. Others provide benefits that are much more highly localized. The regulating services moderate the risks in supply of provisioning and cultural services, and similarly differ in the spatial scale at which they operate. Mangrove protection of coastlines, for example, provides benefits that are highly localized, whereas conservation of landraces and the wild relatives of food crops offer benefits that potentially extend all the way from the local to the global scale.

All ecosystem services depend, in some measure, on the mix of species— and hence on biodiversity. Even monocultures depend on large numbers of interacting species. But the regulating services, especially, depend on the diversity of species performing particular functions. Examples include watershed protection and the mitigation of floods and droughts, waste assimilation, detoxification and decomposition, microclimatic stabilization, the purification of air and water, the generation and renewal of soil and its fertility, the control of agricultural pests, the dispersal of seeds, and the transport of nutrients (Daily, 1997). Since they assure production of provisioning or cultural services over a range of environmental conditions, they tend to be more effective the more species there are that flourish in different conditions. Like any portfolio of assets, diversity within a functional group ensures that the functionality of the system may be maintained in conditions when some members of the group are unable to perform the function. For some services it is important to maintain functional diversity locally. So, for example, subsistence farmers isolated from the market need to select the crops to be cultivated to accommodate the range of environmental conditions they expect to encounter. However, where farmers are able to pool risks through some sort of insurance mechanism, individual specialization may be more appropriate. In this case, however, if all farmers specialize in the same crops, the resulting loss of functional diversity will affect risks over a much wider area, calling for a mechanism to conserve crop genetic diversity that operates at that larger scale.

Aside from the issue of spatial scale, a second challenge is to match the governance structure to the nature of the public good at risk. In most cases, the problem to be addressed relates to the fact that while many of the private benefits of biodiversity change are captured in market prices, many of the social costs are not. Markets for foods and fibres drive specialization in agriculture, forestry, and fisheries but do not generally signal the costs to society of private land conversion and agricultural specialization. Biodiversity in exploited tropical forests has historically been valued for the marketed values of timber and other products including medicinal plants, or for economic activities that depend on forests such as hunting, fishing, recreation, and tourism. But tropical forests also have value for their role in the provision of the global public good (as habitat for endemic species) and a set of local public goods. The point here is that land use decisions in a given location can deliver distinct public benefits and costs at quite different spatial and temporal scales (Perrings and Gadgil 2003). Conservation of watersheds for the supply of clean water, for example, can also provide habitat for endangered species or stimulate the emergence of zoonotic diseases. Indeed, this is the basis for the growing enthusiasm for the Reduced Emissions from Deforestation and forest Degradation (REDD) scheme in developing countries. Conservation groups in particular are persuaded that it offers ancillary benefits in terms of rural poverty alleviation, biodiversity protection, and a range of ecosystem services (Myers 2007; Miles and Kapos 2008; O'Connor 2008; Parker et al. 2008).

Identifying appropriate governance structures accordingly requires an understanding of (1) the interactions between public goods delivered as the joint products of land use decisions; and (2) the nature of each public good. The first of these depends on the degree to which these public goods concerned are complements or substitutes. In the REDD case, studies of the relationship between carbon sequestration and water quality and quantity indicate that the question is far from resolved (Jackson et al. 2005). Yet unless public goods are perfect complements, the development of a mechanism to assure efficient supply of one will not assure efficient supply of another. That is, there is no a priori reason to believe that incentives devised to minimize the cost of carbon sequestration will encourage an efficient pattern of habitat protection. Indeed, there is every reason to believe that the pattern of protection implied by distinct ecosystem services is very different (Chan et al. 2006).

Matching governance to the nature of the public good also requires an understanding of the "supply technology" involved. The social cost of free-riding behavior depends on whether the supply technology for some public good is "additive," "weighted additive," "weakest or weaker link," "best or better shot," and whether it is subject to access restrictions, as in the case of local public goods or club goods. Free-riding behavior is generally most costly in the case of additive-supply technologies and least costly in the case of best-shot technologies. The incentive to supply similarly depends heavily on whether the public good is pure or impure—whether it yields any privately capturable benefits in addition to its non-capturable public benefits (Sandler 1997, 2004). The governance implications of distinct types of public goods are quite different. Since there is no reason to believe that jointly produced environmental public goods—distinct public goods supplied through the same land uses—will have a similar supply technology, it follows that the governance structure may need to correspond to more than one supply technology. Biodiversity conservation, for example, is frequently an impure global public good (a public good yielding both nationally capturable benefits as well as a set of non-exclusive and non-rival benefits to the global community) in which the nationally capturable benefits are either fully or largely private but the international benefits are additive.

The aim of this chapter is to explore the governance of transboundary environmental public goods. While environmental public goods at the national level might share many of the same characteristics as transboundary environmental public goods, their governance is much more straightforward. This is because nation states have the power to assign property rights within their area of jurisdiction, to enact legislation and hence to regulate behavior, and to enforce contracts between resource users. There are certainly important and interesting issues involved in designing governance structures at the national level, the dominant approach to which is a variant of fiscal federalism. In this approach, a central authority assigns environmental functions, fields, or areas of responsibility on the basis of something like the subsidiarity principle behind the devolution of authority in the European Union. Decentralization of authority follows when environmental public goods are local, environmental protection does not exhibit economies of scale, and environmental preferences are heterogeneous (Breton et al. 2009). The same principle applies to the problem of transboundary environmental public goods—that the appropriate scale of governance is determined by the scale at which the benefits of the public good are realized. In the absence of a central authority, however, governance systems at the international level depend on cooperation or coordination between independent actors. The chapter focuses on these systems.

The characteristics of transboundary environmental public goods that need to be reflected in governance mechanisms include their biophysical properties, their spatial and temporal scale, their techonology of supply, the strategic problem they pose, and the structure of property rights. These are reviewed in the next section. To make things concrete, I then focus on governance options and the effectiveness of governance structures for specific types of environmental public good. A final section offers a discussion of the more general issues raised and the implications these have for the resolution of the problems posed by biosphere change.

3.2 CHARACTERISTICS OF ENVIRONMENTAL PUBLIC GOODS AT RISK FROM GLOBAL BIOSPHERE CHANGE

There is no simple way to characterize the numerous environmental public goods at risk from biosphere change. Many are supplied as joint products, some of which are complements, others substitutes. Some deliver benefits locally, others globally. Some involve countries already linked by formal agreements as well as by trade, some do not. To complicate matters further, while some environmental public goods are defined by the biophysical properties of the system itself, many others are socially constructed. That is, the reason they are non-exclusive is not because of the biophysical properties of the ecosystem, but because of a set of socially constructed rules that determine openness of access. Table 3.1 describes the characteristics of some of the environmental public goods at issue. Four features of this are worth noting.

There are few public goods among the provisioning services. The production and consumption of foods, fuels, and fibers is primarily private, involving production either for the market or for direct consumption. At the same time, however, many provisioning services directly depend on ecosystems that are collectively owned—especially in areas beyond national jurisdiction. They are accordingly affected by access rules that regulate private pressure on those ecosystems. I later take sea areas beyond national jurisdiction as a case in point, but the same observations could be made about many terrestrial examples. Collectively owned environmental assets are part of the "environmental infrastructure" that supports private production. Indeed, these are amongst the most important and pervasive environmental public goods.

Many more cultural services than provisioning services are public goods, particularly where they involve the supply of information, have aesthetic appeal, religious significance, and so on. It is not coincidence that the supply of cultural environmental public goods—through conservation, preservation, legal protection, and the like—tends to lie outside the market. The protection of World Heritage Sites, the establishment of international wildlife parks or reserves, and the establishment of ex situ global collections all involve collective action at the international level. This reflects the fact that if left to the decisions of individuals or nation states, such services would be undersupplied. These are often best- or better-shot problems, implying that the benefits to those affected by the public good are provided by individual countries or consortia of countries best able to fund provision of the good.

While there do exist localized regulating services, a characteristic feature of environmental regulation is that it frequently affects many people and processes. Although high levels of diversity amongst nutrient cyclers in soils may confer direct benefits on land users, for example, the insurance offered by diversity in functional groups generally operates at larger scales. Indeed, in the agricultural example cited earlier, the regulatory benefits offered by crop genetic diversity operate all the way from the local to the global scale. Supply technologies for the regulating services can take many forms. The protection offered by disease control measures, for example, is frequently a weakest-or weaker-link supply technology. But the protection offered by redundancy in functional groups is closer to being additive.

Finally, the set of basic ecosystem processes that allow the system to continue to function are defined by the MEA as supporting services. In the problem involved, and the system of governance

Public function	Environmental action	MEA ecosystem service	Geographic scale	Publicness (rivalry, exclusion)	Supply technology	Strategic problem	Governance
Conservation of common environmental resources	Conservation of endangered species	Cultural	Global–local?	Pure public good	Additive (endangered species census or the size of an ecosystem left aside for conservation); better shot (protection of a given endangered species); weaker link (controlling ilegal trade); threshold (maintaining a minimum size habitat, or corridors)	Additive: prisioner's dilemma game if $bi<ci$ or chicken game if no action can have disastrous consequences; better shot: anti-coordination game (although for some countries the incentive may be so strong that it will act unilaterally making it a harmony game); weaker link assurance game	Local–national regulation, PA, MEA
	Conservation of genetic information	Provisioning Cultural	Global	Pure public good	Additive (in-situ conservation policies); better shot (gene banks)	Additive: prisioner's dilemma game if $bi < ci$ or chicken game if no action can have disastrous consequences; better shot anti-coordination game or unilateral action—harmony game	Local–national regulation, PA, MEA
	Conservation of pollinators*	Supporting	Local	Pure public good	Additive	Prisoner's dilemma game if $bi<ci$ or chicken game if no action can have disastrous consequences.	PA, PES
	Conservation of harvested wild living resources	Provisioning	Local–global	Common-pool resource	Additive (harvesting quotas in fisheries)	Prisioner's dilemma game or anti-coordination game, e.g. chicken game	Local–national regulation, PA, MEA
	Protection of sites of special scientific interest, religious or cultural significance	Cultural	Global–local	Joint products	Weighted sum (word heritage protection)	Weighted sum: harmony game—when joint products include significant excludable benefits; weighted sum technology implies a large share of provider-specific benefits	Local protection, PA, SPP

(continued)

Table 3.1. Continued

Public function	Environmental action	MEA ecosystem service	Geographic scale	Publicness (rivalry, exclusion)	Supply technology	Strategic problem	Governance
Control of human, animal, and plant health	Management of infectious disease	Regulating	Local–global	Impure public good	Weaker, weakest link (monitoring and limiting a disease outbreak); threshold	If weaker, weakest link, assurance game; if threshold: chicken game	Local–national regulation, MEA
	Quarantine, port inspections	Regulating	Local–regional	Impure public good	Weaker, weakest link	Assurance game	Local–national regulation, MEA
	Pest control	Regulating	Local–global	Impure public good	Weaker, weakest link (limiting the spread); weighted sum (curbing a pest)	Weaker, weakest link: assurance game; weighted sum a harmony game if provider-specific benefits are large (meaning non-reciprocal cooperation is the best option)	Local–national regulation, MEA
	Eradication of invasive species	Regulating	Local–global	Impure public good	Weaker, weakest link (eradication and containment of any further spread)	Assurance game, or coordination game if it does not pay a country to eliminate as the invasive species exists abroad but it does pay when it has already been eliminated abroad.	Local–national regulation, MEA
	Vaccine development	Regulating	Local–global	Pure public good	Best, better shot (HIV/AIDS vaccination)	Anti-cooperation game	Local–national regulation, MEA
	Information about disease/pest/invasive risks	Regulating	Local–global	Pure public good	Best shot (building a pest database)	Anti-cooperation game	Local–national regulation, MEA

							Local–national regulation
Natural hazard protection	Coastal protection	Regulating	Local	Pure public good	Weighted sum (where coastal barriers protect hinterland), weakest link (where protective dykes need to be intact to deliver benefits)	Weighted sum: harmony game, weakest link: assurance game	Local–national regulation
	Flood protection	Regulating	Local	Pure public good	Weighted sum	Harmony	Local authority
	Avalanche protection	Regulating	Local	Pure public good	Additive, with threshold	Threshold: chicken game; additive: either prisoners dilemma or chicken game	Local–national regulation, MEA
Management of atmospheric quality	Regulation of air quality, control of emissions	Regulating	Local	Impure public good	Weighted sum	Weighted sum implies that a variety of games may be possible depending on the weights. Weights associated with SO_2 seem to be characterized as a harmony game (Helsinki Protocol)	Local regulation, PES
	Microclimatic stabilization	Regulating	Local	Pure public good	Additive	Prisioner's dilemma game or anti-coordination games such as a chicken game	
	Stabilization of ozone	Supporting	Global	Pure public good	Additive (reducing use of ozone destroying chemicals)	Harmony game for the core producers. An EPA report showed benefits > costs for any country acting alone. The pursuit of self-interest without regard to the actions of others leads to unilateral action	MEA, EM, PES
	Carbon sequestration	Supporting	Global	Pure public good	Additive (reducing CO_2 emmissions)	Prisioner's dilemma game or anti-coordination games such as a chicken game	MEA, EM, PES
Management of water quality	Pollution buffering by wetlands	Regulating	Local	Joint products	Additive	Prisioner's dilemma game or anti-coordination games such as chicken game	PA

(continued)

Table 3.1. Continued

Public function	Environmental action	MEA ecosystem service	Geographic scale	Publicness (rivalry, exclusion)	Supply technology	Strategic problem	Governance
	Water supply infrastructure	Supporting	Local–regional	Club good	Additive	If club goods there may be no strategic considerations	Local–national regulation, SPP, MEA
	Water purification and waste treatment	Regulating	Local	Club good	Additive	If club goods there may be no strategic considerations	Local–national regulation, SPP
	Nutrient management	Supporting, regulating	Local–regional	Joint products	Additive, with threshold	Prisioner's dilemma game or anti-coordination games such as chicken game	Local–national regulation, MEA, PES
	Watershed protection	Regulating	Local–Regional	Joint products	Additive (setting standards on water pollution)	Coordination game (such as assurance game, or battle-of-the-sexes game)	Local–national regulation, MEA

* Defined within the MEA as a regulating service—but this is not consistent with the general usage of the term; MEA—Multilateral Environmental Agreement; PA—Protected area; SPP—State–private partnership; PES—Payments for ecosystem services

Source: Touza, J. & Perrings, C., 2011 Strategic behavior and the scope for unilateral provision of transboundary ecosystem services that are international environmental public goods. *Strategic Behavior and the Environment* 1(2): 89–117.

broad context of global environmental change they include the processes of the atmosphere, the hydrosphere, and the biosphere. The beneficiaries of these processes similarly extend all the way from the local to the global scale. The supply technologies for public goods of this type are frequently additive, but similarly operate at very different scales. Mitigation of climate change through carbon sequestration or reduced carbon emissions is additive at the global scale. Mitigation of water pollution risks through reductions in nitrate emissions is also additive, but operates at much more local scales.

Table 3.1 describes two other things. The first is the impact of the distribution of net benefits of different environmental public goods on the incentive to cooperate in their provision. The second is the current governance structure. National contributions towards the provision of international public goods are generally related to the distribution of net benefits—the structure of "payoffs." This determines both the incentive to contribute towards the provision of the public good or to free-ride on others, and the social cost of free-riding. Sandler's (1997, 2004) work on the challenges of cooperative action at the global scale have underlined the importance of free-riding incentives in any additive-supply technology. Wherever the value of environmental public goods depends on the sum of the efforts of all contributors, free-riding imposes a social cost. But the extent of that cost depends on the structure of payoffs. In many cases, the provision of environmental public goods at the international level has features of either the "prisoner's dilemma" or the "chicken" game. Both cases lead to non-cooperative outcomes that are Nash equilibria (no party has an incentive to change their strategy once others have made a decision), but that deliver a social payoff that is less than could be delivered through a cooperative outcome. Because individual countries have an incentive to free-ride on the actions of others, they choose not to contribute to the provision of the public good, with the result that the benefits to all are reduced—potentially with highly undesirable consequences in the case of prisoner's dilemma problems. The best environmental examples are the mitigation of climate change, air, and water quality. However, environmental resources held in common property at all scales induce a similar response. The Nash equilibria in such cases involve overexploitation of the resource—what Hardin (1968) referred to as "the tragedy of the commons." The overexploitation of marine resources in sea areas beyond national jurisdiction is the classic case.

Another common payoff structure occurs when a certain threshold level of provision needs to be secured in order to lead to any benefit at all. Returning a eutrophic international water body to an oligotrophic state, for example, may require more abatement of nutrients than any one country is able to make, so clean up by any one country will yield no benefits at all unless enough other countries make a similar commitment. The existence of such threshold levels of supply gives rise to an assurance game in which there are two Nash equilibria—either no country contributes or all contribute. But it can also prompt individual countries to make a commitment in the hope that other countries will be induced to follow (since the downside risks of that are reduced). The payoff structure associated with assurance games more frequently leads to an efficient outcome than the payoffs associated with other additive supply technologies. But there is still a risk that the public good will be undersupplied.

The two other supply technologies found in Table 3.1, best-/better-shot and weakest-weaker-link have very different implications for free-riding behavior and the costs of that behavior. The characteristics of best- and better-shot problems is that the benefits accruing to all parties are independent of the contributions of the majority. So for example, the information provided by the Center for Disease Control (CDC), the World Health Organization (WHO), the World Organization for Animal Health (Office international des épizooties, OIE) or the United Nations Environment Program (UNEP) is available to all countries, but not all countries bear the cost of its provision. However, even if most countries free-ride on this information, its value to all is not reduced. Free-riding is costless.

Weakest-weaker-link problems, on the other hand, effectively remove any incentive to free-ride. Since the benefits to all are the benefits offered by the least competent provider, no other country has any incentive to do more than the least competent provider. That is, they "match" the behavior of the least competent provider. The best example of this is the control of infectious human, animal, or plant diseases—since the protection offered to each country is no better than the protection offered by the least effective country. In the case of quarantine services, for example, the level of protection offered to the whole community depends on the level of protection offered by the least effective quarantine facility. If one quarantine facility does not contain an invasive pathogen, the fact that all others may do so is irrelevant. The same thing applies to the control of invasive species that have already established themselves. So, for example, if control of an invasive plant involves containment (or eradication) by all landowners, it will only be as good as the containment (or eradication) activities of the least effective landowner. The similarity to the problem of the control of communicable diseases is obvious. Those in poverty are least able to commit resources to control, and so are most likely to undermine the control efforts of others. This is beginning to be seen as one of the most serious and least tractable aspects of the invasive species problem (Perrings et al. 2009a). Against this is the fact that weakest- and weaker-link problems stimulate a collective interest in raising the bar on the least effective country.

The governance arrangements for environmental public goods at the different scales covered by Table 3.1 extend from small-scale partnerships between local government and civil society to the global UN framework conventions

(Climate Change, Desertification, and Biological Diversity). There is some correlation between the scale of the governance structure and the scale of the environmental public good. Clearly local pollution problems are typically addressed at the local scale. However, it remains the case that many of the more remote effects of local public good provision are not reflected in the governance structure—that the subsidiarity principle does not operate. This is especially the case where remote impacts occur beyond national borders, and where there is no multilateral environmental agreement to accommodate those impacts. It is also the case where there is no effective environmental agreement. While the Convention on Biological Diversity (CBD) includes a requirement that countries should take account of any effects that their biodiversity management has on other countries, for example, that requirement is generally ignored. Actions that promote the international spread of animal or plant pathogens should be restricted under the terms of the CBD, but this does not typically happen.

Recurrent elements in governance structures for environmental public goods are a legal framework contained either in national law and regulation (sometimes custom and usage) or international agreement, an authorizing body such as a national legislative council or the conference of the parties to a multilateral environmental agreement, and an executive body, secretariat, or implementing agency. While civil society may be represented in the authorizing body, these are generally dominated by national governments. However, civil society is frequently involved in the execution or implementation of enabling legislation or agreement. In many cases this involves some form of state–private partnership, with the private partners being either corporations or nongovernmental organizations (NGOs).

3.3 CHARACTERISTICS OF GOVERNANCE STRUCTURES

Whatever its form, the test of the effectiveness of a governance structure is its capacity to deliver an outcome that is better than the non-cooperative outcome—the Nash equilibrium. Since no country would consider entering into an agreement unless the outcome was at least as good as they could achieve independently, this is a natural reference point. Governance structures that deliver benefits over and above those obtainable through the independent actions of affected parties are efficient relative to the "no collective action" case. Several factors turn out to influence the relative efficiency of governance structures, including:

- the degree of exclusion,
- the number of parties involved;

- the penalties for defection;
- the frequency of interaction;
- the symmetry between parties.

Recall that many environmental public goods may be said to be "socially constructed," in the sense that they exist because of social rules of access rather than the biophysical properties of the system concerned. There is by now overwhelming evidence that environmental resources that are open access but also scarce (the social opportunity cost of their use is not zero) will be overexploited. This is consistent with the "tragedy of the commons," although the reasons why it occurs are different from those noted in Hardin's original paper on the subject. Environmental public goods that are public only by virtue of the access rules that govern their use are especially vulnerable. At the same time, environmental public goods that are "localized" through access restrictions—such as club goods—are able to deliver benefits to members efficiently. Indeed, there is an equally extensive body of evidence for the effectiveness of local rules of management for common-pool resources that are subject to regulated access (reported in the extensive literature that builds on Ostrom's seminal contribution: E. Ostrom 1990).

A second factor in the efficiency of governance structures—the number of parties to an agreement—is closely related to the degree of exclusion. Barrett's (1994) analysis of the effectiveness of multilateral environmental agreements showed that the benefits they are able to deliver over and above the non-cooperative outcome are related to the number of parties to the agreement. Specifically, taking the case of biodiversity conservation, he showed that there are a maximum number of countries that can sustain cooperation, and that this number is determined by the ratio of the costs and benefits of the transfers needed to secure biodiversity conservation. The larger the net benefits of cooperation, the smaller the number of countries that can sustain the cooperative outcome. This finding was empirically tested by Murdoch, Sandler, and Sargent (Murdoch et al. 1997) for the Helsinki Protocol of the Long Range Transboundary Air Pollution Convention (then 39 parties). They found the outcome of the protocol to be very close to the non-cooperative Nash equilibrium—that is, it merely encoded what countries would have done anyway. While some Millennium Ecosystem Assessments (MEAs) involving large numbers of parties have been acclaimed as successful, there is evidence that the outcome in most such cases is still close to the Nash equilibrium. One frequently cited example is the Montreal Protocol of the United Nations Framework Convention on Climate Change (UNFCCC). However, since cheaper substitutes for CFCs were then coming on to the market, it has been observed that producers were about to reduce the use of CFCs anyway (Sandler 2004).

A third factor is the existence of effective penalties for defection from the cooperative outcome. Since MEAs need to be self-enforcing, it is important that they contain within them disincentives to opt out of an agreed course of action. Penalties for enforcing MEAs generally amount to collective agreements to change the structure of payoffs in ways that make the cooperative solution the dominant solution. Ordinarily this is achieved either by penalties on (or payments to) non-contributors that offset the attraction of defection. In many cases, the adoption of cost-sharing rules can achieve the same effect without incurring any of the substantial costs involved in setting up and implementing transfer systems. In addition, cost sharing does not involve the extra collective action problem in making transfers to change the payoff structure (Sandler 2004). This said, there are a number of examples of MEAs in which the existence of either penalties or compensation arrangements has been sufficient to induce cooperation (Barrett 2003a).

Fourth, in MEAs—as in markets generally—the frequency with which parties interact affects the likelihood of the cooperative outcome. Repeated interactions have a number of consequences for collective action, allowing experience of the outcomes of past interactions to inform future strategies. Even in strategic problems as intractable as the prisoner's dilemma, repeated interaction has the potential to induce a form of cooperation, in that the likelihood that any one party will cooperate reflects their experience of whether other parties have cooperated in the past. The realization that uncooperative behavior is likely to induce tit-for-tat behavior, first observed by Axelrod (1984), has been sufficient to lead a number of long-standing MEAs to generate progressively better outcomes—either through successive protocols or through successive amendments to a given protocol. The bottom line is that the most effective MEAs are those that (1) involve a limited number of signatories; (2) have evolved through repeated renegotiation; and (3) that include effective penalties or disincentives to defect from a precisely defined set of objectives. It is worth emphasizing, though, that repeated interaction by itself is not sufficient to assure stable governance of transboundary resources. In fact the literature on n-dimensional differential games suggests that except in few cases, the Nash equilibrium is likely to be highly unstable (Bressan and Shen 2004).

Finally, understanding the asymmetry between countries is critical to understanding the prospects for the effective governance of international environmental public goods. Many analyses of strategic behavior at the international level assume the symmetry of parties to negotiation, largely to assure tractability of the problem. However, while symmetric two-by-two "games" have provided a useful tool to investigate a number of strategic international interactions, except in the case of some bilateral agreements or multilateral agreements involving a small number of "equal" partners, the assumption of symmetry is far from safe. Indeed, despite the homogenizing effect of globalization, the differences between developed and developing countries are increasing rather than decreasing.

The asymmetry between countries is reflected in differences (1) in the value attached to the national benefits deriving from distinct international environmental public goods; (2) in the capacity of those countries to provide public goods that offer international benefits; and consequently (3) in their willingness to commit to cooperative action through multilateral agreements. These differences are among the most important explanations for the failure of agreements like the UNFCCC to attract general support.

Differences (1) and (3) require some sort of side payment or benefit-sharing scheme as envisaged in the CBD (Touza and Perrings 2011). In the case of the CBD, countries that benefit most from biodiversity conservation are expected to offer side payments to countries that benefit the least, providing the inducement needed to get their participation in an agreement that otherwise offers few advantages (Barrett 2003a). Similar arrangements have been important in, for example, the global eradication of diseases (Barrett 2003b, 2007a).

Difference (2) limits the effectiveness of agreements to provide particular kinds of public goods. In particular, public goods whose benefits depend on contributions by the weaker/weakest amongst all contributors are most heavily affected. In addition to the side payments needed to induce the participation of such countries, asymmetries in the capacity of countries to deliver public goods requires investment in the capacity of the weaker-weakest-link countries (Touza and Perrings 2011).

3.4 GOVERNANCE OF THE HIGH SEAS

While there are a large number of MEAs dealing with the sea areas beyond national jurisdiction aside from the UN Convention on the Law of the Sea (UNCLOS), it remains the archetype for intractable environmental public goods.[1] Despite UNCLOS and the many regional seas agreements governing fisheries in areas beyond national jurisdiction, there are few incentives to comply with the terms of any of the agreements and there is no supranational authority to enforce compliance. The resources of the high seas remain very close to open access. The net effect of open access is a clear decline in yields in many of the world's major fisheries. Worm et al. (2006) identified catches from 1950 to 2003 within all 64 large marine ecosystems (LMEs) worldwide: the source of 83 percent of global catches over the past 50 years. They reported that the rate of fisheries collapses in these areas (catches less than 10 percent of

---

[1] This case study draws on Perrings (2008).

the recorded maximum) has been accelerating, and that 29 percent of fished species were in a state of collapse in 2003. Cumulative collapses affected 65 percent of all species fished. Indeed, the most frequently cited source of stress in marine systems is overfishing (Jackson et al. 2001; Pauly et al. 2002; Myers and Worm 2003; Berkes et al. 2005; Hughes et al. 2005), with bycatch (Lewison et al. 2004), loss of habitat (Pandolfi et al. 2003; Pyke 2004), climate change (Hughes et al. 2005) and the spread of pathogens (Harvell et al. 2004) being contributory factors.

There is a consensus among marine biologists that overexploitation of fisheries is significantly more important as an explanation of declining eco-systems than habitat loss, climate change, pollution, disease, or invasive species (Dulvy et al. 2003; Tittensor et al. 2006). There is a similar consensus about the underlying social causes of overexploitation: the lack of effective institutions and governance mechanisms (Berkes et al. 2003; Hilborn et al. 2005). Given respectively the nature of the public good (that it is additive, the benefits being equal to the sum of the efforts of all contributors) and the strategic problem confronting contributors (that it is a classic prisoner's dilemma, the benefits of cooperation outweighing the benefits of non-cooper-ative behavior, but the incentives driving contributors to the non-cooperative outcome) two conditions on the equilibrium outcome of the strategic game between the resource users can be derived. The first implies that the public good, conservation of stocks, is of the form $Y = \sum_i y^i$, where y^i is the contribution to conservation of the ith country. The second implies that the non-cooperative outcome is a Nash equilibrium, the "open access" equilibri-um, at which rents are exhausted—total revenues are exactly equal to total costs. Open access means that there is nothing to exclude users from the resource, and no incentive to conserve it.

In practice, the only constraints on the behavior of resource users are voluntary. So, for example, the FAO Code of Conduct for Responsible Fish-eries[2] notionally applies to fishing firms, subregional, regional, and global organizations, whether governmental or nongovernmental, as well as those concerned with the management and development of fisheries. However, it is purely voluntary. Although there are four International Plans of Action agreed under the code, and although it embodies the "Agreement to promote com-pliance with international conservation and management measures by fishing vessels on the high seas"[3], these do not create any legally binding obligations upon either nation states or nongovernmental entities.

This said, there is an array of MEAs to protect the global commons; specific agreements to protect fish stocks on the high seas; the development of regional groupings to address specific conservation and management issues (of which

---

[2] http://www.fao.org/figis/servlet/static?xml=CCRF_prog.xml&dom=org
[3] http://www.ecolex.org/en/treaties/treaties_fulltext.php?docnr=3105&language=en

the Regional Fishery Management Organisations (RFMOs) are the most important); the development of Marine Protected Areas (MPAs), and measures to address particular externalities such as oil pollution and invasive species in ballast water. All are designed to mitigate the effects of open access: that is, to solve the problem posed by non-exclusive use of marine resources in areas beyond national jurisdiction. The most encompassing of the MEAs affecting marine resources are UNCLOS and its instruments (the International Seabed Authority and the International Tribunal for the Law of the Sea) and the CBD. Other agreements dealing with the conservation of marine biodiversity range from species-specific instruments such as the North Atlantic Fur Seal Treaty or the International Commission for the Conservation of Atlantic Tuna (ICCAT), through instruments dealing with groups of species such as the International Whaling Commission, to framework agreements such as the Antarctic Treaty which provides a framework for regulating the use of all marine and terrestrial resources south of the 60° latitude. Despite the existence of these agreements, however, the high seas are regarded as effectively unregulated (FAO, 2004).

There are several reasons for this. The CBD, for example, refers to activities and processes carried out under the jurisdiction or control of a signatory that have an impact on biological diversity. Because they have no jurisdiction over biodiversity located in areas beyond the limits of national jurisdiction, the signatories to the convention have no direct responsibility for its conservation and sustainable use. And while the CBD requires signatories to cooperate to achieve the goals of the Convention, there are no penalties for not doing so. Another difficulty is that Article 87 of UNCLOS affirms the principle of the "freedom of the high seas," and specifically "freedom of fishing." While it also refers to a duty to cooperate with other states in the conservation and management of living resources (Article 118) and to maintain populations of harvested species at levels consistent with maximum sustainable yield (Article 119a), many epipelagic and deep-water fisheries are effectively unprotected (FAO, 2004). This is despite the 1993 FAO Compliance Agreement, the 1995 UN Fish Stocks Agreement, the 1995 FAO Code of Conduct for Responsible Fisheries, and an International Plan of Action to Prevent, Deter and Eliminate Illegal, Unreported and Unregulated Fishing. The Fish Stocks Agreement, for example, now extends over the high-seas areas adjacent to the exclusive economic zones (EEZs) of 77 countries (United Nations General Assembly, 2010). Experience with analogous instruments in terrestrial systems suggests that they are seldom effective in conditions where the incentive to defect is significant (Barrett 1994a, 2003a).

Not all marine agreements are ineffective, however. There are examples of marine MEAs that involve a limited number of signatories; have evolved through repeated renegotiation; and that include effective penalties or disincentives to defect from a precisely defined set of objectives (Barrett, 2003a).

Indeed, the importance of the number of signatories to the effectiveness of agreements in this area lies behind Sandler's (2004, 2005) focus on regional agreements involving smaller numbers. The regional seas programs aim to use regional partnerships to achieve conservation goals, to strengthen national property rights, to translate regional seas conventions into national legislation, to coordinate management actions at the regional level (UN, 2004). The RFMOs that similarly involve smaller numbers of partners have more precisely defined remits than the Compliance and Fish Stocks Agreements (Sandler 2005). Yet, as the FAO points out, UNCLOS does not confer any management authority on regional fishery bodies, and many RFMOs are little different from open access regimes (FAO 2004).

While the RFMOs address at least some of the problems of international coordination identified in the literature—in particular they offer scope for repeated negotiation amongst a relatively small number of parties—they cannot effectively establish exclusive rights for member states (Barrett 2003a). Although some RFMOs have developed policies for non-members, they do not have the capacity to deal with unregulated fishing by non-members (Barrett 2003a). Moreover, many regional solutions merely shift the problem from one marine area to another (FAO 2004).

Although the RFMOs are playing an increasing role in respect of illegal, unreported, and unregulated (IUU) fishing, the existence of that problem is itself evidence of weaknesses in the design and enforcement of the FAO Agreement on Stocks (Barrett 2005). RFMOs are being asked to deal with the management of fleet capacity, the effect of the payment of subsidies and the reduction of bycatch, effort reduction, gear restrictions, inspection, and enforcement. However, their capacity to act is limited. Sanctions can only be levied against free-riders amongst the contracting parties. There is nothing that can legally be done to constrain non-contracting parties. Taking ICCAT as an example, although countries have agreed to conserve the tuna passing through their EEZs, none has an incentive to do so. Not only does a reduction in fishing effort that raises the return to fishing effort leave more fish for others to catch, it also provides non-signatories to the Fish Stocks Agreement with an incentive to enter the fishery. At the same time the vessels of compliant countries themselves have an incentive either to withdraw from the agreement or to ignore the agreed catch levels. ICCAT has adopted trade restrictions as penalties against both non-participants and non-complying states, but since there are fewer than 40 signatories, those who are not in compliance are easily able to evade those sanctions (Barrett 2005).

As a result, there is increasing emphasis on the use of MPAs and Particularly Sensitive Sea Areas (PSSAs) as precursors to MPAs. For areas beyond the limits of national jurisdiction, MPAs have the potential to complement regional management agreements. By siting MPAs in spawning areas of high species richness, for example, it is possible to enhance catches in adjoining areas. The location of marine reserves is critical to their effectiveness as both conservation and fishery protection measures and the location criteria accordingly include both biophysical and economic elements. The economic case for MPAs would seem to be strongest for deepwater coral and seamount habitats that directly or indirectly support both deepwater and epipelagic fisheries (Roberts 2002; Roberts et al. 2003). The CBD has since agreed to promote development of a global network of MPAs, building upon national and regional systems and including a range of levels of protection. One candidate for this is the Arctic Ocean, and it is proposed that an arctic MPA should be zoned for specific uses, but that a substantial proportion should be in fully protected reserves (Chapin et al. 2005).

3.5 GOVERNANCE OF GLOBAL DISEASE RISKS

The second global governance issue I wish to highlight appears more tractable, and it is worth considering why. It is the risks to human, animal, and plant health caused by globalization—the closer integration of the world economic system. This problem is analyzed in some detail in Perrings et al. (2009b), and this section summarizes the conclusions reported there. One measure of the closer integration of the world economic system is the ratio of world trade to global GDP, where trade is typically measured by either import or exports. In the past thirty-five years this ratio has grown from not much more than 10 percent to over 30 percent. The proportion of economic activity involving internationally traded goods and services differs from country to country, but across the board it is rapidly increasing.

One of the main effects of this has been to increase the rate of species dispersal, and especially the dispersal of pathogens. The development of new trade routes has led to the introduction of new species either deliberately or accidentally, while the growth in the volume of trade along those routes has increased the frequency with which introductions are repeated (Cassey et al. 2004). As economies have become more open (with respect to imports and exports) they have also become more likely to experience the introduction of potentially invasive species (Dalmazzone 2000; Vilà and Pujadas 2001). Moreover, as trade between bioclimatically similar regions has increased, the likelihood that introduced species will establish and spread has also risen (Levine and d'Antonio 2003). The risks associated with imports differ depending on the source of the exports and the volume of imports, and the cumulative number of introductions from a particular source is a concave function of the volume of imports—it does attenuate over time (Costello et al. 2007). However, at present the number of new trade routes and the volume of trade along those routes are both increasing rapidly.

There is now clear evidence for the role of trade in the emergence of diseases such as West Nile virus (Lanciotti et al. 1999), SARS (Guan et al. 2003; Li et al. 2005), H5N1 avian influenza (Kilpatrick et al. 2006a, 2006b), and a series of key livestock diseases (Rweyemamu and Astudillo 2002; Karesh et al. 2005; Fevre et al. 2006; Smith et al. 2008). More generally, there is a strong positive relationship between the opening of new markets or trade routes and disease risks (Daszak et al. 2000; Hufnagel et al. 2004; Tatem et al. 2006; Jones et al. 2008). The system of governance for managing global disease risks accordingly involves both the trade system and the pathogen-host system, but there are important differences between the governance of plant and animal disease risks and the governance of human disease risks.

Under the World Trade Organization (WTO) and its constituent agreements, particularly the General Agreement on Tariffs and Trade (GATT) and the Sanitary and Phytosanitary (SPS) Agreement, countries have the right to disrupt trade temporarily to protect food safety, animal, or plant health within their jurisdiction. The SPS Agreement implements the clauses on these matters contained in the GATT, and its primary role is to minimize impacts on trade of sanitary and phytosanitary actions taken by countries to protect food safety, animal, or plant health within their jurisdiction. It is supported by three agencies: the Codex Alimentarius Commission for food safety, the World Organization for Animal Health (International Office of Epizootics for animal health), and the International Plant Protection Convention for plant health. The position with respect to human health is rather different. The 2005 International Health Regulations (IHR) administered by the World Health Organization (WHO) mandate both coordinated and cooperative international action to address human health risks globally, independent of the world trade system. The IHR also authorizes actions that disrupt trade to particular countries, but its focus is global risk and its authority does not derive from the GATT.

The IHR (2005) requires member countries to notify the WHO of any event that may have implications for international health, including public health risks due to the movement of people, disease vectors, or contaminated goods. This includes any action or event that is "likely to significantly affect adversely the biological diversity of other States or areas beyond the limits of national jurisdiction" (IHR, 2005; article 14). More particularly, where the potential damage to other states is "imminent or grave," states are required both to notify potentially affected States and to "initiate action to prevent or minimize such danger or damage" and to "encourage international cooperation to supplement such national efforts and, where appropriate and agreed by the States or regional economic integration organizations concerned, to establish joint contingency plans" (Article 14d, 14e).

One reason for the difference in the treatment of human and other disease risks is that the institutional landscape for the latter is much more fractured.

While human health is the responsibility of the WHO and the IFR, institutions concerned with the impact of invasive species on the general environment include the CBD and its Cartagena Protocol on Biosafety, the Ramsar Convention on Wetlands of International Importance, the Convention on Migratory Species (CMS), the Convention on International Trade in Endangered Species (CITES), and with many other multilateral environmental agreements. Institutions concerned with pathways (transport routes) include the International Maritime Organization (IMO), the International Civil Aviation Organization (ICAO), the International Air Transport Association (IATA), and the UN Convention on the Law of the Sea (UNCLOS). Institutions concerned with agriculture, aquaculture, forestry and fisheries include World Organization for Animal Health (OIE), International Plant Protection Convention (IPPC), and the UN Food and Agriculture Organization (FAO), along with its Compliance Agreement and Code of Conduct for Responsible Fisheries. Institutions concerned with trade include the Convention on International Trade in Endangered Species (CITES), but are dominated by the WTO and the GATT, along with supporting agreements such as the SPS Agreement and the Agreement on Technical Barriers to Trade (TBT Agreement). Many of these bodies have overlapping mandates. The CBD, FAO, and WTO, for example, have broad and frequently overlapping coverage. Since environmental, agricultural, and trade issues often overlap, there is at least a prima facie case for coordinated action. In practice, however, the outcome in any particular case is dominated by the body with the strongest set of rules (frequently the WTO's SPS Agreement). In other instances, nobody has explicit responsibility—the invasive species risks of tourism, emergency aid and development assistance, military activity, and inter-basin water transfers are all cases in point.

The net result is that the international community has done more to protect global human health than to protect the health of all other species, including those on which people most depend. Perrings et al. (2009a) argue for bringing the International Health Regulations and the Sanitary and Phytosanitary Agreement into conformity with one another. The intent of the two agreements is currently very different. The IHR is focused on protecting global human health. The SPS Agreement is focused on minimizing the trade restrictions involved in national defensive measures. They argue that the SPS Agreement should be strengthened to offer the same focus on global risks to human, animal, and plant health. They note that the IHR and the SPS Agreement also involve important differences in the approach they take to building the capacity to discharge countries' responsibilities in each case. The IHR both imposes reporting obligations on countries, and requires that they develop the capacity "to meet develop, strengthen and maintain . . . the capacity to detect, assess, notify and report events in accordance with these Regulations" within a period of five years (IHR 2005: article 5(1)). At the same time, it requires the WHO to "assist States Parties, upon request, to develop, strengthen and maintain the capacities referred to." There is nothing equivalent for the SPS Agreement. Instead, it requires member states to "consider" bilateral assistance, or to "facilitate" multilateral assistance "where substantial investments are required in order for an exporting developing country Member to fulfil the sanitary or phytosanitary requirements of an importing Member" (Article 9.2).

Relative to the treatment of the high seas, however, the MEAs governing global risks to human, animal, and plant health are much more effective. This is largely because of the nature of the public good involved. The control of infectious diseases is a weakest-or weaker-link public good (Sandler 2004). At the national level, an inspection and interception policy that protects the residents of a country against invasive pathogens provides benefits that are neither rival nor exclusive. If one person benefits from the protection offered by the policy, it neither affects the costs of the policy nor the benefits it offers to others. The same is true at the international level. If one country is protected by an international inspection and interception regime, it does not reduce the protection offered to other countries. However, the benefits offered by any inspection and interception regime are only as good as the benefits offered by the least effective provider—the weakest link in the chain. In the national case, for example, if one quarantine facility fails to contain an invasive pathogen, the fact that all others may do so is irrelevant. If one landowner fails to control an invasive plant, it nullifies the control efforts of all others. Internationally, if one country fails to monitor, detect, or contain an infectious disease, it compromises the control efforts of all other countries (Perrings et al. 2002).

More importantly, the international control of infectious diseases is an impure public good. If the well-being of citizens in the ith country depends on both international control of infectious diseases, Y, and a set of other things described by the vector x, that is $U^1 = U^i(x, Y)$, and if Y depends on the contributions of n countries, that is $Y = (y^1, y^2, \ldots, y^i, \ldots, y^n)$, then international control of infectious diseases is an impure public good if $U^i = U^i(x, y^i, Y)$. In other words, the ith country derives both a direct benefit from its own contribution to the public good (the direct protection offered to its citizens) and an indirect benefit from the collective contributions of all other countries. The existence of a direct benefit provides a strong incentive to undertake the defensive actions permitted under both the IHR and the SPS Agreement. Note that it is a weakest-link problem if $Y = \min(y^1, y^2, \ldots, y^i, \ldots, y^n)$; that is, the international control of infectious diseases is equal to the control efforts of the least effective provider. The welfare of the ith country is then described by $U^i = U^i(x, y^i, \min(y^1, y^2, \ldots, y^i, \ldots, y^n))$. If that country is not the weakest link in the chain, the direct benefits offered by its own efforts can be compromised by the weakness of the international control of infectious diseases. This provides an incentive to that country to strengthen the capacity of the weakest link in the chain. Indeed, this is the motivation for the capacity-building provisions in the IHR.

Although the international governance of animal and plant disease risks is different from that of human disease risks, the problem has exactly the same structure and hence exactly the same potential to be effective. While evidence to date suggests that control of most non-human pathogens lags significantly behind that of human pathogens, this is not true of all non-human pathogens. Until recently, the OIE distinguished between species according to both growth and damage potential: transmissible diseases that have the potential for very serious and rapid spread and serious socio-economic implications (List A), and diseases which affect countries that trade animals and animal products, but which are less fast growing or damaging (List B). Analysis of the effectiveness of SPS measures in mitigating the risk that exports would be contaminated by these diseases (Perrings et al. 2009b) indicates a striking difference between the two categories. The international control of animal pathogens that have the potential to impose substantial harm is closer to the international control of human pathogens.

3.6 DISCUSSION

Both the high seas and global disease risks are hard problems, and even though I have characterized governance of global disease risks as more effective than governance of the high seas, the outcome in both cases is less than might be achieved through cooperation. The lack of cooperation is not, however, accidental. It is directly related to the nature of the environmental public good at stake, and the structure of payoffs to alternative strategies. Both these cases are global, but beyond that they have little in common. Nor do they necessarily have much in common with the many other transboundary environmental public goods currently governed through MEAs. The central point here is that understanding the scope for effective governance, and the institutional options available, requires understanding of the nature of the problem—its spatial and temporal dimensions, the nature of the public good and its supply technology, the structure of payoffs this gives rise to, and the resulting strategic problem (the form of the game). At the same time, although some problems are harder than others, for most there is still an incentive to implement a system of governance that will yield an outcome that is better than the non-cooperative Nash equilibrium.

The open access to the high seas enshrined in UNCLOS, and the public good nature of conservation activities, make it hard both to coordinate and enforce conservation efforts in areas beyond national jurisdiction. Yet there are three reasons to think that it should be possible to do better. The first is the fact that many countries have a direct interest (for commercial reasons) in the conservation of biodiversity within their own EEZs, and that the effectiveness of these national efforts can be significantly enhanced if there is coordination of effort in areas beyond the EEZs. This provides a positive incentive to explore the benefits of coordination. It does not solve the problem of illegal, unreported, and unregulated fishing by private interests, but it provides countries with significant marine resources adjacent to the high seas to coordinate actions regionally. The second is that marine biodiversity conservation in areas beyond national jurisdiction may be a threshold public good, implying that the effectiveness of individual conservation efforts depends on a minimum level of collective conservation. This reduces the problem posed by free-riding, and increases the incentive for those with the deepest pockets (the USA in the Pacific and the EU in the Atlantic) to underwrite conservation activities beyond their national jurisdictions. The third is that, as Sandler (2005) has noted, by decomposing the global problem into its regional constituent parts, it may be possible to increase the potential for cooperation by reducing the number of parties involved in the agreement, by tightening the objectives, and by increasing surveillance of member states. Taken together these three things give reason to believe that it may be possible to develop self-enforcing regional agreements to coordinate conservation actions that go beyond the RFMOs.

The problem of global public health risks is more tractable precisely because the potential costs of non-cooperation are both near term and severe, while many of the benefits of national defensive measures are capturable. The weakest-link nature of the public good also provides a clear target for action, and the fact that the weakest link can compromise the effectiveness of defensive measures provides a clear motivation for capacity-building. Indeed, building both capacity and commitment in developing countries to reduce the risks they pose to others is a necessary condition for the provision of many other public goods aside from the control of infectious diseases. Bilateral trade agreements can be useful in raising sanitary and phytosanitary standards in exporting countries. Where achievement of particular sanitary and phytosanitary standards is a condition on exporters, they have an incentive to commit resources to the problem. But while bilateral and regional trade agreements have the potential to improve standards, they necessarily neglect the costs or benefits imposed on third parties. So even if a bilateral agreement internalizes the external effects of trade within the two countries involved, it ignores the effects imposed on third parties. Given the "small world" nature of the global trade network, and the fact that many introductions involve re-infection from third parties, this is not acceptable.

Perrings et al. (2009a) argue that improved governance of plant and animal disease risks requires four things: (1) bringing the SPS Agreement into conformity with the IHR; (2) the development of mechanisms to generate and disseminate information on invasive species risks and their impacts in order to enable the more effective use of defensive measures allowed under the SPS Agreement, especially by developing countries; (3) the coordination of actions by different international institutions, and cooperative international action on invasive species that may cause widespread harm to animals and plants; and (4) the development of a global program of investment in building the capacity to identify and respond to trade-related invasive species risks.

Bringing the SPS Agreement into conformity with the IHR is necessary to recognize and respond to the global nature of many trade-related invasive species risks. While some invasive species issues are highly localized in their effects, and therefore best dealt with at a local level, many others are not. This is particularly true of infectious diseases spread through international trade. The two elements involved in bringing the SPS Agreement into conformity with the IHR are a focus on global as distinct from country-level risk, and global support to individual countries to comply with the terms of the regulations. Capacity building to identify and respond to health risks is already called for under the IHR, but is not funded. A similar requirement is needed under the SPS Agreement, along with the establishment of a global fund for both.

At present, countries individually incur very large costs in terms of output lost to pests and pathogens, compromised human, animal and plant health, impacts on ecological functioning and ecosystem services, along with the costs of inspection, interception, eradication, control, and other sanitary and phytosanitary efforts. But while individual country expenditure on invasive species is large—larger than that on almost any other environmental problem—it is significantly less than it should be. Because countries are authorized by the existing institutional and legal structure to neglect many of the external costs of their actions, they do not take these into account in developing their own invasive species management strategies.

The general point is that if there is a payoff to cooperation, then it may be possible for the contracting parties to a MEA to design the agreement such that it yields the cooperative outcome and is self-enforcing. This will not always be true. The side payments needed to induce cooperation, for example, may not be feasible given the gains to all parties (Barrett 1994b; Sandler 2004). But it is clear that many existing MEAs have to be described as failed opportunities. They have failed to deliver benefits over and above those that would have accrued anyway. Sometimes this is because the agreement is consciously negotiated to deliver an outcome that the parties would have achieved anyway (Murdoch et al. 1997; Sandler 2004), but in many cases it is because MEAs that are negotiated to deliver outcomes closer to the cooperative solution fail to include incentives to comply with the terms of the agreement. They are not self-enforcing. In all cases, the form of the agreement will be sensitive to the nature of the public good at issue, its temporal and spatial scale, and the markets and the institutions within which the contracting parties operate. It is these conditions that determine the supply technology of the environmental public good concerned and the strategic options open to the contracting parties. But it is also these conditions that determine the opportunities for constructing a structure of payoffs that induces the contracting parties to cooperate. What makes global health risk a more tractable problem than the high seas despite its global scale is the high potential cost of pandemics, the impure nature of the public good, and the fact that capacity building in the weakest links in the chain offers a positive payoff to all parties. It is these characteristics that provide the architects of the MEAs concerned with the incentive to design agreements that induce cooperation.

4

Navigating the Sustainability Transition: Governing Complex and Dynamic Socio-ecological Systems

Oran R. Young

4.1 WHAT IS THE PROBLEM?

There is a growing gap between reality and our guiding assumptions about the behavior of socio-ecological systems that threatens to undermine efforts to create effective governance systems to manage or steer human–environment interactions. The dominant paradigm regarding institutional arrangements needed to govern these interactions assumes—implicitly, if not explicitly—that the socio-ecological systems of interest are characterized by linear and gradual, rather than discontinuous and abrupt change. We assume that populations of renewable resources (e.g. fish stocks) will grow or decline smoothly and relatively slowly, so that we do not have to worry about dramatic and sudden collapses once thresholds are crossed or tipping points reached. Similarly, we assume that temperatures will increase and sea levels will rise gradually as a result of climate change, so that we will be able to adapt to these changes on an incremental basis when the time comes to take climate change seriously. For the most part, we assume that human responses to biophysical changes are also linear and gradual. We tend to take it for granted, for instance, that economic adaptation to climate change will be incremental in nature and that policy processes relating to environmental change will not involve system flips or rapid and radical state changes once some sort of crisis occurs. When dramatic or abrupt changes do occur, we are taken by surprise.

In analytic terms, our standard assumptions have significant advantages. The tools we have developed for thinking about systems in which change is linear and gradual are far more sophisticated than the tools available for understanding complex and dynamic systems featuring thresholds, abrupt changes, and emergent properties that generate novel challenges for governance. The problem is that there is a large and profoundly important gap between our assumptions and reality in these terms. This is a consequence, above all, of the emergence of coupled systems in which anthropogenic drivers are prominent forces. Human actions have had major impacts on biophysical systems for thousands of years (Turner et al. 1990). Yet the scope and magnitude of the human forces operating in socio-ecological systems up to and including the Earth itself have risen dramatically (Schellnhuber et al. 2004; Steffen et al. 2004), leading prominent scientists to conclude that we have entered a world of human-dominated ecosystems (Vitousek et al. 1997) and even that the planet has transitioned from the Holocene into a new era best described as the Anthropocene in view of the prominent role of human actions on a planetary scale (Crutzen and Stoermer 2000; Crutzen 2002). Dealing with biophysical systems or socioeconomic systems alone is challenging enough. But the resultant socio-ecological systems are far more complex and dynamic than anything we have encountered previously; there is every reason to expect these conditions to intensify in the future. It follows that we must learn to live with nonlinearities and the inevitable uncertainties associated with complex and dynamic systems if we are to build effective institutions to govern human–environment interactions.

The thesis of this chapter is that the use of management tools that assume change will be linear and gradual to manage complex and dynamic socio-ecological systems is a liability that is already costly and that has the potential to generate profoundly disruptive consequences for humans and their communities in the future. We are plagued by a problem of fit that is becoming more severe, despite growing sophistication regarding management tools and practices (Young 2002; Young et al. 2006; Galaz et al. 2008). Or, to use the terminology Vatn employs in Chapter 2, we run a growing risk of relying on policies that do not match the nature of the problems they are intended to address (Vatn this volume). In developing this thesis and analyzing its implications, I proceed as follows. The first substantive section of the chapter provides a brief account of the nature of change in socio-ecological systems and the challenges different types of change pose for those who are responsible for managing human–environment interactions. The next section explores the management tools available to address situations of this kind and asks how the use of these tools in a systematic and sustained manner would lead to management practices that differ from those characteristic of most current governance systems dealing with human–environment interactions. The penultimate section introduces and examines the implications of the proposition that institutional arrangements themselves are complex and dynamic systems characterized by a pronounced tendency to change in nonlinear and abrupt ways. The concluding section then seeks to distill some initial lessons from this account of complex and dynamic systems that support several principles regarding ways to (re)form resource and environmental regimes to achieve sustainable results in a world in which change can be nonlinear, abrupt, irreversible, and often nasty from a human perspective. The result is what I call navigating the sustainability transition.

4.2 SOCIO-ECOLOGICAL SYSTEMS ARE COMPLEX AND DYNAMIC

The systems we are concerned with in efforts to manage human–environment interactions are highly dynamic. They change continually, and there is no reason to take it for granted that homeostatic processes will ensure that they remain within relatively well-defined basins of attraction (Gunderson and Holling 2002; Walker and Salt 2006). One of the few constants in these systems is change itself. But it is useful, at the outset, to differentiate among a number of dimensions or aspects of change occurring in biophysical systems, socioeconomic systems, and—most importantly for our purposes— socio-ecological systems. Although many distinctions regarding types of change are relevant, the dimensions of linearity, speed, and reversibility are particularly important for the purposes of this analysis.

Linearity has to do with discontinuities in rates of change. A population that grows at a constant rate per unit of time (e.g. 5 percent per year) is changing in a linear fashion, even though (other things being equal) compound growth will lead over time to an explosion in the size of the population. Even shifts in rates of change at the margin can be represented in linear terms. Nonlinearities occur when change is discontinuous. To use the example of a population again, nonlinear change occurs when a population reaches a critical threshold or tipping point and then crashes. Similarly, a population that declines beyond some threshold will become non-viable, though it may prove difficult to determine precisely where this threshold lies and how long it will take for extinction to occur. Phenomena of the same type are common in socioeconomic systems as well. Discontinuities occur when otherwise constant rates of change accelerate to produce sustained growth, hyperinflation, or stock market crashes. Some of these changes are also sudden or abrupt in character. But it is the discontinuity in the rate of change rather than the speed of change that is the hallmark of (non)linearity.

The speed of change is a distinct property that may or may not correlate with linearity. Some changes in complex systems are gradual, taking place over long periods of time, while others are sudden or abrupt. Animal populations that grow slowly may cross some critical threshold (e.g. the exhaustion of food or water supplies) and crash seemingly overnight. Human systems that take decades or even centuries to build up may pass some tipping point and collapse like a house of cards (Tainter 1988; Diamond 2005). Much of the recent scientific interest in climate change focuses on abrupt change or what have become known as rapid climate change events or RCCEs caused by trigger mechanisms like the disintegration of major ice sheets or the shutting down of the thermohaline circulation (Alley 2000; Mayewski and White 2002). But some changes in dynamic systems are remarkably slow or gradual. The decline of the Roman Empire, for instance, played out over several centuries (Homer-Dixon 2006). Sea level rise may occur at a rate of 1–2 centimeters per year over a period of decades or even centuries without triggering massive or sudden shifts in related systems.

Looming over these concerns is the issue of reversibility. Some changes are reversible; they may even shift back and forth in some regular or cyclical fashion. But others are irreversible. Many weather patterns are reversible. Seasons follow a prescribed pattern. Droughts come and go. The phenomenon known as El Niño produces change in patterns of precipitation that oscillate between unusually dry and unusually wet seasons. On the other hand, shifts in the Earth's climate system occurring in geologic time are essentially irreversible. We cannot simply go back to the relatively benign conditions prevailing in the Holocene, whether we like it or not. As this example suggests, however, reversibility is often a matter of time scales. What seems irreversible on a human scale may be part of a regular cycle playing out over tens of thousands of years. What is more, there are many cases of partial or perhaps we should say dynamic reversibility. Abandoned farm land typically reverts to forest in short order. But there is no reason to assume that the pattern of succession will produce an assemblage of species in the regenerated forest that is essentially the same as that characteristic of the pre-agricultural forest.

These are analytic distinctions. Actual changes will be linear or nonlinear, slow or fast, and reversible or irreversible at the same time. Some of the resultant combinations will be more benign and easy to adapt to than others from a human perspective. Those changes that are linear, slow, and reversible are comparatively easy to deal with, whereas changes that are nonlinear, abrupt, and irreversible will be difficult or even impossible for humans to anticipate or adapt to without dramatic changes in prevailing social practices. This accounts for much of our current concern about the problem of climate change. So long as we could assume that changes in the Earth's climate system would play out over centuries and involve only modest shifts in temperatures and patterns of rainfall, it was easy to operate on the assumption that adaptation would occur without any need for intervention on the part of the state. But the occurrence of RCCEs is another matter altogether (Linden 2006). We know that dramatic changes in the Earth's climate system have occurred in the past in a matter of years, much less decades or centuries (Alley 2000). What once seemed a good candidate for benign neglect has become a prominent item on public policy agendas around the world.

Changes that are nonlinear, abrupt, and irreversible are common enough in both biophysical systems and socioeconomic systems. Phase or state changes affecting large ecosystems occur in many settings. Much of the current concern about the fate of large marine ecosystems or LMEs, for instance, arises from the growing realization that these systems are susceptible to poorly understood system flips, a condition that calls into question familiar management practices governing consumptive uses of renewable resources (e.g. fish) and efforts to regulate the flow of pollutants into marine systems. Much the same is true of socioeconomic systems. What makes stock market crashes and business cycles so challenging, for example, is the occurrence of changes that are nonlinear and abrupt at the same time.

The argument I develop in this chapter starts with the proposition that coupled or socio-ecological systems are more likely to give rise to changes that are, at one and the same time, nonlinear, abrupt, and irreversible than either biophysical systems or socioeconomic systems on their own. This may seem paradoxical at first. After all, human systems are reflexive, and there is some reason to believe that humans will observe the early stages of major changes and take steps to prevent such changes from getting out of hand (Young et al. 2006). But despite the effects of reflexivity, there is no evidence that humans have acquired the knowledge and the capacity to initiate and coordinate actions needed to manage changes that occur abruptly and on a large scale. Human reactions to changes in complex systems are just as likely to trigger positive or self-reinforcing feedback processes that increase the likelihood of system flips rather preventing such changes.

If this argument is correct, we will need a whole new generation of governance systems or regimes to cope with the challenges of the Anthropocene. The fact that such changes will occur on a large scale means that we will need to address them through international and even global initiatives; uncoordinated national responses will not suffice. The abruptness of many of these changes will call into question current practices in which the formation of international or global regimes—much less their implementation—often takes years and involves numerous false starts before progress is made (Young 1999). And the irreversibility of some of the largest and most nonlinear changes means that efforts to address the resultant problems through some procedure featuring trial-and-error will be risky. In many cases, we will need to get our responses right at the outset or risk severe reductions in human welfare. It is easy to see that this will require dramatic adjustments in the procedures we use to govern or manage human–environment relations at the macro-level. But let me sharpen this issue and turn in into a question. What specific changes in regimes or governance systems will be needed to achieve sustainability in a world of dynamic socio-ecological systems?

4.3 GOVERNING COMPLEX AND DYNAMIC SOCIO-ECOLOGICAL SYSTEMS REQUIRES INNOVATION

The density of problem-specific regimes operating at the international or transnational level has increased dramatically over the period since the end of World War II. Some of these arrangements (e.g. the regime for Antarctica, the ozone regime, the regime for the North Sea, the Rhine River regime) have performed well, at least in terms of fulfilling their stated goals (Haas et al. 1993; Miles et al. 2002; Breitmeier, Young, and Zürn 2006; Breitmeier, Underdal, and Young 2011). Still, as the cases of climate change and the loss of biological diversity make clear, few of these regimes have been constructed to deal with changes that are nonlinear, abrupt, and irreversible. For the most part, they rest on (often implicit) premises that are at odds with the picture of change in socio-ecological systems I sketched in the preceding section. What would it take to reconstruct these arrangements or to build new ones to address the demand for governance arising in dynamic socio-ecological systems? In my judgment, the answer to this question involves three related yet analytically distinct elements that I shall describe as harnessing reflexivity, enhancing adaptability, and coping with uncertainty.

4.3.1 Harnessing reflexivity

Reflexive systems are those in which expectations regarding future developments trigger anticipatory responses. As this statement implies, we normally use the term reflexivity to refer to situations in which human actions are central to the dynamics of the relevant systems. The emphasis is on expectations and anticipatory responses framed in anthropogenic terms. It is possible to argue that other systems are reflexive, too, in the sense that non-human actors are capable of sensing patterns of change and taking actions designed to deal with expected rather than actual changes. But in this discussion of governance involving highly dynamic systems, the emphasis is on the capacity of human actors both to foresee or anticipate impending changes and to react in appropriate ways before the changes in question actually occur.

It is striking how often human actors fail to anticipate nonlinear and abrupt changes that have far-reaching effects on their livelihoods. Studies of the collapse of whole societies emphasize this phenomenon on a grand scale (Tainter 1988; Diamond 2005). But examples dealing with changes that are more limited in scope but closer to home are easy enough to locate. Few observers, much less actual policymakers, foresaw the collapse of cod stocks in the northwest Atlantic during the 1990s prior to the actual collapse. Most observers were taken by surprise by the swift disintegration of the Soviet Union in the run-up to the final collapse in 1991.

Even when human actors recognize prospective changes and take actions based on their expectations, the result may be to increase the likelihood of nonlinear, abrupt, and detrimental changes. We are all familiar with the idea of a run on the bank in which panicky actions on the part of sizable groups of individual actors ensure that widely feared events actually come to pass. But positive feedback processes that generate self-fulfilling prophecies can and do occur in many settings. The results range from fiscal crises that undermine otherwise stable economic systems to the self-generating dynamics of arms races that prove immensely costly, do nothing to enhance security, and may even precipitate wars that no one wants. The phenomenon of reflexivity may emerge as part of the problem rather than part of the solution in efforts to devise governance systems capable of dealing with dynamic socio-ecological systems in which nonlinear and irreversible changes are prominent realities.

Still, reflexivity can emerge as part of the effort to build effective governance systems in such settings. The trick here is to devise negative feedback mechanisms that can alter the trajectory of the system before emerging trends cross a point of no return or tipping point beyond which profound changes become inevitable. Familiar cases involve going on a diet to avoid the onset of obesity leading to fatal illnesses and using monetary policy (e.g. cutting interest rates on the part of the Federal Reserve Bank) to prevent economic downturns from triggering recessions or depressions. As these examples suggest, making use of reflexivity to address problems of governance is complex. It is hard to forecast the consequences of gaining weight, and diets can produce undesirable consequences of their own. Cuts in interest rates on the part of central banks can trigger inflation, whether or not they succeed in their primary objective of stimulating economic activity.

Even so, there is much to be said for efforts to harness reflexivity as a means to maintain the fit between socio-ecological systems and relevant governance systems. Perhaps the most dramatic case in point today involves the looming threat of climate change. Although we do not know what level of greenhouse gases in the Earth's atmosphere will lead to a tipping point making major changes in the climate system unavoidable, it is easy to see that recent trends in emissions of greenhouse gases are unsustainable. Although it is possible that limiting concentrations of carbon dioxide in the atmosphere to 450ppm will suffice to avoid dangerous anthropogenic interference in the climate system, many scientists now take the view that it would be safer to aim for 350ppm. But as our understanding of this system grows, pressure is rising to take actions now to avoid costly impacts in the future (Stern 2007).

Despite its limitations, the development of the climate regime constitutes a significant effort to harness reflexivity. It seeks to mobilize actors who are preoccupied with current problems to expend time, energy, and material resources on avoiding the occurrence of a future development that is hard for most people to understand and that may not generate costly impacts for some time to come. As our experience with integrated assessment modeling suggests, moreover, there is profound uncertainty regarding both the probable costs of a failure to respond to changes in the Earth's climate system in a timely manner and the likely costs of taking effective steps to avoid the impacts of climate change (Stern 2007; Nordhaus 2008).

As this example suggests, three key conditions govern the success of efforts to harness reflexivity to address large-scale problems associated with human–environment interactions. First is the issue of timing. How long should we wait before intervening, knowing not only that irreversible change is a distinct possibility but also that our understanding of the problem will improve over time and that our capacity to respond effectively is likely to grow? Is it accurate, for instance, to say that we have one or at most two decades left to make a determined effort to head off dramatic changes in the Earth's climate system? Second is the matter of collective action. How can we ensure that efforts to address climate change will take the form of concerted or coordinated actions? In cases like climate change where global actions are needed and incentives to free-ride on the efforts of others are substantial, the challenge of coordinating responses looms large. Third is the problem of opportunity costs and avoiding unintended but potentially severe side-effects of the actions we take. As those whose primary concern is the fulfillment of the Millennium Development Goals know well, a desire on the part of wealthy developed countries to accord priority to the problem of climate change can divert attention from problems of poverty, inadequate sanitation, and substandard health care that are central concerns in the developing world (Young and Steffen 2009).

It follows that harnessing reflexivity is easier said than done. Still, this is a unique feature of human systems that can help to avoid the dangers arising when governance systems lack the nimbleness to adapt by reacting quickly and decisively to changes in socio-ecological systems that are nonlinear, abrupt, or irreversible. To the extent that governance systems are unable to adjust rapidly, it makes sense to get a jump on problems by anticipating their occurrence and reacting in advance, rather than waiting until they are upon us before reacting.

4.3.2 Enhancing adaptive capacity

It takes no genius to see that success in governing socio-ecological systems subject to changes that are nonlinear, abrupt, and irreversible will require an ability to detect and interpret correctly the onset of such changes coupled with the flexibility needed to adjust the terms of institutional arrangements to take into account the (anticipated) consequences of the changes. But what does this mean in practice? Is there a danger that the arrangements required to deal with these challenges will necessitate costly compromises in terms of other conditions that are important to the achievement of success in regimes created to govern or manage human–environment interactions? If so, what can we do to limit the impact of such compromises without sacrificing the ability to create and maintain the required level of adaptability? This subsection addressees these questions through an examination of monitoring, early warning, and adaptive management.

Everyone will agree that monitoring is important to any effort to govern or manage dynamic socio-ecological systems. The more these systems are prone to changes that are nonlinear, abrupt, and irreversible, moreover, the greater the need for high-quality monitoring. But what exactly does this mean in practice? Knowing what to monitor may require both a sophisticated understanding of the nature of the socio-ecological system in question and the development of a set of indicators that can track the behavior of the system well and that are widely accepted. Systems featuring natural feedback mechanisms that trigger countercyclical processes require less monitoring than those in which positive feedback mechanisms can lead to runaway processes. For some purposes a one dimensional indicator (e.g. GDP per capita) may suffice. But an index that encompasses several dimensions (e.g. the UN Human Development Index) will prove more useful in other situations (UNDP 2006, 2007).

There are obvious questions concerning both the frequency of observations and the number of independent observations needed to obtain an accurate picture of the status of specific systems. Observations taken annually or even at multi-year intervals (e.g. the typical ten-year census cycle) may be sufficient for some purposes but not for others. A small number of observations may suffice in tracking homogeneous systems yet be inadequate with respect to systems that are characterized by high levels of diversity. In dealing with marine systems, which are three-dimensional and relatively opaque to many forms of observation, monitoring is a much more challenging task than it is in most terrestrial systems. Monitoring systems designed to anticipate abrupt changes (e.g. volcanic eruptions, tsunamis, hurricanes) will require much more frequent observations than monitoring systems in which change is slow, even though it may turn out to be nonlinear. Continuous monitoring may be needed in some cases.

There is much to be said for enhancing monitoring capacity and building redundancy into observing systems. Yet resources are always limited, and monitoring can become an expensive proposition. So we are apt to be caught in the following dilemma. The more we find ourselves dealing with changes that are nonlinear, abrupt, and irreversible, the greater our need for sophisticated and continuous monitoring. But such conditions also give rise to other needs (e.g. a rapid response capacity to cope with the impacts of abrupt events like earthquakes). The result is a need to make trade-offs or, in other words, to decide what to give up or forego in order to free resources to enhance monitoring capacity. Generic formulas that call for allocating more resources to monitoring until the marginal benefits from doing so just equal marginal costs will not get us far in such situations. In cases like the loss of biological diversity where we do not have certain knowledge about the existence of many—perhaps most—species, we do not even know what to monitor (Wilson 2003). On the other hand, when it comes to climate change, where it makes sense to think of the Earth's climate system as a single, integrated whole, the case for monitoring on a planetary scale is compelling.

What are the implications of these observations for specific governance systems like the climate regime or the regime for biological diversity? One response to this question is to design monitoring efforts to maximize returns on our investment. In dealing with biodiversity, for example, there is much to be said for focusing attention on the condition of keystone species or on hot spots that are unusually rich in species. There is a similar argument for paying attention to areas that can function as the canary in the mine with regard to climate change (ACIA 2004). In all cases, we should be on the lookout for thresholds and trigger mechanisms. Such mechanisms produce results that are disproportionate to their role in causal clusters. Their value from the point of view of monitoring lies in the fact that they may help us to identify conditions leading to the onset of changes that are nonlinear in nature. Given the constraints arising from competing demands on available resources (economists would call them income effects), there is a good case for approaching this issue in investment terms, adopting strategies that are both focused and intensive.

These comments lead naturally to the proposition that we are in need of early warning systems. It makes sense to design monitoring systems in such a way as to provide as much warning as possible regarding approaching thresholds or tipping points that can precipitate system flips. But whereas the case for monitoring is always persuasive, early warning becomes important under specific conditions. When changes are linear, gradual, and reversible, we will naturally want to track their trajectories. But there is no particular need to make a large investment in early warning. Even nonlinear changes may occur in slow motion, giving those likely to be affected by system flips ample time to take note of the changes and to act in ways that eliminate or at least alleviate the negative impacts of nonlinear changes on human welfare. But early warning is important in cases involving abrupt changes (e.g. earthquakes, hurricanes, floods, or volcanic eruptions). This leads to the following formula. Monitor changes in all cases, but focus on early warning only in those cases where abrupt changes are expected and the events in question are likely to produce major impacts on social welfare.

Whether or not the case for early warning is compelling, institutional arrangements dealing with highly dynamic socio-ecological systems must have a capacity to adapt or adjust in the face of change. Analytically, we can distinguish among adaptive changes occurring at three distinct levels. First is the operational or micro-level at which managers make adjustments that do not require changes in the prevailing rules of the game or approval on the part of governing bodies. Changes in the length of seasons (i.e. in the use of openings and closings) or adjustments in total allowable catches in the fisheries exemplify adjustments of this sort. At the next or meso-level, adjustments typically involve the introduction of new rules or rights or adjustments in the obligations of subjects, without altering the defining features of the regime itself. The case of the ozone regime in which phase-out schedules can be accelerated without triggering the need for ratification and new families of chemicals can be added to those slated for phase out with the consent of the members provides a prominent example (Parson 2003), At the third or macro-level lie those situations involving the transformation of existing regimes or the creation of new ones in order to meet the rising demand for governance. The replacement of traditional command-and-control regulations in the fisheries with arrangements relying heavily on incentive mechanisms in such forms as individual transferable quotas (ITQs), designated access privileges (DAPs), or catch shares constitutes a prominent case in point. Even broader are proposals calling for the elimination of sector-specific arrangements (e.g. fisheries regimes) and their replacement with more integrated arrangements of the sort envisioned in the idea of ecosystem-based management or EBM (Crowder et al. 2006).

The widely discussed but somewhat vague idea of adaptive management comes into focus here (Lee 1992). Adaptive management applies to the first level and probably the second level identified in the previous paragraph. It makes sense to experiment with the use of specific policy instruments, such as no-take zones and gear restrictions in the fisheries or phase-out schedules in the case of ozone-depleting substances. But when it comes to more transformative changes like the shift from systems focused on maximum sustainable yields (MSY) to EBM in ocean governance or the creation of quasi-markets designed to reduce atmospheric pollution, it is probably better to speak of societal learning (Social Learning Group 2001). At this level, we are replacing existing arrangements with something qualitatively different rather than adjusting arrangements already in place in the light of new information about the problem to be solved or the efficacy of specific policy instruments.

At each level, there is a need for sufficient flexibility to adjust or even to transform existing arrangements in the face of changes that are nonlinear, abrupt, and irreversible. Yet this can become a slippery slope with regard to the effectiveness of governance systems. Any arrangement that changes in response to every little shift in the (perceived) nature of the problem or the behavior of the subjects cannot be effective in governing human–environment interactions. Systems that are extremely difficult or impossible to adjust in the light of changing circumstances, on the other hand, will become brittle and ultimately collapse as circumstances change. The result is a challenge to those charged with (re)designing management systems. In this context, the gap between rules on paper and rules in use may be large. The Antarctic Treaty of 1959, to take a specific example, allows for the convening of a review conference at any time after the treaty has been in force for 30 years (that is, from 1991 onward). But this provision has never been activated, even though there are a number of matters that could and should be revisited in the light of experience with this regime. The problem arises from the fact that many members of the regime believe that holding a review conference would open a Pandora's box of proposed changes and that the overall results of such a conference would constitute a step backward rather than a step forward. Consequently, they prefer to make adjustments in a piecemeal manner rather than engaging in a more comprehensive review process.

The levels of change identified in the previous paragraphs are relevant in this context. It makes sense to increase the stringency of the procedures governing adjustments as we move from the micro-level to the macro-level. Experiments designed to fine tune existing policy instruments (e.g. the details of the cap-and-trade system applying to emissions of sulfur dioxide in the United States) make a lot of sense. But we are understandably cautious when it comes to major adjustments in constitutive agreements or even proposals to replace them with new and substantially different arrangements. Consider the differences among adjusting existing regulations, passing new laws, and adopting amendments to the constitution of the United States as a case in point. Under most circumstances, it makes sense to provide administrative agencies with the discretionary authority needed to adjust regulations in the face of change, while at the same time adopting rules and procedures that make it very hard to enact amendments to the constitution itself.

Another point worth noting in this discussion of adaptive capacity concerns forms of change. While some changes are formalized and codified through constitutional amendments or legally binding agreements, others involve informal adjustments to day-to-day practices. The challenge here is to match forms of change with the circumstances at hand, rather than to ask whether one form of change is preferable to the others. Informal changes have the virtues of being easier to adopt, quicker to implement, and less controversial to adjust. But formal or legally binding changes have greater normative force and put more pressure on subjects to comply with their requirements or adjust their behavior to meet the requirements of new systems of rights and rules. In cases where changes are nonlinear and especially abrupt, relying on informal adjustments is often essential. Changes in constitutions or other constitutive documents involve deliberative processes that cannot be rushed.

There may be good reasons to update constitutions from time to time to formalize major developments in the de facto character of governance systems as well as to adjust to socioeconomic changes. But when changes are nonlinear, abrupt, and irreversible, the case for relying on informal changes—at least in the short run—is compelling.

4.3.3 Coping with uncertainty

No matter how much effort we devote to analysis and other forms of preparatory work, there is no way to avoid uncertainty in governing human–environment interactions involving complex and dynamic socio-ecological systems. Uncertainty involves unknowns occurring at several levels. Ordinary uncertainty is a matter of our inability to provide clearcut answers to questions of the following sort. How many distinct species are there on the planet? For any given species, how low can the population go without turning it into a relic or ghost species? At what level will concentrations of greenhouse gases in the atmosphere give rise to dangerous anthropogenic interference in the climate system? What is the probability that highly disruptive RCCEs will occur during the next few decades? Beyond this, lies what we can call second-order uncertainty, a higher level of uncertainty that has to do with unknown unknowns. Are there as yet undetected forces that can help to explain why the Earth's climate system has behaved in a benign manner over the past 10,000 years and that will determine the likelihood that this situation will continue in the future? Will globalization affect large-scale socio-ecological systems in ways that we have yet to conceptualize, much less to analyze in a systematic manner?

Recent thinking about biophysical systems has emphasized an holistic approach, a perspective that highlights dynamism, nonlinear processes, state changes, and the importance of emergent properties. Similar comments are in order regarding socioeconomic systems. As the stories of numerous failed states attest, these systems can experience state changes that take even attentive observers by surprise. But where uncertainty becomes particularly wide and deep is in efforts to understand the dynamics of socio-ecological systems. Here we face not only uncertainty associated with the behavior of biophysical systems and socioeconomic systems but also the higher-order uncertainty that arises in conjunction with coupled systems in which biophysical and human forces become interactive drivers. This variety of uncertainty is destined to grow in importance as we move deeper into the Anthropocene or, in other words, into an era of human-dominated ecosystems in which it is pointless to attempt to analyze either the biophysical or the anthropogenic forces at work in terms of models that set one or the other of these types of forces aside as exogenous factors.

There is much more to be said about specific types of uncertainty and about the prospects for reducing or even eliminating uncertainty regarding some issues (Kahneman and Tversky 2000). But the important point here is that regimes governing human–environment interactions in complex and dynamic systems must be able to function effectively in situations featuring more or less severe uncertainties. Among the strategies available for coping with these uncertainties are adoption of precautionary measures including insurance, the development of heuristics or rules of thumb, and the conduct of targeted research efforts.

One way to respond to uncertainty is to adopt a precautionary approach. In other realms (e.g. national security), we routinely base policy choices on some form of worst-case analysis. We assume the worst about both the capabilities and the intentions of potential opponents and construct our defense forces with this assumption in mind. Following this logic, we routinely allocate hundreds of billions of dollars—over 4 percent of GDP in the USA—to defense spending every year. This is not to say that we should adopt a worst-case approach to potential problems arising in human–environment interactions; it is worth asking whether extreme forms of worst-case thinking have done more harm than good in the case of national security. Nonetheless, it is striking how reluctant we are to consider and act on increasingly plausible scenarios about threats associated with RCCEs. A precautionary approach in this case would center on making deep cuts in emissions of greenhouse gases justified by the possibility of RCCEs occurring, even though we are not able to forecast either the timing or the consequences of such events with precision. Calculations of the costs of adopting such an approach in the case of climate suggest that taking action would be expensive (costing perhaps 1–2 percent of GDP) but not nearly as expensive as the measures we take in the name of national security.

A related but distinct response to uncertain events centers on the develop-ment of insurance schemes. The purpose of insurance—in such forms as life insurance and home owners insurance—is to avoid ruination in the face of uncertain but catastrophic events, such as a premature death or the destruc-tion of a home by fire (Leggett 2001). Useful as these devices are in their normal applications, they have major limitations as procedures for dealing with problems like climate change that grow out of human–environment interactions under conditions of uncertainty. It is virtually impossible to approach threats like climate change in actuarial terms. We are dealing here with events that are to a large extent one of a kind. The best we can do under the circumstances is to employ subjective probabilities, a procedure that is often contested and requires a willingness to address normative issues, such as whether or how to discount the significance of events that may occur at some time in the future. The strategy of taking out insurance also gives rise to the problem of moral hazard. To the extent that they are confident that either private or public insurance systems will indemnify their losses, individuals may take greater risks than would otherwise be the case. We see this clearly in such cases as the destruction wrought by the impact of hurricanes on homes located on barrier islands or the impact of wild fires on homes located in areas prone to fire. So long as the government is willing to designate hard hit areas as disaster zones and to provide generous financial aid to victims of such destructive events, owners of homes in areas prone to flooding or burning will be more likely to rebuild in the same place rather than to relocate, as would be the case in the absence of public assistance.

Another response to the uncertainties associated with human–environment interactions is to rely on various types of heuristics or rules of thumb (Tversky and Kahneman 1974). The use of heuristics is widespread in situations involving uncertainty, which is to say in most situations that find their way onto the agenda of public policy. There is simply no way to avoid making decisions about a raft of issues (e.g. national defense, macroeconomic policy, education) in which difficulties of measurement abound and uncertainties about the impacts of policies loom large. One way to respond to this situation is to make use of rules of thumb to bridge the gap. Such rules may cover a wide range of situations from expectations about the extent to which subjects will comply with regulatory measures to expectations about the costs of achieving various environmental goals. We may hope that rules of this sort involve inductive reasoning, even in cases where it is impossible to establish causal connections. Thus, rules of thumb can reflect best practices in the sense that they arise from a careful consideration of a number of cases that resemble one another in significant ways (e.g. they all require finding ways to avoid the tragedy of the commons or to deal with externalities that impinge on the welfare of others). Rules of thumb always rest on subjective calculations or qualitative judgments; applying them to specific situations can produce results that run counter to the goals of policy makers. Still, the case for developing such rules is strong. Framing best practices in the form of recommendations relevant to current issues is a better response to uncertainty than a procedure reflecting nothing but ad hoc or "seat-of-the-pants" judgments.

It is naïve to suppose that research can eliminate the uncertainties that plague efforts to make good choices regarding issues that arise in human–environment interactions. Nonetheless, applied research may prove helpful to policy makers responsible for making such choices. One prominent case involves the conduct of scientific assessments of the sort we associate with the work of the Intergovernmental Panel on Climate Change (IPCC) and the Millennium Ecosystem Assessment (MEA) (MEA 2005; IPCC 2007b). These projects strive to synthesize all available knowledge. They do not feature the conduct of new research, and they do not eliminate uncertainty surrounding major issues like climate change or the loss of biological diversity. Yet it is widely acknowledged that these projects have proven helpful to policy makers despite—or perhaps because of—the uncertainties surrounding such issues (Mitchell et al. 2006). The IPCC's assessment reports do not tell us how high concentrations of greenhouse gases in the atmosphere can go without triggering dangerous anthropogenic interference in the climate system. Those responsible for IPCC assessments are careful to give a range of estimates regarding such matters and to stress that these estimates should not be construed as predictions (Bolin 1997). Even so, the work of the panel has generated useful results on issues ranging from the atmospheric processes that give rise to climate change to the probable results of various proposals for carbon sequestration or carbon capture and storage.

Simulations of the sort associated with integrated assessment modeling constitute another useful research endeavor. Such efforts join together bio-physical components (e.g. climate models) with socioeconomic components (e.g. macroeconomic models) to explore the interactions characteristic of coupled systems. The simulations arising from these exercises are not predictive in any meaningful sense. But they are useful in exploring the dynamics of complex systems. They allow us to explore the sensitivity of some components of the system to relatively small changes in other components. A particularly interesting case in point centers on the development of models to explore the effects of alternative discount rates in comparing the costs to society arising from the impacts of projected changes in the climate system with the costs of launching sustained efforts to lower the probability that such changes will occur (Stern 2007; Nordhaus 2008).

4.4 INSTITUTIONAL ARRANGEMENTS ARE COMPLEX AND DYNAMIC SYSTEMS, TOO

The previous section focused on the nature of socio-ecological systems and explored the features of institutional arrangements needed to steer or guide these systems toward socially desirable outcomes. The basic message is clear. The combination of highly dynamic socio-ecological systems and high levels of uncertainty regarding the behavior of these systems calls for the creation and operation of institutional arrangements that differ in significant ways from the regimes we normally think of in our efforts to address environmental and natural resource issues. But there is another source of complexity we must consider in this context as well. Institutional arrangements are systems, too, and there are good reasons to regard them as complex and dynamic systems just like the socio-ecological systems they are created to govern. This means we must be prepared for failure in our efforts to govern or manage specific human–environment interactions. But we also need to redouble our efforts to understand the challenge of governance in this setting and to devise arrangements that are both adaptable in the face of change and able to tolerate high levels of uncertainty.

Consider, again, the issues of linearity, speed, and reversibility as features of change. Nonlinear change is a common occurrence with regard to institutional arrangements. There is a sense in which the creation of a new regime or a fundamental change in an existing regime constitutes a form of planned nonlinearity. Given the complications associated with implementation or, in other words, the shift from paper to practice with regard to institutional arrangements, such changes may be somewhat less dramatic on the ground than they appear to be in theory. Nevertheless, the creation of the regime designed to protect the stratospheric ozone layer through the adoption of the 1985 Vienna Convention and the 1987 Montreal Protocol produced a clearcut break or discontinuity with the situation prevailing prior to the adoption of these agreements (Parson 2003). Although the mechanism was less formal in the sense that it did not involve changing legally binding provisions, we can say also that the adoption in 1982 of a moratorium on the harvesting of great whales gave rise to a nonlinear shift in the character of the regime established under the terms of the 1946 International Convention on the Regulation of Whaling (Friedheim 2001). Similar breaks occur at other levels of social organization as well. The decision in the United States to reduce emissions of sulfur dioxide by roughly 50 percent and to create a cap-and-trade system to achieve this goal under the provisions of the Clean Air Act Amendments of 1990 constitute a nonlinear change at the national level (Bryner 1995).

Institutional arrangements can also pass thresholds or tipping points that precipitate rapid changes. Under normal circumstances, regimes are remarkably path dependent, sometimes remaining in place long after the problems they address change substantially and mismatches between problems and institutional arrangements become prominent. Yet abrupt changes in institutions are also common; they often take even those who are closely involved in their management by surprise. We are all familiar with such cases at the macro level; the collapse of the Soviet Union in the early 1990s is a striking example. But similar changes occur from time to time with regard to environmental and resource regimes. The regime designed to manage the harvesting of northern fur seals, which had a history stretching back to the early years of the twentieth century, collapsed like a house of cards in 1984–1985 when the US Senate refused to approve what previously would have been a routine extension of its provisions. The international regime governing exchange rates and related monetary issues experienced a sea change in 1971 when the USA decided that it would no longer treat the dollar as convertible to gold. Nor is abrupt change confined to the collapse or dramatic restructuring of regimes. Efforts to create regimes that seem stuck and unlikely to bear fruit can experience breakthroughs when diplomatic or legislative logjams are broken.

An interesting case in point is the regime governing the administration of the Svalbard Archipelago. The provisions of the 1920 Treaty of Spitsbergen, adopted almost as an afterthought in the peace settlement following World War I, would have been impossible to adopt in the political environment of the pre-war period (Singh and Saguirian 1993).

Similar remarks are in order regarding the magnitude of change, at least relative to the scale and scope of issues that environmental and resource regimes address. It is hard to imagine a more fundamental change than the shift from a regime designed to manage consumptive uses of whales to an arrangement based on the idea of preservation and intended to terminate harvesting. The decision of the USA to mandate sharp reductions in emissions of sulfur dioxide also deserves to be treated as a fundamental change. It represented a sharp break from a system in which emitters were permitted to use the atmosphere as a repository for wastes free of charge to a system in which this use of the atmosphere is acknowledged to amount to the use of a scarce resource and is priced accordingly. Institutional changes that are incremental or so modest that they are hard to identify are also common. This is especially true regarding contested issues where changes are clothed in language that is so opaque that it is difficult to determine whether or not they will amount to anything over time. It is important to recognize that environmental and resource regimes are not static arrangements; change of one sort or another is a continuous process in such settings.

Most institutional changes are irreversible. Like ecosystems that have been disturbed, regimes that are subjected to more or less severe stresses seldom settle back into patterns that replicate the status quo ante, even after a crisis or a significant perturbation subsides. It is normal to add new provisions to a regime designed to avoid or to cope with the forces giving rise to a crisis. Whether or not they prove effective in specific cases, the introduction of limited-entry schemes to stabilize fisheries suffering from severe depletions reflects such reasoning (Iudicello et al. 1999; Costello et al. 2008). But disturbances can also lead to other types of change, such as the dramatic extension of coastal state jurisdiction reflected in the creation of Exclusive Economic Zones formalized in the 1982 UN Convention on the Law of the Sea (Ebbin et al. 2005). There is no inherent reason why institutional changes should be irreversible; it is possible to imagine tentative or experimental changes that are allowed to expire or are rolled back in favor of the status quo ante. Nonetheless, it is hard to avoid the conclusion that institutional change is usually irreversible. Institutional reforms may fail, and this may generate incentives to move on to yet another effort at restructuring prevailing systems of rights and rules. But a simple reversion to the status quo ante is seldom feasible.

It would be wrong to overdo these arguments. Many—perhaps most—institutional arrangements do have staying power. Regimes often prove sticky and resistant to change, even when they are no longer well matched to the problems at hand (Young 2002). But the important point is this. Not only are socio-ecological systems dynamic and given to changes that are nonlinear, abrupt, and irreversible; the institutional arrangements we create to govern human–environment interactions in such settings are also complex systems that exhibit similar patterns of change. The implication of this is clear: we are operating in a world of flux and uncertainty (Wilson 2006). Our goal is to match governance systems to socio-ecological systems to avoid or minimize the problem of fit. But both sides of this equation are dynamic, so that it is always risky to create institutional arrangements and then to assume that there is no need to monitor the resultant interactions and to make appropriate adjustments on a continuous basis.

4.5 SO, HOW SHOULD WE PROCEED?

What are the implications of this analysis, and how should we adjust our normal thinking regarding the creation and operation of environmental governance systems? There is no way to do justice to this question in a few paragraphs. In my judgment, however, it is possible to identify some principles that should guide our efforts to manage human–environment interactions in the light of the argument I have sketched in this chapter. For starters, I suggest a focus on (1) making good use of various forms of simulation and scenario development to enhance our understanding of the behavior of complex and dynamic systems; (2) monitoring the behavior of these interactive systems closely and establishing procedures that facilitate adjustment to changing circumstances; (3) drawing a clear distinction between basic commitments that must be protected and operating rules that are subject to change; and (4) constructing firewalls and building redundancy into institutional arrangements to minimize the likelihood of systemic collapse.

> Principle 1: Take full advantage of opportunities to improve knowledge through the use of simulations, scenario development, and other procedures that allow us to explore the dynamics and emergent properties of complex and indeterminate systems.

There is much to be said for devoting significant time and resources to using simulations to gain insights regarding the likely results of institutional innovations in efforts to manage complex and dynamic systems. Simulations do not allow us to make firm predictions regarding the behavior of real-world systems; they cannot provide a basis by themselves for selecting rules and decision-making procedures to deal with specific situations. But complex and dynamic systems—both of the socio-ecological sort and of the institutional variety—behave in ways that often generate emergent properties that are counterintuitive. Even simple simulations, like the game known as Fishbanks, can generate insights and understanding regarding the consequences of human uses of common-pool resources that are otherwise hard for most users to grasp. Similar remarks are in order regarding the use of scenarios to direct attention to the dynamics of complex systems. This first principle, then, calls for concerted efforts to use simulations and scenarios in order to enhance awareness of the range of developments that may occur in complex systems and that managers should be aware of in making decisions about the use of specific policy instruments. The fact that institutional arrangements as well as socio-ecological systems are complex and dynamic simply reinforces this principle.

> Principle 2: Monitor closely both the behavior of socio-ecological systems and the performance of institutional arrangements and establish procedures that make it easy to make adjustments or mid-course corrections.

Not surprisingly, there is no alternative in dealing with situations of the type under consideration in this chapter to devoting the resources required to monitor the behavior of socio-ecological systems and the performance of environmental and resource regimes on a continuous basis. In cases where abrupt and potentially nasty changes (e.g. RCCEs in the case of climate change) are a real concern, the need for monitoring will be especially acute. But whenever we are dealing with changes that are likely to be nonlinear, abrupt, and irreversible, the costs of failing to monitor continuously are likely to be high. Our experience in this realm is full of catastrophic but avoidable changes, such as the American Dust Bowl of the 1930s, the collapse of the Northwest Atlantic cod fishery in the 1980s–1990s, and the climate changes occurring in the Arctic today. In each case, the failure arises from an inability to understand changes in socio-ecological systems combined with an unwillingness to introduce significant changes in prevailing institutional arrangements. Even when the prospect of nonlinear and abrupt change becomes evident, path dependence often thwarts efforts to craft timely and appropriate responses. The second principle, then, calls not only for a dedication to continuous monitoring but also for the development of procedures that make it possible to respond to changing circumstances without becoming bogged down in the bureaucratic and political complications that commonly delay processes of institutional reform.

> Principle 3: Draw a clear distinction between the core elements or defining features of governance systems and the operating rules or policy instruments used to implement them.

The point of this principle is to draw a distinction between foundational (typically normative) commitments and policy instruments and to spell out a rationale for treating them differently. In the realm of ocean governance, for instance, we can make a commitment to use ecosystem-based management and provide meaningful opportunities for stakeholder involvement, without deciding in advance whether to create certain types of marine protected areas or to rely on a particular sort of limited-entry system. In the case of climate change, we can commit ourselves to making specified cuts in greenhouse gas emissions over a period of time, without making fixed choices regarding the use of energy taxes, cap-and-trade arrangements, or some other regulatory mechanisms to get there. This third principle can only succeed if those responsible for the administration of the resultant regimes are genuinely committed to pursuing a common goal and are in possession of the resources needed to do so. This is a critical condition; it is easy to imagine circumstances in which interest groups of one sort or another will endeavor to manipulate or corrupt such arrangements to serve their own ends. But there is no substitute for the combination of commitment to foundational principles and flexibility with regard to the selection and adjustment of policy instruments. It is preferable to work hard to hold the line against corruption than to adopt a policy of relying on rigid institutional arrangements in a world of complex and dynamic systems.

> Principle 4: In cases where adaptive capacity is limited, incorporate firewalls and redundancy into institutional arrangements to minimize the likelihood of abrupt systemic collapse.

One way to mitigate the dangers associated with the occurrence of nonlinear, abrupt, and irreversible change is to compartmentalize institutional arrangements to avoid cascading processes leading to systemic collapse or, in other words, to introduce redundancy so that governance systems can remain resilient even when some of their elements are degraded or destroyed. Of course, this strategy will incur costs. As the literature on the currently popular concept of multi-level governance makes clear, coordination can be hard to achieve under such arrangements, and there is a tendency for such systems to privilege the interests of some stakeholders over the interests of others. At a minimum, this response to the dangers of nonlinear, abrupt, and irreversible change will involve significant opportunity costs. This suggests that the prescription embedded in this principle will be most relevant when the likely changes are large scale and the probability of passing critical thresholds is either high or unknown. A current issue that fits this description is the problem of climate change.

4.6 A FINAL NOTE

The articulation of these principles is only an initial step in learning to live sustainably in a world of complex and dynamic socio-ecological systems.

Efforts to manage human-dominated ecosystems will produce failures as well as successes. But the fact that human behavior is reflexive offers some basis for hope. Reflexivity can make matters worse, as the familiar metaphor of a race to the bottom suggests. But reflexivity can also help us to address problems in a timely manner, providing the impetus to innovate when things go wrong and to learn from experience in assessing the results of institutional innovations. Some such approach will be essential if we are to find ways to come to terms with the behavior of the complex and dynamic socio-ecological systems and institutional arrangements that are defining features of the Anthropocene and, in the process, to succeed in navigating the sustainability transition.

Part II

Addressing Global Issues by Articulating Local Governance Frameworks

As was shown in Part I, one of the key challenges of the global commons issue is to define governance structures capable of navigating complex systems, involving multiple scales, and exposed to abrupt and unpredictable changes. This second part is therefore devoted to the question of the optimal level of governance, in particular whether to govern the global commons at the global or the local level. As the contributions of this part will make clear, the answer is not obvious. Although most contributors (Ostrom, Groom et al., Bréchet and Eyckmans) argue in favour of polycentric and localized solutions to overcome problems of country heterogeneity, Ellerman demonstrates that a globalized solution in the form of the European Emissions Trading Scheme (EU ETS) can be successful. Such opposite views can be reconciled in a broader framework that takes into account the nature of the environmental issue, the extent of information asymmetries at various scales, inequalities, and inertia in institutional reforms.

The chapter by Elinor Ostrom makes a strong argument against the existence of a universally best policy regime of environmental governance. Accordingly, the scales of governance need to be matched with the types of collective action problems under consideration. Her claim is supported by empirical field studies of well-established institutions for the governance of natural resources which show that sustainable management of common-pool resources is possible at the local level. Often, such polycentric governance structures offer more flexibility to match institutions with environmental governance problems. Therefore leaving intact lower local tiers of organization pays off due to better availability of specific information on the particular problem. Thus, polycentric systems do often outperform hierarchical top-down agency-based governance structures.

The chapter by Ben Groom, Rupert Gatti, Timo Goeschl and Timothy Swanson analyzes the conditions for the emergence of stable international regimes by considering the joint contributions of countries to the provision of public goods. Their key point is that without prior agreement about the distribution of the gains, the issue of cooperation for providing global public goods may not even be considered. A major difficulty for reaching an agreement is the existence of inequalities with respect to the benefits from the public goods: the most developed states have the capacity—in particular the human capital—to capture benefits from these goods, while the less developed countries do not. Cooperation for biodiversity protection benefits then less to the "South" than to the "North." Not only is the world trapped into an inefficient equilibrium, but this equilibrium tends to be worsened by the game played by the poorest nations to enhance their bargaining positions. It becomes indeed rational for them to threaten to destroy their resources, which are needed by the "North" to innovate (e.g. reservoir of genes, traditional knowledge, etc.). Therefore long-term stable regimes require a better recognition of the actual inequalities in the distribution of assets among nations and sharing agreements on the surplus generated by the international cooperation.

The chapter by Thierry Bréchet and Johan Eyckmans focuses on climate governance, by analyzing the conditions of emergence and stability of coalitions in climate change negotiations. Their analysis, which relies on the integrated assessment model CLIMNEG, shows some of the contrasting features of climate agreements and possible ways to mitigate the less desirable outcomes. Agreements bringing together relatively homogenous countries with similar emission-reduction costs and climate-change characteristics tend to be more stable than arrangements among heterogeneous countries. However, homogeneous coalitions tend to aim for less ambitious greenhouse-gas emissions reduction targets than larger heterogeneous coalitions. Designing appropriate transfer schemes may, however, stabilize the larger coalitions. They also show that a governance structure based on a multitude of small agreements can yield better global results than restricted cooperation in a single large agreement.

In contrast to the previous chapters of Part II, Denny Ellerman's contribution shows how and why a global governance system can work. The EU ETS is an example of a governance arrangement involving a heterogeneous set of national governments in the context of a weak federal structure. Such a pioneering public policy system illustrates the possibility to design large-scale governance architectures, which might be successfully extended at an even larger scale. Ellerman analyzes the ingredients of the EU ETS experience that were potentially amenable to a successful global governance system. He shows that the initial trading periods were characterized by decentralized cap-setting and allocation systems. The period of decentralized experimentation and incremental change played an important role for the success of the system, in spite of the lack of harmonization in the allocation decisions in the various EU member countries. But, once the system was operating, agreements on further development and improvements of the system became easier. The success of the EU ETS is also fundamentally based on the possibility to delegate to an entity of limited power (the European Commission) the enforcement of the agreed policy regime, suggesting that a similar function will also be needed in a global system.

5

Polycentric Systems: Multilevel Governance Involving a Diversity of Organizations

Elinor Ostrom

5.1 INTRODUCTION

Scholars frequently divide the socio-economic world into two broad units—the market and the state. As problems related to global public goods have taken a more prominent place in both policy and academic literatures (IPCC 2007a; Stern 2007), the difficulty with the notion of a unitary sovereign state as the most relevant governmental organization has become more and more obvious. The problem of collective action is the most general problem facing people at all levels of organization. In regard to climate change, decisions are made in a household (about how to heat a home and what type of transportation should be used for various purposes), in a community (about the type of power-generation facilities, transportation systems, and zoning), in regional and national governments (about investments in technologies and policies related to emission levels), and within international regimes (about the future of the Kyoto Protocol, REDD, and other global policies).

This chapter addresses the challenge of matching scales of governance to the types of collective-action problems under consideration. The concept of polycentricity will then be discussed as more relevant for thinking about multiscale governance than "the state." Findings from earlier studies of polycentric systems will then be summarized, including the repeated finding that there is not one blueprint that works well in solving all collective-action problems. Instead of a blueprint, past research has identified design principles that appear to underlay governance systems that have sustained a variety of small- to medium-sized natural resource systems over time. The last section of the chapter addresses the relevance of polycentricity for the study of climate change.

5.2 MATCHING THE SCALES OF GOVERNANCE SYSTEMS FOR SOLVING COLLECTIVE-ACTION PROBLEMS

Collective-action problems occur when the inputs and efforts of multiple individuals are needed in order to achieve joint outcomes—and it is difficult to exclude beneficiaries of these actions from benefiting even if they do not contribute (E. Ostrom 1998a). Collective-action problems vary in scale from very small problems involving only a few individuals to extremely large problems involving global resources, such as the atmosphere and the oceans. Solving collective-action problems requires opening public and private spheres of activities ranging from the small to the very large so as to encourage effective problem solving (Hess and Ostrom, eds 2007).

In regard to the provision and production of private goods—goods that are relatively easy to package and lack major externalities—creating open, competitive markets is conducive to increased levels of investment, innovation, and lower prices to consumers. Entrepreneurship plays a key role in the private sector since entrepreneurs are the ones who must discover strategies to put heterogeneous factors of production together in new and complementary ways given the availability of resources and technology. In the private sector, the profit motive is the driving force for private entrepreneurs.

Providing and producing public goods and common-pool resources—including public safety; conflict resolution at international, national, regional, and local levels; public education; and public health, as well as sustaining natural resource systems—require different institutions than an open, competitive market (Toonen 2010). Even the market itself is not a viable independent institution without being embedded in effective public property arrangements, courts of law, and police.

The language used by many analysts divides the rich world of institutions into a barren dichotomy of "the market" versus "the state." While markets are considered to be open, public realms where many individuals and firms of diverse sizes and assets compete, the public sector is depicted as a top-down hierarchy with little room for problem solving except by top-level, government officials. Whether a system is unitary or not, some scholars prefer to think about governance occurring primarily at the national level when governance is a multiscale activity ranging from small family units all the way to the globe. Even federal countries may need to think about expanding some of their borders to an international level with respect to specific functions that are larger than any of the units within the federal system (Frey 2005).

If we are to solve collective-action problems effectively, we must rethink the way we approach market and governmental institutions (Berkes 2007; E. Ostrom 2007). We need to develop analytical approaches and general principles that are consistent with a public sector that encourages entrepreneurship and innovation at local, regional, national, and international levels (V. Ostrom 2008a,b). Public entrepreneurs are motivated by diverse interests, including improving services to their own communities, sharing the burden for increasing benefits, the stimulus of innovation, the respect they receive from others, as well as the income they derive from their positions in the public service for those who are not entirely volunteer workers (Mintrom 2000; Kuhnert 2001).

Given that the benefits of public goods and common-pool resources are dispersed within a community, many scholars ignore the possibility of local public entrepreneurs devising effective ways of providing, producing, and encouraging the co-production of these essential goods and services. On the other hand, many scholars stress the need for leadership in the public sector. Entrepreneurship is a particular form of leadership focused primarily on problem solving and putting heterogeneous processes together in complementary and effective ways, rather than simply making public speeches and being charismatic.

5.3 POLYCENTRICITY

When governance systems are arranged polycentrically from small to very large, collective-action problems at multiple scales can be tackled. The costs of effective self-organization are lower when authority exists to craft institutions whose boundaries match the problems faced. External financial resources may increase the options available to a local community. External resources are not, however, the essential ingredient for building an effective public sector to provide local public goods and protect smaller-scale common-pool resources. The results achieved, for example, to solve local problems when massive levels of international donor assistances have been allocated, have been grossly disappointing (Gibson et al. 2005).

Extensive studies of urban service delivery (for an overview see McGinnis 1999b) and of common-pool resources (E. Ostrom et al. 1994; Gibson et al., eds 2000) have found communities of individuals in urban and rural areas who have self-organized to provide and co-produce surprisingly good local services given the constraints that they face. Many policy analysts presume that without major external resources and top-down planning by national officials, public goods and sustainable common-pool resources cannot be provided. This presumption is wrong. The opposite presumption that local communities will *always* solve collective-action problems is also wrong. It is a struggle to find effective ways of providing these services. Public entrepreneurs, however, working closely with citizens frequently do find new ways of putting services together using a mixture of local talent and resources (Dietz et al. 2003). And, if governance systems are arranged polycentrically from small to very large, collective-action problems at multiple scales can be tackled.

The presumption that locals cannot take care of public sector problems has led to legislation throughout the world that places responsibility for local public services on units of government that are very large, frequently lacking the resources to carry out their assignments and overwhelmed with what they are assigned to do. Contemporary assignments of regional, national, or international governments with the exclusive responsibility for providing local public goods and common-pool resources remove authority from local officials and citizens to solve local problems that differ from one location to the next. Doug Wilson, Research Director for the Institute for Fisheries Management and Coastal Community Development in Denmark, has recently reflected on the evolution of fisheries policies in the European Union.

> The Common Fisheries Policy (CFP) as it is called is an 'exclusive competence' of the European Union (EU) meaning that all decisions are taken at the level of the Union. . . .
> The CFP is not only politically important within the overall effort to build a new kind of polity in Europe; it is also failing to do a very good job of maintaining sustainable fish stocks. Fisheries scientists tell us that, in 2003, 22% of the fish caught from stocks managed by the CFP were taken from stocks that were smaller than they should have been for sustainable fishing. Neither scientists, fishers, government agencies, nor marine conservation groups are happy with the CFP, and there are myriad attempts to reform it. The reforms include better policy, better data gathering, a reduction in perverse subsidies to the fishing industry and, finally 30 years after most other fisheries management agencies had moved beyond top-down management, some serious attempts at stakeholder involvement. (Wilson 2006: 7)

This emphasis on top-down planning is certainly not the way that Europe developed. Since the eleventh century, thousands of independent waterboards were established in the delta of the Rhine River with their own rules and physical structures, drained the swampy land, and protected the land from being inundated except during extreme storms (Toonen 1996; Andersen 2001). In Switzerland, alpine peasants devised a variety of private and common-property systems to gain profitable income from an extreme and diverse ecology (Netting 1981). More than 1,000 free cities with their own charters and legal traditions flourished in Europe during the Middle Ages and were the foundation for modern constitutional democracies (Berman 1983). Drawing on the rich tradition of European public sector development, we need to think of the public sector as a polycentric system (V. Ostrom 1999), rather than a monocentric hierarchy.

Research has repeatedly demonstrated that high performance is more likely to be achieved in effective, local public economies established within broader national systems where large, medium, and small governmental and nongovernmental enterprises engage in diverse cooperative as well as competitive relationships (Frey and Eichenberger 1996). Local public economies are not markets, nor are they simple hierarchies. Households are not able to engage in a wide diversity of independent quid pro quo relationships with any producer they choose in a local public economy. Decisions are made for collective consumption units—including a wide diversity of self-organized associations as well as governments at multiple levels—that are then held responsible for providing tax revenue and user charges to pay for the provision of public goods and services. Local organizations also enhance the level of citizen co-production of public safety, education, and health. Entities in a public economy engage in extensive horizontal as well as vertical interrelationships. The structure and performance of a public economy must be examined at an interorganizational level of analysis as well as at the level of a single unit (McGinnis, ed. 1999a,b; 2000).

5.4 POLYCENTRIC PUBLIC ECONOMIES IN URBAN AREAS

The basic assumptions of a polycentric theory, when applied to the study of urban areas, are:

1. Public goods and services differ substantially in regard to their production functions and their scale of effects.

2. Individuals with relatively similar preferences for public goods and services tend to cluster in neighborhoods. Preferences will tend to be more homogeneous within neighborhoods than across an entire metropolitan area.

3. Citizens who live in multiple jurisdictions learn more about the performance of any one jurisdiction by seeing or hearing about how problems are handled in other jurisdictions.

4. Multiple jurisdictions with different scopes and scales of organization allow citizens more effective choice in selecting packages of services most important to them, in articulating their preferences and concerns, and if necessary, in moving to other jurisdictions.

5. The presence of large numbers of potential producers of urban goods and services in a metropolitan area allows elected officials more effective choice of producers.

6. Producers who must compete for contracts are more likely to search for innovative technologies, to encourage effective team production, as well as citizen co-production, so as to enhance their own performance (V. Ostrom 1999, 2008b; E. Ostrom et al. 1978).

This modified form of competition—of vying for citizens to resolve problems and procure services in an urban neighborhood—is one method for reducing opportunistic behavior even though no institutional arrangement can totally eliminate opportunism with respect to the provision and production of collective goods. Allowing citizens to form neighborhood-level collective consumption units encourages face-to-face discussion and the achievement of common understanding. Creating larger collective consumption units reduces the strategic behavior of the wealthy trying to escape into tax havens where they could free-ride on the tax contributions of citizens in other jurisdictions. Larger units also more effectively cope with the provision and production of urban goods and services that have large-scale effects.

5.5 THERE IS NO "ONE BEST SYSTEM" FOR ALL LOCAL PUBLIC ECONOMIES

Scholars have conducted rigorous empirical research that has challenged the presumptions that large scale is always the best way to organize to provide public goods. Studies have challenged the assumption that larger public school districts achieve higher performance (Hanushek 1986; Teske et al. 1993), that fragmentation of governments leads to higher costs (Dilorenzo 1983; Schneider 1986; Boyne 1992), that consolidated police departments are more effective (E. Ostrom et al. 1978), and have provided further insights to the way local governments are constituted (Oakerson and Parks 1989; Stephens and Wikstrom 2000). As a result of extensive empirical and theoretical research, the presumed self-evident truth that constructing one government for each metropolitan area is the best way to achieve efficiency and equity, has slowly been replaced with a recognition that judging "structure directly on the single criterion of uniformity contributes little to the advancement of research or reform" (Oakerson 1999: 117). Instead of a single best design that would have to cope with the wide variety of problems faced in different localities, a polycentric theory generates core principles that can be used in the design of effective local institutions when used by informed and interested citizens and public officials (V. Ostrom 2011).

In his conclusion to an in-depth study of urban consolidation efforts in the United States and Canada during the twentieth century, Andrew Sancton reflected:

> Municipalities are more than just providers of services. They are the democratic mechanisms through which territorially based communities of people govern themselves at a local level. . . . Those who would force municipalities to amalgamate with each other invariably claim that their motive is to make municipalities stronger. Such an approach—however well-intentioned—erodes the foundations

of our liberal democracies because it undermines the notion that there can be forms of self-government that exist outside the institutions of the central government. (Sancton 2000: 167)

Sancton is not the only scholar to be concerned about the consequences of consolidation. John Barber (2006) confirms the loss of voice that occurred as an outcome associated with a major consolidation—in this case, the city of Toronto. In an article in the July 19, 2006, *Globe and Mail* concerning the results for citizens' voice of the Toronto amalgamation that had occurred a decade earlier, Barber reflected:

> Every one of the many reports on government reform following amalgamation has identified citizen alienation as the worst consequence of that convulsive and chaotic process.... Toronto today is both huge and hugely centralized. ...
> The only power really worth delegating is power over development. What alienated citizens want, and have come to express clearly and repeatedly, is some small hope that neighbourhoods can begin to exercise a modest degree of formal control over their own futures. But the incumbents have decided that this is precisely the power that Toronto community councils shalt not have. (Barber 2006: A9)

We simply must get over the simple equation of multiple units of government with inefficiency and waste and recognize the importance of units of public service (governments as well as private associations) operating as a part of a polycentric system at multiple scales. On the other hand, creating a large-scale governance unit to help solve the larger-scale problems facing metropolitan areas is also important. The key problem that needs much deeper thought than has been given to many "consolidation" campaigns is how to establish a large, metropolitan-wide unit that does not eliminate the medium- and smaller-sized units that help citizens cope with neighborhood-level public goods and common-pool resources. Those scholars, public officials, and citizens who are concerned with solving collective-action problems effectively, equitably, and efficiently, recognize the importance of authorizing citizens to constitute their own local jurisdictions and associations using the knowledge and experience they have concerning the public problems they face.

5.6 POLYCENTRICITY AND COMMON-POOL RESOURCES

Common-pool resources are systems that generate finite quantities of resource units so that one person's use subtracts from the quantity of resource units available to others (E. Ostrom et al. 1994). The use of forests, pastures, and irrigation systems are among the important types of common-pool resources present in most countries of the world. Most common-pool resources are sufficiently large that multiple actors can simultaneously use the resource system and efforts to exclude potential beneficiaries are costly. When the resource units (e.g. water, fish, trees) are highly valued and many actors benefit from harvesting them for consumption, exchange, or as a factor in a production process, the harvests withdrawn by one individual are likely to create negative externalities for others.

The "tragedy of the commons" will occur in highly valued, open-access commons where those involved and/or external authorities do *not* establish an effective governance regime. Governance regimes regulate one or more of the following:

- who is allowed to appropriate resource units;
- the timing, quantity, location, and technology of appropriation;
- who is obligated to contribute resources to provide or maintain the resource system itself;
- how appropriation and obligation activities are to be monitored and enforced;
- how conflicts over appropriation and obligation activities are to be resolved; and
- how the rules affecting the above will be changed over time with changes in the performance of the resource system and the strategies of participants.

A self-governed common-pool resource is one where actors, who are major users of the resource, are involved over time in making and adapting rules within collective-choice arenas regarding the inclusion or exclusion of participants, appropriation strategies, obligations of participants, monitoring and sanctioning, and conflict resolution. Some extremely remote common-pool resources are governed entirely by users and are not governed at all by external authorities. Thus would have been the case for Swiss Alpine meadows for many centuries (Netting 1981). In most modern political economies, however, it is rare to find any resource systems that are governed *entirely* by participants without rules made by local, regional, national, and international authorities also affecting key decisions (V. Ostrom 1991, 1997). In a self-governed, polycentric system, participants make many, but not necessarily all, of the rules that affect the sustainability of the resource system and its use.

5.7 THE CONVENTIONAL THEORY OF COMMON-POOL RESOURCES

Since the important early studies of open-access fisheries by Gordon (1954) and Scott (1955), and the much-cited work of Hardin (1968), many theoretical studies by political economists have analyzed simple common-pool resource systems using relatively similar assumptions. In such systems, it is assumed that the resource generates a highly predictable, finite supply of one type of resource unit (one species, for example) in each relevant time period. Users are assumed to be homogeneous in terms of their assets, skills, discount rates, and cultural views. They are also assumed to be short-term, profit-maximizing actors who possess complete information. In this theory, *anyone* can enter the resource and appropriate resource units. In other words, there are no property rights established related to the use of this resource. Users gain property rights only to what they harvest, which they then sell in an open, competitive market. The open-access condition is a given and it is assumed that those involved cannot make any effort to change it. Harvesters act independently and do not communicate or coordinate their activities in any way.

> In this setting, as the incisive analysis of Gordon and Scott demonstrates, each fisherman will take into account only his own marginal costs and revenues and ignores the fact that increases in his catch affect the returns to fishing effort for other fishermen as well as the health of future fish stocks.... [E]conomic rent is dissipated; economic over-fishing, which may also lead to ecological over-fishing, is the result. (Feeny et al. 1996: 189)

Many textbooks in resource economics and law and economics present this conventional theory of a simple common-pool resource as the only theory needed for understanding common-pool resources more generally. Field research challenges the universality of this theory.

5.8 COMMON-POOL RESOURCES IN THE FIELD

A sufficient number of empirical examples exists where the absence of property rights and the independence of actors capture the essence of the problem facing users that the broad empirical applicability of the conventional theory was not effectively challenged by field research until the mid-1980s. Until the work of the National Academy of Sciences' Panel on Common Property (National Research Council 1986), the basic theory discussed above was applied to all common-pool resources regardless of the capacity of appropriators to communicate and coordinate their activities. The growing evidence from many studies of common-pool resources in the field called for a serious rethinking of the theoretical foundations for the analysis of common-pool resources (McCay and Acheson 1987; Berkes 1989; Berkes et al. 1989; Bromley et al. 1992). The consequence of these empirical studies is not to challenge the empirical validity of the conventional theory, where it is relevant, but rather its generalizability.

James Acheson, James Wilson, and colleagues (Wilson et al. 1994, 2007; Acheson et al. 1998, 2003) have documented how the lobster fishermen of Maine recovered from a major crash of the lobster stock in their coastal waters during the 1920s and 1930s to experiment with a diversity of ingenious rules well-fitted to important attributes of the relevant resource units—the lobsters—and how fishermen were organized within the harbors where they lived and berthed their boats. The lobster fishers of Maine have lived in shoreline communities for multiple generations and have deep roots in their communities. They have been able to organize locally and develop norms of trustworthiness and reciprocity. Given their long history, they have gained effective knowledge about their local resource system to build an ever more valuable local fishery—with sales of lobster from the state of Maine totaling $186.1 million in 2000 (Acheson 2003: 13).

In the field, many common-pool resources are characterized by different attributes than the base theory of an open-access resource presented in some textbooks as if all resources were well characterized by this universal model. Small- to medium-sized irrigation systems are frequently built by local farmers who develop complex governance systems that specify who can use the resource, when and how much water can be withdrawn, how rules will be monitored, and what sanctions will be imposed. Thus, irrigation systems are one setting in which to examine how diverse types of governance systems perform in the field (Tang 1992; Shivakoti and Ostrom 2001; Meinzen-Dick 2007).

Recent research on small- to medium-sized irrigation systems in Nepal has found a very substantial difference in performance between those systems owned and governed by the farmers themselves as contrasted to those systems owned and operated by a national governmental agency. Colleagues associated with the Asian Institute of Technology in Bangkok have been working with colleagues at Indiana University since the early 1990s (Benjamin et al. 1994; Lam et al. 1994) to develop an extensive database on the performance of irrigation systems in Nepal, as well as comparative studies across Asia (Shivakoti et al. 2005).

Farmers in Nepal have long taken on the responsibility of creating their own water associations, constructing and maintaining their own systems, and monitor and enforcing conformance to their rules. The irrigation systems constructed and maintained by farmers tend to rely on low-tech construction techniques, including building nonpermanent headworks from mud, trees, and stones. International aid agencies have provided considerable funding to government agencies in an effort to upgrade the engineering standards.

In a detailed analysis of data from 150 farmer-governed and national government irrigation systems in Nepal, W. F. Lam (1998) developed three performance measures: (1) the physical condition of irrigation systems; (2) the quantity of water available to farmers at different seasons of the year; and (3) the agricultural productivity of the systems. Using multiple regression analysis techniques so as to control for environmental differences among systems, Lam finds several variables strongly related to these dependent variables. One is the form of governance of the system. Holding other variables constant, irrigation systems governed by the farmers themselves perform significantly better on all three performance measures. This variable has the largest explanatory power of any variable in Lam's analysis, including the physical size of the system, terrain characteristics, and the number of farmers.

We have continued to develop the Nepal Irrigation Institutions and Systems (NIIS) database, which now has information about 231 irrigation systems located in 29 out of the 75 districts in Nepal (Joshi et al. 2000). Our consistent finding, and that of other scholars doing research on irrigation in Nepal (Gautam et al. 1992), backs up Lam's earlier study and finds that, on average, farmer-managed irrigation systems (FMIS) outperform agency-managed irrigation systems (AMIS) on multiple dimensions. Let me provide a very brief overview of our findings from the NIIS database.[1]

Focusing on three measurements of the physical condition of the irrigation system at the time of data collection, as shown in Table 5.1, a larger proportion of the FMIS are able to maintain the overall physical condition of the system in excellent or moderately good condition as contrasted to AMIS, as well as achieving higher technical and economic efficiency (see Lam 1998 for definitions of these concepts). The better physical condition of the canals enables

Table 5.1. Relationships between governance structure and physical condition of irrigation systems

Physical condition of irrigation systems		Types of governance structure		Chi-square value	Sig.
		FMIS (%)	AMIS (%)		
Overall condition	Excellent [37]	18.2	8.4	23.02	0.00
	Moderately good [144]	67.4	45.8		
	Poor [48]	14.4	45.8		
Technical efficiency	Highly efficient [58]	28.9	12.5	27.30	0.00
	Moderately efficient [137]	62.8	50.0		
	Inefficient [33]	8.3	37.5		
Economic efficiency	Highly efficient [66]	33.2	12.5	45.35	0.00
	Moderately efficient [140]	63.5	52.1		
	Inefficient [23]	3.3	35.4		

Note: Number of irrigation systems is in brackets.
Source: Joshi et al. (2000· 78)

---

[1] Readers who wish to dig deeper are encouraged to read Lam (1998), Joshi et al. (2000), Shivakoti and Ostrom (2001), and E. Ostrom et al. (2011) and the extensive references cited therein.

FMIS to achieve increased levels of cropping intensity (the number of crops grown during a year) at both the head end of a canal and the tail end of the canal, as shown in Table 5.2. Thus, the investment of farmers in keeping their systems in good physical condition pays off in regard to significantly more agricultural productivity.

About two-thirds of both FMIS and AMIS have formal written rules that include provisions for imposing fines on farmers for not contributing resources to operate and manage the systems (Joshi et al. 2000: 75). On the other hand, in eight out of ten AMIS, an official guard is hired, while only six out of ten FMIS rely on an official guard (ibid.). The presence of an official guard, however, does not translate into an increased likelihood that fines will actually be imposed. On 75 percent of the FMIS, fines are actually imposed when farmers are observed to break a rule, while fines are actually imposed on only 38 percent of the AMIS (ibid.: 76). Farmers follow the rules of their system to a greater extent on FMIS than on the AMIS, and they also tend to achieve a higher level of mutual trust (ibid.).

The specific rules that the farmers use in governing their systems on a day-to-day basis vary substantially from one system to another since each FMIS has been self-organized. The "official" guard on many of these systems is one of the farmers who "rotates" into this position on a regular basis. The rules specifying allocation rules, responsibilities for monitoring, and punishment, however, are not consistent from one system to the next. Thus, the monitoring of water allocation and contributions to maintenance are largely performed by farmers who have participated in the crafting of the specific rules of their own system and have a strong interest in seeing their system perform well and ensure that others on the system are not free-riding or taking more water than their official share.

Thus, farmers with long-term ownership claims, who can communicate, develop their own agreements, establish the positions of monitors, and sanction those who do not conform to their own rules, are more likely to grow

Table 5.2. Relationships between governance structure and cropping intensity of irrigation systems

Cropping intensity		Types of governance structure		Chi-square value	Sig.
		FMIS (%)	AMIS (%)		
Intensity at head end	High [142]	70.2	52.2	5.27	0.02
	Low [72]	29.8	47.8		
Intensity at tail end	High [123]	65.1	34.1	13.74	0.00
	Low [87]	34.9	65.9		

Note: Number of irrigation systems is in brackets.
Source: Joshi et al. (2000: 80)

more rice, distribute water more equitably, and keep their systems in better repair than is done on government systems. Some of these farmer-managed systems are organized in multiple tiers with the basic organization of 10 to 50 farmers sharing a tertiary distribution channel. At this level, the farmers work together to distribute water and keep the local channel in good repair. Usually, several of these organizations send representatives to a second-level organization that makes somewhat more general policies and resolves conflicts that may arise within or between the lower farmer organizations. For larger systems, there will be a third (or in the case of a very large system, fourth) level where broader planning is undertaken for how to deal with seasonal problems—too little water in some seasons and flooding in others.

While there is variance in the performance of Nepali farmer-managed systems, few perform as poorly as government systems, holding other relevant variables constant. Since many of the government systems rely on high-tech engineering, the capability of farmers to increase agricultural production on their "primitive systems," while they also provide the labor to maintain and operate the system, is particularly noteworthy.[2]

In the past decade, we have been studying diversely organized institutions for managing forests around the world. Again, instead of one model that works well in all types of forests, we have found national government-owned forests that work well and are associated with sustainable forests and government forests that are overrun by illegal harvesting and are unable to stop the poachers (Dietz et al. 2003; E. Ostrom and Nagendra 2006). We have found the same diverse patterns for community-managed forests and privately owned forests. To sustain forests over time requires much more than simply imposing a particular blueprint on all forested areas in the world. The capacity and incentives of those in a forest governance organization have to fit the collective-action problems faced in sustaining forests over time (Moran and Ostrom, eds 2005; Webb and Shivakoti, eds 2008).

5.9 DESIGN PRINCIPLES RATHER THAN BLUEPRINTS

In my effort to speculate why some locally developed regimes for regulating the use of common-pool resources survived for long periods of time while others failed (E. Ostrom 1990), I developed a set of design principles that I posited underlay the robust, long-lasting systems and were rarely observed in the systems that had failed. When I first elucidated these design principles, I urged others to test out these tentative conclusions through further empirical

---

[2] For an important study of Philippine irrigation systems with findings consistent with our findings in Nepal, see Araral (2005, 2009).

research that would help ascertain if these principles distinguished between robust and failed systems. Since *Governing the Commons* was published, other scholars have responded to the challenge. As discussed in E. Ostrom (2005a) and Cox et al. (2010), many scholars have examined the relevance of these principles for helping to explain the performance of resource governance systems (such as fisheries, irrigation systems, pastures, and forests) throughout the world.

For example, Abernathy and Hilmy (2000) studied nine small, but long-surviving, irrigation systems in the dry areas of Burkina Faso and Niger. They measured system performance using both physical and nonphysical factors and found that an average measure of performance based on six indicators was highly correlated with governance arrangements conforming to the design principles listed in Table 5.3 (Merrey 1996; Crook and Jones 1999, who have also found strong supporting evidence). Let us briefly review the design principles and their relevance for multilevel governance.

Table 5.3. Design principles derived from studies of long-enduring institutions for governing sustainable resources

---

1. *Clearly defined boundaries*
The boundaries of the resource system (e.g. irrigation system or fishery) and the individuals or households with rights to harvest resource units are clearly defined.

2. *Proportional equivalence between benefits and costs*
Rules specifying the amount of resource products that a user is allocated are related to local conditions and to rules requiring labor, materials, and/or money inputs.

3. *Collective-choice arrangements*
Most individuals affected by harvesting and protection rules are included in the group who can modify these rules.

4. *Monitoring*
Monitors, who actively audit biophysical conditions and user behavior, are at least partially accountable to the users and/or are the users themselves.

5. *Graduated sanctions*
Users who violate rules-in-use are likely to receive graduated sanctions (depending on the seriousness and context of the offense) from other users, from officials accountable to these users, or from both.

6. *Conflict-resolution mechanisms*
Users and their officials have rapid access to low-cost, local arenas to resolve conflict among users or between users and officials.

7. *Minimal recognition of rights to organize*
The rights of users to devise their own institutions are not challenged by external governmental authorities, and users have long-term tenure rights to the resource.

For resources that are parts of larger systems:
8. *Nested enterprises*
Appropriation, provision, monitoring, enforcement, conflict resolution, and governance activities are organized in multiple layers of nested enterprises.

Source: Based on E. Ostrom (1990: 90).

5.9.1 Clearly defined boundaries

The first design principle is that the boundaries of a resource system, as well as the individuals or households with property rights, are clearly defined. The boundary rules relate to who can enter, harvest, manage, and potentially exclude others' impacts. Participants then have more assurance about trustworthiness and cooperation of the others involved. If those rules are not well-defined, strangers who discover a valuable resource may start to use it. Because they are strangers, they may simply overuse it. When long-standing participants fear that others may start using a resource of value to them, creating well-defined boundary rules helps immensely in increasing the probability that if one is cooperating in limiting harvests and in providing maintenance, one is not being a sucker because others are overharvesting and not contributing to the maintenance.

Having a clear boundary for the resource itself is important for a different set of reasons. It clarifies what is meant by a particular resource system. Where may I go and where may I not go? The problem that is addressed by systems that do define their boundaries is free-riding. If a group of users can determine their own membership—including those who agree to use the resource according to their agreed-upon rules and excluding those who do not agree to these rules—the group has made an important first step toward limiting access and developing greater trust and reciprocity. Using this principle enables participants to know who is in and who is out of a defined set of relationships and, thus, with whom to cooperate. It is also important that the boundaries of larger and smaller resource and governance systems than any particular system are also well defined.

Just defining the boundaries carefully, however, may not be sufficient in and of itself, especially when the boundaries are drawn by external officials. The boundaries of the Maya Biosphere Reserve are very well defined on many maps of the reserve located in the capital city of Guatemala, in the relevant national parks, and in many tourist brochures. Sundberg (1998: 402) reports on a survey of residents of an agricultural community in one of the buffer zones of the reserve, however, and finds that almost 80 percent of the farmers did not know anything about the reserve or its boundaries in which they were located (see also the supporting online material (SOM) for Dietz et al. 2003).

5.9.2 Proportional equivalence between benefits and costs

The second design principle is that the rules-in-use allocate benefits proportional to inputs that are required. If a group of users is going to harvest from a resource over the long run, they must devise rules related to how much, when, and how different products are to be harvested. They also need to assess the costs of operating a system on users. The design principle related to proportionality of benefits and costs relates to the likelihood that participants will feel that the rules they are using are equitable. If some people pay low costs but they get high benefits over time, this inequity is a matter of frustration for the participants and may lead to more and more participants refusing to abide by the rules because they are unfair. Thus, this design principle is directly related to the types of attitudes that are necessary to sustain a system over the long run. If some users get all the benefits and pay few of the costs, few of the others are willing to follow rules over time (Ensminger 2000, 2001).

5.9.3 Collective-choice arrangements

The third design principle is that most of the individuals affected by a resource regime are authorized to participate in making and modifying the rules related to boundaries, assessment of costs, authorization to harvest, etc. Resource regimes that use this principle should be able to craft rules to fit local circumstances and to devise rules that are considered fair by participants. As environments change over time, being able to craft local rules is particularly important as officials located far away do not know of the change. Some local common-property institutions do empower a local elite to make most of the collective-choice decisions. In such cases, one can expect that the policies adopted primarily benefit the elite and then are not consistent with the second design principle (e.g. Ensminger, 1990; Platteau 2003, 2004).

5.9.4 Monitoring

Few long-surviving resource regimes rely only on levels of trust and reciprocity among appropriators to keep rule-breaking levels down. Evidence of the importance of monitoring is presented by Schweik 2000; Gibson et al. (2005); Hayes and Ostrom (2005); and E. Ostrom and Nagendra (2006). A recent multivariant analysis by Coleman and Steed (2009) of around 130 forests located in a dozen countries finds that when local forest users are recognized as having a right of harvesting (having at least the position of an authorized user), they are more likely to monitor patterns of harvesting by other appropriators. When this happens, the resource conditions are themselves better than when local users do not monitor each other (see also Coleman, 2009).

Most institutional analysts do assume that rules must be enforced in some manner to achieve robust governance but not always on who should select the monitors. Most self-organized resource regimes select their own monitors. The monitors are accountable to authorized users and are expected to keep an eye on resource conditions as well as on harvesting activities. By creating official positions for local monitors, a resource regime does not rely only on the norms of local right-holders to impose personal costs on those who break a rule. The community creates an official position. In some systems, users rotate into this position so everyone has a duty to be a monitor. In others, the monitors are paid from a fund collected from all authorized appropriators. With monitors appointed, those who want to cooperate with the rules so long as others also cooperate are assured that someone is generally checking on the conformance of others to local rules.

5.9.5 Graduated sanctions

The fifth design principle is the use of *graduated* sanctions. This was a very puzzling finding as I had devoted 15 years of empirical research to the study of policing in metropolitan areas and was deeply familiar with the literature on the economics of crime. This literature stressed the importance of costly sanctions so that the expected value of breaking a law was higher than the benefit that could be obtained even when the probabilities of being caught were relatively low. In many self-organized systems, the first sanction imposed by a local monitor is so low as to have *no* impact on the expected benefit–cost ratio of breaking local rules (given the high payoffs that could be achieved by harvesting illegally, for example).

The initial sanction can be thought of more as information to the person who is "caught" as well as to others in the community. A user could always make an error or could face difficult problems leading them to break a rule. Letting an infraction pass unnoticed could generate a downward cascade of cooperation in a group that relies only on conditional cooperation and has no capacity to sanction. When graduated punishments are used, a person who purposely or by error breaks a rule is notified that others notice the infraction (thereby increasing the individual's confidence that others would also be caught). Further, the individual learns that others basically continue to extend their trust and want only a small token to convey a recognition that the mishap occurred.

5.9.6 Conflict-resolution mechanisms

The sixth principle is that there are rapid, low-cost, local arenas to resolve conflict among users or between users and officials. Rules have to be understood in order to be effective. Some participants may interpret a rule that they have jointly made in different ways. By devising simple, local mechanisms to get conflicts aired immediately and resolutions that are generally known in the community, the number of conflicts that reduce trust can be reduced.

5.9.7 Minimal recognition of rights

Whether local users can develop more effective regimes *over time* is affected by whether they have at least minimal recognition of the right to organize by a national or local government. Participants in resource regimes that are not recognized by external authorities have operated over long periods but they have had to rely almost entirely on unanimity as the rule used to change rules (Ghate 2000). Otherwise, disgruntled participants who voted against a rule change can go to the external authorities to threaten the regime itself! Changing rules using unanimity imposes high transaction costs and prevents a group from searching for better-matched rules at relatively lower costs. When external governmental officials presume that *only* they can make authoritative rules, then sustaining a self-organized regime is very difficult (Johnson and Libecap 1982).

5.9.8 Nested enterprises

When common-pool resources that are being managed by a group are part of a larger set of resource systems, an eighth design principle is usually present in robust systems. The nested enterprise principle is that governance activities are organized in multiple layers of related governance regimes. In addition to some small units, larger institutions exist to govern the interdependencies among smaller units. The rules allocating water among major branches of an irrigation system, for example, may differ from the rules used to allocate water among farmers along a single distributory channel (Yoder 1994).

The reason many scholars focus on prescribing large-sized, governmental institutions for governing and managing resources is that many resource systems are relatively large. But, most large systems do have smaller ecological systems within them that have distinct dynamics, as well as being a part of large ecological systems. Ecologists are deeply familiar with the need to study diverse niches within ecological systems. The focus on the analysis of simple systems by social scientists has overlooked complex, nested systems as occurring frequently in nature and needing a nested set of governance arrangements at each major level. Among long-enduring self-governed regimes, smaller-scale organizations tend to be nested in ever larger organizations and resource users are used to handling some problems at a very small scale and other problems at ever larger scales.

5.10 IS POLYCENTRICITY RELEVANT FOR GLOBAL CLIMATE CHANGE?

Some readers of this chapter may well ask: what is the relevance of the polycentric approach for the analysis of *global* public goods? The initial relevance of the polycentric approach is the parallel between the theoretical presumption that *only* the largest scale is relevant for the provision and production of public goods for metropolitan areas, and the contemporary presumption held by many analysts that only one scale is relevant for policies related to global public goods. Extensive empirical research has found, however, that while large-scale units were part of effective governance of metropolitan areas and common-pool resources, small- and medium-scale units were also necessary components. An important lesson is that simply recommending a single government unit to solve global collective-action problems—because of global impacts—needs to be seriously rethought and we also need to rethink the important role of smaller-scale effects.

While many of the effects of climate change are larger scale, many of the causes of climate change operate at a much smaller scale. To solve climate change eventually, the day-to-day activities of individuals, families, firms, communities, and governments at multiple levels will need to change substantially. Many of those who need to change, however, have not yet accepted the reality of the threat and their need to act locally in a different manner.

Decisions within a family as to what form of transportation to use for various purposes, what car to purchase, and what investments to make for power consumption within the home all impact the global atmosphere. Similar decisions within firms are also important, as buildings in general account for "more than 70 percent of the electricity use and almost 40 percent of greenhouse gas emissions in the United States" (Fuller et al. 2009). Proposals for substantial increases in energy taxes at a national level (to comply with proposed international agreements) are strongly urged as the only way of changing the decisions of individuals and families, as they theoretically make decisions based primarily on individual and family household budgets and do not take the external costs they generate into account. However, many local projects have been adopted as more and more communities are becoming aware that their actions cumulatively affect the threats of climate change.

Retrofitting buildings to add insulation, solar photovoltaics, and more efficient heating systems is a local-level strategy that can be pursued and may generate long-term energy cost savings for the firm or family, as well as reducing greenhouse gas emissions. The up-front costs of such efforts are frequently high even when the investment will reduce private costs over the long run. Some communities are now finding ways of reducing those up-front costs. By a public ballot approved by 81 percent of the voters, for instance,

Berkeley, California, has adopted a general policy to reduce emissions substantially over time. One of the programs is called Berkeley FIRST (Financing Initiative for Renewable and Solar Technology). To participate in the program, the owner of a commercial or residential building asks a contractor for an estimate of the costs of new solar energy equipment or energy-efficiency improvements to the building that would likely cost between $4,000 and $20,000 (Pope et al. 2009). The owner then submits an application to the city, and city staff members review the estimate to be sure that it will reduce greenhouse gas emissions.

> After the municipality approves the application, the work is completed, a lien is placed on the property, and a check is issued to the property owner. A special tax is added to future property bills. If the property is sold before the end of the 20-year repayment period, the new owner pays the remaining special taxes as part of their property's annual tax bill. The interest component of the special tax payments will be tax deductible, similar to a home equity line or home mortgage....
>
> The City of Berkeley started accepting applications through its Web site on 5 November 2008, and applications to claim $1.5 million available for the pilot were submitted within 10 minutes. (Pope et al. 2009: 25)

Obviously the demand for making investments in improving buildings so as to reduce energy consumption is very high. The city of Berkeley has already increased the funds available to support this program over time.

Other cities have now started a variety of "green" initiatives. The city of Toronto, for example, has announced more than a dozen current city policies, related publications, and meetings that are focused on climate change. The city of Toronto has been increasing the budget for its "Live Green Toronto" program since starting this program. Mayors of other large cities are also banding together to discuss actions to reduce carbon emissions that can be taken locally but that if taken jointly can have a much bigger impact. In 2005, eighteen large cities sent representatives to London to examine actions that could be taken at a municipal level; to reexamine urban policies that could be revised, including their own purchasing policies; and to discuss ways of encouraging more investment in climate-friendly technologies in their cities. In October 2008, a merger with the Clinton Climate Initiative was arranged to create the C40 Cities Climate Leadership group, whose members have jointly pledged to reduce emissions in each of their cities to meet or even improve on Kyoto standards. A similar league, the World Mayors Council on Climate Change, was initiated by the mayor of the city of Kyoto (Japan) in December 2005. Currently, there are twenty members of this alliance, from all regions of the world.

Other local-level efforts to overtly increase the level of alternative energy production or reduce the level of automobile use have been reported for many cities around the world—including Sorsogon, Philippines; Esmeraldas,

Ecuador; Maputo, Mozambique; and Kampala, Uganda, where efforts are supported by the Cities in Climate Change Initiative, funded by the government of Norway and the UN Development Account (UN-Habitat 2008). A complete inventory of local actions is not available, but the major point is that many local governments and community organizations have recognized that actions undertaken at a local level are a major source of carbon emissions and that a need exists to tackle these at the local level as well as at higher scales.

The extensive empirical research on collective action has repeatedly identified a necessary central core of trust and reciprocity among those involved to be associated with successful levels of collective action (Poteete et al. 2010). If the *only* policy related to climate change were adopted at the global scale, it is particularly difficult to increase the trust that citizens and firms need to have that other citizens and firms are taking similar actions to those being taken "at home."

Given that the recognition of the danger of climate change among citizens and public officials is still relatively recent, and given the debates about who is responsible for the problem and for finding solutions, one cannot expect that an effective polycentric system will be constructed in the near future. Given the slowness and conflict involved in achieving a global solution, however, recognizing the potential of building more effective ways of reducing energy use at multiple levels is an important step forward (E. Ostrom 2010).

Given the complexity and changing nature of the problems involved in coping with climate change, there are no "optimal" solutions that can be used to make substantial reductions in the level of greenhouse gases emitted into the atmosphere. A major reduction in emissions is, however, needed. A polycentric approach can encourage experimental efforts at multiple levels and the development of methods for assessing benefits and costs of diverse strategies. Building a strong commitment to finding ways of reducing individual emissions is an important element for coping with this problem. Building such a commitment, and the trust that others are also taking responsibility, can be more effectively undertaken in small- to medium-scale governance units that are linked together through information networks and monitoring at all levels.

Thus, our own and other scholars' consistent finding across empirical studies is that while there are general design principles, there are no magic formulae for solving collective-action problems. Collective-action problems come in a wide diversity of sizes and shapes. The design principles elucidated above are an effort to identify core principles rather than blueprints for how best to govern environmental goods and services—especially in federal systems of governance. Applying these principles to small- and medium-sized resource systems is a challenging task, but one that is simpler than designing effective institutions for global resources. The tough task ahead is the exacting empirical and theoretical work needed to identify which of these principles scale up and what new principles have to be added.

6

Bargaining over Global Public Goods

Ben Groom, J. Rupert Gatti, Timo Goeschl, and
Timothy Swanson

6.1 INTRODUCTION

On many occasions it is overlooked that negotiations over global problems are simply bargaining problems. This means that there is a joint gain that may be achieved through cooperation, but it is first necessary to agree on the distribution of the cooperative surplus before that surplus can be achieved. Without that agreement, there is little chance of moving toward cooperation. With that agreement, there is little reason why such a move would not occur immediately. This aspect of the negotiations over climate change or biodiversity is often lost in the rhetoric surrounding "climate-friendly" behaviour or "biodiversity-destroying" activities. In fact, there is no behaviour that is climate friendly without an agreement on how the benefits from that friendliness are to be distributed, nor is biodiversity destruction any more unfriendly than any other form of development until the distribution of benefits from nondestruction is agreed. The point we are making here is that the first objective of negotiations over global public goods must be to achieve consensus on how the gains from cooperation are to be distributed. Without that foundational agreement, the essential problem of global public good creation is not being addressed. For example, the global public good of climate stabilization concerns the question of the agreed limits on the amount of fossil fuel-based development. The cooperative surplus from climate stabilization may be achieved only by means of agreeing how the aggregate gains from fossil fuel-driven development are distributed. The latter is the primal problem. If it is agreed that each state in the world is to receive an equal share of the benefits from fossil fuel-based development, then the movement to the cooperative outcome is guaranteed. Upon agreement, it would then be to every state's individual benefit to move directly to the frontier of optimal climate management immediately to realize the joint gain. Similarly, in the case of biodiversity (which concerns the aggregate limits to be placed on land conversion activities), the issue is how to distribute the gains that have been achieved from such land conversions. Once the agreement on benefit distribution is achieved, there is nothing that would prevent the states from wanting to move immediately to jointly optimal land use management. Resolving the distributional problem of global public good provision is especially complicated by the fact that states do not have a common initial position in these negotiations. Some states have the capacity to capture benefits from these goods, while others do not. Some states have already banked large amounts of development surplus in regard to these global goods, while others have barely commenced their use of the same. Some states have large and experienced sectors already reliant upon these goods, while others have mere designs upon attaining this some day. For these reasons, distributional issues are caught up in both the differential capacity of states to harness flows of benefits from global resources and the differential histories of states in having done so. These are the essential issues we address here in this chapter. We wish to look at how bargaining theory can explain how the distributional question is at the core of the global public good problem. We also wish to look at how bargaining theory is at the core of any solution to the same. Bargaining theory explains that negotiations over global public goods must focus upon the fundamental problems of distribution, before being able to move to the question of efficiency. Both aspects are necessary conditions to conclude negotiations over global public goods, and the need for an agreement to at least address both of these aspects is well recognized. It is given recognition in the concepts of "differentiated treatment," "burden sharing," and "benefit sharing."[1]

Ultimately, the great environmental and development conventions associated with climate change and biodiversity have all the trappings of classic bargaining problems. That is, the resolution of the problem requires that resources are allocated efficiently and there is a consensus concerning the distribution of the cooperative gains. While predicting the precise bargaining solution in any context is extremely difficult, and subject to the vagaries of human and state behaviors, viewing global environmental problems as bargaining problems can certainly cast light on the nature of a solution. Equally, bargaining theory can tell us something about what the bargaining *process* and outcome might look like. For instance, bargaining theory tells us that the source and magnitude of bargaining power are the key determinants of a rational bargaining solution. Commonly such powers are to be found in

---

[1] The Convention on Biological Diversity (CBD, 1992) has equitable benefit sharing as its third principle. The Montreal Protocol also makes reference to benefit sharing. The Kyoto Protocol distinguishes between the responsibilities of Annex I and Non-Annex I countries based on historical resource use and current income levels. The Pacific Salmon Treaty specifically has the equitable sharing of resources as one of its guiding principles (see Article III).

prevailing sharing norms and customs. On other occasions bargaining power can be found in a particular location, in the timing of a decision, or in a particular resource endowment. All of these aspects are important in determining the outcome of negotiations over global environmental problems. Indeed, devising durable agreements to address such global problems, what some have referred to as "regime formation," requires the building of consensus among negotiating parties in respect of solving the externality and distributing the cooperative gains (Young 1994). One part of this process is sometimes called institutional bargaining, in which negotiating parties strive to find an institutional arrangement which is most likely to uphold consensus cooperation (Young 1994). Indeed, the strength and durability of consensus depends on the legitimacy of the emerging institutions (Labatte 2008). To a great extent this will depend upon perceptions of fairness in the light of the "raw endowments," rights, entitlements, and bargaining power that parties bring to the negotiating table (Howarth 2007). In the absence of this kind of legitimacy, the nature of international environmental agreements and their institutions will have to change in order to avoid conflict. What makes global bargaining problems, and the construction of international institutions and instruments to uphold cooperation, more difficult is that the global nature of the problem introduces significant asymmetries between the negotiating parties. These can include large disparities in current national or per capita income, endowments of resources, current and historical resource use, and so on. Such asymmetries can greatly affect both the likelihood of cooperation, the precise terms of any international agreement, and bring to the fore issues of equity and fairness (Munro and Stokes 1989; Barrett 2003a). Indeed, one need only look at the Annex I and non-Annex I signatories of the Kyoto Protocol, which broadly reflect developed and developing countries respectively, to see how asymmetries in current income levels and historical resource use have lead to an agreement which treats different parties differently. In particular, the agreement reflects past contributions to the global bad (CO_2), disparities in current incomes, and consequently strong notions of fairness in the allocation of mitigation costs (Barrett 2003a, 2005: ch. 14).[2] Asymmetries in resource endowments are also important. For instance, if countries have different endowments of natural resources with public good characteristics, and differing costs of conserving them, this too can determine the likelihood and nature of cooperative agreements. At a more regional level, consider the case of the Pacific salmon fisheries shared by Canada and the United States. Here, the reciprocal nature of spawning grounds and fisheries in each country, and the different costs of resource provision that this entails, meant that equity considerations in the sharing of fishing rights have been enshrined

---

[2] Interestingly, another difficulty with the Kyoto Protocol is the question of the distribution of resources over time, in particular, between present and future generations.

in the Pacific Salmon Treaty.[3] Indeed, cooperation has failed on several occasions whenever levels of catch for one or other party were perceived to be unfair, even when this resulted from exogenous changes in fishery productivity (Munro and Stokes 1989; Miller et al. 2000). Perhaps the starkest example of this kind of asymmetry in the provision and exploitation of global public goods is in the context of global biodiversity conservation. By far the majority of biodiverse ecosystems are found in developing, particularly equatorial, countries. However, while biodiversity provides a wide range of environmental and economic services locally, developed countries harbor a significant proportion of the global value of these resources (Droege and Soete 2001; Gatti et al. 2010). A similar situation exists in relation to the mitigation of carbon through "avoided deforestation": deforestation occurs mainly in developing countries, while the willingness to pay for its prevention stems mainly from developed countries. This asymmetry in the location of resources and the location of their demand is frequently stylized as being between a value rich "North" and a biodiversity rich "South" (Droege and Soete 2001; Sarr and Swanson 2009b; Gatti et al. 2010). In addition, there is considerable demand from the biotech industry for the genetic material found in biodiverse habitats which acts as a stock of evolved information and offers potential solutions to various agricultural, medical, and other problems facing humankind. These resources provide intermediate inputs to the process of research and development (R&D). This introduces two additional sources of North–South asymmetry. First, by and large, it is only the North that has the human capital necessary to undertake R&D of this type. That is, there is a "gene-rich" South and a "technology-rich" North. Second, the domestic institutions relating to these capital endowments are very different, with clear property rights institutions in most forms of capital but few in regard to biodiversity. The informational nature of the goods means that a market solution is unlikely to be efficient, and so this is another important case in which cooperation is required (Goeschl et al. 2005). Indeed, the incentives for

---

[3] Principal 2 of Article III (Miller et al. 2000). Note that our contribution in this chapter has methodological and conceptual similarities with Chapter 7 by Thierry Bréchet and Johan Eyckmans on climate change agreements, in Part II of the volume. First, both are concerned with the heterogeneity of the actors and the role of differentiated treatment in international agreements. Second, both are concerned with the stability of agreements. Indeed, in our analysis of the CBD we will argue that currently enshrined mechanisms are not stable given the nature of the bargaining problem associated with biodiversity. Lastly, both are concerned with the nature of the appropriate transfers to uphold agreement among heterogeneous actors. On the latter point, our chapter also overlaps in terms of the subject matter with Chapter 14 by Graciela Chichilnisky in Part IV. Both contributions argue that the appropriate mechanisms for international payments for environmental services are not incorporated in the current systems and go on to describe some of the qualities that these payment instruments ought to embody. Indeed, the use of bargaining theory in this chapter exposes a potential failure in the current mechanism of the CBD.

cooperation appear to be strong in this case, since both parties stand to gain from biotech innovations in agriculture and pharmaceuticals. However, the asymmetric yet complementary contributions of these regions to the production process suggests that any bargaining solution will have a strong emphasis on equitable sharing of the cooperative surplus. What these examples make clear is that one of the more interesting phenomena that occurs within global negotiations concerns the need to develop durable agreements and contracts that are able to handle gross asymmetries between the states concerned. The focus on the "raw materials" of the bargaining problem that these asymmetries tend to engender makes it more difficult to construct the international agreements required to uphold cooperation. Failure to account for asymmetries and equity issues in the cooperative agreements over global public goods may undermine the legitimacy of the institutions, causing the eventual breakdown in consensus and failure of cooperation. In the language of Young (1994) this would indicate that regime building has been unsuccessful and the process of institutional bargaining would continue. The question is, how would this breakdown in cooperation manifest itself? Here once again, viewing global environmental problems as bargaining problems can shed light on the likely nature of the bargaining process. Recent years have borne witness to some extremely interesting strategic behaviour in relation to global and transboundary natural resources. Indeed, the inherent destructibility, often irreversibly so, of natural resources has tended to make them a credible bargaining chip. For instance, in the case of the Pacific Salmon Treaty, the breakdown of cooperation and the apparent recalcitrance of the USA led Canada to engage in what can only be described as strategic destruction of fish stock via a period of extremely intensive fishing (Miller et al. 2000).[4] This is an unusual case of *actual* destruction. More telling perhaps, and indicative of the gross asymmetries introduced in the context of global biodiversity conservation, are the recent announcements by the Governments of Cameroon and Ecuador. In both cases, announcements were made specifying both a fee, the consequences of non-cooperation, and a deadline, making clear the respective governments' views of the bargaining problem facing them.[5] These are interesting cases in the process of bargaining over global public goods which deserve more analysis. For instance, to what extent are the asymmetries inherent in many global public goods driving these bargaining strategies? How do these asymmetries affect the contract which will sustain cooperation? To what extent are the cooperative solutions embodied in international agreements informed by these asymmetries? And are these contracts perceived to be fair by all parties?

---

[4] Miller et al. (2000) question the success of this strategy. Nevertheless, the treaty has been renegotiated (several times) since this action was undertaken.

[5] See: The price of conservation: the unkindest cut. *The Economist* print edition, 14 February 2008.

In this chapter we address these issues in the context of global biodiversity conservation. We draw upon the theoretical literature stemming from Nash (1953) and Rubinstein (1982) to analyse the bargaining solutions in the presence of the asymmetries commonly found in relation to global public goods.[6] To make the bargaining framework concrete we model a particularly complicated case, that of the biotechnology industry. In so doing we lay bare the gross asymmetries between negotiating parties, their mutual interdependence, and the implications for bargaining strategies and solutions in this context. We then analyze the bargaining solutions of two rational agents in this global bargain, the North and the South, and describe the optimal contracts. What emerges is a description of how unfair solutions to the bargaining problem can induce rational agents to employ strategic threats and/or engage in strategic destruction of natural resources, as witnessed in the case of Cameroon, Canada, and Ecuador described above. We are also able to characterize the nature of the contracts which can sustain an efficient solution in the presence of credible threats, as well as providing the conditions for credible threats. Importantly, this allows us to assess the likely longevity of the current negotiated solution to global biodiversity conservation: the Convention on Biodiversity.

In short the biotechnology case study illustrates the importance of addressing equity issues alongside efficiency issues. It shows that contractual solutions which inadequately reflect the contributions to global public goods can lead to strategic behavior. Where environmental resources are concerned, strategic destruction can be credible. The remainder of the chapter unfolds as follows. The next section presents a simple land use model of North–South interdependence in the biotechnology sector, with biodiversity as a global public good. After establishing the efficient allocation we employ Nash Bargaining theory to illustrate the factors that determine the cooperative solution within this framework. Section 6.3 investigates a "rational" solution to the bargaining game (the Nash bargaining solution) and discusses the expected solution in the case of global biodiversity. Section 6.4 discusses the efficient contractual solution and compares this to the solution contained in the Convention on Biodiversity. The role of bargaining power in the form of strategic threats is discussed in Section 6.5, while Section 6.6 discusses the importance of efficiency and fairness in implementing long-term solutions to global problems. A conclusion follows.

---

[6] The theoretical contexts in which strategic destruction can take place are numerous. See Karp (1996) in the context of non-renewable resources and see Copeland (1990) for the case of international fisheries. Finally, see Busch et al. (1998) for an asymmetric model of bargaining with the destruction of surplus.

6.2 THE CASE OF BIODIVERSITY BARGAINING

In this section we explore cooperation in the supply of global public goods as a bargaining problem in the context of the biotechnology sector. There are several reasons why this is a useful case study. The need for global cooperation in the conservation of biological diversity is generally agreed (Barrett, 1994). There is increasing recognition of the important role to be played by genetic resources in addressing problems in the life sciences (health, agriculture) even as the decline of biodiversity continues apace (Leakey and Lewin 1995). It is recognized that genetic resources will likely play a crucial role in supplying the solution concepts within the life sciences industries (Goeschl and Swanson 2003; Kassar and Lasserre 2004). Biodiversity does this by supplying genetic resources to R&D sectors supplying the life sciences industries (Sarr et al. 2008). In short, this is an important case study. Second, this industry displays stark asymmetries between negotiating parties in relation to both natural and human capital: a natural capital-rich South confronts a human capital-rich North. Lastly, this industry captures the complicated mutual interdependence of the North and South arising from the specialized and sequential nature of the R&D process. It is only the South that contains the genetic inputs required for the R&D process. It is only the North that contains the expertise to convert these into the protected intermediate goods (patented products) that contain these valuable genes. Although both North and South may then use the intermediate goods to advance production and welfare, it is the North that appropriates the value of the R&D process through its exclusive rights in the intermediate goods. This vertical structure to the R&D industry renders the industry susceptible to the "hold up problem" and makes it difficult to coordinate the activities of the parties concerned (Sarr and Swanson 2009b).

This mutual independence and the complementary contributions of each party to aggregate welfare suggests that equity issues and benefit sharing will take an important place alongside efficiency issues in determining acceptable cooperative agreement. In summary, like many global public good problems, the case of global biodiversity conservation has all the trappings of a bargaining problem, rather than solely a mechanical problem of resolving an externality. The following section outlines the analysis taken by Gatti et al. (2010) in this regard. As well as defining contractual solutions to the problem, couching global biodiversity conservation as a bargaining problem can help to explain why observed solutions to this problem need not be long lasting, despite being ostensibly efficient. Indeed, as we will see, there are both efficiency and equity reasons for making a bargaining framework the starting point of the analysis of global environmental problems and international environmental agreement.

6.2.1 Biodiversity and biotechnology: the fundamentals of the North–South bargain

Before moving towards an analysis of any solution to a bargaining problem, it is important to define the underlying structure and limits thereof. The essence of the bargaining problem associated with global biodiversity conservation has been outlined above and they consist of gross asymmetries between North and South. We will make these fundamental aspects of the problem more concrete by looking at this question in the context of the agricultural plant breeding dimension of the biotechnology industry. This case study captures the asymmetries and mutual dependence in this sector in a stylized manner by assuming that the agents are distinctive in three fundamental respects: capital endowments, industrial structures, and land use choices. The asymmetry in capital endowments refers to the relative richness of the North in human capital but poverty in natural (genetic) capital, while the South retains its relative richness in genetic capital but without a very rich human capital base. The differential industrial structure refers to the unique existence of an R&D sector in the North specialized in the production of intermediate goods containing embedded innovations, in contrast to the focus on primary production in the South.[7] The distinct land use choices refer primarily to the South's unique capacity for supplying a biodiversity reserve sector, but also to the fact that the South's alternative land uses include both an intensive agricultural sector that is technology-dependent and a traditional sector which is not; whereas the North's land uses are relatively undifferentiated and involve mainly various forms of modern intensive agricultural production. These asymmetries in capital endowments, industry structure, and land use are described schematically in Figure 6.1.

These asymmetries give rise to a coordination problem associated with the mutual interdependence between the North and South. In Figure 6.1 the arrow running from the Reserves sector to the agricultural biotechnology sector reflects that the North uses its relatively abundant human capital within its R&D sector in combination with genetic resources from the South to produce intermediate goods within which innovations are embedded. However, the North has no land use choice regarding the retention of genetic resource reserves (as losses of genetic resources are irreversible), but only has choices over different productive uses of its own agricultural lands, one use employing the intermediate goods from the R&D sector and the other not.[8] The South, on

---

[7] Of course, this stylization is somewhat weakened by the nascent yet important biotech industries in China, India, and Brazil. Nevertheless, it remains broadly descriptive of this industry (Goeschl et al. 2005).

[8] Gatti et al. (2010) represent the northern land endowment as L_N and the output as $y_N = \pi(R)n + b(L_N - n)$, where $\pi(R)n$ is the production function in intensive agriculture

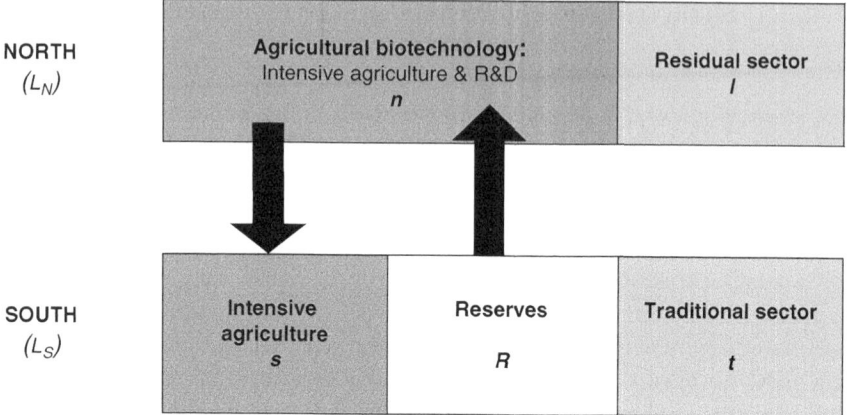

| NORTH (L_N) | Agricultural biotechnology: Intensive agriculture & R&D n | Residual sector l |

| SOUTH (L_S) | Intensive agriculture s | Reserves R | Traditional sector t |

Figure 6.1. Schematic representation of the biotech industry

the other hand. has a natural capital, endowment reserve lands (R) endowed with diverse genetic resources which produce a flow of information which is useful when embedded within the intermediate goods of the R&D sector of the North. The South's land use choice consists of both reserve retention and two methods of agricultural production, one of which uses the intermediate goods from the North, s (arrow running from North to South in Figure 6.1) and the other traditional production, t, which does not. The transfer of genetic material from South to North, and the transfer of technology from North to South, captures the mutual independence arising from these regional asymmetries.[9] The extent of the transfer of these resources depends on the extent of cooperation between the two regions. The global problem now becomes one of optimal allocation of land in the South to Reserves, and hence the supply of genetic material to enhance productivity in the North, and the optimal allocation of technology transfer to the South. Of course, the expansion of intensive agriculture in the South is a means by which cooperative surplus might be shared between the North and the South, but this strategy is

which captures the North's dependence on Reserves R as a productivity enhancing input since $\pi(0) = 1$ and $\pi'(R)>0$. The costs of R&D are assumed to rise with the quantity of the intermediate output, i.e. $c(ns)$. The North can also make a transfer payment, T, to the South. Northern utility is then given by:

$$U_N(n, s, t) = (\pi(R) - b)n - c(n + s) - T + bL_N.$$

[9] The South is endowed with land, L_S, which is originally rich in genetic material. It can be maintained as Reserves with area R, or converted to either a traditional sector, t, or to an intensive agricultural sector using seed imported from the North, s. The traditional sector incurs a labour-related cost $k(t)$ ($k(0) = 0, k'(\cdot)>0, k''(\cdot)>0$). Lastly, land can be used in an intensive sector which, like in the North, is augmented by the presence of Reserves, R: $\pi(R)s$. Therefore, Southern utility is then given by:

$$U_s(n, s, t) = \pi(R)s + t - k(t) + T, \text{ where } T \text{ is any transfer from the North.}$$

potentially in conflict with the objective of retaining the maximum amount of genetic resources for the R&D sector. The problem we examine is how the North and South might simultaneously determine land uses to maximize global surplus and distribute this surplus within such an asymmetric bargaining environment.[10] This defines the asymmetric environment over which bargaining can take place in relation to global biodiversity. However, this begs several questions about the bargaining process. First, will bargaining in this environment be optimal in any sense? Second, against this asymmetric background, what is the expected distribution of a global surplus? In order to answer these questions we must define the limits of the bargain in this case.

6.2.2 The limits of the North–South biodiversity bargaining problem

The outcomes of any bargaining problem among rational agents are confined by two important limits: the conflict point and the bargaining frontier. These measure the outcomes for each agent in the absence and presence of cooperation. The conflict point provides the benchmark against which all bargaining solutions are measured, whereas the bargaining frontier represents all possible distributions of the cooperative surplus between the negotiating parties. Figure 6.2 provides a general illustration of these points.

   On each axis is measured the outcomes for two agents, here the North and South, in terms of "utility": U_S and U_N. The conflict point reflects their respective levels of utility in the absence of cooperation, and is represented by point U^a. In this case the North and South receive low levels of utility given by U_N^a and U_S^a, respectively. The bargaining frontier is shown by the thick black line running between (U_N^E, U_S^a) and (U_N^a, U_S^E). Rational agents will not accept any bargaining outcome with a lower payoff than at the conflict point, since non-cooperation is always available to them. Moreover, outcomes yielding joint utility greater than that obtained by the efficient allocation of resources are impossible. The limit of the cooperative possibilities is given by the bargaining frontier. These points define the limits of the bargaining possibilities. We are interested in the outcome of the bargaining game described above over global biodiversity. So how is the conflict point and the bargaining frontier defined in this case? We assume that the conflict point is an autarkic state in which there is no exchange of biotechnological outputs—that is, new plant varieties—and no transfers are used to transfer any surplus or contract over or coerce land allocations. When cooperation fails, the South benefits

---

[10] As will become clear, this is in effect an assumption of a linear bargaining frontier with perfect transfers of surplus. Miller et al. (2000) discuss some of the implications of this assumption in relation to the Pacific Salmon Treaty. We avoid this discussion here.

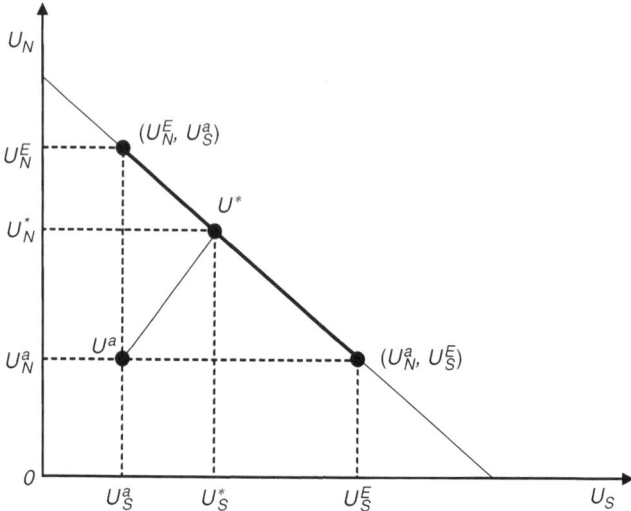

Figure 6.2. The conflict point and the bargaining frontier

only from traditional agriculture. Reserves which contain genetic material are simply a residual land allocation, since the South does not internalize their value embedded in new technologies or receive any related payments. For this reason there is undersupply of the global public good. The precise conditions which describe the conflict point are shown in Appendix 6.1.[11]

The North, on the other hand, still benefits from the presence of any residual reserves (R) due to spillovers arising from their public good nature. So, despite being autarkic, the non-excludable nature of genetic resources contained in the reserves is captured in this solution. Modelling the conflict point in this way captures the fact that the North is dependent upon the South's selection of reserves to generate productivity in the intensive sector, while the South has no reason to supply reserves in the absence of a flow of intermediate goods or contracted payment from the North. Acting in isolation, the South makes land use decisions which lower the marginal productivity of the North's intensive sector, (n). This stylization of the conflict point represents the solution in the absence of a cooperative agreement, with the South undersupplying reserves, since it has no reason to consider the positive externality on the North, and the North benefitting from Southern biodiversity as a spillover from residual lands only. This allows us to define the bargaining frontier as the solution to the "social planner problem": the integrated or cooperative solution for this industry. This is akin to solving the production

---

[11] We assume that the North and the South are single entities. This reflects the idea that the countries in the South are sufficiently large to influence the North in the bargaining solution.

problem of a single vertically integrated industry in which the issues of sovereignty and asymmetry are ignored, and all cooperative opportunities are exploited. The solution maximizes the global surplus and the bargaining frontier then reflects all the Pareto efficient shares of the global surplus between North and South. This is shown by the thick line between (U_N^E, U_S^a) and (U_N^a, U_S^E) in Figure 6.2.[12] The triangle formed by the bargaining frontier and the conflict point is called the bargaining set and reflects all the possible cooperative agreements that could arise making each party at least as well off as in conflict. Given the positive social value of genetic diversity in the biotechnology sector, the globally efficient solution would result in more southern land allocated to Reserves than under autarky $(R^* > R^a)$. In short, to attain the Pareto optimal bargaining frontier requires greater levels of conservation (see Appendix 6.3 for a proof). In some instances these regions specialize completely, with the South specializing in the provision of reserves, and the North in R&D and intensive production.[13] Specialization here results from the fundamental asymmetries: the fact that only the South can provide Reserves while the value from intensive production may be pursued in either region. Although both are necessary for the production of joint surplus, under these conditions the emphasis is on the South providing that which only it can provide (i.e. Reserves). This is indicative of the importance of cooperation in this context: when acting separately each pursues a similar mix of relatively unproductive activities, when acting cooperatively the two generate a vertical industry in which the South specializes in Reserves and the North specializes in final production. The incentive to cooperate is found in the enhanced productivity emanating from the industry. We turn now to defining the level of that cooperative surplus.

6.2.3 The cooperative surplus

In terms of Figure 6.2 the optimal welfare under the social planner solution is given by any value of $U_S + U_N$ on the bargaining frontier. Suppose that negotiations result in an agreement at U^*. In that case optimal welfare is given by $U^* = U_N^* + U_S^*$. A comparison with the outcomes of the conflict point provides a definition of the cooperative surplus, U^C, as the difference between the welfare under the social planner and that under autarky, $U^C = U^* - (U_N^a + U_S^a)$. Since the social planner is always able to select the autarky/non-cooperative outcome, it is safe to say that the social planner

---

[12] The social planner problem is defined as follows (Gatti et al. 2010):

$$\max \quad U(n, s, t) = U_S + U_N = \pi(R)(n + s) - bn + t - c(n + s) - k(t) + bL_N$$
$$s.t. \quad R = L_S - s - t \text{ and } l = L_N - n \text{ and } s, n, t, l, R \geq 0.$$

[13] The detail of this can be found in Proposition 1 in Appendix 6.1.

solution will yield positive gains from cooperation: $U^C \geq 0$. The parties are able to achieve any point along the frontier so long as they can agree on which point they wish to attain (see Appendix 6.4). Although the social planner is not concerned with the distribution of cooperative gains from biodiversity preservation, a system of lump sum transfers ordered by the social planner can facilitate any desired distribution.

Now that the nature of the biodiversity bargaining problem has been established, the indeterminacy of the solution is obvious. Each one of the points along U^* can be sustained as the Nash Equilibrium of a cooperative bargaining game. Choosing among these Nash equilibria depends upon the specifics of the bargaining process: the individual characteristics of the two agents and the institutions that determine their interaction. We turn now to the theoretical solutions to this problem and then to their relation to existing institutions.

6.2.4 A digression into fisheries

Figure 6.2 is a surprisingly useful tool in its own right in discussing potential bargaining outcomes and the failure of cooperation. Miller et al. (2000) use this simple construct to discuss the travails of the Pacific Salmon Treaty between Canada and the US state of Alaska. Over the past twenty or so years a cycle of cooperation and conflict has unfolded between these two parties in relation to their fish. In brief, the problem here is that each country provides the spawning grounds for the other's fisheries, and yet each has the capacity to harvest a proportion of the others main fishery as the fish migrate along their respective coasts. Conflict in this case entails unregulated fishing, while cooperation entails limited harvesting in migratory zones and enhancement of habitat for spawning; that is, efficient resource use and investment. The Pacific Salmon Treaty represents the negotiated agreement to ensure cooperation in this regard. Interestingly, the agreement explicitly recognizes not only efficiency, but also equity concerns. That is, contributions to the aggregate stock through maintenance of spawning grounds should be rewarded equitably. The agreement provides the following principles in relation to efficiency and equity to guide the Pacific Salmon Commission in the management of the fisheries: *each party will conduct its fisheries and its salmon enhancement programmes so as to:*

(a) prevent over-fishing and provide for optimum production; and

(b) provide for each party to receive benefits equivalent to the production of salmon originating in its waters (Article 3 of the Pacific Salmon Treaty quoted in Miller et al. 2000: 3).

The agreement attempts to facilitate cooperation in reciprocal resource use and investment between these sovereign states and effectively determine a point of agreement on the bargaining frontier rather like U^* in Figure 6.2. There are a number of differences, however, in this case. First, there are no mechanisms to redistribute aggregate surplus other than via fishing rights and hence production. That is, there are no side payments. This means that the bargaining frontier is more like the frontier shown in Figure 6.3 between U'_S and U'_N. Due to differences in production costs or diminishing marginal utility, redistribution is therefore costly. Second, Miller et al. (2000) argue that when considering natural resources, the conflict points may be subject to random exogenous shocks due to changing environmental conditions. In combination, these two features can explain much of the cycle of cooperation and conflict witnessed in this case. For instance, as shown in Figure 6.3, suppose that the threat point moves from U^{a1} to U^{a2}, thereby increasing the conflict payoff for the South and reducing it for the North. Any agreement made along bargaining frontier 1 will now not be acceptable for the South and if the terms of the agreement do not adjust to such a change, conflict will ensue, as the South is better off at the new conflict point. Indeed, this is apparently what happened in the mid 1990s in the Pacific Salmon case: Alaskan salmon became much more abundant than the Canadian salmon due to climatic changes, giving a natural advantage to Alaska in the negotiations, and less

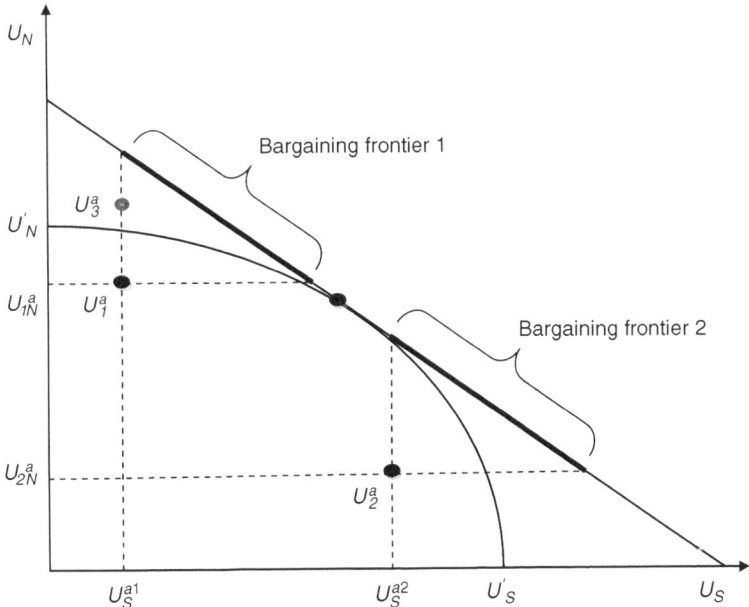

Figure 6.3. Conflict points and bargaining frontiers

benefit to them from cooperation. On the other hand, given that yields have declined and yet enhancement costs remain fixed, the Canadians felt that they were no longer being fairly remunerated. Miller et al. (2000) also suggest that cooperation was further hampered by the absence of side payments. For instance, suppose that a point such as $U^a_{\frac{a}{3}}$ in Figure 6.3 is the conflict point. Clearly this is not attainable in the absence of side payments, which can place the parties on the linear bargaining frontier. Indeed, partly as a consequence of these issues, cooperation broke down in 1993, only eight years after the agreement had been signed. Figures 6.2 and 6.3 help us begin to think about bargaining problems over shared natural resources and provide lessons that can be applied to global public goods also. So far, however, we have not characterized a solution to the bargaining problem, we have only indicated the limits of the bargain. By doing so we will be able to say more about the bargaining outcomes and the agreements that support them. Also, the fact that exogenous changes in the conflict point may improve the bargaining position of a party indicates that strategic manipulation of the conflict point could be employed. The following sections explore these ideas.

6.3 NASH BARGAINING: THE DETERMINANTS OF A "RATIONAL" SOLUTION

6.3.1 The Nash solution

Now that we have laid out the fundamental structure of the biodiversity bargaining problem, we can move towards a discussion of how the resolution of this problem might be determined. To this end we first illustrate the family of solutions to a conventional Nash Cooperative Bargaining Game (NCBG). In Nash cooperative bargaining theory, there are primarily two determinative characteristics of the outcome to any bargaining game: (1) the parties' respective conflict points; and (2) the parties' respective bargaining powers. The key insights from the Nash bargaining solution are first that rational agents will attain a Pareto optimal solution; that is, they will agree on some point on the bargaining frontier such as U^* in Figure 6.2. This indicates the set of outcomes that can be eliminated from consideration. Second, the specific solution depends on the bargaining power of the respective parties. If bargaining power cannot be determined, then any point on the bargaining frontier can be a solution to an NCBG.[14]

---

[14] Formally, the general solution to an asymmetric NCBG is given by the maximization of: $(U_N - U^a_N)^\alpha (U_S - U^a_S)^{(1-\alpha)}$ s.t $U_N + U_S = U^*$, where the parameter $\alpha \epsilon [0, 1]$ is an index of relative bargaining power. The outcomes of this bargaining problem for the North and the

Nash proposed a solution concept that would select a single outcome on the bargaining frontier. In order to do so, he hypothesized that specific characteristics of the bargaining agents would contribute to their capacity to capture a share of the surplus, assuming an outcome along the bargaining frontier. These relative "bargaining strengths" would then determine the share of cooperative surplus acquired by each agent in the game. Framing the solution of the bargain over global biodiversity as an NCBG can then provide some insights concerning the anticipated solution. The limits of the bargain—the conflict point and the bargaining frontier—have already been determined above. The key question to be answered if we are to determine a solution is: how is bargaining power distributed between the North and the South in relation to global biodiversity?

6.3.2 Nash bargaining over global biodiversity: the distribution of bargaining power

All that has been demonstrated is that the solution to the bargaining problem is not determinate in the absence of crucial information about the attributes of the negotiating parties. Indeed, the entire range of efficient solutions remains possible. What the Nash solution shows, however, is that the resolution of a cooperative bargaining game depends upon two crucial features: (1) the relative bargaining "strength" of the two agents; and (2) the conflict point. But what determines bargaining strength in this case?[15]

Bargaining strength may derive from many factors that are characteristic of the agents. The parameter α represents a "sharing rule" or norm which determines the share of the overall cooperative surplus that will accrue to each party. In the original Nash formulation, in which individuals were considered, the sharing norm was implicitly assumed to be 50:50. Indeed, there is evidence to suggest that this is a focal point for many individual bargaining situations.[16] Nevertheless, these norms are contextual and evolve in many different ways. In certain parts of India for instance, the norm in sharecropping agreements appears to more closely resemble a 1/3:2/3 split

---

South are then: $U_N^* = (1 - \alpha)U_N^a + \alpha(U^* - U_S^a)$ and $U_S^* = \alpha U_S^a + (1 - \alpha)(1 - \alpha)(U^* - U_N^a)$. See e.g. Nash (1953).

[15] Where the share of the surplus commanded by the North is given by the parameter a, and for the South (1- α).

[16] See, for instance, Bowles and Gintis (2000), who discuss norms in the context of the ultimatum game. Here large deviations from a 50:50 split are frequently rejected. There is also evidence to show that sharecropping agreements frequently take the form of 50:50 shares (e.g. Bardhan 1984).

between tenant and landlord (e.g. Burke and Young 2000).[17] In Pakistan a variety of sharing rules exist in fisheries and in agriculture (Bardhan and Singh 1987; Ray 1998). Such norms are also important in international agreements. We need only look at the specific guidelines on equity in the Pacific Salmon Treaty, as well as the references to "benefit sharing" appearing in, inter alia, the Montreal Protocol and the Convention on Biodiversity to see this (King 1994; Goeschl et al. 2005). In some cases explicit sharing agreements have arisen, as in the case of The Rhine Treaty on the Emission of Chlorides. Here, a specific cost-sharing agreement was negotiated between negotiating parties. This consisted of the downstream "victim," the Netherlands, paying a significant share (30 percent) of the costs of abatement. It also consisted of Switzerland, an unaffected upstream party, agreeing to bear 15 percent of the costs of abatement on the basis of "solidarity" with the other members of the Rhine River Basin Commission (Barrett 2003a). This provides an important example of how particular sharing rules can arise on the basis of norms of international cooperation. What can we say about the sharing norms in the case of global biodiversity? The main international agreement concerning biodiversity conservation is the Convention on Biological Diversity (CBD). Other related agreements include the International Treaty on Plant Genetic Resources for Food and Agriculture and the agreement on Trade Related aspects on Intellectual Property Rights (TRIPS).[18] In each case "benefit sharing" is a principle objective. Indeed, benefit sharing is the third objective of the Convention on Biodiversity:

> the fair and equitable sharing of the benefits arising out of the utilisation of genetic resources, including by appropriate access to genetic resources and by appropriate transfer of relevant technologies, taking into account all rights over those resources and how benefits are shared based on a set of agreed norms and principles derived from ethics and equity (UNEP 2008).

It is clear from this text that international norms on sharing are in principle being brought to bear on the issue of global biodiversity conservation. In terms of the bargaining outcome, one would expect a more or less equitable sharing of the global surplus in this regard between the supplier, the South, and the source of demand, the North. Furthermore, in the context of the Nash solution, it would be expected that rational bargaining behavior would drive the outcome out towards the bargaining frontier and toward an allocation consistent with the respective contributions that the agents bring to the bargain: reserves from the South, and innovations from the North. The

---

[17] Of course, the context and economic motive for sharing is slightly different here and is frequently understood to reflect the resolution of a principal–agent problem. Nevertheless, the agreed share often reflects the characteristics of the problem, including relative bargaining power and environmental conditions, in addition to risk aversion.

[18] We return to these agreements below.

analysis of global biodiversity as a bargaining problem shows that the antici-pated Nash bargaining solution applied to global biodiversity could easily be consistent not only with basic axioms of rationality in bargaining, but also with basic conceptions of fairness in the recognition of contributions to joint production.

6.4 SEALING THE DEAL: CONTRACTUAL SOLUTIONS TO RATIONAL BARGAINING

To settle on the outcome is not enough in practice of course. To uphold the solution will require the conclusion of some sort of a contract between the North and the South, and the agreement of its terms. This contract will then specify the precise point within the NCBG that is agreed to be the implemen-ted outcome. In this section we specify the general nature of these contracts for the NCBG over global biodiversity. We then ask the question, how has the main international agreement for biodiversity, the CBD, attempted to resolve the bargaining problem? It turns out that there is a disjunction between the theoretically anticipated bargaining solution and contract, and reality. This is something that we discuss later in this section.

6.4.1 Contractual solutions to the bargaining problem

One wrinkle to the contracting process is the question of which party offers the contract. Without any prior information about the problem at hand it is difficult to say which party has the power to offer the contract. Are the contracts offered by the North to the South or vice versa? Ordinarily this would be another source of power, effectively defining a principal–agent problem. However, where we are contracting over an agreed bargaining solution, the ability to offer the contract simply defines the residual claimant to the surplus in the vertical industry and the precise sectors that must be compensated for cooperating in the agreed bargaining solution. From the perspective of the fundamental bargaining game, under certainty this aspect is arbitrary and immaterial.

The "general" contracts specify the efficient land allocations and contain a number of transfers to place the parties at some point along the bargaining frontier. Where the North offers a contract to the South, for instance, the contract contains three components. First, the North, as residual claimant, reclaims the surplus accruing in the South from the intensive agriculture sector. Second, the South is compensated for the costs of participation in the

agreement. This involves compensation for the lost output from the traditional sector incurred as a consequence of the efficient, rather than autarkic, land
allocation. Together these two components place the South back at the conflict
point in terms of welfare, albeit with efficient land allocations. In Figure 6.2
this is reflected by a point such as (U_N^*, U_S^E). Lastly, the contract must contain
a component which transfers the agreed share of the global surplus.[19] The
precise form of these contracts is described in Appendix 6.2. An analogous
contract can be specified for the same agreed bargaining solution, only with
the South as residual claimant. There are, of course, two special cases of this
general contract which reflect the complete absence of bargaining strength for
one or other party. These "extreme point" contracts, in which one or other
party receives the entire cooperative surplus would simply place the South at
point (U_N^*, U_S^E) in Figure 6.2 if it had no bargaining strength, or North at point
(U_S^E, U_S^*) in the opposite case. Therefore, extreme point contracts support
distributions that correspond to the limits of the bargaining frontier, in which
one party is devoid of all bargaining power ($\alpha = 1$ or $\alpha = 0$), and such
contracts must only satisfy the participation constraint: the contracted payoff
must be greater than or equal to the conflict payoff (U_S^a, U_N^a).

It is important to realize that all of these contracts are in fact efficient in the
sense that they allow the agents to attain the bargaining frontier, but each
merely compensates the party receiving the offer for the costs of its participation. As discussed, these extreme point outcomes may result from the bargaining process where all the bargaining power resides in either the North or the
South, respectively. It is obvious, however, that not all international negotiations are approached and resolved by reference to a rational bargaining
solution. It is quite possible that negotiations place the parties at one or
other of the extreme points as a consequence of a process which is independent of bargaining power. This may occur where the identity of the party
making the offer of the extreme point contract is determined by some institutional or structural factor that pre-determines the contractual outcome in
advance of the bargaining process. This is the case, for example, if the identity
of the party able to give the first offer—the first-mover advantage—is determined by structural reasons from outside of the bargaining process. In this
way, the first mover views the problem as a principal–agent problem and
focuses solely on resolving the externality, and ignores the distributional
issues. If taking a bargaining approach to the analysis of global public goods
tells us anything, it is that this possibility does not obviate the bargaining
power of the second mover, it merely makes it irrelevant to the outcome of this
particular bargaining process.

---

[19] Gatti et al. (2010) specify the general North–South contract as follows:

$$T_N(t) = \int_t^{t^a} [1 - k(z)]dz - \pi(L_S - s^* - t)S^* + (1 - \alpha)U^C.$$

6.4.2 Incremental costs: an "extreme point" contract

Clearly, there is range of efficient contracts available to solve the bargaining problem over global biodiversity. Although we have pointed towards the likelihood of an equitable outcome, by reference to fair remuneration for inputs to the productive process, any of the solutions along the bargaining frontier could be upheld in practice. The mechanism for paying for these inputs could be of the nature of a property rights solution (Sarr and Swanson, 2009a). Or it could be of the nature of some sort of global fund. It might also be some agreed formula for contractual compensation. In any event, any solution concept must address the fundamental bargaining problem outlined above.

Indeed, just such a contractual solution can be found under the terms of the CBD and its financial instrument the Global Environment Facility (GEF) in the form of the concept of "incremental costs." These international environmental agreements established the framework within which the North and South agreed that biodiversity should be provided as a global good, and further established the basis for determining how states providing biodiversity should share in the benefits of the global public good they provide. Implicit within the terms of the CBD is the idea that the South must provide much of the biodiversity resource, and the focus of the agreement is the means by which they will be compensated for doing so—the answer to which is found in the concept of *incremental costs* (IC):

> [the North] shall provide new and additional financial resources to enable *[the South]* to meet the agreed full incremental costs to them of implementing measures which fulfil the obligations of this Convention. [Art. 20, CBD]

The meaning of the term "incremental costs" is further defined within the founding instrument of the GEF as:

> [the costs of] additional national action beyond what is required for national development [the baseline] that imposes additional [or incremental] costs on countries beyond the costs that are strictly necessary for achieving their own development goals, but nevertheless generates additional benefits that the world as a whole can share . . .(GEF/C.7/Inf.5: para. 2 & GEF/C.2/6 para. 2)

Thus, the terms of the agreements establishing the CBD and the GEF impose an obligation on those states hosting biodiversity to supply it for the global good, and dictate that the North shall share the benefits of such public goods with the South *by paying the amounts required to compensate it for the costs of its participation.* Of course, the third objective of the CBD is to ensure benefit sharing in accordance with some international norms. The Bonn agreement of 2004 outlines recent mechanisms and instruments (such as up-front payments, revenue sharing rules, and royalties) that can be used to facilitate benefit sharing. Indeed, many of these are directed specifically towards the use of genetic resources in biotechnology. Despite these mechanisms and some small successes, difficulties remain for implementation and enforcement in developing countries. It is widely agreed that these mechanisms are very much in their infancy in terms of efficacy (UNEP 2008). Moreover, these mechanisms are devoted largely to the private economic values held by pharmaceutical and plant breeding companies. While these values are thought to be significant, they do not reflect the social value of the stock of genetic resources arising from the ability to overcome well-known phenomena associated with pathogen adaptation and resistance. These values are likely to significantly outweigh private values. In the end, the main contractual solution for global biodiversity can be found in the IC contract of the CBD. Furthermore, the use of the IC principle is not limited to the CBD, but also underpins funding for the resolution of other global environmental problems. The GEF, which implements the IC contracts, is also the key financial institution for the Framework Convention on Climate Change (FCCC) and the UN Convention to Combat Desertification (UNFCCD). The IC principle was first used in the Montreal Protocol. The IC principle appears to be widely accepted and the GEF has become the largest source of multilateral funding for the global environment (Labatte 2008). So, where does the IC contract place the negotiating parties in the bargaining set? In terms of the preceding analysis, the IC contract requires the North to compensate the South for the additional costs it incurs by electing the cooperative development path rather than its baseline development strategy. There is no allusion to or provision for enhanced sharing by the South in the cooperative surplus by reason of this election, but only provision for the compensation of its costs incurred to generate additional benefits that the world as a whole can share. The South will, of course, obtain its share of this cooperative surplus, but the IC contract does not provide for any enhanced share in exchange for its cooperation. Despite this, the IC contract is efficient in the sense that it pinpoints a solution on the bargaining frontier, albeit an unequal one. Importantly, neither does the contract condition payment on the level of the South's Reserves. In short, the IC contract does not bear any of the hallmarks of the contract that would be anticipated to arise out of the NCBG. Instead, the IC contract is a straightforward offer of the extreme point contract, in which the North offers the South compensation for its costs incurred in participating in the cooperative outcome. In terms of Figure 6.2, the IC contract places the parties at point (U_N^*, U_S^E), in which the North receives the entire global surplus. The puzzle of this NCBG is how an outcome so at odds with the contributions made by the negotiating parties, and hence at odds with usual norms of fairness and equity, could result from this sort of bargaining problem. It is a solution which solves the externality problem, of course, but fails to recognize the fundamental nature of the bargaining problem. Of course, the IC contract is, on the face of it, cost effective. That is, it appears to obtain the biggest "bang for the buck", since the North pays the lowest possible level of compensation to the South. In principle at least, this means that more global environmental projects can be funded. Building on this, some have argued that the IC principle is an example of successful "regime formation" and has some moral content when viewed from a "contractarian" perspective. That is, the IC contract provides the basis for consensus on the provision of global public goods because of its cost effectiveness (Labatte 2008: 220). While an appealing interpretation of the IC contract, as well as a valid explanation for its prevalence in many international environmental agreements, the disjunction of the IC contract with the solution anticipated, when viewed from the perspective of a bargaining problem, suggests that the legitimacy of this institution, and hence the strength of the consensus, might ultimately be lacking. Indeed, it seems unlikely that this can be a lasting solution to the problem. There have been several critiques undertaken of the IC contract in recent years, most of which refer to the difficulties in defining baselines, and other administrative issues. However, in the following section, we show that there are likely to be perverse repercussions from selecting this particular contractual outcome.

6.5 REFRAMING THE GAME: RATIONAL THREATS AS A SOURCE OF BARGAINING POWER

6.5.1 Rational threats

The asymmetric yet complementary inputs provided by the North and the South, and the presence of recognized international norms of fairness, point to the unlikely nature of the IC contract as the Nash bargaining solution. The discord between underlying realities of the bargaining problem and the incremental cost contract, suggests that the IC contract is unlikely to represent a lasting solution. Inequitable distributions such as this are frequently at the bottom of non-cooperation, as in the case of the Pacific Salmon Treaty, the European Sulphur Protocols of the late 1980s, and so on (Miller et al. 2000; Mason and Swanson 2003). In terms of the bargaining framework, the IC contract leaves the South indifferent between cooperation and non-cooperation. Indeed, the South is free to simply revert to "autarky" and select the conflict point. But are there any strategies or responses available to the South that can dislodge the current solution and improve their outcome? By analysing this negotiation from a bargaining perspective it is possible to show that the answer to this question is to be found in the asymmetries between the North and the South.

First, note that the sharing norms or bargaining power shown to be important by bargaining theory, and represented by the parameter α, determine the solution on the bargaining frontier from any given conflict point. However, a complete description of the anticipated Nash bargaining solution for global biodiversity also includes an analysis of the conflict point. The analysis of the Pacific Salmon Treaty shows how the outcome of negotiations can be affected by exogenous changes in the position of the conflict point. However, in the case of the Nash solution, the ability to shift the conflict point by one or other party confers the ability to "re-frame" the bargaining game to their own advantage. Nash (1953) analysed precisely this type of problem, in which shifting the conflict point, or threatening to do so, can be a rational bargaining strategy. In short, the ability to reframe the bargaining problem represents another form of bargaining power. More specifically, one feature of many solution concepts to bargaining games, including the NCBG, is that the value received by one player, say the South (U_S^*) is not only increasing in the value of any outside option available to that player—that is, the conflict outcome U_S^a—but it is also increasing in the maximum value of cooperation to the *other* player, the North $(U_N^* - U_N^a)$. In essence, any actions available to one player that can increase the value of cooperation to the other player, without a negative impact on their own outside option, will increase the payoffs to that player within the cooperative bargaining game. In essence, such a strategy would reduce the other player's potential benefits more than

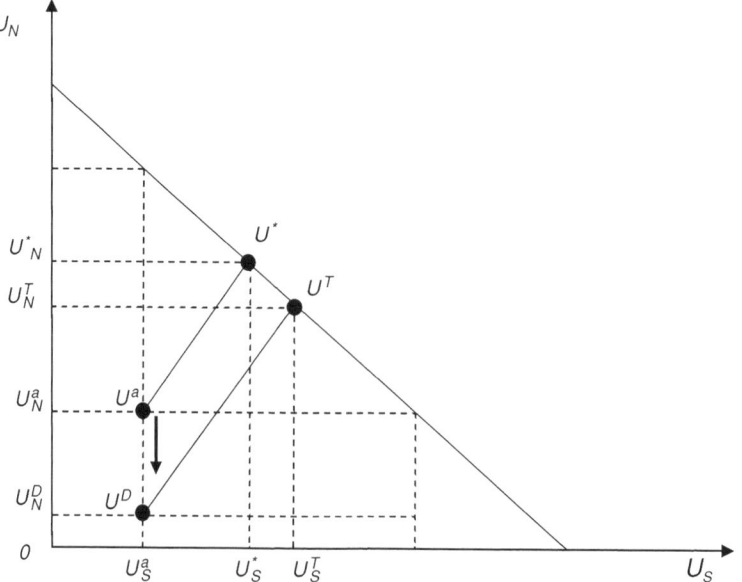

Figure 6.4. The bargaining problem with strategic threats

their own, if the game were to be played non-cooperatively, and so makes it possible to use this threat as the basis for more power within the cooperative game. Figure 6.4 illustrates how this might work. In this case the South now threatens to push the conflict point from U^a to U^D, reducing the North's conflict payoff without affecting its own. Reframed in this way, the Nash solution now becomes (U_N^T, U_S^T), which confers a greater share of the global surplus to the South. Such threats are not made because of an interest in the conflict outcome, but rather because of their impact on the agreed bargaining solution.

So, how is bargaining power of this type distributed in the case of global biodiversity? Our portrayal of a "gene-rich" South and a "technology-rich" North is one of specialized yet interdependent regions. At first glance it would appear that the asymmetric endowments would result in equivalent and reciprocal threat capacities: the North could threaten to reduce R&D, while the South could threaten to limit the supply of Reserves, resulting in no real bargaining advantage. However, this ignores the question of credibility. In any application of the NCBG parties must be able to commit to their threats, via irreversible actions. One obvious means of making a credible commitment is for the party concerned to threaten destruction of the required assets, should the parties fail to reach agreement on the basis for cooperation. Here there is a clear asymmetry in bargaining capacities: the South can credibly threaten destruction of its environmental resources, but the North cannot credibly threaten to destroy human capital or information. Furthermore, the assumption of irreversibility means this threat contains a "natural" commitment mechanism. In short, the asymmetry in capital endowments means only the South can satisfy the necessary conditions for a credible threat in this bargain, and it is a threat of strategic destruction.

6.5.2 Strategic destruction as a rational threat

While the destruction of resources as a bargaining ploy sounds alarming, it has been noted in other contexts as a ploy to secure bargaining power. Nevertheless, what can strategic destruction mean in the context of biodiversity? For concreteness, strategic destruction of Reserves can be understood as a literal threat to destroy resources, as witnessed in Latin America (World Bank 2003). Here, farmers offered an IC contract in Latin America retorted "bueno, corto todo" when no compensation was offered for the existing stock of forest resources. Barrett (2003a: ch. 2) also describes how threats of destruction were issued in the protracted negotiations surrounding the Fur Seal Treaty. Indeed, Canada's response to the unfavorable distribution of surplus in the Pacific Salmon Treaty was to embark upon an "aggressive" fishing policy (Miller et al. 2000). This appears to have been a case of actual destruction of resources, which Copeland (1990) describes as strategic. More generally, in the case of global biodiversity, strategic destruction could be understood as a threat to allow on-going and irreversible land conversion in the absence of cooperation. Gatti et al. (2010) employ the Nash model with strategic threats to analyse the implications for the Nash bargaining solution of the South's ability to reframe the bargaining game via strategic destruction. The description of the conflict point above shows that since "reserves" have public good qualities they affect the outcome for the North in Autarky. For the South this is a residual land allocation. This means that the destruction of reserves can be exploited as a strategic threat and reframe the bargaining problem as described in Figure 6.4. Of course, in order for threats to be taken seriously by the North, they must be credible. Beyond the South's unique capacity for credibly threatening destruction that is embodied in the irreversibility of natural resource destruction, Gatti et al. (2010) suggest that a further necessary condition for credible threats is that the South must not be able to "shoot itself in the foot" if forced to undertake the destruction it has threatened. That is, the South must be at least as well off in both the conflict outcome or in any cooperative solution subsequent to destruction taking place. This can be understood by reference to Figure 6.5.

If strategic destruction is not just threatened but is actually undertaken, the global surplus will diminish. In Figure 6.5 this is reflected by the conflict point shifting downwards *and* the bargaining frontier shifting inwards as socially valuable reserves are destroyed. In any bargaining game subsequent to this the two parties will negotiate over a smaller "pie." The definition of credibility

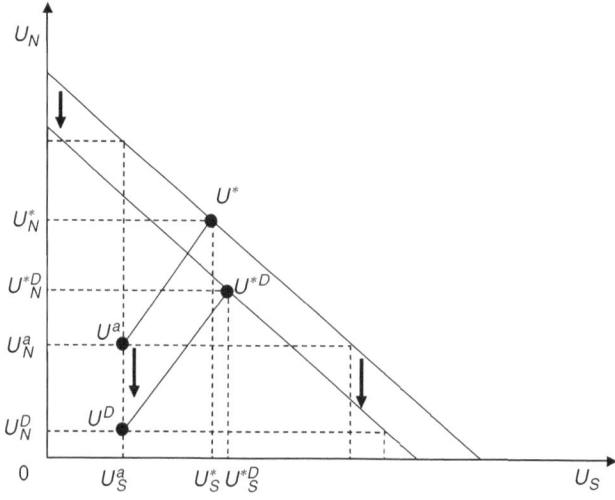

Figure 6.5. Credible strategic threats

used by Gatti et al. (2010) means that the new conflict outcome should not lie to the left of U^a, and the outcome of any Nash bargaining solution subsequent to destruction should not lie to the left of U^c, like U_S^{*D}. If these conditions hold, the South cannot "shoot itself in the foot." But are these conditions satisfied in the case of global biodiversity? Since Reserves are residual to the South in Autarky, reflecting the informational nature of the goods they supply and the market failure in the Reserves market, the new conflict point will not lie to the left of U^a so long as no disproportionate amount of ancillary resources is expended in choosing to destroy Reserves. Assuming cost-neutrality, strategic destruction will not reduce the South's conflict payoff. But what about the bargaining outcome in any future bargaining game? In fact, this question can be rephrased as: can the South increase the value of cooperation to the North? Given the interdependence of the North and South in the biotech industry, it seems unlikely that the South could gain from this exercise, and likely that this will be an extremely stringent condition. Nevertheless, Gatti et al. (2010) show that this will be the case if the social marginal value of reserves increases rapidly as reserves become scarce. Specifically, the social marginal value of reserves must be higher in conflict than on the bargaining frontier. This is an extremely plausible condition. A Nash bargaining solution with credible strategic threats could be represented by a point such as U_S^T in Figure 6.4, where this yields a larger share of the surplus than in the absence of threats: U_S^*, as the South's ability to reframe the bargaining problem is remunerated. Another implication is that if the South satisfies the no "shooting-oneself-in-the-foot" conditions for strategic threats, this opens up the possibility that *actual* destruction would increase the benefits of cooperation for the North, therefore increasing the payoff for the South in any subsequent Nash bargaining game. That is, conditions exist in which destruction might be undertaken, rather than simply threatened. In sum, from the perspective of a bargaining problem, strategic destruction can be a rational response to an inequitable bargaining solution like the IC contract of the CBD. Each party brings asymmetric yet complementary inputs to the negotiating table. This in itself suggests an equitable resolution to the bargaining problem. An inequitable outcome would leave one party, the North, vulnerable to strategic destruction in the South.

6.5.3 Sealing the deal properly: contracts to avoid strategic destruction

How can a North–South bargaining solution be sealed both fairly and efficiently in the presence of such important asymmetries? That is, how can strategic destruction be precluded? The details of the efficient contract in the presence of credible strategic threats differ radically from those without strategic threats. Crucially, they show that efficient contracts must have payments which are conditioned on the stock of genetic resources or reserves. In particular, with perfect information, the South must be compensated for the reserves that could be credibly destroyed, while the size of the transfer reflects the value to the North of the spillover/externality provided by the South in the absence of cooperation. In terms of Figure 6.5, this is a payment for the resources that would be lost shifting the conflict point from U^a to U^D. How do the details of this family of efficient contracts compare to those in the absence of this asymmetric bargaining power discussed above in relation to Figure 6.2? The crucial deficiency of these contracts is that they do not condition on the stock of reserves. They merely contain a transfer reflecting the costs of participation and, in the general case, an agreed share of the cooperative surplus. The "extreme" IC contract of the CBD is as guilty of this as any, and has the additional deficiency, in all likelihood, of being perceived as unfair. Failure to condition payments on the stock of reserves means that reserves have strategic value and strategic threats can be employed where credible. In practice this means that contracts which ignore this stark asymmetry in bargaining power between the North and the South will fail to halt biodiversity loss, and moreover, could induce it.

6.6 DISCUSSION: FAIRNESS AND EFFICIENCY, THREATS AND CONTRACTS

By analysing the case of global biodiversity as a Nash bargaining problem, rather than simply an externality problem, it has been possible to show the need for both the equity and efficiency aspects in the search for a long-lasting solution. The stark asymmetries between the two parties, and the allocation of bargaining power that this confers, suggests that one observed contractual solution, the IC contract of the CBD, is an unlikely one. Although both parties make important contributions to the creation of the cooperative surplus, the fact that the endowment (the Reserves) of the South is inherently and irreversibly destructible provides the South with a significant bargaining advantage. Since irreversibility is a sufficient condition for a threat to be credible, the South has the unique capacity in this context to shift surplus towards itself. The idea that the South could have much of the bargaining power in this case is interesting in its own right. Second, the asymmetry in physical endowments indicates the nature of the process by which it would be expected that the South could drive a bargaining process based upon them. It would appear that the South should be able to exercise its unique advantage to drive the bargaining outcome in its favour. In terms of the NCBG, we would anticipate that the

South would be able to command a substantial share of the cooperative surplus. In addition, as Section 6.5 shows, an efficient solution to the problem would imply that the contractual terms explicitly base compensation upon the existing level of Reserves.

Why is it the case that the current (incremental cost) contract is likely to be able to be a lasting one? Consider the bargaining process. One possibility is that the parties engaged in bargaining, and that the North offered these terms of contract in the context of the NCBG. The problem with this explanation is that the South could have the option of destruction, once bargaining has commenced, and destruction is a possible outcome in the face of an offer that fails adequately to compensate the South for its bargaining position. Contracts which are silent on the commitment to any level of reserves can induce the South to commit (undertake) strategic destruction, with no cost in the case of conflict, and an improved share of the global surplus in any future bargain, as shown in Figure 6.5. In contrast, optimal contracts condition payments explicitly on the optimal stock of genetic reserves in the South, hence removing the incentive to destroy. This general recommendation accords with findings elsewhere (e.g. Lensink and van Soest 2000).

In sum, far from being an example of successful "regime building" it is unlikely, given the observed distribution of bargaining power, that we are at present only part way through the institutional bargaining process and are yet to find the legitimate institution which will form a lasting consensus between negotiating parties (Young 1994). This is likely to be the case despite the fact that the extreme point contract is efficient. Even if the North has the capacity to make the initial offer of the IC contract, it is not a stable outcome of the bargaining game. The South retains bargaining leverage that would imply that outcomes will take into account its unique endowments. We would expect that the rational threats of destruction will, in due course, move the contractual solution nearer to the outcomes shown in Figure 6.4. We have already cited, inter alia, the Pacific Salmon Treaty as an instance in which strategic destruction is thought to have taken place in the form of an aggressive fishing strategy, but have we witnessed any such responses from Southern countries? The answer to this is, yes, we have. Furthermore these cases can easily be interpreted from this bargaining perspective. The best documented examples concern the Governments of Cameroon and Ecuador. In Cameroon in 2008 the Minister of Forestry, Joseph Thatta, made a clear statement of what the government perceived to be a fair share of the cooperative surplus, while effectively redefining the conflict point in the negotiations with international conservation organizations over the Ngoyla-Mintom forest. An annual fee of US$1.6m for 830,000 ha of biodiverse tropical forest was requested to prevent the concessions being sold to logging companies. Rough calculations suggest that the global value in terms of carbon sequestration alone is double the value of the logging concessions, so conservation is on the bargaining frontier. In the absence of any offers, in March 2009 the Government made good on its threat and the process of determining forest concessions began. In terms of the bargaining framework, the process appears to be stuck at the conflict point.

Similar threats were issued by President Rafael Correa of Ecuador in relation to the Yasuni National Park at a meeting of the United Nations in September of 2007. Again, the conflict point and the share of the surplus were clearly defined, albeit under different circumstances to Cameroon. The conflict point was defined as the development of the oil fields beneath the National Park. The share of the cooperative surplus, arising from leaving the oil in the ground, included compensation for lost oil revenues from the international community, which resembles the incremental cost component, and carbon credits amounting to the forgone carbon emissions, reflecting a payment for the stock of carbon. This contractual solution bears more than a passing resemblence to the optimal contract under strategic threats. This approach has been more successful than in the case of Cameroon, and has received numerous pledges of finance. Nevertheless, to date the threat remains on the table until sufficient finance is attracted. Both of these examples represent attempts to dislodge the status quo and certainly represent an active use of threats, or at the very least, a laying bare of the structure of the bargaining game. Threats are not the only responses to the status quo that have been witnessed in the realm of biodiversity. The formation of the Group of Like Minded Mega-Diverse Countries (LMMC) represents an alternative means by which to garner bargaining power, dislodge current solutions, and improve benefit sharing. In the context of the bargaining problem discussed here, this could represent an attempt to develop a credible threat, or, an attempt to influence the sharing rule, α. In sum, these recent responses support the main finding here, that current solutions are unlikely to be long lasting, despite ostensibly solving the externality problem for now.

6.7 CONCLUSION

This chapter has set out to make three basic points regarding institution building for global environmental management. First, it is important to begin thinking about global environmental problems as questions of cooperation over the production of joint surplus. The basic problems of biodiversity and climate change have little to do with preventing externalities or with conserving amenities. These are problems dealing with the fundamental notion of the division of the surplus available from certain forms of production. Biodiversity concerns the product available from the life sciences industries. Climate change concerns the product available from fossil fuel-based production. A basic problem of global cooperation concerns how the states will agree to divide up the product from these basic industries. These are the basics of bargaining problems. The NCBG is the appropriate way to think about these problems. Second, these problems are made fundamentally difficult by reason of the asymmetries between the states concerned. In the context of biodiversity, the South holds the genetic resource capital while the North holds the vast majority of the human capital. The South has very few property rights over its capital, while the North holds extensive rights over its inputs. The North sells the R&D outputs of the life sciences industries, while the South provides the inputs to it. These fundamental differences mean that institution building must be directed toward dealing with them. International institution building is about dealing with these differences in an efficient fashion. It is about finding ways to move toward the bargaining frontier in the presence of these fundamental asymmetries.

Third, the essence of the Nash cooperative bargaining approach is that important differences between the parties must be part of the ultimate solution concept for the bargaining problem. That is, the notion of a fair distribution—that is capable of resolving the bargaining game with finality—will emanate from these essential differences. Any contractual outcome can be efficient, but only in a short-term sense. Divisions of surplus that are not based upon the essential characteristics between the parties will provoke a rational response for that characteristic to be recognized. Any lasting contractual outcome will consider the potential for such rational threats, and offer divisions of surplus that incorporate them. This means that efficient contracts offering lasting solution concepts to the NCBG will be based upon the characteristics identified within the Nash framework. In conclusion, the most interesting result obtained here is the observation that global contracts must be based on the real characteristics and real contributions of the bargaining parties. We have shown that, although any contracted outcome on the bargaining frontier is possible, those contracts that fail to anticipate the potential for rational responses will necessarily be short-lived solution concepts. Real bargaining power derives from real differences—those important to the production of cooperative surplus. Contracts chosen on the basis of perceived political power that fail to recognize inherent economic power must fail. What will turn out to be "efficient" (in the form of a long-run cooperative equilibrium) will also turn out to be "fair" (in the sense of Nash theory).

Appendix 6.1: The conflict point and bargaining frontier

In the absence of cooperation, the North and South act independently and Reserves R benefit the North only.

The South

The South maximizes utility with respect to t.

$$\max_{t} \quad U_S(s = 0, T = 0) = t - k(t)$$

$$s.t.: L_S = t + R \text{ and } 0 \leq t \leq L_S$$

If $k'(0) \leq 1 < k'(L_S)$, the South's optimal use of land under Autarky, t^a, will be an interior solution and satisfy the first-order condition:

$$1 - k'(t^a) = 0$$

Let $R^a = L_S - t^a$ be the South's Reserves under Autarky.

The North

The North takes the behavior of the South as given and maximizes utility over its choice of n and l. The North's problem is as follows:

$$\max_{n} \quad U_N(s = 0, T = 0) = \left(\pi(R) - b\right)n - c(n) + bL_N$$

$$s.t.: 0 \leq n \leq L_N$$

If $c'(0) = 0$ and $c'(L_N) > \pi(L_S)$, the North's optimal land use, n^a, will be an interior solution satisfying the first-order condition:

$$\pi(R^a) - b - c'(n^a) = 0$$

Proposition 1: If the Autarky solution is interior, and the social planner wishes to hold positive levels of Reserves (i.e. $R^* > 0$) then:

(a) intensive agricultural production will always be positive, i.e. $(n^* + s^*) > 0$;
(b) optimal traditional production in the South will be less than under Autarky, (i.e. $t^* < t^a$);

(c) whenever there is intensive production in the North, the optimal Reserve sector increases with global intensive agriculture

$$\text{(i.e. } R^* > (<) R^a \Leftrightarrow n^* + s^* > (<) n^a \text{); and}$$

(d) if profits are equal to zero in the baseline sector ($b = 0$), then $s^* > 0$ only when $n^* = L_N$.

Proof: Whenever $L_S > R^* > 0, \frac{\delta R}{\delta S} = \frac{\delta R}{\delta T} = -1$ and the first order Kuhn–Tucker conditions yield:

$$s^* \geq 0 : \pi(R) - \pi'(R)(s^* + n) - c'(n + s^*) \leq 0$$

$$n^* \geq 0 : \pi(R) - b - c'(n^* + s) \leq 0$$

$$t^* \geq 0 : 1 - \pi'(R)(n + s) - k'(t^*) \leq 0$$

The proof follows in parts: (a) From Equation (c) if $(n^* + s^*) = 0$ then $t^* = t^a$ and so $R^a = R^a$. When $R^* = R^a$, we have that $(n^* + s^*) = n^a > 0$, which is a contradiction; (b) If $t^* = 0$ then $t^* < t^a$ by assumption. If $t^* > 0$ then $1 - k'(t^*) = \pi'(R^*)(n^* + s^*) > 0 = 1 - k'(t^a)$, thus $t^* < t^a$ as $k''(.) > 0$; (c) Comparing Equations (10) and (b), if $n^* > 0$, then $n^* + s^* > (<) n^a \Leftrightarrow R^* > (<) R^a$; (d) Given $b = 0$, comparing Equations (a) and (b); $n^* < L_N \Rightarrow s^* = 0$ and therefore $R^* > R^a$.

Proposition 1(b) shows that the optimal size of the traditional sector in the South is smaller than under Autarky; however, 1(c) shows that the overall level of Reserves will rise and fall with the size of the global intensive sector. How the socially optimal allocation compares with the Autarky state will depend upon the parameters of the model, particularly the relative productivity of the baseline sector in the North and the traditional sector in the South. A low value for b increases the likelihood that the socially optimal level of Reserves is higher than under Autarky. Proposition 1(d) shows that in the extreme case where the profits from the baseline sector are equal to zero ($b = 0$), the ambiguity is resolved and $R^* > R^a$ whenever the North's baseline sector remains active. In sum, the social planner is reluctant to have intensive agriculture in the South due to the loss of socially valuable Reserves this land use would entail, and where $b = 0$, the social planner would choose for each region to specialize in its own function for agriculture: intensive production in the North and Reserves in the South. Specialization here is the result of the fact that only the South can provide Reserves, while the value from intensive production may be pursued in either region. Although both are necessary for the production of joint surplus, under these conditions the emphasis is on the South providing that which only it can provide (i.e. Reserves).

Appendix 6.2: Proposition 2

Proposition 2: "General" and "extreme point" contracts:
Extreme point contracts: (North to South): if framed as an offer by N to the S, the optimal contract to uphold an asymmetric Nash bargaining solution would have the North specify the contractual terms S^* and n^* and the transfer:

$$T_N(t) = \int_t^{t^a} [1 - k(z)]dz - \pi(L_S - s^* - t)s^* + (1\alpha)U^C \qquad (6.A.1)$$

Proof: Given the above, the South's utility is given by:

$$U_S(t : \tilde{n}, \tilde{s}) = \pi(L_S - \tilde{s} - t)\tilde{s} + t - k(t) + T_N(t)$$
$$= t^a - k(t^a) = U_S^a$$

which is independent of t. Thus the South is willing to produce at any level of t, including $t = \tilde{t}$. Given that the South selects $t = \tilde{t}$, the North's problem is to select the values of $(\tilde{n}, \tilde{s}, \tilde{t})$ to maximize

$$U_N(n, s, t) = \left(\pi(R) - b\right)n - c(n + s) - T_N(t : n, s) + bL_N$$
$$= \pi(R)(n + s) - bn - c(n + s) + t - k(t) - [t^a - k(t^a)] + bL_N$$
$$= U(n, s, t) - [t^a - k(t^a)]$$

which, as $[t^a - k(t^a)]$ is a constant, is equivalent to the social planner's problem, and has solution (n^*, s^*, t^*) as required.

Extreme point contracts: (South to North): if the South selects output level $t = \tilde{t}$, the desired output levels $(n, s) = (\tilde{n}, \tilde{s})$ and the extreme point contract to the North is:

$$T_S(n, s : \tilde{t}) = [\pi(L_S - s - \tilde{t}) - b](-n) + c(n + s) + [U_N^a - bL_N] \qquad (6.A.2)$$

Proof: Given the contract above, the North's utility is given by

$$U_N(n, s, t) = \left(\pi(R) - b\right)n - c(n + s) + T_S(t : n, s) + bL_N$$
$$= U_n^a$$

which is independent of (n, s). Thus the North is willing to produce at any output levels, including $(n, s) = (\tilde{n}, \tilde{s})$. Of course, a small deviation penalty could be included to ensure compliance. Given that the North will select $(n, s) = (\tilde{n}, \tilde{s})$, the South's problem is to select the values of $(\tilde{n}, \tilde{s}, \tilde{t})$ to maximize

$$U_S(n,s,t) = \pi(L_S - s - t)s + t - k(t) - [\pi(L_S - s - t) - b](-n) - c(n+s) - [U_N^a - bL_N]$$
$$= \pi(L_S - s - t)(n+s) - bn - c(n+s) + t - k(t) - [U_N^a - bL_N]$$
$$= U(n,s,t) - U_N^a$$

which, as U_N^a is a constant, is equivalent to the social planner's problem and has solution (n^*,s^*,t^*) as required.

General contracts: the only difference between the extreme point contracts and the general contract is the inclusion of a constant term $(1 - \alpha)U^C$ in the transfer payment. A constant transfer payment has no impact on the optimizing decisions of the agents, thus the solution remains unchanged. QED

Appendix 6.3: Strategic Destruction

Proposition 3: Strategic Destruction: if cooperative and autarky solutions are interior and autarky independence holds, strategic threats are viable in terms of definition 1 if:

$$\pi'(L_S{}^* - t^a)(n^a) > \pi'(L_S{}^* - s^* - t^*)(n^* + s^*). \tag{6.A.3}$$

Let $U^*(L_S)$ and $(U_N^a(L_S), U_S^a(L_S))$ represent the optimal social planner and autarky payoffs for particular values of L_S, with the payoffs to the Nash bargaining solution given by:

$$U_N^*(L_S) = (1 - \alpha)U_N^a(L_S) + \alpha\left(U^*(L_S) - U_S^a(L_S)\right)$$
$$U_S^*(L_S) = \alpha U_S^a(L_S) + (1 - \alpha)\left(U^*(L_S) - U_N^a(L_S)\right).$$

We are interested in finding conditions for $\dfrac{dU_S^*(L_S)}{dL_S} < 0$ at $L_S = L_S^*$, so that a reduction in L_S improves the South's payoff after the bargaining game. From the above equations, we have

$$\frac{dU_S^*(L_S)}{dL_S} = \alpha \frac{dU_S^a(L_S)}{dL_S} + (1 - \alpha)\left(\frac{dU^*(L_S)}{dL_S} - \frac{dU_N^*(L_S)}{dL_S}\right)$$

As $\dfrac{dU_S^a(L_S)}{dL_S} = 0$ whenever $L_S > t_a$, we have that

$$\frac{dU_S^*(L_S)}{dL_S} < 0 \Leftrightarrow \frac{dU^*(L_S)}{dL_S} - \frac{dU_N^*(L_S)}{dL_S} < 0.$$

From these, and the Envelope Theorem, for any interior solution we have that:

$$\frac{dU^*(L_S^*)}{dL_S} - \frac{dU_N^*(L_S^*)}{dL_S} = \pi'(L_S^* - s^* - t^*)(n^* + s^*) - \pi'(L_S^* - t^a)(n^a)$$

Thus:

$$\frac{dU_S^*(L_S^*)}{dL_S} < 0 \Leftrightarrow \pi'(L_S^* - S^* - t^*)(n^* + s^*) < \pi'(L_S^* - t^a)(n^a). \text{ QED}$$

Appendix 6.4: Efficient contracts with strategic threats

The Nash bargaining solution for each party with strategic threats is:

$$U_N^T = (1 - \alpha)U_N^D + \alpha(U^* - U_S^a) \text{ and } U_S^T = \alpha U_S^a + (1 - \alpha)(U^* - U_N^D).$$

This differs from the fixed-threat solution only by the presence of U_N^D: the conflict point for the North under strategic threats (see Figure 6.4). As above, a contract offered by the North to the South would take the form:

$$T_N(L_S, t) = \int_t^{t^a} [1 - k'(z)]dz - \pi(L_S - s^* - t)s^* + (1 - \alpha)(U^{CD}). \quad (6.A.4)$$

where $U^{CD} = U^* - (U_N^D + U_S^a)$. Note, this differs from the general contract in the right-hand side term $(1 - \alpha)U^{CD}$, which contains the North's new conflict payoff, U_N^D rather than U_N^a. The difference between the contracts is therefore equal to $(1 - \alpha)(U_N^a - U_N^D)$; which measures the increased North–South transfer which is mobilized by the presence of strategic threats. Closer inspection of this term reveals that it is equal to:

$$(1 - \alpha)(U_N^a - U_N^D) = (1 - \alpha) \int_{L_S^D}^{L_S^*} [\pi'(x - t_a)n^a]dx. \quad (6.A.5).$$

This clearly shows that the contract which upholds the Nash bargaining solution with strategic threats is now dependent upon the existing stocks of Reserves through the specification of the interval L_S^* to L_S^D.

7

Coalition Theory and Integrated Assessment Modeling: Lessons for Climate Governance

Thierry Bréchet and Johan Eyckmans

7.1 INTRODUCTION

Since Hardin (1968) we know that people facing a common do not have the correct incentives for contributing efficiently to its preservation. Individual interest leads to overexploitation and degradation, or even destruction, of the commons. However, Hardin missed the point that some of these people may have an incentive to join forces for managing that commons (or part of it) together. Why is this? Because they may be better off by combining their efforts in a group rather than standing alone. Finding a rationale for this behavior is the very aim of *coalition theory* in economics. Why do people collaborate when they have no obligation to do so? Conversely, is the all-together strategy necessarily doomed? Despite the fact that we all know that there is a problem, why can we not solve it together?

Climate governance is a natural application of this stream of literature. First, there is no worldwide authority capable of enforcing some policy that would be good for the whole. Second, even if there were some worldwide government, a form of worldwide parliament and voting process would also most probably be necessary. So, understanding the motives of each country for agreeing to some global climate governance rules is key. Consequently, and third, identifying the very characteristics of each country and the role these characteristics play for explaining its position in the negotiation process may help to design effective policy agreements for solving the climate problem.

The purpose of this chapter is to show how coalitional theory helps to answer these questions and to derive some insights for climate governance. For that purpose, instead of relying on a purely theoretical discussion, we will make use of an applied integrated assessment model, the CLIMNEG World

Simulation model (CWS) developed under the Belgian CLIMNEG research project. This model will allow us to numerically illustrate the concepts used in coalition theory and their usefulness for guiding climate governance.

The chapter is organized as follows. In the following section, the tools to be used will be briefly presented: coalition theory and the CWS applied integrated assessment model. In both cases the basic concepts will be explained without any mathematical formalization and the emphasis will be on their economic interpretation and usefulness for climate governance. Then, two representative applications will be provided. In section 7.3 we first discuss the issue of *stability* and *effectiveness* of climate agreements, both in terms of climate and welfare. We do this by comparing the *cooperative* and *non-cooperative* theory of coalitions, two compelling streams in the economic theory literature today. In this section we also question the composition of coalitions. What favors an agreement's stability: *homogeneity* (in terms of stage of development of the coalition members) or *heterogeneity*? Section 7.4 discusses the link between stability and the design of climate agreements. The first question is: should we seek one single large agreement or some smaller, but sufficiently numerous, fragmented agreements? Can we say something about that in terms of stability and, again, effectiveness? The second question addressed is about exclusive membership versus open membership: which rule favors stability? Is it always beneficial for a coalition to welcome newcomers? For every issue, the discussion will be both theoretical and based on numerical simulations made with the CWS integrated assessment model. Section 7.5 concludes.

7.2 COALITION FORMATION THEORY AND INTEGRATED ASSESSMENT MODELING: TWO COMPLEMENTARY TOOLS FOR CLIMATE GOVERNANCE

The methodological innovation of our approach is to combine both integrated assessment modeling and game theoretical arguments to answer the policy questions raised above. We first present the background concepts from coalition theory that we will use. Then, the main characteristics of integrated assessment modeling are described.

7.2.1 Key background concepts from coalition theory

Game theory analyses choice behavior in settings where these choices are interdependent; that is, the outcome of the strategic interaction for one particular subject depends on the strategy choices made by other subjects.

A game consists of players (all countries in the world in the context of climate change), strategies (greenhouse gas emission levels and the decision to join or not to join international climate agreements limiting these emissions) and payoff functions (functions that predict the welfare level countries can achieve for given emission levels of their own and all other countries in the world).

Broadly speaking, two counteracting forces drive the payoff structures. On the one hand, forming larger coalitions leads to higher aggregate welfare. Given the particular nature of climate change damage functions and greenhouse gas emission reduction cost functions, members of a coalition could jointly achieve better outcomes than if its members were to act individually (provided outsiders to the coalition do not change their strategy choices). In game theory, this property is called superadditivity and it is this process that provides the incentive to form larger coalitions.[1] On the other hand, however, outsiders to a coalition benefit from the efforts made by coalition members. In transboundary pollution problems like global climate change, outsiders—that is, non-members of an agreement—typically enjoy more benefits if they can free-ride on the efforts of a big coalition compared to a small coalition. This property is called *Positive Externalities to coalition formation* (PEP in the sequel; see for instance Finus and Rundshagen 2009) and induces countries to free-ride, especially if a big coalition is forming. The combination of both forces results in a tendency to cooperate for some countries but this collaboration usually falls short of the full cooperative potential that could be achieved if all countries were to participate.

Two categories of games are considered in the literature, namely *cooperative* and *non-cooperative* ones. In either case the players are countries; each player's strategies are the values chosen for the economic decision variables (for instance, investment in physical capital, emission abatement, and adaptation efforts) and the players' payoffs are the countries' welfare level over their whole decision horizon. A family of strategies, one for each player, defines what we call a *scenario*. Among the many conceivable scenarios, we shall deal with (1) the Nash equilibrium scenario; (2) scenarios of partial agreement Nash equilibrium with respect to given coalitions; and (3) the Pareto efficient scenario.

Non-cooperative games are those that consider strategies enacted by individual players. The Nash equilibrium concept is the dominant solution concept in this setting. Cooperative games, by contrast, typically consider, in addition, the strategies chosen jointly by groups of players, usually called "coalitions;" that is, subsets of players (including singletons and the grand

---

[1] It should be noted that superadditivity of games of multilateral environmental externalities is not always guaranteed. The benefits of expanding a given coalition can be eroded by the strategic free-riding reaction by the outsiders, non-members of the coalition; see Eyckmans and Finus (2006a).

coalition of all players). In either case the behavioral assumption is that the strategy chosen by individual players, as well as the strategies chosen by coalitions, results from payoff maximization between alternative options: the individual payoffs in the non-cooperative setting and the joint payoffs of the coalition members in the cooperative setting (this joint payoff being called the *worth* of the coalition). This illustrates the basic hypotheses of game theory: players are assumed to be rational (i.e. maximizing some objective function) and serving their own (in case of non-cooperative games) or a group (in case of cooperative games) interest. By doing so, they compare the costs and the benefits of joining a coalition, where costs are emission abatement efforts, and benefits are a better climate and fewer climate change damages.

7.2.1.1 Stability concepts

First, the cooperative approach focuses on strategies chosen jointly by the members of the grand coalition, the set of all players. This scenario, and the grand coalition that generates it, are then said to be *stable in the core sense* if the scenario belongs to the core of a suitably defined cooperative game (see Chander and Tulkens 1995, 1997 for a precise definition of the gamma core in the context of environmental externalities); that is, if it is such that:

1. no individual player can reach a higher payoff by *not* adopting the strategy assigned to him in the efficient scenario and choosing instead the best individual strategy he could find if none of the other players form a coalition; this property is called *individual rationality*;

2. no subset of players can similarly do better for its members—that is, by rejecting the strategies assigned to them by the efficient scenario and adopting a group optimal strategy of their own assuming that all non-members play an individual Nash strategy against them; this property is called *coalitional rationality*.

Second, the non-cooperative approach considers some strategies and the resulting individual payoffs that can be reached by every player in that scenario according to whether he is *inside* or *outside* of the coalition.[2] Being *inside* means for the player to follow the strategy he is assigned to within the coalition he is a member of, whereas being *outside* means behaving as a singleton. The internal and external stability concept was introduced by D'Aspremont et al. (1983) in the context of cartel formation in industrial organization and was later applied by Carraro and Siniscalco (1993) and Barrett (1994b) in the context of international environmental agreements.

---

[2] It is assumed that a player can only either join the coalition or remain alone.

A coalition and the Partial Agreement Nash Equilibrium (*PANE*)[3] scenario it generates are then said to be stable in the internal–external sense if the scenario is such that no insider prefers to stay out of the coalition (internal stability, denoted by *IS*) and no outsider prefers to join the coalition rather than stay outside (external stability, denoted by *ES*). The set of all internally and externally stable coalitions corresponds to all Nash equilibria of a simple announcement game in which players have to state "Yes" or "No" and where a coalition is formed among all players who have stated "Yes." This announcement game is said to be an *open membership game* since players can join coalitions without explicit approval of fellow coalition members.

7.2.1.2 Predictions regarding stability of international climate agreements

It should be pointed out that these two approaches rest on different views regarding the behavior of players and coalitions in light of the defection of a coalition member. On the one hand, the core-stability approach assumes that, if one or several countries attempt to free-ride on an efficient agreement with transfers, the other countries will no longer cooperate among themselves and cooperation unravels completely, leading to the Nash non-cooperative scenario. Clearly, this prospect of a complete lack of cooperation constitutes an important threat for potential free-riders. Put differently, the threat to revert to the non-cooperative Nash equilibrium induces core stability.

In the internal–external stability approach, on the other hand, the stability of an agreement within a coalition is obtained if no country attempts to free-ride on it, assuming that the other countries continue cooperating among themselves. The defection of a player from a coalition does not make the remaining players split up further. Therefore, potential defectors can benefit from the efforts of the remaining coalition members, even though the remaining players will re-optimize their economic strategies (i.e. their emission level) to take into account the new coalitional setting. It is clear that this assumption makes free-riding a more attractive option compared to the assumption in the cooperative approach that coalitions dissolve after defection of one, or several, of its members.

Given the different assumptions behind both approaches, it should not come as a surprise that these two approaches lead to different conclusions. The main message of the cooperative approach is that the grand coalition can be stabilized (by appropriate transfers; see Chander and Tulkens 1995, 1997), whereas the non-cooperative approach stresses that, most likely, the grand

---

[3] A Partial Agreement Nash Equilibrium is a game theoretic concept describing which strategies will be chosen by all players when a coalition of players interacts with a set of non-members; see Chander and Tulkens (1995, 1997).

coalition will not be able to generate enough surplus to compensate the free-riding claim of all of its members (see, for instance, Carraro and Siniscalco 1993; Barrett 1994b; or more recently Diamantoudi and Sartzetakis 2006).[4]

7.2.1.3 The need for appropriate transfer schemes

Whatever equilibrium concept—cooperative or non-cooperative—is used, an internatinal environmental agreement can only be sustainable if the participants perceive the distribution of individual benefits and cost as balanced. For instance, according to Ostrom at Chapter 5 in this volume, proportional equivalence between benefits and costs is an important design principle for robust and long-lasting resource management regimes. In order to restore the balance between the benefits and costs of emission reduction efforts in an international environmental agreement, financial transfers can play an important role.

In the context of the cooperative approach, transfers schemes were proposed by Chander and Tulkens (1995, 1997) for the standard game with multilateral externalities used to deal with international environmental agreements. Chander and Tulkens proved that appropriate transfers can induce the core stability property. These transfers guarantee that each player receives a payoff at least equal to what it would be in a case of non-cooperation, and it divides the surplus of cooperation over non-cooperation according to some pre-determined weights. In the multilateral environmental model, the weight of each player is given by its share in marginal climate change damage costs.

The non-cooperative approach proposes no specific transfer formula, but introduces instead the notion of *potentially internally stable* coalitions; see Eyckmans and Finus (2004). A coalition is potentially internally stable (*PIS*) if it guarantees to all its members at least their free-rider payoff. For a given coalition, the free-rider payoff of any of its members is the payoff the member would obtain in the *PANE* scenario *w.r.t.* that coalition if it would stay out and behave as a singleton in the face of that coalition. The free-rider payoff assumes that if a player defects from a coalition, the remaining players will continue to cooperate, though after re-optimizing their economic strategies as a function of the new coalitional setting.

The free-rider payoff of a player vis-à-vis some coalition may be seen as the minimum payoff that a player requires to remain a member of the coalition. Coalitions whose worth under their *PANE* is large enough to meet this requirement for all their members can thus be potentially stabilized, at least

[4] It should be noted that successful attempts were made to reconcile both approaches. For instance, Chander (2007) shows that core stability is consistent with internal and external stability if one assumes "farsighted," i.e. a more sophisticated notion of rationality, behavior by the players. In particular, in the farsighted approach, players are assumed to anticipate further deviations by other coalition members when assessing the benefits of defecting from a coalition.

internally. Eyckmans and Finus (2004) show also that using this type of transfer scheme makes it possible to stabilize, both internally and externally, the coalition that generates the highest global welfare among all *PIS* coalitions. Hence, adopting transfers of the Eyckmans–Finus type allows one to achieve the best possible global welfare as a *PANE*, constrained by the requirement of internal and external stability.

One may wonder what these transfers represent, in practice. Actually, in such a generic framework they only represent abstract wealth transfers. In practice, one should specify the transfer mechanisms, that is the policy instruments leading to wealth transfers. Any policy instrument yielding wealth transfers among countries could be identified as such. Some examples are endowments of emission permits in an international system of tradable pollution licences (see, for instance, the contribution by Ellerman in Chapter 8 of this volume), technological transfers, or an international carbon tax with redistribution of the revenues.

7.2.2 Integrated assessment modeling: the CWS model

Our integrated assessment model, named CWS (CLIMNEG World Simulation model), closely resembles the original RICE model by Nordhaus and Yang (1996) or variations on it as in Eyckmans and Tulkens (2003), Yang (2008), or Bréchet et al. (2010).[5] The model is worldwide and distinguishes six regions or countries (USA, EU, China, Japan, Former Soviet Union, and Rest of the World).[6] An essential characteristic of an IA model is that it contains an endogenous feedback between economic decision variables like emission levels and the rate of capital accumulation and ensuing changes in the global climate system leading to climate change damages that decrease consumption possibilities. This is illustrated in Figure 7.1. The block on the left contains the economy module which consists of a description of the physical production process, climate change damages, emission reduction costs, capital accumulation process, and a material balance equation linking these different concepts. The block on the right-hand side describes the carbon cycle and temperature change module. Basically, this block translates all individual countries' emissions of greenhouse gases into changes in atmospheric carbon concentration and ultimately changes in global mean temperature. This change in temperature feeds back into the economy module via the climate change damage function.

---

[5] See Kolstad and Toman (2005) for an introduction and overview of integrated assessment climate-economy models and Bréchet and Luterbacher (2011) for a discussion on their usefulness for policy support.

[6] A new version of the model distinguishes 18 regions: see Gérard and Holzweber (2008) and Bréchet et al. (2012).

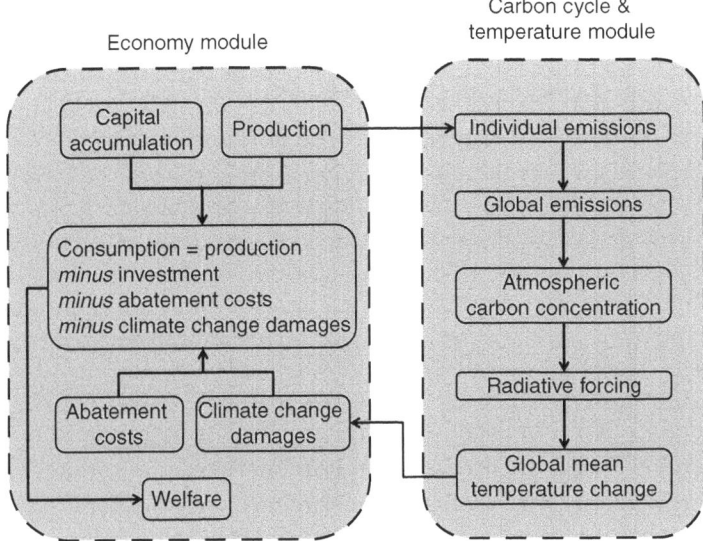

Figure 7.1. Overview of the CWS integrated assessment model

While choosing climate policy actions, countries' policy makers weigh the benefits (avoided future climate change damages) and costs (costs of re-orientating their economies towards lower carbon emission levels). While speaking about welfare, we will refer to some notion of Green National Product that takes into account both climate change damages and emission reduction costs. More precisely, welfare in a country is given by the stream of discounted consumption net of damage and mitigation costs. In every region and time period, the budget constraint holds; that is, consumption equals production *minus* investment *minus* abatement costs *minus* climate change damages. Because climate change has long-term impacts, the time horizon considered in the model is 300 years.

Production is assumed to be a function of labor and capital. Total factor productivity increases exogenously over time and capital accumulation is endogenous in the model. Production causes emissions of greenhouse gases according to an exogenous intensity parameter. Still, emissions can be reduced by means of some specific measures, like replacing a coal-fired power plant by renewable energy sources, investment in more fuel-efficient cars, or energy demand management, what is called *emission abatement* in the model. The abatement costs are increasing with the emission reduction rate. Emission abatement cost functions are relatively well-known and easy to estimate (see chapter 11 in the IPCC (2007a) Working Group II Report for a recent overview on cost estimates). We use cost estimates taken from the RICE model by Nordhaus and Yang (1996).

Emissions of greenhouse gases accumulate in the atmosphere, thereby disturbing the global carbon cycle and ultimately causing climate change. The physical processes are captured by a simplified carbon cycle and climate model. Temperature change has a variety of physical impacts, among which are a rise in the sea level, changes in precipitation patterns, and extreme weather events. The economic valuation of the damages caused by these impacts is summarized in a damage function. This function represents the loss due to some temperature increase expressed in terms of GDP. Estimating damage functions is quite a tricky task (see, for instance, the Stern Review (2007) or IPCC (2007a) Working Group II Report), but it is necessary in order to implement integrated assessment. First, *physical* impacts must be estimated, and several studies are now available on how to do that. Second, damages must be evaluated in monetary terms, including non-market damage like biodiversity loss and changes in living amenities. This remains challenging, for there are no market prices available for their valuation. Further, weighting costs and benefits requires normative judgments regarding intergenerational justice and intragenerational justice (i.e. weighting costs and benefits accruing to different generations over time or to citizens that differ strongly in wealth position within one particular generation).

We can now turn to two applications. These applications provide a good illustration of the kinds of lessons that can be drawn for climate governance.

7.3 STABILITY AND EFFICIENCY OF CLIMATE AGREEMENTS: TWO COMPELLING OBJECTIVES?

The purpose in this first application is to shed some light on the properties of potential coalitions in three respects: stability, climate performance, and global welfare.[7] By doing so we make use of the two theoretical strands mentioned in Section 7.2. Assessing the properties of alternative climate coalitions in a concrete numerical context gives a powerful justification for recommendations as to the size and nature (homogeneity versus heterogeneity) of possible climate coalitions. Moreover, by explicitly showing which transfers among countries are appropriate to stabilize efficient coalitions, we also identify more space in which to negotiate. It is important to keep in mind that, in the following numerical simulations, the agreements are supposed to hold forever.[8]

---

[7] For the complete analysis, see Bréchet, Gerard, and Tulkens (2011).

[8] This clearly constitutes a shortcoming of this type of analysis. It will be discussed further later in the chapter. Because of that, the figures might be considered as an optimistic view of the agreement, in the sense that stability is checked over the whole time horizon considered in the CWS model.

7.3.1 Stability analysis of climate agreements

Given the six regions identified in the CWS model, 63 coalitions can potentially form, for each of which we compute the worth at a Partial Agreement Nash Equilibrium (PANE) of the model.

Focusing first on the cooperative approach, it appears that, without transfers, the Pareto solution, which needs the grand coalition to be achieved, is not core-stable: 18 smaller coalitions (out of 63) can improve upon it. Still, the grand coalition can be stabilized with adequate transfers among countries.[9] This first result is especially important, as it confirms the possibility of achieving the core stability of the world efficient allocation, thanks to adequate transfers.

As far as this non-cooperative approach is considered, the results can be summarized as follows. Without transfers the following appears: (1) few coalitions are internally stable (7, out of 57, i.e. excluding singletons) and the grand coalition, in particular, does not pass this test; (2) only one coalition is both internally and externally stable: the USA + the EU. Complementary to the *IS* and *ES* tests, the *PIS* test is one that implicitly refers to transfers within the coalitions, with the purpose of inducing internal stability. With transfers among countries, applying the *PIS* concept leads to the following outcomes: (1) the grand coalition does not pass the test; (2) four five-country coalitions and five four-country coalitions do not pass the test, whereas one five-country and all other coalitions of four countries or less do pass it.

Summarizing, the numerical results obtained with the CWS model confirm the theoretical insights put forward by Chander and Tulkens (1995, 1997) for the cooperative approach: appropriate transfers are capable of stabilizing the grand coalition in the sense of the core; and it also confirms the results of Barrett (1994b) and Carraro and Siniscalco (1993) for the non-cooperative approach: very few coalitions are stable in the internal–external sense.

Although it is in theory possible to stablize the grand coalition in the cooperative game theory approach by means of transfers, these monetary flows may be difficult to implement in practice. The amount of financial wealth to be transferred often exceeds by far any current level of, for instance, development assistance flows. For this reason it may be more realistic to focus on smaller-scale cooperation regimes within a non-cooperative theoretical framework and allowing for multiple agreements to coexist. It is usually easier in small-scale, and often already existing, regional cooperation regimes to build up sufficient trust and reciprocity to organize substantial financial transfers; think, for instance, of the example of the European Union. We

---

[9] See Germain et al. (2003) for the adequate type of transfers.

will come back to this in Section 7.4, where we will explicitly discuss the question of single versus fragmented climate agreements.

7.3.2 Stability and environmental performance

Can some policy implications be derived from the above stability discussion and simulation results? In particular, how important are the coalitional stability properties we have identified? Should they serve as an argument to support or advocate specific structures for climatic international agreements such as small coalitions rather than large ones, or homogeneous rather than heterogeneous ones? To answer these questions, we consider two criteria measuring the global outcome resulting from an agreement:

- the aggregate welfare level reached at the world level;
- the environmental performance achieved, expressed by atmospheric carbon concentration (in the year 2200).

The results for some representative coalitions are gathered in Table 7.1. Environmental and welfare performance are measured by so-called "closing the gap" indices that assign the value 0 percent to the non-cooperative Nash scenario and the value 100 percent to the cooperative (i.e. the grand coalition) PARETO scenario.

The first striking result from Table 7.1 is that the Kyoto agreement, characterized by Annex B commitment, is quite close to the non-cooperative NASH situation, both in terms of welfare and climate. This agreement has virtually no positive effects. It is actually reinforced when considering the Annex B group without the USA. The second result is that some coalitions are rather close to the PARETO situation. Interestingly, withdrawing the EU from the grand coalition makes it potentially internally stable, with a very good record regarding welfare (92 percent of PARETO is achieved). Substituting the

Table 7.1. Performance and stability for some coalitions with transfers

PANE	Welfare index (%)	Environmental index (%)	Stability
NASH	0	0	—
Annex B[a] without USA	2	1	PIS
Annex B[a]	8	3	PIS
USA + China	20	15	PIS
China + FSU + ROW	24	49	Not PIS
USA + Japan + China + FSU + ROW	92	80	PIS
USA + EU + China + ROW	97	92	Not *PIS*
PARETO	100	100	—

[a] In the CWS model Annex B gathers USA, EU, FSU, and Japan.

EU by Japan gives an even higher ranking (97 percent of PARETO), but this coalition cannot be stabilized. If one is interested in small coalitions, one example is that formed by China and the USA: it can be stabilized, but its performance is rather low. Other examples of this type may be provided.

Clearly, accepting or recommending small coalitions because of their potential internal stability virtues entails a loss on both counts that striving for an efficient and core stable alternative could avoid. Internal stability per se thus appears to be a weakly desirable objective. What matters is the effectiveness of the agreement, and effectiveness increases sharply with coalition size and/or composition, for countries are not symmetric. The rationale behind this result is that the larger the coalition, the stronger the internalization of the climate externality. But, on the other hand, including large emitters provides the coalition with strong climate benefits. So the debate on the kind of agreement that is desirable cannot be reduced to a single question, such as size. Actually, size does matter. But the size of what remains an open question.

7.3.3 Should coalitions be homogeneous?

A common argument in the climate policy debate is that developed countries should engage themselves first, after which developing countries would be invited to join the agreement and participate in the mitigation of global warming. Although this argument seems reasonable on the basis of historical responsibilities,[10] one may question its effectiveness. We can analyze how the composition of a coalition—that is, its degree of homogeneity (which is to be defined)—affects its stability. The regions/countries considered in the CWS model can be split into two categories:

- on the one hand, developed Annex B countries (USA, EU, and JPN), with high per capita emissions and GDP level, steep emission abatement cost, and climate change damage functions;

- on the other hand, developing non-Annex B countries (CHN and ROW), with low per capita emissions and GDP level, relatively flat abatement cost functions, and relatively low valuation of climate change damages.

In what follows, a *homogeneous coalition* will designate a coalition formed by countries from a single category. Conversely, a *heterogeneous coalition* will designate a coalition formed by countries coming from the two categories. A special case is the FSU, as it displays the characteristics of both a developed

---

[10] This is the principle of common but differentiated responsibilities of countries set out in the UN Framework Convention. Notice that this argument will be no longer valid for some countries in a future that may be close: Botzen et al. (2008) show that China could overtake the USA as a major cumulative contributor to GHG concentrations.

country (high emissions per capita) and a developing one (low cost abatement opportunities, low GDP per capita). According to these definitions, the 57 possible coalitions (i.e. excluding singletons) can be organized into 42 heterogeneous coalitions and 15 homogeneous ones.

The question we can now address is the following: is there any relation between the composition of a coalition and its stability? Computing the CWS model reveals the following.

Without transfers, all four homogeneous coalitions involving FSU and developing non-Annex B countries are internally stable, and the coalition USA + EU is both internally and externally stable. So homogeneity seems good for stability. On the other hand, none of the coalitions involving at least one of the two main polluters of each category (that is, USA or EU, on the one hand, and CHN or ROW on the other hand) is internally stable. Integrating a major polluter to an agreement seems detrimental to its stability. Finally, in the same spirit, the largest heterogeneous coalition, which is the grand coalition, is not core-stable without transfers, with four more blocking coalitions. Intuitively, the reason for the instability of coalitions involving high marginal climate change damage and low marginal abatement cost players is clear. The high marginal climate change damage coalition members (for instance, the EU) ask for important emission reduction commitments by the coalition but most of the emission reduction burden falls on the low marginal abatement cost coalition members (for instance, China) in a cost-efficient *PANE*. Without compensation, the additional abatement costs outweigh the reduction in climate change damages for the low marginal cost countries, hence they are bound to lose from coalition membership compared to nonparticipation.

When the possibility of transfers is introduced, stability also appears to be enhanced by homogeneity. All homogenous coalitions are *potentially internally stable*.[11] Furthermore, the Annex B coalition turns out to be more stable than the "Annex B without the USA" coalition.[12] Paradoxically, this latter coalition does not satisfy the *external stability* property: the CWS model suggests that the United States would be better off by coming back to the Annex B coalition. Out of the 42 possible heterogeneous coalitions, 11 are not stable in the *PIS* sense. Indeed, no four-country, or more, coalitions involving simultaneously the USA and the EU and at least one non-Annex B country passes the *PIS* test.

The homogeneity versus heterogeneity debate can also be analyzed by looking at Table 7.1. One can see that the *best* (in terms of global welfare)

[11] In the previous version of the CWS model, calibrated on 1990 data, only an Annex B coalition {USA, JPN, EU, FSU} out of the 15 homogeneous coalitions did not pass the *PIS* test (the so-called *Old Kyoto* coalition in Carraro, Eyckmans, and Finus, 2007). So it seems that there is more room for cooperation between these countries today than ten years earlier.

[12] The so-called *Present Kyoto* coalition in Carraro et al. (2007).

homogeneous coalition (CHN + FSU + ROW) leads to far lower global welfare and far higher carbon concentrations than both the *best* heterogeneous coalition (the grand coalition) and the *best* heterogeneous coalition satisfying the *PIS* property (USA + JPN + CHN + FSU + ROW). As a consequence, promoting homogeneous coalitions may lead to very low mitigation policies at the world level, unable to tackle climate change issue in the way heterogeneous (larger) coalitions could do. Intuitively, appropriately designed transfers are able to overcome the participation problem that we sketched above for the no-transfer case. Combining high marginal climate change damage countries with low marginal abatement cost countries leads to ambitious coalitional emission abatement targets, and potential imbalances of costs and damages for individual coalition members can be mitigated by means of appropriate transfers.

By way of a conclusion, there seems to be a trade-off between stability and environmental effectiveness. Homogeneity in climate coalitions fosters stability but is detrimental to climate effectiveness. Heterogeneity in cost and damage structures leads to more ambitious abatement targets but requires substantial redistribution of the surplus to keep all countries on board in the climate agreement boat.

7.4 STABILITY AND THE INSTITUTIONAL DESIGN OF CLIMATE AGREEMENTS

Besides the crucial importance of transfers to sustain stable climate agreements, economists have also pointed out the importance of more specific design features of global climate agreements. Several institutional aspects have been investigated in this respect in the literature, but we focus only on two of them: first, the question whether one broad agreement (single coalition agreement) is better than several smaller agreements (multiple coalitions agreement), and second, the question whether external stability can be promoted by making the accession of newcomers conditional on the approval by existing coalition members (open versus exclusive membership).

7.4.1 Single versus fragmented climate agreements

The first question is of major importance for climate governance. Should one strive for one broad, single agreement signed by as many countries as possible, or should one allow that several small agreements coexist? We will not enter the debate on the legal status of such sub-agreements in relation to the existing UNFCCC legal framework.[13] Instead, we will focus on the impact of stable coalitions when allowing for multiple coalitional agreements on their size and their environmental and welfare performance.

At first sight one might argue that it is better to have one single large agreement instead of several small agreements coexisting, based on arguments of economies of scale. In many economic production processes, the average unit costs of production decrease for bigger production volumes generating so-called economies of scale. The intuition behind this observation is that fixed costs—that is costs that are independent of the scale of production—are preferably spread out over larger instead of smaller production volumes. Likewise, one might argue that one big climate agreement is to be preferred over a collection of small ones because it allows for cost savings, for instance, in the degree to which the externality is internalized or in the set up and practical operation of a system of tradable emission permits. In addition, a broad agreement is to be preferred also if carbon leakage—the phenomenon that CO_2-intensive industries would relocate to regions with loose environmental regulation—is a serious concern; see Victor (2007).

Although there are surely some aspects of scale related to climate agreements, one should also take into account strategic issues; that is, the stability and level of commitment of coalitions. Carraro (2007) uses game theoretical arguments to make a case for a bottom-up approach to the formation of new climate agreements. Eyckmans and Finus (2006a,b), using numerical simulation results from CWS, demonstrated that multiple coalition structures can emerge as internally and externally stable equilibria and can lead to higher welfare levels than some single coalition agreements. Table 7.2 shows stable coalition structures for a variety of agreement architectures. Without transfers, the results are basically the same: open membership games, be it single or multi-coalitional, do not lead to stable climate agreements. Heterogeneity among regions is simply too strong to overcome conflicting incentives. However, it appears that more coalitions are stable and they lead to better welfare and ecological performances in the multiple coalition setting compared to the single coalition setting without transfers. For instance, we observe that coalition structure ({USA, JPN}, {EU, ROW}, {CHN}, {FSU}) consisting of two couples, performs better than any single coalition structure with *Exclusive Membership Majority Voting* framework (see below). Basically, allowing for multiple coexisting agreements in coalition formation increases the chances of building more stable and effective agreements.

---

[13] In fact, one might argue that the 1997 Kyoto Protocol is already of a multicoalitional nature since only a subset of parties (Annex B countries) accepted quantified greenhouse gas emission limits. The other countries ratified but did not commit to emission targets.

Table 7.2. Stable coalition structures in the no-transfer case

No. (1)	Coalition structure (2)	OM (3)		EM—MV (4)		EM—UV (5)		Welfare (6)	Concentration (7)
		S	M	S	M	S	M		
203	{USA, JPN, EU, CHN, FSU, ROW}·	n	n	n	n	n	n	100.00	100.00
26	{USA, FSU, ROW}, {JPN}, {EU}, {CHN}	n	n	n	n	y	y	60.71	43.17
156	{USA, JPN, ROW}, {EU}, {CHN}, {FSU}	n	n	n	n	y	y	59.03	41.50
155	{USA, JPN}, {EU, ROW}, {CHN}, {FSU}	—	n	—	y	—	y	58.11	40.98
4	{EU, ROW}, {USA}, {JPN}, {CHN}, {FSU}	n	n	y	n	y	n	57.46	40.79
20	{JPN, FSU, ROW}, {USA}, {EU}, {CHN}	n	n	n	n	y	y	54.20	34.21
6	{USA, ROW}, {JPN}, {EU}, {CHN}, {FSU}	n	n	y	y	y	y	54.13	35.18
153	{USA, JPN}, {FSU, ROW}, {EU}, {CHN}	—	n	—	y	—	y	47.89	26.94
2	{FSU, ROW}, {USA}, {JPN}, {EU}, {CHN}	n	n	y	n	y	n	47.22	26.75
5	{JPN, ROW}, {USA}, {EU}, {CHN}, {FSU}	n	n	y	y	y	y	46.44	24.72
196	{USA, JPN, EU, FSU}, {CHN}, {ROW}	n	n	n	n	n	n	5.07	1.58
87	{JPN, EU, FSU}, {USA}, {CHN}, {ROW}	n	n	n	n	n	n	2.94	0.75
1	{USA}, {JPN}, {EU}, {CHN}, {FSU}, {ROW}	n	n	n	n	n	n	0.00	0.00

Abbreviations: n = not stable, y = stable, and – = not defined; OM = open membership, EM—MV = exclusive membership majority voting, EM—UV = exclusive membership unanimity voting; S = single coalition game, M = multiple coalition game. Source: Eyckmans and Finus 2006b, Table 7.2.

These results are also in line with the argument put forward by Barrett (1994b) that there is often a trade-off in international environmental agreements. Either one observes agreements with many members but with little more commitment than in the plain non-cooperative Nash equilibrium, or one observes small, stable agreements with a substantial commitment to reduce emissions, but since their participants constitute only a small part of the total number of polluters, global environmental quality is not enhanced significantly either.

These results show that (1) allowing for flexibility in coalition formation might lead to more participants in stable coalition structures; (2) these multi-coalition structures might lead to a substantial improvement of global environmental quality. In practice, multi-coalitional agreements can also be thought of as agreements that allow for heterogeneity in commitments by the participants. As in the 1997 Kyoto Protocol, one could perfectly allow for differentiated commitments among, for instance, developing countries and industrialized countries under the common umbrella of, for instance, the UNFCCC. These multiple-agreement coalition structures can also be interpreted as an example of the so-called polycentric approach to global climate governance, as suggested by Ostrom in Chapter 5 of this volume.

7.4.2 Is everybody welcome to join the climate club?

Concerning the second question, it is easy to see that the problem of external stability—that is, outsiders wanting to join an existing agreement and thereby upsetting the internal stability of the agreement—can be mitigated to some extent by making the accession of newcomers conditional on the approval of existing coalition members. Games in which no approval for accepting newcomers is required are called *open membership games*. On the contrary, *exclusive membership games* require some form of approval, though there is a large variety in the degree of consensus required; for instance, majority versus unanimity voting procedures. What is important from a conceptual point of view is that the general belief that unconditional accession of newcomers promotes cooperation might prove to be false if one accounts for coalitional stability considerations.

Table 7.2 nicely illustrates how different degrees of exclusive membership result in different degrees of effective and stable climate policy. Under open membership (*OM*), no coalition is stable, in neither a single nor a multi-coalitional setting. Requiring that newcomers can join a coalition only if a 50 percent majority of existing members agrees to it (i.e. is better off in welfare terms after accession of the newcomer) leads to several stable coalition structures (both single and multi-coalitional), some of which are able to close the gap between cooperation and non-cooperation by more than half. The even stricter accession requirement that all existing members have to agree (unanimity voting, *UV*) leads to additional stable coalitions and better environmental and welfare performances.

Practically speaking, exclusive membership is widely used in many international cooperative structures. For instance, in NATO and in the EU, new members can only join after a formal approval procedure in which existing members can have their say on the accession. Again, this simple modification of agreement architecture, which at first sight would hamper the accession of newcomers unnecessarily, might in the end lead to broader and more effective global climate agreements.

7.5 CONCLUSION

In this chapter we have combined results from game theory and an integrated assessment climate-economy model to derive conclusions for global climate governance. We have pointed out that agreements that bring together countries with similar emission reduction costs and climate change damage characteristics—homogeneous agreements—tend to be more stable than heterogeneous agreements. However, heterogeneous agreements have a tendency to aim for more ambitious greenhouse gas emission reduction targets. We showed that appropriately designed transfer schemes can stabilize such ambitious heterogeneous climate agreements, both in the cooperative and non-cooperative game theory frameworks. Crucial for the transfer schemes is that they should be designed in the first place to limit free-riding behavior. We realize, however, that large transfers of wealth between sovereign nations are unrealistic in the short run. In the short term, this type of transfer is more likely to emerge in smaller coalitions because it takes time to build the trust and institutions to govern them.

We also showed that small institutional changes of climate agreements can have important stability implications. For instance, allowing for co-existing multiple agreements can yield better global welfare and environmental results compared to a situation in which we would limit from the outset cooperation to a single agreement only. Finally, making membership to international climate agreements exclusive—that is, conditional upon the consent of the other members—can foster, instead of hamper, the stability of a future climate agreement.

8

Governance Issues in a Multinational Cap-and-Trade System: Centralization and Harmonization

Denny Ellerman

8.1 INTRODUCTION

The past two decades have witnessed the appearance of a radically new approach to environmental regulation in the form of tradable permit systems of the cap-and-trade variety, most prominently for air emissions. These systems have been applied at various governance levels, from the subnational focused on conventional local pollutants, such the RECLAIM NOx and SO_2 programs for the Los Angeles Air Basin (Harrison 2004) or the Chicago Volatile Organic Compound program (Kosobud et al. 2006), to the national level addressing regional pollutants, such as the US Acid Rain or SO_2 Trading Program (Ellerman et al. 2000) and the NOx Budget Program, and most recently to the multinational level aimed at global pollutants, such as the European Union's CO_2 Emissions Trading Scheme (EU ETS) (Ellerman and Joskow, eds 2008; Ellerman et al. 2010). While the feasibility of local, regional, and national cap-and-trade programs is rarely challenged, the practicality of a global system spanning nations is more open to question due to the issues discussed in the preceding chapters in this part of the book.

Notwithstanding these difficulties, the EU ETS, now in its seventh year, demonstrates that a multinational system can be adopted and implemented. Its creation benefited from specific facilitating conditions and mechanisms that indicate what will be required in any broader global system. Explaining these features and their differences from those that are standard in national programs is the subject of this chapter, which proceeds as follows. The next section discusses the advantages and unique requirements of a cap-and-trade system. The following section considers US precedents and points out some key features that distinguish the US experience from what can be expected in a multinational context. The fourth section turns to the EU ETS and explains the features that allowed it to succeed as a multinational system. The final section concludes.

8.2 CAP-AND-TRADE IN A MULTINATIONAL SETTING

8.2.1 The advantages of cap-and-trade

Cap-and-trade enjoys a distinct advantage when compared with its rival instruments of a tax or prescriptive regulation: it can deal with equity without compromising efficiency (Stavins 2007a: 52–3). Pleas for equitable consideration in a cap-and-trade program are dealt with by lump-sum, free allocations of tradable allowances, whereas the same pleas in a tax system are commonly resolved by exemption, usually in the form of a reduced tax rate. Exemption changes the price of the regulated emission for the beneficiary—and thereby creates inefficiency—whereas the allocation of a free tradable allowance does not. Surrendering a freely allocated allowance to cover emissions implies forgoing the opportunity to sell it at the market price and thereby imposes a cost as surely as if the allowance had been purchased. The same defect of being unable to deal with equity without compromising efficiency applies to prescriptive regulation, which has the added disadvantage of being always inefficient because there is no mechanism to equalize marginal costs. When legal mandates are used, equitable considerations also lead to a similar loosening of the constraint for those most adversely affected, thereby diminishing the mandate's effectiveness and usually exacerbating inefficiency.

It might be argued that side payments out of revenue collected from a tax could achieve equity with compromising efficiency, but the explicitness of the transfer makes it politically impractical, and probably more so in an international context. Thus, in the heterogeneous case considered by Bréchet and Eyckmans (Chapter 7), the requisite transfers posited by Groom et al. (Chapter 6) would require one government to transfer some of its tax revenue to another. With a cap-and-trade approach, the same transfer can be arranged by agreeing to caps that differ in stringency based on ability to pay, historical responsibility, etc., or by other arrangements, such as have been devised for the EU ETS. All else being equal, caps of differing stringency imply differing marginal costs before the trading that equalizes those costs and effects the resulting flows of permits and payments. The politically necessary transfer is not so much the result of government direction as it is the result of the actions of decentralized agents pursuing the cheapest sources of abatement, much as those same agents might look abroad for cheaper sources for other inputs.

This reveals the second disadvantage of the tax approach: the incentive faced by agents must be decided directly and explicitly by the government, whereas in the cap-and-trade approach, the agents themselves determine the price by their pursuit of cheap abatement. Tax and cap-and-trade approaches share the advantage of a pervasive price that does a far better job at ferreting out cheap emission reductions than does any mandate. However, only in the cap-and-trade case can the direct responsibility for that compelling incentive be deflected. Theoretically, any cap implies an equivalent tax, and vice versa, but this applies only in a world in which everything else is held constant. In the practical world where uncertainty reigns, the cap is only one of many factors determining the price that agents face. In what can be seen as an instance of the polycentricity advocated by Ostrom (Chapter 5), governments agree on the conditioning constraint, but the operative incentive is determined largely by the decentralized agents themselves.

8.2.2 The requirements of cap-and-trade

While a cap-and-trade regime presents certain advantages, it also has specific requirements that can cause problems in a multinational setting. These can be summarized as institutional capacity, cap-setting, and allocation.

8.2.2.1 Institutional capacity

All approaches to environmental regulation presume a degree of institutional integrity to ensure that whatever is decided is not ignored through neglect, incompetence, or corruption; and each has specific prerequisites that must be met if it is to succeed. Consequently, arguing that a general institutional incapacity invalidates a cap-and-trade approach misses the point. The same defect invalidates any approach. Instead, attention must be focused on the specific institutional capabilities that are required by different approaches. In the case of a cap-and-trade system, these are the measurement of emissions, allowance tracking, and the existence of markets.

Measurement is a prerequisite that is shared with a tax approach. If emissions cannot be reliably measured, then neither market-based approach is possible and the only alternative is conventional, prescriptive regulation. What is unique to cap-and-trade is allowance tracking and the emergence of an allowance market to ensure the creation of a uniform price and the efficient exchange of allowances. Both of these requirements can be a concern where banking or market institutions are non-existent or weak; however, any economy that is developing and thereby becoming a major source of emissions will have developed accounting and computer capabilities in the banking sector similar to those required for allowance tracking, as well as a means of exchange that can accommodate allowances.

8.2.2.2 Cap-setting

A cap-and-trade approach requires governments to make qualitatively different decisions from those required in a command-and-control or tax approach. The first is deciding the cap. The relevant political authority must decide a precise, quantifiable level of emissions over a given set of emitting sources and over some time horizon. This decision becomes more difficult in the case of a global pollutant or in a multinational system when the nature of the environmental problem extends beyond the reach of any single participating government.

When a pollutant's effects are local or regional, as has been the case for all early cap-and-trade systems in the USA, the relevant political entity spans the environmental problem being addressed. There is some level of emissions that creates "pollution" and, at least in theory, that level determines the cap. Deciding this level may be less precise than is typically assumed, and more political than usually recognized, but the pretense is there and some rational, scientific support can usually be marshaled to support the choice of the cap.

The problem with a global pollutant is that the motivating problem exceeds the effective span of the deciding institution. While it can be argued with some scientific basis that an appropriate level of global greenhouse gas emissions exists, that argument breaks down completely when applied at the decision-making level of the nation state. Consequently, there is no scientific rationale for the level of emissions that an individual nation might choose in adopting a GHG cap-and-trade program. No decision made by the United States or the European Union alone can limit the increase in average global temperature to two degrees Centigrade. That goal will be achieved only if a sufficient number of other nations take similar action. Consequently, the choice of a national cap for a global pollutant is purely political and it can be justified only in strategic terms: how it might lead to sufficiently wide participation that the underlying global problem would be effectively addressed.

8.2.2.3 Allocation

Another qualitatively different decision required by a cap-and-trade approach is the distribution of the tradable allowances. At a national level, this can be either by free allocation, which has been the general practice, or by auctioning, which is increasingly advocated, or by some combination of the two. Free allocation has both facilitated and complicated the adoption of cap-and-trade systems. It can provide a ready means of dealing efficiently with the equity issues that are inevitably raised by a new constraint, but the very transparency and explicitness of the allocation can become so contentious that adoption of the system is imperiled.

The facilitating role of free allocation was dominant in the early cap-and-trade systems; however, from what can be observed in the EU ETS and in the debate about a comparable GHG system in the USA, allocation is far more controversial now. In the case of the EU ETS, free allocation was a requirement of gaining agreement to proceed with the program (Skjaerseth and Wettestad 2008: 125–38), but the resulting outcry concerning "windfall profits" led to amendment of the initial agreement in December 2008 to make auctioning the predominant means and basic principle of allocation. In the US debate, positions concerning allocation appeared at times so irreconcilable as to call into question the likelihood of any agreement or perhaps a turning to other approaches that avoid addressing distributive issues explicitly.

As the first multinational cap-and-trade system, the EU ETS has revealed a new problem in allocation: harmonization. This term refers to the differences that arise in the allocation of free allowances to like facilities in different participating nations. At the very least, these differences are seen as unfair and invariably the argument is also made that they create competitive disadvantages for the less favored. This argument must be distinguished from the similar one concerning competition with competing sources outside of the system that do not bear a CO_2 cost. Harmonization is fundamentally a demand for equality of treatment within the system, usually through the use of some benchmark in allocation so that all plants with similar output, capacity, or some other technical characteristic receive like allocations.

8.3 THE LIMITED APPLICABILITY OF US CAP-AND-TRADE PRECEDENTS

The United States was the first country to adopt cap-and-trade systems to deal with environmental problems and these precedents have had considerable influence. Nevertheless, their applicability in an international setting is limited. Two systems, the SO_2 Trading Program and the NOx Budget Program, can be used to illustrate important features of these US precedents and the limits of their applicability in a multinational context. The SO_2 Trading Program is the most widely known and it is often cited as the canonical cap-and-trade system (Ellerman et al. 2000). It is, however, less relevant because of its completely centralized structure. A better example is the NOx Budget Program, which is both more decentralized and voluntary as regards trading (Aulisi et al. 2005).

Still, it enjoyed advantages in adoption and implementation that do not exist in a multinational setting.

8.3.1 The SO_2 trading system

The US SO_2 trading system had enormous influence in showing that a large cap-and-trade system could be constructed and that it would operate more or less as theory predicted. However, when viewed from an international perspective, the individual states played no role whatsoever in the adoption or implementation of this program, despite enjoying significant prerogatives in the American union. The decisions to create the system and to allocate allowances were taken by legislative act at the national level. Differing state interests had to be accommodated in gaining a consensus to adopt the system, and some states and installations received more allowances than others, but that was it. Once created, the national SO_2 cap-and-trade system was an entirely federal program. The registry was created and is maintained by the US Environmental Protection Agency (USEPA); emission reporting is done directly from installation or operating company to the USEPA in Washington; and enforcement is a federal matter.

Two other features of allocation are also important in considering the value of the US SO_2 Trading Program as a precedent: public awareness and pre-existing standards. Allocation played an important role in building the "majoritarian consensus" that made enactment on the SO_2 program possible (Joskow and Schmalensee 1998), but public awareness of allocation was never high when the program was being proposed and debated. In particular, "windfall profits" did not emerge as an issue because the electric utilities, which were the only affected companies, were then subject to cost-of-service regulation. The value of the freely allocated permits would, in theory, be passed on to consumers in the form of lower electricity rates, and the only costs that consumers would bear would be those of purchased permits and of abatement measures less any revenue from permit sales. This regulatory treatment made it easier to allocate allowances entirely and freely to incumbent fossil-fuel generators and thereby helped to avoid the allocation controversies that have bedeviled later cap-and-trade proposals.

Allocation was made easier by a pre-existing standard that could serve as the benchmark for free allocation to covered facilities. This was the New Source Performance Standard (NSPS), an emission rate limit that applied to all new coal-fired power plants that were built after enactment of the Clean Air Act Amendments of 1970. New plants were subjected to this federally determined, uniform emission rate limit that reflected what could then be attained by the best available technology and which was generally lower than the emission rates imposed by states on existing plants.

In 1970, the expectation was that all existing plants would be retired and replaced by new plants subject to the NSPS within thirty years or so. For several reasons, this did not occur and the debate about acid rain legislation in the 1980s was a response to the recognition that the pre-1970 plants would not be retired as had been expected. Moreover, since nearly all regions of the country were in compliance with the national ambient air quality standards for SO_2, no further reductions could be expected under the existing Clean Air Act. The trading program succeeded in capping national SO_2 emissions at a level that would have obtained if all the plants existing in 1970 had been retired and replaced by new plants meeting the NSPS. The emission equivalent of the original expected outcome was achieved by giving the older, non-retired plants a free allocation equal to the NSPS emission rate times their average output from 1985 to 1987.

This regulatory history—and the fact that the NSPS applied to 60 percent of the electricity generation in 1990 when the program was adopted—made the initial NSPS an obvious choice as a benchmark for the free allocation of allowances to cost-regulated electric utilities. Since emission rates at the pre-1970 plants ranged from a little above the NSPS to as much as four times greater, this benchmark did not "harmonize" allocations by treating all plants equally, but the institutional presence and force of the NSPS was such that its use as the benchmark for allocation was accepted. The absence of a comparable regulatory precedent made free allocation in the EU ETS more difficult and led to the calls for harmonization.

8.3.2 The NOx Budget Program

The NOx Budget Program has received much less attention than the US SO_2 Trading Program, but it is more interesting from a multinational point of view because of the greater role of the states. They allocate allowances to facilities within their borders, issue the implementing regulations, and ensure compliance, much as is the case for the EU ETS. Moreover, participation in the trading program is voluntary; and over time the program has grown in size from the original core of northeastern states, much as one might hope for in a global system.

The NOx Budget Program started out as a smaller trading system limited to the northeastern states that were part of the Ozone Transport Commission (OTC), an interstate compact charged with addressing the persistent ozone non-attainment status of the heavily urbanized Northeastern Corridor running from Washington DC to Boston. The legislative provisions establishing the OTC encouraged the collaborating states to develop a regional plan that could serve as an alternative to the individually developed State Implementation Plans that had failed previously to eliminate non-attainment with the ozone standard in these states. This authorizing legislation did not require the adoption of cap-and-trade; that was a decision of the participating states. In fact, the first phase of the regional OTC program took the form of the usual legal mandate to install Reasonably Available Control Technology, but the second and third phases consisted of a progressively more demanding inter-state cap-and-trade system.

Federal action then enlarged this initial core. In response to regulatory findings that tightened the national ambient air quality standard for ozone and required more action on the part of all eastern states (not just those in the northeast), the USEPA issued a regulation in which a much larger group of eastern states were each given a USEPA-determined NOx emissions "budget" and two alternative choices. One was to submit a State Implementation Plan in the conventional manner that would limit emissions to the budget. The other was to adopt a federal "Model Rule" that would make affected installations in the state part of a regional cap-and-trade program. All but one state opted for the trading alternative. Evidently, it provided a preferable regulatory mechanism for allocating responsibility for reducing NOx emissions among the state's sources.

While the origins and structure of the NOx Budget Program resemble what might be expected of an international trading program, the role of the federal government was still very strong. For instance, cap-setting—determining how many allowances a state could allocate—was determined centrally by the federal EPA. More importantly, these programs were firmly embedded in the pre-existing structure of the national Clean Air Act, which empowers the federal government to compel states to take actions to achieve national environmental goals. Participation in the trading part of the NOx Budget Program was voluntary, but addressing the problem of ozone precursor emissions was not. The participating states remained under a fundamental obligation to come into compliance with the required limit on emissions, if not through participation in the trading program, then by adopting conventional prescriptive measures to reduce NOx precursor emissions to the level required by the state's NOx "budget." A comparable requirement to act is notably lacking in a global context.

8.4 THE EU ETS

Both the United States and the European Union are federations of states, but the balance between the individual states and the federal center is significantly different. Both are alike in the reservation of powers to the constituent states unless specifically delegated to the federal level, but the delegation to the center is much greater in the Constitution of the United States than in the Founding

Treaties of the European Union. This weak federal structure makes the EU ETS a far better laboratory for testing the viability of cap-and-trade in a multinational setting.

EU directives, such as those governing the EU ETS, are as much international agreements as they are legislation. The role of the European Parliament in the decision-making process gives directives the appearance of legislation; however, the ultimate decision to adopt rests solely with the European Council, which is a body of the participating governments with voting rights that have been carefully negotiated in the basic treaties creating the European Union. The Parliament plays an important role: a directive must be debated in the Parliament, parliamentary amendments are typically made to proposed directives, and the Parliament can veto a directive if its views have not been taken sufficiently into account. Still, the European Parliament cannot enact a directive. If a proposed directive fails to gain the required votes in the European Council, or the Council fails to take up the measure, the proposal dies. Thus, EU directives are ultimately the result of agreement among the participating governments.

8.4.1 Completing the Kyoto Protocol

A notable feature of the EU ETS is that it partially achieves the efficient abatement that the Kyoto Protocol held forth as a possibility (but did not require) and thereby anticipates how an efficient multinational trading system might work. The signatory nations of the Kyoto Protocol agreed to individual emission caps on all emissions and allowed trading of those emissions in the form of Annual Assigned Units (AAUs); however, the primary agents in this system are governments, not the individual firms who undertake abatement. It is theoretically possible that the participating governments might undertake measures to reduce emissions and trade AAUs in a manner than would equalize marginal costs both domestically and internationally, but the grounds for believing that they would do so are not compelling.

The EU realized the potential efficiency of trading by tying each European Union Allowance (EUA) to an AAU for those parts of the European economy that are covered by the EU ETS. To use the jargon of emissions trading, AAUs were "downloaded" to the agents who take abatement actions and possess the information to do so efficiently. When individual firms trade EUAs across national borders, they are also redistributing AAUs among the member states of the EU. Thus, compliance with the ETS not only goes a long way towards meeting member states' international obligations under the Kyoto Protocol, but it also ensures efficient abatement in the traded sectors across Europe (although not in the sectors not included in the EU ETS).

8.4.2 Institutional capacity

The European Union should not be viewed as a homogeneous set of nations sharing a common historical experience, institutional development, and standard of living. The Iron Curtain separated the west and east European nations for almost a half century and provided very different historical exposure to markets. More generally, the differences in general institutional development between EU15 member states, such as the Netherlands, Germany, or the UK, and east European new member states are significant, as are the differences in per capita income levels. When calculated on a purchasing power parity basis, Ireland's per capita income is five times greater than that of Bulgaria or Romania, the poorest of the new member states. Furthermore, the per capita income level of Bulgaria and Romania is only about 50 percent higher than that of China, while Irish per capita income is comparable to that of the United States. In many important respects, the East–West divide in Europe mirrors the global North–South divide that will have to be bridged in any global trading system.

To date, the evidence indicates that these differences are being bridged and that the more institutionally challenged new member states are capable of implementing the measures required to maintain the integrity of the whole system. Accession to the European Union presumes and indeed requires the development of the general institutional capability that would be required to participate in a multinational trading system, but the speed and ease with which these member states (with the exception of Bulgaria) have been integrated into the ETS is surprising. In less than three years, they have developed the cap-and-trade infrastructure needed to ensure integrity; and the owners of affected facilities in these countries are participating in the resulting multinational market almost as fully as those in the EU15 (Trotignon and Ellerman 2009). Arguably, the integration of these countries into the trading system has proved quicker and less problematic than their integration into European labor, capital, goods, and services markets.

This encouraging experience raises the question of whether the experience in eastern Europe presages what might occur on a global scale. There are several reasons to think that this might be so. First, a general institutional transformation is not necessarily required for participation in particular forms of global trade, as evidenced by the many countries with a general institutional capacity that would be considered deficient, but which manage nevertheless to meet the required quality specifications for various exported goods. Second, economic development itself requires and enables a more general improvement in the required institutional capabilities. Countries like China, which are both big emitters and rapidly developing, will be more likely to develop the institutions that will facilitate integration in a global system for reducing global GHGs than stagnant economies for which such integration is less likely and less necessary. Finally, the contribution of creditable CO_2-reducing projects, such as those developed under the Clean Development Mechanism (CDM), familiarize agents in developing countries with emissions trading and effectively promote the development of the requisite trading infrastructure through the monitoring, reporting, and verification procedures that are required of these projects.

8.4.3 Cap-setting and centralization

The toughest challenge in implementing a cap-and-trade system in a decentralized, multinational setting is deciding the cap and its apportionment among the participating members. In its brief life, the EU ETS has provided a model for what might occur in a global system by evolving from an initial, highly decentralized cap-setting process to a considerably more centralized one.

In the first and second trading periods, extending from 2005–07 and 2008–12, respectively, member states developed National Allocation Plans (NAPs) which specified the total number of allowances each member state would issue and their distribution to installations within their borders. This process for cap-setting was cumbersome and it has been much criticized; but it reflected what was possible given the underlying political realities. It did result in a cap for a common system consisting of 27 largely sovereign nations and that cap did create a scarcity, a price for carbon, and the necessary infrastructure to make the EU ETS the primary means by which the EU member states will meet their obligations under the Kyoto Protocol.

Two features of the initial NAP process were essential to the success of the EU ETS. The first was the carefully crafted, special delegation of power to the European Commission to review and to reject member state NAPs. The second was the reference point provided for cap-setting by the Kyoto Protocol and the subsequent European Burden-sharing Agreement, which redistributed the undifferentiated European targets of limiting greenhouse gas emissions to 8 percent below 1990 levels among the EU15.

The ETS Directive's special grant of authority to the Commission to review and to reject NAPs is unusual. Normally, the Commission's role is to monitor member states' "transposition" of a directive into national law and, if the directive is not being implemented properly, to notify the European Council and to initiate legal proceedings in the European Court of Justice. In this instance, there was a short-circuiting of the usual process and a subtle shift of prerogative. By requiring NAPs to be reviewed and allowing them to be rejected in part or in whole, member states set up a mechanism giving greater assurance that the commonly agreed criteria for cap-setting and allocation specified in the Directive would be observed. If member states disagreed with the Commission's decisions, the burden was now on them to appeal the Commission's decision to the European Court of Justice.

This provision turned out to be an important one in creating the ability to counteract what was a clear tendency to inflate caps. In both the first and second periods, most of the NAPs submitted for review were rejected and required to reduce the number of allowances that the member state proposed to distribute. Without this provision, the aggregate first-period cap would have been higher by about 100 million tons annually, or a little less than 5 percent of the final cap. In the second period, the additional required reduction was 200 million tons or about 10 percent. Inflated totals were not the only reason that NAPs were rejected, but it was the most important one and the one that got the most attention.

The second important feature for cap-setting in the first two periods was the reference point provided by the Kyoto Protocol and the European Burden-sharing Agreement (BSA). Since the EU ETS is the EU's primary means for meeting its internationally binding obligations under the Kyoto Protocol, the criterion for cap-setting was obvious for most EU members: emissions should be set at a level that would not jeopardize compliance with the Kyoto/BSA targets, taking into account other measures that the member state would be adopting. This criterion was included in the ETS Directive and amplified by increasingly specific guidance applicable to the NAP submissions for the first and second periods.

Nevertheless, the application of this criterion to the new member states in Eastern Europe was not obvious. All were signatories of the Kyoto Protocol; but none in danger of exceeding their targets, except Slovenia. Further-more, the guidance concerning cap-setting could be interpreted as allowing member states with anticipated surpluses to have a cap higher than expected emissions. Indeed, Poland and some other east European member states adopted this position (Jankowski 2007). However, the Commission prevailed in taking a position that business-as-usual emissions would be the reference point for member states with non-constraining Kyoto targets. This interpre-tation ruled out the intentional inclusion of excess AAUs or "hot air" by new member states. In the event, the first period cap provided plenty of room for the new member states because predicting business-as-usual emissions proved to be difficult and not very accurate.

While this decentralized NAP structure of cap-setting has worked, there has been a distinct evolution away from it in the second trading period and in what is now the agreed post-2012 third period. In the second period, the formal structure did not change, but the tone did. What could best be described as a set of negotiations between the individual member states and the Commission concerning cap levels in the first period became for the second period a much more one-sided determination of those levels by the center. This change of tone could perhaps be expected since the second period was a more serious affair in which the obligations of the Kyoto Protocol mattered, whereas the first, "trial" period was outside of the legally binding Kyoto Protocol. More importantly, the revelation, shortly before NAP submissions for the second period were due, that emissions were lower than expected and that the system would likely be over-allocated led the Commission to adopt a much tougher stance on cap-setting. Member states still proposed totals, but there was little to negotiate. Rejection of the proposed total depended on how closely it conformed to emission levels developed by the Commission based on a consistent modeling exercise using the recently available, verified 2005 emissions data.

The amendments to the ETS Directive for the post-2012 periods, which were agreed by the European Council and Parliament in December 2008, have changed the cap-setting structure entirely (European Union 2009). From 2013 on, the EU-wide cap will no longer be the sum of member state totals. Instead, it is established up-front in the amended directive, that is, as agreed by the participating governments. In addition, the apportionment of that total among the member states is also pre-specified, albeit in the form of rights to sell allowances at auction instead of for free allocation to affected facilities. The amendments include various derogations that allow free allocation to industry in all member states and to the electricity sectors in some East European member states for a transitional period, but the new structure of a centrally agreed aggregate cap and apportionment of allowances to be auctioned by member states is clear. An important aspect of the agreement is that it provided sufficient differentiation to the less advantaged, who were now part of the decision-making process, to gain their agreement (Ellerman 2010). The December 2008 amendments effectively discarded the decentralized NAP structure that had been used to get the system started. Cap-setting and allocation are now centrally determined by the EU equivalent of an international agreement and the Commission's new task is developing the benchmarks and other transitional provisions associated with the transitional free allocation.

The European example suggests that, if decentralization is initially required, as seems likely in a global system, the problem will be developing an institution to exercise the essential functions provided by the European Commission. The Commission was conveniently at hand to perform this role for the EU ETS, but there is no obvious candidate on the global stage. Perhaps a similar facilitating and coordinating role will emerge out of the existing framework of the UN Framework Convention on Climate Change or the several "major emitter" forums that have been formed. Such an organization might also evolve out of the negotiations that would be needed for mutual recognition between independently developed systems, such as might be envisaged in attempting to link the EU ETS with comparable systems in other nations.

8.4.4 Allocation and harmonization

As noted above, the EU's initially decentralized approach to allocation re-vealed a new problem—harmonization—which will likely recur in any cap-and-trade system in a multinational setting. This problem in allocation be-came an issue despite a remarkable degree of "soft harmonization" as a result of similar circumstances, the sequential submission of NAPs, and outright copying among member states (Zapfel 2007: 35).

Not least among the problems created by the demand for harmonization was what defines equal. The standard prescription for achieving harmoniza-tion is benchmarking, but no concept was more advocated and less practiced in the first and second period allocations than benchmarking, which foun-dered on the shoals of product and process heterogeneity. Installations with the same capacity may not be equally utilized and even if so, they may use different processes because the final product at one factory is more finished than at another, thereby requiring more processing, or the fuels used may be different because of national energy policies or local resource availabilities. In the few cases where benchmarking was used for allocation in the first and second periods, such as in the electricity sectors in Germany and the UK, the benchmarks are differentiated by fuel or other characteristics deemed important.

An even bigger problem is that much of the lack of harmonization in the EU ETS can ultimately be traced to the criterion for cap-setting and the implied differentiation of responsibilities among the participating member states. While common but differentiated responsibilities—as called for in the UN Framework Convention on Climate Change—are routinely acknowledged, and actually implemented in the EU ETS, it is hard to see how differentiation would not lead to differences in the allocation to like facilities in the respective jurisdictions so long as free allocation to installations is present. In Europe, the issue may have been whether installations in Poland should receive the same allocation as otherwise similar installations in Germany, but the issue globally would be whether facilities in China or India and similar ones in Europe or the USA should receive identical allocations based on capacity, output, or some other attribute.

With the 2008 Amendments, the EU member states were able to reconcile harmonization with differentiation by adopting auctioning as the basic prin-ciple of allocation, while allowing some transitional free allocation. This reconciliation occurred because of two effects of auctioning. The first was establishing zero as the eventual uniform benchmark for free allocation to affected facilities. This was not the benchmark that advocates had in mind, but it performed wonders in facilitating agreement among heterogeneous facilities spanning national boundaries on a common, positive benchmark for the remaining free allocation. The second effect was to create a new right—to auction allowances—that enabled a change in the means of effecting differentiation. Auctioning implies some auctioning authority, which in a multinational system will likely be decentralized to the participating governments. Allocating "auction rights" (and the implied revenue) allows differentiation at the national level without creating the within-sector differences that led to the call for harmonization.

The post-2012 transitional free allocation in the EU ETS still called for some standard for allocation to the eligible facilities, which were all industrial facilities and electricity generating plants in some east European member states. This benchmark is to be centrally determined and EU-wide for the more than 50 industrial sectors with essentially similar facilities and equal to the emission rate of the 10 percent most efficient plants times baseline output. Over time, the free allocation is progressively phased out by 2020 for electricity-generating plants in eastern Europe and by 2027 for industrial facilities, except for industrial sectors deemed to be trade-impacted; that is, subject to competition from countries without equivalent carbon charges. At the installation level, differentiation will still occur, but it will be by sector not by nation. Overall, phased-in auctioning allowed both differentiation at the national level and benchmarking at the sector level. To return to the comparison of Germany and Poland, cement installations in these two countries will henceforth be treated alike, but the government of Poland will receive a more than proportionate allocation of the increasing share of system-wide allowances that are to be auctioned.

Such an approach may not be feasible initially in setting up a cap-and-trade system, but the EU ETS demonstrates that initial free endowments need not be permanent. For many, the endowments will end in 2013, eight years after the start of the program, and for others, depending on industry and circumstance, the phase-out may continue for another 14 years.

8.5 CONCLUDING OBSERVATIONS

The EU ETS provides a unique opportunity to test the applicability of a cap-and-trade system in a multinational and potentially global setting. Heretofore, the advocacy of a global trading regime has been based either on theoretical legal and economic considerations or on the success of cap-and-trade systems in the United States, where the governance structures are less applicable.

The main contribution of the EU ETS has been to show that a cap-and-trade system can be implemented in a multinational setting. In doing so, the ETS has shown that international agreements, which often times express aspiration as much as commitment, can be turned into specific and efficient mechanisms for reducing greenhouse gas emissions. In Europe, this was accomplished despite significant differences in historical, economic, and institutional circumstances. This experience suggests that these differences may pose less of a problem to implementing a broader global system than is often thought.

More importantly, the evolution of cap-setting in the EU ETS provides an example of how a cap can be determined where a strong center does not already exist. In remarkably few years, the over-all cap evolved from being the sum of loosely coordinated, nationally determined caps to a mutually agreed upon aggregate cap with differentiation in the allocation of the value created by that cap. This could not have been accomplished without the ability to separate the distribution of the scarcity value created by the cap from the cap itself. Doing so allowed the bargaining over equity, emphasized by Groom et al. (chapter 6), to occur. Similar bargaining over the distribution of revenue from a uniform carbon tax could have achieved an equally efficient outcome, but where there is no central tax-collecting agent, explicit and politically sensitive transfers of revenue from more to less well-off member states would have been required. The European experience suggests that distributing auction rights ex ante may be more politically palatable than redistributing tax revenues ex post.

The EU ETS has also made an important contribution in resolving the problem of harmonization, an issue not encountered in US precedents, but shown by the EU ETS to be a problem in a multinational setting. Here again, auctioning provided a solution. In creating rights to auction allowances, a means of differentiation was created that did not necessarily extend to the installation level within constituent member states. Auction rights are attractive to negotiating governments, allowing them to dispose of the scarcity value created by the cap as they choose, while holding out a zero emission benchmark for installations that facilitated agreement on transitional sector-wide benchmarks. Here too the EU ETS has shown how seemingly intractable conflicts can be resolved.

Perhaps the most important question raised by the EU ETS is whether it is a Europe-only phenomenon because of the European Union. The pre-existing institutions of the European Union were enormously valuable in facilitating the adoption and implementation of the EU ETS. The absence of similar institutions at the global scale seems obvious, but we should be wary of making too much of this difference. It was not so long ago that cap-and-trade was viewed as an approach that could work "only in America" because of the presumed greater openness to markets in the USA. While widespread, such a perception ignored the long history of heavy-handed, command-and-control regulation that had dominated the environmental realm in the USA.

It would be similarly misleading to view the European Union as a strong federal state with a center able to impose its view on recalcitrant member states. The heterogeneity, bargaining, and polycentric decision making that go on within the European Union are far more like those that must occur in the global context than the more centralized processes that exist within unitary nation states. The differences between the EU and the global stage are of degree only, reflecting a willingness by the member states of the EU to use pre-existing institutions created for a very different purpose, and an earlier start made possible perhaps by a greater concern for the global commons. A similar willingness to create or adapt appropriate facilitating institutions, to bargain seriously over division of the gains achievable through cooperation, and to embrace polycentric decision making will be required in the broader global context. These are not small tasks, as made clear by the preceding contributions in Part II of this book, but the European experience with the EU ETS shows that they are feasible and no more implausible than a market-based cap-and-trade system in Europe.

Part III

Designing Institutions Taking into Account Social Preferences

In contrast to Part II, which relies on the standard behavioral assumption of selfish rational agents, Part III examines the issue of designing governance instruments for agents who exhibit social preferences. Agents are said to have social preferences whenever they value differently their consumption or assets, depending on the consumption and assets of other agents. Social preferences might account for trusting and cooperative behavior, but also for envy or lust, which can lead to destructive actions or sabotage. Today there is ample evidence that social preferences are widespread and researchers from various disciplines recognize that individuals' preference systems are based on at least two components which we call for simplicity "selfish" and "social," respectively. How these two components interact within individuals remains partly unclear and has not yet been completely satisfactorily understood and modeled. However, the existence of the social component as such, affects agents' decisions in predictable ways and should therefore be taken into account when evaluating the possible impacts of policy instruments and governance systems on individuals' behavior and their interactions. For instance, monetary incentives might crowd out individuals' intrinsic motivation (Deci 1971; Frey 1997; Nyborg and Rege 2003), preventing public policies from reaching their expected target. More generally, failure to take into account the right preferences may lead to inappropriate policy objectives and to the design of inefficient incentive systems and governance structures (see Bowles 2008).

Hiroe Ishihara and Unai Pascual consider the role of social capital (Putnam 1993) in governing common-pool resources, and particularly as a means to prevent their over-exploitation. Social capital and social preferences are tightly related, although the causality is unclear. Whatever the direction of the relation, social capital shapes the individuals' perception and preferences for their environment and for public goods in general. The consequence is that preferences are no longer given but are the product of social relationships, and they therefore reflect these relationships. While this does not lead to a radical relativism, it does imply that there are no "natural" or "physical" imperatives. Preferences for environmental goods (such as biodiversity and clean air) can be balanced against other preferences (such as equality and development for the poorest).

Chapter 10 by Andries Richter and Daan van Soest focuses on the interaction between voluntary action and government intervention. Individuals' moral motivation to contribute to public goods may be crowded out by government's incentives to foster agents' contributions, for example through rewards and penalties. The authors provide an overview of the literature on the circumstances under which formal interventions can crowd out voluntary contributions to the common good. They draw policy implications concerning the design of policy instruments which both increase policy effectiveness and preserve agents' intrinsic motivation to contribute to public goods and preserve social capital. In particular, communication plays a key role because introducing a new policy may send ambiguous messages to some agents. Decoding the signals conveyed by formal institutions can therefore clarify the underlying intentions or beliefs and prevent crowding-out.

Chapter 11 by Paulo Nunes and Laura Onofri addresses the warm-glow motive for contributing to public goods. According to the warm-glow hypothesis, individuals contribute voluntarily to improve their feeling of moral satisfaction and to foster their self-esteem by beautifying their self-image. From an empirical point of view, separating voluntary contributions that are altruistically motivated from those that are grounded on other reasons—such as impure altruism—is a tricky exercise. The authors present an econometric analysis and an empirical classification of warm-glow effects from a contingent valuation study.

9

Social Capital and Collective Action in Environmental Governance Revisited

Hiroe Ishihara and Unai Pascual

9.1 INTRODUCTION

Since the 1990s a growing number of authors have argued that social capital[1] has a positive impact on achieving desirable environmental outcomes, especially in the context of community-based natural resource management and collective action dilemmas (e.g. Katz 2000; E. Ostrom 2000a; Pretty 2003). More recently, it has been argued that policies based on market instruments, such as Payment for Ecosystem Services, could negatively affect social capital at the community level in relation to the crowding-out effects of such conservation instruments (Vatn 2009; Chapter 10 by Richter and Soest in this book). In this chapter we argue that despite this plethora of social capital literature, the connection between social capital and collective action is far from clear, and we offer a framework to shed light on the connection. By drawing on a pluralistic perspective; that is, ecological economics, sociology, and anthropology—and introducing two key concepts, *common knowledge* and *symbolic power*, we aim to unravel the links between social capital and collective action or coordination. By introducing these two concepts we aim to recapture a recursive relationship between social structure and human agency. Human agents are not born into a social vacuum, but rather born into a certain social structure which forms their preferences and agencies and enables/restricts their actions (Giddens 1984; Hodgson 1999). We point out that such a pluralistic

---

[1] This chapter does not argue whether social capital should be termed as "capital" or not. Arrow (1999) and Solow (1999) argue that social capital is a by-product rather than deliberate investment, thus it does not qualify to be termed as capital. We agree with McNiell's (2007) recent proposition that the concept should be termed *sociality* rather than social capital. However, considering the popularity of the concept and the fact that it is one of the fields where interdisciplinary conversation is taking place, the chapter uses the former term.

perspective, especially that of sociology and anthropology, is instrumental for improving environmental governance. These perspectives deepen our understanding of the fact that individual preferences are socially constructed, leaping from the standard model of human agents typical in the welfare economics literature which defines agents as welfare maximizers having stable individual preferences. We also explicitly acknowledge that different types of rationalities exist depending on the social context (Vatn 2009; Chapter 2 by Vatn in this book). The focus of this chapter is mainly on environmental governance and the function of social capital at the community level. We strongly believe that it will still provide useful insights about global environmental governance.

The next section looks into two sister disciplines in the social sciences, namely economics on one hand and sociology and anthropology on the other. Then, in Section 9.3, we introduce the concept of "social embeddedness" proposed by Granovetter, which gave birth to the original theory of social capital; we also briefly address how social capital is regarded by new institutional economics. We point out that standard social capital theories suffer from both "over-socialized" and "under-socialized" models of human agency. This section thus identifies some deficiencies of the standard social capital theory. In Section 9.4, we present an alternative conceptual model of social capital. The model links social capital and collective action by introducing two key concepts, "common knowledge" and "symbolic power." We argue that the potential for creating and fostering collective action cannot be considered to be just the result of pure rational calculation by individual members of a given community. Rather, it ought to be understood as a process of social construction where some groups in the community have the power to impose their view on collective action as legitimate "common knowledge" due to their position in the social structure. This discussion leads us to explore how common knowledge can be diffused among community members and also how common knowledge may be challenged by marginalized groups. This implies that the existence of social capital does not necessarily lead to the creation of collective action. It could also increase the chances of failure in fostering collective action. The final section concludes by addressing the implication of this argument in the context of global environmental governance.

9.2 TWO SISTER DISCIPLINES IN SOCIAL SCIENCE

With the respect to the future, my feeling is that sociologists don't know game theory and economists, who do, are hopelessly naïve about social structure. The best work remains to be done by those who have mastered both disciplines (Bonacich, quoted in Swedeberg 2001).

As Bonacich expresses himself in the personal communication with Swedeberg quoted above, the conversation between two sister disciplines in social science—economics and sociology/anthropology[2]—has not been successful due to epistemological differences that they embrace regarding human agency (Appadurai 1989; Bardhan and Ray 2008). On the one hand, economists tend to view human agents as rational welfare maximizers making choices according to their stable preferences. On the other hand, anthropologists/sociologists view agents as socialized beings who follow rules and norms that the social structure determines. Despite the establishment of ecological economics as an interdisciplinary field (Kapp 1976; Söderbaum 1992; Røpke 2005) and some serious attempts to facilitate this conversation (Vatn 2005; Bardhan and Ray 2007), the conversation itself has been less than fruitful (Ray 2008).[3] One of the very few areas where the conversation has been occurring is in the social capital debate (Lehtonen 2004). This concept has been used by various authors from different intellectual backgrounds, creating confusion and attracting criticism from both sides, from both economists and sociologists/anthropologists alike (e.g. Arrow 1999; Cleaver 2000; Harriss 2001). In this chapter, we aim to unravel some of the confusion and to facilitate the conversation between these disciplines as we deem it necessary for a better understanding of collective action towards environmental governance,[4] especially in common property management.

With the seminal work by Putnam (1993) the concept of social capital has proliferated not only in academia but also in the policy arena, especially with regard to development policy (Harriss 2001). Putnam has defined social capital as "features of social organization such as networks, norms and trust that facilitate coordination and co-operation for mutual benefit" (Putnam 1993: 35–6). This concept was introduced into the literature about common-pool resource (CPR) management as an incentive mechanism or institutional arrangement to curb individuals' incentive to free-ride regarding the provision of public goods (E. Ostrom 2000a; Aoki 2001). It is also generally argued that the existence of networks among the agents and a dense flow of information

---

[2] We note that there is a difference between anthropology and sociology; however, when juxtaposed to economics, we believe that they are in a same camp.

[3] This type of conversation has been especially impeded by their different positionalities in social science, i.e. economists preoccupying a more dominant and more influential position while anthropologists/sociologists preoccupy a more marginalized position. As a result, the anthropologists/sociologists have a tendency to be more defensive against economic theory and have even developed a school inside their discipline which specializes in criticizing economics (Ray 2008).

[4] In this chapter we will limit our argument to the collective action problem in CPR management and environmental governance at community level. Although we notice that a broader application of social capital and collective action or environmental governance is possible, that will be our future challenge.

lower the transaction costs of collective action (Putnam 1993; E. Ostrom 2000a; Pretty and Ward 2001; Collier 2002; Paavola and Adger 2005).

However, these institutionalist arguments have also been criticized by both economists and anthropologists/sociologists. Economists argue that the institutional angle cannot explain why some communities succeed in creating collective action while others fail to do so despite the existence of networks and dense flows of information. As governments and markets fail, communities can fail as well (Bowles and Gintis 2002; Bulte and Engels 2007). Additionally, anthropologists and sociologists argue that the explanatory power of social capital has been destroyed by divorcing social capital from social structure (Harriss 2001; Cleaver 2003; Mosse 2006). It is argued that what is missing in these game theorist and institutionalist approaches is the explicit recognition of the power relations and its implication for sustainable cooperation (Ray and Bijarnia 2007). The relationship between social capital and environmental outcomes and governance through collective action is far from clear (Lehtonen 2004). According to these critics, existing social capital theories have left social capital as a black box (Harriss 2001) and do not explain how it is associated with collective action towards CPR management (Ray and Bijarnia 2007).

By introducing two key concepts, namely, common knowledge as defined by Chwe (1999) and symbolic power, sensu Bourdieu (1990), this chapter indentifies the connection between social capital and collective action. By bringing these two concepts together, we argue that the creation of collective action is not just the result of rational calculation about how much to invest in collective action by individuals, but also a social construction of what the community perceives as being optimal. In other words, we argue that the creation of collective action involves social perception or knowledge which is in turn crafted by power relations.

The existence of power in the creation of knowledge has been fiercely debated between Habermas and French post-modernists such as Foucault, Derrida, and Deleuze (see Kelly 1994). Foucault (1965, 1977) analyzed how rationality was socially constructed by looking into modern institutions, such as mental hospitals, prisons, and discourse in psychiatry, which divided humans into those who are rational and those who are irrational (insane/mad/guilty), and gave the power to speak to those who are rational, excluding the others. He argued that the creation of rationality, which disciplines the human agency from within and monitors their action from inside, legitimizes existing power relations (Dreyfus and Rabinow 1982). Later, his argument was further developed by the authors of Subaltern studies and post-colonial studies, where they revealed how Western academics have deprived the oppressed of their voice, especially in the non-Western colonized world, and their ability to express and represent themselves in the "public sphere," thus legitimizing the colonization process or racial/sexual discrimination (Said 1979; Spivak 1988). For these authors power is not just about physical dominance but also depriving the voice of the subjected/colonized. Power is about determining what is rational and what is not and defining the legitimate knowledge in the "public sphere" (Foucault 1965, 1977; Bourdieu 1990). By defining rationality, the voices of the subjected/colonized are jettisoned as "unthinkable" (Bourdieu 1971).

On the other hand, Habermas argued that it is possible to make a normative distinction between legitimate and illegitimate use of power using communicative rationality (Habermas 1984). According to him, if agents can communicate with each other on equal footing and come to agreement, this can be legitimate use of power. This argument has led to the discussion on discursive democracy, which has been recently introduced in environmental evaluation methodologies (e.g. Dryzek 1990; Goodin 1996). Further, institutional economists tend to use the Habermasian concept. However, from a Foucaudian point of view, the Harbermasian argument has been criticized harshly. For example, the "public sphere," modelled after the Greek democracy, was only sustainable with the institution of slavery and women working at home (Benhabib 1996). Participation in the deliberative processes by the male elites was only possible due to the sacrifice made by the slaves and the women. In such a society, the women and the slaves were stigmatized as irrational and of being not worthy to express themselves in the public debate.

At the same time, anthropologists and sociologists, who often rely on the Foucauldian concept, are not without problem. They often fall into agnosticism and absolute cultural relativism, where they cannot distinguish legitimate power (Karalayali 2004). While this debate is outside the scope of this chapter, we argue that power relations influence the way preferences by individuals are shaped through the creation of so-called "common knowledge" (Ray and Bijarnia 2007). Moreover, we aim to bring in some of the Foucauldian argument of power by using the terminology of symbolic power.[5] In this vein we hope to contribute to the analysis of power within the pluralistic perspective of ecological economics which tends to be more reliant on the Habermasian approach.

9.3 WHAT IS THE PROBLEM WITH STANDARD SOCIAL CAPITAL THEORY?

9.3.1 Social embededness and human agency

Since the 1950s, gradually, social scientists have started to recognize that economic activity is embedded in the social structure; that is, individual

---

[5] Note that Bourdieu fiercely refuted being termed as post-modernist (Bourdieu and Wacquant 1992).

rational calculation and stable preferences are not the only driving forces that determine certain individual choices (Polanyi 1944). For example, Geertz (1992) analyzed that businesses by merchants in Moroccan bazaars are dictated by social networks and the connections that they have, not just by market principles or rational calculation of cost and benefit. Similarly, Granovetter (1973, 1985), who was the leading author concurring with this view, argued that the "weak ties," the ties outside the immediate circle of families and close friends, have a significant impact on the amount of information individuals can obtain regarding job opportunities. To take into account the influence of social structure, he put forward the argument of "social embeddedness," that is "the argument that the behaviour and institutions to be analyzed are so construed by ongoing social relations that to construe them as independent is a grievous misunderstanding" (Granovetter 1985: 481).

These arguments by economic sociologists had a profound influence on some institutional economists, who have conceptualized economic activity as an institutional process (Williamson 1981; North 1990). Throughout the 1990s ecological economics, as an alternative to neoclassical economics, has recognized the "embeddedness" of the economic system not only within the broader ecological but also within social systems (Spash and Villena 1998; Paavola and Adger 2005; Røpke 2005). Out of this embeddedness in the social structure and the relationship between the social structure and environmental outcomes, the idea of social capital has been developed in particular by the expanding common property literature (E. Ostrom 1990; Aoki 2001; Lehtonen 2004). But what was the original proposition by Granovetter? Have these institutionalists who succeeded him taken his proposition as he originally intended?

According to Granovetter, sociology tends to regard human agents as basically constructed by a social structure through the internalization of symbolic systems, social norms, and customs. On the other hand, economists often assume humans as rational welfare maximizers. He regarded the sociological view as being "over-socialized" and the utilitarian economic model as "under-socialized." However, he also recognized that both disciplines share a key common trait in that they see human agents as atomized actors; that is, as automata of rational calculation and norms/rules. Granovetter (1985) eloquently clarifies this point by saying that "fruitful analysis of human action requires us to avoid automation implicit in the theoretical extremes of under- and over-socialized conception. Actors do not behave or decide as atoms outside social context, nor do they adhere slavishly to a script written for them by the particular intersection of social categories that they happen to occur. Their attempts at purposive action are instead embedded in a concrete, ongoing system of social relations" (ibid: 487).

It is through the concept of social embeddedness that Granovetter attempts to avoid both the "over-socialized" approach of generalized morality and the "under-socialized" one of impersonal, institutional arrangements. Later Giddens (1984) and Archer (2003) developed Granovetter's idea of social embeddedness into that of human agency. Human agency arises from the agent's control of resources, which means the capacity to reinterpret or mobilize an array of resources creating a new meaning of resources and a new position inside the social structure (Giddens 1984; Bourdieu 1990; Sewell 1992). Human agents are born into a social structure and are constrained by the social structure. However, the fact that they are constrained does not deprive them of their ability to change and transform social structures (Giddens 1984; Bourdieu 1990).[6] Here, we use the term "human agency" to refer to the capacity of individual agents to reinterpret and transform the social norm/ rules within certain limits (Giddens 1984; Bourdieu 1990). This agency and ability to manipulate the social structure varies among the agents according to the social position that they occupy (Sewell 1992; Lin 2001).

Current theories of social capital, especially after Putnam (1993), who is said to follow Granovetter's main tenets, keep succumbing to the pitfall of either the "under-socialized" or "over-socialized" model and fail to capture the embeddness of institutional outcomes in the social structure. As a result, the standard social capital theories assume that human agents can craft social capital based on their rational calculation. They do not acknowledge the fact that human agents are constrained by social structure (Giddens 1984) and are blind to the power relation involved in creating collective action (Ray and Bijarnia 2007). At the same time, standard theories assume that once the institutional arrangements are established, human agents follow the norms/ rules automatically. They do not take into account that human agents are able to reinterpret/misinterpret and transform the social structure (Giddens 1984; Taylor 1993). Social structures are not just constraining, but can be enabling as well (Giddens 1984; Vatn 2005). This makes it impossible to understand why collective action sometimes succeeds and at other times fails with regard to common property (Cleaver 2003). In the next section, we briefly revise how the concept of social capital has been introduced into the common property literature.

9.3.2 Social capital in common property management

The debate on the commons and common property management was stimulated by Hardin's (1968) seminal work, although he was referring to the issue

---

[6] However, we must admit that the argument of these sociologists is weak in terms of theorizing the structuring aspect of human agency (Kouchi 1995).

of open access resources rather than common properties (McCay and Jentoft 1998). Empirical evidence has demonstrated that coordination norms/rules do exist inside communities that may reinforce the expectation of collective behavior, leading a critical mass of individuals to adopt cooperative strategies. In other words, there is an institutional mechanism inside social groups where Hardin's misplaced tragedy can be avoided (E. Ostrom 1990; Runge 1992).

The existence of coordination mechanisms is explained through the concept of interdependency. That is, any dominant strategy would fail to capture the essence of the motivation of individual decisions if the importance of changing the expectation of others' behavior is not analyzed. In this sense, decision making regarding the use of common properties involves interdependent choices in which not only the benefits and costs of using common properties becomes a function of the aggregate action of individuals, but the decision to use (or overuse/underuse) is also affected by the expected decisions of others (Paavola and Adger 2005). That is, agents do not act in a social vacuum; rather, they are surrounded by a web of social networks, which gives them information about others' actions. These networks also function as a mechanism to monitor and sanction each other's actions. This web that surrounds agents is termed "social capital". In other words, social capital was originally used to explain how communities are able to impose certain coordination norms without relying on external coercive regulation, such as states or legal systems. Here we briefly review the history of the social capital concept in the common property literature after Putnam's (1993) contribution and also in ecological economics (e.g. Lehtonen 2004; Rodrıguez and Pascual 2004).

Although there were precursors of social capital theory to Putnam—for example, Bourdieu and Coleman[7]—it was Putnam's (1993) influential work which popularized the notion of social capital. For Putnam, social capital refers to those "features of social organization, such as trust, norms, and networks that can improve the efficiency of society by facilitating coordinated action" (Putnam 1993: 167). For example, Putnam applied this concept to explain the difference in the institutional performance between the north and the south of Italy. However, the concept of social capital, which was introduced as a logical framework that explains institutional performance in his first book, later makes an unexpected turn, as he also refers to social capital as the object to be fostered by public policy (Putnam 2000; Morotomi 2003). It is this twist in his conceptualization of social capital that has made his argument most popular, especially in the policy arena (Fine 2001). Since then, the idea of social capital has become divorced from social structure and has become a resource that can be crafted and manipulated by agents to

---

[7] Portes (1998) traces back the origin of the concept to Marx and Durkheim.

obtain favorable economic and political outcomes. As a result, the dark side of social capital, such as social exclusion or the reproduction of unequal social structure, has often been ignored (Portes 1998; Carroll and Stanfiled 2003; Dolfsma and Dannreuther 2003; van Steveren 2003).

This trend has continued when imported into the common property management literature, most notably by Ostrom (2000a), for whom the concept of social capital is mainly interpreted as consisting of coordination norms or institutional incentive mechanisms used to explain the potential for collective action inside communities. In this vein, social capital is understood as "shared knowledge, understanding, norms, rules and expectation about the pattern of interaction that a group of individuals bring to recurrent activity" (E. Ostrom 2000a: 176) and as "an attribute of individuals and of their relationship that enhance their ability to solve collective-action problems" (E. Ostrom and Ahn 2002: xiv). Ostrom's view goes even further when she argues that "to create social capital in a *self-conscious manner*, individuals must spend time and energy working with one another to craft institutions—that is the set of rules that will be used to allocate the benefit derived from an organized activity and to assign responsibility for paying the cost" (E. Ostrom 2000a: 178, *emphasis added*). Ostrom thus argues that human agents have the capacity to craft and invest in social capital to provide the (socially and ecologically) efficient amount of collective action according to some predetermined rational calculation.

Ostrom's view has been reinforced by game theorists. For example, Aoki (2001) applies a "linking game" to exemplify how in the Edo period (1603–1868) in Japan farmers were able to create collective action. They needed to coordinate their actions to maintain the functioning of the communal irrigation system in a context in which each farmer had the incentive to free-ride on such communal effort. Since it was technically difficult to punish or exclude cheaters in order to foster collective action coercively, Aoki argues that farmers linked this irrigation game with a social exchange game of ostracism. He shows that the linkage between both games overcomes the incentive to free-ride, especially when the cost of ostracism is high enough.

Another important strand of the institutionalist approach puts more emphasis on social capital in relation to its ability to reduce transaction costs (Katz 2000; Pretty and Ward 2001; Paavola and Adger 2005). For example, Pretty and Ward (2001) define social capital as "the structure of relations between actors and among actors" that encourages productive activities. These aspects of social structure are called social capital because they act as a resource for individuals to use in order to realize *their personal interest*. Local institutions are effective because "they permit to carry on our daily life with *minimum repetition and costly negotiations*" (ibid: 211, *emphasis added*). Within this tradition, it is commonly assumed that social capital is useful as it lowers the transaction cost of acting cooperatively for individuals' mutual benefit. For example, Pretty and Ward (2001) have shown that recent programmes to formulate watershed and catchment management groups based on individual communities have been more successful compared to previous programmes that included whole river basins where more than one community were involved. When the whole river basin was included and multiple numbers of communities were involved, people involved had no social networks, making it difficult to monitor the actions of others. As a result, programmes at the local community level have made substantial, often two- to threefold, improvements in catchments.

In summary, standard social capital theories, especially those stemming from institutional economics and game theory tend to assume that social capital is a resource that can be invested in order to circumvent the incentives of free-riding and to lower the transaction cost associated with collective action. Furthermore, some economists have also gone on another step to develop proxy indicators for social capital and have measured the correlation between the institutional outcomes and impacts of social capital empirically (e.g. Narayan and Pritchett 1999; Whiteley 2000; Guiso et al. 2007). Their underlying assumption is that individuals rationally calculate the cost and benefit of collective action and can self-consciously invest and disinvest in social capital.

9.3.3 Under- and over-socialized human agents

There are two major problems in these standard social capital theories. First, the concept of social capital is too vague to be operationalized econometrically (Manski 2000; Durlauf 2002). Bourdieu, one of the founders of this concept, did not propose this concept for economic methodology (Sobel 2002). Second, they cannot explain why social capital has that ability to circumvent the incentive to free-ride (Cleaver 2000, 2003) or why indeed it can lower transaction cost (Ballet et al. 2007). A theory that explains why agents feel more obliged to comply with "coordination norms" when there are interpersonal networks or dense information flows is missing.

If the role of social capital is reduced to institutional arrangements as argued by game theorists and reduced to proxy indicators in econometric analysis (e.g. Narayan and Pritchett 1999; Guiso et al. 2007), then it becomes an independent variable that could in principle help to explain the existence of collective action (Cleaver 2000, 2003). However, the capacity of social capital to create collective action resides in being part of a hierarchical social structure. Social capital itself should be also treated as a dependent variable of social structure (Sobel 2002). Thus, at the very least, it should be instrumental in an endogenous system of equations. As a result of this ignorance, it cannot explain independently how the common understanding of collective action, which we name as common knowledge in the next section, is formed and shared in the community. The rationalist approach ignores the influence of interdependency and thus holds the under-socialized model of human agents with stable preferences. This under-socialized approach to social capital ignores the role of the social structure and its coercive character (Mosse 1997; Cleaver 2003; Mosse 2006).

At the same time, paradoxically, when game theory is applied to problems such as common property management, it also suffers from an over-socialized model of human agency. This is because it is often assumed that once self-enforcing incentive mechanisms are built, agents would automatically follow the commonly agreed rules/norms and reach a Nash equilibrium which can be an efficient solution (Hodgson 1997). However, empirical evidence shows that CRP management is also associated with resistance and struggle, despite the existence of networks and a dense flow of information (Cleaver 2000; Agrawal 2001). As Ballet et al. (2007) put it, social capital can also be dangerous to the management of common property, leading to collective action failure.

As mentioned above, generally economists and political scientists debating about social capital overlook the recursive relationship between human agency and social structure (Giddens 1984; Bourdieu 1990). Human beings are born into certain social structures, however; they have the ability (agency) to change and transform the social structure. This agency varies among the agents according to their position in the social structure (Sewell 1992; Lin 2001). In other words, human agents are constrained by social structure but they are also structuring the social structure within certain limits (Giddens 1984; Bourdieu 1990). Lacking this notion of human agency, the standard social capital literature falls into the under- and over-socialized models. Social capital should be considered to forge a link between the social structure and agents, rather than just being a part of an institutional arrangement per se (Paavola and Adger 2005).

If social capital is to be a factor explaining collective action, its interpretation as the density of the networks and rate of these information flows is clearly insufficient. We align with Cleaver's (2000) view that the existence of networks and information flow do not necessarily lower the transaction cost, nor guarantee that agents would follow an institutional arrangement. Thus, there is still a need to identify the nature of networks and information flows that can lower transaction costs, and how would this come about? We need to open the black box of social capital and reveal the process that allows it to foster collective action.

9.4 TOWARDS A NEW CONCEPTUAL MODEL OF SOCIAL CAPITAL AND COLLECTIVE ACTION

To open the black box of social capital and collective action, we propose that social capital positively contributes to (1) the creation of "common knowledge," identified with the link "L_1" in Figure 9.1; and (2) its sharing or diffusion among community members (L_3),[8] allowing collective action to be fostered in order to solve environmental governance problems (L_4).

The model also focuses on the often neglected negative pathway between social capital and collective action, shown by the link $L_1 - L_5 - L_6$. This complex pathway is mediated by "symbolic power," or the capacity to represent social preferences (L_2) in communities affected by collective environmental problems. In this section we will explain two key concepts: common knowledge (Chwe 1999, 2001) and symbolic power (Bourdieu 1990). Table 9.1 summarizes the main concepts used in our argument, which form the building blocks of the

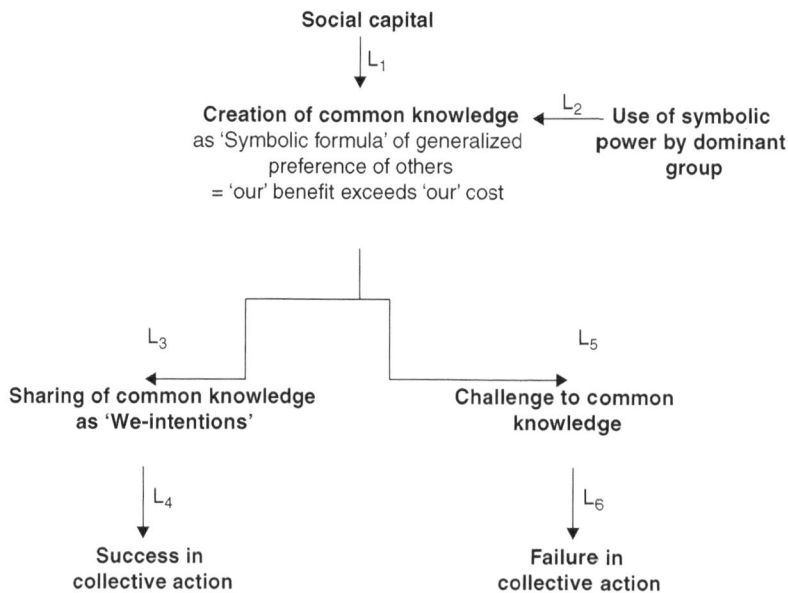

Figure 9.1. Conceptual framework of the role of social capital in fostering collective action

---

[8] Although we are aware of the fact that the two processes—creation of common knowledge and its sharing—are not two separate processes, rather one process progressing in parallel. The domination of certain preferences is established through both the creation of common knowledge and the diffusion of common knowledge, and in both processes symbolic power is the key.

Table 9.1. The main concepts as a roadmap between social capital and collective action for CPR management

Concepts	Definition	Seminal literature
Symbolic formula	Frame of reference that provide agents with understanding of the world	Douglas (1986)
Common knowledge	Symbolic formula that represents the generalized preference of the others	Chwe (1999; 2001)
Symbolic power	Power that legitimizes the certain "symbolic formula" as common knowledge	Bourdieu (1990)
Internalization	A long-term process of consolidating and embedding one's own beliefs, attitudes, and values, when it comes to moral behavior	Berger and Luckman (1966)
We-intentions	An individual agents' attribution of an intention to a community that the agents believe is reciprocally held by other agents in the same community	Tuomela (1995; 2007)
Human agency	Ability of human agents to change and transform social structure	Giddens (1984) Bourdieu (1990)

conceptual model that connects social capital and collective action in the context of the governance of complex environmental public goods such as common properties.

9.4.1 Creation of common knowledge

9.4.1.1 Node L_1: what is "common knowledge"?

Even "super-rational" game theorists assume that individual agents do not make their decision in a social vacuum but that they take into account other agents' preferences and decisions. In other words, it is acknowledged that human agents are interdependent with each other (Gächter and Fehr 1999). The understanding of the preferences of others is referred to as "common knowledge" (Chwe 1999, 2001). Here we define common knowledge as the understanding embedded in the social structure, which enables us to put resources to a particular use (Newell et al. 2004), thus enabling agents to take into account the preferences of the other agents in the community (Chwe 1999, 2001). Common knowledge may be about who has the right to access and who has the responsibility for conservation of natural resources in the context of common property management (Cleaver 2000). Community members may tend to act collectively when they can formulate a common knowledge that acting collectively creates benefits that outweigh the costs of such effort at the individual level. This common knowledge is especially important in environmental governance as the decision by one agent often affects those of the others (Paavola and Adger 2005; Vatn 2005).

However we depart from standard game theorists' understanding of common knowledge in claiming that the creation of common knowledge is not a simple process of averaging out the preferences of members of the community. Rather, it is a process of influencing (or in an extreme case imposing) certain arbitrary forms of individual preferences, often by a dominant group[9] in the community. Even in small communities where common property is at stake, the preferences of individual members are often highly heterogeneous and varied according to their gender, cast, ethnicity, etc. Agents with different social positions have different preference structures (Leach et al. 1999; Agrawal and Gibson 2001). Given our cognitive limitations, it is not possible to deal with all such different preferences in a instrumentally rational way (Hodgson 1999). To avoid this overload, we economize our cognitive capacity by relying on what Douglas (1986) calls "symbolic formulae."[10] For an individual member of the community the symbolic formulae represents the generalized preferences of the other members and as such the preference of the whole community as common knowledge. In other words, we need to account for the need to *socially construct* a "symbolic formula" as common knowledge that shows that "our" benefit (benefit for the community as whole) of collective action exceeds "our" incurred cost (cost as a community as a whole) from engaging in collective action.

This goes beyond the argument of bounded rationality and embraces the notion that common knowledge needs to be socially constructed (Berger and Luckmann 1966; Bourdieu and Wacquant 1992). Social construction implies that agents interacting together form, over time, a typification or "symbolic formula" of each other's preferences, and that these typifications eventually become "habitualized" into reciprocal roles played by the actors in relation to each other (Berger and Luckmann 1966). It is important to note that this process of social construction is neither a process of averaging out the existing preferences in the community nor a purely rational calculation, as often modelled in game theoretical approaches. Rather, it is a process of political struggle over who has the legitimacy to represent their preference as common knowledge.

[9] Here the dominant/marginalized group does not necessarily mean a dominance/subordination in terms of demographic weight; rather, it has a political/social connotation linked to the idea of power. Here we define "dominant group" as a group that seizes economic, political, and social resources and occupies a superior position in the hierarchical social structure. In other words, there is always an alternative discourse to the common knowledge held by the marginalized group and there is a possibility for these alternative discourses to become common knowledge. Legitimacy of common knowledge is challenged through daily struggles (Bourdieu 1984; Giddens 1984). However, for the simplicity of the argument, in this chapter, we will simply state dominant group and marginalized group. But this does not exclude the possibility of the dominant group falling to the marginalized group or vice versa.

[10] This concept is similar to the Veblenian notion of "habit of thought" (Hodgson 1997; 1999).

9.4.1.2 Node L_2: what is symbolic power?

Whose calculation of benefits and costs are represented as common knowledge out of the manifold preferences existing in a heterogeneous community? The answer should focus on those who have the power to influence what is a legitimate and what is not (Bourdieu 1990; Swartz 1997).[11] This is where the notion of symbolic power comes in, interpreted by Bourdieu (1990) as "world-making power." The creation of common knowledge is not just the result of rational calculation, but mostly the result of a hierarchical power relation existing within a given social structure, which in turn legitimizes certain groups in the community and can even monopolize symbolic power (Mosse 1997, 2006; Cleaver 2000, 2003). For example, if we come back to Aoki's (2001) linking game of the Edo period in Japan, there are numerous games in society and which game is to be linked to which one is an arbitrary decision. Deciding that the irrigation game is to be linked with the social exchange game might be the result of the fact that this specific type of linking game gives an advantage to the dominant group in the society. In this sense, there is no guarantee that the preferences that gain such common character would achieve the level of collective action needed for the socially desired (ecological or economic) outcome. The dominant preference which becomes common knowledge is arbitrary. In addition, by legitimizing the arbitrary symbolic formula as common knowledge, other preferences become "unthinkable" or "irrational" (Bourdieu 1971).

However, it is not enough just to create common knowledge. This has to be diffused and shared among the members of the community (L_3). Even when this commonly shared preference regarding the collective provision to a public good effectively becomes common knowledge, some individuals, especially from powerless or marginalized groups may be implicitly forced to act collectively despite their real preferences not coinciding with that of common knowledge. In such cases, the possibility of challenging the common knowledge arises (L_5), leading to a possible failure of cementing collective action (L_6).

9.4.2 Sharing of common knowledge—Node L_1-L_3-L_4: towards the success of collective action

For common knowledge to function as an incentive mechanism for collective action, it is not enough to create it, but it also has to be shared or diffused

---

[11] In similar way, Habermas (1986) argues "the fundamental phenomenon of power is not the instrumentalization of another's will, but the formulation of a *common* will in a communication directed to reach agreement" (ibid: 76, *emphasis added*).

effectively among the members of the community; that is, common knowledge has to be internalized. According to Berger and Luckman (1966) in their argument about social constructionism, such internalization is a long-term process of consolidating and embedding one's own beliefs, attitudes, and values, when it comes to moral behavior. Through this process, the arbitrary symbolic formula becomes the "natural order" of things, distancing itself from its origin and jettisoning other possibilities as illegitimate (Bourdieu 1971, 1990). While the common knowledge becomes a frame of reference for the community members to decide upon their action, there is also the possibility that common knowledge is interpreted differently or misinterpreted from the original content. If it is assumed that internalization automatically creates collective action without any form of challenge, we would fall into the pitfall of over-socializing the model of human agency. To understand either possibility—that is, common knowledge being shared by the members of community (L_3) or being challenged by community members (L_5)—we call this process where common knowledge is internalized the creation of "*we-intentions.*"

According to Tuomela (1995, 2007), "we-intentions" can be defined as individual agents' attribution of an intention to the whole community when agents believe such attribution is reciprocally held by other agents in the community. Additionally, this belief needs to be mutually held and shared among the majority of the community members (Tuomela 1995; Davis 2002). "We-intention" implies that each individual member in the community would agree with the given common knowledge showing that "our" benefit exceeds "our" cost of investing in the collective action. However, while in reality all individual agents deliberate on the content of the common knowledge, it is not necessarily shared by all, thus allowing room for interpretation/misinterpretation and for a challenge to the common knowledge to arise from within the community. For collective action to be successful, an effective number of members have to share the common knowledge and consider it to be the legitimate symbolic formulae.

Fundamentally, it is the capacity to diffuse the idea of common knowledge within a social group that ultimately enables social capital to reduce the level of transaction cost that arises in collective action. This is especially so when there is a heterogeneous set of preferences within the community, associated with groups that are hierarchically related in terms of the power they have to impose what would become common knowledge. Symbolic power plays a key role in reducing transaction costs. It also follows that the existence of networks and information flows does not on its own guarantee the reduction of such costs. Rather, we argue that networks and information flows can also become instrumental and enable dominant groups to spread their (rational and self-legitimated) vision of the costs and benefits associated with collective action.

McKean (1992) shows, in a very similar manner to Aoki, how common property was managed in the Edo period in Japan. McKean (1992) claims that its success was due to a sufficient level of homogeneity in the community.[12] The village chief had the exclusive right to decide when to open and close the mountain for the extraction season to fetch fodder or wild edible plants. The regulations were so strict that it went so far as to identify the equipment to be used for collecting those resources from the communal land. Those who violated the rules were punished with a form of ostracism called "Mura-hachib,"[13] which had serious effects upon the survival strategy of the household which breached the rules. Such a harsh punishment was only possible because villages in the Edo period had an strict hierarchical social structure between the village chief and the peasant farmers (Takeuchi 1990). As a result, it was possible for the common knowledge to be created and shared effectively. This is an example of power-mediated collective action at work in environmental governance. Common knowledge was self-legitimized and effectively shared in the community.

9.4.3 Challenge to common knowledge—Nodes L_1-L_5 -L_6: possibility of failure of collective action

Despite community members tending to share common knowledge as "we-intention," it does not usually go without challenge. This is due to the sharing process of the common knowledge process, as "we-intention" is not perfect due to alternative discourses that exist in society. It includes both the problem of interpretation/misinterpretation of common knowledge and the challenges created according to the alternative discourses. In other words, the marginalized group may accept the dominant common knowledge—using the authorized language—and make of it something quite different (Mosse 2004). It is in this sense that we agree with the argument on the existence of "hidden transcript" and "public transcript" as discussed by Scott (1990) and we will term the common knowledge held by the dominant group who tries to impose their view as "public" common knowledge and that of the marginalized group as "hidden" common knowledge. The relationship between the "public" common knowledge and the "hidden" common knowledge is shown in

---

[12] From the ecological point view, whether this was an optimal amount of collective action or not is questionable. For example, Mizumoto (2003) points out that the landscape of Japanese mountains was quite different from what we see today. Most of the mountains were deforested during this period due to a high demand for grassland and fodder production. This has resulted in the increased frequency of floods, which has lead the succinct Meiji-government to promote tree plantation projects to regulate the water.

[13] "Mura-hachibu" literally means 80 percent separation from the village. There were 10 main events in the traditional Japanese society, among them weddings, celebration of coming-of-age, and celebration of a new-born. The ostracized household were excluded from 8 ceremonies and were allowed to participate in only two events: funerals and fire-fighting.

Figure 9.2. This is because, first, not all members can always interpret the common knowledge as the dominant group would wish, but rather they can reinterpret and misinterpret its content according to the context they face. We call this "interpretation failure"; it can be unintentional or intentional, depending on the situation that agents face. If the agents do not have enough power to challenge the common knowledge, those same agents may intentionally choose to misinterpret or displace the content of common knowledge. Second, there is also the possibility that alternative discourses challenge the common knowledge in cases of strong social capital within the marginalized groups. We call this "legitimacy failure." It can be observed in cases where marginalized groups claim power by denying the legitimacy of "public" common knowledge. However, the distinction between "interpretation failure" and "legitimacy failure" is not clear cut in reality. There may be cases where "interpretation failure" occurring due to the existence of "hidden" common knowledge, may lead to "legitimacy failure" as the challenges progress.

9.4.3.1 *"Interpretation failure"—possibility of reinterpretation/ misinterpretation of common knowledge*

With regard to the first point, Hodgson (1999) quotes Wittgenstein to argue that, "there are all sorts of interpretive problems involved in moving from the existence of rule to behavior that follows the rule. The feeling that one is being

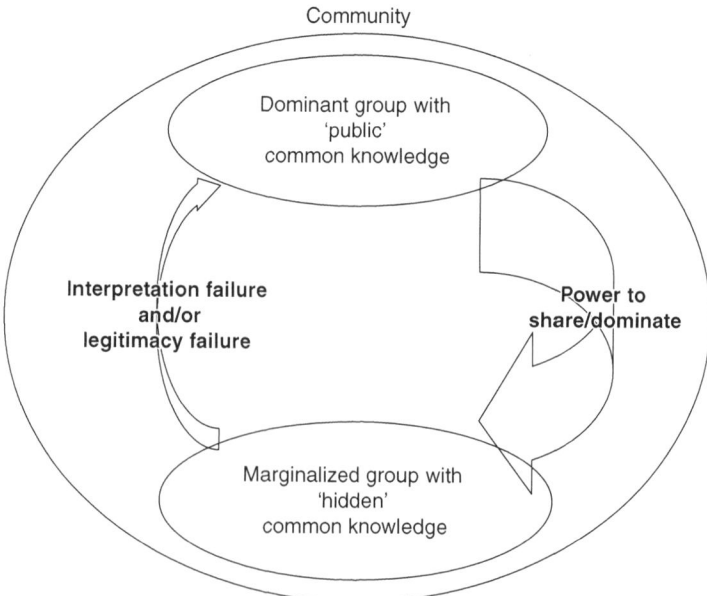

Figure 9.2. Interpretation failures and legitimacy failures

guided by rules does not guarantee that the rules are being followed" (ibid: 61). Community members reinterpret/misinterpret common knowledge according to their position inside a certain social structure, even if such social structure is continuously being transformed by them. There is always a possibility that community members displace the original content of common knowledge and create a new interpretation of it (Sewell 1992; Lin 2001). This implies that whether common knowledge is shared by individuals as "we-intention" depends on the circumstances of the interaction between them in the community. Hence, even if "public" common knowledge exists, there is no guarantee that community members would accordingly accept it. Rather, it implies that common knowledge cannot be directly associated with collective action through the process of internalization.[14] There are always those who interpret the dominant common knowledge according to more "hidden" common knowledge, making the dominant common knowledge something quite different. Community members are not mere rule/norm followers, but rather improvisers of rule/norms (Taylor 1993).

For example, Cleaver (2003) mentions the case of a poor woman in a Tanzanian village who broke common property management rules but went without punishment. In this village, the villagers have to pay for water according to how much water they consume in order to maintain the pumping facility. This woman consumed more water than she paid for. However, her action was justified by the fact that she was poor and hard-working. In other words, this case shows that such women are able to exercise their agency by bringing in other virtues such as being hard-working, and to reinterpret the common knowledge. This is an example that helps to illustrate that the most vulnerable groups in society, for example poor females, are capable of exercising agency despite their constraints. In other words, human agents can sometimes reinterpret/misinterpret common knowledge intentionally or unintentionally according to the context they face.

9.4.3.2 *"Legitimacy failure"—possibility of the survival of alternative discourse*

"Legitimacy failure," where some members maintain an alternative discourse which may in turn challenge the legitimacy of common knowledge, is of great importance. It is possible that marginalized groups do not share the common knowledge and do not accept its legitimacy or that the dominant groups do

---

[14] The concept of internalization applied by institutional economists regarding social/institutional embeddedness suffers from this oversimplification. It is also important to note that social constructuralism is criticized because human agents are born into a certain social structure and are not free to construct it as they wish (Bourdieu 1984; Giddens 1984). This is the basis of structuration theory (Tanabe 1995).

not have enough power to consolidate the legitimacy of common knowledge and diffuse it effectively. According to their alternative discourse, marginalized groups may challenge the arbitrary nature of common knowledge, especially when they have to bear a disproportionate cost derived from it, for example collective action (Taylor 1993).[15]

However, these cases are rare because marginalized groups face difficulties in raising their voices within a public discourse which favours the dominant group's interests (Spivak 1988). It is important to note that human agency varies according to the position that human agents occupy in the social structure. Often, dominant groups have more freedom in terms of creating new interpretation and new common knowledge because they have more access to resources, technology, and information (Sewell 1992; Lin 2001). However, this does not mean that the arbitrariness of common knowledge cannot be disclosed. Disclosure does occur and thus the legitimacy of common knowledge is implicitly negotiated in everyday social life practice (Willis 1977; Bourdieu 1990; Cleaver 2003).

For example, Agrawal (2001) reports cases from Nepal and India where females do challenge the common knowledge they face by intentionally violating the rule of common property management determined by the males who are dominant in the communities. Despite the fact that the females are the daily users of the common property and have accumulated valuable knowledge on how to manage it effectively, such knowledge is not reflected in the dominant rule of common property management. Common knowledge is instead dominated by male preferences. However, due to the high level of social capital inside their female communities, they are able to maintain and stick to an alternative discourse that challenges the imposed common knowledge by the males.[16] It is rather easy to imagine that this female alternative discourse may gain some attention and overcome the marginalized position of women within the social structure as regards international development policy for participatory forestry management or in the global discourses of feminism.[17] Thus social capital does not guarantee a

---

[15] It should be noted that this challenge does not arise from a neoclassical rationality. It is the dominant group which defines what is "rational" and what is not (Foucault 1965; Bourdieu 1990). Those who challenge have to start by constructing a new rationality that approves of their claims.

[16] It would be interesting to relate the debate on bonding social capital and "subaltern counter-public," which enables the oppressed to form their own voice by forming their own public sphere (Benhabib 1992; Fraser 1992) and also to relate the argument of "environmentality" coined by Agrawal (2005) to these arguments. However, that is beyond the reach of this chapter.

[17] But at the same time it is worth noting that this may lead to subjugation to another power relation: the power relation between the feminists in the Western world and those in the Third World (Abu-Lughod 2002). Power relations are multi-layered and deliverance from one may lead to subjugation to another.

creation of collective action, rather even in the presence of social capital; society may fail to create it due to "interpretation failure" and "legitimacy failure."

9.4.4 Some policy implications

What are the implications of this chapter regarding environmental governance, especially at the global level? Our argument on social capital, common knowledge, and symbolic power can be connected to the issue of environmental governance at the global level in an indirect way. We can provide some hints based on an alternative understanding of the crowding-out effect in relation to power structure. Multiple common knowledges exist at various levels and various compartmentalized parts of our everyday life, for example inside communal institutions, or inside a private company's moral ethics, or national legislation. In other words, common knowledge held by the dominant group which functions as a "public" transcript at the communal level, will function as a "hidden" transcript on another scale; that is to say national policy. This implies that the relation between policy and practice is not as straightforward as the dominant neoclassical economics presumes (Mosse 2004).

Crowding-out occurs when there is a discrepancy or poor fit between the common knowledge held among the political elite who formulate the national policy and common knowledge at the community level, as shown in Figure 9.3. For example, economic incentives created by schemes such as those based on payments for environmental services (PES) may be interpreted in a very different manner from that of the "public" common knowledge, which is based on "the rationality of maximizing individual utility" (Vatn 2009). Led by "hidden" common knowledge at the community level, community members may consider PES as illegitimate, or at least as an instrument that reduces the legitimacy of their "own" common knowledge. For example, PES, especially as a payment for communal activities, might demean their livelihoods, since the maintenance of common property resources does not reside in the realm of the market where individual preferences prevail; rather, it could well reside in the civic obligation leading to crowding-out effects of the PES. This might in turn lead to policy failure. At the same time, at the community level, policy intervention could mean something else. Policy intervention could cast some light on the arbitrariness of the common knowledge held by the dominant group at the communal level and a marginalized group may start to doubt the legitimacy of the "public" common knowledge held by the dominant group.

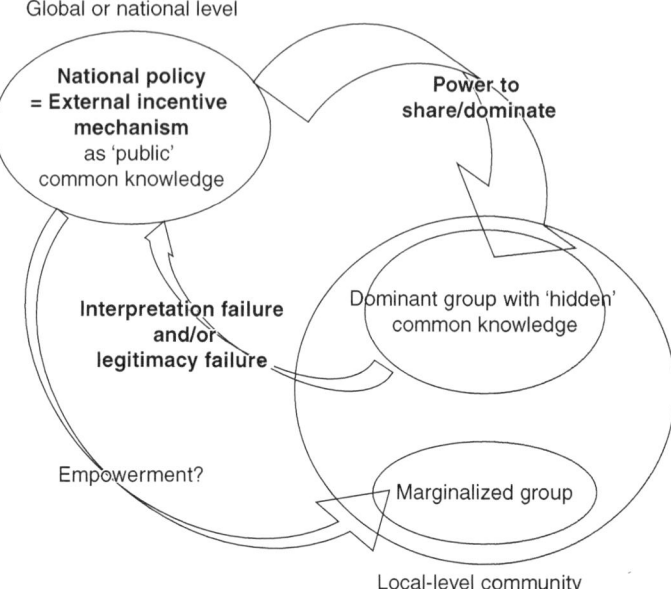

Figure 9.3: Interaction between "public" and "hidden" common knowledge

9.5 CONCLUSION

In this chapter we concur with Harriss (2001) in that the standard social capital theory becomes an *anti-politics machine*,[18] given that the theories are depoliticized, even if it is the very political nature of social capital that can be instrumental in creating collective action. To put it differently, social capital can help to foster collective action because it has the ability to impose certain visions as legitimate in a given social context, despite the fact that it does not represent the heterogeneous preferences existing in the community. We have thus attempted to bring into our model of social capital and collective action the concepts of common knowledge and symbolic power in order to capture the intrinsic political nature of social capital.

At the same time we have argued that standard social capital theory, as it stands, fails in so far as human agency falls into either an "over-socialized" model or an "under-socialized" model; that is, whether an individual becomes

---

[18] This concept was coined by Ferguson (1994), who has analyzed the poverty alleviation policies in Lesotho. He analyzed why these policies were renewed despite their "failures" in reaching their objectives. He argued that "uncompromisingly, reducing poverty to a technical problem, and by promising technical solutions to the suffering of the powerless and oppressed people, the hegemonic problem of 'development' is the principle means through which the problem of poverty is depoliticized in the world today" (ibid: 256).

an automaton that follows the social norms and rules or is a rational agent with stable preferences outside any social structure. We prefer to leave some room for interpretation/misinterpretation and challenge by the alternative discourses and create a space for human agency to play a role. In other words, we argue there exists the possibility of: (1) success in creating collective action, which will give benefits to the dominant group in reproducing the social structure that they dominate; and also (2) failure in its creation, which may lead to the dominant group being challenged and thus for the social structure to change.

In this chapter, we have identified two main processes by which social capital contributes to the creation and the sharing of common knowledge. Here we interpret the common knowledge as an understanding of the preferences of others, which enables agents to act together and to bear the costs and responsibility of collective action. In the face of limited cognitive capacity, such common knowledge needs to be socially constructed by generalizing preferences, in turn represented by symbolic formulae. This has led us to address the question of whose preference should be represented in that common knowledge. We have argued that the process of the creation of common knowledge is not a simple process of averaging out the preferences of all community members. Rather, symbolic power (Bourdieu 1990) plays a key role in the creation of such common knowledge. In this sense, the ability of social capital to create collective action is political in nature (Cleaver 2003; Mosse 2006).

We have also addressed the issue of how common knowledge is shared among community members. By sharing or internalizing common knowledge, the predictability of behavior by other agents is enhanced and the social structure is more likely to remain stable (Sewell 1992). When common knowledge is shared by a majority of the community members who also agree to bear the cost of collective action, collective action can be created. However, since the common knowledge is susceptible to "interpretation failure" and "legitimacy failure," the common knowledge can be challenged and thus collective action may fail, despite the level of social capital in a given society. Also at the end of the chapter, we have discussed some policy implications regarding the relationship between policy and practice.

Finally, we would like to emphasize again the importance of understanding the power relations inside the community when designing a policy of common property management, especially as the dominant groups are not necessarily the primary common property users and the holders of the knowledge about common property management (Agrawal 2001). Moreover, even when the common knowledge is shared among community members, this does not mean that it would provide the efficient amount of collective action or may force the marginalized groups to bear a disproportionate cost of the collective action (Boyce 2007). In the latter case, social capital would serve only the objectives of the powerful, to the detriment of the disadvantaged groups of the community.

After a decade, we concur with Gale (1998) that ecological economics is still lacking a suitable concept of power and in particular a concept of power that incorporates not just the material aspects but the symbolic aspects (Bardhan and Ray 2008). Currently it is mainly sociologists and anthropologists, especially Foucauldians, who discuss power relations and the symbolic aspect of power relations (Ray 2008). They are reluctant to generalize their arguments, which is making it difficult for economists to incorporate these ideas into their theorizing (McNiell 2007). As a result, the literature linking social capital, collective action, and common property may be overly dominated by political scientists and economists who overlook the issue of power (Fine 2001). By bringing the concept of symbolic power into social capital theory, we hope to bring back the contributions of sociologists and anthropologists to the issue of common property management.

While our argument has been limited to common property management and environmental governance at the community level, we do believe that some of the arguments on power relations are also relevant to other aspects of environmental governance issues, especially at the global level, given the hierarchical power relation between developed and developing countries (Hajar 1995; Escobar 1996). We would like to come back to the quote by Bonacich from Swedeberg (2001) that we cited at the beginning of Section 9.2. It is our understanding that we still fundamentally lack communication between the two sister disciplines in the social sciences, which has resulted in a lack of understanding of the relationship between policy and practice. We sincerely hope that our chapter will contribute to such communication and that other authors will continue our endeavor.

10

Global Environmental Problems, Voluntary Action, and Government Intervention

Andries Richter and Daan van Soest

10.1 INTRODUCTION

Climate change, the depletion of (high sea) fisheries, and biodiversity loss rank high on the list of environmental problems the global community is confronted with. Over the past decade these problems have received ample attention in the media (at least in developed countries), and as a result firms and consumers are very much aware of their existence and also—albeit to a varying degree—of the necessity to take mitigating action.

Even if individual agents are well aware of these problems, it is not necessarily the case that they do take protective action. Environmental quality depends on the aggregate behavior of all agents on this planet, while each individual agent's actions have a negligible impact on any of the global environmental problems mentioned above. Indeed, all these problems are classic examples of the so-called "tragedy of the commons," as the benefits of protective actions are enjoyed by everyone, while the costs of taking them are private.

This analysis suggests that without government intervention, the prospects for mitigating or preventing climate change, fisheries depletion, and biodiversity loss are bleak. However, casual observation of the behavior of people around us reveals that many people take at least some protective action. When buying a new electric appliance people do take into account the energy consumption of the various competing brands: energy efficiency and amounts of CO_2 emitted per kilometer driven are among the criteria on the basis of which people choose a new car, and many households voluntarily separate their waste flows for recycling purposes. Also within the business community, the concept of corporate social responsibility receives increasing attention (Khanna 2001).

These examples of private mitigation activities suggest that people are motivated to take protective environmental action even if extrinsic incentives—such as environmental taxes or quota—are absent. This raises two questions. The first is whether or not the amount of action taken is equal to the socially optimal level; and if not, the second question is how government intervention should be designed to bring protective action to its socially optimal level.

The first question is easy to answer—for most environmental problems we cannot rely on the voluntary actions of consumers and firms alone. If we could, these environmental problems would have been solved a long time ago. But the second question is much more relevant, for the following reason. In the standard game-theoretic framework—that is, assuming that all agents are exclusively self-interested—government intervention is always welfare enhancing, as own-profit maximizing agents do not voluntarily contribute to the common good (if there are net costs involved in doing so). However, because we observe that at least some people voluntarily undertake protective action, the possibility arises that government intervention may be countereffective, because it may result in a crowding-out of the agent's intrinsic motivation to voluntarily contribute. And this is what this chapter aims to analyze; under what circumstances does government intervention strengthen ("crowd-in") or weaken ("crowd-out") the regulated agents' intrinsic motivation to act pro-socially, and under what circumstances is the change in behavior permanent?

While the issue of stimulating crowding-in and preventing crowding-out of intrinsic motivation is important in all policy domains, it is especially important when facing global environmental problems like climate change, depletion of large-scale fisheries, and biodiversity loss. These are all examples of environmental problems with many stakeholders (virtually everyone on the planet), and both the benefits and costs of reducing the problem are substantial. Typically, benefits and costs are distributed unevenly across countries and citizens, which makes striking international agreements very difficult (Finus 2008). In general, governments are unwilling to impose large costs on their citizens (Nordhaus and Yang 1996), and hence regulations are unlikely to be very strict, in spite of the fact that most citizens perceive these to be serious problems. Due to this problem-awareness, citizens are willing to undertake voluntary actions to solve large-scale problems, such as sustain the global climate (Milinski et al. 2006, 2008). The combination of a high willingness to solve a problem voluntarily and rather mild government regulations are the circumstances under which crowding-out is most likely to occur, and hence analyzing how crowding-out can be prevented is especially important in these global commons problems.

The set-up of this chapter is as follows. In Section 10.2 we provide an overview of the economic and psychological literature on the interaction between formal government intervention and the regulated agents' intrinsic motivation to contribute, resulting in either crowding-in or -out. In Section 10.3 we turn to examples of crowding-out in (real-world) environmental problems. Having established that crowding-out is observed to occur in the real world, we analyze how this is related to the institutional setting, and we do so in Section 10.4. In Section 10.5 we identify the factors that may lead to crowding-out. Section 10.6 shows how these factors affect formal and informal institutions. The corresponding policy recommendations are provided in Section 10.7, and finally Section 10.8 concludes.

10.2 INTRINSIC MOTIVATION AND CROWDING-OUT

One is said to be intrinsically motivated to perform an activity when one receives no apparent reward except the activity itself (Deci 1971). Employees in firms may not be just motivated to work hard to capture incentive payments; they also take pride in their work. In a similar vein, people are willing to abstain from certain activities that are harmful to their environment, even if the private returns to these activities are negative (think of voluntarily reducing the amount of waste produced by one's household, which requires effort to search for environmentally friendly products that are, in many cases, more expensive than other products).[1] The intrinsic motivation to contribute to the provision of public goods (like reducing one's emissions of greenhouse gases, or purchasing sustainably produced tropical hardwoods to prevent species extinction) may arise because of moral considerations (Ayala 2010) or because of a sense of fulfillment of having contributed to something constructive (cf. Ariely et al. 2008 for experimental evidence on this).[2]

The reason why the introduction of extrinsic incentives does not always result in increased provision of public goods is because the extrinsic reward may negatively affect an individual's intrinsic motivation "to do the good." This is best illustrated using Figure 10.1. In this figure, an agent's contribution to a public good is measured along the horizontal axis, while the vertical axis reflects the incentives provided by the government to induce the agent to act

---

[1] Clearly, the extent to which people are willing to voluntarily contribute to a specific public good varies with its characteristics, such as the amount of private benefits the good provides, how costly it is to contribute to its provision, the number of stakeholders involved, whether the benefits and costs of the good are distributed uniformly over the stakeholders or highly unevenly, etc. For an overview, see Barrett (2007b) and E. Ostrom (2003).

[2] The utility derived from the process of contributing to something constructive is closely related to the idea that people may derive a "warm glow" from contributing to public goods, expressing a positive willingness to pay for projects in valuation studies. That these preferences should be taken seriously is forcibly argued in Chapter 11 by Nunes and Onofri in Part III of this volume.

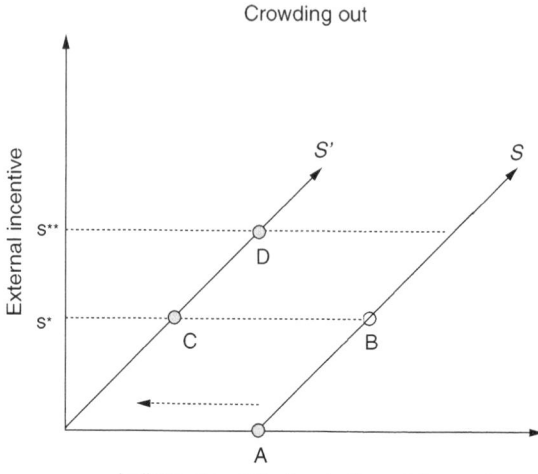

Figure 10.1. The concept of crowding-out

cooperatively (a subsidy per unit of contribution to the public good, or a tax per unit of pollution generated). If the agent is intrinsically motivated to contribute to the public good, her contributions will be non-zero even if there are no incentives provided by the government to do so. Suppose that this contribution level is equal to point A in Figure 10.1. Now the standard line of reasoning in economics would be: "We do not know why the agent provides a non-zero contribution to the public good, but if the government provides incentives (in the form of a subsidy or a tax), the stimulus for the agent to contribute is larger and hence contributions will go up" (see also E. Ostrom 2000b). Assuming that the agent's contribution schedule is stable, the policy maker would expect that contributions would be increased to point B if the incentive (on the vertical axis) is set equal to, for example, s^*.

However, the assumption of a stable contribution schedule is often not met in practice. External intervention may crowd-out the intrinsic motivation to contribute, resulting in a leftward shift of the individual's contribution schedule from S to, for example, S'. If so, setting the incentive equal to s^* would result in contributions ending up in point C rather than in point B. The monetary incentive itself increases the marginal cost of shirking and/or increases the marginal benefit of good provision, but this does not only result in a movement along the original contribution schedule (from A to B), but also in a leftward shift to point C. Hence, crowding-out occurs because external incentives are not separable from intrinsic motivation (Bowles 2008).

This simple figure suggests two things. First, government intervention is effective if the incentive is sufficiently strong, but it may be countereffective if the external incentive is too small (see also Frey 1997, and Nyborg and Rege

2003). In our example, introducing s* results in contributions falling from A to C, but if s ≥ s**, contributions end up in D, or better. This implies that the issue of preventing the crowding-out of intrinsic motivation is of special importance in cases of global environmental problems—as argued in the introduction. Absent any international agreements effectively addressing the issues of climate change, species extinction and fisheries depletion in the oceans, governments may still decide to unilaterally implement policies—but they will necessarily be less stringent or encompassing than if proper international agreements were in place. For example, emissions of CO_2 may be taxed at about 15 euro per ton (the current price at which tons of CO_2 are traded on the European Trading System), while a nonnegligible share of the currently available global damage estimates 80 euro or higher (Tol 2008). If the tax rate imposed is too low to counteract a possible leftward shift of the "emission reduction supply schedule," the government's unilateral intervention may even be countereffective. And the same holds for possible interventions regarding trade in tropical hardwoods (to reduce the rate of species extinction) or regarding the consumption of high sea fish species.

The second conclusion is that it is probably cheaper to use policy instruments that preserve the agent's intrinsic motivation to contribute; when preserving the agent's intrinsic motivation, the same level of contributions can be achieved at much lower costs. This is because (1) the loss of intrinsic motivation constitutes a direct decrease in utility; and (2) the enforcement costs are likely to be an increasing function of the level of stimulus provided.[3] And clearly government intervention would be even more effective if it were able to crowd-*in* the agent's intrinsic motivation to contribute, inducing her supply curve *S* to shift to the right. Hence, governments should be interested in finding out which policy instruments are likely to result in crowding-out, and which are able to increase contributions by strengthening the agent's intrinsic motivation to contribute.

According to psychologists, crowding-out is likely to occur if external intervention is perceived to reduce people's self-determination and/or their self-esteem because they feel that their involvement and competence is not appreciated (Frey and Jegen 2001: 8). But the extent to which crowding-out occurs in actual practice is hard to establish because of the many confounding factors. Kreps (1997) gives the example of the difficulty of identifying the existence of intrinsic motivation in the workplace. Employees may work long hours because they take pride in their work, but also because they respond to

---

[3] Note that this is even the case if the stimulus is provided in the form of taxes. For the same level of monitoring, higher taxes make tax evasion more profitable and hence enforcement needs to be increased. This is a welfare cost, while the tax revenues themselves are a transfer from the agent to the government, and hence do not constitute a welfare gain.

fuzzy extrinsic motivators, including fear of discharge, scrutiny by fellow employees, or even the desire for their coworkers' esteem.

Whereas strong empirical support of the crowding-out theory is hard to find, anecdotal evidence abounds. Children are willing to mow the lawn, but after they have been paid once to do it, they are only willing to do it again if they receive monetary compensation (Deci 1971). The pharmaceutical company Merck decided to invest in developed an unprofitable drug against river blindness in order to increase its workforce's intrinsic motivation for research (Murdock 2002). Imposing a fine on parents arriving late to collect their children at day care increased the number of late-coming parents (Gneezy and Rustichini 2000a). Small honoraria for seminar speakers may increase the probability of them declining the invitation (Gneezy and Rustichini 2000b). Unit pricing of unsorted waste does not necessarily result in a substantial increase in the amount of material offered for recycling (Ackerman 1997; Berglund 2006). Survey results suggest that people may actually decrease their contribution to voluntary work if a fee for non-participation is introduced (Brekke et al. 2003). Opposition against the implementation of "not in my backyard" (NIMBY) projects may increase when monetary compensation is offered to the local community. An example is the case with a mid-level radioactive nuclear waste repository in Switzerland (Frey et al. 1996; Frey and Oberholzer-Gee 1997).

10.3 CROWDING-OUT IN ENVIRONMENTAL PROBLEMS

As Kreps (1997) argues, "abundant smoke signifies a fire, and the assertion is too strongly rooted in folk wisdom to be entirely hot air." While monetary incentives do not crowd-out intrinsic motivation per se (Cameron and Pierce 1994), it is by now well established it can happen for a wide range of conditions (Deci et al., 1999, 2001; Frey and Jegen, 2001; Gintis et al., 2005; E. Ostrom, 2005a; Frey and Stutzer, 2006; Bowles, 2008; Vollan, 2008).

However, this list of instances of crowding-out raises two questions. The first question concerns the circumstances under which crowding-out is observed to take place. The examples presented are of a parent who wants his lawn mowed by his child, a boss of a firm who wants a project to be implemented, an owner of a day-care centre who wants to induce the parents to pick up their children on time, etc. These are all examples of so-called principal–agent problems, where the principal has certain objectives for which she is dependent on the efforts of someone else (the agent) to have them achieved. In these situations the interests of the principal and the agent do not completely coincide. So how does this relate to environmental problems where there is not just one principal to be "served," but a larger group—or even society? Indeed, failing to take protective action in environmental problems results in damages accruing to a large and diverse group of agents (citizens, firms, or consumers) as is the case with, for example, overharvesting of fisheries, failing to invest in water capture in arid regions, destroying biodiversity by converting forests into arable land, and the use of fossil fuels contributing to global warming. These environmental problems have in common that all the agents involved would be better off if they collectively undertook protective action, but given that all others do so, it is in each agent's private interest not to do it. In that sense, they are all examples of social dilemmas where the objective functions of individuals and society are not perfectly aligned—see below. The second question regarding the examples presented refers to the temporal nature of the change in motivation: if crowding-out occurs, is this change permanent and (largely) irreversible, or is it just transitory?

Before addressing the issue of whether crowding-out may occur in (global) environmental problems too, we investigate whether social interaction in multiplayer social dilemma situations is properly described by the neoclassical assumption of selfish actors. Here, social dilemmas are situations in which actions that maximize the sum of payoffs of all stakeholders do not coincide with the actions that maximize the payoffs of an individual agent, and vice versa. Hence, in a social dilemma the social and private objectives are not perfectly aligned. Consider the fishery. After every fishing trip, the agent pockets the sales revenues of his harvests, but he bears only part of the costs. When catching a fish one does not only remove that fish from the pond or sea, but also all the offspring generated by that fish. If all fishermen decided to catch fewer fish, more offspring would be produced and all fishermen would be better off. However, given that all other fishermen restrained their fishing effort, each individual fisherman would profit from increasing his fishing effort. And similar considerations apply to other environmental problems such as global warming and biodiversity loss.[4]

Whether or not agents are willing to voluntarily contribute to a public good is often difficult to observe in practice. Data on individual harvests or catch, for example, are hard to obtain, and also it is difficult to establish what baseline level to compare actual harvests with. One more easily observable act of

---

[4] While the term "crowding-out" typically refers to government interventions reducing *individual* agents' motivation to contribute to public goods directly, it can also refer to the situation where the self-regulatory capacity of a *community* is negatively affected. Indeed, even if not all members of a community contribute to the (local) public good, some may decide to form a coalition to enhance its provision; see van Soest et al. (2010). In that setting, the policy issue is how to design government interventions that strengthen, rather than weaken, the self-regulatory capacity of the community. For an analysis of coalition formation regarding climate change and biodiversity conservation, see Chapter 7 by Bréchet and Eyckmans in Part II of this volume.

voluntary cooperation is agents' propensity to discipline their peers. For example, Brazilian fishermen in the Bahia region destroy the nets of fellow fishermen who do not respect the catch quotas (Cordell and McKean 1992). Sanctioning one's peers is an example of a second-order public good provision because there are often—hidden—costs associated with imposing punishments (e.g. because one exposes oneself to retaliation) while—if effective—the benefits of the punished individual restraining his fishing effort level accrues to all individuals having access to the fishery. When agents impose punishments on their peers to improve public good provision, they offer a benefit to the rest of the group while they themselves incur a personal cost. Hence, disciplining one's peers is a second-order public good.

Because it is hard to establish to what extent observed pro-social behavior is the result of intrinsic motivation or of other considerations (including the threat of social punishment or the presence of hidden rewards), economists and psychologists alike have studied this behavior by means of controlled experiments. In social laboratory experiments subjects are confronted with a (computerized) game that captures the essence of the decision problem the researcher wants to analyze (such as the fishery problem described above). Subjects are induced to think carefully about how to behave as decisions have actual financial consequences. The propensity of humans to act cooperatively has, among others, been studied in Public Goods (PG) games and in Common-Pool Resource (CPR) games. In both games the costs of contributing to the common good is larger than the private benefits but smaller than the resulting increase in aggregate payoffs (i.e. the sum of the payoffs of all group members). In the PG game the decision to be made is how much to contribute to a public good, where the associated benefits accrue to all members of the group. In the CPR game subjects need to decide whether they are willing to put in less than the privately optimal amount of harvesting effort in order to reduce the negative consequences of their catch on the payoffs of their peers. It is easy to see that homo economicus would act non-cooperatively, deciding not to contribute to the public good in the PG game and choosing the privately optimal extraction effort level in the CPR game. This prediction also holds in cases of multiple rounds of interaction as long as the number of periods for which the game is played is finite (and subjects are informed about this). In such a finitely repeated setting, there is no reason to "invest" in trying to maintain cooperation in the last round (because there are no future decisions to be affected), and hence also not in the round before that (because there will be zero cooperation in the last round anyway). But that means that there is no reason to invest in maintaining cooperation in the second-but-last round either, and hence, on the basis of backward induction, the conclusion is that it does not pay to invest in even the first round. The typical pattern that emerges when PG games and CPR games are played over multiple rounds is that cooperation declines quite steeply over time (see, for example, E. Ostrom et al. 1992; Fehr and Gächter 2000; Gächter et al. 2008). This pattern emerges if university students are used as subjects, but it is also observed with a wide variety of other subject pools too. This suggests that humans are willing to act cooperatively, but that defection by others results in cooperation declining over time.

Interestingly, both Fehr and Gächter (2000) and E. Ostrom et al. (1992) also implemented treatments in which subjects can punish their peers for acting non-cooperatively. In these treatments, each round consists of two stages. The first is the "social dilemma stage" as described above (i.e. modeled in the form of either a PG game or a CPR game), and the second is the sanctioning stage. In the latter stage, subjects can decrease the payoffs of any of their peers at positive costs to themselves. Game theory predicts that sanctioning would never occur because of a backward induction argument very similar to the one above. In the last period there is no reason to sanction because the punisher incurs costs while it is impossible to affect the punished individual's behavior because the game ends. Hence there is no incentive to act cooperatively in the first stage (the social dilemma stage) of the last round either. That means that there is no reason to punish one's peers in the second stage (the punishment stage) of the one-but-last round, which implies that there is also no incentive to act cooperatively in the first stage (the social dilemma stage) of that one-but-last round. Continuing reasoning backwards, the standard assumption of players being purely selfish results in the prediction that there will be zero contributions to the common good and also no sanctioning in any of the rounds the game lasts. The experimental evidence gathered by E. Ostrom et al. (1992) and Fehr and Gächter (2000), however, refute these predictions. Punishments do take place, and the threat of being sanctioned raises the level of cooperation almost to the level that maximizes group payoff. And similar results are found when self-regulation is by means of rewards (as opposed to punishments), although the results tend to be a little less strong (Vyrastekova and van Soest 2008).

Given that humans (fishermen in the real world, student subjects in controlled economic experiments) act more cooperatively than predicted by standard economic theory, the question is to what extent formal government intervention can be counterproductive by crowding-out the regulated agents' propensity to cooperate voluntarily. In the environmental economics literature several cases have been documented of crowding-out occurring in environmental problems. One of the earliest examples is by Anderson and Lee (1986: 690), who observe that "the suggestion that policies be implemented assuming that people will not comply with them has the potential for eroding social capital which depends on respect for the law." This claim has been corroborated by, among others, Hatcher et al. (2000) and Sutinen and Kuperan (1999).

A second example of formal rules crowding-out informal norms is provided by Cárdenas et al. (2000). In this study experiments were run with people in rural Colombia who are confronted with a common-pool problem in their daily life. The game used by Cárdenas et al. was a CPR game in which subjects were asked to decide how much timber to extract from a forest. The scenario presented was that harvesting had an adverse effect on water quality (as is actually the case in the study region), posing a cost on everyone in the group. The game was first played without any regulations, while at a later stage an extraction norm was introduced that was enforced by a mild probabilistic fine. Cárdenas et al. (2000) find that subjects reduce their extraction level after the regulation is introduced, but start extracting more aggressively after realizing that consequences are rather mild. Strikingly, in the last rounds, extraction levels were higher with the regulation than without. As a result, payoffs are significantly lower when individuals are confronted with a formal rule than in its absence; the weak official rule interacted with the internal norms of the subjects and crowded-out their intrinsic motivation to cooperate. Therefore, it can be seen as a warning towards indiscriminately introducing regulatory intervention without a proper understanding of how it might undermine norms already operating in the field.

These examples suggest that crowding-out can occur in multiperson environmental problems too, but the studies presented above do not answer the question whether crowding-out is likely to be permanent or just transitory. Some evidence on the issue of the irreversibility of crowding-out is available from Bouma et al. (2008). This study addresses the issue of farmers' propensity to invest in the construction (as well as the maintenance) of soil and water conservation structures. The study sites were five villages in three different watersheds in (predominantly arid) rural India. Investments in soil and water conservation structures (as well as in their maintenance) provide private and public benefits, and one can hypothesize that the same set of factors determines whether households invest in the structures themselves, or whether they put effort into maintaining them. In practice there is a crucial difference between the two activities, though. The investments themselves are highly subsidized (either by government organizations or by NGOs), whereas the maintenance activities are not. As expected, the households' propensity to invest depends on the extent to which they are dependent on income from agriculture, on the size of their land holdings, etc. Interestingly, the authors found that the decision to invest also depends on the community's amount of social capital. To measure social capital the authors use several proxies, including social homogeneity (as given by the relative size of the largest caste in the community), but social capital was also quantified by having villagers participate in a simple game, a so-called

Trust game. This game is played by two players and is set up as follows. The player that moves first, the investor, has to decide how to allocate an amount of money between him-/herself and the second mover, the trustee. The investor can keep all money, give the total amount to the trustee, or anything in between. The amount of money sent—if any—is tripled by the experimenter, and given to the trustee. The trustee then has to decide how to divide the amount received between him-/herself and the first mover, the investor. The trustee can keep all the money, give the total amount to the trustee, or anything in between.

Behavior in the Trust game is expected to reflect social capital because the standard game theoretic prediction is that the investor will not send any money. The reason is that the trustee will not give back any money if he/she is purely selfish, and hence the investor will pocket the investment fund him-/herself. The Trust game therefore provides two measures of social capital—trust/altruism as measured by the amount sent by the investor, and altruism/reciprocity as measured by the share returned by the trustee; see also Cox (2004).

Bouma et al. (2008) use straightforward regression analysis to analyze the villagers' propensity to invest in soil and water structures themselves, as well as in their maintenance. Explanatory variables include the various measures of social capital (social homogeneity, amount sent, and share returned) as well as a large vector of subject-specific and village-specific control variables. In the results of the regression explaining the villagers' propensity to invest in the structures themselves, only variables that reflect private stakes are significant (per capita land holdings, household size) and none of the "social capital" variables. In contrast, the "social capital" ones are the most significant variables explaining the propensity to undertake maintenance activities. This is salient because the former investment activities are subsidized, whereas the latter maintenance activities are not. Interestingly, the probability of a household contributing decreases substantially if there are maintenance funds that support material costs but that do not compensate individual effort.

These results reflect two things. First, it seems that the formal intervention by the government organizations and NGOs crowded-out the households' propensity to voluntarily contribute to a public good—given that social capital indeed matters, as evidenced by its role in the maintenance activities. Second, it is noteworthy that this crowding-out in the investment phase did not spill over to maintenance activities, suggesting that crowding-out may be highly context-specific, but also does not result in permanent crowding-out (as the maintenance activities obviously took place after the investments in the structures had been made).

10.4 CROWDING-OUT AND THE DESIGN OF ENVIRONMENTAL POLICIES

Having established that indeed formal intervention may be counterproductive in terms of resource conservation objectives, the question arises whether government policies can be designed such that formal and informal institutions are mutually reinforcing. It seems that three institutional characteristics are especially important: (1) the extent to which the external intervention is perceived to be legitimate and adequate (or proportional); (2) the extent to which participation is voluntary; and (3) to what extent the institution is perceived to be supportive (rather than restrictive).

When an institution is perceived to be legitimate and fair, participants are much more inclined to obey the rules (Frey 1997: ch.6). A striking example supporting this finding comes from Danish fisheries, where "fishers feel they are taken hostage by an illegitimate management system, and thus feel it is morally correct not to comply" (Raakjær and Mathiesen 2003). Somanathan (1991) describes how state intervention in Central Himalaya "directly weakened villagers' incentives to allow regeneration and conserve forests." As a result, a well-functioning informal system based on social arrangements was crowded-out. Similar phenomena can be observed in many African societies (Vatn 2007). This raises the question how legitimacy can be achieved. Sometimes it seems to be enough to convince the individuals about the usefulness of the rule and that obeying it is in everyone's interest (Rodriguez-Sickert et al. 2008). Reeson and Tisdell (2008), however, found that moral persuasion does indeed promote cooperation, but only in the very short run.

One way to achieve legitimacy is involving stakeholders in the process of designing formal institutions (Jentoft et al. 1998; Hatcher et al. 2000; Dankel 2009). This does not only include the set-up of the monitoring and enforcement mechanisms, but also the way in which the benefits and costs of the institution's interventions are allocated between all stakeholders (see also chapter 6 by Groom, Gatti, Goeschl, and Swanson in Part II of this book). Such a participatory approach may build trust between users themselves, but also between users and central authorities. This may crowd-in stewardship motives, and increase compliance. This form of co-management has the additional advantage that stakeholders possess important knowledge which may help to craft better institutions (Jentoft et al. 1998). An active dialogue between stakeholders and decision makers can also help to identify and overcome potential conflicts of objectives and stakeholders (Dankel 2009). Many economists are somewhat skeptical about involving stakeholders too closely in the process of designing institutions, as it gives them the possibility to seek rents (Johnson and Libecap 1982; Bergland et al. 2002). This is indeed problematic, especially when stakeholders differ in the amount of resources they have to lobby for their interests. In many cases, the voices that shout loudest are most heard (Hatchard, 2005). One could overcome this by making stakeholders more responsible and accountable (Mikalsen and Jentoft 2008). This is especially necessary when the local users value various aspects of the environment differently than society does. For example, local users may be interested in having a well-functioning ecosystem (which ensures income in the future), while they do not necessarily care about biodiversity as such.

Regarding this, several economic experiments have been conducted to test whether user participation does indeed increase the effectiveness of the institution under consideration; that is, does it mitigate the extent to which agents' intrinsic motivation are being crowded-out? In a laboratory setting, this can be tested by allowing regulated subjects to vote on the details of the enforcement institution's design, and subsequently compare their behavior in the social dilemma activity to the behavior of agents participating in a treatment in which regulation is exogenously imposed. Voting serves a dual purpose. First, the voting outcome (e.g. based on a majority voting rule) affects the design of the institution, and hence its direct effectiveness. But voting outcomes also provide information about the intentions and preferences of the community's majority to effectively protect the resource and to maximize group payoff (as opposed to trying to non-cooperatively maximize one's individual payoff). Therefore, in voting experiments we can observe whether a group of people is able to find consensus on designing effective institutions, but also whether voting itself affects the compliance of the institution that has been agreed upon.

Sutter and Weck-Hannemann (2004) provide an example where a failure to obtain majority agreement for the socially optimal action is detrimental to social welfare, as behavior in the social dilemma activity becomes significantly less cooperative. In their experimental study, subjects have the possibility to vote on a minimum contribution level to a public good, upon which they make their decisions about how much to contribute. When the group fails to achieve a majority vote in favor of the rule, contributions are significantly lower than in the treatment without. This makes intuitive sense because even though there are no binding rules in either treatment, a failure to reach consensus reveals information about the lack of cooperativeness of the co-players.

Obviously, the consequences of not achieving a majority vote are even more detrimental if the voting outcome results in the abolishment of formal institutions, as is uncovered by Tyran and Feld (2006). In this study, subjects can vote on the level of a (deterministic) sanction in a public goods environment. As is the case in Sutter and Weck-Hannemann (2004), subjects tend to contribute significantly less (more) when the majority vote is against (in favor of) the presence of an enforcement institution empowered to impose fines on those who contribute less than a certain level.

Having established that introducing voting with respect to details of the enforcement institution's design can either improve or reduce welfare and conservation, depending on the voting outcome (directly via the change in the institution, but also indirectly by crowding-in voters' intrinsic motivation to contribute to the common good), the question arises what factors determine voting behavior. Vyrastekova and van Soest try to answer this question in two related papers (Vyrastekova and van Soest 2003 and van Soest and Vyrastekova 2008). In these two papers, subjects were allowed to vote on whether the enforcement institution should be provided with sufficient incentives to actively sanction excessive extraction, or not. More specifically, one subject was assigned to take the role as policy enforcer. The other subjects voted on whether or not the subject representing the enforcement institution was allowed to keep the fine revenues. If a majority voted against this, any collected fines were removed from the game. In this case, the enforcer is not expected to actively impose fines when observing violations of the formal rule because there are fixed costs associated with punishing. In this setting the weakly dominant strategy is to vote in favor of the enforcer receiving the fine revenues. In Vyrastekova and van Soest (2003) two treatments were compared. In the first treatment, the policy enforcer always received the revenues of her sanctioning activity (i.e. the fines imposed on those resource users who extracted more than was prescribed by a rule). In the other treatment, the enforcer was only allowed to keep the fines if the majority voted in favor of this, as described above. Vyrastekova and van Soest find support for the hypothesis that voting actually improves efficiency of resource use, as compared to the treatment in which incentives are assigned exogenously. Casting their vote serves as a means for resource users to communicate their stance with respect to the need for reduced aggregate extraction. Conditional on a majority having voted in favor of implementing an appropriate incentive structure, extraction behavior was significantly more cooperative in the voting treatment (i.e. much closer to the level that maximizes group welfare) than in the treatment where the enforcer is always allowed to pocket the fine revenues. Hence, allowing subjects to vote on the regulatory regime crowds-in their propensity to act cooperatively.

In a companion paper, van Soest and Vyrastekova (2008) analyzed to what extent actual voting outcomes depended on the characteristics of the enforcement institution. The specific characteristic they focused on was the probability that when engaging in enforcement, the institution is indeed able to successfully impose fines. Keeping the expected fine constant, they compared the impact of a 50 percent chance of conviction (and a specific fine level) on voting behavior to that in the case of a 90 percent chance of conviction (and a lower fine level). In both cases, the weakly dominant strategy was to always vote in favor of the enforcer receiving the fine revenues, because of the arguments given above. Van Soest and Vyrastekova actually found marked differences between the 50 percent and 90 percent probability treatments. Whereas in the latter treatment resource users almost always voted in favor of the enforcer receiving the fines, a favorable majority voting outcome was achieved in less than 40 percent of the cases in the former treatment.

These results are striking as they imply that trying to save on enforcement costs by reducing the probability of conviction (with a concomitant increase in the fine level such that the expected fine is kept constant) is hazardous if the enforcement institution's effectiveness is at least to some extent dependent on the support of the regulated individuals. If the intervention is insufficiently effective, intrinsic motivation to contribute to the public good is reduced and the regulated agents decide to vote against the government regulation. These findings suggest that individuals will not support an institution that is perceived to be unfair. A similar study has been undertaken by Kosfeld et al. (2009), where individuals could choose to become a member of a sanctioning institution. The authors show formally that a likely equilibrium outcome will be that such an institution is formed, resulting in increased efficiency. These findings have been corroborated in an experimental setting. This study showed that institution formation can be an effective tool for solving a social dilemma, but fairness issues can be serious obstacles, confirming the results obtained by van Soest and Vyrastekova (2008).

An interesting case arises when individuals can communicate with their peers regarding what they perceive to be appropriate behavior. An experimental regularity is that communication alone is often sufficient to promote cooperation, even if any agreements made are non-binding. In many instances the social pressure arising from "cheap talk" is more effective in correcting behavior than a fine that could serve as a price. Even more surprising is the fact that voluntary participation can foster cooperation even without social pressure. Di Falco and van Rensburg (2008) analyzed the effect of governmental subsidies on livestock farmers in Ireland. Farmers receive livestock premiums based on the number of cattle, but they can choose to sign up for a rural environmental protection scheme (REPS) as well. The authors analyzed the effect of both payments on cooperation, but also on conservation effort. While the livestock premiums had no effect on cooperation and a negative effect on conservation, the payments from REPS lead to more cooperation and higher conservation effort. This is remarkable, as encouraging cooperation is not an explicit aim of REPS. An open question remains whether the voluntary nature of the program makes users more cooperative, or just attracts users that have more cooperative attitudes. While it is well established that there are important feedbacks between institutions, preferences, and economic outcomes, further research is needed to identify the causal relationships between those elements.

10.5 THE THEORETICAL FOUNDATIONS OF CROWDING-OUT

In the previous section we have documented that the occurrence of crowding-out is determined by (1) the legitimacy of the institution and the level of involvement of the individuals; (2) the voluntary nature of it; and (3) the enforcement structure. While these are all properties of an institution, the mechanisms behind crowding-out must be identified at the individual level. Microeconomic models that assume agents to be exclusively motivated by material interests are undoubtedly very useful, but they are not necessarily capable of describing the behavior of the average person, who is concerned about her identity, embedded in social structures, and equipped with a moral compass. Even worse, "policies designed for self-interested citizens may undermine the moral sentiments," as Samuel Bowles (2008) has pointed out. Therefore, formal models of moral motivation help us to understand the interactions between extrinsic and intrinsic motivations, while taking into account the corresponding feedbacks between the individual and the institution.

The fact that voluntary contributions to public goods are so omnipresent suggests that individuals derive some benefit from it. This raises the question whether people care about the public good itself or whether they enjoy the act of giving. The first is sometimes referred to as "pure" or output-oriented altruism, while the second is referred to as "impure" or action-oriented altruism (Francois and Vlassopoulos 2008). This form of altruism is "impure" because it is not the result that makes people happy, but the act of giving itself (see also the discussion of "warm glow" in Chapter 11 by Nunes and Onofri in Part III of this volume). Whether this makes the deed less altruistic is part of a lively ongoing debate,[5] and may explain why some people find the term "altruistic" misleading and prefer to use terms like pro-social or other-regarding behavior.

Behavior is always the result of preferences and beliefs, embedded in certain institutions (Bowles 2003). One way to account for pro-social behavior is to assume that agents have "social preferences," such as inequity aversion or care about the payoff of other people in general (Fehr and Fischbacher 2002). Some authors have criticized that explaining social behavior with social preferences is a tautology (see, for example, Baland and Platteau 1996: ch 6). This is certainly a valid concern for any model with a limited strategy space and does, of course, also apply to models of moral constraints—if the researcher imposes them, it is

---

[5] This is nicely illustrated in the American sitcom "Friends," in the following conversation between Joey and Phoebe. Joey: Look, there's no unselfish good deeds, sorry. Phoebe: Yes there are! There are totally good deeds that are selfless. Joey: Well, may I ask for one example? Phoebe: Yeah, it's . . . Y'know there's . . . no you may not! (Friends, Season 5, Episode 4).

no surprise that model outcomes reflect "moral behavior." One could overcome this problem by developing very flexible models that allow for a whole array of strategies, such as pro- or anti-social preferences. Nyborg and Rege (2003) analyze how different models of moral motivation, based on altruism, social norms, fairness considerations, and conditional cooperation can explain crowding-out. In the literature several mechanisms have been suggested that give rise to crowding-out (Bowles 2008). First, a loss of self-determination triggers some loss of motivation. We hypothesize that this is linked to the fact that humans may undertake voluntary action to signal their pro-social stance and trustworthiness. Second, incentives convey information which changes the beliefs, and hence, the choices of an agent. And finally, incentives change the context frame of a decision or trigger a complete preference change. Let us discuss each of them in more detail.

10.5.1 Crowding-out and costly signals

Costly signaling theory suggests that behavior which seemingly fails the cost–benefit test occurs because such behavior conveys reliable information from the sender to the receiver. Contributing to the "common good" can improve one's reputation in the community (or one's social status), which may yield future benefits. In this view acting pro-socially is an investment in one's reputation or self-image, which can be profitable because it gives cooperative individuals the possibility to identify each other in social interactions, thus avoiding being exploited by non-cooperators. Trust plays a crucial role in economic exchange (Fehr 2009), and one's contributions to public goods can be interpreted as a signal that the person is likely to be trustworthy in bilateral exchange situations too. Dynamic models have been developed that show that investing in one's reputation or self-image can enhance one's long-term payoff and hence contributing to the common good can be rational after all (Nowak and Sigmund 1998; Gintis et al. 2001; Brandt and Sigmund 2005).

Costly signals have been attributed to crowding-out before, though often implicitly as impaired expression possibility (Frey 1997), but also explicitly (Posner 2000a, 2000b; Smith and Bird 2005). When this signal gets blurred one may as well stop investing in it. This can be illustrated with a simple example. Consider a population that consists of three types of people: pure altruists, "strategic altruists" and selfish individuals. In society, being an altruist is perceived to be a good thing, and it leads to a good reputation or high social status (at least within the group of the altruistically minded individuals). The pure altruists care only about the result—that is, the public good—but not about the social consequences, while selfish individuals are purely financially motivated. Strategic altruists contribute to the public good when it leads to higher social status and reputation. When no material incentives are attached to the provision of a public good, the selfish would free-ride, while the pure and strategic altruists would contribute. When a material incentive is introduced, the selfish increase their contributions. This implies that altruists can no longer be distinguished from selfish individuals. This could be one reason for the strategic altruists, who are concerned about their reputation, to stop signaling their good intentions. The same would occur if, more realistically, individual preferences are determined by material interest, altruistic motivations, and reputational or self-image concerns. Bénabou and Tirole (2006) have shown formally how such a model can explain several aspects of crowding-out. These theoretical predictions have been confirmed not only in laboratory settings, but also in a field experiment: a financial incentive increases the willingness to contribute to a good cause in private (i.e. when nobody is watching), while it actually decreases contributions in public when it is an observable signal (Ariely et al. 2009).

In reality, the benefits from a good self-image are not constant, but more realistically depend on the composition of the population. Janssen and Mendys–Kamphorst (2004) modeled a situation where individuals are either altruists or egoists and choose whether to contribute to a public good. Social rewards depend positively on the number of contributing cooperators and negatively on the number of selfish people. A financial incentive for contributing induces more selfish people to contribute and hence lowers the social reward for altruists. As a result, altruists may cease contributing and aggregate provision may decrease.

10.5.2 Crowding-out and beliefs

The information content of an incentive is related to beliefs, which have often been attributed to the crowding-out phenomenon. This is especially the case in traditional principal–agent settings, where contracts are usually incomplete, and an extrinsic reward or control could change the perceived nature of the task. One reason for this to occur is that the reward reveals that the task requires much more effort or is much less fun than previously thought (Bénabou and Tirole 2003). Therefore, beliefs play a big role in explaining crowding-out in bilateral interactions, and it is possible to extend this line of reasoning to the delivery of public goods. In most societies there is much debate on the scope of civic duties and therefore people may update regularly what they are expected to do as committed citizens. If one receives payment for donating blood one may infer that it is something one is not expected to do by default. Scientists, politicians, or celebrities may accept an invitation to give a talk without any compensation, but after having received a honorarium a couple of times, they may think twice about whether or not to give a free talk. Brekke et al. (2003) have developed a model in which utility depends on leisure, the consumption of a private good, the consumption of a public good, and a self-image as a socially responsible person (given by how actions deviate from some socially desired effort level). A sufficient extrinsic incentive will make individuals feel that they are no longer morally obliged to contribute, and hence contributions may go down if the unit value of leisure is higher than the unit value of private consumption.

In certain cases, beliefs are linked to the pro-social signals described in subsection 10.5.1. If people are conditionally cooperative, not trusting reveals information about the expected share of selfish individuals in the population, making conditional cooperators not cooperate (Sliwka 2007). In a similar vein, Ellingsen and Johannesson (2008) show how crowding-out can easily occur in bilateral interactions, where players are either altruistic or selfish. Utility depends on material payoffs and on the warm glow from giving, but also on how actions are perceived by the others. Actions depend on one's own preferences, on one's beliefs about the preferences of the persons one is matched with, and on their observed prior actions. A key mechanism is that one obtains a higher utility by being nice to a good person (i.e. an altruist), and hence signaling to be an altruist may pay back.

10.5.3　Crowding-out and context-dependent preferences

In many situations behavior is observed to be context-dependent and takes place in a "decision frame" that "is controlled partly by the formulation of the problem and partly by the norms, habits, and personal characteristics of the decision maker" (Tversky and Kahneman 1981). Evidence from social experiments and the field suggests that many social preferences are conditional (Cox et al., 2008; Fischbacher et al. 2001). For this reason many people play fair only as long as the opponent reciprocates. More generally, preferences depend on the situation the agent faces and also on the process that has led to the situation (Bowles 2003). Situation-dependent preferences are not unique for social preferences, as choices are always the result of given preferences in a certain environment. Process-regarding preferences, however, are special in the sense that they do not depend only on the outcome, but also on the chain of events that led to this outcome (Ben-Ner and Putterman 1998). People may be reluctant to help someone who took some foolish decisions that brought him into trouble while they do help someone who was just extremely unlucky or unfortunate. Thus, one may conclude that preferences are higher-dimensional.

While many studies draw attention to the multidimensional nature of preferences verbally, they are hardly used in formal analyses, as the results may be rather complex. Assuming preferences to be higher-dimensional implies that the corresponding equilibria are higher-dimensional as well.

When an individual stops cooperating, we may be inclined to detect a preference change. This may be the correct inference in some cases, but not in all. An alternative explanation is that preferences are stable but the environmental context has changed, thus resulting in the agent changing his/her behavior. That means that people may decrease their contributions to the public good in response to the introduction of formal government intervention if they interpret the regulation as reflecting a lack of trust (Fehr and Fischbacher 2005).

Laboratory experiments are useful for unraveling many of these situations. One example is the fact that players make different choices when they face a human opponent or a computer. Another frequent observation is that cooperative individuals cease cooperating after having been exploited by defectors. What looks like a true preference change may just be a change in behavior given that a subject finds herself in a less cooperative environment than expected or believed.

This implies that it is very difficult to identify a true preference change. This is illustrated in Figure 10.2, which plots an individual's contribution to the public good on the horizontal axis against the sum of contributions of his/her fellow group members on the vertical axis. In this stylized example we assume that the decision maker's contribution to the public goods is conditional on the number of other people contributing—she is assumed to be conditionally cooperative.

Suppose that an experimenter observes a high level of cooperation by both the individual and by the rest of the group (say point H) in the early stage of a game; see the left-hand side panel of Figure 10.2. During the game, the sum of contributions by the rest of the group (on the vertical axis) decreases and the individual agent reduces his/her cooperation too, resulting in a move to point L. The experimenter thus observes the shift from point H to point L in the left-hand panel, but she cannot determine whether this change in behavior is only a response to a change in the environment, or whether the individual is so frustrated that his willingness to contribute in general has changed; see the

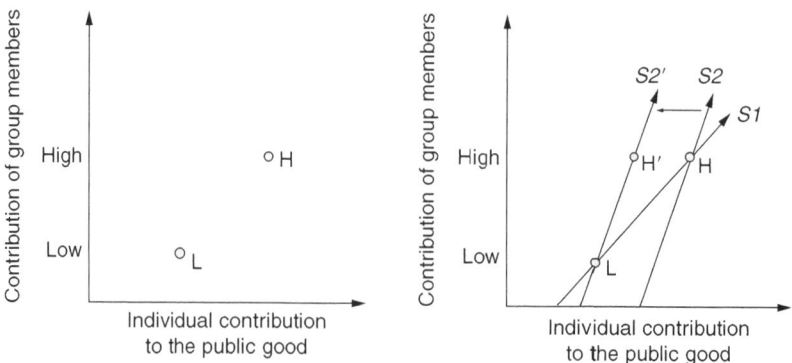

Figure 10.2. Reversible and irreversible changes in behavior

right-hand side panel in Figure 10.2. The first situation is represented by a shift along the contribution schedule *S1*, where one could speak of a reversible change. If the number of cooperators returns to the initial high level, individual contribution will also be high again. An irreversible change would occur if the contribution schedule shifts to the left, from *S2* to *S2'*. This implies that a return to the initial level of cooperation in the group will not be sufficient to restore the initial level of contribution, because the new level will be at H'. Note that observing a drop in cooperation followed by lower individual contribution, is not sufficient to recognize which situation applies, because one does not know the slope of the contribution schedule. To be able to do so, one would need sufficiently detailed data for single individuals, and that is typically not available. In real-world behavior it is even more difficult to distinguish temporary change from a long-lasting "once bitten, twice shy" effect.

Another way of capturing the context dependency of decisions is to assume that individuals hold multiple preferences that are weighted according to the situation. A good example is the model by Nyborg (2000), where individuals hold a preference as consumers, but also as good citizens. Individuals apply different preferences in different contexts. Therefore, choices depend highly on the situation. It is a priori unclear how consumers weigh these different preferences. In any case, an external intervention may lead to a shifting of weights. This is especially relevant when intervention influences the perception of a social dilemma. If an individual faces several co-players that are "in the same boat" she may be more inclined to infer some form of Kantian moral imperative: "if everyone cooperates, we will all be better off." If, however, a government regulator is imposing some law, the agent probably views the game very differently. The stage is now completely set, so her actions will most likely neither affect her future payoff, nor the rules set by the regulator. Therefore she would probably try to get the best out of the situation, given the presence of the regulator.

10.6 REPERCUSSIONS ON INSTITUTIONAL CONSTRAINTS

Let us now try to map these microeconomic fundamentals to the experimental results in order to understand the implications for institutional design—focusing on how these microfoundations interact with the institution's legitimacy, voluntariness, and enforcement structure.

Legitimacy is strongly linked to context-dependency, but also to the endogeneity of preferences. When the institution lacks legitimacy, individuals may infer that being cooperative does not pay off, or even lose all confidence in cooperative behavior altogether. Note that it matters whether the institution is perceived to be legitimate, not whether it is legitimate by objective standards. Raakjær and Mathiesen (2003) present a case from Danish fisheries, where rule-compliance went down after the fishermen felt decoupled from the decision-making process. Fairness issues should be taken seriously as they may not only influence the distribution of rents, but also the success of the institution, and therefore, its efficiency. In South Africa the government intended to reduce illegal fish landings by establishing *de jure* rights for the local fishermen. Some fishermen had the feeling that the process was not very fair and expressed their discontent by "protest fishing" (Hauck 2008).

The voluntary nature of an institution is important for three reasons. First, it reveals important information about the intentions of other individuals. Second, it gives individuals the opportunity to signal their social attitude or build up a good image or reputation. These can only work when individuals actually have the choice to do so, otherwise it would be impossible to distinguish true signals or images from forced ones. Because of this loss of information, individuals may as well cease investing in a social image at all. The third reason why a voluntary institution may perform better than a compulsory one has been pointed out by Hauert et al. (2007). When individuals have the opportunity to withdraw from some joint activity, it is much harder for others to take advantage of them. Therefore, self-determination provides an escape route to being exploited by defectors. An example where a new law crowded-out existing norms of reciprocity is presented by Borges and Irlenbusch (2007). When the German government introduced a law that made it possible to return any product just bought (for example, via the Internet), the number of products returned upon purchase increased sharply. This happened in spite of the fact that most sellers offered the same refund opportunity even before the introduction of the law.

Concerning the importance of the enforcement structure, it is difficult to pinpoint the exact microfoundations, as many mechanisms are at work, making the interaction between incentives and enforcement a complex one. Chhatre and Agrawal (2008) analyzed 152 forests that were common property in nine countries. They found, as expected, that the more valuable forests were depleted faster when local enforcement was absent. Interestingly, in the presence of enforcement the opposite holds, as regeneration is higher when forests are more valuable.

It seems to be important to distinguish enforcement mechanisms that are centralized from decentralized ones. Most experiments focus on the role of punishments and rewards in decentralized peer-to-peer enforcement. While most studies show that peer-to-peer enforcement is very effective in inducing cooperation, its impact on welfare is more ambiguous (Egas and Riedl 2008). Dreber et al. (2008) found that costly punishment raises cooperation, but the cost may be so high that the community as a whole may be worse off and therefore "winners don't punish." This finding has been challenged by Gächter et al. (2008), who found that punishment pays off, but only in the long run. Nikiforakis (2008) finds that adding a second stage of peer-enforcement may reduce all efficiency gains. This happens because the possibility of counter-punishments induces most players not to punish in the first place, because they fear retaliation. The same breakdown can be observed when rewards are used as an enforcement mechanism, albeit for different reasons. A second stage of rewarding gives defectors the chance to build a profitable rewarding network (Stoop et al. 2008).

Hence, both the punishment and reward mechanisms have their drawbacks, as the desire to punish non-cooperators can be very resource consuming, while rewarding or reputation does not always help in sanctioning the bad guys. Rockenbach and Milinski (2006) have looked at this issue in detail, and concluded that it is the combination of punishment and rewarding based on reputation that performs best in an experimental setting. Ohtsuki et al. (2009) have analyzed a model where two players of the population randomly meet and can either cooperate, defect, or punish. Individuals have a good reputation, or a bad one. There is, however, the chance that someone mistakenly identifies a partner as good when he is bad, or the other way round. They find that when the probability to correctly identify someone is high, defecting with the bad guys is the best strategy, while one should cooperate with the good ones. When the probability of correctly identifying someone is low, always defecting is superior. When the probability is in a very narrow parameter space between these two cases, punishing defectors and cooperating with cooperators is the winning strategy. This may indicate that increasing information (either through monitoring or gossip) makes punishment redundant, provided that one can actually refuse to interact with bad people. If one cannot, as is typically the case in a common-pool problem, the answer is less straightforward. In such a case, an appropriate weapon against defectors is needed, be it either punishment or ostracism. This theoretical finding is confirmed by Rustagi et al. (2010), who combine laboratory experiments and field data to reveal the key factors that determine success in forest management in Ethiopia. The authors identify the interplay of norm-compliance, costly monitoring, and a sufficiently large share of cooperatively minded individuals to explain whether forests are successfully preserved or not—hinting at a complex interaction between social preferences, institutions, and the renewable resource at stake.

10.7 RECOMMENDATIONS FOR POLICY DESIGN

The previous sections have shown that crowding-out actually occurs in the real world, and they also give hints regarding the way in which the phenomenon can be prevented from occurring. The most important ones are that the external intervention must be such that (1) it does not reduce people's sense of self-determination; (2) it is perceived as legitimate and fair; and (3) it is supportive of the social norms in place. In many instances the most effective way to meet these three criteria is to allow for direct stakeholder participation. That means that there are various fairly simple recommendations to prevent crowding-out from occurring.

First, communication and monitoring are important mechanisms for self-regulation, and often gossip suffices as an enforcement instrument. If this is not the case and more drastic punishments are needed, the welfare effects are more ambiguous. Therefore, a lack of communication or monitoring possibilities can form an obstacle to the evolution of effective social norms. In such a case, formal institutions may be more efficient. When a central authority steps in, a lack of involvement, but also fairness considerations can be an important reason why individuals actively try to undermine the institution. Including individuals in the rule-designing process is often a solution, but may sometimes have drawbacks. This is especially the case when some individuals perceive the institution to be unfair; either no consensus is reached or individuals who opposed the rule do not feel committed to follow it. Sometimes the social norms in place are maladaptive, because the environment or the technology has changed, while the social norms have not (Posner 1996). In such a case, government intervention may be necessary, but should be done very carefully. Any attempt to manage or regulate social norms may backfire, because the authority is perceived to be part of the "game" (Posner 1998). In the same vein, any attempt made by a central authority to strengthen existing social norms or "invest in social capital" may be well intended, but may have unpredictable consequences.

Financial incentives are problematic because individuals take into account that this will affect their self-image. Incentives in the form of public goods could be a solution, because individuals can then signal that they have a pro-social attitude. Indeed, the provision of compensation in the form of publicly provided goods is more effective than money in increasing support for "not in my backyard" projects, such as a noisy road (Mansfield et al. 2002).

Once the government decides to impose an external incentive, it is important to identify the nature of the product/task that is targeted. Subsidizing a good that has signaling character, like a hybrid car, may be countereffective, as pointed out by Ariely et al. (2009). If a small symbolic tax tries to underline the fact that a certain behavior is unacceptable, this may work especially well with goods that have a signaling character. For example, the use of plastic bags in Ireland dropped by 94 percent after the introduction of a small tax on their purchase because using them became highly stigmatized (Bowles 2008).

In general, the regulated agents' perception of the institution is crucial. In the famous child-care study by Gneezy and Rustichini (2000a), a small fine was perceived as a price that parents were more than happy to pay. Therefore, the conventional economic wisdom of "getting the incentives right" only works as intended if governments send an unambiguous message. In that sense, tradable emission rights, for instance, may be especially susceptible to crowding-out, because the owner holds the "right" to do something, taking away the negative connotation from polluting (Frey and Stutzer 2006). This seems to be relevant as well in the recent discussion on the effectiveness of individual transferable quotas (ITQ) in fisheries (Costello et al. 2008). When social issues are important, as is typically the case in small-scale fisheries, ITQs may undermine local stewardship (Ban et al. 2009). In the worst case, ITQ regimes crowd-out ecosystem responsibility of the ITQ holders (who hold the "right" to fish), while leading to "protest fishing" among the non-holders.

10.8 CONCLUSIONS

In this chapter we have presented evidence that we can neither rely on external regulation, nor on voluntary actions alone to solve many environmental problems—especially so when global environmental problems are at stake. Absent rigorous and effective international cooperation governments are likely to undertake unilateral environmental policies that are insufficiently stringent from a global point of view. Introduction of a lenient policy may be countereffective because the increase in "public good provision" by purely extrinsically motivated citizens or agents may not compensate the decrease in voluntary provisions by the citizens or agents who are intrinsically motivated to care for the global commons.

The first-best solution would be that governments take their responsibilities and start cooperating at the international level to address the global commons problems that currently confront us. Increasing public goods provision to the socially optimal level requires a substantial increase in efforts of all agents in the economy. A substantial increase in the stringency of national policies will most likely not prove to be countereffective. First, intrinsically motivated agents would welcome a strong worldwide shift towards environmental policy that seriously attempts to save the global commons. Second, extrinsically motivated agents are confronted with such a substantial increase in policy stringency that it is in their best interest to obey the law and take the necessary actions. Absent effective international cooperation, however, the probability of crowding-out intrinsic motivations is non-negligible. This may especially happen if the environmental costs are not shared fairly among citizens or countries, or regulations are so weak that governments fail to convince citizens that they are willing to craft effective regulations. In this case, intrinsically motivated citizens may lose their motivation for voluntary action, while the incentives for extrinsically motivated agents are not strong enough.

While there is not one standard recipe for solving diverse social dilemmas, the overview provided by this chapter identifies several regularities that determine the success or failure of policy design. These regularities can help to synthesize important core principles for designing effective governance structures. While it is unlikely that global problems will be solved without active government actions, any governmental actions will be much more effective if these are linked to lower institutional scales.[6] Therefore, it is imperative that governments are aware that any implemented law will affect the complex motivational structure of its citizens.

Experimental and theoretical work has shown that decentralized arrangements, based on voluntary action, communication, peer control, and reputation can be very effective, but also highly fragile. As a warning, it must be emphasized that imposing external interventions may not strengthen these arrangements, but replace them, leading to crowding-out and a loss of social capital. Even when a certain regulation is established to formalize a certain right that *de facto* already exists, unexpected outcomes may materialize. In any case, governments need to be aware that institutional changes imposed may lead to unintended consequences that will be very difficult to reverse.

---

[6] See Chapter 5 by Ostrom in Part II of this volume.

11

De Rationibus est Disputandum: Profiling "Warm-glowers"

*Paulo A. L. D. Nunes and Laura Onofri**

11.1 INTRODUCTION

"De gustibus non est disputandum" claims the ancient Latin proverb and the seminal economic paper by Becker and Stigler (1977).[1] This means that every rational individual can rank preferences the way she prefers. No *ex-ante*, axiomatic ranking can be imposed to individuals'choices, taste formation, and preferences structure. However, if one cannot discuss individuals' preferences structure, one can investigate the inner motivations that drive individuals to choose. Therefore, paraphrasing the Latin motto, we can add that *"de rationes disputandum est."* It is possible to discuss inner motivations that inspire economic agents' choices, actions, tastes, and preferences. Investigating economic agents' motivations to contribute for the private provision of a environmental public good is the topic of the chapter. We do not address the issue of whether an economic agent wants to contribute (or not) for a public good; of whether that agent expresses (or not) a preference (in monetary terms) for the good. We want to investigate why an economic agent chooses (or not) to privately contribute for a public good. *"De gustibus disputandum non est."* However, *"de rationibus est disputandum."*

In a seminal paper, Andreoni (1989: 464) states: "When people make donations to privately provided public goods, such as charity, there may be many factors, influencing their decisions other than altruism." As Olson

* The research leading to the results in this chapter has received funding from the European Union's Seventh Framework Programme (FP7/2007–2013) under grant agreement no. 226675 (KnowSeas—knowledge-based Sustainable Management for Europe's Seas).

[1] The Latin tradition attributes the origin of the sentence to Julius Caesar. The General and his officers were invited to dinner by a gentleman in *Mediolanum* (today Milan). The gentlemen offered asparagus dressed with butter to his guests. Caesar's officers disliked the preparation, since in Rome, butter was used as a body lotion. Caesar shut up his army, claiming that *"de gustibus non disputandum est."*

(1965: 60) noted, "people are sometimes motivated by a desire to win prestige, respect, friendship, and other social and psychological objectives," or as Becker (1974: 1083) observed, "apparent 'charitable' behaviour can also be motivated by a desire to avoid scorn of others or to receive social acclaim." Clearly social pressure, guilt, sympathy, or simply a desire for a "warm glow" may play important roles in the decision of agents. While such warm-glow giving has been acknowledged in the literature, the most common approach has been to assume that preferences depend only on private consumption and the total supply of the public good, and not on the individual donations per se.

In this chapter, we want to empirically identify, measure, and discuss that peculiar psychological motivation (based on warm glow) that spurs individuals to privately contribute for the provision of a public good. In our framework, "warm glow" is defined as the feeling of moral satisfaction that economic agents experience when contributing to the private provision of public goods. Warm glow is the enjoyment derived by contributors to public goods, when they consider the benefits realized by the beneficiaries, since, in Andreoni's framework, giving produces a pleasurable feeling.

In our opinion, understanding and targeting the warm-glow effect allows the researcher to be more rigorous when attempting to analyze economic agents' behavior and choices. Understanding, targeting, and measuring the inner motivations that spur actions and choices may allow better design and implementation of public policies, including for the governance of the global environmental commons.

This empirical research adopts the dataset gathered by Nunes and Schokkaert (2003). The authors report the results from a contingent valuation (CV) study (see Appendices 11.1 and 11.2) designed to investigate the influence of warm glow in willingness-to-pay (WTP) responses for the provision of a public good (a National Park in Portugal). The authors measure inter-individual differences in warm-glow motivations through a factor analysis, performed on a list of attitudinal items. Socio-economic variables and motivational factor scores are significant in the explanation of the individual reported WTP values. The authors compute "cold" WTP measures by taking out the effect of the warm-glow motivation.

In this chapter, we extract Nunes and Schokkaert's computed individual motivations factor scores, in order to estimate warm glow. We empirically capture the relationship between contributors' warm-glow motivation and a set of socio-economic and attitudinal/behavioral variables. Econometric analysis allows us to elicit different motivational profiles, based on survey-reported WTP values. In particular, we empirically capture the profile of those respondents, whose contributions to the environmental public good is motivated and inspired by warm glow. We name that type of contributor "warm-glowers". Therefore, our results represent a significant contribution to the analysis of the governance of the global environmental commons, including, for the case at issue, the protection of biodiversity provided by national protected areas.

There is a large body of experimental literature trying to identify and profile types of contributors (and related motivations for contributing). When studying the issue of the private provision of public goods (PG), standard economic theory (based on the model of a selfish and perfectly rational representative agent) is able to profile and explain free-rider behavior. However, standard economic theory is unable to account for many phenomena of giving, such as, for instance, the existence of cooperators, over-contributors, and reciprocators, observed in experiments. Quoting Burlando and Guala (2005): "The most obvious departure from the standard approach consists in relaxing the selfishness and the full rationality assumptions." This can be done by introducing altruism and error parameters (Palfrey and Prisbey 1996, 1997). Empirical estimates of these augmented models, however, have discovered a considerable heterogeneity among the subjects participating in PG experiments. The implications and relevance of heterogeneity has generated a lively discussion of PG experiments pointing in this direction and include, among others, Fehr and Gächter (2000), Fischbacher et al. (2001), and Andreoni and Miller (2002).

We can highlight two relevant streams of literature for warm-glow motivation:

(a) papers trying to perform experiments in order to identify and measure the extent of warm glow (among others, Palfrey and Prisbey 1996, 1997; Andreoni and Miller, 2002);

(b) papers trying to perform experiments in order to define and identify contributor types and estimate their proportion in a subject population (among others, Keser and van Winden 2000; Fischbacher et al. 2001).

This work follows the above literature only because it adopts the economic definition of warm glow, as defined in the seminal paper by Andreoni (1989).

The chapter differs in crucial ways from the surveyed stream of research for several reasons. First, to our knowledge, it is the first attempt to "profile" respondents with particular motivational characteristics (warm-glowers) based on survey-based WTP values. Second, the consumer motivational profile (warm glow) is given a quantitative dimension by making use of factor analysis. Moreover, we do not only "separate," identify, and measure a particular motivational category (warm-glowers), but we look deeper into the "motivational box," trying to empirically capture the relationship between individuals' socio-economic characteristics and individuals' warm-glow motivational latent construct. Finally, the chapter discusses some implications of the presence of warm-glow motivation for the governance of public environmental goods and commons. The latter point is very important because it is related to the crucial theme of the implementation of CV results. We discuss possible answers to several questions. When a typical warm-glow profile is identified, and once we have disentangled the warm-glow valuation component from the reported WTP values, which of the valuation results should be taken into account to perform (social) cost–benefit analysis and the design of the governance architecture of environmental commons? The reported WTP values? Or alternatively, the "cold" WTP results, which are corrected for warm glow? Or, in a broader context, how should a governance architect behave? Should reported WTP values be respected, or not? And what are the respective implications in terms of public policy design? Why should reported WTP be corrected for warm glow? If a factor increases utility and does so from a welfare perspective, is that what counts as aggregate utility? So every increase in utility should be counted when considering a change according to a standard cost–benefit analysis. The same is true for altruism. The usual argument against counting altruistic preferences in benefit aggregation is double counting. But isn't it the case that in a more altruistic society, welfare is larger, all other things being equal? Why, therefore, should there be a need to correct the naturally expressed preferences whenever they are accurately measured?

The remainder of the chapter is organized as follows: Section 11.2 presents an overview of Andreoni's theoretical model on impure altruism. Section 11.3 reports the methodology that underpins the identification of the latent warm-glow motivation. Section 11.4 reports the empirical results and Section 11.5 contains a discussion regarding the assessment of the profile of the warm-glower. Discussion about the implications for the governance of environmental commons and the importance of embodying motivational structures in the provision of environmental public goods is provided in Sections 11.6 and 11.7, respectively. Section 11.8 concludes.

11.2 THEORETICAL FRAMEWORK: ANDREONI'S IMPURE ALTRUISM MODEL

Andreoni (1989, 1990) developed a general model of private contributions to provide public goods that includes impure altruistic considerations derived from giving. This model assumes that individuals contribute to the provision of a specific public good for two reasons: first, because they simply want more of it; second, because they derive some private benefits from giving to the good. The latter reason signals the presence of impure altruistic considerations and is often interpreted in terms of a warm glow or feeling of satisfaction derived from the act of giving per se. From this perspective, the contribution to the good enters an individual's utility function twice: once as a private good and once as a public good.

In this section, we present an overview of Andreoni's model to provide a theoretical framework for our work. Following Andreoni, individuals may have different preference mappings with respect to the private provision of public goods and therefore a number of utility functions can be derived to take account of possible different underlying preferences. Suppose that U_i is the utility function of individual i ($i = 1, \ldots, n$); x_i is the private goods consumption of individual i, G is the level of provision of (services from) the public good and g_i is the individual's donation to the provision of the public good. The sum of the individual contributions equals the total supply of the public good:

$$G = \sum_{i=1}^{n} g_i \tag{1}$$

From these assumptions, we can distinguish three different types of utility function, corresponding to three different possible underlying preferences and related psychological profiles:

$$U_i = U_i(x_i, G) \tag{2}$$

$$U_i = U_i(x_i, g_i) \tag{3}$$

$$U_i = U_i(x_i, G, g_i) \tag{4}$$

Equation (2) describes the utility function of a pure altruistic individual, where there are no warm-glow benefits from contributing to the public good G. For such an individual, the private donation g_i only enters the utility function as part of the level of public benefits G. This utility function profiles a purely altruist contributor, whose motivation only depends on the desire to provide the good for the sake of the good's existence. The contributor cares about the well-being of the recipients.

Equation (3) describes the utility function of a pure egoistic individual, where private benefits are the only benefits received by the individual i. Such an individual does not consider the total level of public good G, but only his personal contribution (and benefit) for the provision of G. In this case, the contributor's motivation may only depend on the possibility (or not) of making private use of the provided public good. The contributor does not care about the well-being of the recipients.

Finally, equation (4) describes the utility function of an individual for whom both the level of G and the amount of g_i become explicit arguments in individual i's utility function. The contributor cares about the well-being of the recipients but also derives pleasure form giving per se. Andreoni (1989) calls impure altruism this combination of pure altruism and warm glow. This latter motivational profile can be described and explained in terms of different elements, such as social pressure, feelings of sympathy and moral satisfaction, or simply the desire for a warm glow.

11.3 IDENTIFYING THE WARM-GLOW CONTRIBUTOR PROFILE

The present study focuses on the impure altruistic model formulation. The purpose of our research work is twofold. First, we aim to "look into warm glow," in order to identify the elements affecting such a psychological attitude towards private contributing for a public good. Second, we want to get some empirical information about the profile of people having a utility function, as described by equation (4).

In this section we provide an econometric analysis of individuals' warm-glow motivational profile. In order to do so, we regress warm-glow motivation against a series of variables containing information about the respondents' characteristics.

In formal terms we propose to estimate the following equation,

$$\hat{f}_{wg,i} = a_0 + \sum_k a_k x_{ki} + u_{wg,i} \text{ for all } i - \text{respondents} \tag{5}$$

where $\hat{f}_{wg}$, the dependent variable, is the vector with all the individual observations for the level of warm-glow motivation, x_k is a vector with the observations of all individuals for the socio-economic characteristic k, $u_{wg,i}$ is a vector with disturbance terms and a is the coefficient to be estimated.

In our econometric analysis, the dependent variable "warm glow" is a latent variable. Warm glow is not observable and, before estimation, must be "built" in a two-step operational procedure.[2] The first step consists in eliciting reported WTP responses from the CV study, and distinguishing the main components of a respondent's willingness-to-pay. In the study, reported WTP values are obtained from a nationwide CV to assess the economic value of protecting the Portuguese Alentejo Natural Park, a coastal protected area, from tourism development.[3] In short, the Alentejo Natural Park, and its

---

[2] For a detailed description of the operationalization procedure see Nunes and Schokkaert (2003) and Nunes (2002b). See also the appendix.

[3] Contingent valuation, a survey-based valuation method, was selected because it is the valuation technique capable of including the non-use value component, when measuring the total value of the public good/natural resource. State-of-the-art techniques were used in developing questionnaires and the guidelines recommended by the National Oceanic and Atmospheric Administration panels (see Arrow et al. 1993) were closely followed, including the use of focus groups, field pre-testing and one-to-one interviews. In the fall of 1997, the survey department of the Portuguese Catholic University executed a national survey. The interviewer

environmental benefits, were described in terms of the Wilderness Area (WA) and the Recreational Area (RA). The first refers to the geographical area of the park that is allocated to the protection of the local wildlife diversity; the Wilderness Area is not open to visitors. The Recreational Area is open to visitors, who can enjoy a set of recreational activities in a natural environment. Respondents' *WTP* for the Alentejo Natural Park mainly depends on the possibility of seeing the wilderness area protected from any human exploitation (*WA*), the opportunity to exercise recreational activities (*RA*), and warm glow (*WG*), i.e.:

$$WTP = WTPf\ (WA, RA, WG) \tag{6}$$

where *WTP* is the dependent variable and three different motivational dimensions are the independent variables. In particular, *WA* can be interpreted as the "existence" motivational factor score;[4] *RA* can be interpreted as the "use" motivational factor score,[5] and *WG* can be interpreted as warm glow.

The second step refers to identifying and disentangling warm glow from the *WTP* regression line and from the other motivational factor scores or other motives of giving, described by equation (6). In this case, the task is to obtain quantitative data regarding individual warm-glow motivation and get quantitative information with respect to the individual preferences, related to the psychological motivation of warm glow. In order to detect the latent motivational variable, factor analysis is adopted (Table 11.1; see the Appendix for technical details about the procedure).

Whilst the dependent variable is a latent variable, which had to be constructed by making use of factor analysis, independent variables are directly elicited from the surveys. They mostly refer to individual respondents' (1) personal features; (2) recreational-consumption characteristics; (3) ideological profile; (4) charitable behavior; (5) material wealth indicators; and (6) sociological profile.[6]

---

teams paid visits to 3,597 households but 21 percent of them were not reachable since nobody answered the door. From households that were successfully contacted, a total of 1,678 completed interviews were received. To better mimic price taking in market behavior, the respondents were asked whether they were willing to pay a given monetary amount in order to continue the protection of the Alentejo Natural Park. For detail, see Nunes (2002a)

[4] This motivational factor score inspires altruist contributors, whose motivation only depends on the desire to provide the good for the sake of the good's existence. The contributors care about the well-being of the recipients. In the case at issue, the contributor pays because she cares for the (actual and future) preservation of the public good per se.

[5] This motivational factor score spurs pure egoistic contributors, whose motivation may only depend on the possibility (or not) to make the private use of the provided public good. The contributor does not care about the well-being of the recipients. She pays, for instance, because she can use the public good or take direct benefits related to personal consumption of the good.

[6] The respondents were asked to provide information about (1) gender, age, marital status; (2) whether they practice surfing, biking, trekking, and camping activities; (3) their political orientation, religious direction, and their political position regarding different public policy issues; (4) whether they practice donation activities, give blood, or are committed to other charitable

Table 11.1. Warm-glow factor loadings after varimax rotation

Estimate	Survey motivational question
0.56	Our family admires the individuals who, on a voluntary basis, participate in collecting contributions for national programs for social aid and solidarity.
0.60	There are some funding campaigns to which my family and I feel very close and therefore we do not hesitate to contribute with a donation.
0.47	It is difficult for me to decline my help to other individuals who, either in the streets or at my door, beg for charity.
0.57	I am happy with myself whenever I give a financial contribution to national fund-raising campaigns.
0.58	My family and I like to contribute to good causes such as the protection of the environment, and whenever we can afford it, we do not decline our help to such fund-raising campaigns.

Source: Nunes (2002b)

11.4 ESTIMATION RESULTS

Table 11.2 reports the estimation results. We can point out that for this model only a small part of the variance of the realized warm-glow motivation factor can be explained by the selected characteristics—the respective R^2 is less than 20 percent. From an impure altruistic literature perspective, such a low R^2 is good news. Such an apparent paradoxical result indicates that this motivational factor score, when contrasted to the individual socio-economic characteristics, contains additional empirical information for the characterization of the individual consumer profile. In contrast, a high R^2 would say that most of the individual characteristics influence the individual motivation factor, indicating that the individual motivation factor per se would convey redundant information.

In other words, warm-glow factor scores are meant to reflect psychological dispositions, containing additional information that is not fully captured by other socio-economic characteristics, as well as indicators. On the other hand, from a strict econometric perspective such a low R^2 signals a weak explanatory power of the selected model specification.[7] For these reasons, we interpret the estimation results carefully, following from the first attempt to explore the empirical analysis of the individual warm-glow profile and its steering components.

Perhaps unsurprisingly, estimated coefficients of material wealth indicator variables (income level, living in a luxurious apartment, etc.) are not statistically

activities; (5) income level and housing conditions; and (6) education level, job type, and location of their dwelling.

[7] However, the adopted model specification presents a much higher explanatory power (in a strict econometric sense) than the empirical model used by Nunes (2002b).

significant. We may interpret this set of results as demonstrating that actual contributory/financial capability does not represent the driving force affecting contribution decisions and, therefore, warm-glow feelings.

Other personal features, however, appear to have a robust econometric role in explaining the individual warm-glow effect and profile. In particular, we can highlight the following variables:

(a) *personal feature variables*—being a male has a negative impact on the warm-glow motivation. The feeling of satisfaction provided by the act of giving reveals itself to be stronger among women. In particular, this effect is stronger among young women, given that age has an effect on warm glow too;

(b) *recreational-consumption feature variables*—higher warm-glow factor scores occur among the respondents who present a stronger propensity for recreation in general, and undertake recreational activities in the Alentejo Natural Park, such as surfers, bikers, and trekkers, in particular;

(c) *ideological variables*—respondents caring for the implementation of *"Medical Assistance-Social Security"* present a positive estimated coefficient for warm glow. On the contrary, individuals who state a high concern regarding the *"Quality of the public education system"* reveal weaker warm-glow effect. Both results are statistically significant. Catholics (mainly located in the northern area of Portugal) present negative estimated coefficients for warm glow. Finally, left-wing taxpayers, mainly voters for the Portuguese Communist Party, are associated with negative warm-glow estimated coefficients;

(d) *charitable behaviour variables*—respondents who report having participated in donation and charity schemes are more likely to have positive estimated warm-glow coefficients;

(e) *sociological variables*—the inhabitants of Portugal's rural areas present positive estimated coefficients for warm glow. This means that the satisfactory feeling derived by the act of contributing to the provision of an environmental good is stronger among those populations leaving near the good. Alentejo local inhabitants present positive warm-glow estimated coefficients. The nature of the job held by the respondent, also affects the warm-glow motivational profile: the feeling of satisfaction provided by the act of giving is weaker among professionals, including lawyers, architects, and other liberal professions. Finally, education level has a negative impact on "warm glow": individuals holding graduate degrees derive less satisfaction from the act of contribution for the public good.

Warm glow is a feeling; it has a psychological dimension. This characteristic is captured by our estimation results: among all considered variables, it is mainly psychological and ideological variables that matter in the regression line (i.e. they are statistically significant), when determining warm glow. The warm-glow profile that emerges from analysis of Table 11.2 is rather blurred and difficult to bring back to a unified figure. Hence, some "scientific warnings" are due. We analyze data and results that are derived from a study conducted in Portugal, with Portuguese taxpayers. The public good at issue is a national park; the payment scheme is a voluntary contribution. It is important to highlight all these factors, since we are aware the institutional setting plays an important role as the platform that underpins the current valuation exercise. Therefore, caution is needed when interpreting the results, since one could expect a different outcome if we had considered another range of sociological characteristics, juridical frameworks, and social norms. Further-more, the nature of the public good itself (whether a hospital or a bridge or a public park) may generate a different reaction in the respondents, depending on the (personal or social) importance (and related WTP) they attribute to the good at issue. Having said this, we will now proceed with the identification and analysis of possible types of warm-glow(ers).

Table 11.2. Warm-glow estimation results

Variables	Parameter estimate	Standard error	p value
Intercept	−0.2746	0.142	0.054**
Personal features			
Gender = male	−0.2114	0.050	0.001*
Age	−0.1244	0.066	0.059**
Recreational consumption features			
Recreationists	0.1317	0.030	0.001*
Ideological features			
Catholics	−0.0646	0.023	0.005*
Medical assistance and social security	0.0669	0.038	0.084**
Taxpayers with a left-wing orientation	−0.0714	0.053	0.043*
Quality of public education system	−0.0385	0.023	0.013*
Charitable behavior			
Financial donation (via organizations)	0.3172	0.067	0.001*
Charity (on the streets)	0.5293	0.070	0.001*
Sociological features			
Household dimension	−0.0233	0.021	0.183
Rural areas	0.1684	0.102	0.101**
Unskilled workers	0.1497	0.140	0.136
Professional workers	−0.2153	0.096	0.025*
Education level	−0.5903	0.019	0.002*
Local inhabitants	0.3205	0.101	0.001*
$R^2 0.183$			

Note: The estimated results are computed in SAS®. The model was estimated by the use of the STEPWISE procedure in SAS®. Variables are included in the equation if the probability associated with the F-test for the hypothesis that the coefficient of the entered variable is statistically significant at 15 percent. Other model specifications are available upon request. *(**) Significant at 5% (10%)

11.5 INTERPRETATION OF THE ESTIMATION RESULTS: ANALYSIS OF THE WARM-GLOW PROFILE

In this particular setting, and according to our empirical estimates, we can sketch two different types of warm glow. This distinction comes from an economic interpretation of the empirical results. Both classes may overlap. The feeling of satisfaction, provided by the act of contributing for a public good, appears to be stronger in those respondents who:

(1) derive moral satisfaction because they want to obtain a direct personal advantage or a direct personal sense of pride from their contribution;

(2) derive moral satisfaction because the contribution makes them experience an indirect personal sense of price, mostly dependent on the sentiment of social-cohesion, which the choice of contribution generates in the donator.

We name the first category *"ego-driven"* warm glow; we call the latter category *"social-oriented"* warm glow.

11.5.1 "Ego-driven" warm glow

In the first situation, the warm-glow profile is mainly sketched by looking at the estimation results for individual ideological variables. Respondents who express a strong positive feeling towards social programs, for example related to medical assistance and social security, highlight a personal interest and personal advantage in contributing for the public good and have, therefore, estimated positive coefficients for warm glow. This result may be explained by the fact that the social programs under consideration have direct impacts in the personal sphere of the respondents. The efficient working of the medical system, for instance, is a fact that affects society in general, and the respondent in particular. When stating that he cares for the promotion of such a social program, the respondent is caring for and protecting his own interest as a user of the public medical assistance scheme. This is the essence of impure altruism *à la* Andreoni (1989).[8]

If we extend this reasoning to the provision of the public good under consideration, we can infer that the *"ego-driven"* warm glow drives the individuals to contribute for the protection of the Natural Park in order to satisfy a personal interest from the act of giving. In the same way, these types

---

[8] According to Andreoni's impure altruism model, giving is a private good. Therefore, a warm-glow contributor does not change her contribution whenever the population size changes (more or less beneficiaries of her contribution), nor if the marginal value of the public good changes (see Palfrey and Prisbey 1996). It is the utility provided by the act of giving itself, independently of how much people will benefit from it and the marginal value that matters.

of contributors care for social programs because they want to derive a personal advantage from the effective working of those policies. The sense of satisfaction derived by the act of giving is, in this case, animated by the desire to get advantages from the good itself. In short, if the public medical assistance system works, it will also work for the "*ego-driven*" warm-glower. If the public good is provided, it will also be provided for the "*ego-driven*" warm-glower. Therefore, he is willing to pay for it.

Individuals committed to charitable operations also present an "*ego-driven*" type of warm glow. In this case, the satisfaction provided by the act of giving is inspired by the sense of pride, borne by feeling useful to society. Furthermore, respondents who are committed to donation and charitable activities may be driven by the desire to feel "good" towards others, including people in need. This feeling of "personal goodness" can be extended to the case at issue, in order to interpret the econometric results and define the warm-glower profile. We may recognize a different source of warm glow: respondents are willing to pay for the public good, simply because the provision makes them feel "good," as when participating in charitable activities.

11.5.2 "Social-oriented" warm glow

In the second case, warm glow features are, somehow, related to social exclusion elements. In particular, the warm-glower belongs to more marginalized categories (caveat: in the Portuguese society as a reflection of a standard Western capitalist democracy), among which we can point out residents of rural areas, unskilled workers, people holding a low level of education. The feeling of satisfaction generated by the act of contributing for a public good is strongly present in such categories.

In our framework, the socially driven warm-glow type is not the commitment and/or reciprocal type according to the existing literature, as adopted in the framework of Richter and van Soest (Chapter 10 in this volume). The socially driven person does not feel a kind of moral obligation to contribute. Contribution for the public good at stake is not a Kantian categorical imperative. The socially oriented warm-glowers are not altruist either, and their act of giving is not motivated by the desire to improve social welfare. They are social warm-glowers because they feel impure altruism from contributing and improving the society where they live. The sense of satisfaction from the contribution is not generated by an awareness of improving society by giving (otherwise, it would not be warm glow but altruism or reciprocity), but by the sensation of feeling useful and socially recognized, thanks to the contribution.[9]

---

[9] This type of warm-glower can also be defined as ego-driven, where the ego satisfaction from living is borne by social instances.

We may explain this as an attempt to feel more involved in social activities and in society as a whole, not for the sake of society's welfare, but for the sake of personal satisfaction. The socially oriented warm-glowers derive utility by the act of giving itself, independently of how much people will benefit from it and the marginal value of the contribution. Roughly speaking, the socially oriented warm-glower derives a sense of satisfaction from the act of giving because the personal returns will (also) be in terms of "social recognizability" (implemented though the donation). *Do ergo sum.* The social warm-glower contributes so that she can be better considered in the environment where she lives (at the margins). The social warm-glower does not contribute for the welfare of the social community where she belongs. She donates so that the social community, where she belongs and lives, recognizes that she is doing something good for the society. The sense of warm glow derives from the (impurely altruistic) sense of self that contributing for the welfare of society may increase. The contributor does not care about the well-being of the recipients; she cares about the personal, selfish feeling of satisfaction that contributing (for the well-being of recipients and society) will bring about.

If we consider, for instance, high-profile jobs or a high level of education, we notice that the warm glow variable has a negative estimated coefficient for the respondent's choice whether to contribute for the public good. These results are statistically significant and can strengthen our thesis that socially marginalized respondents desire to feel a sense of satisfaction from the contribution, because this may spur them to (selfishly) feel better integrated ito the community. Table 11.3 summarizes our analysis.

According to our interpretation of the results, the overlapping effect is strong when considering Alentejo local inhabitants. Respondents, living in the Alentejo region (locals) are both *"socially oriented"* and *"ego-driven"* warm-glowers. Local inhabitants, in fact, may derive moral satisfaction because they will feel directly related and responsible for the provision of the public good and, in this way, experience a tighter sense or sentiment of social cohesion withother members of the commuity. This sentiment of social cohesion is not inspired by reciprocity, nor altruism, but by warm glow. At the same time, the feeling of satisfaction derived from the act of giving, can be inspired (and explained) by the fact that the act of contributing for the public good may have a positive impact on the local reputation of the respondent, in terms of personal prestige.[10]

---

[10] This empirical result is well founded and explained by the theoretical literature in signalling (see Laffont and Tirole 1993). According to such literature, the stated WTP answers for a public good can signal different classes and typologies of contributors. In our survey, however, we did not specify that if the respondents were willing to pay for the public good, their name would have been published or made public. In our opinion, such choice renders the result even stronger, when interpreting "local" warm-glowers. The personal feeling of satisfaction derived by the act of paying for the public good can be interpreted as driven by the desire to increase the respondent

Table 11.3. The profile of warm glow and respective inspiration factors

"Ego-driven" warm glow	*"Socially oriented"* warm glow
Inspiration factors	Inspiration factors
Derive a personal advantage or satisfy a personal interest	Feel more socially integrated
Derive a feeling of usefulness or goodness towards society and oneself.	Feel more cohesion with society as a whole
Strengthen personal reputation in the local community	Feel less socially marginalized

11.6 IMPLICATIONS FOR THE GOVERNANCE OF ENVIRONMENTAL COMMONS

Our exercise, aiming at the identification of a "warm-glower," does not aim at a technical "*art pour l'art*" operation. On the contrary, it offers us the basis for a discussion of a very practical implementation problem. Our analysis may be useful for critically tackling CV results in the implementation perspective of environmental public policies and the architecture of the governance of global environmental commons. In fact, once the warm-glow effect is targeted and the warm-glower is identified, what should a designer of the governance of global environmental commons do?

Suppose reported WTP estimates are compared with "cold" WTP estimates; that is, those corrected for a warm-glow effect. Two scenarios are available. One is characterized by having both reported and "cold" WTP estimates larger than the social costs of the provision of the public good under consideration. The second is characterized by having reported WTP estimates larger than social costs and the social costs larger than "cold" WTP estimates. In the first scenario, one should not have much discussion in agreeing that the environmental public good should be provided. The second scenario, however, calls for a further reflection. How should one design a governance architecture that underpins the provision of the common public good? Should such an architecture support the provision of the environmental good or not? In other words, should the architecture embed the individual respondent's sense of satisfaction, or not? This is a relevant and complex public policy question, the answer to which is anchored to a better understanding of the "black box" of preferences and to the nature of the designer of the governance architecture of global environmental commons. In order to discuss the answers to these questions, we propose to reason along the following lines:

personal prestige in the local community. Even if their name is not rendered public, respondents can communicate their participation in the provision in the local environment in other ways, or feel that the local community acknowledges their contribution.

(1) the governance architect does not take into account the warm-glow effect and does not provide the public good;

(2) the governance architect takes into account the warm-glow effect and provides the environmental public good.

11.6.1 Governance architecture that does not embed the warm-glow effect

In the first case, efficiency principles, suggest that the governance architect will not pay for the environmental public good under consideration, since the social public benefits do not cover the social public costs of is provision. If cost-effectiveness principles inspire the decision-maker policy, the warm-glow effect will have a final, preponderant weight on the decision whether or not it is providing the environmental public good. In particular, such motivational factor, when disentangled from the "cold" WTP values, will have a negative impact on the provision of the environmental public good. In this situation, one may infer that the decision maker does not respect individual consumers' preferences. However, the warm-glow motivational element can be interpreted by an efficiency-oriented decision maker as an irrelevant valuation effect, not directly expressing the real WTP (only "cold" WTP matters). If reported WTP values consist of two different components—one relating to the value attributed by the respondent to the environmental public good (and to the strict economic preference[11]), the second relating to the psychological feeling of "warm glow,"—a decision maker oriented by efficiency criteria may strictly focus on the stated economic preference and never let the social costs of the provision overcome the social benefits.

11.6.2 Governance architecture that embeds the warm-glow effect

Suppose now that the governance architect decides to take into account the "warm-glow" valuation mechanism and provides the good. In this case, the profiling of the "warm-glower" may create support in pursuing and targeting public policies and governance, in addition to the provision itself of the environmental public good. By considering the individual consumer's well-being related to the individual's personal participation in the provision of the public good, the decision maker can (voluntarily or involuntarily) increase the overall welfare. This may constitute an important aspect that underpins

---

[11] Or, in the Andreoni sense, self-interest agents are only money-maximizing.

the global environmental commons governance architecture in the provision of environmental public goods.

The decision maker, for instance, may be willing to provide the public good because, by taking into account a "warm-glower of the social oriented type," she can promote social cohesion, supporting minorities or the integration of more marginalized social groups of the population. In the study at issue, for instance, the feeling of satisfaction provided by the act of giving is stronger among low educational categories. By contributing to the public good, the warm-glowers may feel more socially integrated. Alternatively, in the scenario where the "warm-glow" valuation mechanism is mainly due to "ego-driven" profiles, we can interpret the decision about public good provision as signaling the presence and respect of an "invisible hand." Every "warm-glower," by pursuing his/her own personal interest, can contribute to achieving Pareto optimal outcomes. Suppose, for instance, that people engaged in charitable activities are mostly driven by the desire to fulfill their own (impurely altruistic) desire to feel good, when helping needy categories of people. By pursuing an egoistic interest, these people, somehow, improve society. If we reason in Pareto principle terms, we may say that the needy person is better off after being helped (for instance, because she receives food or clothes that she could not otherwise afford) and the donor or charity giver is better off because she feels a good person. Let us extend this reasoning to "*ego-driven*" warm-glowers. Suppose that the respondents are willing to pay for the public good because this strengthens their social reputation. Once again, society may be better off with the provided public good and the "*ego-driven*" warm-glowers are better off because they fulfill their personal goal.

11.7 DE RATIONIBUS EST DISPUTANDUM: A DISCUSSION

We are aware that our exercise is, somehow, limited and cannot assume a certain "universal truth" dignity. The survey was implemented in Portugal and was designed for Portuguese citizens. As already remarked, every national reality differs because of its socio-economic, institutional, cultural, and juridical setting. Different factors, like the nature and type of the public good to be provided, the payment scheme (voluntary contribution), and the signaling incentives defined in the survey have an influence on the CV respondents. If the same exercise were performed in the Netherlands or in the United States, we may expect different results, and maybe, different warm-glower profiles. Nevertheless, our study wants to represent a starting point for further CV and experimental exercises and for the definition and targeting of public policies.

We want to stimulate a debate about the understanding of the "black box of preferences." Our study stresses that psychological motivation, driven by impure altruistic forces, finds room in the utility function definition and is strictly related to particular socio-economic profiles (the warm-glower). Moreover, the identification of the proper public policy represents another important issue: if the estimated demand function for the public good disregards one of the underlying driving forces—such as the warm-glow valuation component (or any other motivational issue)—the demand function is misspecified, and the respective value predictions are not correct. Moreover, we highlighted how the identification of a warm-glower and its consideration when designing a public policy may be useful in pursuing public objectives, other than the simple provision of the public good.

Despite the above scientific "warnings," when discussing whether to use (or not) reported WTP estimates in policy making and cost–benefit exercises, in our opinion, the survey responses do reflect true WTP responses—the empirical results confirm the validity of the proposed impure public good model formulation—and, in this way, the original WTP responses constitute correct information to be used in the estimation of the demand for the public good. Therefore, warm glow is a legitimate valuation component and the original WTP estimates can (and should) be used in cost–benefit analysis. In our opinion, there are several reasons to believe that the use of the "*cold*" WTP—, that is, correcting WTP estimates from warm glow—in cost–benefit analysis does not constitute a compelling argument.

The statement that (impure) altruism motives are incompatible with economic theory is hardly consistent with the notion of consumer sovereignty, a cornerstone in a modern theory of social choice. It violates a long-standing tradition that one takes people's preferences as one finds them. The modern theory of social choice has always emphasized that it was immaterial whether individual's preferences reflected selfish interest or moral judgment. According to Arrow, "the individual may order all social states by whatever standards he deems relevant" (Arrow 1951: 17). In a similar vein, we can find the work of Becker, who always defended the premise that "individuals maximize welfare as they conceive it, whether they be selfish, altruistic, loyal, spiteful, or masochistic" (Becker 1992: 1).

Our empirical evidence confirmed Andreoni's impure altruism model formulation. Therefore, we could interpret the demand for the public good as characterized by two driving forces:

(a) the individual consumer's well-being derived from the provision of the environmental public good;

(b) the individual consumer's well-being related to the individual personal participation in the provision of the environmental public good.

Therefore, the correction of WTP estimates from warm glow would be associated with a valuation bias when assessing the demand for the public good and thus the use of such a WTP measure in policy decisions or cost–benefit analysis would be associated with a misleading allocation of resources.

The governance architecture may not take into account the warm-glow effect (and therefore, the environmental public good is not provided), because the policy design can interpret warm glow as a strategic misreport. Contingent valuation critics argue, in fact, that reported WTP responses do not reflect real economic preferences and, for this reason, should not be used in cost–benefit analysis (see Diamond et al. 1993; Milgrom, 1993). This position can be interpreted as a "narrow interpretation" of the concept of consumer preferences. Many economists disagree with this position. Since Kahneman and Knetsch (1992), the idea that CV respondents express only "narrow economic preferences" in their WTP responses has been questioned. According to these authors, individuals' contributions to the public good are explained by two driving forces. The first is that individuals want the provision of the public good. The second is that contributing per se makes individuals feel good (for any psychological motivation, different form the simple money-maximizing behavior). According to Kahnemann and Knetsch (1992) embedding is not in conflict with the standard value theory, because embedding can be explained in terms of an impure altruistic motivation of the individual consumer, and that aspect of consumer behavior was not considered in the standard valuation framework. The authors proposed an explanation that maintains that the WTP for public goods is also an expression of WTP to acquire moral satisfaction. "Respondents express a willingness to contribute for the acquisition of many public goods and there is no reason to doubt their sincerity or seriousness ... what is the good that respondents are willing to acquire in CV surveys? We offer the general hypothesis that responses to CV questions express a willingness to acquire a sense of moral satisfaction (also known as warm glow of giving)" (Kahneman and Knetsch 1992: 62–4).

Therefore, warm glow, altruism, and other dimensions of preferences can be considered as true values in contrast to strategic misreports, and should be considered when performing cost–benefit analysis.

11.8 CONCLUDING REMARKS

This chapter explored econometric analysis for capturing the relationship between a motivational variable, "warm glow" for the provision of an environmental public good, and socio-economic characteristics of individual consumers. We use microeconomic data provided by a national contingent valuation survey that was performed in Portugal, in order to value the provision of a coastal, national protected area. Estimation results show that "warm glow" is mostly affected by four main effects: (1) the charitable habits of respondents; (2) level of social participation in the community of the respondents: (3) degree of importance attributed to social policies by the respondents; and (4) the religious belief of the respondents.

In this context, the interpretation of our estimates allowed us to categorize and profile two types of "warm-glowers": the "ego-driven" and the "socially oriented" ones. A critical discussion on whether embodying (or not) the latent estimated motivational structures (and underlying determination factors), when performing cost–benefit analysis for the provision of environmental public goods followed the interpretation of estimation results and profiling exercise.

Finally, we would like to conclude with the words of Andreoni and Miller:

> not all 'non-economic' behavior is beyond economic analysis. Our maintained assumption as economists is that individual behavior is consistent with self-interest. At its weakest, self-interest only means that choices conform to some underlying preference ordering that is complete, reflexive and transitive, and, hence, some utility function can be used to describe behavior. However, the assumption of self-interest does not tell us what variables are in that utility function. What does? Our methodology is that people themselves, through their actions, will do so. (Andreoni and Miller 1998: 15)

This chapter has shown that motivational profiles can indeed be captured by econometric analysis and the use of surveys that highlight and elicit respondents' behaviors. This summarizes the motivation of the research at issue and represents the basis for every research investigating human motivations to choices. *De gustibus non est disputandum.* We all agree with that. On the contrary, *de rationibus est disputandum.* The psychological and motivational dimensions of choice matter. Much work has to be produced along these lines.

Appendix 11.1: The complete list of attitudinal items as stated in the original Cv survey

1. My family and I would have great pleasure in knowing that the SIC, RTP, and TVI together have agreed in introducing in their TV schedule more documentary films about wildlife and its natural habitats. ("use")

2. My family and I think that the preservation of the Alentejo coast line is important because this is a place which all of us can visit and where we can see very beautiful natural landscapes. ("use")

3. My family and I like to see the Portuguese government giving more support to the national organizations that are promoting work in the field of environment conservation. ("warm glow")

4. My family and I think that the preservation of the Parks is important because these are privileged places where everybody may enjoy a walk or a picnic in a relaxed environment. ("use")

5. My family and I take great satisfaction in knowing that it is today guaranteed that our children, and future generations, will continue to have the possibility of observing wildlife in its natural habitat. ("use")

6. Despite the fact that my family and I may never see an otter in its natural habitat, we would be very worried if the total population of otters in Portugal became extinct. ("existence")

7. My family and I like to spend the weekends at home or going to the movies rather than going out for a walk in the countryside or by the beach. ("use")

8. Our family admires the individuals who, on a voluntary basis, participate in collecting contributionsfor national programs for social aid and solidarity. ("warm glow")

9. My family and I take great pleasure in knowing that we are still able to visit villages in Alentejo which keep their true identity and their typical houses, facades, and streets. ("use")

10. Despite the fact that my family and I may never see an Iberian lynx in its natural habitat, we are very happy to know that we have the guarantee that the lynx is kept safe from extinction in Portugal. ("existence")

11. My family and I think that the preservation of the natural areas is important since they are privileged sites for recreational activities like sightseeing or biking in a natural environment. ("use")

12. There are some funding campaigns to which my family and I feel very close and therefore we do not hesitate to contribute a donation. ("warm glow")

13. Despite the fact that my family and I may never visit a Natural Park, we are very happy to see these natural areas protected so that other Portuguese citizens may also have the possibility to observe wildlife in its natural habitat. ("use")

14. My family and I think that the preservation of the Alentejo coast line is important because this is a privileged place where all of us may enjoy going to the beach in a relaxed environment and being in contact with nature. ("use")

15. It is difficult for me to decline my help to other individuals who, either in the streets or at my door, beg for charity. ("warm glow")

16. Whenever I am approached by identified personnel, it is not difficult for me to refuse to make a financial contribution to a national fund raising campaign. ("warm glow")

17. The protection of the forests is very important because for Portugal they are a very important source of wealth. ("use")

18. With the increasing use of the media in our elementary schools as well as an increasing number of school visits to the Zoo, it will no longer be important to take the children on educational trips to the Natural Areas. ("use")

19. *Sometimes our help in national fund-raising campaigns is explained because we come under observation and feel "socially pressed" to contribute, and therefore we do not decline to make a contribution.* ("warm glow")

20. *I am happy with myself whenever I give a financial contribution to national fund raising campaigns.* ("warm glow")

21. *With the Portuguese participation in the EU, the preservation of our national diversity is no longer so important since we are constructing a common and shared European culture.* ("existence")

22. *Despite the fact that my family and I may never observe an eagle in nature, we take great pleasure in knowing that the eagles are kept safe from extinction.* ("existence")

23. *My family and I like to contribute to good causes such as the protection of the environment, and whenever we can afford it, we do not decline our help to such fund-raising campaigns.* *(warm glow)*

24. *Giving blood is giving life.* ("warm glow")

25. *During the holidays, my family and I prefer to stay home or to go to the beach rather than travelling around Portugal visiting our traditional villages.* ("use")

26. *My family and I think that the preservation of the Alentejo coast line is important because in this way we are protecting a typical lifestyle of the local inhabitants, which belongs to our national identity.* ("use")

Source: Nunes and Schokkaert (2003)

Appendix 11.2: The Latent Factor Model

The CV survey contains a list of 26 attitudinal items. Each item is represented by a sentence as presented in the instrument survey. The respondent expresses her opinion by classifying each sentence using a five-point semantic differentials or Likert scale: "I completely agree," "I agree," "Sometimes I agree, sometimes I disagree," "I disagree," and "I completely disagree" (see Appendix 11.1).

From a formal point of view, equation (11.A.1) describes the fundamental regression of the econometric latent model (in a matrix notation and for all individuals): (11.A.1)

$$\mathbf{av} = \wedge \mathbf{f} + \varXi$$

where **av** captures the matrix giving the answers of the sample respondents on the attitudinal items as presented in the instrument survey; **f** captures the matrix of factor scores giving the position of the sample respondents on the retained motivation; $\varLambda$ captures the matrix of factor loadings showing the correlations between the answers for the 26 items and the respondents' factor scores, and $\varXi$ captures the matrix of the residual terms. Since **f** is not observed, we must estimate them as functions of the observed **av**'s. It is assumed that the structure of the latent factor scores is characterized by the standard Gauss–Markov conditions.

$$E(\mathbf{f}) = \mathbf{0} \qquad\qquad \text{A1}$$

$$\operatorname{cov}(\mathbf{f}) = \mathbf{I} \qquad\qquad \text{A2}$$

$$E(\varXi) = \mathbf{0} \qquad\qquad \text{A3}$$

$$\operatorname{cov}(\varXi) = \varOmega = \begin{pmatrix} \omega_1 & 0 & \cdots & 0 \\ 0 & \omega_2 & \cdots & 0 \\ \vdots & \vdots & & \vdots \\ 0 & 0 & \cdots & \omega_{26} \end{pmatrix} \qquad\qquad \text{A4}$$

$$\operatorname{cov}(\mathbf{f}, \varXi) = \mathbf{0} \qquad\qquad \text{A5}$$

Assumptions A1 and A2 state that the underlying consumer factor scores are normalized or standardized variables; therefore they have mean zero and variances of one. Moreover, A2 declares that the consumer motivation factor scores are uncorrelated with each other—as such, the consumer motivations do not overlap. Assumptions A3 and A4 assert that the residual part is assumed to have a zero mean and specific variance—given by the main diagonal of $\varOmega$. Assumption A4 also declares that the residual parts are uncorrelated with each other. These assumptions imply that the motivation factors account for all the correlations among the observable variables. Finally, A5 assigns that the residual component and the constructed motivation factors scores are uncorrelated with each other.

Bearing in mind such premises, we obtain the following expression for the covariance matrix of the observed attitudinal items,

$$\text{cov}\,(\mathbf{av}) = \Lambda\Lambda' + \Omega \tag{11.A.1}$$

where the covariance matrix is broken down into two components: a common component, called the *communality* ($\Lambda\Lambda'$) and a unique component, called the *specific variance* (Ω). Therefore, we can describe the proportion of variance in the observed variables that is determined by the consumer motivation factors by analyzing the communalities scores matrix. The communalities, however, are not known, since they are the elements of information based on the unobserved factor loadings. The main objective, then, is to estimate the communalities such that the underlying motivational structure is able to reproduce these correlations as well as possible. The first step consists of attempting to find an estimator Λ that will approximate the fundamental expression (11.A.1) with S, the sample correlation matrix, in place of cov (av), i.e.,

$$S \cong \hat{\Lambda}\hat{\Lambda}' + \hat{\Omega} \tag{11.A.2}$$

We propose to estimate the communalities using the squared multiple correlation. This way we are able to neglect Ω and factor S into $S = \hat{\Lambda}\hat{\Lambda}'$. Finally, and as to find a frame of reference where the warm-glow retained factor is more interpretable, the estimated matrix Λ will be submitted to a rotation and $\hat{\Lambda}^* = \Lambda\,T$ (where T is orthogonal) will be obtained. We propose the varimax method as the selected orthogonal rotation procedure because this method is characterized by seeking rotated loadings that maximize the variance of the squared loadings in each column of $\Lambda *$. Therefore, varimax attempts to make the loadings either large (in absolute value close to one) or small (close to zero) so as to assist in the interpretation of the motivational structure.

The procedure first involves the extraction of the initial common factors[12] and second, the performance of a confirmatory analysis exercise; that is, a test of whether the motivation factor structure is supported by the data.[13]

Taking into account the computed factor loadings for warm glow and the respondent's answers to the attitudinal questions, we can estimate warm-glow motivation scores using a least squares estimation method,

$$\hat{f} = (\hat{\Lambda}^{*'}\Lambda^*)^{-1}\hat{\Lambda}^{*'}\text{av} \tag{11.A.3}$$

where $\hat{\Lambda}^* = \hat{\Lambda}\,T$ (T is orthogonal) and $\hat{\Lambda}$ is the matrix of factor loadings showing the correlations between the answers to the attitudinal questions and the position of the respondents on the warm-glow motivation.

---

[12] The factor loadings are analogous to the standardized regression coefficients as obtained in regression analysis. The matrix of factor loadings represents the product–moment correlation between the observable variable and the underlying factor.

[13] We used the maximum likelihood technique to test H_0 and run a Kaiser test (Kaiser 1960). The rationale for the Kaiser test is as follows: each observed variable contributes one unit of variance to the total variance in the data set. Thus, any component that displays an eigenvalue greater than one accounts for a greater amount of variance than had been contributed by one variable. In addition, a component that displays an eigenvalue less than one accounts for less variance than had been contributed by one variable. Since the purpose of the factor analysis is to assess a number of reduced components (or factors), this cannot be effectively achieved if one retains factors that account for less variance than had been contributed by individual variables.

Part IV

Designing Incentives Mechanisms under the Constraints of the Socio-political Game

Part IV provides an in-depth discussion of how to design policy instruments to solve the global commons problem. All three papers by Faure, Libecap, and Chichilnisky focus strongly on incentive-based approaches and concentrate on the governmental toolkit and the real-world design of regulatory policies.

Michael Faure reviews the various policy instruments that have been proposed by economists, political scientists, and lawyers to reach environmental targets: liability and tort law, ex-ante regulation, environmental taxation, and emissions trading schemes. He shows that the gap between command and control instruments versus market-based instruments may not be as deep as usually thought but at the same time none of the instruments belonging to either category is perfect. There is therefore plenty of room for combining policy instruments. However, even if optimum mixes exist, they might not be implemented because of policy obstacles or interest groups and such obstacles are stronger when transboundary issues are involved.

The chapter of Gary Libecap addresses the property rights solution. He shows that even in some of the simplest problems (local common-pool resources), the establishment of property rights involves serious shortcomings. There is often a war of attrition between the stakeholders, who expect that the cost of the privatization process be undertaken by the rival parties. Thus the establishment of property rights arrives often too late, that is once overexploitation and mismanagement of the resource has already happened. Sometimes, property rights are even implemented too late to prevent resources depletion. Moreover, to build political support, politicians mold the assignment of property rights in a manner that achieves other distributional objectives or meets the demands of those who claim to be harmed. These adjustments, which attenuate the property rights that are granted, weaken the ability of the rights regime to reduce the losses of open access.

The contribution by Graciela Chichilnisky analyzes the question of how to design effective environmental governance architectures to overcome the commons problems. This chapter identifies three core principles that a functioning environmental governance scheme is to be based on. Mechanisms need to ensure sustainable usage of the resource, they must be self-funded mechanisms that assign property rights in economic markets, and they must seek to decrease the gap in welfare between developed and less developed countries. For managing the commons problem with international watersheds, she suggests that assigning property rights to private–public corporations and bundling all water-related eco-services into bonds can be a way to resolve the commons problem. By doing so, prices are attached to otherwise costless resources. These policy instruments can, thus, mitigate the paradox of high actual, but low economic values for unpriced resources due to a lack of clearly defined property rights.

12

Designing Incentives Regulation for the Environment

Michael Faure

12.1 INTRODUCTION

In this chapter, which will more particularly focus on how incentives regulations can be designed for environmental protection, the central question of this book, being which governance is desirable for which environment, plays a crucial role. Indeed, most of the environmental law and economics literature has rightly pointed at the fact that in the past (but sometimes still today) one heard a general reference about the necessity to "protect the environment" apparently without any awareness of the fact that economic growth almost unavoidably brings about some pollution of the environment.

The statement of some traditional environmental lawyers that the goal of environmental law and policy would be to prevent environmental pollution (implying that this would be an absolute goal) is therefore not realistic. The question is rather what type of environmental protection (*inter alia* given its state of development and the corresponding preferences) a particular society desires. A crucial question with which environmental law and economics scholars therefore have often been engaged within the context of the determination of "Which environment?" is therefore indeed how one can usefully determine the desired level of environmental protection. To some extent this is then translated into an environmental standard. In legal terms, this is then referred to as an environmental quality or an ambient quality standard.

A second equally important question which has kept environmental law and economics scholars busy is indeed "which governance" can lead to the particular desired environmental protection? This has led to a detailed literature on the design of optimal instruments and institutions to provide this environmental protection. Economists have, moreover, held that to an important extent, it may be possible to provide this environmental governance at lowest costs (and probably most effectively) when institutions and instruments are designed in such a way that appropriate incentives are provided to the market participants to reach the desired environmental result. This idea has led to a broad literature on the use of incentive-based (also referred to as "economic") instruments to reach environmental goals. Strikingly, economic literature usually only reserves the term "economic" instruments for those that only specify a particular goal to be reached, but subsequently leave it (via financial incentives) to market participants to decide how to reach that particular outcome. That is why, traditionally, environmental taxes and emission trading were considered as the examples of market-based or "incentive-based" instruments.

However, to the extent that one takes this notion literally, one can also hold that probably more traditional legal policy instruments like liability rules and regulation are also "incentive-based" in the sense that they aim at providing incentives to market participants to reach a particular policy goal (such as reducing particular emissions). The main difference is usually in the amount of flexibility allowed and in the sanctions or enforcement if the particular goal is not reached. Increasingly, it has also appeared from the literature that there is therefore not that clear a dividing line as one would probably suppose between, on the one hand, economic instruments and, on the other hand, what is sometimes referred to as command-and-control regulation. Indeed, various policy initiatives introducing economic instruments have made clear that the particular form of legal design of the economic instrument is crucial for its success. Hence, also an economic instrument like taxation or emission trading requires an amount of regulation (and enforcement) for its functioning.

Moreover, also traditional regulatory instruments should not necessarily be of the static command-and-control type, but can also be more flexible, dynamic, and provide incentives for emission reductions at lowest costs. In addition, various policy initiatives with different instruments showed that both economic instruments as well as more traditional forms of regulation have their own strength and weaknesses. That has led many to hold that the key issue is not to find the one and only incentive-based instrument that could optimally provide environmental protection, but rather to look for the strengths and weaknesses of various instruments and to use them in combination. Much of the recent environmental policy literature therefore pays a lot of attention to so-called optimal mixes of a variety of (economic and more traditional) policy instruments.

The goal of this chapter is to provide an overview of the various types of incentive-based regulations from an environmental law and economics perspective by addressing their relative strengths and weaknesses as far as, for example, allowing sufficient flexibility and providing optimal incentives for a cost-effective reduction of environmental harm. A crucial issue in that respect is, of course, that incentive mechanisms will always have to be designed within a particular socio-political context where (as public choice has powerfully shown) industry will unavoidably lobby in favor of regulations which may reduce costs for them. A crucial design issue is therefore how incentive-based regulations can successfully be designed in such a way that either lobbying by industry (at the legislative level) or capturing (of administrative agencies) can potentially be reduced.

Even though it may not seem too ambitious to provide an overview of the strengths and weaknesses of various instruments based on existing literature, this attempt can still be useful for the simple reason that between but also within the various disciplines dealing with environmental policy design, there are still many (seemingly conflicting) approaches, or at least different accents. Just to mention a few: among economists one can clearly distinguish between those who would favor a more Coasian-based contractarian approach and would therefore stress that environmental protection can to a large extent result from efficient negotiations between potential polluters and victims. Also, liability rules forcing a potential polluter to compensate victims for environmental harm inflicted upon them can to a large extent still fit into this approach. Under a liability regime, the courts basically force polluters to compensate for damage done either in all cases (under strict liability) or if a certain level of care was not followed (under negligence), but compliance with a particular standard under a liability rule is not mandatory. The polluter is still free to deviate as long as he is able to pay the price in the sense of paying damages to the victim. The basic idea is that this flexible system (under particular strong assumptions, such as the solvency of the polluter and an adequate assessment of damages by the judge) will provide appropriate in-centives without the need to determine the type of measures to take to reduce the pollution. Traditional text books in environmental economics, on the other hand, deal to a large extent with environmental taxation and to a minor extent with emission trading as well. Even though economists pay that much attention to Pigouvian taxes, this stands in strong conflict with the reality of environmental policy in most countries, where environmental taxes either only play a modest role or are usually set at much lower levels than desired by economists for an optimal internalization of the externality caused by the pollution. Traditional environmental lawyers, in contrast, in their handbooks on environmental law pay most attention to what economists would refer to as the command-and-control type of regulation, being the structure of the traditional environmental statutes and the corresponding administrative system based on licenses, permitting, and standard setting by administrative agencies.

Notwithstanding these seemingly different approaches to policy design, I will try to show in this chapter that it is to a large extent not surprising that there are so many differing approaches, since none of the policy instruments (contracts, liability rules, regulation, or economic instruments) may alone be optimal to provide adequate incentives for pollution control. More particularly, since each approach has its own strengths and weaknesses, a combination may be necessary (which can also often be found in policy practice), ideally making optimal use of the advantages of each particular policy instrument. To show the relevance of these instruments in practice I will also address how particular instruments (environmental liability, emission trading) have been implemented in European environmental policy and discuss these evolutions from an economic perspective.

The remainder of this chapter will be structured as follows: first in Section 12.2 I discuss the well-known dichotomy between command-and-control versus "market-based" instruments, addressing some of the limits of command-and-control regulation. It is on the basis of the criticisms of command-and-control regulation that incentives and "market-based" mechanisms have been designed and implemented. Next, the potential of environmental liability as incentive-based instrument is explained in Section 12.3, while the particular weaknesses which may make a regulatory intervention necessary are the subject of Section 12.4. The traditional instrument proposed by environmental economists to govern environmental issues is environmental taxation, but the question, of course, arises why it has therefore been used so little in practice, and this is considered in Section 12.5. Increasingly, there is also experience with the model of emission trading. Both in the USA and in Europe (but also in other jurisdictions) emission trading is now used as an instrument to control greenhouse gases (the emission of which is supposed to contribute to climate change). These recent experiences show that notwithstanding the incentive-based character of such an emission trading system, legal design issues are crucial for the success of such a particular instrument, which is the topic of Section 12.6. Having discussed these five seemingly different approaches to environmental policy design issues, Section 12.7 addresses the question of whether it is useful to determine which instrument is "best" or whether one could rather opt for a combination of particular types of instruments.

12.2 COMMAND-AND-CONTROL VERSUS "MARKET-BASED" INSTRUMENTS

12.2.1 "Market-based" or "economic" instruments?

Below it will be shown that environmental externalities can be internalized through liability rules and regulation. It should, however, be mentioned that, traditionally, environmental law for the largest part consisted of regulation of what was referred to as "command-and-control" type of regulation. However, economists have increasingly pointed to the fact that this traditional approach of imposing pollution standards via government regulation may have several disadvantages as well (see for further details Faure, Peeters, and Wibisana 2006). Thus, they have in recent years picked up the classic message of the 1920s from Pigou that taxation could be a good instrument to use to internalize externalities. Moreover, since the 1960s Dales has pointed to the fact that social welfare could be increased if pollution rights were to be allocated to those parties that would be able to reduce pollution at the lowest costs. In order to effectuate this idea, trading in pollution rights should be made possible. These ideas are now referred to in the literature as the use of so-called economic instruments, sometimes also referred to as market-based instruments.

Many policy analysts interested in environmental policy have, for a number of years, advocated the increasing use of these economic or market-based instruments, more particularly as a reaction to regulation. Regulation is in that respect often referred to as a "command-and-control" approach. Economic instruments are today, at least in the literature, but increasingly also at the policy level, very popular. The use of market instruments, instead of relying on regulation, sounds modern and flexible and hence politicians will increasingly argue that environmental policy should be market-oriented instead of merely relying on top-down regulation by government. However, many talk about economic or market-based instruments without clearly defining what precisely is meant by the term. Indeed, one could, from an economic perspective, argue that all legal and policy instruments can be considered as "economic" as long as they give appropriate incentives to polluters for an efficient reduction of the externality caused by the pollution. Hence, as we have shown above, to an important extent also liability rules can be considered as "economic" instruments in the sense that the foresight derived from being held liable will also give incentives to polluters to prevent environmental harm.

Nevertheless, in the literature liability rules are traditionally not referred to when "economic" instruments are discussed. This concept usually refers to instruments whereby only the environmental targets are defined, but whereby it is largely left to the polluters to find the optimal instruments necessary to reach the particular targets. Hence, key notions in the use of so-called economic instruments are, on the one hand, the fact that they are incentive driven and, on the other hand, that they allow for more flexibility than the traditional command-and-control approach under regulation. Many instruments within that broad definition could qualify as "economic." Thus one could, for instance, argue that environmental management systems (EMAS) and the promotion of environmental care systems or environmental audits are surely also "economic." This chapter is going to focus more particularly on two examples of economic instruments: environmental taxes and emission trading.

12.2.2 Weaknesses of command and control

Before looking at environmental taxes and emission trading in more detail, it would be interesting to briefly summarize the criticisms on the command-and-control approach as they have been formulated in the literature, since these constituted the basis for experiments with economic instruments. First, a traditional command-and-control system focuses on a permit or licensing system. Within this system, traditionally, permits set emission standards, but these often disregard the effect of the aggregate level of emissions on the environmental quality of the receiving environmental medium. This was a criticism that was formulated, particularly in the 1970s, in situations where the approach was heavily focusing on emission systems. Whereas environmental policy had indeed been focusing on the control of emissions, the total effect of the emissions on environmental quality was disregarded. As a result, the effect was that, notwithstanding severe emission controls, total environmental quality was seriously reduced. It is indeed striking that in the USA, emission trading could develop within the context of the Clean Air Act, which had set target standards referred to as National Ambient Air Quality Standards (NAAQS) (Hahn and Hester 1989). Hence, the focus should, of course, be on target standards or environmental quality standards. However, this criticism on the use of emission standards is not necessarily a criticism on the use of command and control as such. Indeed, even within a system that would largely focus on target standards, one could still have either command-and-control or economic instruments. However, there are several other criticisms that can be formulated.[1]

A second criticism of command and control is that it requires high information and enforcement costs. Indeed, each industry must be scrutinized in detail to determine the appropriate level of emission control. Hence, on the one hand, the government needs to set optimal standards. It must be remembered that the traditional regulatory approach only works optimally if there is also optimal enforcement. In many cases polluters will balance the possibility of being fined (when they breach a regulation) against a marginal profit that can be realized with additional pollution. However, enforcement costs are often very considerable. If controls are too strict, the social enforcement costs will be too high. If, on the other hand, the level of control is too low, the damage costs for society as a result of the environmental pollution will be too

---

[1] For a summary of these criticisms see also Faure and Ubachs (2003).

high (Tietenberg 2000). Of course, one could argue that the authorities may reduce enforcement (and information) costs by relying on information provided by industry. However, the private interest theory of regulation will teach that it is still likely that the industry will distort the information in favor of its own interests.

Third, it has often been argued that the command-and-control approach has in many cases failed to generate sufficient incentives for polluters to reduce their pollution levels. The problem is that a command-and-control type regulation only requires a polluter to follow the regulatory standard, as this is, for instance, incorporated in a permit. However, as soon as the polluting firm complies with the regulatory standard there is no additional incentive to invest in, for example, research and development towards further innovative environmental technologies.

A fourth criticism is that the command-and-control approach has the disadvantage that it cannot equalize the marginal costs of pollution control among the different polluters that produce the same pollution. This has to do with the fact that a command-and-control approach is often too general. Indeed, with regulation the standard set by the regulatory agency will often be similar for each polluter and will therefore not take into account the fact that, for example, an efficient pollution reducer could reduce pollution at much lower costs. This constitutes a major shortcoming of a command-and-control system. This failure to equalize the marginal pollution costs will excessively increase the costs of pollution control. This, of course, has to do with the difficulty that administrative agencies will in many cases not be able to determine what the efficient emission for each individual polluter is. Indeed, the efficient pollution will vary from case to case. Ideally, authorities should be able to identify the polluters and should also determine the efficient pollution for that specific polluter. For certain factories the efficient pollution level will probably be higher than the imposed standard; for other factories it may be lower. If the authorities are not able to acquire correct information about the actual pollution of certain polluters, they might demand that all polluters reduce their emissions by the same percentage. This will inevitably lead to inefficiency and thus to welfare losses because the possibilities for pollution abatement will be different for each polluter.[2] The essential problem with the command-and-control approach is that those polluters that have the capacity to abate the pollution above the regulatory standard do not have any financial incentive to do so under a command-and-control system.

Fifth, under a command-and-control approach the polluters will only pay the prevention costs required to comply with the regulatory standard. However, polluters will not necessarily be required to pay for the costs of residual

---

[2] This point has also been made by Rosen (1999).

damages associated with the pollution that they have produced in conformity with the standard.

These criticisms show that there are considerable disadvantages with the traditional command-and-control approach, which can be summarized by the fact that the regulatory standard is often too general and not flexible or differentiated enough. An optimal environmental policy would need flexible (and hence often referred to as market-based) instruments, which both provide more flexibility (taking into account the individual possibilities of optimal pollution abatement of each polluter) and provide optimal incentives toward environmental technological innovation and not merely compliance with a regulatory standard. After having addressed the disadvantages of the traditional command-and-control approach, we can better understand why environmental policy analysts are increasingly interested in the so-called economic instruments.

12.3 ENVIRONMENTAL LIABILITY AS AN INCENTIVE INSTRUMENT

An important function of environmental liability is, at least from an economic perspective, to provide incentives for risk creators to look at prevention. The way liability rules aim at prevention can to a large extent be considered as a market-oriented approach or, if one wants, as the use of soft law instead of hard law. Indeed, the way tort law functions in providing these incentives is that it fixes a price for a specific violation of norms (negligence) or for reaching a certain consequence (strict liability), but it generally leaves it up to the parties to find the optimal way to prevent environmental harm. In the next three subsections we will have a look at how this regulatory function of environmental liability is seen from an economic perspective, how the two major liability rules, negligence and strict liability, function and finally we will consider the actual policy of the European Union in this domain.

12.3.1 Economic principles of accident law

The economic analysis of law in general and of accident law more specifically starts from the belief that a legal rule and more particularly a finding of liability will give incentives to potential parties in an accident to undertake careful behavior.[3] Thus, economists tend to stress the deterrent function of

---

[3] For excellent overviews of the role of liability and insurability as "engineering instruments" see Gimpel-Hinteregger 1994; Endres and Staiger 1996; Wagner 1999; Monti 2001.

tort law. Lawyers mention this deterrent function sometimes, but tend to attach more value to the compensation goal of accident law. This "victim protection" argument is discussed in the economics literature as well,[4] but more often it is stressed that the best form of victim protection is to avoid victimization in the first place. Of course, no one will argue that the prevention of accidents is not a form of victim protection as well. The difference in the two approaches is also characterized as an ex ante versus an ex post vision. Whereas lawyers tend to be more interested in the accident problem ex post, taking the view that there is a victim to be compensated, economists look at the accident problem from an ex ante perspective by asking the question how an ex post finding of liability will influence ex ante the incentives of potential parties to adopt care-taking behavior.

Of course, the differences in the approaches of the lawyers and the economists are not really that black and white. There are lawyers who stress the deterrent function of tort law as well (Koziol 1997) and some economists pay attention to compensation issues by stressing that accident law should also aim at equitable loss spreading (Veljanovski 1981). Moreover, lawyers also argue that tort law should lead to duties of care, which require preventive behaviour. From an economic perspective, the main goal of liability rules is the minimization of what was called by Guido Calabresi (1961, 1970) the primary accident costs: the costs of accident avoidance and the expected damage. Indeed, from a social point of view, accidents do not only cause costs from the moment an accident occurs and harm is suffered; potential parties in an accident setting, both injurers and victims, make investments in care to avoid the occurrence of an accident.

Sometimes the costs of care-taking are very clear and visible. We can refer, for instance, to the investments made by firms to reduce environmental pollution by purchasing water-cleaning equipment or installing safety controls to avoid product defects. But, in addition, the mere fact that in a traffic accident case both injurer and victim are limited in their freedom of movement, for instance because they have to drive or work carefully, is considered as a cost by economists.

A further distinction is made between unilateral accidents, in which only the care taken by one of the parties (the injurer) can influence the accident risk, and bilateral accidents, in which the behavior of both parties can influence the accident risk.[5] In a bilateral accident, the goal of accident law should therefore be to put in place incentives to minimize the total costs of care-taking by the potential injurer and the potential victim and the expected damage that will occur in case of an accident.

---

[4] Schwartz showed that rules of tort law may serve both the aims of deterrence and corrective justice: Schwartz (1997).
[5] This distinction has been made by Shavell (1987).

Economists use classic cost–benefit analysis to determine what the level of care is that will lead to such a minimization of the social costs of accidents. Not surprisingly, this can be found where the marginal costs of care-taking equal the marginal benefits in accident reduction (Shavell 1987). Indeed, since care-taking has a price as well, a legal rule should not give incentives to avoid every possible accident that could occur, but only those accidents that could be avoided by investments in care, of which the marginal costs are lower than or equal to the marginal benefits in accident reduction. It might well be that an extremely high level of care could additionally contribute to a reduction of the accident risk, but the marginal costs of care-taking might be higher than the additional benefit in accident reduction. Investments in care would in that case be inefficient and scarce resources would be spoiled.[6] These levels of care where the marginal costs of care-taking equal the marginal benefits in accident reduction are referred to in the literature as optimal or efficient care levels (Landes and Posner 1981; Polinsky 1983).

12.3.2 Strict liability versus negligence

12.3.2.1 Basic model

After having defined the regulatory function of liability rules—that from an economic perspective they should provide incentives to risk creators to take optimal care—the next question (which has been extensively addressed in the literature) is which liability rule may provide these appropriate incentives and can, in other words, be considered appropriate in an incentives-based strategy to optimally prevent environmental damage. The two legal rules distinguished in this respect are the classic fault or negligence rule (e.g. the one incorporated in art. 1382 of the Civil Code) and the strict liability rule. The basic difference between them is that under a fault or negligence regime the risk creator is only due to compensate the victim when his behavior falls short of a certain level of due care, to be determined by the court. Strict liability, on the other hand, lays a duty upon the injurer to compensate the victim irrespective of his behavior.

A strict liability rule only requires that there is a causal relationship between the activity of the injurer and the damage of the victim. The economic literature holds that if a negligence rule is adopted, the injurer will take optimal care, provided the due care required in the legal system is equal to the optimal care as defined in the model (Calabresi 1975; Shavell 1987). This can be easily understood. If the judicial system sets the due care standard

---

[6] This finding only holds in a risk-neutral setting. In case of risk aversion, higher investments in care might well be efficient, since a reduction of accident risk will also remove the disutility of risk from a risk-averse person.

correctly, the injurer can avoid liability by taking due care. Thus, he will have to take care to avoid the accident, but if he does so he can avoid paying the expected damage. Since the optimal care standard was defined as exactly that level of care where the marginal costs of care equal the marginal benefits in accident reduction, taking less than the due care standard will not be interesting for the individual injurer, since it will increase his total expected costs. Thus a negligence rule will lead to an efficient outcome as long as the legal system defines the due care as equal to the optimal care of the model. A strict liability rule will also lead to the optimum in a case where only one party can influence the accident risk. The reason is quite easy. A strict liability rule basically states that the injurer has to compensate in any case, no matter what care he took. It is sometimes argued that this will lead the injurer to take excessive precautions or to take no care at all since he is liable anyway. Neither of these statements seems true. By making the injurer strictly liable, the social decision is in fact shifted to the injurer. In a unilateral accident it simply means that he has to bear all the social costs of accidents, that is his own costs of care-taking and the expected damage (Polinsky 1983; Shavell 1987). Therefore, he will take exactly the same decision, that is to minimize his total expected accident costs. We discussed in the model that this could be reached at the optimal care level. Therefore, the injurer will take optimal care, since this is the way to minimize his total expected costs. Spending more on care would increase his costs of care-taking inefficiently and spending less on care would increase the expected damage inefficiently.

12.3.2.2 Refinements

This leads to the conclusion that in this particular setting where we only considered the influence of the injurer's care on the accidents, both negligence and strict liability will provide incentives to take optimal care. Of course, important nuances to this difference can be added. For instance, the administrative costs of applying both rules differ. The strict liability rule seems to have the disadvantage that a legal case will follow with every accident, since the injurer is always bound to compensate. Court costs can therefore be expected to be high. On the other hand, the negligence rule seems to have high information costs for the judge, since he will have to determine in a particular case what the marginal costs and marginal benefits of care-taking were (Brown 1973; Calabresi 1975; Shavell 1987).

The analysis, of course, can be much more refined if one goes into the bilateral accident situation. In that case, a contributory or comparative negligence defence has to be added to a strict liability rule to give victims as well an incentive to take optimal care. In other words: since victims would be fully compensated under strict liability, some defence should be added if the victim can equally influence the accident risk. Otherwise the victim would lack the incentive for prevention. The advantage of the negligence rule in that case is that the victim will anyway assume that he has to bear the loss, so he will always have an incentive for taking optimal care. The simple reason is that a fully informed victim (which is obviously a strong assumption) will be aware of the fact that the injurer will take due care to avoid liability. Hence the victim is left with his loss and will automatically have incentives for prevention, even if no defences are added. A further refinement can be found when attention is given to factors other than care that can influence the accident risk. In the literature, attention has especially been paid in that respect to the influence of the activity level (Diamond 1974; Shavell 1980; Adams 1989).

12.3.2.3 Strict liability for environmental harm?

How does this test apply to the issue concerned in this chapter, environmental liability? Environmental pollution can in most cases be considered a unilateral accident; that is, an accident whereby only the injurer can influence the accident risk. In this case we noted that the economic model predicts that the advantage of the strict liability rule is that it will give the injurer an incentive both to adopt an optimal activity level and to take efficient care. Since the victim cannot influence the accident risk, strict liability seems to be the first-best solution to give the potential polluter optimal incentives for accident reduction in those cases.[7] There may, however, obviously be cases where parties other than the polluter could influence the risk of environmental degradation. These are not always the victims in the traditional sense. One can imagine cases where, for example, public or private actors would be responsible for managing a natural resource area. It might be desirable in those cases that liability also aims to give them appropriate incentives to take those preventive measures. In that case environmental pollution would constitute a bilateral risk on the condition that one considers that third party a victim.[8]

However, since, in the example given, the influence of the polluter is probably still far more important than the influence of the other parties, the outcome doesn't change: a strict liability rule is still warranted to give the party who has most influence on the accident risk (the polluter) the incentive to take preventive measures. It is, however, important to remember that in bilateral cases a defence should always be added to victims as well. Moreover, if parties other than the polluter can influence the accident risk as well, they might additionally be held liable to the amount in which they contributed to the loss. That is, however, not an argument against the strict liability of the polluter. If

---

[7] See Faure (1995) for an application to nuclear liability.

[8] Although it is then probably more likely that more parties can influence the accident risk (and should therefore be given appropriate incentives), since the actors in the example given cannot be considered traditional victims who suffer the loss personally. See also Niezen (2000).

we apply these criteria determining the choice between negligence and strict liability to the environmental case, there seem to be strong arguments in favor of an introduction of strict liability. In many cases environmental pollution will be truly unilateral in the sense that only the injurer's activity can influence the accident risk, which constitutes a strong case for strict liability.[9]

There is another important aspect of the difference between negligence and strict liability which should be mentioned. This concerns the fact that the application of negligence requires high information costs from the judge, who will have to set the due care standard. The information necessary to weigh costs and benefits and to fix the optimal care may not be readily available to the judge. Strict liability shifts all costs to the injurer, who will then have to define the optimal care level. If one therefore assumes that, as may be the case with environmental harm, the information on optimal precaution is better available with industry than with the judges, this constitutes an argument for strict liability. Note that obviously, in some cases, there may be an information advantage with the regulator. This is, as we will discuss below, an argument in favor of regulation, but not necessarily against strict liability. This information advantage may therefore constitute an additional argument in favor of strict liability for environmental harm. One should, however, remember that this finding only holds in the models, such as the one which has been developed by Shavell, which start from an assumption of risk neutrality. If risk aversion is introduced and the potential injurer is risk averse, Endres and Schwarze correctly argue that strict liability is only efficient if in some way risk can be removed from the risk-averse injurer, for example through insurance (Endres and Schwarze 1991). Moreover, we assume that the judge has accurate information on the amount of the damage. If courts err in assessing damages, strict liability will lead to underdeterrence.[10]

12.3.3 Environmental liability in European private law

Of course, any discussion of the incentive function of liability rules within the context of a project on European private law should also pay some attention to recent developments in this respect at the policy level. The question more particularly arises of the extent to which the preference for strict liability (at least in unilateral accident cases) can also be found in legal practice. First of all, it can be held that the move towards strict liability for environmental damage

[9] In some cases it will be the victim's activity that caused the harm, e.g. if the victim knowingly came to the nuisance. This may then lead to a denial of a claim for compensation. This follows the discussion on the coming to the nuisance doctrine by Wittman (1980).

[10] If, in other words, courts can more easily observe the socially desirable level of precaution than the exact amount of external harm, a negligence rule should be favored. This point has been made by Cooter (1984).

can be discovered in many legal systems in Europe. This is more particularly the case when it concerns liability for soil pollution. Indeed, one can point at developments in legislation and case law in many countries which indicate a general trend towards strict liability.

Strict liability rules could already be found in many international conventions, for example in the civil liability Convention of 29 November 1969 with respect to oil pollution damage (Vanden Borre 2007) and in the nuclear liability conventions (of Paris and Brussels), which equally impose a strict liability on the licensee of a nuclear power plant (Verhey 2007; Wang 2007). Strict liability has also been introduced in the legislation of many countries. For instance, section 12.7 of the 1995 Environmental Act in the UK imposes strict liability for soil pollution.[11] Chapter 32 of the 1998 Swedish Environmental Code provides for a strict joint and several liability regime and a duty to compensate for those whose activity would cause bodily injury, material damage, and pecuniary losses, while chapter 10 of the same environmental code equally imposes a strict liability rule for soil contamination. The 1990 German Environmental Liability Act similarly introduced a statutory strict liability.[12] In other countries the move towards strict liability did not result from formal changes in legislation, but from developments in case law. This is the case in France, where a broad interpretation of Article 1384 of the Civil Code leads effectively to a strict liability, for example for polluted soils.[13]

This European-wide tendency towards strict liability now seems to have reached the European Union with its Directive 2004/35/CE of 21 April 2004.[14] Of course, this is not the place to discuss the contents of the Directive in any detail. It is mentioned here to verify the extent to which the approach in the directive follows the lessons from economic analysis enabling environmental liability to exercise its function of providing incentives for prevention. Although the Directive is formulated in a rather complicated way the policy options seem to correspond with economic analysis. For environmental damage, as defined in Article 2(1) of the Directive, a strict liability rule applies when this damage is caused by any of the occupational activities listed in Annex III. Annex III contains a number of hazardous activities such as waste management operations, the operation of installations subject to specific

---

[11] For more details on the UK soil pollution regime see Jones (1999). For an overview of the liability system for environmental damage in the UK, see also the 1996 McKenna Report, Study of Civil Liability Systems for Remedying Environmental Damage and the 2001 Chris Clarke Report for the European Commission, Update Comparative Legal Study.

[12] For an overview of environmental law in Germany. See also the 1996 McKenna Report, Study of Civil Liability Systems for Remedying Environmental Damage and the 2001 Chris Clarke Report for the European Commission, Update Comparative Legal Study. See also Hager (1993).

[13] For a critical discussion of French tort law from an economic perspective, see Faure (2001).

[14] *Official Journal* L143/56 of 30 April 2004.

permits, etc. For other activities, Article 3(1)(b) of the Directive provides that there is liability only when the operator has been at fault or negligent. This distinction, applying a strict liability rule mainly to damage resulting from hazardous activities, seems to be in line with economic principles. Moreover, Article 17 of the Directive provides that it shall not apply to damage caused by an emission, event, or incident that took place before the implementation date of the Directive. Hence, an inefficient retrospectivity of the Directive has been avoided. However, what is more problematic is that many issues are still left to the member states. This concerns for example:

- the fact that member states may allow the operator to be excluded from liability in cases where an emission or event was covered by a permit (Article 8(4)(a));
- as far as cost allocation in cases of multiple party causation is concerned, the Directive also refers to national regulations (article 9);
- as far as financial security is concerned, member states are only asked to take measures to encourage the development of financial security instruments and markets by the appropriate economic and financial operators (Article 14 (1)), but an outright duty to insure or provide other financial guarantees has not been imposed. This is problematic, since under insolvency strict liability may lead to underdeterrence.

12.4 REGULATION

12.4.1 Environmental liability versus regulation

It is not difficult to argue that although environmental liability undoubtedly has an important task as an instrument to prevent environmental damage, it also has serious inherent limitations. Given these limitations, some scholars therefore qualify the public law approach as "the preferred approach" to prevent environmental damage (Bergkamp 2001). However, it would be intellectually incorrect to qualify the fact that liability law cannot be applied to many cases of environmental damage as a shortcoming or limitation of tort law. The limitation of this instrument is that it can only be used when there is an identifiable victim and injurer and when a causal relationship can be established between an activity of the risk creator and the damage of the victim. If the injurer cannot be identified or the cause of the environmental damage cannot be established, liability law cannot be applied to this particular type of damage. This can hardly be considered as a "shortcoming" of liability law; it simply means that the conditions for the application of liability law are not fulfilled. However, this does justify the conclusion that if one wants to achieve the prevention of environmental harm, instruments other than liability law will have to be used.

Law and economics have paid a great deal of attention to the question of whether safety in society can best be reached through liability rules or through regulation. An important contribution to this debate comes from Steven Shavell (1984a, 1984b, 1987), who examined the choice between liability rules and regulation. Both liability rules and regulation can be used to reach the same goal—the optimal prevention of environmental harm. However, the way in which both instruments reach this goal is totally different. If tort law is used, the risk creator remains free to choose the way in which environmental damage can be prevented. Tort law assumes that the preventive function of liability rules will give incentives to the potential risk creator to introduce optimal preventive mechanisms. This is the case either because it is the optimal way for him to prevent the damage (under strict liability) or because it is a way to avoid having to pay compensation to the victim (under a negligence rule). Under regulation, the government will ex ante impose the use of a particular standard. Non-compliance with this standard will also be enforced and can lead to the imposition of administrative or criminal sanctions. Regulation is therefore considered to be an ex ante system aiming for prevention, whereas liability rules mainly intervene ex post after the damage has occurred. The criteria advanced by Steven Shavell that influence the choice between safety regulation and liability are:

- information asymmetries;
- insolvency;
- the underdeterrence of tort law;
- empirical evidence;
- the necessity of combining liability and regulation.

These are discussed in turn in the following subsections.

12.4.2 Information asymmetries

Information deficiencies have often been advanced as a cause of market failure and as the justification for government intervention through regulation.[15] For the proper operation of a liability system, information on the existing legal rules, the accident risk, efficient measures to prevent accidents, etc. is a precondition for an efficient deterrence. According to Shavell, the parties in an accident setting generally have much better information on the accident risk than that possessed by the regulatory body (Shavell 1984a). The parties

[15] See the basic article by Stigler (1961); Schwartz and Wilde (1979); Mackaay (1982).

themselves have, in principle, the best information on the costs and benefits of the activity that they undertake and of the optimal way to prevent accidents. This "assumption of information," however, will be reversed if it becomes clear that some risks are not readily appreciated by the parties in an accident setting. This may be more of a problem if costs are external, as they cannot always be easily assessed by the parties involved.

12.4.3 Insolvency

If the potential damages can be so high that they will exceed the wealth of the individual injurer, liability rules will not provide optimal incentives. The reason is that the costs of care are directly related to the magnitude of the expected damages. If the expected damages are much greater than the individual wealth of the injurer, the injurer will only consider the accident as having a magnitude equal to his wealth. He will, therefore, only take the care necessary to avoid an accident equal to his wealth, which can be lower than the care required to avoid the total accident risk (Shavell 1984a). This is a simple application of the principle that the deterrent effect of tort liability works only if the injurer has sufficient assets to pay for the damages he causes. If an injurer is protected against such liability, a problem of underdeterrence arises.[16] Safety regulation can overcome the problem of underdeterrence caused by insolvency. (If insurance were to come into the picture, it could overcome the problems of underdeterrence, provided that the moral hazard problem, caused by insurance, can be solved.) In that case, the efficient care will be determined ex ante by regulation and will be affected by enforcement instruments which induce the potential injurer to comply with the regulatory standard, irrespective of his wealth. Therefore, a problem might still arise if the regulation were also enforced by means of monetary sanctions. Again, if these were to exceed the injurer's wealth, the insolvency problem would remain. Hence, if a safety regulation is introduced because of a potential insolvency problem, the regulation itself should be enforced by non-monetary sanctions (Shavell 1985).

12.4.4 Underdeterrence of tort law

Some activities can cause considerable damage, but even so a law suit to recover these damages may be never brought. If this were the case, there would be no deterrent effect of liability rules. Therefore, the absence of a liability suit would again be an argument to enforce the duty of efficient care

---

[16] Shavell (1986). It was mentioned above that insolvency causes a problem under a strict liability rule, but less so under negligence.

by means of safety regulations, rather than through liability rules (Shavell 1984a). There can be a number of reasons why a law suit is not brought, even though considerable damage has been caused. Sometimes an injurer can escape liability because the harm is thinly spread among a number of victims. As a consequence, the damage incurred by every individual victim is so small that he has no incentive to bring a suit. In particular, this problem will arise if the damage is not caused to an individual but to common property, such as the surface waters in which each member of the population has a minor interest. In addition, a long time might have elapsed before the damage becomes apparent; in this case, much of the necessary evidence may be either lost or not obtained. Another problem is that if the damage only manifests itself years after the activity, the injurer might have gone out of business. A related problem is that it is often hard to prove that a causal link exists between an activity and a type of damage (Landes and Posner 1984; Kunreuther and Freeman 2001). The burden of proof of a causal relationship becomes more difficult with the increasing passage of time since the damaging incident took place. Often a victim will not recognize that the harm had been caused by a tort, but might think that his particular ailment, for example cancer, had a "natural cause," associated with general ill health. For all these reasons, a liability suit might not be brought and hence safety regulation is necessary to ensure that the potential polluter takes efficient care.[17]

12.4.5 Empirical evidence

For these reasons it is clear that some form of government regulation of environmental pollution is necessary. To reformulate: this shows that liability rules alone cannot suffice to prevent environmental harm, but there might be other, publicly imposed, instruments than the command-and-control type regulation which can be used to reach this goal. Taxes are obviously such an alternative. But these are also publicly imposed and can hence also be considered as "regulation." Although it is difficult to examine whether the environmental regulation is generally effective in reducing environmental harm, some studies have attempted to examine the effectiveness of safety regulation in controlling environmental harm. These studies do not address the specific quality of every environmental law, but examine whether regulation has generally been more important in reducing environmental harm than liability rules. Dewees demonstrated that in North America the quality of the environment has improved substantially as a result of regulatory efforts, not so much

---

[17] For alternatives to liability suits see Bocken (1987,1988).

in response to legal action in tort (Dewees 1992). This empirical evidence of the success of regulation, compared to tort law, has also been stressed by Dewees, Duff, and Trebilcock 1996. They hold that the large regulatory effort to improve the environment has met with considerable success when measured by the reduction of emissions, but that it is more difficult to argue that the environmental regulations of the 1970s in the USA equally had a considerable influence on the ambient environmental quality. Moreover, they also stress that while environmental regulation is a determining factor in pollutant emissions and ambient concentrations, other non-regulatory factors such as economic growth and even the weather also influence environmental quality (Dewees et al. 1996).

12.4.6 Necessity of combining liability and regulation

We have just stressed that according to Shavell's criteria there is a strong argument for controlling the environmental risk through ex ante regulation (or taxes). However, in individual cases there can still be damage to the environment. Then liability under tort comes into the picture and the question has been addressed in the literature how regulation influences the liability system and vice versa. The complementary relationship between tort law and regulation has been examined in detail by Rose-Ackerman (1992a, 1996), Kolstad et al. (1990), Faure and Ruegg (1994), and recently by Burrows (1999) and Arcuri (2001). Rose-Ackerman also compared US and European experiences in using regulation versus tort law in environmental policy. The first point which is often stressed is that the fact that there are many arguments in favor of ex ante regulation of the environment does not mean that the tort system should not be used any longer for its deterring and compensating functions. One reason for still relying on the tort system is that the effectiveness of (environmental) regulation is dependent upon enforcement, which may be weak. In addition, the influence of lobby groups on regulation, to which public choice theory has rightly pointed, can to some extent be overcome by combining safety regulation and liability rules. Moreover, safety regulation, for example emission standards in licenses, can become quickly outdated and often lack flexibility, which equally merits a combination with tort rules. Hence, from the above it follows that, although there is a strong case for safety regulation to control environmental risk, tort rules will still play an important role as well.[18] This obviously raises the question of whether compliance with regulation will affect the liability issue. These interdependencies

---

[18] For a recent different analysis, leading to the same result that liability and regulation should be combined, see Schmitz (2000).

between regulation and tort law raise a number of interesting questions that have been extensively addressed in the literature.[19]

12.5 ENVIRONMENTAL TAXATION

12.5.1 Basic principles

The Pigouvian tax for environmental pollution is a concept of pollution tax first developed by the British economist, Arthur C. Pigou. This concept states that in order to reduce the output of goods or the pollution level to its socially optimal level, the government may impose a tax which equals the damage cost of the pollution, namely the level where the marginal private benefit is equal to the marginal social cost (pollution damage cost resulting from an extra unit of the private polluting activity). Theoretically, we could argue that the marginal benefit (MB) of the firm will decrease as its activity continues, while the marginal social cost (MSC) will increase as the activity continues, since we assume that more pollution will be produced. Hence, without a tax, the firm will have no incentive to reduce its activity level to the socially optimal level. In this case, the firm will continue its activity as long as its marginal benefit is larger than zero. Consequently, the optimal pollution tax should be set at a point where MB is equal to MSC. This will induce the firm to reduce its activity to the socially optimal level of activity (Turner et al. 1994; Groosman 2000).[20] Why will the firm be induced to carry out this activity up to the optimal level? Apparently, whenever the MB is greater than the tax, the firm will prefer to carry out this activity and pay the tax to reduce its activity. However, for any activity level higher than the optimal level, the MB is less than the amount of tax that the firm should pay to the government. Therefore, in the latter case, the firm will be better off if it reduces its activity up to the optimal level.

12.5.2 Potential advantages of environmental taxes

First, a pollution tax entails less total abatement costs than the emissions standard does. Second, since pollution taxes could be administered by the

---

[19] See e.g. Schmitz (2000).

[20] Other authors suggest that sometimes it is more useful to illustrate the figure in terms of an abatement cost for the firm. Instead of showing the benefit of polluting, it would be better to show the cost of pollution abatement. Here, MB will be replaced by MCA (marginal cost of (pollution) abatement) for the firm. See Pindyck and Rubenfield (2001); Perman et al. (2003).

government's existing tax framework, there is a lower risk of evasion compared to fixed emission standards that are controlled via irregular on-site inspections. (This particularly applies to taxes that have employed input substances rather than output emissions as their tax bases. One could argue that the opposite result, namely the higher risk of evasion, seems to be more likely where emissions are used as tax bases. In this case, the effectiveness of some emission taxes can be guaranteed only if we have sufficient control and monitoring from the authority. Unfortunately, such control and monitoring are no cheaper or less demanding than control and monitoring under regulatory standards). Third, pollution taxes will provide an incentive for further emissions abatement, as reducing the amount of emissions means a reduction in the amount of tax and abatement cost. This leads to the fourth advantage of pollution taxes, namely that they might induce the firm to invest in research and development to search for new pollution abatement technologies or lower pollution production methods. Fifth, taxes upon some pollutants may induce the reduction of some other related pollutants; for example, a carbon tax may induce producers to use a non-fossil fuel, which would reduce the sulfur dioxide emissions that are also associated with fossil fuel.

12.5.3 Critical issues

(A) The tax rate should be set at a level that appropriately expresses the environmental objectives to be achieved. This requires that the function of marginal benefit and marginal cost should be defined accurately: if the tax rate is set at a level that is less than optimal, too much pollution might be produced. Therefore, we could argue that failure to set an appropriate tax rate would undermine the effectiveness of the tax as a means to achieve environmental objectives.

(B) The assessment basis of environmental taxes must reflect emissions as closely as possible. Emissions are not always easy to monitor or may comprise a complex combination of different substances. To avoid such a difficulty, an approach called "proxy variables" could be employed. The basis of the tax will be linked as closely as possible to emissions: the closer the linkage between the tax rate and emissions, the greater the effectiveness of the tax. However, one could argue that when consistently applied, the "proxy variables" could result in a situation where a firm finds itself amidst "piles of taxes." For example, if the government sets several taxes in relation to different assessment bases such as BOD (biological oxygen demand) level, used water, and various different toxic wastes, then a company, say a mining company, will face a number of different environmental taxes just for its waste water. This could significantly increase administrative costs, especially in terms of monitoring costs, which would undermine the efficiency of tax. Therefore, we often find taxes that combine several assessment bases, such as the combined industrial water emissions taxes applied in Germany, France, and the Netherlands, or the combined industrial air emissions taxes in Latvia and China.[21] If it is impossible to align the assessment basis with pollution emissions, indirect indicators or a flat rate are usually used as basis.[22]

(C) It is often argued that taxes have regressive effects on some income categories. In some cases, for example in energy tax, taxes will have stronger effects on poorer households. Although it is highly debatable, the effects of taxes on distribution need to be given due consideration.

(D) The effectiveness of pollution taxes will depend heavily on the shape of the demand and supply functions of the goods produced. When the demand curve of a good is very steep, indicating the inelasticity of the demand for that good, a substantial increase in its price can only slightly reduce the consumption of that good. This has been the situation, for instance, of a tax imposed on cigarettes. On the other hand, the availability of alternatives or substitutes will change the demand curve to a flatter (more elastic) profile, indicating that a small increase in the price will reduce consumption substantially. The illustration above indicates that a pollution tax will be more effective if demand for the polluting good is elastic. The basic idea of the Pigouvian tax is therefore simple: economists claim that pollution should be taxed and the tax will reflect the true social costs of the pollution. The effect will be that the correct price is charged for pollution. The theory behind this is, as was just mentioned, that this will create an incentive-based mechanism which will drive the polluter towards alternative technologies. However, as we pointed out, the application of an efficient tax also requires the government to have optimal information in order to fix the correct tax rate.

12.5.4 Empirical evidence

As far as empirical material relating to experiences with taxes is concerned, it is notable that much more evidence seems to come from Europe than from the USA. This is the reverse of situation for marketable pollution permits, which were (until recently) more popular in America than in Europe. Dewees et al.

---

[21] See Stavins (2003).

[22] The use of indirect measurement refers to indirect effects that are expected when assigning a tax for a particular basis. For example, by using carbon as an assessment basis for fuel tax, we could expect that it would also indirectly influence the reduction of sulfur emissions. However, using indirect measurement as an assessment basis is more likely to create errors, and hence it becomes a burden on the authority to minimize these errors. One could also argue that the use of a flat rate is not consistent with the idea of Pigouvian tax, since different people have different marginal cost functions and therefore, more importantly, a flat rate will not create an appropriate incentive for further emissions reduction.

(1996) note that charges are rarely introduced "in the text book form." Hahn (1989), moreover, claims that most emission charges or fees are used as a revenue-generating device for public services, rather than as instruments of environmental policy, as was prescribed by economists. The reasons why taxes are relatively rarely used in the USA are discussed in a report drafted by Oates (1994) for the OECD.

Most of the empirical evidence concerning the effectiveness of environmental taxes and charges comes from Europe. Dewees et al. (1996) argue that in the Netherlands water pollution by 14 industries responsible for 90 percent of total water pollution decreased by 50 percent between 1969 and 1975 and by another 20 percent by 1980, and that half of this reduction was due to an effluent charge. Similar success stories come from Germany (Brown and Johnson 1984: 929), where water effluent charges brought about significant increases in water treatment, allowing most firms to comply with the existing emission standards. Since Germany (and indeed most European countries) still has a combination of effluent charges and emission standards, it is, however, hard to argue that the significant investment in water treatment plans were mainly due to the charges system and not, for example, to the threat of administrative and/or criminal sanctions for violation of emission standards. These findings concerning the success of effluent charges in Germany comply with reports by Frey (1992), who argues that environmental taxes lead to a considerable reduction of emissions into the aqua system and into the air. A study by Bongaerts and Kraemer (1987: 12–19) comparing water pollution charges in France, the Netherlands, and the Federal Republic of Germany, came to the same conclusion: that effluent charges provide a strong incentive to invest in water pollution abatement equipment, but that it is impossible to disentangle the separate effects of charges and emission standards. The latter effect is especially strong in Germany, where the charges are halved for emitters who meet the effluent standards.

12.5.5 Influence of private interest

So far it has been assumed that government regulation and choices with respect to particular environmental policy instruments are always made "in the public interest." Reality is, of course, very different, as has been convincingly demonstrated by economists belonging to the public choice school. Often, regulation primarily serves the private interests of rent-seeking interest groups, rather than the public interest. Rent-seeking behavior may equally explain why the "economic prescriptions" (Hahn 1989) are not always followed, particularly as far as environmental taxation is concerned. In the USA emission taxes are seldom used and policy still relies to a large extent on the command-and-control approach. The reason is that firms will prefer emission standards to taxes, because standards serve as a barrier to entry to new firms, thus raising the profits of existing firms. Charges, on the other hand, do not preclude entry by new firms and represent an additional cost to the existing firms on the market (Buchanan and Tullock 1975; Coelho 1976: 976–8; Yohe 1976: 981–2). This basic point made by Buchanan and Tullock has been extended by other scholars, examining the implication of rent seeking for pollution taxation (Lee 1985: 731–44 and Brooks and Heijdra 1987: 335–42). As a result of the influence of private interest, there are also clear examples of regulatory failure as far as environmental taxation is concerned. For instance, in the Netherlands in 1996 a regulatory energy tax was introduced in the Act concerning taxes on an environmental basis. It is a regulatory charge that has as its primary goal the realization of certain ecological goals. However, this energy tax is only addressed towards small consumers, since it imposes a system of digressive taxes. This simply means that the larger the energy use, the lower the tax. This curious model therefore seems to give an incentive to increase the use of energy instead of decreasing it.[23]

12.6 EMISSIONS TRADING

12.6.1 Basic principles

We have already mentioned that the lack of flexibility and incentives was often considered to be a particular disadvantage of the traditional command-and-control approach. Some firms could abate pollution at relatively low costs or would innovate and invest in cleaner technologies, whereas others would not. The problem is that the traditional command-and-control approach in the form of standards is too general and does not allow for differentiation between polluting firms. And, in addition, fine-tuned regulation, such as permit schemes, requires a lot of (expensive and burdensome) bureaucratic work.

These problems could potentially be solved by using marketable permits as a policy instrument. Such an instrument was introduced in the 1960s by Dales (1968a) and has become increasingly popular, originally especially in the United States.[24] In this system, marketable permits that, for instance, allow a certain quantity of CO_2 to be emitted during a certain period in a certain area are issued to polluters, for instance, factories. Once again the authorities will have to set a certain environmental target; for example, limiting carbon

---

[23] For a critical analysis, see Faure and Ubachs (2002, 2005).

[24] One can think of the National Sulfur Dioxide Trading Program and Regional Nox Trading Programs: see Nash and Revesz (2001). For more discussion on the instrument, see Oates (1990: 290–3). See also Barde (1995: 218–20).

dioxide emissions to quantity X. The government will subsequently issue permits until quantity X is reached. The issuing of these permits takes place according to a certain distribution formula. Many different distribution schemes are possible; if the permits are issued for free, companies that pollute less than is allowed by their permit can sell their remaining quota to companies that wish to pollute more than their assigned quota. If government chooses to auction the permits, factories simply buy units of pollution at the equilibrium price, depending on the total amount of their pollution.

Interestingly, the efficiency of emissions trading could also be linked to Coase Theorem. According to Coase Theorem, polluters have a mutual interest in trading permits; a polluter who pollutes less has the opportunity to receive payment by trading his remaining pollution rights, while the polluter who would like to pollute more, is willing to pay for extra pollution rights (provided that transaction costs are low). This way, a possible loss of welfare—which arises if regulation is used as an instrument for environmental policy—can be reduced. If the government introduces a system in which permits are sold to the polluters, the government acts like a broker and should be able to control the functioning of the system. Marketable emission permits have several major advantages: first, they give the environmental regulator direct control over the quantity of emissions; second, contrary to the tax system, marketable permits will enable automatic adjustment for the inflation; third, marketable permits may gain more acceptance simply because of familiarity, namely that the trading originates from a permit, a system which the regulators have experience of and are therefore more comfortable with.

Marketable permits may also have a number of disadvantages: first, there is a disadvantage with respect to the initial allocation of the permit (in practice, permits are usually granted via grandfathering (and are thus free of charge) according to past emissions records, hence it can be assumed that initial rights to use the environment are assigned to the polluters); second, there are often public concerns that the system will cause pollution to be transferred to another region; third, marketable permits are also criticized in relation to revenue. It is argued that under marketable permit schemes, the industry's profit will increase while pollution levels remain the same, in contrast to a tax system, which will not only improve the level of pollution but also raise revenue for the government.

12.6.2 Design issues

Even though on paper the system of emissions trading sounds very promising, there are potential problems that cannot be neglected. These have partly to do with the legal and institutional design of the system, issues that are sometimes overlooked by economists.

12.6.2.1 Allocation method

First there is the issue of the choice of allocation method. Ideally (at least from an economic perspective) auctioning would be chosen.[25] However, in practice, grandfathering is often chosen whereby a de facto reward for (old) polluters takes place. Grandfathering has been criticized as a way used by incumbent firms to prevent new firms from entering a competitive market (Ogus 1999: 169). However, Turner et al. (1994) argue that marketable permits, whether the initial allocation is auctioned or grandfathered, are already vulnerable to being used as an entry barrier. This could occur if existing firms retain as many Emission Reduction Credits (ERCs) as possible and then refuse to sell them to the newcomers or will only sell only at a high price (Turner et al. 1994: 186).[26]

Another objection is that grandfathering runs counter to the basic meaning of the polluter pays principle. Indeed, with grandfathering the bigger firms who polluted the most would be "rewarded" with tradable emissions rights corresponding to their historic emissions. In this sense, it seems that it is not a "polluter pays," but a "polluter earns" principle that is being applied (Peeters 2003). New, cleaner companies might face a situation where they have to buy emissions rights from existing firms that have polluted more. Companies that had already started environmentally friendly activities before the market in ERCs started (the "early actors") would be in a disadvantageous position. To avoid these negative effects, alternative criteria for the initial allocation of the rights must be considered. But it should be recognized that the government must respect to a certain extent the legitimate expectations firms may have of continuing their activities allowed by a traditional permit. The (partial) revocation of such a permit must therefore correspond to legal criteria, such as taking into account a reasonable transition period. Choosing to correct for the undesirable outcome of grandfathering in the context of the polluter pays principle can also probably be done with an additional financial instrument. It could, for instance, be considered whether or not setting a maximum price on the tradable rights should be recommended (Victor 2001: 102).

12.6.2.2 Enforcement

A system of marketable permits requires effective control—which places a strong demand on government institutions. Indeed, emitting without surrendering a corresponding emission right must be prohibited and this prohibition must be controlled and enforced. Much of the debate on emissions trading

---

[25] On the allocation methods in the EU emissions trading scheme, see Chapter 8 by Ellerman in this volume.

[26] The relationship between interest group lobbies and the emission trading system in the USA has been discussed by Svendsen (1998: 133–44).

concerns the first steps that have to be made in introducing and applying the instrument: how will it fit into the existing legal system (especially the existing permit procedures or other policy instruments) and how will the allocation of permits be conducted? Apparently, the focus on the enforcement of an emissions trading scheme has been debated less than the other topics mentioned. Even Dales did not pay much attention to the enforcement aspects of emissions trading, but nowadays we know that environmental legislation often has an enforcement deficit. However, policy makers should be very alert to the enforcement task that belongs to an emissions trading system. It can be assumed that with the introduction of a financial incentive for reducing emissions, a simultaneous incentive for not following the rules is included. One should note that there could be an attraction for firms to camouflage the real emissions data in order to arrange that fewer rights can be surrendered to the government. We may assume that firms, to a large extent, will focus on minimizing their expected costs, among which are emissions control costs, receipts, or expenditure from permit market transactions, and expected penalties from reporting and emissions violations (Stranlund et al. 2002: 343–61).

12.7 BALANCE

The central question in this chapter is through what kind of legal or policy instruments a "pricing" of environmental pollution take place. This is an important element of the search for the optimal instrument that will give a potential polluter the incentive to prevent environmental harm. Indeed, the issues of cost–benefit analysis and environmental standard setting give an indication of the level of pollution that should be internalized; they do not explain the kind of instrument through which these optimal standards should be implemented.

12.7.1 Not one single optimal instrument

It appears from an examination of some of the environmental policy instruments that there is no one single optimal instrument that will internalize environmental externalities in the most effective way. Depending upon particular circumstances, they all have their specific strengths and weaknesses.

Consider, for example, the first instrument discussed: environmental liability. Its strength is undoubtedly that it can provide an excellent incentive to potential polluters to take optimal measures to reduce pollution, still leaving industry with sufficient flexibility. Indeed, in a liability regime, there is no intervention by government determining, for example, what type of standard has to be followed. Potential polluters are, in principle, allowed to neglect the optimal standard, provided they are willing to pay the "price" in terms of damages to the victim. The economic idea is that precisely this duty to compensate the victim will prevent the polluter from taking care below the required standard. Under liability, it is either the judge (under a negligence setting) or the potential polluter himself (under strict liability) who will determine the optimal care to be taken. The advantage is that an adaptation—for example, to technological changes—can take place dynamically and that incentives are given (especially under strict liability) to innovate in order to reduce pollution even further in a cost-effective way. Liability rules are relatively cheap, since no standards need to be determined ex ante through government agencies and enforcement takes place via private parties (the victim) and not via government.

However, notwithstanding these advantages it was then demonstrated in the discussion of regulation that liability rules will have this incentive effect only if the value of the expected harm to be caused by the potential polluter is not higher than his wealth. Moreover, it is supposed that a potential victim can always identify the potential polluter and can prove that the harm stands in a causal relationship with the polluter's activity caused the harm and that it stands in a causal relationship with his activity. When all of these conditions fail (which may often be the case with environmental harm, also due to latency) liability rules will fail to have a deterrent effect. That is the major justification of regulation.

However, it was equally shown that regulation cannot be idealized either for the simple reason that it may not be flexible enough (too static), not able to adapt quickly to changing circumstances, does not provide enough incentive for innovation, and (probably most importantly) it can be subject to influence by private interest groups. The latter may lead to the setting of inefficient care levels by regulatory agencies. Also, as far as market-based instruments are concerned, we found that on paper they look wonderful and theoretically have many advantages compared to regulation (or command and control). By focusing on the way that, for example, environmental taxation and emission trading function in practice, many scholars have shown that in practice certain legal and institutional design issues may reduce the efficiency of these so-called economic instruments: environmental taxes never reflect marginal environmental costs correctly and are only used to a limited extent; emission trading may suffer from grandfathering and other design issues, which can reduce their effectiveness.

The reason why these economic instruments are never introduced in textbooks is well-known: the influence of private interest also affects instrument choice and the design of particular policy instruments. One can see the influence of interest groups in the way in which even market-oriented instruments such as emission trading are organized. Notice in this respect the fact that when an emission trading system is introduced, the legislator will often prefer a grandfathering of emission rights to existing polluters, rather than an auctioning system. Grandfathering is, of course, in the interests of the existing firms and it effectively grants them a right to pollute and may create barriers of entry for new firms.

12.7.2 Search for "optimal mixes"

Given the fact that (for a variety of reasons) all policy instruments seem to have particular advantages, but also suffer from particular weaknesses, it may be best to use the strength of particular policy instruments in an optimal way in combination with other instruments. There is an abundant law and economics literature on this optimal combination of various policy instruments. It discusses the comparative benefits of various instruments in a given situation. Polinsky (1979) builds on the Calabresi and Melamed model, which discusses the optimal use of property rights and liability rules, by adding a tax subsidy approach to this classic comparison between property rights and liability rules. Polinsky argues that when the government has full information about the externality problem, only a tax subsidy approach can control the externality efficiently and protect both parties' entitlements. This remains the case, in a positive transaction costs world. Polinsky also addresses the more realistic setting in which the government has limited information. In that case, the approaches can be ranked to some extent (Polinsky 1979: 1–48). A comparison of Pigouvian taxes and the liability rule approach is also provided by Brown and Holahan (1980: 165–78). Polinsky (1979) claims that the tax approach will be inferior to the liability approach in a wide range of circumstances, but that in terms of entitlement protection there is a clear preference for the property rights approach. Hence, a distinction is made between, on the one hand, common law remedies such as property rights and liability rules and, on the other hand, incentive-based mechanisms such as taxes and charges. Some attention has also been paid to the problem of combining tort recovery and effluent fees or tradable rights. Rose-Ackerman (1992b) has argued that incentive schemes require a fundamental rethinking of the relationship between tort law and statutory law. She argued that incentive-based regulatory statutes should pre-empt tort actions: if fee schedules have been set to reflect social costs, tort actions would be redundant or even counterproductive (see Rose-Ackerman 1992b: 128; see also above subsection 12.4.6). This goes to the fundamental point mentioned above, that a combined use of instruments is useful when the instruments have complementary benefits. However, if both instruments in fact achieve the same goal, applying two instruments may only lead to increased administrative costs or to overdeterrence.

In terms of the choice of various instruments we should point to the law and economics literature, where a combined use of a variety of instruments such as property rights, liability rules, emission and target standards has been advocated. Once more, we should stress that such a combined use of instruments does not mean that all instruments should be used at the same time, but that the comparative benefits of every instrument should be used in a complementary approach.[27] One issue relating both to environmental taxation and to emissions trading is that environmental policy instruments may have a so-called double dividend (Paulus 1995). For example, both environmental taxation and emission trading schemes (in case of auctioning) can be revenue generating and aim at the reduction of emissions as well. Hence, this revenue-generating feature of environmental instruments can play an important role in the optimal design of policy instruments as well.

Finally, it may be clear that an important element in the choice (and probably mixes) of instruments also concerns the role of uncertainty about the marginal abatement cost and the marginal damage cost curve (Weitzman 1974). Uncertainty about firms' clean-up costs can be an argument in favor of a mixed system whereby the use of licenses is supplemented by an affluent subsidy and a penalty (Roberts and Spence 1976).

12.7.3 Optimal instrument mixes in practice

In practice environmental policy may be based on a combination of economic instruments (such as environmental taxes) with regulatory solutions (such as emission standards in permits).[28] Given the weaknesses of both liability rules and regulation in many legal systems, environmental pollution is controlled primarily via (command-and-control) regulation, but liability rules still apply as well. That means that even when a particular regulatory standard was followed by a potential polluter he can still be held liable in tort. That would give him additional incentives to follow an optimal care level, even when this is higher than the required regulatory standard. There is undoubtedly more potential in actual environmental policy to make such an optimal use of a combination of the strength of various policy instruments. Take the example of climate change: it is somewhat remarkable that the EU chooses emissions trading as the main (and in fact only) instrument to achieve the emission reductions required by the Kyoto Protocol. This is striking, given that other classic instruments to internalize environmental externalities (taxation being

---

[27] See Skogh (1982: 67–80; 1989: 87–101); Gravelle (1987: 115–31); and Hansson and Skogh (1987: 132–44), and more particularly Gunningham and Grabosky (1998).

[28] On the instrument mixes in environmental policy, see Gunningham and Grabosky (1998: 422–53).

an obvious one) are not used. There is undoubtedly room to examine whether in the EU environmental taxation could achieve (instead of or in combination with the ETS) similar or even better results than emissions trading.

An interesting combination of environmental taxation and emissions trading can be found in the UK. The UK introduced a so-called climate change levy the revenues of which are recycled back to business in the form of a 0.3 percent cut in employers' national insurance contributions. What is particularly attractive about this UK system is that the tax does not increase the total costs for business, since its revenues are recycled back to industry.

An interesting example of a combination solution can be found in Switzerland, where companies that participate in an emissions trading scheme are exempted from the domestic CO_2 tax. However, one should be careful when introducing taxes as the golden solution to reduce CO_2 emissions (if it were at all politically feasible to introduce such a mechanism). Baldwin (2008), for example, stresses that a cap on emissions in a cap-and-trade ETS at least has the advantage that it provides more predictable outcomes, since the overall level of emissions is fixed. In a taxation system, emission levels will be contingent on individual firm's cumulative responses to incentives, which makes the outcome (in terms of reducing CO_2 emissions) less predictable (Baldwin 2008: 6).

12.7.4 Limits of instrument mixes

One has to stress once more that the potential mixes of policy instruments may not always be used to the optimal extent, for the simple reason that this may be determined by political choices and by political interest groups. The fact that a certain command-and-control instrument is introduced rather than another (market-oriented) instrument will often be the result of effective lobbying by an interest group. This is undoubtedly the case in the EU, where emissions trading was the preferred option rather than environmental taxation. This should not come as a surprise, since emissions trading obviously serves the interest of industry better than costly taxation measures. To a large extent the shape of the EU ETS Directive can therefore be considered as the result of effective lobbying by industry.

There is, however, one particular warning one has to formulate against a combination of different types of instruments. In this respect it is interesting to discuss the work of Bruno Frey. Frey (1997, 1999) pointed out the importance of the intrinsic motivation of citizens in the form of an environmental morality. He argued that some instruments might encourage an intrinsic motivation, whereas others rather undermine it (consider governmental crowding-out of voluntary provision of public goods and Chapter 10 by Richter and Van Soest in this volume). Frey argues that an environmental policy which is solely based on controls and commands undermines environmental morality, because it reduces the self-determination of the people. Moreover, complex and abstract regulations are unlikely to improve environmental morality. The same is, however, true according to Frey for tradable emission rights. To pay for being able to undertake an undesired activity—the pollution of the environment—can be compared with the indulgences sold in the Middle Ages: the sense of punishment induced by sinning is lost as a result of the "license to pollute." Emission rights, of course, tend to reduce pollution because they make violation costly, but they also destroy the intrinsic motivation to safeguard the environment. The best way to promote environmental morality in the short term is by appeals and participation procedures and in the long run by education. Moreover, when legal regulations have an expressive function, this supports environmental morality. This is the case with easily comprehensible regulations whose punishments fit exactly the damage done to nature. Because the market-oriented policy instruments such as tradable licenses do not always support an environmental morality, Frey suggests using complementary environmental policies. However, a complementary policy should not be identified with a "system's approach" in the sense that everything should be done at the same time. The aim must be, as we equally held above, to exploit the strong points of each instrument while at the same time compensating for the approach's negative aspects (Frey 1997: 56–79; 1999: 395–417). An important lesson from this literature is that choosing an optimal combination of the strengths of various policy instruments should not result in an imposition of all instruments at the same time, which may lead to an ineffective and costly overdeterrence and potentially adverse results.

It is also interesting to mention that the Coase Theorem still plays an important role for one domain which was not explicitly addressed within the context of this chapter: transboundary environmental harm. In a recent study of large environmental disputes between states, it was shown that courts (more particularly the International Court of Justice) in fact rarely provide for a final allocation of property rights for the simple reason that (due to limited information) the probability of misallocation by courts is large. Courts seem, rather, to provide a few indications to the parties in order to further facilitate Coasian bargaining between them. More particularly, transboundary pollution cases between states could provide the type of potentially low transaction cost setting where bargaining could possibly achieve better results than court- imposed solutions (Faure and Johnston 2008). A typical element of environmental pollution is without any doubt that they have in many cases a transboundary nature. In some cases (as with climate change) environmental goods can even be considered as global public goods. The transboundary character of the externalities caused by environmental pollution have therefore often been stressed as an important reason for a type of multilevel regulation required by international treaties. Once again, this raises important questions concerning not only the effectiveness of treaty mechanisms, but also how compliance with international environmental agreements can be guaranteed (see Faure and Lefevere 1999).

12.7.5 Importance of multidisciplinary research

Experience with the European Emission Trading Directive has shown the importance of multidisciplinary research and cooperation to better understand the strengths and weaknesses of an instrument like emissions trading. For lawyers it is undoubtedly important to have a grasp of economics (or at least cooperate with economists) in order to understand the incentive function of a typical economic instrument like emissions trading. However, a close analysis of the emissions trading directive is not only an invitation to lawyers to take economic analysis seriously. Economic efficiency and the effectiveness of an emissions trading scheme may well to a large extent depend on what some non-lawyers would refer to as "legal details." It is more particularly these "legal details" or, to put it more politely, legal design issues that will have an important bearing upon the economic effects of an emissions trading scheme. It is more particularly these institutional design issues of particular (economic) instruments that may crucially influence the effectiveness of that particular policy tool. These examples show that in order to better understand the effectiveness of environmental policy instruments, close cooperation between various scholars interested in "environmental social engineering," such as lawyers and economists (preferably brought together in the law and economics discipline) is of crucial importance.

13

Property Rights as Solutions to the Problems of Open Access: Options and Constraints

Gary D. Libecap

13.1 INTRODUCTION

Even though property rights in some form are the theoretical response to open-access losses involving natural and environmental resources, formal property rights typically come late, after considerable waste has been endured. Prescriptive government regulation that calls for uniform rules and standards as a means of constraining behavior generally comes first. Only later, when these actions have failed to address the problem effectively is there a resort to property rights.[1] This chapter summarizes the theoretical reasons why this pattern exists and presents three empirical examples of overfishing, over-extraction from oil and gas reservoirs, and excessive air pollution to illustrate the main points. The key explanation for this pattern is that early, *formal* property rights involve high resource and political costs relative to their expected gains; they have formidable information and input requirements in allocation, measurement, bounding, and enforcement; and they have substantial distributive effects when there is too much uncertainty as to how these might impact key constituencies. Accordingly, there is delay in the assignment of property rights to address open access. During this period of transition, asset rents are dissipated, but enduring these losses does not necessarily imply inefficiency when the resource costs of developing the institutional response are considered. As I argue elsewhere, when the value of the resource or the cost of the externality is relatively low, prescriptive regulation to limit exploitation through uniform restrictions can be cost-effective and politically acceptable.[2]

---

[1] There are exceptions when the resource is of very high value, information costs regarding the problem are low, and rights can be relatively easily assigned. Consider gold and silver and other hard rock minerals. For a discussion see Libecap (2007).

[2] Libecap (2008).

Information demands are limited and aimed at administering general rules and standards; regulation does not involve obvious redistribution; and reliance upon standardized restrictions reduces uncertainty regarding the impact on constituencies. The various parties involved can predict how they might be affected and their current political and wealth standings are unlikely to be importantly altered. At the same time, however, these policies incompletely address the externality, leaving many margins for rent dissipation unconstrained. Over time as the problem becomes more serious, information is generated about the benefits and costs of property rights; information asymmetries are reduced; and overall uncertainty is diminished. At that point more parties see that they will be made better off, and it becomes more economically rational and politically feasible to adopt property rights.

Property rights address the externality directly and link individual incentives with social objectives for resource use. And property rights institutions have impressive records of success in addressing open-access losses.[3] Nevertheless, they are adopted only when their costs are offset by the aggregate rents that are saved from overexploitation. Because the transaction costs involved in assigning, measuring, and enforcing formal property rights can be large, the value of the resource and the nature of uncertainty determine the optimal time for introducing them. Crises that suddenly and sharply raise benefits and lower uncertainty speed this process.[4]

13.2 THE LOSSES IN "THE TRAGEDY OF THE COMMONS"

The losses inherent in "The Tragedy of the Commons" occur because there are no clear property rights (informal or formal, group or individual) to the resource and open access prevails.[5] Social and private costs and benefits diverge so that individuals do not bear the full costs of their actions in resource use decisions. Aggregate short-term production or use levels are too high and investment is too low. The parties inflict harm on one another with costly technological and pecuniary externalities. In anticipation of these spillovers, there can be a competitive rush to exploit the resource. Because exchange is not possible within large groups in the absence of property rights, the parties cannot bargain with one another to constrain behavior or to re-allocate the resource to higher-valued uses currently or across time.[6] There are no price signals to reveal opportunity costs. Valuable labor and capital inputs are

---

[3] See, for example, a summary of the gains in fisheries in Costello et al. (2008).
[4] See Krier and Ursin (1977) and Krier (1994).
[5] Garrett Hardin (1968).
[6] Bargaining of the kind discussed by Ronald Coase (1960).

diverted from productive use to predation and defense. The losses involved in this process can be very large, and the social savings from avoiding them provide incentives for collective action to secure more official group or government action. In the following section, a framework is presented to describe the collective action problem in bargaining within and across groups to address the wastes of open access.

13.3 ANALYTICAL FRAMEWORK

In collective action negotiations, each party determines whether or not to participate by comparing their current welfare situation with what is forecast through group efforts. If individual expected net gains are positive, the parties will choose to take action within the group. These net gains are a function of the predicted aggregate benefits and costs of eliminating the externality and their proposed distribution among group members. The greater the uncertainty associated with cost and benefit calculations, the lower the anticipated returns. The benefits of collective action also depend upon monitoring and enforcement. If the costs are so high that free-riding is prevalent, then the advantages of collective action are reduced.

Generally, collective action is promoted if the number of parties is small; if they are homogeneous in the expected net gains of agreement; if there is little uncertainty regarding the size and distribution of costs and benefits (information, measurement, bounding, and compliance costs are small); and if the aggregate gains of taking action are large relative to the costs.[7] Important deviations from these criteria can hinder group efforts. If the common resource is of low value and/or the transaction costs of addressing the problem are high, there are few incentives for action until values increase or costs fall. As group size grows, bargaining and compliance costs increase. If the aggregate benefit is a public good (high bounding costs) whereas the costs of taking action are private, free-riding and defection are encouraged. High information costs lead to uncertainty in calculating aggregate net gains and their distribution, and hence, in estimating how individuals or larger constituencies will fare from group action. If the uncertainty is uniformly distributed across group members, agreement on measures to be taken can still be reached. But asymmetric information and related differences in publicly available and privately held information about costs or benefits result in divergent views of the overall advantages of addressing the externality and sharing the resulting net returns. Collective action can become more practical after delay as

---

[7] E. Ostrom (1998b).

transaction costs fall; as new information emerges regarding the severity of the problem; as the resource becomes more valuable; as new technology or techniques are developed to lower the costs of closing the externality; and when the number of parties declines as the private returns to exploitation fall. At this point, distributional concerns become subordinate to the overall need to respond to open access, and group efforts follow. These general principles regarding collective action and delay in the assignment of property rights apply whether bargaining occurs within groups to address the externality; across groups to lobby politicians for state intervention; or across countries to elicit international responses to global externalities.[8]

The arguments suggested here regarding the response to open access are similar to those described by Krier and Ursin.[9] They listed six themes associated with government environmental policies:

1. Politicians (and agency officials) adopt regulations that take the path of least resistance; they are reactive, rather than precautionary in order to garner political support for regulation and to minimize the political risk of adopting inappropriate or extremely costly policies.

2. Politicians place the burden of uncertainty on those parties seeking policy change. Since new regulations potentially impose vague costs on other constituencies, politicians insure that proposed standards and other controls are based on reliable data through additional research.

3. Political action follows crises that clarify the benefits of new policies through the generation of additional information and a broader sense of immediacy among citizens.

4. Politicians rely on technological solutions, rather than more fundamental programs to change citizen behavior, which can be controversial, with costs spread unevenly. Since technology mandates can be applied uniformly, they appear to maintain existing distributions of wealth and political support and avoid divisive distributional issues, especially in the design of transfer payment schemes.

5. Politicians take action only after research and learning reveal what is most likely to work, lowering uncertainty and the costs imposed on constituents.

6. There is a lag or a seemingly "unwarranted delay in government resolution of a social problem."

In group, national, and international actions to reduce the losses of open access, the parties involved are more likely to reach agreement when uncertainty is reduced, when differences in expected costs and benefits across constituencies are narrowed, and when the aggregate benefits of collective

---

[8] Constituent-group politics is discussed by Peltzman (1976) and Becker (1983).
[9] Krier and Ursin (1977: 11–13, 252–304).

efforts exceed the transaction costs involved. These points suggest that there will be widely differing views regarding the extent of early open-access problems and the importance of confronting them. These conditions encourage group members and politicians to wait. When action is taken, it will involve general rules, regulations, and standards that involve the fewest costs and information demands and raise the least allocation concerns. These acts will be insufficient so that the problem will intensify. Only then will formal property rights be implemented, and their ability to address the externality will depend upon how distribution demands were overcome in their design and allocation. This is not to say that crises are always required to implement property rights. But the arguments outlined here suggest that crises generate sufficient information to make property rights adoption more feasible than otherwise might be the case.

13.4 APPLICATION

13.4.1 Fisheries

In fisheries the implications of open access have been understood for a very long time by fishers and by pioneering students of the problem, such as Scott Gordon, Anthony Scott, and Vernon Smith.[10] Nevertheless, in 2000, Quinton Grafton, Dale Squires, and Kevin Fox described the continuing dramatic wastes of overfishing and inappropriate regulation in the Pacific Northwest halibut fishery; in 2003, Ransom Myers and Boris Worm warned that the world's major predatory fish populations were in a state of serious depletion; and in 2006, Jennifer Devine, Krista Baker, and Richard Haedrich provided a similar dire assessment for other deep-sea fisheries.[11]

The patterns of response are clear. The first government reaction to open access has been the implementation of uniform restrictions on access and fishing effort that minimize information requirements and avoid significant deliberate changes in *status quo* economic and political rankings among the parties involved. Uniform regulations, however, do not align the incentives of the parties with the objectives of reduced harvest and conservation of the stock. Accordingly, if the fishery is sufficiently valuable, at some point there has been a turn to property rights of some type. But these typically have come late, only after the stock has collapsed and declining returns have made existing practices untenable. Rognvaldur Hannesson, Ragnar Arnason, and Ross Shotton, among others, outline a common process of open-access losses,

---

[10] Gordon (1954), Scott (1955), and Smith (1969).
[11] Grafton et al. (2000); Myers and Worm (2003); and Devine et al. (2006).

delayed regulation, and finally, a limited adoption of individual transferable quotas (ITQs) or individual vessel quotas (IVQs).[12] Further, Ronald Johnson and Gary Libecap (1982) describe the contracting problem among fishers, who differ in skill and returns under both open access and regulation. These heterogeneities determine the kinds of regulations and property rights that can be agreed to and limit their timely adoption.[13]

For migratory offshore fisheries, the closing of the commons has required the existence of political jurisdictions and/or international agreements on fishing restrictions. These institutions were assembled with the establishment of 200-mile exclusive economic zones (EEZs) by coastal states, but this process did not occur until the 1970s following the Law of the Sea negotiations. Iceland staked its claims in 1975; the US Congress did so in 1974, followed by Presidential Proclamation in 1983; and Canada acted in 1977.[14] These national ocean claims, however, were not made part of international law until 1994. There was nothing biologically or environmentally significant about 200-mile zones in fisheries, beyond which many stocks migrate. Efforts in 1993 to extend them to more effectively address over-harvesting in the open seas under the UN Conference on Straddling Stocks and Highly Migratory Fish Stocks failed due to disputes among coastal states over the size of allotments. An international agreement was reached in 1995, but it did not extend the exclusive zones; rather, it avoided the issue by vesting management in regional fisheries' organizations that lacked any real enforcement power.

The 200-mile limit, however, made regulation possible within it, and by the 1970s important, valuable fisheries were already seriously overexploited. Among these were the British Columbia salmon fishery, the North East Atlantic, Icelandic, and North Sea Herring fisheries, and the Norwegian cod fishery.[15] In response to these conditions, ITQs were suggested by fishery economist Francis Christy in 1973 as a means of raising fishing incomes and of motivating fishers to conserve stocks.[16] The response to over harvest, however, was not the assignment of property rights through ITQs, but rather the adoption of generalized season, vessel, and equipment controls. With diverse interests, ranging from inshore and offshore fishers, large and small boat owners, fishers from different locales, sports and commercial fishers, processors, equipment sellers, labor groups, and regulatory officials, there could be agreement only on standardized rules and not on the more difficult task of assigning and monitoring individual property rights. While attractive for

[12] ITQs are the most widely applied form of property right in fisheries (Hannesson 2004: 56). See also Shotton (2000) and Arnason (2002).
[13] Johnson and Libecap (1982).
[14] Hannesson (2004: 38, 107, 116).
[15] Hannesson (2004: 69–71, 103, 116–17).
[16] Hannesson (2004: 71).

technological and distributive reasons, these regulations did not successfully address open access. Boat capitalization increased, stocks plummeted, and fishing seasons were shortened drastically. For example, in the British Columbia halibut fishery, when regulation began in 1980, total capacity was set at 435 vessels, and new entry to meet that target was rapid, with the number of vessels rising by 31 percent within 9 years. Increased fishing pressure, however, brought a fall in the stock, and regulators gradually reduced the season from 65 days to 6 days by 1990. The shortened season led to further investment by fishers in larger and more powerful vessels and a competitive fishing derby to harvest as many fish as possible in the limited time available. Harvests had to be processed and frozen, and more valuable fresh halibut were not available for market after the season closed. In response to these conditions, IVQs were adopted in 1991.[17] After that, the number of vessels fell as quotas were purchased and consolidated and the season was expanded to 245 days by 1993 as stocks rebounded. With longer seasons fresh halibut could again be offered for most of the year.[18] Similar problems with uniform regulation occurred in other fisheries.

Under ITQs and IVQs, regulators set the total annual allowable catch based on assembled biological information, anticipated environmental conditions, and expected harvest impacts. Each authorized fisher or vessel is granted a share in the annual catch based on the allocation rule, and the quotas generally can be traded, although with varying restrictions. The most common allocation rule is first-possession or historical catch. Past investment in vessels and equipment is often taken into account. The advantage of ITQs is that they better align the harvest practices of fishers with practices that protect or enhance the stock. The value of their quotas, which often can be major sources of wealth, depends upon the long-term health of the stock. Hence, there are incentives for self- and group monitoring of compliance, and importantly, ITQs, as a property right, are the basis for further contracting among fishers to reduce fishing pressure. The dramatic improvement of fishery stocks after the introduction of some form of property right through catch quotas has been illustrated by Costello, Gaines, and Lynham (2008) in their analysis of global fisheries institutions and catch statistics in 11,135 fisheries from 1950 to 2003. They found that by 2003, the fraction of ITQ-managed fisheries that were collapsed was about half that of non-ITQ fisheries. Their results probably underestimate ITQ benefits, because most ITQ fisheries are young. The analysis suggests that well-designed property rights instruments may prevent fishery collapse across diverse fisheries.[19] Even so, there is resistance to their adoption until late in exploitation.

---

[17] Hannesson (2004: 111), Grafton et al. (2000: 686).
[18] Grafton et al. (2000: 685). See their Table I for vessel numbers and fishing seasons.
[19] Costello et al. (2008).

13.4.2 Oil and gas extraction

Oil and natural deposits that lie under private lands in the USA also are open-access resources. They are lodged in subsurface reservoirs under great pressure. When any part of the surrounding geologic formation is punctured by a well bore, a low-pressure area is created. Natural gas and oil migrate rapidly toward the opening. Migration potentially allows adjacent landowners to extract their neighbor's oil.

In the USA, because of the fugitive nature of subterranean oil and gas, in situ property rights are not assigned to surface landowners, as is done with fixed subsurface mineral resources, but instead are granted only upon extraction or capture, as is done with wild animals (minerals *ferae naturae*).[20] This ownership rule creates conditions for competitive withdrawal. Owners lease exploration and production rights to oil and gas firms, and these firms have incentives to drill and drain to increase their shares of oil field rents, even though these individual actions lead to aggregate open-access losses. Rents are dissipated as capital costs are driven up with the drilling of excessive numbers of wells (more than geologic conditions require or price and interest rate projections warrant) and with the construction of surface storage, where the oil can be held safe from drainage by other firms. Rapid extraction also increases production costs as subsurface pressures are vented prematurely, forcing the early adoption of pumps and injection wells. Total oil recovery falls as pressures decline because oil becomes trapped in surrounding formations, retrievable only at very high extraction costs. Finally, rents are dissipated as production patterns diverge from those that would maximize the value of output over time.

As with fisheries, the problem of competitive withdrawal has been recognized for a long time. It was observed when oil was first discovered in the United States in 1859. The nature and extent of the externalities involved, however, were not well enough understood to attempt coordinated strategies to constrain them. By the early twentieth century, however, the economic value of oil was high enough to raise concerns about waste. These losses stimulated scientific research on subsurface reservoir mechanics and on how production practices could affect overall recovery. With this knowledge, there was a basis for negotiations among private parties to reduce the losses of open access. Buyouts of all but one party on a reservoir to place it under single ownership or unitization for cooperative production were the most complete solutions. Neither property right solution was widespread, however. As a result, as with fisheries, initial formal efforts to address open access turned to state regulation. State regulation focused on limiting the drilling of wells and the

---

[20] The problems of open access in oil production are discussed by Libecap and Smith (2002).

extraction of oil and gas from them. The Texas Railroad Commission and other state regulatory agencies set monthly statewide production levels and allocated the total among regulated wells as quotas under a system termed prorationing. These production rules were applied uniformly to all oil fields, even though each field had a unique physical configuration and optimum production potential.

Subsequent dissatisfaction with state regulation led larger oil and natural gas firms to consider either private collective action through buyouts or unitization of fields. Unitization was the preferred solution for many firms because it maintained their lease ownership in the field at a time of considerable uncertainty about long-term lease values that prevented agreement on sales prices. But lease valuation problems also hindered unit agreements.[21] With unitization production rights are delegated through negotiation to a single firm, the unit operator, with net revenues apportioned among all parties on the field (including those that would otherwise be producing). As the only producer on the field and a residual profit claimant, the unit operator has an incentive to maximize field rents. Accordingly, unitization results in important economic gains: a time stream of output that more closely approximates the rent-maximizing pattern, increased oil recovery, and reduced wells and other capital costs. Unit agreements, especially during primary production when natural subsurface pressures could force oil to the surface, however, were very difficult to complete. Unitization during secondary recovery was easier because of existing coordination among producers for injecting water, gas, or other fluids to push oil out of the ground. Otherwise field output would plummet. Accordingly, secondary recovery and unit agreements could be written jointly, but the losses of competitive production during primary recovery remained. The key issue of contention in these collective efforts has been the allocation of of oil-field rents through shares of the net proceeds of unit production.[22] These shares are property rights to the unit rents and are based on estimated pre-unit lease values. Contingent updates are not possible because once the unit is formed individual leases lose their meaning and reservoir production dynamics change.[23] The bargaining problem arises due to disagreement on lease values.

Because of conflicts over allocation, unit agreements can take a very long time to negotiate or they breakdown and result in incomplete units that cover only part of a field. In their detailed analysis of seven units in Texas and New Mexico, Steven Wiggins and Gary Libecap (1985) found that they required

---

[21] For discussion of unitization see Smith (1987); Libecap (1998); Libecap and Smith (1999).

[22] For discussion, see Libecap (1989: 93–114). Wiggins and Libecap (1985) examined the bargaining problem underlying unit formation, and Libecap and James Smith (1999) described the nature of a complete unit contract.

[23] Updates are possible during certain pre-agreed events such as the shift from primary to secondary recovery. See Libecap and Smith (1999: 535–7).

from four to nine years from the time negotiations began until agreements could be reached. Moreover, in five of the seven cases the acreage in the final unit was less than that involved in the early negotiations. With incomplete units, part of the reservoir remained open access or was organized into competitive subunits with significant losses.[24]

The problems of negotiation are more difficult for reservoirs that involve mixtures of oil and natural gas. Differences in price volatility for the two substances make it difficult to agree upon conversion factors. Such reservoirs are frequent, since 63 percent of the largest US oil fields contained significant volumes of natural gas along with oil.[25] Oil lease owners prefer to re-inject gas into the formation to expel the oil, whereas gas lease owners prefer to sell their gas. To promote unitization, states have intervened with compulsory or forced unitization statutes. These statutes relaxed the unanimity voting rule on share allocations. In Oklahoma, compulsory unitization legislation was enacted in 1945. In Texas, however, small firms resisted the loss of the regulatory advantages afforded them through the state's prorationing regulation, and because of their large number and political influence, Texas was never able to adopt a compulsory unitization law.[26] Not surprisingly, Texas has had a lower share of production from fully unitized fields than do other states. Accordingly, the pattern of responding to open access in oil and gas reservoirs is similar to that which occurred in fisheries: tolerance of open access until the costs became large compared to the expected benefits of minimally addressing it; adoption of uniform production rules, molded by political factors; finally, resort to property rights, in this case through buyout or field unitization. Uncertainty in estimates of how the parties would fare under new regulations or property rights regimes, relative to the *status quo*, delayed action.

13.5 AIR POLLUTION

The use of the air as a disposal outlet for pollution is also an open-access problem. Emissions arise from manufacturing plants, utilities, vehicle exhaust, as well as a myriad of other sources that are part of a modern economy. Because there are no property rights to the atmosphere, which is fugitive and virtually impossible to bound, there is the potential for too many emissions. If the emitted particles are relatively large or they interact with local sunlight and geographical factors, as with urban smog, air pollution has localized effects. Where the emissions travel larger distances, as with SO_2, the external effects

---

[24] Wiggins and Libecap (1985: 377–83).
[25] Libecap and Smith (2002: S597).
[26] Libecap and Wiggins (1985: 706–12).

are more broadly cast, and if they migrate to the upper atmosphere, global externalities result, as with chlorofluorocarbons (CFCs) and CO_2. When releases are limited and the airborne stock is small relative to the atmosphere affected, there is little adverse impact. As emissions grow and the stock of pollutants increases, however, air pollution becomes a more serious problem. As concerns about air pollution have risen, the regulatory response has been slow and the adoption of property rights to mitigate the problem has come even later. The notion of tradable emission permits as a property rights solution to address air pollution was put forward by Thomas Crocker in 1966 and by J.H. Dales in 1968, but their adoption took another 30 years.[27] James Krier and Edmund Ursin (1977) and Krier (1994) describe the sluggish pace of government response to air pollution in Southern California. Although there had been growing persistence of smog in the Los Angeles Basin by the early 1940s, it took approximately 35 years before regulations were enacted to directly attack the major source of the problem—auto exhaust. The primary regulatory response was on technological adjustments to reduce emissions as a condition for licensing new vehicles and some used cars, and the establishment of uniform emissions standards for stationary sources, rather than on behavioral changes, such as restrictions on driving.[28] Most mobile pollution sources remained relatively unregulated by the state of California. The Federal Clean Air Act of 1963, the Motor Vehicle Control Act of 1965, the Federal Air Quality Act of 1967, and the Federal Clean Air Act Amendments of 1970 allowed for more direct federal government regulation. The 1970 law established uniform air quality standards across the country and identified non-attainment areas where more restrictive controls were to be implemented.[29] Market-based pricing approaches, such as emissions taxes, were not adopted.[30] Although pollution levels were reduced in some areas, states consistently failed to meet targeted standards during 1970–90, and in many areas air quality actually worsened.[31] Finally, in 1994, some 50 years after the first concerns about smog, California implemented a property rights approach to reduce NOx and SO_2, the major sources of smog, in the Los Angeles Basin with the Regional Clean Air Incentives Market, RECLAIM. Unfortunately, RECLAIM applied only to certain stationary facilities—utilities, refineries, and manufacturing plants—and not motor vehicles. These facilities were granted emissions quotas, based on historical releases and annual reduction rates. The South Coast Air Quality Management District (SCAQMD) set total annual allowable releases, with each facility's quota a share of the aggregate. The

---

[27] Crocker (1966: 61–8); Dales (1968a).
[28] Krier and Ursin (1977: 8, 277–9).
[29] Krier and Ursin (1977: 2–3).
[30] Dewees (1998: 597).
[31] Krier and Ursin (1977: 258, 296–307).

quotas were a property right to emit pollutants, and they could be traded to encourage those organizations that could reduce pollution at lower cost to do so while selling the residual to sources with higher abatement costs.

There is a similar pattern of delay, reliance upon uniform standards, and finally on property rights in national efforts to lower SO_2 pollution. In the 1960s there was growing awareness of the damage caused to lakes and forests from acid rain downwind from power plants that released SO_2 into the atmosphere. The 1970 and 1977 Clean Air Act Amendments set national maximum concentrations of SO_2 and the states were charged with meeting those standards. The regulations specified the equipment to be used, such as types of scrubbers, even if the utility used low-sulfur coal, and setting new source performance standards that applied to new plants. Nevertheless, acid rain continued to be a problem, and much more significant reductions in SO_2 releases were determined to be necessary, particularly new ones aimed at controlling emissions from the dirtiest units.[32] The political and economic costs, however, were viewed as being prohibitive unless policies were changed to allow for more cost-based approaches. By 1990 US pollution control costs had reached $125 billion annually, nearly a 300 percent increase in real terms from 1972 levels.[33] Existing uniform rules generally did not recognize that the costs of controlling emissions varied across and within firms. Since traditional regulation gave advantages to old plants and technology, there were few incentives for those firms to develop new technologies to reduce emissions at lower cost. Newer units were forced to adopt the technology specified by the regulator, rather than that which might have been more cost-effective.[34] In response, Title IV of the 1990 Clean Air Act Amendments, finally authorized electric utilities to trade allowances to emit SO_2 while reducing total allowed emissions by approximately 50 percent.

This was the first large-scale, long-term US environmental program to rely on tradable emission permits.[35] Under the permit system, an annual targeted level of emissions was set and prorated across permit holders, who were allowed to discharge a specified amount of the gasses. Emission permits were allocated to utilities through first-possession rules, based on past electricity production, heat generation, fuel use or emissions, free of charge, and hence grandfathered in existing utilities. As in the RECLAIM program, the permits were a tradable property right to discharge a specified amount of SO_2 and NO_x. Rather than equating pollution levels across firms as in past regulation, by trading these instruments marginal abatement costs could be equalized across firms. Those firms that could reduce emissions at lower cost could

---

[32] Joskow and Schmalensee (1998: 46–50).
[33] Stavins (2007b: 34).
[34] Freeman and Kolstad (2007: 5).
[35] Joskow and Schmalensee, (1998: 38); 1990 CAAA, Public Law 101-549; Stavins (2007b: 23).

do so and sell the residual emission rights, apply them to offset excess emissions in other parts of their operations, or bank them. An active market in emission permits developed.

Adoption of tradable emission permits has been viewed as a successful means of lowering overall air pollution with a cost saving of over $1 billion relative to what might have been possible under previous regulation.[36] But as with similarly successful ITQs in fisheries and unitization in oil and gas reservoirs, tradable emission permits were not adopted until existing regulation proved both to be too costly and too ineffective in mitigating the losses of open access. Moreover, by that time the benefits and costs of adopting property rights were sufficiently clear to allow side payments in the allocation property rights to address distributional demands.

There have been even more extreme problems in efforts to address global air pollution externalities. The very nature of global environmental externalities presents incentive problems. Abatement by any country benefits others as a public good, but if abatement is costly to a country's citizens, its politicians have an incentive to invest less in reduction efforts than would be globally optimal and to free-ride on cutbacks taken elsewhere.

The most successful effort to address international air pollution has been the Montreal Protocol of September 1987 on Substances that Deplete the Ozone Layer.[37] Concern about the build up of chlorofluorocarbons in the upper atmosphere surfaced in 1974 when two studies hypothesized that chlorine released from the breakdown of CFCs had destructive effects on stratospheric ozone.[38] In the 1970s the imperative of taking unilateral action that could involve substantial economic costs in the USA was not compelling for key constituencies, such as the chemical industry. The actual atmospheric mechanisms involved were incompletely understood, and the extent of ozone depletion and its consequences were unclear. Indeed, in 1983, under the Reagan Administration, the EPA advised Congress that no action should be taken until the relationship between CFCs and ozone depletion was more clearly determined. In March 1988, the NASA Ozone Trends Panel released additional scientific information suggesting that the ozone "holes" were larger than previously believed and that there were tighter links between ozone layer deterioration and CFC emissions. This new information helped to shift the US position on international collective action. It also changed because domestic political opposition to regulation had diminished. The chemical industry, with new technologies for CFC substitutes, no longer resisted domestic CFC controls, and it lobbied for international restrictions to phase out CFC production

---

[36] Stavins (2007b: 23).

[37] Montreal Protocol on Substances that Deplete the Ozone Layer Treaty Doc No. 10, 100th Congress, 1st Sess., 1987.

[38] Stolarski and Cicerone (1974) and Molina and Rowland (1974).

and trade. But opposition remained among European firms, who would be disadvantaged by CFC controls and from representatives of undeveloped countries, who saw restrictions on CFCs as being particularly costly.

The first international action was launched 11 years after the ozone "holes" were first detected. The Vienna Convention for the Protection of the Ozone Layer was completed in 1985 and ratified by the USA one year later, in 1986.[39] Disagreements, especially between representatives of developed and developing countries, blocked any actual CFC control measures. In response, representatives from the USA, Canada, Japan, and Europe offered countries with low per capita consumption of CFCs various exemptions from international regulations. This concession led to the agreement on the 1987 Montreal Protocol. Under the Protocol, developed countries were to cut production and consumption of CFCs by 20 percent of their 1986 levels by 1993 and by 50 percent by 1998. CFC trade with countries not adopting the restrictions was to be stopped. With the notion of "common but differentiated responsibilities," developing countries were allowed an extra 10-year delay to reach reduced production targets and were authorized to exceed their 1986 levels of production by up to 10 percent to satisfy "basic domestic needs."[40]

Overall, it took 16 years to reach general international agreement on controlling the production and dissemination of CFCs. Regulation has been based on production bans and technological substitution. There has also been use of tradable emission permits for achieving compliance with the Montreal Protocol, and a tax on CFCs was introduced later to accelerate the phase out. CFC emissions have declined, and taxpayers in developed countries have born most of the costs of the regulations.

The second example of international air pollution control efforts to limit greenhouse gas (GHG) emissions, however, faces even more difficult problems. There have been delays, differential responses among countries to calls to address the externality, and no success in reducing overall emissions. It seems unlikely that any effective, coordinated response will take place until crises increase perceived benefits and mitigate international distributional concerns. The issues are quite similar to those that have arisen regarding CFC control.

Global warming has been a concern in many quarters at least since the 1990s and perhaps earlier.[41] With unrestricted access to the atmosphere, gases such as carbon dioxide (CO_2), nitrous oxide (N_2O), chlorofluorocarbons (CFCs), and methane (CH_4) are released as by-products of human activities and other natural sources across countries. Regardless of their origin the gases are spread around the globe with potential external effects. The gases retard

---

[39] Vienna Convention for the Protection of the Ozone Layer, May 2, 1985, Treaty Doc. No. 9, 99th Congress 1st Sess., 1985.

[40] Benedict (1991: 241).

[41] Krier (1994: 857–9).

the re-radiation of the sun's energy from the Earth's surface back into space. There are many sources of uncertainty regarding aggregate effects of global warming, their distribution among countries, and the costs of reducing GHG emissions.

The magnitude of global warming and associated climate change remains generally undetermined, although there is more of a consensus on the issue than even a few years ago. The scientific uncertainty comes in estimating the rate at which greenhouse gas concentrations will increase, the corresponding impact of rising GHG concentrations on temperatures, the patterns of climate change across the globe, and their impact on the regions affected. The resulting scientific uncertainty regarding global warming allows politicians to chose among conflicting evidence for justifying positions desired by critical constituencies with more certainty than actual understanding may merit. The necessary emission reductions in response to possible climate change and the associated economic costs involved are similarly unclear.

The magnitude of the costs depends upon the amount of the reduction required for each country and its pace. The costs are the greatest for the countries that produce the most CO_2 and other greenhouse gases. Within countries abatement efforts will have differential impacts, with the transportation, manufacturing, and utility sectors incurring higher costs. There are many estimates of the costs of emissions controls in the USA with the results dependent on the assumptions made regarding timing, magnitude, and the instruments used. Those countries and interests that anticipate bearing more of the costs of regulation understandably resist action until compensating arrangements are implemented, but agreement on them is subject to disputes over who should pay and receive the amounts involved, and the forms and timing of compensation. Further, as with the Montreal Protocol, there is no underlying enforcement mechanism within the Kyoto Protocol of 1997, which was the first formal international treaty to reduce GHG emissions.[42]

Given the unclear and uneven distribution of the costs and benefits of international action and a general lack of immediacy in taking it, it is understandable that progress has been slow regarding global warming. As of December 2006, 169 countries had ratified the Protocol, but the USA and Australia had not, and China and India, as well as other developing countries which have ratified it, are not required to take direct action.

To lower the costs of GHG abatement, the Kyoto Protocol incorporated tradable emissions permits based on their success in SO_2 regulation in the USA. In response, the European Union, which ratified the Protocol, created a multinational GHG emissions trading scheme, the largest in the world. Emissions were capped, and permits were allocated for virtually all stationary

---

[42] Kyoto Protocol to the United Nations Framework Convention on Climate Change, http://unfccc.int/resource/docs/convkp/kpeng.html.

industrial and electricity-generating units in the EU. A market developed with two trading periods, 2005–07 and 2008–12. This is an unusual case where property rights have been established relatively early in the process of responding to an open-access externality. Whether this case represents a true outlier to the pattern described in this chapter remains unclear. I am not an expert on the EU ETS as described by Ellerman in chapter 8, but I can offer some conjectures as to why cap-and-trade was adopted early and why this action may still be consistent with the overall hypothesis of this chapter.

First, as Ellerman notes, the cap is purely political, in that no single country or group of countries can affect the global externality unless all of the major emitting countries are involved. The 1997 Kyoto Protocol represented an important international effort by the EU as a unified body, and it wanted the Protocol to be successful. The Kyoto Protocol adopted cap-and-trade in emissions allowances, building on the successful experience of the US SO_2 trading scheme. In that regard, information costs had been lowered regarding the use of emission rights as compared to reliance upon uniform standards. This would have reduced uncertainty for politicians and internal country constituencies within the EU. It is not obvious how individual country regulation of emissions without trading would have worked, given the great heterogeneity in emissions and production costs across the EU. It may be that cap-and-trade involves the lowest risks to politicians in member states. It allows for the trading of allowances. Second, the EU ETS involves two phases, with the first granting emission allowances freely and loosely. Indeed, the first phase has been very decentralized and flexible, as Ellerman emphasizes. In many ways it is more symbolic than binding. This setting is also consistent with the desire of politicians to avoid more rigid costly arrangements when the returns from doing so are unclear. Adoption of a low-cost trading scheme in phase I allows for new information to be gathered and for firms (and politicians) to adjust to the more stringent restrictions proposed under phase II in 2013.

Phase II is more centralized in the EU rather than in member states, allowing local politicians to blame the EU should costs be greater and outcomes be less than expected, as is likely. Further, it remains to be seen whether ETS will be renegotiated if international competitors—China, the USA, India, Brazil, and so forth—remain outside of major international emission controls. In that regard, the experience of phase II may also turn out to be consistent with the general arguments of this chapter. It is too early to tell.

13.6 CONCLUDING REMARKS

Collective action in addressing open-access resource problems comes when there is a consensus on the aggregate benefits to be gained, that the parties perceive positive net gains from agreement, and that they are homogeneous with respect to bargaining objectives and in the distribution of the costs and benefits to be incurred. Agreements reached under these conditions tend to be self-enforcing because it is in the interest of all parties to insure success. Uncertainty in predictions regarding aggregate benefits and costs of collective action and their distribution among constituencies complicates this process by raising transaction costs.

Uncertainty makes it more difficult for parties to determine how they will fare with formal arrangements to mitigate open-access externalities. Accordingly, the incentives are for delay and for subsequent adoption of policies that involve the least cost and minimize distributive effects. Property rights, which are the fundamental solution to open access, however, are more costly and they can result in a major redistribution of wealth and political influence. In this case, it may be efficient to wait to assign property rights as we have seen in fisheries, common oil pools, and air-pollution control. This suggests that despite their theoretic appeal, property rights are often the solution of last resort to "The Tragedy of the Commons."

14

Managing the Global Commons:
Principles and Practice

Graciela Chichilnisky

14.1 THREE FUNDAMENTAL PRINCIPLES FOR THE GLOBAL COMMONS

We are in the midst of one of the largest extinction events in the planet, the first major extinction that is caused by human action. This chapter proposes the creation of global market mechanisms to forestall the rapid and possibly irreversible loss of species and ecosystems that is taking place on the land and seas. The aim is to organize the use of the global commons, in principles and in practice, during a period of rapid disorganized and potentially dangerous globalization that is stretching the limits of the Earth's resources.

Several distinct mechanisms are proposed here, each addressing a different aspect of the global environment challenge: watersheds, biodiversity, indigenous knowledge, and the global spectrum. All the mechanisms proposed here address the same overall topic and follow the same fundamental principles. The global commons is the overriding topic, and each mechanism addresses one aspect of this. All the mechanisms proposed here are based on the same fundamental principles or imperatives: (1) promoting sustainable use of the Earth's resources, a harmonious relationship between humans and ecosystems; (2) using market-based and self-funded mechanisms that require no donations for their implementation; and (3) decreasing the wealth gap between rich and poor nations and more generally between high- and low-income people, women, men, and children.

Timing is of critical importance. New global financial mechanisms are needed because we face challenges that never existed before. For the first time in human recorded history we are modifying the Earth's metabolism: the planet's atmosphere, its water bodies, and the complex web of species that makes life on Earth. This new development creates new global risks and introduces new constraints on our behavior, how we use and produce energy, how we use land, and how we relate with other living species. We are in the midst of a transition from a world where resources such as water and air appeared to have no limits, to a world with critical scarcities, for example of drinkable water, and where important living species disappear daily on land and in the seas. To make a successful transition we must find ways to re-examine economic value so as to guide our economic behavior in a way that is consistent with the new scarcities. This in turn requires that we learn to measure economic success in a different way, a way that is consistent with the new scarcities we face, since until now critical resources such as clean water and clean air were considered unlimited and therefore had no economic value.

The standard measure of a nation's success that has been used since the mid 1950s is its gross domestic product or GDP, namely the sum of all the goods and services the nation produces valued at market prices. Whether we like it or not, GDP is based on markets, and this creates a fundamental problem in measuring the new scarce commodities because important environmental commodities such as the concentration of gases in the atmosphere, the composition of biodiversity, the clean water produced by a watershed, have no market prices and therefore no economic value in today's world. The GDP is mute on these important items; economic success measured by GDP disregards key Earth resources that have no price and do not appear in the GDP. This obvious problem has led to many calls for updating the measure of GDP in a way that is sensitive to accounting for the use or abuse of environmental resources. Over the years many laudable efforts have been initiated in this direction, but it seems fair to say they have achieved limited success. The reason for this lack of success is that it is difficult to achieve a new measure of GDP that values critical resources when we do not have market prices for the new resources to be measured. Trees provide a stark example. Under current economic accounting measures, cutting down all US forests to produce wood plank or even toilet paper would be an unequivocal improvement of GDP, a measure of success. Yet few people would agree with the desirability of cutting down all the trees in the USA. The problem is that social values are not appropriately represented by today's market prices. This problem is disorienting and the source of enormous social stress. There is no real economic value attached to a living tree or to a tree's environmental services today, such as its role in purifying the air. The origin of the problem is the slow pace of change of social institutions with respect to the new global scarcities we face. Economic value comes from market prices, which is fair enough. But we are missing critical markets, because we are not taking appropriate account of new scarcities. Lacking markets, we lack market prices, and the GDP measures are out of whack with reality. An important signal for scarcity—higher prices—is missing.

Rather than suggesting the introduction of new accounting measures for GDP, which met with limited success before, this chapter proposes instead the creation of actual markets or market mechanisms that recognize the new scarcities. The new markets create new market prices that change our notion of economic value in the GDP. These are prices for environmental commodities such as a clean atmosphere, clean water, clean air, and biodiversity composition, on which human survival depends. Some of these markets have already been created, for example the carbon market of the Kyoto Protocol, and they are having the desired effects: re-valuing the new commodities such as the gas content of the atmosphere and recognizing, for the first time, and through national limits on carbon emissions, the scarcity of the atmosphere as a sink to absorb the products of burning fossil fuels to produce energy across the world. The task is daunting but important, and the proposals presented here represent merely a first step in what could be a process involving many years of scientific and diplomatic work, judging by the time it took so far for the UN Climate Convention to reach global agreement. But the scope of the problem deserves the effort, and there seems to be no choice. We know that 99.9 percent of all species that ever existed are now extinct, and with the sea change we are precipitating in the metabolism of the planet, the survival of our own species could be at stake. The current loss of species and ecosystems is comparable to only five other extinctions on the planet, one being the period 65 million years ago when dinosaurs went extinct.

This chapter proposes global systems of tradable property rights on the use of global environmental assets that seem necessary at this stage of human evolution and related markets that encompass and extend the Kyoto Protocol, its emission caps, its carbon market, and its Clean Development Mechanism. We focus on the challenging issue of *how to extend a system like the carbon market to manage other sharply different global commons—such as biodiversity.*

The chapter outlines the transmission mechanisms through which the proposed solutions would generate an appropriate flow of revenues to allow developing nations to benefit from biodiversity conservation and clean technologies, and the process by which global property rights could be allocated within and across nations, including how initial endowments can be decided. It shows how the creation of new global property rights can generate revenues to fund R&D efforts to the benefit of all, in particular, developing nations. It builds on prior published work by the author listed in the bibliography at the end of the book, starting from the beginning of the 1990s and during the Kyoto Protocol negotiations in 1996 and 1997, including the author's proposal leading to the creation of the global carbon market of the Kyoto Protocol, and of an *International Bank for Environmental Settlements* (IBES) to regulate this. It discusses specific mechanisms to guarantee the adequate level of funding and the appropriate selection of R&D projects, as well as the governance conditions for adequate performance.

In order to establish the background for the proposals in this chapter, it is necessary to explain by means of a few practical examples the global and the local nature of the environmental assets under consideration, such as watersheds, forests, indigenous knowledge, and the global spectrum. Once these examples are presented, the chapter suggests specific ways in which substantial revenues can be obtained for the benefit of all and examples of the mechanisms to ensure the successful implementation of the three fundamental principles already stated: (1) securing adequate levels of funding, through the selection of projects that are self-funded; (2) encouraging sustainability; and (3) redistributing income and wealth in fair and efficient ways across the world. These conditions are steep but not impossible, as they are satisfied by the Kyoto Protocol's market mechanism, the Carbon Market created by the author (Chichilnisky 1996; Chichilnisky and Sheeran 2009), and its CDM, as discussed below.

14.2 GLOBAL NEEDS AND LOCAL ASSETS: CRITICAL EXAMPLES

The global environmental issues described in this chapter are both local and global, and the chapter provides a careful consideration of both aspects, as they are both critical to the success of the market mechanisms proposed here.

Biodiversity loss as a whole undermines the basic needs of human societies and at the limit can cause our own extinction. *Water services* are a critical example of this phenomenon. The biodiversity in watersheds includes micro-organisms and plants that help provide water supply, flood and erosion control, and purify the water that is essential for human survival. Yet poorly managed watersheds are unable to provide water filtration and erosion control for the regulation of flood waters, resulting in today's global water crisis. Human-built filtration systems require billions of dollars to replace the natural filtration services that biodiversity provides at no cost, so the ecosystem destruction in watersheds makes little economic sense. Yet a malfunctioning watershed problem is common to most large cities in the world, and over a trillion dollars in artificial filtration plants would be required to replace what the natural services can provide at no cost. The situation makes no economic sense and yet no steps have been taken to resolve the issue. The problem is a malfunctioning of the international market that leads to inferior global solutions. It is truly a "prisoner's dilemma" where each trader is rational and yet the solution is inferior for all. The problem appears most frequently when natural resources that are national property or common property within a nation become actively traded in international markets. This leads inevitably to a global tragedy of the commons. The author has shown that the local problem of the commons can only be resolved by redressing the institutional framework at the global level (cf. Chichilnisky, 1994, 1996a, b, 2010a, b).

Why are such institutions needed now when they were not needed before? This question has a simple answer. We are in a unique period of human evolution. The problem is new, that is why. This is the first time that humans have dominated the planet and can change its fundamental metabolism—including the atmospheric composition of gases and the complex web of species that makes life on Earth. The change has been swift—mostly occurring in the second part of the twentieth century, after World War II, together with rapid industrialization and globalization led by the Bretton Woods Institutions. We have not yet adapted our global institutions to suit. We still use the global institutions that were introduced after World War II, the Bretton Woods Institutions such as the IMF, the World Bank, and the WTO. The situation has changed fundamentally, and along with it rationality requires that we adapt to the change.

A similar problem arises with the *biodiversity in forests*, and valuable *traditional knowledge* about how to use it for medicinal purposes, which by itself generates over $100 billion in annual revenues for the global pharmaceutical industry (Chichilnisky 1993a). As forests disappear or are replaced by new growth this valuable ecosystem resource ceases to provide its enormous value to humankind. The attendant ecosystem destruction undermines the health needs of populations around the world, in rich and poor nations alike. A similar issue arises with the *management of the global spectrum* that is discussed at the end of this chapter. We show how managing the commons properly can only increase global welfare. It can be self-funded, sustainable, and can redistribute global gains fairly and efficiently. Yet no action has been taken so far in this direction. Once again, the situation makes no economic or human sense, yet to date no steps have been taken to resolve this issue either.

What explains this lack of action?

This chapter seeks a positive explanation for the situation, and solutions to overcome the gap between the current biodiversity loss and the value of conserving biodiversity and ecosystem services, suggesting global financial mechanisms that can realize their economic value in practical and sustainable ways and benefit lower-income groups and communities across the world. The chapter starts from the premise that the preservation and maintenance of ecosystems and the services they provide often makes good economic sense, but we lack institutional ways to realize this economic value. The emphasis is therefore on the institutional changes that are needed to accommodate and manage change in the physical assets of the planet that took place since the middle of the twentieth century, when industrialization in the rich nations and globalization took on a life of their own.

Other chapters in this book elaborate on practical and concrete examples of problems surrounding the value of local ecosystem services to human societies, and how this value could be realized in practice. Yet most chapters share a concern about the inability of current economic systems to realize this local value in practice. The purpose of this chapter is to tackle a critical missing element, namely the global aspect of the problem of biodiversity loss and ecosystems and the global financial mechanisms that could overcome the enormous gap between the human value of these services for our species as a whole—and the lack of financial resources that are available today for conserving these valuable resources and ensuring their fair and sustainable availability across the world. As we discuss below and have discussed elsewhere (Chichilnisky 1994, 1996a, b, 2000, 2009, 2010a, b), property rights are essential to resolve the problem, and if properly handled they can help create efficient new markets, redress erroneous market prices and the weakness of GDP, and even redistribute resources as needed to overcome the global divide between rich and poor nations. The chapter does not attempt to aggregate local ecosystem values into global values. The purpose of this chapter is rather to explain why a local solution is often unable to resolve a local problem, requiring a nation-by-nation global treatment instead. At the same time the chapter explores (1) what is missing in our local and global economic systems that lead to lack of action; and (2) how to fill this gap with practical global financial mechanisms that can help realize the value of biodiversity and ecosystems in profitable, effective, and sustainable ways.

The UN Kyoto Protocol is an example of a global solution to this problem; this requires substantial extension to apply it to different environmental issues such as biodiversity. The task, as pointed out earlier, is daunting but possible. The carbon market provides a successful illustration of the type of governance we have in mind, involving the allocation and trading of global property rights on the global commons. We must extend this governance to the most important assets on the planet, which are our environmental assets and knowledge. These assets are unique types of economic goods—they are *privately produced* global *public goods*. Economic institutions, such as markets, must be adapted to the change. Markets that trade global public goods are different types of market with new challenges and opportunities for action.

It must be acknowledged from the onset that there is a clear and sharp contrast between carbon emissions and biodiversity assets. Biodiversity is made of a complex collection of heterogeneous pieces scattered around the biosphere that we do not fully understand how to measure, while carbon is a homogeneous product that can be measured at any point in the world. Indeed, carbon concentration in the planet atmosphere is the same all over the world, a unique property of CO_2 as a gas that ensures the same air concentration of CO_2 in Madrid, New York, and Kuala Lumpur on any given day or season, and makes carbon emissions a global public good (bad).

For this reason, the carbon market is the most developed solution for the theoretical issue of how to obtain value from payments for ecosystem services (PES), operating at the international level. Article 4 of the UN Climate Convention requires that developing nations be exempt from limiting emissions unless they are compensated for this, so they cannot trade in the carbon market. However, through the Clean Development Mechanism (CDM) of the United Nations Framework Convention for Climate Change (UNFCCC) Kyoto Protocol, projects that deliver carbon offsets in developing countries receive payments from carbon emitters in industrial nations. Thus the CDM together with the carbon market can be seen as an international payment for ecosystem services (IPES). As the author of the carbon market in the Kyoto Protocol and a lead author of the IPCC, I helped provide the scientific basis for this market, as well as the basis for the favorable treatment of poor nations that is embodied in it (Chichilnisky 1993b, 1996a,b, 2009). The principle is enshrined in Article 4 of the 1992 UNFCCC and has been critical for the creation of IPES financial mechanisms such as the carbon market and the CDM.

The carbon market and the CDM offer a unique combination of market efficiency and equity that is appealing to industrialized and developing nations alike. The carbon market trades the rights to use of a global public good that is privately produced—the carbon concentration in the atmosphere. Such markets are fundamentally different to the private goods markets we know and have used until now. For these new markets link equity and efficiency in unexpected ways that certainly do not hold in standard markets for private goods. This unusually challenging but attractive combination made the signing of the Kyoto Protocol possible in 1997, and helped achieve its ratification into international law in 2005. The same combination of equity and efficiency will be essential to the future of the carbon market of the Kyoto Protocol and its attendant CDM after 2015, when the COP17 extended their carbon limits.

Furthermore, as this chapter shows, a similar blend of equity and efficiency is critical for designing successful systems for international payments for ecosystem services (IPES) solutions to conserve other important global commons such as biodiversity and ecosystem services. The blend of equity and efficiency exemplified in the Kyoto Protocol's CDM is essential to achieve successful global financial mechanisms for international payments for ecosystem services. This chapter shows why IPES mechanisms will take the form of markets with special characteristics which—as the carbon market—are quite different from the markets used until now. Because of the critical importance of biodiversity and ecosystem services for human survival, these new types of markets will become increasingly important over time and eventually alter the core of the global economy. I predict that they will transform capitalism during the twenty-first century.

14.3 FOUNDATIONAL PRINCIPLES FOR GLOBAL GOVERNANCE

Experience with innovative incentive for combating climate change provides an inspiration for addressing other global environmental issues, even while we acknowledge the sharp contrast between carbon emissions and biodiversity. While proposing the creation of the global carbon market to combat global warming as part of the Kyoto Protocol (Chichilnisky, 1996a; Chichilnisky and Heal 1998, 2000, 2009) the author also proposed a number of other global financial mechanisms for the conservation of biodiversity and ecosystem services, including watersheds and water services generally, forests and their biodiversity, genetic resources including traditional knowledge, and the use of the global spectrum for telecommunication services (Chichilnisky 1996b). In 2006 the United Nations Environment Program and the international union launched an initiative for research options for an international payment for ecosystem services (IPES) mechanism with special emphasis on biodiversity and a broad range of ecosystem services. Following this initiative, in February 2008 at a meeting of United Nations Environment Program IPES group in Geneva, the author proposed the following principles to be followed by any successful IPES mechanism:

- it should foster sustainable development;
- it should be self-funded, no donations needed, and incorporate local communities, governments, and the private sector;
- it should address basic needs and reduce the gap between the poor and the rich.

The three principles just presented are demanding, and they may seem impossible to achieve. But the Kyoto Protocol shows the way. The Carbon Market of the Kyoto Protocol is an example of a successful Global Market Mechanism that satisfies all three principles. The Carbon Market provides a price signal that "rewards" carbon reducers and "penalizes" excessive emitters, thus helping to avert climate change. It is self-funded—requiring no donations to be executed, and through its CDM it reduces the gap between the poor and the rich nations—which I have called the Global Divide. This is consistent with Article 4 of 1992 Climate Convention.

According to the World Bank "Status and Trends of the Carbon Market" (2006–2011), by 2011 the carbon market had traded "US$ 200 billion" and its CDM executed US$ 50 billion in productive investment on the soil of developing nations, while reducing by 20 percent EU annual emissions. In sum, the Kyoto Protocol thus satisfies the three key operating principles:

– it fosters sustainable development;
– it is self-funded—it requires no donations to execute;
– it helps reduce the gap between the poor and the rich—the Global Divide—since it transfers significant productive resources to lower-income communities.

The following are examples of global financial mechanisms that emulate the Kyoto Protocol in the sense of helping to realize the economic value of biodiversity and ecosystem services—while conserving the resources in a sustainable fashion.

14.4 HOW TO ACHIEVE ECONOMIC VALUE FROM BIODIVERSITY: BASIC PRINCIPLES

There is a gap between the enormous value that biodiversity offers to humans, satisfying our basic need for water, food, and medicines, and the economic value that can be realized today from biodiversity in dollars and cents. A clear example is provided by *watersheds and their services*. They have enormous economic value to humans: water is essential for survival, and the biodiversity within a watershed. For example, the microorganisms in the soil, can perform valuable services such as purifying water at no cost. Indeed, watersheds' biodiversity can save us trillions of dollars in terms of artificial purification plants (Chichilnisky and Heal 1998).

While these values are real, they are not concretely realized anywhere in the world today. There is no real action taken anywhere to capture the value of watershed services. Why? The reason is simple. In today's world economic value derives from *market prices*. This is how the Gross National Product of a nation is computed: as the sum of goods and services it produces computed at market prices. But markets for watershed services do not exist today; they never existed. So there are no market prices for such assets. This is why there is no economic value for watersheds and their ecosystem services in today's economies. It is really as simple as that. One may ask—why don't these markets exist? The answer is equally simple. It is because markets require "property right" allocations to function. Unless we know "who owns what"—namely unless we know what are the prevailing property rights—we cannot and do not trade, markets do not exist, and there are no market prices. Think of the automobile market. Nobody buys a car without a clear title. The "property rights" for a car must be defined before there is a sale. There would be no automobile markets if people had no property rights on cars. As simple as that. And without an automobile market, there would be no market price for automobiles, and nobody would gain from producing cars—we would barely produce any cars. We would have few or no cars.

This is the problem we face with biodiversity: we lack property rights on biodiversity; therefore we lack markets and market values. Nobody "produces" biodiversity because there is no way to assign value and no way to gain from that activity. This is why biologists' good intentions about creating payments for ecosystem systems are just that—good intentions—and have failed so far to raise the funding needed to preserve ecosystem services. They will continue to fail. They have no basis of reality without well-defined property rights. In sum, since most of the world lacks property rights on watershed services, a market on watershed services does not exist and cannot exist. And since the market does not exist, there are no market prices for watershed services. And without market prices there is no way to translate an abstract notion of economic value derived from human needs into a practical economic reality of dollars and cents. The implications are also simple. We need to allocate property rights on biodiversity and ecosystem services before their market value can be realized. Property rights are needed before markets can exist, before their services can be traded, and before market prices and real economic value can emerge. This is the simple point that is missing in all the studies and projects around the world that attempt to put voluntary values on ecosystem services. They will eventually fail without well-defined property rights. Experience shows that voluntary carbon markets fail as well (World Bank 2006–2011). Payments for ecosystem services cannot be "voluntary"—that is not going to work reliably and on a scale that matters. This is the reason why we have such problems realizing the true value of ecosystems and their services. It is not lack of rationality, it is lack of institutions that are needed for the new world in which we live.

The Kyoto Protocol provides a good example of this phenomenon: of the problem and the solution. Until the Protocol became international law in 2005, there had never been a value on carbon emissions, a value that reflects the cost to society of emitting carbon and possibly changing the planet's climate. Why? Because there was no market for trading such values. We could emit unlimited amounts of emissions at no cost: there was no way to assign a cost to carbon emissions. Clearly, to create the carbon market we first had to limit the rights on the use of the atmosphere of the planet to emit carbon dioxide by the nations of the world. We had to agree on emissions limits before the carbon market could be created. These limits are what are called "property rights"—they are in fact rights to emit by the various nations. Bear in mind that this is not the same as invoking free markets and capitalism everywhere. The property rights we are concerned about are the rights of nations to use the planet's atmosphere. Within a nation, the limits can be ensured by decree, or by taxes, or by carbon markets. It does not matter how the national limit is achieved. For this reason, very different economic systems are compatible with the carbon market of the Kyoto Protocol. The emissions limits appear in the Appendix of the Kyoto Protocol as numerical limits or decreases from existing levels. The enormous contribution of the Kyoto Protocol was to create an international agreement that allocates tradable property rights on the use of the global commons, the planet's atmosphere, nation by nation.

The limits on emissions required in the Kyoto Protocol may have to be reduced for the Protocol to be effective in forestalling climate change, but the concept of the Protocol is right. Only when the limits on emissions are well-known and agreed trade can take place and market prices emerge. Only then can the carbon market emerge. Only then can carbon prices (the negative value of emissions) be determined from the forces of supply and demand. Of course, voluntary markets in which traders have no emissions limits may emerge—and in fact they do emerge—as part of this phenomenon. But without global emission limits—without property rights on the use of the global commons—voluntary markets will be short lived and little will be achieved (World Bank 2006–2011).

In a nutshell: the inaction with respect to watersheds derives from the lack of property rights on watershed services, and therefore no market prices for those services. Without market prices the value of a watershed exists in a physical and a metaphysical sense, but not in an economic sense. To overcome the problem we need the equivalent of the Kyoto Protocol in terms of the use of watershed services across the world. This is a difficult task because of the enormous diversity of the watersheds and the services they provide, which are generally local. There is a fundamental difficulty in assigning such property rights without further consideration to equity issues. Nothing could be more destructive than to define private property on the watersheds in a way that prevents access to lower-income groups. The following sections will suggest a way to overcome these problems. A critical aspect of the solution will be to find ways to define ecosystem services as a uniform global commodity that can be traded, to allocate property rights and to design markets in a way that satisfies the overriding principles of equity and efficiency as presented above.

14.5 A SHARP DIFFERENCE BETWEEN BIODIVERSITY AND CARBON EMISSIONS

It has been pointed out that there is a sharp contrast between carbon emissions and biodiversity. Conserving biodiversity and ecosystem services is fundamentally different from limiting or reducing carbon concentration in the planet's atmosphere. Carbon dioxide concentration in the atmosphere is the same the world over. This is a unique property of CO_2: as a gas it distributes uniformly and stably over the entire planet's atmosphere. This has nothing to do with economics or politics. This scientific fact is favorable to the creation of the global carbon markets.

The carbon market is a financial market where the "underlying commodity" is rather simple. One trades the right to emit one ton of carbon, the same right anywhere in the world. Since the concentration of carbon dioxide is the same in all nations, if one ton of carbon is emitted in Beijing it has the same effect on the world's atmosphere as if one ton were emitted in New York City. There is one and the same commodity all over the world: a ton of CO_2 emitted. This provides a simple and unifying unit.

The situation with biodiversity and ecosystem services is different. In sharp contrast, there are many measures of biodiversity and no universal agreement exists on "commodity" called biodiversity. The same is true about ecosystem services: they are idiosyncratic by nature. A watershed's service is generally different from the next. A problem in creating a market approach for IPES is therefore to achieve a uniform commodity to be traded. The solution is to aggregate the entire stock of biodiversity services, bundling it and dividing it into uniform units. For example, we could bundle all the services from all the watersheds in the world, or those from all European watersheds into what is called a "bundle" of assets. This bundle can be used to "back" a financial instrument such as stock or bonds, whose role is to divide the total asset into little uniform pieces for trading purposes.

For a concrete illustration of this approach in a completely different area, consider Freddie Mac and Ginnie Mae, important financial institutions in the USA that were created following the recession in the 1930s to encourage home ownership for low-income families. They were the largest and most profitable financial institutions in the USA for many years, owning almost half of the housing assets in the USA. The two institutions were created to be partly private and partly public. Now nationalized since the onset of the 2008 financial crisis, these institutions were previously the second most profitable financial institutions in the USA after Citibank. Yet they had a public objective, to encourage home ownership by lower-income groups in the USA after the Great Depression.

These institutions sell bonds that are "backed" by bundles consisting of millions of home mortgages across the entire USA—about 40 percent of all mortgages in the USA of a total of $13 trillion in assets, are part of their portfolio of assets. Each individual mortgage is backed typically by a single house as an asset and, importantly, each *house is sharply different from the next*. Yet by bundling millions of different assets, institutions such as Ginnie Mae and Freddie Mac are able to create a market for a uniform commodity; their corporate bonds, which for many years were successfully traded in global markets and created enormous liquidity for their operations. The bonds are backed by the entire bundle of assets, consisting of millions of home loans. Since the 2008 financial crisis these institutions have been under severe stress, as have most or all financial institutions across the world, mostly lacking proper risk management and solid regulation. Yet the concept behind these institutions—if properly managed—is sound and suggestive. It is called *the law of large numbers*. Essentially it means that there are ways to "bundle" assets so as to favor consumers, by reducing risks and giving access to an appropriate system of property rights (in this case, home ownership for low-income groups).

The problems are very different, yet a similar approach can be used to create a single uniform commodity that can be traded globally based on a different type of asset: the services of many different watersheds across a region, a nation, or a continent. The following sections will use this approach to suggest examples of global financial mechanisms for the International Bank for Environmental Settlements (IBES) that could implement a system of international payment for environmental services.

14.6 EXAMPLE 1: WATERSHED CORPORATIONS AND A GLOBAL WATERSHED FUND

The principle is to aggregate the services of large numbers of different watersheds across a region or the world, bundled into one global financial asset that can be called "global watershed services". Typically, the watersheds considered for this scheme would include those providing water services to cities with populations of more than 1 million people. The precise mechanism of implementation for the proposed solution involves creating a system of property rights on the use of the global environmental asset (a global "bundle of watersheds") and related markets that can generate an appropriate flow of revenues and allow people to trade and benefit. One way to build a national financial system for the profitable conservation of watersheds is to create a public–private corporation that owns rights to all the *watershed services* under consideration, with strict covenants. The property rights are the *ownership of the watershed services*—and not on the land nor on the biodiversity itself.

A nation can create property rights to use the watershed services to a number of watersheds that provide services to cities with at least 1 million inhabitants in the nation. These are *new* property rights—rights that do not exist today. How does this work in practice? Below is a precise, step-by-step process to be followed, part of which was proposed earlier by the author in other publications (Chichilnisky 1996b), a specific mechanism. The first step is to determine the role of each nation within itself, with respect to its own watersheds. The second step is to describe how this extends to an international system of watershed rights, and the third step is to show how an international agreement offers financial possibilities to cover costs and produce profits for a watershed solution to satisfy the three principles we proposed (1) encouragae conservation of the asset; (2) benefit local communities and lower-income groups; (3) be self-funded. Each step contains incentives to help implement the other steps—they all work together to achieve the global objective of the institutions we propose.

Before going into details, it is worth explaining how the creation of a financial mechanism creates incentives for the conservation of an asset. The owner of a valuable home who needs cash. Without a mortgage market, the only solution is to sell the house, or to chop its bricks one by one and sell those, thus diminishing or destroying the value of the asset. This is analogous to the situation in developing nations today with respect to their valuable biodiversity, as the Yasuni initiative of President Carreras, Ecuador's plight to the international community has recently made abundantly clear. However, once a mortgage system is introduced, the home-owner can borrow money based on the value of the house. And the creation of mortgage markets as a financial institution encourages the conservation of the asset, since now the bank who offered the mortgage loan and the owner have an incentive to preserve the house's value. A similar situation arises with the financial mechanisms proposed here.

Here are step-by-step details. A first logical step is for a nation's government to allocate property rights to a newly created corporation(s)—the "watershed corporation"—which should be owned as a public/private commercial venture(s). Recall that the property rights we propose are not to rights to the watershed nor the watershed land itself—such rights would make the problem almost impossible to resolve—but rather the rights to benefit commercially from *the services of the watershed in producing clean, drinkable water* and *under strict legal conditions*, also called "covenants," which ensure that the corporation will restrict the use of the land in the watershed area to avoid all agricultural, residential, and/or commercial. This means all uses that could conflict with the production of the watershed's services. This covenant may seem restrictive but in fact it is similar to what was done in New York City for its watershed in the Catskills, in New York State, in the 1990s. The "covenants" described above will typically forbid or limit (1) the use of fertilizers and pesticides; (2) other environmental effluents and stress factors that can damage the biodiversity in the watershed; and yet (3) allow unimpeded the continuation of the watershed's biodiversity services for the purpose of water catchment, filtration, and erosion control. This is also similar to the process followed in the Catskills' watershed for New York City (Chichilnisky and Heal 1998).

In terms of the equity and the efficiency of the initial distribution of rights, the corporation could be owned and managed by its stockholders and these should include representatives from (1) the local communities; (2) the government; (3) the private sector, represented for example by private investors and possibly also; (4) environmental groups representing the interests of the "future." This implies that local communities and low-income groups will automatically participate in and benefit from, the commercialization of the watershed services. All stockholders (including private investors, local communities, the "future," and the government) will share the profits or gains from the corporation. The initial endowments are to be decided by law makers in each nation—in the context of international agreements for the purpose of these allocations. This is described in more detail below.

The creation of the new property rights in itself can generate substantial revenues to fund R&D efforts, to the benefit of biodiversity conservation, and of low-income communities in each nation. Here is the exact mechanism I have in mind to guarantee the adequate level of funding and the appropriate selection of R&D projects. A watershed corporation should be endowed with the rights to sell water including, if appropriate, sell water to the government for distribution to its citizens. In reality, water provision services are a profitable business worldwide, and the allocation of property rights on the watershed services is in each nation a valuable asset that the government can allocate in exchange for demanding covenants for the protection of biodiversity. To obtain funds to subsidize R&D operations, the corporation that is endowed with the watershed services can sell bonds and equity that are backed by its assets, so as to be self-funded. Indeed, this is a generalization of what happened in the case of the New York City watershed, where the government of New York sold bonds to pay for the R&D, the purchase of land, and the operations of the watershed protection in the Catskills, including the covenants already described that protected biodiversity (microorganisms that purify water in the soil of the watershed).

For equity and efficiency, the government can allocate the property rights to ensure that the public–private watershed corporation would have rights to own—and to profit from—the savings created by using ecosystem services, rather than artificial plants to capture and filtrate water. Such savings can be considerable. For example, in the Catskills watershed the creation of an artificial filtration plant was valued at about $6 billion, while the watershed could do the filtration if unimpeded, at no cost (Chichilnisky and Heal 1998).

This means that the watershed corporation would own from the outset an asset valued at $6 billion—which will help the sale of bonds or equity in the world's capital markets. The next step is to explore the participation of the international community in facilitating the national system of watershed corporations mentioned above, and in particular the execution of the three overriding principles enunciated above, which should be at the core of international agreement. This includes Article 4 of the UNFCCC that is at the core of the "shared but differentiated responsibilities" in the 1992 Climate Convention. The international community can provide incentives for an international agreement that will require each nation to take action and create watershed corporations as described here, in the form of financial incentives for the international system as a whole. This is described below.

So far we described the role of a government restricted to the national watersheds. In cases of ambiguity, for example if a watershed extends across nations, the issue falls naturally into the realm of international agreements. In general, government action towards its watersheds (as explained above) requires international action, similar to the action taken in the Kyoto Protocol. The biodiversity in the world's watersheds is of international value to humankind as a whole, even though it is distributed across nations, cities, and towns, and is different in each case. Think of the polar bear, the dolphins, and the penguins. Their genetic survival is recognized to be of international importance. The same is true for the microorganisms that populate watersheds and provide water services globally.

How can the international community provide incentives for each nation to take action and create watershed corporations as described here? There are substantial financial incentives for the "bundling" of watershed corporations and their assets across the world. It is the "law of large numbers" at work; its financial desirability is demonstrated by the existence of successful hedge funds (e.g. the Swiss Pictet Water Fund) that specialize in water services investment across many nations. Observe that in each nation, the watershed corporation(s) will own substantial assets and can be substantially profitable. The financial assets that it creates, such as bonds and equity on the corporation, can be sold in the global capital markets—they can be called, for example, Water Hedge Funds. The corporation can create liquidity for its services through an Initial Public Offering (IPOs) and secondary markets. In general, the bundling of several watershed assets is even more profitable than each is on their own, since the risks become lower as more watersheds are considered at the time. For this reason, international agreements can help regulate groups of various national watershed funds. They can require nations to provide property rights and the infrastructure specifically defined above, in exchange for financial participation in the global profits of the watershed sector created by international agreement.

For example, a nation such as India may not be willing or able to create a watershed corporation on its own. This may require financial expertise and funds availability and access to global capital markets that it cannot provide on its own. Furthermore, allocation of land may not be possible for political reasons. But in conjunction with a number of other Asian nations, India could participate in the creation of a $1 trillion Asian watershed fund that provides access to capital markets to sell bonds, and equity in each nations' watershed corporations (as described above). There are already profitable water funds that own hundreds of millions in watersheds assets, showing that the activity can be and indeed is profitable; their main objective is private profits and not conservation.

The procedure just described shows how the creation of the new property rights nation by nation—in the context of international agreements on watersheds—can generate substantial revenues to the benefit of the private and the public sectors in each nation. This is true in particular in developing nations where water supplies are under stress. The process can (1) support the conservation of biodiversity in watersheds; (2) protects the fair access to clean water services by low income groups within each nation; (3) provide profitable returns to the private and the public sector, and specifically to local communities that participate and co-own the watershed corporation; and (4) encourage private/public investments in this crucial global water infrastructure. The negotiation of how each nation's system of watershed corporations integrates into the international watershed fund is left to diplomatic routes, but it is no different to any other international negotiation[1] with costs and benefits for all involved.

By creating an appropriate corporate design, the three overriding principles presented above can be satisfied in this example. First of all, watershed corporation can be *self-funded*. It is relatively easy to attract global funding for water funds: the "PICTET Water Hedge Fund" in Switzerland has a similar

---

[1] The urgently needed new organizations for managing the global commons must be subject to transparency laws and regulation as needed to function properly and as required equally by the best functioning capital markets in the world. The global crisis of 2008–10 was an example of how deregulation that took away basic protections ended up damaging financial markets the world over, as well as the real economies that they are designed to serve. For example, just before 2000, in the USA Alan Greenspan, Robert Rubin, and Larry Summers successfully dismantled the US Glass–Steagal Act that was passed after the 1930s recession and prevented the use of individual bank deposits for highly risky investment banking trading by the banks, including derivatives and "naked" short trading, as well as the requirements of bank deposits similar to "marking to market" operations that essentially ensure the ability of the traders to carry out the terms of their transactions and thus decrease "counter-party" risk. In this way, the US capital markets functioned during most of the first decade of the twenty-first century with fewer controls and regulations that those imposed by the casinos in Las Vegas, which are careful in requiring proof of ability to pay before allowing very risky transactions. Transparency of operations is also critical. These and other organizational principles for private–public corporations must be established and followed in order not to fall into the same traps of mismanagement as Fannie Mae and Freddie Mac suffered in the USA.

structure (but it operates only as a private hedge fund, as mentioned above) and it is proof of the fact that water services are a profitable line of business that attracts considerable global investment. Yet, no nation has created property rights as proposed here, and so far the profits have gone only to the private sector. Furthermore, having no covenants, as described above, current water service providers do *not* protect the biodiversity of the watershed. The second principle, *sustainable development and sustainable use of the watershed* is guaranteed by the covenants described above, and its biodiversity can ensure substantial profits for the corporation by offering filtration and water flow services at no cost (as in the Catskills watershed example, Chichilnisky and Heal 1998). Finally through international agreements that encourage an *appropriate distribution of property rights on the stockholders of the corporation*—including local communities, government and the private-sector entities—one can ensure that both equity and efficiency conditions are met. The above proposal is difficult to implement—as it could be rather innovative—but it benefits all, including the private sector. It can be done, and the sooner we start the better. The critical aspect of this scheme is an international effort to ensure that the nations of the world offer their support in the form of designing and enforcing the covenants described above, and allocate property rights to corporations and stakeholders on the savings derived from using natural capital rather than artificial plants. Artificial water filtration plants can run into the trillions of dollars for the world as a whole, a cost that can be saved by the natural process proposed here, with the savings providing start-up capital.

14.7 EXAMPLE 2: A GLOBAL FOREST FUND

A second example of a global financial mechanism would be a private–public corporation that aggregates the services of large numbers of forests across the world, bundled into a global financial asset that can be called "global prospecting services." A blueprint for this is a development of the Costa Rica–Merck InBIO agreement, which is discussed in Chichilnisky (1993a, b, 2000, 2010a, b, Chichilnisky and Heal 1998, 2000) and has led to substantial forest conservation results so far in that small and innovative nation.

The financial mechanism proposed here can be structured in several ways. In analogy with the case of the watershed corporation, international agreements are needed to reap the benefits of the financial mechanisms proposed. Without them, the Costa Rica example will remain limited and a great opportunity will be lost, perhaps an irreversible loss. How to encourage and create an international agreement for the "global bioprospecting" of ecosystem services? The first step is to define nation-by-nation limits (or covenants) on the use of forest-based biodiversity. This can be achieved by computing the per capita "forest biodiversity content" of consumption in each nation, based on so-called "forest footprints" local or national. Rather than computing the use of forest biodiversity for local production, say, in the USA or the EU, one would compute the consumption of forest biodiversity per capita by the average US or EU citizen—including the forest content of imports from other nations, directly and indirectly. Such measures exist in rudimentary form and it is difficult but not impossible to generalize them and create a unit that can be agreed internationally as a first step. The next step is to achieve an international agreement on the limits that science will find appropriate to achieve sustainable development. This may require legislating a rate of extinction that is closer to evolutionary standards rather than to exceptional extinction events globally, such as our period in the history of the planet. The UN Millenium report finds that current rates of extinction are 1,000 times larger than those found in fossil records. Of course, this is to be expected. An institution that parallels the IPCC in the Climate Convention can be created to provide input from scientists all over the world to reach a minimum consensus on biodiversity limits as soon as possible. Such proposals (for a Biodiversity version of the IPCC) have already been advanced by France within the Convention for Biological Diversity and all efforts must be made to advance the knowledge needed and the consensus required to move forward. Our own extinction as a species could be at stake.

In advancing towards this goal, it will be helpful to encourage economic motives and align market objectives so that there can be gains as well as losses for the private sector. This will encourage the type of institutions that need to be created worldwide. How can we align business interests and profit motives to encourage the institutional changes needed?

A public–private corporation can be created which is assigned property rights on the services of a forests' biodiversity—with *strict covenants*, which restrict their use for commercial, agricultural, or residential purposes, or any use that threatens conservation of the asset. The new corporation owns the property rights on the health services that can be produced from the intellectual property obtained from the forests specimens, worldwide. As in the case of the watershed corporation, to become self-funded, the forest corporation can sell bonds and/or equity that is backed by its assets in global capital markets. To achieve success in global capital markets, and it may be necessary to aggregate the assets across many nations, as this enhances the value of the assets, decreases financial risks, and increases their attractiveness to global investors. The global investor will be offered bonds or equity based on the global biodiversity of the world's forests, and their derived health benefits used for commercial purposes. We know these health services have a large commercial value, involving hundreds of billions in sales worldwide.

The forest corporation can also do an Initial Public Offering and become a "public corporation," in order to trade in secondary capital markets, thus acquiring further liquidity and access to larger pools of capital worldwide. As an example, consider a public–private corporation that owns and profits from bioprospecting services around the world (Costa Rica's example involves a partnership with Merck, who share the property rights on the use of the samples derived from the forest for medicinal purposes) (Chichilnisky 1993a).

The corporation will own prospecting rights but not property rights on the land or the biodiversity itself. This is important, since otherwise sovereign interests could be violated. It owns rights to "land use" and "biodiversity resource use" rather than the rights to land or biodiversity—namely the services of its assets and not the underlying assets themselves. The "services" can be owned by local communities, as well as by private investors, and government can share an interest in the corporation in exchange for imposing the appropriate covenants that create the biodiversity conservation and its commercial value. Financial assets such as bonds or equity on the world's forest corporations can be sold in global capital markets—called, for example, Forest Hedge Funds. The Forest Hedge Fund could become public through an IPO to obtain liquidity and finance its operations, as well as trade its equity in secondary markets. In addition to being self-funded, appropriate corporate design is needed to allocate, by international agreements, the ownership or stockholding in the corporation(s) to (1) governments; (2) local communities; and (3) the private sector (private investors). Such forest corporation(s): can ensure not just the sustainable conservation of the asset—namely the forests' biodiversity services—but can also make substantial profits. Some of these returns will return to the local communities who are shareholders, thus satisfying the three overriding principles of (1) sustainability; (2) self-funding; and (3) equity and efficiency that were proposed above. It should be noted that some of the structure proposed here can be put in place at the national level before international agreements are achieved, and these can provide useful case studies or pilot plants for the ultimate international agreement that is sought.

14.8 EXAMPLE 3: TRADITIONAL KNOWLEDGE

An international agreement by the nations of the world can seek sustainable conservation of a valuable global public good: "traditional knowledge". This is usually transmitted verbally and is at risk of disappearing at present due to the fragmentation and rapid extinction of local cultures and languages around the world. In addition to health services, one includes historic and cultural assets such as poetry, literature, and music, as well as anthropological knowledge and human systems and their genetic backgrounds. The critical step is to find a way to make the owners of traditional knowledge participate and initiate the process, and make knowledge widely available while honoring through modest license fees the contributions of the authors, thus satisfying the three principles stated above: (1) to be self-funding; (2) promoting sustainability; and (3) equity and efficiency.

There are several ways to generate flow of revenues to allow communities to benefit from the conservation of the knowledge assets at stake, and to create and allocate appropriate property rights on the asset across nations and within nations. One way is to create a public–private corporation that owns the assets of a Digital Database that is developed to record and prevent permanent loss of verbally transmitted traditional or indigenous knowledge, together with records of the sources (or initial authors) of the knowledge itself. It is worth repeating for clarity that the rationale is to avoid the permanent loss of traditional or indigenous knowledge that is currently threatened by the segmentation of traditional communities and the encroachment of industrial societies into their territory, as well as by the migration of its populations. Since traditional knowledge is verbally transmitted, it is particularly vulnerable and at risk of permanent loss.

One way to deal with the initial allocation of property rights is for the Database to record the original sources and thus ensure licensing revenues to the source according to international agreement. This issue has been the subject of heated debate in the Convention of Biological Diversity. However, the purpose here is not to limit the use of the world's knowledge, as is usually feared—for example, through patents—but rather through the use of new systems of property rights proposed elsewhere by the author that allow universal use and moderate income sharing by small license fees (Columbia University and Brookhaven National Laboratories L.I., "The Pegram Lectures" by G. Chichilnisky). The author has proposed replacing patents (which are a form of monopoly, for a limited period of time) by so-called "compulsory licenses," so the knowledge cannot be removed from public use and yet its creators can be moderately compensated to encourage production and sustainable recording and use.

The knowledge itself continues to be owned by the originating sources but is licensed for global use. The public–private corporation sells knowledge services to the private sector. Medicinal knowledge alone represents over $100 billion in annual sales for pharmaceutical companies, and therefore the Database would own the license rights on a valuable asset. The development of the Database itself would encourage digital training and job creation for indigenous youngsters, mentored by community elders, thus helping to heal the fragmentation of the communities.

With the appropriate corporate structure—as discussed earlier for the case of watershed and forest corporations, the corporation that develops the Database could sell bonds and equity, placing its shares in global capital markets, and an IPO could create liquidity to kick start the operations, making the entire enterprise self-funded and profitable, while encouraging sustainable use and redistributing gains towards low-income groups and communities across the world.

14.9 EXAMPLE 4: THE GLOBAL SPECTRUM

There is enough "bandwidth" available for a global spectrum that assigns a unique wavelength to each of 10 million people on the planet. Such a system would improve communications across the world and organize them, and could play the role of a "traffic light system" that avoids accidents and produces enormous efficiency values simply by organizing traffic on highly transited roads. The basis of this example is a new type of property right— the use of the global spectrum that is owned by each nation within its territory.

The financial mechanism proposed could create efficiencies in global communication systems, while compensating nations for the use of their own property: the electronic wavelengths that go through their territory. A financial mechanism could create private–public corporation(s) to exploit the services of the global spectrum. Owned as appropriate by local communities, with bonds and shares sold in global capital markets, this mechanism would be self-funded and sustainable, and furthermore, as already explained, it would recognize the valuable property of all nations small and large, and thus help to overcome the global divide. Developing nations (Latin America and Africa) are the largest expansion markets for wireless services in the world today, thus they have the potential to become a very profitable. The rest of the structures discussed here apply to this example and do not require repetition.

14.10 CONCLUSIONS

We proposed specific global financial mechanisms to forestall the rapid and irreversible loss of species and ecosystems that is taking place on the land and the seas, and more generally to help organize the global commons in a period of rapid globalization. The proposals represent merely a first step in what could be several years of scientific and diplomatic work. Through the sea change we are precipitating in the metabolism of the planet, the survival of our own species could be at stake. This chapter has proposed global systems of tradable property rights on the use of global environmental assets that seem necessary at this stage of human evolution, market mechanisms that encompass and extend the Kyoto Protocol, its emission caps, carbon market, and the CDM. We focused on the challenging issue of *how to extend a system like the carbon market to manage other different global commons—such as biodiversity and the global spectrum.*

To summarize, the chapter focused on four prominent examples: (1) watersheds; (2) forest biodiversity; (3) indigenous knowledge; and (4) the global spectrum. Each presents an aspect of the global environmental dilemmas. All require the three fundamental principles that we proposed for governing the global commons: (1) to be self-funded; (2) to promote sustainability; and (3) to be fair and efficient and geared towards decreasing the global divide between the rich and poor nations, and the rich and poor communities across the world. These are challenging principles, but the Kyoto Protocol satisfies all three, and the chapter showed how they can be achieved in the examples chosen here. The chapter outlined the transmission mechanisms through which the proposed solutions would generate an appropriate flow of revenues to allow developing nations to benefit from biodiversity conservation and clean technologies, and the process by which global property rights could be allocated within and across nations, including how initial endowments can be decided. It showed how the creation of new global property rights can generate revenues to fund R&D efforts to the benefit of all, in particular of developing nations. The rationale for these proposals is based on prior published work by the author starting from 1993, during the Kyoto Protocol negotiations in 1996 and 1997, and include the author's proposal leading to the creation of the global carbon market of the Kyoto Protocol.

The chapter discussed specific mechanisms to guarantee the adequate level of funding and the appropriate selection of R&D projects, as well as the governance conditions for adequate performance. By means of a few practical examples, the chapter explained the global and the local nature of the environmental assets under consideration, such as watersheds, forests, indigenous knowledge, and the global spectrum. The examples are diverse but they all share the same principles of how to organize the global commons. The chapter suggested specific ways in which substantial revenue can be obtained for the benefit of all and examples of the mechanisms to (1) guarantee adequate levels of funding; (2) identify a selection of projects that are self-funded; (3) encourage sustainability; and (4) redistribute income and welfare in fair and efficient ways across the world. The proposals presented are ambitious. But the sea change taking place in the world economy requires a corresponding change in institutions from the Bretton Woods orientation that prevailed in the world economy since World War II. We need to create new institutions with principles that are harmonious with planetary resources, and can be consistent with the survival of our species. The proposals in this chapter address this challenge.

15

Conclusion: Governance and Environment: Policy Challenges and Research Questions

Eric Brousseau, Tom Dedeurwaerdere, Pierre-André Jouvet, and Marc Willinger

Global warming, depletion of species and natural resources, nuclear crises, North–South imbalance, and the environmental cost of development, pollution of closed seas, international watersheds management, global pandemic diseases... There is no doubt that environmental challenges exist and that, in most cases, their scale requires transboundary action. Moreover, the potentially catastrophic and irreversible evolution of socio-ecological systems can turn these issues into crises requiring an immediate fix—even though these crises have a number of facets and are characterized by interdependencies within natural and socio-economic systems both. Environmental challenges and the potential solutions to address them have a direct effect on living standards, economic organization, infrastructure, and modes of urbanization. Successfully addressing these complex and multidimensional problems will require reforms in our current institutional frameworks. First, existing institutions that are imprinted by national sovereignty seem too fragmented to cope with the multiple dimensions of many environmental issues. Hence many actions and policies fail to address the issues at stake in a comprehensive way. Second, such institutions rely on crude mechanisms that reflect an insufficient understanding of how individuals and groups react to constraints and incentives. As a consequence, many policies are either ineffective or counterproductive.

Environmental challenges and their global dimensions have become more visible since the 1980s, and many initiatives have been taken that attempt to address them. Both within and across national boundaries, many innovations in governance and policy have been tried; examples include tradable emission quotas, citizen juries to establish complex societal norms, multistakeholder committees to manage common resources, and the Intergovernmental Panel on Climate Change (IPCC)—which aims to inform international negotiations and create global standards. Given the knowledge accumulated so far, one of this book's goals is to take stock of that knowledge and use it (1) to determine what factors should be considered when designing policies; and (2) to identify the questions that should be answered both by practitioners and the research community.

This concluding chapter synthesizes the policy lessons drawn from this book and summarizes the research paths needing further exploration. Clearly, these two goals should be adopted not only by policy makers and the research community, but also by stakeholders. Policies should be based on a thorough understanding of global environmental challenges and the properties of governance mechanisms, an understanding that will expand only by combining wide-scale experimentation with the systematization of "reflexivity"—that is, the ability to assess the actual consequences of existing practices in order to reform them if needed—in matters of governance.

First, in Section 15.1, we identify the specific characteristics of the governance challenge in issues involving the environment. In Section 15.2 we describe the dilemmas associated with establishing collective goals in matters of sustainable development. In Section 15.3, we discuss the properties of the mechanisms available for deciding to frame our individual and collective behaviors. Finally, in Section 15.4 we discuss the policy toolkit that could be used to implement commonly agreed solutions.

15.1 THE SPECIFICITY OF ENVIRONMENTAL GOVERNANCE

Three main features characterize environmental governance: its scale, its strongly political nature, and the irreversible character of its failure.

15.1.1 Scale effects and the challenge of cooperation

The scale of environmental issues stems from three intertwined processes: industrialization, an expanding human population, and the globalization of economics and society. As a result, the consumption of natural resources and the load on ecological systems have reached levels that threaten their ability to regenerate. Because of the interdependencies among components of biological systems, resource depletion in one area can result in the depletion of other resources, chains of population extinctions, and loss of natural resources far beyond the initial geographical area (as discussed by Charles Perrings in

Chapter 3). Hence, from the viewpoint of human society, the scope of an environmental problem is typically much greater than the scope of the community that generated it—because that community either mismanaged its resources or simply externalized the costs of consuming them. In other words: most jurisdictions do not include all the stakeholders affected by a given resource, so mechanisms must be created that take their interests into account. Such mechanisms range from the establishment of a global government (indeed, a quite unrealistic target) to the development of various forms of cooperation among individuals and/or the mechanisms that now govern and coordinate them, whether they be formal governments or nonstate organizations.

Cooperation failures and coordination dilemmas, as well as the building of institutions aimed at modifying the structure of these problems are thus at the heart of environmental governance. Of course, not all environmental issues raise the same coordination problems: individual contributions to their solutions can aggregate differently as a function of the "technology" by which an environmental good (e.g. clean air, preservation of species, risk avoidance) is produced. This is the *aggregation technology* dimension of providing environmental goods (Hirschleifer 1983; Cornes and Sandler 1984). With *summation* goods, each unit contributed to the public good adds identically and cumulatively to the overall level of the good available for consumption—for example, contributions to reduced CO_2 emissions. Because individual contributions are substitutes for each other, it is essential that the largest possible contributors (i.e. the large polluters in our example) be induced to contribute. In general, neither unanimity nor majority are required to ensure minimal provision of the good. A notable exception is that of *weakest-link* public goods, where the smallest contribution fixes the quantity of the public good available for the entire group (as in, e.g., contamination security control). In such cases, unanimity is required, yet each decision maker has a strong incentive to contribute: free-riding would likely induce retaliation in addition to the deprivation of the good's benefits. With *best-shot* public goods—for which the overall level of a public good (e.g. innovation in environmentally friendly technology) is determined by the largest individual provision—it is essential to ensure that those most likely to contribute are facilitated and encouraged to do so.

Between these extreme types is a wide set of intermediary cases. These include *weighted-sum* public goods (where different contributions can have different impacts, as with pollution's "point of injection" into a river or biological cycle) and *threshold* public goods (where a minimum level of provision must be reached, as in population dynamics when attempting to protect endangered species). Moreover, the provision of actual environmental goods often depends on combining various actions characterized by different aggregation technologies. For example, reducing greenhouse gas emissions will probably require major technical innovation as well as massive emission abatements. Understanding the necessity, feasibility, and effectiveness of international agreements, is dependent on establishing the patterns of coordination needs and incentive structures of the different environmental issues.

15.1.2 Cumulative irreversibilities and the need for agility

The potentially irreversible character of governance failures lies in the "generalized interdependencies" among biosphere components and in the central features of evolution: nonlinearity, discontinuity, and abruptness (as discussed by Oran Young in Chapter 4). Such failures may result in cumulative irreversibilities and catastrophic evolution that—beyond a certain threshold— cannot be controlled. The point is that most current policies presume that changes occur in a linear, gradual, and reversible fashion. These policies may stipulate an ex post cure for some identified negative outcome or advocate a gradual implementation to manage acceptability by current stakeholders. Today, it is essential to determine whether the human species has developed a socio-economic dynamic that is too demanding of the biosphere and whether we are witnessing the beginning of a catastrophic evolution due to a growth process that is too physically demanding. Our present state of knowledge does not allow an unqualified answer, but there is clear evidence of resource depletion and associated disequilibria. However, the current generation will likely not be much affected in comparison with future generations. From this fact follow two specific dimensions of environmental challenges: (1) biases in the current generation's incentives to address those challenges; and (2) high levels of uncertainty regarding the speed, scope, and interdependencies of the various processes of natural resource depletion. It will be difficult to agree on solutions to these problems, although designing such solutions is an urgent need.

As revealed by paradoxes in emerging property rights systems (see the analysis by Gary Libecap in Chapter 13), governance solutions often emerge when increased human activity makes scarce a resource that was naturally abundant. Yet implementing solutions is delayed by the conflicts that inevitably arise when property rights (or other governance solutions) entail exclusion and rationing. In some cases the delay is so long that the "solution" comes too late to prevent depletion of the resource.

To avoid such a fate, governance solutions should first reduce uncertainty by stimulating the production and diffusion of knowledge among the stakeholders; thus, decisions will be arrived at by better-informed agents. In this regard, the IPCC is certainly a model for how the scientific community's efforts could be better integrated in governance regimes. Second, reflexivity in governance should be promoted: governance mechanisms should regularly assess the state of the systems and resources within their purview. This recommendation would support the development of knowledge about the mechanisms of transmission (between policies and targets) and, most importantly, the early identification of catastrophic evolutions. Even so, uncertainty combined with the potential catastrophic character of systemic crises could well delay cooperation and coordination in managing them, which in turn might accelerate collapse of the socio-ecological system we now occupy.

15.1.3 Sharing a finite resource: clearly, a political issue

The third dimension of environmental issues is that environmental resources are limited—or, at least, cannot expand at the growth rate of the global economy, or even the global population. In short, per capita consumption cannot grow indefinitely. How should humankind share a given amount of natural resources? It is most difficult to agree upon a reply because this could be a zero-sum game.

As discussed in Chapter 6 (by Ben Groom, J. Rupert Gatti, Timo Goeschl, and Timothy Swanson), agreements are difficult to reach also because of inequalities among social groups within nations (and among nations at the global level). The current distribution of access to natural resources is largely the result of historical processes characterized by predation, wars, and injustice, to say the least. It is obviously unacceptable to expect the poorest and least-developed countries to slow their consumption growth for the benefit of other, more advanced countries. Conversely, the wealthy are seldom convinced to change their standard of living significantly or even to reduce their wealth in the slightest. For these reasons, most environmental issues can be characterized as a severe conflict over how the organized groups of a rapidly growing population will share a limited amount of resources. Technical and organizational innovations will certainly contribute to alleviating the burden of this equation. Also needed, however, is a major evolution in our understanding of the constraints and in our acceptance of the solidarity needed to address the issue: redistribution of the effective access to natural resources and wealth. In particular, those living in the world's wealthiest countries must recognize that resolving fundamental asymmetries between parties is critical for solutions involving international cooperation—because (1) such asymmetries are typically the result of past injustice (especially colonization); and (2) the accumulated financial, human, and organizational capital in the most developed countries enables them to draw higher benefits from common resources than their least-developed partners. This issue is one of ethics and of effectiveness. Indeed, cooperation will fail in the absence of redistributive efforts toward the less endowed, whose first-best strategy would then be threating the wealthiest with strategic destruction of resources or relying on terror to modify the balance of bargaining power.

15.2 ESTABLISHING NORMS FOR SUSTAINABLE DEVELOPMENT

When combined, the three sets of governance challenges raised in Section 15.1 translate into constraints on establishing norms and principles of governance. In what follows we build on the research presented in this book—which demonstrates that there are no well-established solutions for managing these constraints—in order to suggest some governance principles worthy of being implemented, as well as some research questions that should be addressed.

15.2.1 Agility in practice

Socio-ecological systems are subject to abrupt change and to "cascade" effects; they also feature emergent properties and potentially irreversible processes of destruction. Therefore, it is essential to conceive of solutions within a dynamic perspective. What worked well enough in the past and in a specific context might no longer be effective when conditions change. Moreover, since systems can collapse quickly in certain circumstances (as a function of thresholds, tipping points, and "system flips"), quick reactions are necessary to avoid catastrophic evolution. This explains the need for flexibly adjusting policies to match system evolution, including the case of abrupt and discontinuous change. Thus, the key elements of "agility" are reflexivity and adaptive capacity.

Agility begins with the building of information mechanisms that aim to collect and distribute information on the state of the system so that all stakeholders can develop knowledge about possible adaptations. Knowledge creation is boosted by recombining current knowledge, so it is essential to develop mechanisms that favor the spread and the sharing of information and knowledge. In concrete terms, the principles of "open science" are clearly preferable to those of "industrial property." Governments, Intergovernmental Organizations (IGOs), Nongovernment Organisations (NGOs), and corporations should support the development of epistemic communities, such as those operating in the information technology and creative industries (Open Source Software, Creative Commons, etc.). Such communities are already involved in the sharing of biological and genetic resources (Dedeurwaerdere 2010). Not only do these communities favor all kinds of innovation, they also might establish a common infrastructure for developing and preserving the material basis of sustainability (as has been done for crops).

With sufficient information in hand, the next task is to assess the performance of existing policies and to amend them when needed. All too often, policies are not properly assessed—or assessment is limited to checking the degree of compliance with the policy. What is needed instead is a regularly scheduled review of the policy's performance in terms of its initial goals: resource preservation, system restoration, pollution abatement, and so forth. Information on results should be widely available for purposes of benchmarking and making comparisons. One must bear in mind that, once implemented, a policy is often difficult to amend; those who established it or adapted to it are reluctant to make additional efforts. Likewise, organizations tend not to question their existence and, to the contrary, often seek to extend the scope of their activity beyond the organization's initial goal. This is why it is so difficult to "reform the reform" and to adapt policies to evolving circumstances (or even in response to poor performance). Therefore, any information generated to analyze policy performance should be distributed to all stakeholders, allowing them to call for changes if needed.

The combination of transparency and agility is typical of independent agencies (e.g. those set up in some countries to monitor nuclear safety), which are therefore well suited to the governance of environmental domains. Ideally, the agencies would themselves be subject to oversight by committees composed of a wide diversity of stakeholders and organized at the international level. Such arrangements would reduce the strategic manipulation of information, as occurred in France during the 1980s, and more recently in Japan with regard to nuclear safety. The European Union could prove to be a relevant framework for establishing such agencies in Europe, though excellent support might also be provided by such UN institutions as the World Meteorological Organization, which hosts the IPCC.

Beyond the development of institutional principles that favor disseminating information and sharing knowledge, research in environmental governance should more thoroughly investigate how our socio-ecological systems could better cope with the risks of systemic collapse. Following Shannon's (1948) principle, this research should explore the means by which firewalls and redundancies could be implemented to minimize the likelihood of such collapse. Also worthy of further exploration is the building of self-reforming institutional frameworks along the lines of the reflexive governance movement (Brousseau, Dedeurwaerdere, and Siebenhüner, eds 2012). According to Habermas (1996, 2001) and many followers, democratic systems based on the election of representatives in central assemblies—which were developed in the nineteenth-century Western world—are in crisis because of society's increasing complexity, the multinational character of many social issues, and the interplay between mass media and the polity. A more democratic and effective governance would rely on a more direct and pluralistic form of involvement of citizens in collective decision making, as is evident in many environmental domains that feature cooperation among heterogeneous entities (e.g. governmental agencies, NGOs, businesses, citizens' committees, local referenda). Systematic research is needed on these alternative modes of governance, especially regarding the environmental issues to which they are best matched and the conditions under which their learning capacity could be increased. Moreover, the greater ability of alternative governance modes to accommodate institutional and political innovation (as well as radical choices, when needed) should be analyzed to determine whether such modes could successfully address the other governance challenges identified in this book.

15.2.2　Valuing and managing the future

Because threshold effects and irreversibilities characterize many environmental goods, it is essential for the present generation to preserve fundamental resources for future generations. In turn, some redistribution from the future to the present generation might be justified in terms of making the former's contribution more palatable. One clear implication is that we must consider distribution of the *costs* of a transition to a more sustainable economy and society. For instance, public debt to fund research or investment in cleaner technologies could be acceptable to many (provided public funds are not wasted on useless projects), and it might be possible to set up mechanisms for guaranteeing long-term investments by private equity firms. As suggested by Graciela Chichilnisky in Chapter 14, such mechanisms could be based on a delineation of property rights over natural resources that allows the economic valorization of all related services. The resulting flow of income would then enable a guarantee of long-term loans and the funding for investments necessary to develop or maintain the eco-resources. Of course, these various mechanisms would require international cooperation in order (1) to avoid speculative attacks against those who will eventually invest more; and (2) to implement strong control mechanisms aimed at avoiding the speculative drifts to which private–public corporations are subject.

That being said, a critical issue when dealing with intertemporal redistribution is agreeing on how the future should be discounted. The question is complex because its answer depends on how the interests of the various generations are balanced and also on expectations about the evolution of productivity and relative prices. Resolving this question is a matter of expertise, of beliefs about how systems evolve, and of ethics (since the issue involves balancing the contrary interests of different generations and social classes, of rich and poor nations, etc.). The chapters in this book have highlighted how far we are today from any consensus (even scientific consensus) on how best to account for the intertemporal value of environmental assets; yet this accounting is a prerequisite to comparing alternative projects or R&D programs and to implementing mechanisms that manipulate relative prices—through reduced interest rates, subsidized investments, taxes, and guaranteed prices—so that economic agents will use environmental resources more efficiently. Clearly, an avenue of research is open. The ethical dimensions of the issue preclude it from being considered simply as an economic problem. Moreover, resolving matters should not be left exclusively in the hands of the research community: ordinary citizens should certainly be able to express their preferences. These elements call again for reflection and experimentation in matters of collective decision mechanisms.

15.2.3 Establishing collective preferences

Although environmental goods are public goods and many of them have a global dimension, choices remain to be made; that is, we must decide on both the quality and the volume of the provision. If public goods are localized and do not benefit all on an equal basis, then also localization becomes a problem to be solved. Finally, it is necessary to establish priorities among various goods and the basis for arbitrage between public and private goods.

Beyond the difficulties of achieving consensus and cooperation in large and heterogeneous communities (to be discussed in Section 15.3), an important issue is that many citizens and stakeholders do not have access to the information and knowledge needed to "rationally" rank their preferences. Indeed, doing so requires an understanding of the structure and dynamics of socio-ecological systems. A lack of this understanding clearly hampers our ability to establish collective preferences and to justify the sacrifices that may be required in order to avoid the various tragedies of the commons that threaten humanity.

A traditional reply to this insufficient diffusion of knowledge is advocating cooperation between the scientific and the political elite. Yet questions immediately arise concerning the legitimacy of those elites to make choices on behalf of other citizens, potential manipulation of the decision in favor of the elites' inevitably biased interests, and the acceptability of any solution they might seek to implement. Once again, the answer is building collective decision mechanisms that address the crisis of current representative democracies. However, these mechanisms must be commensurate with the scope of environmental issues, which is often regional or global.

The experience of local communities, international networks of activists, NGOs, IGOs, and (of course) governments and corporations has generated an extensive array of innovative governance practices in all kinds of domains—not only the environment but also the information society, human rights protection, and humanitarian crises. Among the lessons that can be drawn from these practices is that establishing a rationally designed hierarchy of norms is simply not possible: the norms could not be implemented (given conflicting interests and the pre-existing distribution of power) and it is far from certain that such systems could cope with the complex issues at stake. In this case, a more feasible and effective approach (as advocated by Arild Vatn in chapter 2) is to employ more "biological" processes of decision that are based on a state of permanent negotiation and cooperation among groups built according to different logics. This approach requires understanding mutual interdependencies and involves implementing and revising solutions to concrete problems. Therefore, our knowledge must be increased so that we can identify the extent to which more centralized governance is needed in specific cases (such as catastrophic evolutions or crises) and how it can be operationalized. Another important question is: to what extent are mechanisms inducing compliance compatible with the dynamic of these initially voluntary processes? Resolving this question is crucial for aggregation technologies that make free-riding problematic.

Because the rise of a dominant middle class in Western democracies exhausted the redistribution capacity of representative democracies, one could also question how well collective decision mechanisms that are based on voluntary adherence could manage a sizable redistribution. As mentioned previously, the origins of inequalities that are evident worldwide make it most unlikely that cooperation in the name of the global environmental good will evolve in the absence of strong efforts to redistribute not only wealth but also various kinds of capabilities. Thus, we need to determine whether the organization of a more global polity is necessary to facilitate the process of redistribution. Observe that, within each Western nation state, strong mechanisms of redistribution and of reducing inequalities (not only in wealth but also in education) were implemented to enhance social cohesion and to support the ruling elite's legitimacy; the result was a huge economic benefit in terms of macrodynamics and growth (Brousseau, Schemeil, and Sgard 2010). Hence we must ask whether a more integrated polity at the global level (in contrast to decentralized voluntary cooperation) would favor the needed redistribution and increase the provision of environmental goods, *while also* satisfying ethical objectives. We are not here advocating the establishment of a global government together with an integrated bureaucracy. However, there may be more effective modes of collective decision making than those based on purely voluntary networks, and such additional modes might be needed in some circumstances (Brousseau, Sgard and Schemeil 2012). The combination of academic research and societal experimentation should allow us to make some progress in understanding the governance solutions to these problems.

15.3 DESIGNING NORMS AND POLICIES

There is often a mismatch between the scales of ecological systems and the scope of humanly built jurisdiction. This mismatch is a central constraint in the design of governance mechanisms aimed at establishing norms and policies. However, the relationships among various levels of government is not the only issue in the matter, since environmental goods usually have several facets. Indeed, such goods do not benefit all contributors in the same way. An ecological system provides various services; some of them (e.g. biodiversity) automatically benefit all, whereas others (e.g. landscape and clean water) can be appropriated. Given this mix of public and private goods in the provision of certain environmental resources, it is essential to consider the resulting heterogeneity among stakeholders when governance arrangements are designed. Finally, we emphasize that the development of knowledge is necessary not only for many solutions to environmental issues, but also for a more accurate assessment of the stakes involved. A central question is how best to incorporate the research community into the decision process.

15.3.1 Cooperation failures and opportunities

As this book makes clear, pre-existing political orders are a strong constraint in the governance of transboundary issues. No international power has the legitimacy to represent the general interest and impose actions on the public's behalf. Therefore, any multilateral agreement on transboundary service provision rests on compliance and so raises the question of adequate enforcement. Upstream, potential noncompliance can reduce the will to settle agreements, thereby reinforcing the status quo. The likelihood of strongly diverging and conflicting interests makes it even more difficult to reach agreements—between, for example, past colonial empires and their former colonies, the most and the least developed countries, countries that are and those that are not immediately endangered by climate change, etc.

Yet there are also some reasons to be optimistic, for paths exist by which sustainable cooperation processes can emerge. First, since not all environmental goods are pure public goods, many second-best solutions are able to provide a reasonable level of provision. In fact, the agreement of a perfect and complete coalition at the global level would be necessary only for weakest-link public goods, such as the control of pandemic diseases or invading species. In Chapter 7, Thierry Bréchet and Johan Eyckmans demonstrate that, for many public goods, minimal coalitions are sufficient. Combining this result with the greater ease of establishing coalitions among partners with common characteristics and observing that the size of minimal coalitions is strongly dependent on the partners' relative weights, we can see that such coalitions as the EU, the OECD, and the G-20 are examples of groups of countries that are well positioned to address global environmental issues and settle agreements. Nation states that are part of such coalitions have little incentive to free-ride because they are also involved in other complex networks of mutual interdependencies and linked issues. Today, these coalitions' members are a reasonable proxy for an "international order," and they cooperate also in dissuading other parties from too much free-riding. Thus, the exemplary or admonishing behavior of national "agents" can initiate a ratchet effect.

Nonetheless, in many cases it seems that more heterogeneous coalitions are more environmentally effective (because resources are localized and may also be complementary, and because an essential feature of ecological systems is their diversity); thus we have a trade-off between stability and effectiveness. On the one hand, differences in endowment create mutual incentives to cooperate. On the other hand, inequalities can result in an unequal distribution of the benefits of cooperation, discouraging the slighted party from seeking agreement. In fact, when combined with a negative moral evaluation of the origin of inequalities, feelings of injustice and humiliation may well engender *refusal* to cooperate and other counterproductive results. As mentioned in Section 15.1, this possibility should motivate most developed countries to implement redistribution using the framework of their current agreements with developing countries. This approach should also reinforce the incentives of developed countries to form coalitions aimed at implementing unilateral schemes of public goods provision. A constraint, however, is the need to gain the support of public opinion, which is necessary because such policies (e.g. the EU road map for reducing CO_2 emission levels by 80 percent from 1990 to 2050) translate into redistribution from the North to the South. These transfers will have an impact on each country's capacity for growth, if not also on its citizens' standard of living. For this reason, such policies will be accepted only if (1) they are openly discussed within a democratic arena; and (2) accompanying policies are implemented that aim to distribute the costs fairly (this would likely involve redistribution *within* Western societies).

From this perspective, we certainly should not underestimate the role of beliefs, culture, and knowledge (as argued by Hiroe Ishihara and Unai Pascual in chapter 9). At micro-levels within families, local communities, and social networks—and also at more macro-levels within nations and societies—one witnesses many forms of pro-social behavior, including acceptance of sacrifice and voluntary contribution to the public good. Pro-social norms can evolve not only through education and information but also though democratic debates that increase one's understanding of others' viewpoints, of interdependencies that exist, and of possible cooperative solutions. And if social norms are generally shared or at least mutually understood, then conflicts are easier to resolve and cooperation is easier to establish. Moreover, shared beliefs and common cultures are strong supporters of a cooperative process because deviation is discouraged by the fear of (even symbolic) retaliation such as ostracism, the pressure of public opinions on leaders, and the questioning of legitimacy. As indicated by the slow but measurable evolution of public opinion in most developed countries and in the elites of emerging countries, the transformation of beliefs is a major driver of political evolution. It could be fostered by the evolution of democratic debates, by a wider dissemination of scientific evidence, and by innovative social practices.

The preceding remarks lead to questions about the timing of a needed transformation. A pessimist would contrast the need for urgent and radical reforms (e.g. to combat environmental degradation) with the slow pace of evolution in socio-political systems. However, not all environmental resources and ecological systems are approaching exhaustion, so there may be time available to implement some reforms. An unfortunate consequence is that, with "early" attempts to preserve a resource, the potential gains are too low (relative to the economic and political costs) to allow an appropriate incentive structure. Hence policies should focus on stimulating the development of information and knowledge about the problem's structure and evolution. In this way, the actual value of the resource—and the methods of preserving, renewing, or extending it—are established early enough to allow the various stakeholders to reach an agreement long before the resource is actually threatened with depletion. This approach will require support for (1) research and the development of international agencies seeking to ensure that all stakeholders are informed; and (2) experimentation in all kinds of settings.

Of course, with resources for which depletion is near and potentially catastrophic, rapid decision making and implementation are clearly favored. In this case, minimal coalitions and leaders might be the only viable solution (given the time constraint), even if that solution is not satisfying with respect to stakeholder involvement or democratic agreement. For instance, a massive reduction in CO_2 emissions mandated by the OECD (or, *a fortiori*, by the G-20) would be an effective way to address the issue of climate change—and would certainly be preferable to striving for a more global agreement that is, for the moment, beyond reach.

These considerations are linked to the debate over the need for centralized versus decentralized governance, which is traditionally approached—within the framework of fiscal federalism—in terms of the optimal match between an issue's scope and the available levels of government (cf. the introduction to this book). We argue here, in line with many related contributions in the field of environmental governance, that many second-best solutions to providing environmental goods rely on decentralized solutions, which are feasible when allowed by relevant aggregation technologies. This does not mean, of course, that decentralized governance is always the most efficient or even sufficient. Besides the weakest-link case, there are obviously all kinds of emergency situations that might lead one to prefer centrally coordinated intervention. Moreover, as in the case of emissions trading (see Chapter 8, by Denny Ellerman), centralized decision and centralized enforcement make it easier both to set the most efficient abatement targets and to allocate efficiently the rights to achieve them. Indeed, the constraints of international agreements often result in objectives of the sovereign states that cannot be justified on objective grounds and result instead from power politics and political bargaining. Increased centralization can therefore reduce the collective costs for provision of transnational goods, which would facilitate international agreement on how this burden should be shared. In sum, the short-term necessity of building minimal coalitions and unilaterally providing public goods should not obscure the long-term effectiveness of better adapting less centralized governance structures to the regional or global scope of environmental issues.

15.3.2 Toward more inclusive processes of decision

The need to manage collective decisions in an international context should not focus all our attention and efforts on reaching global conventions and international treaties. Indeed, national governments are far from being the sole (or, in some cases, the most relevant) stakeholders. In many countries, it is not only the government that has the capacity to deal with complex issues involving a diversity of stakeholders and requiring scientific expertise and legitimacy to constrain citizens. Furthermore, many governments are relatively powerless with regard to some businesses—whether they be multinational corporations or national companies in the hands of some fraction of the local elite. Note also that governments in some of the poorest countries rank industrial development and political stability much more highly than protecting the environment or efficiently managing natural resources. Even in the most developed countries, governments may be severely hampered in their ability to deal properly with environmental issues. Lobby groups will rail against the necessity of any sacrifice to accommodate environmental regulations or international agreements. Finally, because many environmental resources rely on the contribution of several categories of goods and involve many kinds of expertise, it might be necessary to involve private businesses, active citizens, scientific institutions, communities, NGOs, and IGOs.

These issues are addressed by the concept of polycentric governance (as developed in Chapter 5 by Elinor Ostrom), which involves a diversity of organizations at multiple levels of governance. This promising approach offers an efficient way to match the scale and style of governance with the types of collective-action problems. It also enables an heterarchic system in which checks and balances result from the existence of de facto authorities that have been legitimized by their ability to address environmental governance issues (on the notion of heterarchy, see Brousseau, Marzouki, and Méadel 2012). Polycentric governance is less of a choice than a fact of life. A polycentric system often outperforms hierarchical, top-down, agency-based governance structures because it better manages the heterogeneity of incentives and the adaptation of solutions to the particular socio-natural problem. However, we must recognize that there are many types of strategies for bypassing or constraining governments when they are stuck (individually or collectively) in equilibria that prevent them from acting efficiently in matters of the environment. Federations of local initiatives, successful local experimentation, responsible citizens, NGOs promoting agendas at the international level, IGOs picking up popular agendas, private businesses investing in the development of technologies and turnkey solutions—all these factors can improve the provision of environmental services. They can also lead to changes in the political equations constraining governments and public bureaucracies.

In addition, polycentric governance is one way to manage, on an open-ended basis, the question of democratic debate that has been raised several times in this conclusion. By construction, polycentric systems promote the involvement of stakeholders because decisions do not rely on convincing a single, powerful ruler; that is, decisions must be agreed upon by a wide variety of stakeholders. This requirement could conceivably hinder action. Yet participation in governance is voluntary and is largely based on legitimate achievements; most participants in applied environmental policies are well aware of interdependencies. The structure of polycentric games requires exchange of information, sharing of knowledge, and the will to reach an agreement—all features that favor accountability, openness, acceptance of compromises, and exploring all possibilities for win–win agreements. Thus, leaders of the various social groupings involved in polycentric forms of governance have not only internal incentives (empowerment, legitimacy) but also external incentives (ability to convince others in collective decisions) to promote the involvement of stakeholders in decision making and enforcement. These incentives also have an impact on the long-term dynamic of governance issues in favor of knowledge diffusion, stakeholder awareness, civic consciousness, organized action, and the expression of new ideas. All these features have been identified as essential to addressing global environmental issues.

15.3.3 Reflexive governance and scientific knowledge

We have emphasized the central role of knowledge in the governance of environmental issues. Despite its diffusion to all kinds of stakeholders, the genesis of knowledge is central. We remark that the scientific community is hardly the sole producer of knowledge. All types of communities (local, epistemic, etc.) and organizations (businesses, NGOs, governments, etc.) are involved in processes of knowledge building, and all embody know-how and tacit knowledge. That being said, science and its institutions (e.g. research teams as a mode of organizing projects, peer review as system of assessment, awards, and career goals to stimulate individuals) play a strong role in transforming localized knowledge into elements that can be integrated with a more general corpus, in facilitating the recombination of ideas through universal systems of codification and storage, in systematizing benchmarks among concepts and technologies (including social ones), and in favoring collective action as a means to advance knowledge. The role of the scientific community is therefore central. Yet we must still establish the conditions under which the scientific community can issue credible alerts, propose legitimate solutions, and structure the debate to avoid (1) major collective errors; and (2) the promotion of illegitimate solutions in the name of theories that remain conjectural. Recall that, throughout history, the scientific community has repeatedly been keen to embrace collective wrong opinions.

Replies to these questions are complex because they must address the organization of the scientific community itself as well as its interaction with society. Internal mechanisms at play within the community—in particular, the attention paid to the logic of argumentation and the strength of evidence—allows reversal of even the most dominant paradigms. These mechanisms are efficient in the long run but not always in the short term, even though decisions may benefit from incorporating the most recent advances. Hence the scientific community should seek to minimize this inevitable time lag by (for instance) reinforcing in-depth peer reviewing, replicating experiments, and/or classifying results in terms of the stringency of tests to which they have been submitted. Also needed are strong efforts to educate stakeholders so they can interpret scientific results more easily and understand debates better. Everyone must recognize that scientific knowledge is, in essence, "provisional" and that solutions proposed by scientists rely on assumptions that must be verified to check how well they fit the problem's actual nature.

In order to reduce the chances of the scientific community coming to a wrong or biased consensus, alternative modes of funding science should be encouraged. Along these lines, the concern that many stakeholders feel about environmental issues should serve as fuel for funding research related to these issues.

It remains an open question how scientists should be involved in the decision process. The progress signified by creation of the IPCC is accompanied by some failures in its performance. Nonetheless, scientists are also needed in the less formal and more decentralized processes of governance. Thus a wide avenue of research is open on the best way to articulate "the academy" with politicians, private decision makers, and citizens (whether or not they are organized into communities).

15.4 IMPLEMENTING NORMS AND POLICIES

An important aspect of the progress made in recent years is a better understanding of the properties of alternative policy tools. To a certain extent we have witnessed the failure of both "command-and-control" and "market-based" tools. Traditionally, so-called hierarchic modes of coordination were implemented after market failures in the provision of public goods. These modes included regulation, governmental provision of environmental services, and the like. Economists (among others) developed a broad set of theoretical and applied analyses highlighting the drawbacks and often the failures of those instruments, which too often missed their target because the motivation of actors—and their ability to bypass all kind of constraints—were not well understood. Another problem is that public bureaucracies and political decision processes may lead to diverted action, misappropriation of assets, corruption, and abuse of authority because there are incentives and organizational slack that serve special interests instead of the collective good. A frequently recommended solution was to implement a set of economic tools aimed at changing incentives by manipulating rights, relative prices, and the conditions of access to resources. Yet the design and implementation of these tools proved to be an extremely complex challenge. Indeed, what may cause the failures of command-and-control solutions could also lead to the downfall of market-based solutions. For instance, we know that a well-designed property rights system eliminates the problem of externalities, for then all relevant interactions among agents can be managed on a quid pro quo basis; parties can contract to rearrange their initial rights, and they can "internalize" all costs of using resources (if transaction costs are low enough). However, the process by which the rights are initially distributed may be costly and time-consuming. This can lead to incomplete property rights or to an absence of their distribution (which means that the resource in question remains a commons, threatened by the well-known tragedy). In concrete terms: political conflict, bureaucratic errors, or corruption can prevent the organization of effective markets for rights and permits. Hence these factors can perpetuate or even worsen the environmental problem that was to be solved.

Our current knowledge of policy tools is informed by a vast amount of scientific analysis and actual experience. We shall open this brief discussion on tools by explaining why there is no silver bullet—which means that all practical policies are based on combinations of imperfect tools (Section 15.4.1).

We then return to the complex issues of compliance and crowding-out; some policies could actually have counterproductive effects (Section 15.4.2). This fact leads us to conclude on the benefits of cooperative approaches to policy implementation (Section 15.4.3).

15.4.1 Targets and tools

This book has demonstrated that, ideally, environmental governance combines at least three targets. In particular, any implemented mechanism should ensure sustainable use of natural resources, should be self-funding, and should reduce gaps in welfare. As is well-known in matters of economic policy, it is seldom easy to achieve more than one objective with a single tool.

There have obviously been many attempts to do so. Recall that management of the commons could be based on assignment of property rights to private–public corporations responsible for all eco-services related to each natural resource; these corporations would trade those services with market value, enabling cross-subsidies to fund the provision of all eco-services. As such corporations are created, the sale of their bonds would fund the investments necessary to manage these resources (and secure property rights) efficiently. Note also that selling property rights over the resources could generate the means needed to manage redistribution. The problem with such a mechanism is that it presupposes a benevolent and nearly omniscient state that would virtuously assign redistribution responsibilities to the most efficient public–private corporations, all of which behave in an exemplary manner. Given the economic stakes and the anticipated financial flows thereby generated, it is doubtful that such a process could remain free of misconduct, bureaucratic drift, organizational capture, or political manipulation.

We have mentioned that another difficulty when designing policies is that it may not be possible to implement the "best" solution. This is well illustrated by the case of property rights. With respect to environmental resources, political and cultural factors tend to work against the settlement of property rights. Moreover, even when property rights are implementable, their proper design and distribution faces a long row of hurdles. When there are pre-existing private rights, vested interests will oppose any redistribution or re-design unless costly compensation is offered. In the absence of pre-existing property rights, any system—including auctions and "first come, first serve"—may be biased in some ways. In the real world, assignation is usually imperfect and costly; this leads to inefficiencies, delays, and sometimes a total lack of action.

In such a context there is clearly no optimal policy—or, more precisely, no implementable policy leading to an environmental optimum. The four most prominently relied-upon policy instruments discussed in Chapter 12 by

Michael Faure (i.e. liability and tort law, ex ante regulation, environmental taxation, and tradable permits) should be combined to reflect the scope and relevant incentive structure of each environmental issue. In light of the information gaps, the strategic games, and the missing knowledge that influence the establishment of all governance mechanisms and policies, it is clear that they should undergo frequent and systematic testing to assess (given the evolution of relevant parameters) whether they could evolve to reach the targeted goals more efficiently. Since reforms cannot safely rely on the renegotiation of complex compromises, creating additional tools to compensate for revealed weaknesses of existing frameworks is certainly not a solution that minimizes transaction costs and ensures full consistency, but it is often the most pragmatic way to address the multitude of objectives typically assigned to environmental policies.

The preceding logic dictates that policy and research agendas match in the sense that better policies rely on more systematic, comparable, independent, and wide-ranging assessments of environmental policies. Transparent and informed evaluation of alternative policies along multiple criteria would certainly clarify the benchmarks for stakeholders and encourage debate on those alternatives. Such evaluation could erode the status quo's legitimacy when governance regimes are clearly underperforming, but it could also favor consensus and compromise in that the impact on collective welfare would be more certain. The resulting data could be used by researchers to study the properties of complex combinations of tools, to clarify their conditions of successful implementation, and to assess their dynamic and cumulative effects. Finally, these research efforts could contribute to clarifying the relative costs (and benefits) of reaching environmental policy objectives.

15.4.2 Transcending incentives

As with social sciences in general and policy making in particular, a limitation of traditional approaches to environmental policies stems from their assumptions about individual and collective behavior. Too often, individuals are viewed as selfish maximizing agents (i.e. as *homo œconomicus*). This explains the historical focus on manipulating monetary incentives (relative prices, taxes, ownership, and liability, etc.) to reach policy goals. As demonstrated in this book, that viewpoint fails to take into account the social nature of human beings, whose actions reflect a wide set of social motivations. The design of efficient policies should therefore account for the interplay between motivations and incentives. Otherwise, results may actually be worse than doing nothing because policies that appeal to economic self-interest do affect the salience of ethical, altruistic, and other social preferences, as is well documented by Bowles (2008). Indeed, policies designed to incentivize self-interested citizens may undermine the moral sentiments of those who have other motivations. For instance, as discussed by Andries Richter and Daan van Soest in Chapter 10, voluntary contributions to the common good from intrinsically motivated individuals might be crowded-out by external incentives aimed at stimulating contributions from selfishly oriented individuals. Policy design should therefore be based on careful ex ante studies that examine the motivations of a given resource's various stakeholders, and include cost–benefit analyses of each alternative option. Only then can decision makers reasonably decide whether policies should be based on incentives or on "crowding-in" through transformation of norms and beliefs. Therefore, replacing versus combining communication and education efforts with incentives policies should be analyzed systematically.

We are clearly at the beginning of a learning phase, so our knowledge on these issues is quite incomplete. Despite the recurrent call for policies more grounded in actual human nature and the policy paradoxes highlighted by social scientists, there have been few clear policy prescriptions, and even fewer assessments of actual policy experiences. Hence there is a crucial need for research that can help us better understand the various motivations behind the voluntary provision of public goods and the willingness to cooperate (as exemplified by Paulo Nunes and Laura Onofri in Chapter 11). Such research would yield a more comprehensive understanding of individual decision making in general. It should also make possible policy-oriented profiling of various subpopulations. Increased understanding of social heritage, of collective belief formation and transformation processes, of legitimacy building and erosion, and of political and moral leadership are all important directions for the research needed to build the next generation of policy tools. It is not sufficient merely to recognize that crowding-out exists or that humans can be altruistic. Rather, the various types and causes of crowding-out and altruism must be identified in order to evaluate under what conditions they should be avoided or encouraged. Here we have hinted at the large increase in our knowledge base that is certainly needed before we can adequately address many issues in the vast domain of research on individual versus collective or selfish versus pro-social motivations and actions.

15.4.3 From policy to cooperation

All in all, the evolution of the research frontier in environmental policy leads one to question whether the very notion of "policy" is still relevant in matters of the environment. Indeed, this notion entails governmental intervention that seeks solutions within the framework of a given vertical relationship between citizens and stakeholders (on the one hand) and governments (on the other). Governments attempt to establish collective decision processes that are increasingly more legitimate and more informed, as well as to devise more subtle and effective ways of managing compliance, of ensuring cooperation on a wide scale through a renewed version of federalism, and so forth. This vision is both realistic and useful.

However, the approach proposed in this conclusion suggests that there are alternative paths to better management of our common socio-ecological system. Indeed, governmental intervention (from the local to the global level) is both possible and legitimate when crises occur. In that case (as several contributions to this book have pointed out), the prevailing resistance to collective action, when combined with the need for rapid and massive mobilization of means, leads citizens and stakeholders to accept major policy measures and reforms. This sudden burst of government legitimacy (and action) is certainly better than no reaction, but the resulting emergency plans seldom result in the optimal measures being implemented and seldom avert all consequences of the crises. The recent financial crisis is an excellent example.

Therefore, a major goal of human collectivities should be crisis avoidance. An important step in this direction is to view the environment as a cooperative common goal and not as a policy target (or constraint). In a cooperative process, all stakeholders are accountable for the joint result and should feel so. Since there is no "benevolent dictator," all parties must consider their individual responsibility in contributing to the public good and, more generally, to the process of cooperation. Hence, no party should play myopically. The call for more "reflexive" governance of environmental issues is not only a question of pragmatism in better managing dispersed knowledge and the heterogeneity of human motivation. It is also a means to change the structure of many social dilemmas examined in this book so that we might better control the Earth system's possibly catastrophic evolution in the context of a growing human population with huge gaps to fill in living standards.

Glossary

Allocation mechanisms (pollution permits): When a regulator sets up a cap to limit aggregate emissions of some pollutant (e.g. CO_2, SO_2, NOx) he needs simultaneously to provide an allocation mechanism to divide the emission limit among the potential polluters. The choice of an allocation mechanism can have important efficiency and distributional impacts, and needs therefore to be carefully designed. Furthermore, ethical issues are usually involved because the history of past emissions inevitably comes into play. From an economic point of view, at a given point in time the mechanism should allocate emission rights according to efficiency: each permit should be allocated in a way to make the largest possible contribution to social welfare. Technically, each allocated permit should be welfare improving, in the sense that the social benefit is larger than the social cost of the polluting activity, and that no alternative allocation of the permit could generate a larger welfare gain. In practice three candidates have been under consideration: grandfathering, output-based allocation, and auctions. Under the grandfathering rule, the initial allocation of emission quotas depends on past emissions, and is usually inefficient. This is the main reason why most EU member states adopted this system by allowing for a periodic revision to take into account the evolution of the productive system. Output-based allocation methods take into account current production rather than past production, but can lead to inefficiencies as well. The most efficient system is the auction system, since there are some auction institutions that are perfectly demand revealing (e.g. second price auctions) and therefore allocate auctioned permits efficiently, according to theory.

That said, as discussed extensively in Chapter 13 by Gary Libecap, the problem of efficient allocation of property rights pretty much depends on the nature of the resource (and generated externalities) and most of the time allocation is strongly impacted by conflicts among the various stakeholders.

References and further reading: Cason et al. (2003), Ellerman et al. (2010), Goeree et al. (2009), Harris and Raviv (1981), Klemperer (2002), Montgomery (1972), Tietenberg (2003).

Altruism/impure altruism: Altruistic preferences are a special case of social preferences. A pure altruist prefers to increase others' material resources rather than her own material resources. Parental altruism is often taken as an illustration of pure altruism. However, according to biologists, parental altruism is a special case of selfishness because of the genetic common pool shared among parents and offspring. According to evolutionary biologists, pure altruism cannot survive because of its lack of fitness. A more realistic variety of altruism is impure altruism. Impure altruism relies on the observation that donations are likely to be motivated by many different factors such as the "desire to win prestige, respect, friendship, and other social and psychological objectives" (Olson 1965), rather than altruism. Impure altruism provides a possible explanation about why organizations such as the "Red Cross" or the "Salvation Army" exist, despite the apparent contradiction with the standard selfish rational behavioral assumption. Warm-glow giving is a private good which improves an individual's self-image.

References and further reading: Andreoni (1990), Olson (1965).

Collective action: Collective-action problems occur whenever individuals in interdependent situations face choices in which the maximization of short-term self-interest yields outcomes which leave all participants collectively worse off than feasible alternatives (Sandler 2004). These problems are often presented in the form of so-called "social dilemmas," where the optimal collective outcome is contrasted with the outcome resulting from the pursuit of individual self-interest.

One subcategory of social dilemmas are public-good dilemmas (Kaul et al. 2003). In a public-good dilemma, all those who benefit from the provision of a public good—such as clean air or security—find it costly to contribute and would prefer others to pay for the good instead. If everyone follows the selfish dominant strategy, then the good is not provided or is underprovided. Yet, everyone would be better off if everyone contributed. In those situations of social dilemmas, institutions introduce a certain level of collective constraint, whether through formal or informal rules, with the aim of producing better outcomes. Because the creation of institutions is costly, however, it is important to assess the relative costs and benefits of the different types of formal and informal institutional arrangements that can alleviate the collective-action problems. In particular, the creation of formal legal institutions creates a new collective-action problem (a so-called "second-order social dilemma"), because, even if all will benefit from the rule, not everybody has an incentive to contribute to its creation and maintenance (E. Ostrom 2005b).

References and further reading: Sandler (2004), Kaul et al. (2003), E. Ostrom (2005a, 2005b)

Club goods: Club goods share one property with public goods—non-rivalry—but not non-excludability. Club goods are therefore enjoyed only by club members who have paid for their adhesion to the club or who are members of a de-facto club like a local community. Examples of club goods include cable and satellite television, on-line libraries, social clubs, the European Union, . . . Club goods avoid the free-riding problem at the expense of the privatizing of an otherwise publicly available good to the exclusive benefit of the club members. The welfare gain of such privatization is therefore not obvious; although the production of the good might be increased through the efforts of the club members, the club good is enjoyed only by them, in contrast to an open-access good, which benefits all members of the society. Buchanan (1965) was among the first scholars to investigate the efficiency properties of clubs, essentially because clubs are able to exploit economies of scale but also because they can better share the production costs of collective goods (see also Olson 1965 and Tiebout 1956). The reasons why clubs are voluntarily formed remains puzzling: similarity of tastes and strategic alliances are obvious reasons, but remain controversial.

References and further reading: Buchanan (1965), Cornes and Sandler (1996), McNutt (2002), Olson (1965), Pauly (1967), Scotchmer (2002), Swope (2002), Tiebout (1956).

Collective good: *see Public good.*

Commons: The commons is a non-technical term that designates a wide variety of non-private goods. As such it covers both common-pool resources, which are shared resources (non-exclusive) but depletable (each person's use makes less of the resource available for others), and public goods, which are also shared resources, but non-depletable such as knowledge (my use of your knowledge does not make less knowledge available for others).

Much thought has recently been given to the positive role of the commons in modern economies, in response to what had become conventional wisdom concerning a supposedly ineluctable "tragedy of the commons" (Hardin 1968). The seminal work of Elinor Ostrom and her colleagues focused on commons-based management of natural resources, as regulated by a clearly defined group of local users (E. Ostrom 1990). Empirically, the formal proprietary scheme underlying the administration of such resources varied in practice, from a purely private property regime to various forms of collective ownership, including direct state ownership (E. Ostrom 1990; E. Ostrom et al. 2002; Platteau 2000). Ostrom's work accordingly sought to establish the possibility of a sustainable intermediate economic alternative, situated midway between market-regulated exchanges of private entitlements and pure public goods that typically depend on state-based governance of resources.

More recently, the commons concept has been applied to a wide range of tangible resources in the life sciences, such as pooled genetic resources (Byerlee 2010) and to intangible information goods that are pooled and distributed through digital networks (Benkler 2006; Boyle 2008; Hess and Ostrom (eds) 2007; Lessig 2001). In this context, and after much discussion, the term "commons" as used with regard to both scientific research resources and the production of information goods is generally understood to refer to any resource that is shared on a non-exclusive basis by a discrete group of people at any level, whether local or global, or somewhere in between (Hess and Ostrom (eds) 2007).

References and further reading: Benkler (2006), Boyle (2008), Byerlee (2010), Hardin (1968), Hess and Ostrom (eds) (2007), Lessig (2001), E. Ostrom (1990), E. Ostrom et al. (2002), Platteau (2000).

Coordination dilemmas: *see Coordination failures.*

Coordination failures: Popular examples of coordination failures are choosing on which side of the road to drive or choosing a route to commute (congestion game). In game theory a coordination failure might occur in games where there exist multiple pure strategies Nash equilibria. In such games a coordination failure arises if not all of the agents choose the same strategy which corresponds to one particular equilibrium. They therefore end up in a non-equilibrium situation, which involves lower payoffs than in the equilibrium situation for at least one of the players. Well-known examples of coordination games involving such a possible issue are battle-of-the-sexes games, stag-hunt games, and weakest-link games. An illustration is given by the provision of a step-level public good with non-refundable contributions. If contributions fall short of the provision point, money is lost and the public good is not provided because of underinvestment. If contributions are above the threshold level, the public good is provided but money is wasted because of overinvestment. Coordination failures can lead to resource overexploitation, inefficient macro-economic policies, inefficient management of the workplace, low-performance organizations, ... How agents coordinate their actions is still a largely unsolved puzzle. Schelling (1960) shows the importance of focal points (e.g. norms, common beliefs, ...). Experimental findings highlighted the key role of communication to prevent coordination failures in simple games (Cooper et al. 1989, 1992; Brandts and Cooper 2006).

References and further reading: Brandts and Cooper (2006), Cooper et al. (1989, 1992), Harsanyi and Selten (1988), Schelling (1960).

Crowding-out: Crowding-out arises when the manipulation of economic incentives generates counterproductive effects. A popular example is the decrease in public revenues after an increase in the income tax rate, because of a higher incentive for taxpayers to evade taxes. Internal motivations may be related to religious beliefs, ethical values, or more generally to moral or philosophical arguments. Crowding-out occurs when internal motivations are conflicting with external (economic) incentives. Examples of such conflicts have been documented by Frey and Oberholzer-Gee (1997) for example. Clean examples of conflicts between economic incentives and motivation to act have been documented by Frey and Oberholzer-Gee (1997) and by Gneezy and Rustichini (2000a, 2000b). Such conflicts are hardly accounted by the standard behavioral hypothesis of economic theory, according to which agents are self-interested and motivated solely by their material payoff. Therefore, agents react to monetary incentives by adjusting their decision variables accordingly. For instance, if individuals are rewarded for taking socially desirable actions, more of them will act in the desired way. But behavioral economics and the psychological literature have largely documented that most people take their economic decisions on the basis of several, sometimes conflicting, motivations. In particular, many people have an intrinsic motivation to act (for instance, preserving the quality of the environment) based on some moral or categorical (Kantian) imperative. "The critical assumption in the conventional approach is not that other-regarding motives are absent but that policies that appeal to economic self-interest do not affect the salience of ethical, altruistic, and other social preferences" (Bowles 2008). In other words, moral sentiments are still active when standard policies are activated, a prediction that is actually rejected by the crowding-out literature.

References and further reading: Bowles (2008), Brekke et al. (2003), Deci and Ryan (1985), Frey and Jegen (2001), Frey and Oberholzer-Gee (1997), Gneezy and Rustichini (2000a, 2000b), Harsanyi (1955).

Environmental federalism: Environmental federalism points out that the provision of many environmental goods can be performed on a decentralized basis, especially as many natural resources are localized in particular regions. There is therefore a theory (and a practice) of the optimal devolution of the provision of public goods to the right level of governance that depends both upon natural characteristics (watersheds, forests, etc.), and societal ones (in particular shared culture, political organization, and integration of the economy) (Oates 2002).

This is aptly illustrated in the research on institutional design for environmental governance, which addresses the question of matching scales of governance to the types of collective-action problems under consideration (Young 2002). The central question is how the principles characterizing successful decentralized resource-management schemes can be scaled up to address problems on a global scale, and what new principles need to be added (Keohane and Ostrom (eds) 1995). The example of polycentric metropolitan governance, which has a long history of working arrangements that typically range from the very small to large, overarching metropolitan governance units, is used in the literature as a model to address problems of institutional fit at a regional scale (McGinnis 1999b). At the other end of the spectrum, for those environmental goods that have to be provided at the global level, coordination mechanisms at higher levels and new, regional, collective entities may be needed to create the best fit between governance mechanisms and the problems being considered. The main challenge here is to establish larger units that do not eliminate the medium- and smaller-sized units that help citizens to cope with neighborhood-level public goods and common-pool resources. An important lesson for environmental governance is the importance of encouraging experimental efforts at multiple levels. By structuring decision making in this way, the level of public-good provision can be tailored to the specific circumstances—the tastes of residents, the costs of production, and other peculiar local conditions—of each jurisdiction.

References and further reading: McGinnis (1999a, 1999b), Keohane and Os-trom (eds) (1995), Oates (2002), Young (2002).

Externalities: *see Property rights.*

Free-rider/-riding: A free-rider is someone who consumes or uses a costly good without paying for it or without contributing to its production. Classical examples refer to the use of public transportation without paying the fare, or taking a free lunch on a shared diner. The problem of free-riding is that it might lead to underprovision of voluntarily provided public or club goods. If people expect others to free-ride on a voluntarily provided good, they will contribute less effort or resource to produce it than the socially optimum level of contribution would require. For instance in the case of a step-level public good—that is, a good that should be provided at a minimum level to be valuable—the aggregate voluntary contributions might be insufficient to reach the threshold level to make the good feasible, although it would be efficient to provide it. Also, in the absence of a well-defined institution, free-riders are likely to over-harvest common-pool resources, leading to the well-known tragedy of the commons or commons dilemma (Hardin 1968). In a more general sense, free-riding means, therefore, neglecting one's influence on others' well-being, in contrast to the predictions of social preferences theories.

References and further reading: Cornes and Sandler (1986), Hardin (1968).

Governance regimes: *see Institutions (formal/informal).*

Incentive mechanisms: An incentive mechanism is a way to favor a particular course of action by economic agents. By changing the trade-off that agents are facing through bonuses or penalties, an incentive mechanism induces reasons for preferring one choice over the alternatives.

Mechanism design is the technique at the heart of incentives implementation. It attempts to figure out all the options an agent considers when making a decision, how they interact and result in alternative costs and benefits (and risks). Then the designer of the system—for example, a principal in a principal–agent relationship—manipulates the expected payoffs of the agent to induce him to choose the preferred action of the designer. This is done by conditioning payments to specific observable actions or outcomes. The difficulties lie in the fact that in many cases, what is wished—typically an effort—is not observable—a third party generally sees the result of the action but not the care or the intensity with which it was taken—inducing distortions between the incentive mechanism and its outcome. The goal of the social scientist (and of the decision maker) is to reduce this distortion (qualified as information rent in the litera-ture) as much as possible. The 2007 Nobel Memorial Prize in Economic Sciences was awarded to Leonid Hurwicz, Eric Maskin, and Roger Myerson "for having laid the foundations of mechanism design theory."

The study of incentive mechanisms is central for policy making since fiscal instruments, contracts with private operators, or changes in the relative prices of commodities influence individual decisions, generally with the aim of reconciling individual behavior with a given collective objective. That said, economists tend to focus essentially on financial incentives, while a usual taxonomy divides incentives into three categories: financial, moral, and coercive. The latter two tend to be studied more by sociology and political science, respectively (Gauthier 1986). Recently, however, economists have attempted to enrich their understanding of human motivations, by taking into account the way individuals consider others' satisfaction or others' beliefs (See the entry *Social preferences*).

References and further reading: Aumann and Hart (2002), Faruk (2008), Gauthier (1986), Myerson (2008).

Incentive schemes: *see Incentive mechanisms.*

Institutions (formal/informal): Institutions are sets of rules of the game or codes of conduct that serve to define social practices, assign roles to the participants in these practices, and guide their interactions (Young 1994). They also have been qualified as rules of the game (North 1990) and mutually reinforced patterns of behaviors (Aoki 2007; Greif 2006) to point out the fact that, while created by human beings, they are imposed to individual decision makers who cannot individually change them or escape the constraints they put on their possible behaviors and strategies. Structures of property rights, on this account, are institutions. So are electoral systems used to choose representatives, or more informal rules governing kinship relationships for example.

In general, institutions are created by human beings to cope with problems of coordination and cooperation that arise in social groups. A common feature of the various research traditions on institutions is the recognition of the complementarities between formal institutions (such as formal legal statutes and contracts), and informal rules (community norms, customs, and intrinsic values). Indeed, from the point of view of institutional analysis, it is the combination of formal legal rules and informal rules that produces effective governance regimes (E. Ostrom 2005b; Williamson 1996). In the context of institutional analysis, formal rules can be understood as prescriptions that are imposed and enforced in an organized manner by a designated entity, such as the state, the head of an organization, or parties in a contract. Informal rules are prescriptions that are followed because of the existence of certain social or individual norms, without any formal agreement on the sanctions to be applied.

As stressed by Cooter (1994), the complexity of modern economies is so great that centralized law creation cannot effectively cope with the need to achieve normative regulation among communities of individuals who repeatedly face collective-action problems. Hence the need for different types of institutions.

References and further reading: Aoki (2007), Cooter (1994), Greif (2006), North (1990), E. Ostrom (2005b), Williamson (1996), Young (1994).

Mechanism design: *see Incentive mechanism.*

Moral and intrinsic motivation: Intrinsic or moral motivation refers to the internal reward system that leads individuals to act without any external incentive. For instance, some people may take economically meaningful actions, simply because they think it is the right thing to do. Such motivation may be grounded on religious beliefs, ethical values, or more general moral or philosophical arguments. For instance, the Kantian categorical imperative belongs to this category of internal motivation, which leads to moral norms of behavior. However, such "moral norms" must be carefully distinguished from social norms, since the individual imposes them on himself even though the norms of the society might be weaker or different.

Moral motivation theory provides an explanation as to why most people contribute voluntarily to the private production of public goods (e.g. sorting waste), which contrasts with the explanation of the impure altruism model based on the warm-glow motivation (see the entry *Altruism/impure altruism*).

References and further reading: Bowles (2008), Brekke et al. (2003), Deci and Ryan (1985), Frey and Oberholzer-Gee (1997), Harsanyi (1955).

Moral hazard *(see also Free-riding):* Moral hazard arises because an individual or institution does not take the full consequences and responsibilities of its actions, and therefore has a tendency to act differently than it otherwise would. Moral hazard occurs in situations of information asymmetry on key inputs (Brousseau and Glachant 2002). One major example is the case of precaution in cases of risk, when individuals are less careful since they do not fully bear the consequences of their actions, for instance because they are insured (Arrow 1985; Holmstrom 1979), but the theory of moral hazard has also been applied to a wide variety of problems of asymmetric information. This is particularly the case in a principal–agent problem, where one party, called an agent, acts on behalf of another party, called the principal. The agent usually has more information about his or her actions or intentions than the principal does, because the principal usually cannot completely monitor the agent.

Moral hazard plays an important role in the context of the management of environmental risks. To the extent that actors are confident that either private or public insurance procedures will indemnify their losses, individuals may take greater risks than would otherwise be the case. This is often observed in such cases as the destruction brought by the impact of hurricanes on barrier islands or the impact of wild fires on homes located in areas prone to fire. So long as the government is willing to designate hard hit areas as disaster zones and to provide generous financial aid to victims of such destructive events, owners of homes in areas prone to flooding or burning will be more likely to rebuild in the same place rather than to relocate, as would be the case in the absence of public assistance.

References and further reading: Arrow (1985), Brousseau and Glachant (2002), Holmstrom (1979).

Norms: *see Social norms.*

Preference aggregation: Social choice theory relies on the assumption that there exist a meaningful way to aggregate individual preferences into a collective preference on which society's choices might be grounded. Preference aggregation is also relevant for multi-criteria decision making and voting. There exist many possibilities to aggregate individual preferences in order to construct a collective preference. An extreme possibility consists simply in the selection of the preferences of a single member of the society whose preferences arbitrarily represent the society's preference. This corresponds to dictatorship. At the other extreme one can think of an aggregation for which the preferences of each society's member are counted equally, as in egalitarian utilitarianism.

To provide a meaningful representation of individuals' preferences the aggregation technique should satisfy some desirable criteria: non-dictatorship, universality (each member is represented), independence of irrelevant alternatives (expansions and contractions of the choice set should not affect the ranking), Pareto efficiency, and non-imposition (any social ranking is feasible). The famous Arrow (1951) impossibility theorem shows that for each member of the society has an individual ranking (preference) over a set of alternatives it is impossible to construct a social ranking (aggregation) of these alternatives that satisfies all these criteria at the same time. At least one of the criteria will not be met (e.g. it is easy to construct a social ranking that satisfies all criteria except non-dictatorship). Harsanyi (1955) and Sen (1970) showed, however, that if one admits at least partial comparability between individual welfare, the aggregation dilemma raised by Arrow's theorem can be circumvented.

References and further reading: Arrow (1951, 1963), Harsanyi (1955), Sen (1970, 1979).

Property rights: A property right is a set of rules establishing how a resource can be accessed, used, preserved, or destroyed. The definition and allocation of property rights has a strong impact on efficiency, since it determines how individuals consider the resource. In particular, property rights define how the individual wealth of a given potential user of a resource will be impacted when he/she will decide to access, use, or invest in it, or when others will do.

Property rights can concern any physical or intangible resource and can be granted to individuals or groups. Depending upon the nature of the right, an owner can decide how to use the resource. He can also, by means of a contract, transfer temporary or permanently, some rights of use to third parties.

When the use of a resource by an individual (he) impacts upon the utility of another individual (she) who has no right to control over it, one speaks of externality; which can be positive or negative. Externalities result in economic issues since resources tend to be misused, hence the attempt to design more precise and sometimes new property rights—as emission permits in the case of pollution—to allow a re-internalization of externalities; that is, a clear delineation of decision rights to those who produce goods or bads so that they bear the consequences of their decisions. This was the line proposed by Coase in 1960 to resolve many issues linked to externalities. Settling and securing property rights, however, has a cost, that comes in addition to the costs of managing transactions. These "transaction costs" should be balanced with the benefits of a "better" property rights system; that is, a system that reduces distortions between the distribution of decision rights and the distribution of costs and benefits.

Some philosophers such as Proudhon (1840) or Bastiat (1850) asserted that property rights arise from social conventions. Many economists, in the line of Douglass North (1990), studied how property rights systems emerge and evolve along historical processes. This is a way to better understand how property systems can be amended and reformed to provide better incentives to agents in the society so as to result in a better use of resources (Barzel 1989; De Soto and Chevenal 2006). The economics of property rights attempts to weigh the benefits and the costs of alternative scopes and alternative bundling of decision rights over resources.

References and further reading: Ackerman et al. (2002), Alchian and Demsetz (1973), Barzel (1989), Bastiat (1850), Coase (1960), De Soto and Cheneval (2006), North (1990), Proudhon (1840).

Public goods: Public goods have two peculiar properties compared to private goods: non-rivalry and non-excludability. Non-rivalry means that the consumption of the good by one individual does not affect its availability for consumption by others. Non-excludability means that no one can be excluded from the consumption of the good. Typical examples of public goods are lighting (e.g. a lighthouse), national defense, national parks, public television, FM radio . . . A key issue with public goods is that if they are voluntarily provided by private agents, they will generally be underprovided with respect to the socially optimum level of provision. The reason is that selfish-oriented utility-maximizing agents have an incentive to free-ride on others' contributions to the public good (see the entry *Free-rider/riding*). For instance, public goods with a provision point might simply not be provided by private agents, an extreme case of market failure. Governmental provision of public goods, or some alternative institutional arrangement can, however, restore efficiency.

An important qualification concerns the extent of the public good (global or local). A local public good benefits the citizens located in the district, but there might exist spillovers to non-resident citizens; local public lighting or landscape are examples. Such a situation involves a "decentralization dilemma." If the provision of the public good is decentralized at the local level, it might be underprovided because local governments/communities maximize only the welfare of the residents in the jurisdiction, neglecting spillovers to residents of neighboring districts. In the case of global public goods—for instance, the environmental goods to be provided at the biosphere level—they should be provided by a centralized authority. Such an institution does not, however, exist, and the provision dilemma is therefore how to provide in a decentralized way a global public good, a situation called the Westphalian dilemma (see Nordhaus 2005).

The rigorous definition of "public good" by economists relies on the intrinsic quality of the good. However, in many social debates there might exist some confusion because some argue that certain goods—for example, education or wealth—that "technically speaking" are private goods (they are excludable and (partly) rival) should be provided by the society for moral and political reasons. Economists would argue that this might be (partly) grounded on the existence of spillover effects. Indeed, an individual's ability to value her education is partly dependent upon the level of education of others. Similarly, one's own health is also partly dependent on others' health. Since such spillovers result from interdependencies on both the demand and the supply side, it justifies the need for public intervention.

References and further reading: Cornes and Sandler (1996), Nordhaus (2005).

Social dilemma/cooperation failure: The prisoner's dilemma illustrates a general issue in social interaction systems. Each individual of a group would be better off if all other members of the group chose to cooperate, but no one has the material incentive to do so. In other words, assuming that all members of the group agree to cooperate, if a single member deviates from the cooperative agreement, he receives a payoff that is even larger than if the cooperative agreement could be enforced. Knowing that each member of the group has such an incentive, the worst outcome arises: no one cooperates; that is, a general cooperation failure. The prisoner's dilemma illustrates a major paradigm of economics that has been generalized through the notion of social dilemma. There exist numerous examples of such dilemma situations in the environmental domain (e.g. the voluntary contributions to provide some amount of public good, the exploitation of a common-pool resource or the ratification of an emission reduction treaty) but also in other domains (doping in sports, humanitarian aid, tax evasion, . . .). While standard theory predicts an extreme outcome of such dilemma situations (no cooperation), the empirical and experimental evidence is mixed. For instance, many agents (countries, companies, households, . . .) take voluntary actions to curb greenhouse gas emissions, although they are aware that others do not cooperate even if they benefit from it. Elinor Ostrom gathered many examples throughout the world, documenting that such cooperative agreements might be sustainable. However, in these examples many factors, which are not accounted for by the theory, can actually account for such cooperative agreement. The experimental literature, which is less controversial since it allows these factors to be isolated, essentially shows that cooperative outcomes arise depending on individuals' preferences and beliefs. Individuals who are not solely motivated by their material payoff but who have social preferences (see relevant entry) are more prone to agree to cooperate, and individuals who believe themselves to be in a cooperative environment are more likely to cooperate as well. These observations recently gave rise to a fast-growing literature on conditional cooperation based on social preference theories.

References and further reading: Fehr and Fischbacher (2002), Gächter and Fischbacher (2010), Keser and van Winden (2000), E. Ostrom et al (2005, 2010).

Socio-ecological systems: The term "socio-ecological system" is used to model situations where social and ecological systems are linked through a set of dynamic interactions, which makes the delineation between the social and the natural system artificial and arbitrary (Berkes et al. 2003). Human actions have had major impacts on biophysical systems for thousands of years. Yet, the scope and magnitude of the human forces operating in socio-ecological systems have risen dramatically, leading prominent scientists to conclude that we have entered a world of human-dominated ecosystems (Vitousek et al. 1997), even on a planetary scale (Crutzen 2002; Crutzen and Stoermer 2000).

The specific objective of the research on socio-ecological systems is to investigate how human societies deal with changes in these coupled systems, and how capacity can be built to adapt to future changes. Dealing with biophysical systems or social-economic systems alone is challenging enough. But the resultant socio-ecological systems are far more complex and dynamic than any ecosystem human societies have encountered previously. It follows that nonlinearities and the inevitable uncertainties associated with complex and highly dynamic systems need to be taken into account in the analysis of institutions to govern human–environment interactions.

References and further reading: Berkes et al. (2003), Crutzen (2002), Crutzen and Stoermer (2000), Vitousek et al. (1997).

Social norms: Social norms are customary rules of behavior that coordinate our interactions with others. Once a particular way of doing things becomes established as a rule, it continues in force because we prefer to conform to the rule given the expectation that others are going to conform (Lewis 1969; Schelling 1960). This definition covers simple rules that are self-enforcing at a primary level, such as which hand to extend in greeting, and more complex rules that trigger social sanctions against those who deviate from the rule.

Social norms may play an important role not only in the explanation of individual behavior (Bernstein, 2001; Ellickson 1991; Greif 2006; Posner 2007), but also in the decisions of national governments in the diplomatic arena (Hoel and Schneider 1997). Governments may fear being labeled as opportunistic and non-cooperative, and therefore sign and stick to an environmental convention, even when, in purely economic terms, free-riding pays off. Formally speaking, taking such motivations into account amounts to expanding the set of arguments in the utility (or welfare) functions of the players. This non-environmental cost is likely to be higher the larger the number of cooperating countries. Psychosocial interventions are essential to deliver the widespread changes in social norms needed to initiate the changes in the economy and in lifestyles that are essential to address global environmental issues

References and further reading: Bernstein (2001), Ellickson (1991), Greif (2006), Hoel and Schneider (1997), Lewis (1969), Posner (2007), Schelling (1960).

Social preferences: Economists' standard behavioral hypothesis, which is based on self-interested and self-centered agents, has been partially rejected by the huge amount of experimental data that was accumulated over the past decade. This data showed that other-regarding or so-called social preferences are widespread, and failure to take them seriously into account leads to misconceptions and unexplained facts. Social preferences refer to a particular case of interdependency among agents according to Fehr and Fischbacher (2002): "A person exhibits social preferences if the person not only cares about the material resources allocated to her but also cares about the material resources allocated to relevant reference agents." In terms of utility representation, "social preferences" means that an agent's utility depends not only on his own income or consumption but also on other agents' incomes or consumptions. Altruism, envy, spite, inequity aversion, preference for reciprocity, are special cases of social preferences. For instance, an agent's utility or well-being may be negatively affected by an increase in other's income or consumption, a manifestation of envious behavior. On the other hand, an agent's well-being may be positively affected by an increase in others' income or consumption, because of empathy. Social preferences have strong implications for the understanding of cooperation, competition, and incentives (see Fehr and Fischbacher 2002). Several models have been developed to account for such preferences, among which Fehr and Schmidt (1999) and Bolton and Ockenfels (2000) are the most prominent.

References and further reading: Bolton and Ockenfels (2000), Fehr and Fischbacher (2002), Fehr and Schmidt (1999), Rabin (1993).

Tragedy of the commons: *see Commons.*

Transaction costs: According to a narrow and standard definition, transaction costs are the costs of interactions on the markets. Transaction costs include the costs of discovering market prices, a buyer or a seller, and settling an arrangement. The notion has been progressively extended in modern economic thinking to the cost of interacting and coordinating among agents. Transaction costs refer, therefore, to the costs incurred by individual agents or the society in using alternative "social technologies" to coordinate; that is, alternative contractual, organizational, or institutional solutions.

Alternative "social technologies" establish and allocate decision-making rights to agents, stating what they can or cannot decide concerning the use of resources or their interaction with other agents in various circumstances. They state "rules"—which define authorized, forbidden, or mandatory actions—and ensure compliance thanks to enforcement mechanisms. Transaction costs are the costs of performing these two sets of tasks. In the view of Barzel (1989) and Allen (1999), they refer to the costs of resources and efforts dedicated to defining and enforcing rights of access and of use over resources, and the costs of establishing and managing agreements to reorganize and transfer these rights.

The transaction, as unit of analysis, was introduced by the institutional economist John R. Commons in 1931 to designate the interactions occurring among individuals in the society. Ronald Coase relied on the notion of transaction cost, to propose a theoretical framework aimed at determining when transactions would be internalized in firms, or performed via the market. Transaction cost reasoning was extended by Oliver E. Williamson to analyze any contractual and organizational arrangement, including market and non-market forms of coordination. The notion was then extended not only to analyze single dyadic relationships, but also to study the way institutions impact on the cost of coordinating a wide set of individuals at the societal level. In particular, Douglass North was the first to propose analyzing how institutions shape the ability to divide labor and organize exchange at the level of the whole society (North 1990).

References and further reading: Allen (1999), Barzel (1989), Coase (1937), Commons, (1931), Klaes (2008), North (1990), Williamson (1981, 1996).

References

Abernathy, C.L. and Hilmy, S., 2000. Experiments of some government-sponsored organizations of irrigators in Niger and Burkina Faso, West Africa. *Journal of Applied Irrigation Studies*, 35(2): 177–205.

Abu-Lughod, L., 2002. Do muslim women really need saving? Anthropological reflections on cultural relativism and its others. *American Anthoropologist*, 104 (3): 783–90.

Acheson, J., 2003. *Capturing the Commons: Devising institutions to manage the Maine lobster industry*. New Haven: University Press of New England.

Acheson, J., Wilson, J., and Steneck, R., 1998. Managing chaotic fisheries. In: F. Berkes and C. Folke (eds) *Linking Social and Ecological Systems: Management practices and social mechanisms for building resilience*. Cambridge: Cambridge University Press, 390–413.

Ackerman, A., Ellickson, R., and Rose, C.M. 2002. *Perspectives on Property Law*, 3rd edn. New York: Aspen Law and Business.

Ackerman, F., 1997. *Why Do We Recycle: Markets, values, and public policy*. Washington, DC: Island Press.

Adams, M., 1989. New activities and the efficient liability rules. In: M.F Aure and R. Van den Bergh (eds) *Essays in Law and Economics. Corporations, accident prevention and compensation for losses*. Antwerpen: Malku Uitgevers.

Agrawal, A., 2005. Environmentality: Community, intimate government, and the making of environmental subjects in Kumaon India. *Current Anthropology*, 46(2): 161–90.

Agrawal, A. and Gibson, C.C., 2001. The role of the community in natural resource reservation. In: A. Agrawal, and C.C. Gibson (eds) *Communities and the Environment: Ethnicity, gender, and the state in community-based conservation*. New Brunswick: Rutgers University Press, 1–31.

Agrawal, B., 2001. Participatory exclusion, community forestry and gender: An analysis for South Asia and the conceptual framework. *World Development* 29(10): 1623–48.

Alchian, A. and Demsetz, H. 1973. The property rights paradigm. *Journal of Economic History*, 33(1): 16–27.

Allen, D.W. 1999. Transaction costs. In B. Bouckaert and G. De Geest (eds) *Encyclopedia of Law and Economics*. Aldershot: Edward Elgar, 893–926.

Alley, R., 2000. *The Two-mile Time Machine: Ice cores, abrupt climate change, and our future*. Princeton, NJ: Princeton University Press.

Almer, Ch. and Goeschl, T., 2010. Environmental crime and punishment: Empirical evidence from the German penal code. *Land Economics*, 86(4): 707–26.

Alston, L.J., Libecap, G., and Mueller, B., 2010. Interest Groups, information manipulation in the media, and public policy: The case of the landless peasants movement in Brazil", NBER Working Paper No. 15865, April.

Andersen, M.S., 2001. *Economic Instruments and Clean Water: Why institutions and policy design matters*. Paris: OECD.

Anderson, L.G. and Lee D.R., 1986. Optimal governing instrument, operation level, and enforcement in natural resource regulation: The case of the fishery. *American Journal of Agricultural Economics*, 68(3): 678–90.

Andreoni, J., 1989. Giving with impure altruism: Applications to charity and ricardian equivalence. *Journal of Political Economy*, 97(3): 1447–58.

Andreoni, J., 1990. Impure altruism and donations to public goods: A theory of warm-glow giving. *The Economic Journal*, 100: 464–77.

Andreoni, J., 1993. An experimental test of the public goods crowding-out hypothesis. *American Economic Review*, 83(5): 1317–27.

Andreoni, J. and Miller, J., 1998. Analyzing choice with revealed preference: Is altruism rational? Ch. Plott and V. Smith (eds) (Manuscript prepared for *The Handbook of Experimental Economic Results*), pp. 1–16.

Andreoni, J. and Miller, J., 2002. Giving according to GARP: An experimental test of the consistency of preferences for altruism. *Econometrica*, 70: 737–53.

Andreoni, J., Harbaugh, W., and Vesterlund, L., 2007. Altruism in experiments. In: S.N. Durlauf and L.E. Blume (eds) *The New Palgrave Dictionary of Economics*. Basingstoke: Palgrave Macmillan.

Aoki, M., 2001. Community norms and embeddness: A game-theoretic approach. In: Y. Hayami and M. Aoki (eds) *Communities and Markets in Economic Development*. Oxford: Oxford University Press, 97–128.

Aoki, M., 2007. Endogenizing institutions and institutional changes. *Journal of Institutional Economics*, 3(1): 1–31.

Appadurai, A., 1989. Small-scale techniques and large-scale objectives. In: P. Bardhan (ed.) *Conversations between Economists and Anthropologists: Methodological issues in measuring economic change in rural India*. Delhi: Oxford University Press.

Araral, E., 2005. Bureaucratic incentives, path dependence, and foreign aid: An empirical institutional analysis of irrigation in the Philippines. *Policy Sciences*, 38 (2–3): 131–57.

Araral, E., 2009. What explains collective action in the commons? Theory and evidence from the Philippines. *World Development*, 37(3): 687–97.

Archer, M.S., 2003. *Structure, Agency, and the Internal Conversation*. Cambridge: Cambridge University Press.

Arctic Climate Impact Assessment (ACIA), 2004. *Impacts of a Warming Arctic*. Cambridge: Cambridge University Press.

Arcuri, A., 2001. Controlling environmental risk in Europe: The complementary role of an EC environmental liability regime. *Tijdschrift voor Milieuaansprakelijkheid*, 15(2): 39–40.

Ariely, D., Kamenica, E., and Prelec, D., 2008. Man's search for meaning: The case of legos. *Journal of Economic Behavior & Organization*, 67(3–4): 671–7.

Ariely, D., Bracha, A., and Meier, S., 2009. Doing good or doing well? Image motivation and monetary incentives in behaving prosocially. *American Economic Review*, 99(1): 544–55.

Arnason, R. 2002. A Review of International Experiences with ITQ. In: *Annex to Future Options for UK Fishing Management, Report to the Department for the Environment, Food and Rural Affairs*. University of Portsmouth, UK: CEMARE.

Arrow, K., 1951, 1963. *Social Choice and Individual Values*. New York: Wiley.

Arrow, K.J., 1981. Optimal and voluntary income redistribution. In: S. Rosenfield (ed.) *Economic Welfare and the Economics of Soviet Socialism: Essays in honor of Abram Bergson*. Cambridge: Cambridge University Press.

Arrow, K.J., 1985. The economics of agency. In: J. Pratt and R. Zeckhauser (eds) *Principals and Agents: The structure of business*. Boston: Harvard Business School Press.

Arrow, K.J., 1999. Observation on social capital. In: P. Dasgupta and I. Serageldin (eds) *Social CAPITAL: A multifaceted perspective*. Washington, DC: World Bank, 3–6.

Arrow, K.J., Solow, R., Portney, P.R., Leamer, E.E., Radner, R., and Schuman, E.H., 1993. Report of the NOAA Panel on Contingent Valuation, Federal Register, 58, 4602–14.

Aulisi, A., Farrell, A.E., Pershing, J., and Van Deveer, S., 2005. *Greenhouse Gas Emissions Trading in U.S. States: Observations and lessons from the OTC NOx Budget Trading Program*. Washington, DC: World Resources Institute.

Aumann, R.J. and Hart. S. 1992, 1994, 2002. *Handbook of Game Theory with Economic Applications*. The Hague: Elsevier.

Axelrod, R., 1984. *The Evolution of Cooperation*. New York: Basic Books.

Ayala, F.J., 2010. The difference of being human: Morality. *Proceedings of the National Academy of Sciences*, 107: 9015–22.

Bakan, J., 2004. *The Corporation—The Pathological Pursuit of Profit and Power*. New York: Free Press.

Baland, J.M. and Platteau, J.P., 1996. *Halting Degradation of Natural Resources*. Oxford: Clarendon Press for FAO.

Baldwin, R., 2008. Regulation lite: The rise of emissions trading. *Regulation & Governance*, 2(2): 193–215. Available at: http://www3.interscience.wiley.com/journal/119423171/issue (accessed 2 October 2008).

Ballet, J., Sirven, N., and Requier-Desjardin, M., 2007. Social capital and natural resource management: A critical perspective. *The Journal of Environment and Development*, 16(4): 355–74.

Ban, N.C., Caldwell, I.R., Green, T.L., Morgan, S.K., O'Donnell, K., Selgrath, S., Lynham, J., Costello, C., Gaines, S.D., Grafton, F.D., and Prince, J., 2009. Diverse fisheries require diverse solutions. *Science*, 323(5912): 338–9.

Barber, J., 2006. Citizens powerless in the mighty megacity. *Globe and Mail*, July 19, p.A9.

Barde, J.P., 1995. Environmental policy and policy instruments. In: H. Folmer, H.L. Gabel, and H. Opschoor (eds) *Principles of Environmental and Resource Economics: A guide for students and decision-makers*. Aldershot: Edward Elgar, 218–20.

Bardhan, P., 1984. *Land, Labor, and Rural Poverty: Essays in development economics*, Oxford: Oxford University Press.

Bardhan, P. and Ray, I., 2007. *The Contested Commons: Conversations between economists and anthropologists*. Oxford: Blackwell Publishing.

Bardhan, P. and Ray, I., 2008. Economists, anthropologists, and the contested commons. In: P. Bardhan and I. Ray (eds) *The Contested Commons: Conversation between economists and anthropologists*. Oxford: Blackwell Publishing.

Bardhan, P. and Singh, N., 1987. On moral hazard, incentive and risk in cost-sharing under sharecropping. *American Journal of Agricultural Economics*, 69: 382–3.

Barrett, S., 1994a. The biodiversity supergame. *Environmental and Resource Economics*, 41: 111–22.

Barrett, S., 1994b. Self-enforcing international environmental agreements. *Oxford Economic Papers*, 46: 804–78.

Barrett, S., 2001. International cooperation for sale. *European Economic Review*, 45(10); 1835–50.

Barrett, S., 2003a. *Environment and Statecraft. The strategy of environmental treaty-making*. Oxford: Oxford University Press.

Barrett, S., 2003b. Global disease eradication. *Journal of the European Economic Association*, 1: 591–600.

Barrett, S., 2005. Managing the global commons. Stockholm: Sweden (Background working paper for the Task Force on Global Public Goods).

Barrett, S., 2007a. The smallpox eradication game. *Public Choice*, 130: 179–207.

Barrett, S., 2007b. *Why Cooperate? The incentive to supply global public goods*. Oxford: Oxford University Press.

Barro, R.J., 1974. Are government bonds net wealth? *Journal of Political Economy*, 82(6): 1095–117.

Barth, F., 1967. Economic spheres in Darfur. In: R.W. Firth (ed.) *Themes in Economic Anthropology*. London: Routledge, 149–74.

Barzel, Y., 1989. *Economic Analysis of Property Rights*. Cambridge: Cambridge University Press.

Bastiat, F., 1850 [1996]. *Economic Harmonies*. G.B. de Huszar, trans. and W. Hayden Boyers, ed. Irvington-on-Hudson, NY: Foundation for Economic Education, Inc.

Becker, G.S., 1974. A theory of social interactions. *Journal of Political Economy*, 82: 1063–93.

Becker, G.S. 1983. A theory of competition among pressure groups for political influence. *Quarterly Journal of Economics* 98(3): 371–400.

Becker, G.S., 1992. Habits, Addictions and Traditions. *Kyklos*, vol. 45(3), Wiley Blackwell, 327–45.

Becker, G. and Stigler, G.J., 1977. De gustibus non est disputandum. *American Economic Review*, 67: 76–90.

Ben-Ner, A. and Putterman, L.G., 1998. *Economics, Values, and Organization*. Cambridge: Cambridge University Press.

Bénabou, R. and Tirole, J., 2003. Intrinsic and extrinsic motivation. *Review of Economic Studies*, 70(3): 489–520.

Bénabou, R. and Tirole, J., 2006. Incentives and prosocial behavior. *American Economic Review*, 96(5): 1652–78.

Benedict, R.E. (1991) *Ozone Diplomacy: New Directions in Safeguarding the Planet*. Cambridge, MA: Harvard University Press.

Benhabib, S., 1992. Models of public sphere: Hannah Arendt, the liberal tradition and Jurgen Habermas. In: C. Calhoun (ed.) *Habermas and Public Sphere*. Cambridge MA: MIT Press.

Benhabib, S., 1996. *Democracy and Difference*. Princeton, NJ: Princeton University Press.

Benjamin, P., Lam, W.-F., Ostrom, E., and Shivakoti, G., 1994. *Institutions, Incentives, and Irrigation in Nepal.* Decentralization: Finance & management project report. Burlington, VT: Associates in Rural Development.

Benkler, Y., 2006. *The Wealth of Networks.* New Haven, CT: Yale University Press.

Berger, P. and Luckmann, T., 1966. *The Social Construction of Reality: A treatise in the sociology of knowledge.* Garden City, NY: Doubleday.

Bergkamp, L., 2001. *Liability and Environment.* The Hague/London: Kluwer.

Berglund, C., 2006. The assessment of households' recycling costs: The role of personal motives. *Ecological Economics,* 56(4): 560–9.

Bergland, H., Clark, D.J., and Pedersen, P.A., 2002. Rent-seeking and quota regulation of a renewable resource. *Resource and Energy Economics,* 24(3): 263–79.

Bergstrom, Th.C., Blume, L.E. and Varian, H.R., 1986. On the private provision of public goods. *Journal of Public Economics,* 29: 25–49.

Berkes, F., 1989. *Common Property Resources: Ecology and community-based sustainable development.* London: Belhaven Press.

Berkes, F., 2007. Community-based conservation in a globalized world. *Proceedings of the National Academy of Sciences,* 104(39): 15188–93.

Berkes, F., Feeny, D., McCay, B., and Acheson, J., 1989. The benefits of the commons. *Nature,* 340: 91–3.

Berkes, F., Colding, J., and Folke, C., 2003. *Navigating Social–Ecological Systems: Building resilience for complexity and change.* Cambridge: Cambridge University Press.

Berkes, F., Hughes, T.P., Steneck, R.S., Wilson, J.A., Bellwood, D.R., Crona, B., Folke, C., Gunderson, L.H., Leslie, H.M., Norberg, J., Nyström, M., Olsson, P., Österblom, H., Scheffer, M., and Worm B., 2005. Globalization, roving bandits, and marine resources. *Science,* 311(5767); 1557–8.

Berman, H.J., 1983. *Law and Revolution: The formation of the western legal tradition.* Cambridge, MA: Harvard University Press.

Bernheim, B.D., 2002. Taxation and saving. In: A.J. Auerbach and M. Feldstein (eds) *Handbook of Public Economics.* The Hague: Elsevier, vol. 3: 1173–249.

Bernheim, B.D. and Bagwell, K., 1988. Is everything neutral? *The Journal of Political Economy,* 96(2): 303–38.

Bernstein, L., 2001. Private commercial law in the cotton industry: Creating cooperation through rules, norms and institutions. *Michigan Law Review,* 99: 1724–90.

Biermann, F., 2007. Earth system governance as a crosscutting theme of global research. *Global Environmental Change,* 17(3–4): 326–37.

Bloch, F., 1997. Non-cooperative models of coalition formation in games with spillovers. In: C. Carraro and D. Siniscalco (eds) *New Directions in the Economy of the Environment.* Cambridge: Cambridge University Press, 311–52.

Bocken, H., 1987. Alternatives to liability and liability insurance for the compensation of pollution damages. *Tijdschrift voor Milieuaansprakelijkheid,* 1: 83–7.

Bocken, H., 1988. Alternatives to liability and liability insurance for the compensation of pollution damages. *Tijdschrift voor Milieuaansprakelijkheid,* 2: 3–10.

Bolin, B., 1997. Scientific assessment of climate change. In G. Fermann (ed.) *International Politics of Climate Change: Key issues and critical actors*. Oslo: Scandinavian University Press, 83–109.

Bolton, E.K. and Zwick, R., 1998. Dictator game giving: Rules of fairness versus acts of kindness. *International Journal of Game Theory*, 27: 269–99.

Bolton, G. and Ockenfels, A., 2000. A theory of equity, reciprocity and competition. *American Economic Review*, 100: 166–93.

Bongaerts, J.C. and Kraemer, R.A., 1987. Water pollution charges in three countries. Control through incentives. *European Environment Review*, 1(4): 12–19.

Borges, G. and Irlenbusch, B., 2007. Fairness crowded out by law: An experimental study on withdrawal rights. *Journal of Institutional and Theoretical Economics*, 163: 84–101.

Botzen, W.J.W., Gowdy, J.M., and Van Den Bergh, J.C.J.M., 2008. Cumulative CO_2 emissions: Shifting international responsibilities for climate debt. *Climate Policy*, 8 (6): 569–76.

Bouma, J., Bulte, E., and van Soest, D., 2008. Trust and cooperation: Social capital and community resource management. *Journal of Environmental Economics and Management*, 56(2): 155–66.

Bourdieu, P., 1971. The thinkable and the unthinkable. *Times Literary Supplement*, 15 October, pp. 1255–6.

Bourdieu, P., 1984. *Distinction: A social critique of the judgement of taste*. Cambridge MA: Harvard University Press.

Bourdieu, P., 1990. *The Logic of Practice*. Stanford, CA: Stanford University Press.

Bourdieu, P. and Wacquant, L., 1992. *An Invitation to Reflexive Sociology*. Chicago, IL: University of Chicago Press.

Bowles, S., 1998. Endogenous preferences: The cultural consequences of markets and other economic institutions. *Journal of Economic Literature*, XXXVI (March): 75–111.

Bowles, S., 2003. *Microeconomics: Behavior, institutions and evolution*. Princeton, NJ: Princeton University Press.

Bowles, S., 2008. Policies designed for self-interested citizens may undermine "the moral sentiments": Evidence from economic experiments. *Science*, 320(5883): 1605–9.

Bowles, S. and Gintis, H., 2000. Walrasian economics in retrospect. *Quarterly Journal of Economics*, 115: 1411–39.

Bowles, S. and Gintis, H., 2002. Social capital and community governance. *The Economic Journal*, 112(483): 419–36.

Boyce, J., 2007. Inequality and environmental protection. In: J.M. Baland, P. Bardhan, and S. Bowles (eds) *Inequality, Cooperation, and Environmental Sustainability*. Princeton, NJ: Princeton University Press, 314–48.

Boyle, J., 2008. *The Public Domain*. New Haven, CT: Yale University Press.

Boyne, G., 1992. Local government structure and performance: Lessons from America. *Public Administration*, 70: 333–57.

Brandt, H. and Sigmund, K., 2005. Indirect reciprocity, image scoring, and moral hazard. *Proceedings of the National Academy of Sciences*, 102(7): 2666–70.

Brandts, J. and Cooper, D. 2006. A change would do you good. An experimental study on how to overcome coordination failure in organizations. *The American Economic Review*, 96(3): 669–93.

Bréchet T. and Luterbacher, U., 2011. Computational models for policy support in climate issues. In: U. Luterbacher and D.F. Sprinz. *The Evolving Climate Change Regime*. Cambridge, MA: MIT Press (eds).

Bréchet, T., Eyckmans, J., Gérard, F., Marbaix, P., Tulkens, H., and J-P. van Ypersele, 2010. The impact of the unilateral EU commitment on the stability of international climate agreements. *Climate Policy*, 10: 148–66.

Bréchet, T., Gerard, F., and Tulkens, H., 2011. Efficiency *vs.* stability in climate coalitions: A conceptual and computational appraisal. *The Energy Journal*, 32(1): 49–76.

Bréchet T., Thénié, J., Zeimes, Th., and Zuber, S., 2012. The benefits of cooperation under uncertainty: The case of climate change. *Environmental Modelling and Assessment*, 17(1–2): 149–62.

Breitmeier, H., Young, O.R., and Zürn, M., 2006. *The Analysis of International Environmental Regimes: From case study to database*. Cambridge, MA: MIT Press.

Breitmeier, H., Underdal, A., and Young, O.R., 2011. The effectiveness of international environmental regimes: Comparing and contrasting findings from quantitative research. *International Studies Review*, 13(4): 579–605.

Brekke, K.A., Kverndokk, S., and Nyborg, K., 2003. An economic model of moral motivation. *Journal of Public Economics*, 87(9–10): 1967–83.

Bressan, A. and Shen, W., 2004. Semi-cooperative strategies for differential games. *International Journal of Game Theory*, 32: 561–93.

Breton, A., Brosio, G., Dalmazzone, S., and Garrone, G., 2009. *Governing the Environment: Salient institutional issues*. Cheltenham: Edward Elgar.

Bromley, D.W., 1990. The ideology of efficiency: Searching for a theory of policy analysis. *Journal of Environmental Economics and Management*, 19: 86–107.

Bromley, D.W., 1991. *Environment and Economy: Property rights and public policy*. Oxford: Blackwell Publishing.

Bromley, D.W., 2006. *Sufficient Reason: Volitional pragmatism and the meaning of economic institutions*. Princeton, NJ: Princeton University Press.

Bromley, D., Feeny, D., McKean, M., Peters, P., Gilles, J., Oakerson, R., C., and Thomson, J., 1992. *Making the Commons Work: Theory, practice, and policy*. San Francisco, CA: ICS Press.

Brooks, M.A. and Heijdra, B.J., 1987. Rent-seeking and pollution taxation: An extension. *Southern Economic Journal*, 54(2): 335–42.

Brousseau, E. and Glachant, J.M., 2002. *Economics of Contracts*. Cambridge: Cambridge University Press.

Brousseau, E., Schemeil, Y., and Sgard, J. 2010. Bargaining on law and bureaucracies: A constitutional theory of development. *Journal of Comparative Economics*, 38: 253–66.

Brousseau, E., Sgard, J., and Schemeil, Y. 2012. Delegation without borders: On individual rights, constitations and the global order. Global Constitutionalism.

Brousseau, E., Marzouki, M., and Méadel, C., 2012. *Governance, Regulations, Powers on the Internet.* Cambridge: Cambridge University Press.

Brousseau, E., Dedeurwaerdere, T., and Siebenhüner, B. (eds), 2012. *Reflexive Governance and Global Public Goods.* Cambridge, MA: MIT Press.

Brown, G. and Johnson, R. 1984. Pollution control by effluent charges: It works in the Federal Republic of Germany, why not in the US? *Natural Resources Journal*, 24: 929–66.

Brown, J.P., 1973. Toward an economic theory of liability. *Journal of Legal Studies*, 2(2): 343.

Brown, J.P. and Holahan, W.L., 1980. Taxes and legal rules for the control of externalities when there are strategic responses. *Journal of Legal Studies*, 9: 165–78.

Bryner, G., 1995. *Blue Skies, Green Politics: The clean air act of 1990 and its implementation.* Washington, DC: Congressional Quarterly Books.

Buchanan, J., 1965. An economic theory of clubs. *Economica*, 32: 1–14.

Buchanan, J. and Tullock, G., 1975. Polluters' profits and political response: Direct controls versus taxes. *American Economic Review*, 65: 139–47.

Bulte, E. and Engels, S., 2007. Conservation of tropical forests: Addressing market failure. *IPD Working Paper Series.*

Burby, R.J. and Paterson, R.G., 1993. Improving compliance with state environmental regulations. *Journal of Policy Analysis and Management*, 12: 753–72.

Burke, M. and Young, H., 2000. The terms of agricultural contracts: Theory and evidence. CSED Working Paper #16.

Burlando, R. and Guala, F., 2005. Heterogeneous Agents in public goods experiments. *Experimental Economics*, 8(1): 35–55.

Burrows, P., 1999. Combining regulation and liability for the control of external costs. *IRLE*, 19: 227–42.

Busch, L.A., Shi, S., and Wen, Q., 1998. Bargaining with surplus destruction. *Canadian Journal of Economics*, 31(4): 915–32.

Byerlee, D., 2010. Crop improvement in the CGIAR as a global success story of open access. *International Journal of the Commons*, 4(1): 452–80.

Calabresi, G., 1961. Some thoughts on risk distribution and the law of torts. *Yale Law Journal*, 70: 499–553.

Calabresi, G., 1970. *The Costs of Accidents. A legal and economic analysis.* New Haven, CT: Yale University Press.

Calabresi, G., 1975. Optimal deterrence and accidents. *Yale Law Journal*, 84: 656–71.

Cameron, J. and Pierce, W.D., 1994. Reinforcement, reward, and intrinsic motivation: A meta-analysis. *Review of Educational Research*, 64(3): 363–423.

Cardenas, J.C., Stranlund, J., and Willis, C., 2000. Local environmental control and institutional crowding-out. *World Development*, 28(10): 1719–33.

Carraro, C., 2003. *The Globalization of the World Economy: Governing the global environment.* Cheltenham: Edward Elgar.

Carraro, C., 2007. Incentives and institutions: A bottom-up approach to climate policy. In: J.E. Aldy, and R.N. Stavins (eds) *Architectures for Agreement. Addressing global climate change in the post-Kyoto world.* Cambridge: Cambridge University Press, 161–72.

Carraro, C. and Siniscalco, D., 1993. Strategies for the international protection of the environment. *Journal of Public Economics*, 52(3): 309–28.

Carraro, C., Eyckmans, J., and Finus, M. 2007. Optimal transfers participation decisions in international environmental agreements. *Review of International Organizations*, 1(4): 379–96.

Carroll, M.C. and Stanfiled, J.R., 2003. Social capital, Karl Polanyi, and American social and institutional economics. *Journal of Economic Issues*, 37(2): 397–404.

Cason, T., Gangadharan L., and Duke C. 2003. A laboratory study of auctions for reducing non-point source pollution. *Journal of Environmental Economics and Management*, 46: 446–71.

Cassey, P., Blackburn, T.M., Russell, G.J., Jones, K.E., and Lockwood, J.L., 2004. Influences on the transport and establishment of exotic bird species: An analysis of the parrots (Psittaciformes) of the world. *Global Change Biology*, 10: 417–26.

Chan, K.M.A., Shaw, M.R., Cameron, D.R., Underwood, E.C., and Daily, G.C., 2006. Conservation planning for ecosystem services. *Public Library of Science: Biology*, 4: 2138–52.

Chander, P., 2007. The gamma-core and coalition formation. *International Journal of Game Theory*, 35: 539–56.

Chander, P. and Tulkens, H., 1995. A core-theoretic solution for the design of cooperative agreements on transfrontier pollution. *International Tax and Public Finance*, 2; 279–93.

Chander, P. and Tulkens, H., 1997. The core of an economy with multilateral environmental externalities. *International Journal of Game Theory*, 26(3); 379–401.

Chapin, F.S., Hoel, M., Carpenter, S.R., Lubchenco, J., Walker, B., Callaghan, T. V., Folke, C., Levin, S., Mäler, K.G., Nilsson, C., Barrett, S., Crépin, A.S., Danell, K., Rosswall, T., Starrett, D., and Xepapadeas, A., 2005. Building resilience and adaptation to manage arctic change. Beijer Institute Working Papers, Stockholm.

Chhatre, A. and Agrawal, A., 2008. Forest commons and local enforcement. *Proceedings of the National Academy of Sciences*, 105(36): 13286–91.

Chichilnisky, G., 1993a. Property rights on biodiversity and the pharmaceutical industry. Columbia Business School, case study.

Chichilnisky, G., 1993b. The abatement of carbon emissions in industrial and developing countries. paper presented at the OECD/IEA Conference on The Economics of Climate Change, Paris, June 14–16, 1993.

Chichilnisky, G., 1994. North–south trade and the global environment. *American Economic Review*, 84 (4): 851–74.

Chichilnisky, G., 1996a. The greening of the Bretton Woods. *Financial Times*, January 10: 8.

Chichilnisky, G., 1996b. Development and global finance: The case for an International Bank for Environmental Settlements. *United Nations Development Program Publication No 10*, and UNESCO.

Chichilnisky, G., 2000. An axiomatic approach to choice under uncertainty with catastrophic risks. *Resource and Energy Economics*, 22 (3): 221–31.

Chichilnisky, G., 2009. Avoiding extinction: Equal treatment of the present and the future. *Economics: The Open-Access, Open Assessment e-Journal*, 3: 2009–32.

Chichilnisky, G., 2010a. Managing the global commons: Principles and practice. European Environmental Agency.

Chichilnisky, G., 2010b. The missing signal: How ecological prices change markets and decision making. UNESCAP 6th Ministerial Conference on Environment and Development in Asia and the Pacific.

Chichilnisky, G. and Heal, G.M. 1994. Who should abate carbon emissions: An international perspective. *Economic Letters*, Spring 1994, 443–9.

Chichilnisky, G. and Heal, G.M. 1995. Markets for tradable emission quotas: Principles and practice. OECD Publication no. 153. Paris: OECD.

Chichilnisky, G. and Heal, G.M. 1998. Economic returns from the biosphere. *Nature*, 391: 629–30.

Chichilnisky, G. and Heal, G. M. 2000. *Environmental Markets: Equity and efficiency*. New York: Columbia University Press. Available at: http://www.chichilnisky.com "Books and Writings."

Chichilnisky, G. and Sheeran, K. 2009. *Saving Kyoto*. London: New Holland.

Chwe, M.S.Y., 1999. Structure and strategy of collective action. *American Journal of Sociology*, 105(1): 128–56.

Chwe, M.S.Y., 2001. *Rational Ritual: Culture, coordination, and common knowledge*. Princeton, NJ: Princeton University Press.

Clark, W., Mitchell, R., Cash, D.W., and Alcock, F., 2002. *Global Environmental Assessments: Information, institutions and influence*. Cambridge, MA: MIT Press.

Cleaver, F., 2000. Moral ecological rationality, institutions and the management of common property resources. *Development and Change*, 31(2): 361–83.

Cleaver, F., 2003. Reinventing institutions: Bricolage and the social embeddedness of natural resource management. In: T.A. Benjaminsen and C. Lund (eds) *Securing Land Rights in Africa*. London: Frank Cass, in association with EADI, European Association of Development Research and Training Institutes.

Coase, R., 1937. The nature of the firm. *Economica*, 4: 386–405.

Coase, R., 1960. Problem of social cost. *Journal of Law and Economics*, 3: 1–44.

Coase, R.H., 1992. The institutional structure of production. *American Economic Review*, 82: 713–19.

Coelho, P.R.P., 1976. Polluters' profits and political response: Direct control versus taxes: comment. *American Economic Review*, 66: 976–8.

Coleman, E., 2009. Institutional factors affecting ecological outcomes in forest management. *Journal of Policy Analysis and Management*, 28(1): 122–46.

Coleman, E. and Steed, B., 2009. Monitoring and sanctioning in the commons: An application to forestry. *Ecological Economics*, 68(7): 2106–13.

Collier, P., 2002. Social capital and poverty: Microeconomic perspective. In: C. Grootaert, and T.V. Bastelaer (eds) *The Role of Social Capital in Development: An empirical assessment*. Cambridge: Cambridge University Press.

Commons, J.R., 1931. Institutional economics. *American Economic Review*, 21: 648–57.

Commons, J.R., 1934. *Institutional Economics. Its place in political economics*. New Brunswick: Transaction Publishers.

Cooper, R., DeJong, D., Forsythe, R., and Ross, T. 1989. Communication in the battle of the sexes game: Some experimental results. *RAND Journal of Economics*, 20: 568–87.

Cooper, R., DeJong, D., Forsythe, R., and Ross, T. 1992. Communication in coordination games. *Quarterly Journal of Economics*, 107: 739–71.

Cooter, R. 1984. Prices and sanctions. *Columbia Law Review*, 84: 1343–523.

Cooter, R.D., 1994. Structural adjudication and the New Law Merchant: A model of decentralized law. *International Review of Law and Economics*, 14: 215–31.

Copeland, B.R., 1990. Strategic enhancement and destruction of fisheries and the environment in the presence of international externalities. *Journal of Environmental Economics and Management*, 19(3): 213–26.

Corbera, E., Brown, K., and Adger, W.N., 2007. The equity and legitimacy of markets for ecosystem services. *Development and Change*, 38(4): 587–613.

Cordell, J.C. and McKean, M.A., 1992. *Sea Tenure in Bahia, Brazil*. San Francisco, CA: ICS Press.

Cornes, R. and Sandler, T., 1984. Easy riders, joint production, and public goods. *Economic Journal*, 94(3): 580–98.

Cornes, R. and Sandler, T. 1986. *The Theory of Externalities, Public Goods, and Club Goods*. 2nd edn. New York: Cambridge University Press.

Costello, C., Springborn, M., McAusland, C., and Solow, A., 2007. Unintended biological invasions: Does risk vary by trading partner? *Journal of Environmental Economics and Management*, 54: 262–76.

Costello, C., Gaines, S.D., and Lynham, J., 2008. Can catch shares prevent fisheries collapse? *Science*, 321(5896): 678–81.

Cox, J., Sadiraj, K., and Sadiraj, V., 2008. Implications of trust, fear, and reciprocity for modeling economic behavior. *Experimental Economics*, 11(1): 1–24.

Cox, J.C., 2004. How to identify trust and reciprocity. *Games and Economic Behavior*, 46(2); 260–81.

Cox, M., Arnold, G., and Villamayor Tomás, S., 2010. A review of design principles for community-based natural resource management. *Ecology and Society*, 15(4): 38.

Crocker, T.D., 1966. The structuring of atmospheric pollution control systems. In: H. Wolozin (ed.) *The Economics of Air Pollution*. New York: W.W. Norton, 61–8.

Crook, D.S. and Jones, A.M., 1999. Design principles from traditional mountain irrigation systems (Bisses) in the Valais, Switzerland. *Mountain Research and Development*, 19(2): 79–122.

Croson, R., 2007. Theories of commitment, altruism & reciprocity: Evidence from linear public goods games. *Economic Inquiry*, 45: 199–216.

Crowder, L., Osherenko, G., Young, O.R., Airamé, S., Norse, E.A., Baron, N., Day, J. C., Douvere, F., Ehler, C.N., Halpern, B.S., Langdon, S.J., McLeod, K.L., Ogden, J. C., Peach, R.C., Rosenberg, A.A., and Wilson J.A., 2006. Resolving mismatches in U. S. ocean governance. *Science*, 313(5787): 617–18.

Crutzen, P., 2002. Geology of mankind—The Anthropocene. *Nature*, 415: 23.

Crutzen, P.J. and Stoermer, E.F., 2000. The "Anthropocene". *IGBP Newsletter*, 41: 17–18.

D'Aspremont C., Jacquemin, A., Gabszewicz, J.J., and Weymark, J.A., 1983. On the stability of collusive price leadership. *Canadian Journal of Economics*, 16: 17–25.

Daily, G., 1997. *Nature's Services: Societal dependence on natural ecosystems*. Washington, DC: Island Press.

Dales, J.H., 1968a. *Pollution, Property and Prices: An essay in policy*. Toronto: University of Toronto Press.

Dales, J.H., 1968b. Land, water and ownership. *The Canadian Journal of Economics*, 1: 791–804.

Dalmazzone, S., 2000. Economic factors affecting vulnerability to biological invasions. In: C. Perrings, M. Williamson, and S. Dalmazzone (eds) *The Economics of Biological Invasions.* Cheltenham, Edward Elgar, 17–30.

Dankel, D.J., 2009. *Building Blocks of Sustainability in Marine Fisheries Management: Stakeholders, objectives, and strategies.* Norway: University of Bergen.

Daszak, P., Cunningham, A.A., and Hyatt, A.D., 2000. Emerging infectious diseases of wildlife: Threats to biodiversity and human health. *Science,* 287(5452): 443–9.

Davis, D.D. and Holt, C.A., 1993. *Experimental Economics.* Princeton, NJ: Princeton University Press.

Davis, J., 2002. Collective intentionality and individual behavior. In: E. Fullbrook (ed.) *Intersubjectivity in Economics: Agents and structures.* London: Routledge, 11–27.

De Soto, H. and Cheneval, F., 2006. *Realizing Property Rights.* Zurich: Ruffer & Rub.

Dearlove, J., 1989. Neoclassical politics: Public choice and political understanding. *Review of Political Economy,* 1: 208–37.

Deci, E.L., 1971. Effects of externally mediated rewards on intrinsic motivation. *Journal of Personality and Social Psychology,* 18(1): 105–15.

Deci, E.L. and Ryan, R.M. 1985. *Intrinsic Motivation and Self-Determination in Human Behavior.* New York: Plenum Press.

Deci, E.L., Koestner, R., and Ryan, R.M., 1999. A meta-analytic review of experiments examining the effects of extrinsic rewards on intrinsic motivation. *Psychological Bulletin,* 125: 627–68.

Deci, E.L., Koestner, R., and Ryan, R.M., 2001. Extrinsic rewards and intrinsic motivation in education: Reconsidered once again. *Review of Educational Research,* 71(1): 1–27.

Dedeurwaerdere, T., 2010. Global microbial commons: Institutional challenges for the global exchange and distribution of microorganisms in the life science. *Research in Microbiology,* 161(6): 407–13.

Delmas, M.A. and Young, O.R., 2009. *Governance for the Environment: New perspectives.* Cambridge: Cambridge University Press.

Demsetz, H., 1967. Toward a theory of property rights. *The American Economic Review,* 57(2): 347–59.

Denzau, A.T. and Munger. M.C., 1986. Legislators and interest groups: How unorganized interests get represented. *American Political Science Review,* 80(1): 89–106.

Devine, J.A., Baker, K.D., and Haedrich, R.L. 2006. Fisheries: Deep-sea fishes qualify as endangered. *Nature,* 439: 29.

Dewees, D.N., 1992. Tort law and the deterrence of environmental pollution. In: T.H. Tietenberg(ed.) *Innovation in Environmental Policy, Economic and Legal Aspects of Recent Developments in Environmental Enforcement of Liability.* Aldershot: Edward Elgar, 139–64.

Dewees, D.N., 1998. Tradable pollution permits. In: P. Newman (ed.) *The New Palgrave Dictionary of Economics and the Law.* Basingstoke: Palgrave Macmillan, vol. 3, 596–601.

Dewees, D., Duff, D., and Trebilcock, M., 1996. *Exploring the Domain of Accident Law: Taking the facts seriously.* Oxford: Oxford University Press.

Di Falco, S. and van Rensburg, T.M., 2008. Making the commons work: Conservation and cooperation in Ireland. *Land Economics,* 84(4): 620–34.

Diamantoudi, E. and Sartzetakis, E.S., 2006. Stable international environmental agreements: An analytical approach. *Journal of Public Economic Theory*, 8: 247–63.

Diamond, J., 2005. *Collapse: How societies choose to fail or succeed*. New York: Viking.

Diamond, P., 1974. Single activity accidents. *Journal of Legal Studies*, 3: 107–64.

Diamond, P., Hausman, J., Leonard, G., and Denning, M., 1993. Does contingent valuation measure preferences? Experimental evidence. In: J. Hausman (ed.) *Contingent Valuation: A critical assessment*. New York: North-Holland.

Dietz, T., Ostrom, E., and Stern, P., 2003. The struggle to govern the commons. *Science*, 302(5652): 1907–12.

Dilorenzo, T., 1983. Economic competition and political competition: An empirical note. *Public Choice*, 40: 203–9.

Dolfsma, W. and Dannreuther C., 2003. Subject and boundaries: Contesting social capital-based policies. *Journal of Economic Issues*, 37(2): 405–13.

Douglas, M., 1986. *How Institutions Think*. Syracuse, NY: Syracuse University Press.

Dreber, A., Rand, D.G., Fudenberg, D., and Nowak, M.A. 2008. Winners don't punish. *Nature*, 452: 348–51.

Dreyfus, H. and Rabinow, P., 1982. *Michel Foucault: Beyond structuralism and hermeneutics*. Chicago, IL: Chicago University Press.

Droege, S. and Soete, B., 2001. Trade-related intellectual property rights, north–south trade and biological diversity. *Environmental and Resource Economics*, 19: 149–63.

Dryzek, J.S., 1990. *Discursive Democracy: Politics, policy, and political science*. Cambridge: Cambridge University Press.

Dryzek, J.S., 2002. *Deliberative Democracy and Beyond. Liberals, critics, contestations*. Oxford: Oxford University Press.

Dulvy, N.K., Sadovy, Y., and Reynolds, J.D., 2003. Extinction vulnerability in marine populations. *Fish and Fisheries*, 4: 25–64.

Durlauf, S.N., 2002. On the empirics of social capital. *The Economic Journal*, 112(483): 459–79.

Ebbin, S., Hoel, A.H., and Sydnes, A. (eds), 2005. *A Sea Change: The exclusive economic zone and governance institutions for marine living resources*. Dordrecht: Springer Verlag.

Eckel, C., Grossman, P., and Johnston, M., 2005. An experimental test of the crowding out hypothesis. *Journal of Public Economics*. 89(8): 1543–60.

Egas, M. and Riedl, A., 2008. The economics of altruistic punishment and the maintenance of cooperation. *Proceedings of the Royal Society B: Biological Sciences*, 275(1637): 871–8.

Ellerman, A.D., 2010. The EU's emissions trading scheme: A proto-type global system? In: J.E. Aldy and R.N. Stavins (eds) *Post-Kyoto International Climate Policy*. Cambridge: Cambridge University Press.

Ellerman, AD. and Joskow, P.L. 2008. *The European Union's Emissions Trading System in Perspective*. Washington, DC: Pew Center on Global Climate Change.

Ellerman, A.D., Joskow, P.L., Schmalensee, R., Montero, J.-P., and Bailey, E., 2000. *Markets for Clean Air: The U.S. acid rain program*. Cambridge, UK, and New York: Cambridge University Press.

Ellerman, A.D, Convery, F., and De Perthuis, C., 2010. *Pricing Carbon: The European Union emissions trading scheme*. Cambridge: Cambridge University Press.

Ellickson, R.C., 1991. *Order Without Law: How neighbours settle disputes*. Cambridge, MA: Harvard University Press.

Ellingsen, T. and Johannesson, M., 2008. Pride and prejudice: The human side of incentive theory. *American Economic Review*, 98: 990–1008.

Endres, A. and Schwarze, R., 1991. Allokationswirkungen einer Umwelthaftpflicht-versicherung. *Zeitschrift für Umweltpolitik und Umweltrecht*, 14: 1–25.

Endres, A. and Staiger, B., 1996. Ökonomische Aspekte des Umwelthaftungsrecht. In: M. Ahrens and J. Simon (eds) *Umwelthaftung, Risikosteuerung und Versicherung*. Berlin: Erich Schmidt, 79–93.

Engel, S., Pagiola, S., and Wunder, S., 2008. Designing payments for environmental services in theory and practice: An overview of the issue. *Ecological Economics*, 65: 663–74.

Ensminger, J., 1990. Co-opting the elders: The political economy of state incorporation in Africa. *American Anthropologist*, 92: 662–75.

Ensminger, J., 2000. Experimental economics in the bush: Why institutions matter. In: C. Menard (ed.) *Institutions, Contracts and Organizations*. Cheltenham, UK: Edward Elgar, 158–71.

Ensminger, J., 2001. Reputations, trust, and the principal agent problem. In: K.S. Cook (ed.) *Trust in Society*. New York: Russell Sage Foundation, 185–201.

Escobar, A., 1996. Construction of nature: Elements of post-structuralist political ecology. *Future*, 28(4): 325–43.

Etzioni, A., 1988. *The Moral Dimension: Toward a new economics*. New York: The Free Press.

European Environment Agency, 2001. Late lessons from early warnings: The precautionary principle 1896–2000. Environmental issue report No 22. Copenhagen: European Environment Agency.

European Union, 2009. Directive of the European Parliament and of the Council amending Directive 2003/87/EC so as to improve and extend the greenhouse gas emission allowance trading system of the Community. Brussels, PE-CONS 2727/08, 26 March 2009.

Eyckmans, J. and Finus, M., 2004. An almost ideal sharing scheme for coalition games with externalities. CLIMNEG Working Paper #62. Leuven, Belgium: Katholieke Universiteit Leuven.

Eyckmans, J. and Finus, M., 2006a. Coalition formation in a global warming game: How the design of protocols affects the success of environmental treaty-making. *Natural Resource Modeling*, 19: 323–58.

Eyckmans, J. and Finus, M., 2006b. New roads to international environmental agreements: The case of global warming. *Environmental Economics and Policy Studies*, 7: 391–414.

Eyckmans, J. and Finus, M., 2007. Measures to enhance the success of global climate treaties. *International Environmental Agreements: Politics, Law and Economics*, 7: 73–97.

Eyckmans, J. and Tulkens, H., 2003. Simulating coalitionally stable burden sharing agreements for the climate change problem. *Resource and Energy Economics*, 25: 299–327.

FAO, 2004. *The State of World Fisheries and Aquaculture*. Rome: FAO Fisheries Department, FAO.

Faruk, G. 2008. Behavioral economics and game theory. In: S.N. Durlauf and L.E. Blume (eds) *The New Palgrave Dictionary of Economics*. Basingstoke: Palgrave Macmillan.

Faure, M., 1995. Economic models of compensation for damage caused by nuclear accidents: Some lessons for the revision of the Paris and Vienna conventions. *European Journal of Law and Economics*, 2(1): 21–43.

Faure, M., 2001. Tort liability in France: An introductory economic analysis. In: B. Deffains and T. Kirat (eds) *Law and Economics in Civil Law Countries*. London: Taylor and Francis Group, 169–81.

Faure, M. and Lefevere, J., 1999. Compliance with international environmental agreements. In: N.J. Vig and R.S. Axelrod (eds) *The Global Environment. Institutions, law, and policy*. Washington: CQ Press, 138–56.

Faure, M. and Ruegg, M., 1994. Standard setting through general principles of environmental law. In: M. Faure, J. Vervaele, J. and A. Weale (eds) *Environmental Standards in the European Union in an Interdisciplinary Framework*. Antwerpen-Apeldoorn: Maklu uitgevers, 39–60.

Faure, M. and Ubachs, S., 2002. Environmental taxation in the Netherlands: A Dutch treat? In: L.A. Kreiser (ed.) *Critical Issues in International Environmental Taxation. Insights and analysis for achieving environmental policy goals through tax policy*. Chicago, IL: CCH, 301–29.

Faure, M. and Ubachs, S., 2003. Comparative benefits and optimal use of environmental taxes. In: J. Milne, K. Deketelaere, L. Kreiser, and H. Ashiabor (eds) *Critical Issues in Environmental Taxation. Vol. I: International and Comparative Perspectives*. Richmond: Richmond Law and Tax: 29–49.

Faure, M. and Ubachs, S., 2005. Harmful tax measures and greying of taxation in the Netherlands: What went wrong? In: H. Ashiabor, K. Deketelaere, L. Kreiser, and J. Milne (eds) *Critical Issues in Environmental Taxation: International and comparative perspectives. Volume II*. Richmond: Richmond Law and Tax, 521–32.

Faure, M., Peeters, M., and Wibisana, A. 2006. Economic instruments: Suited to developing countries? In: M. Faure and N. Niessen (eds) *Environmental Law in Development. Lessons from the Indonesian Experience*, Cheltenham, UK: Edward Elgar, 8–262.

Feeny, D., Hanna, S., and McEvoy, A., 1996. Questioning the assumptions of the "tragedy of the commons" model of fisheries. *Land Economics*, 72(2): 187–205.

Fehr, E., 2009. On the economic and biology of trust. Institute for Empirical Research in Economic, University of Zurich, Working Paper Series, No. 399.

Fehr, E. and Fischbacher, U., 2002. Why social preferences matter—The impact of non-selfish motives on competition, cooperation and incentives. *Economic Journal*, 112(478): C1–33.

Fehr, E. and Fischbacher, U., 2005. The economics of strong reciprocity. In: H. Gintis, S. Bowles, R. Boyd, and E. Fehr (eds) *Moral Sentiments and Material Interests: The foundations of cooperation in economic life*. Cambridge: MIT Press, 151–91.

Fehr, E. and Gächter, S., 2000. Cooperation and punishment in public goods experiments. *American Economic Review*, 90(4): 980–94.

Fehr, E. and Gintis, H., 2007. Human motivation and social cooperation: Experimental and analytical foundations. *Annual Review of Sociology*, 33(3): 1–22.

Fehr, E. and Schmidt, K., 1999. A theory of fairness, competition and co-operation. *Quarterly Journal of Economics*, 114: 817–68.

Feldman, A.M., 2008. Welfare economics. In: S.N. Durlauf and L.E. Blume (eds) *The New Palgrave Dictionary of Economics*, 2nd edn. Basingstoke: Palgrave Macmillan.

Ferguson, J., 1994. *Anti-politics Machine: "Development," depoliticization, and bureaucratic power in Lesotho*. Minnesota: University of Minnesota Press.

Fevre, E.M., Bronsvoort, B., Hamilton, K.A., and Cleaveland, S., 2006. Animal movements and the spread of infectious diseases. *Trends in Microbiology*, 14: 125–31.

Fine, B., 2001. *Social Capital Versus Social Theory: Political economy and social science at the turn of the millennium*. London: Routledge.

Finus, M., 2008. Game theoretic research on the design of international environmental agreements: Insights, critical remarks, and future challenges. *International Review of Environmental and Resource Economics*, 2(1): 29–67.

Finus, M. and Rundshagen, B., 2009. Membership rules and stability of coalition structures in positive externality games. *Social Choice and Welfare*, 32: 389–406.

Fischbacher, U. and Gächter, S., 2006. Heterogeneous social preferences and the dynamics of free riding in public goods. CeDEx Discussion Paper No. 2006/01.

Fischbacher, U., Gächter, S. and Fehr, E., 2001. Are people conditionally cooperative? Evidence from a public goods experiment. *Economics Letters*, 71: 397–404.

Fischer, M.E., Irlenbusch, B., and Sadrieh, A., 2004. An intergenerational common pool resource experiment. *Journal of Environmental Economics and Management*, 48(2): 811–36.

Folke, C., Hahn, T., Olsson, P., and Norberg, J., 2005. Adaptive governance of social–ecological systems. *Annual Review of Environmental Resources*, 30: 441–73.

Foucault, M., 1965. *Madness and Civilization: A history of insanity in the age of reason*. New York: Pantheon Books.

Foucault, M., 1977. *Discipline and Punish: The birth of the prison*. New York. Pantheon Books.

Francois, P. and Vlassopoulos, M., 2008. Pro-social motivation and the delivery of social services. *CESifo Economic Studies*, 54(1): 22–54.

Fraser, N., 1992. Rethinking the public sphere: Contribution to actually existing democracy. In: C. Calhoun (ed.) *Habermas and Public Sphere*. Cambridge MA: MIT Press.

Freeman J. and Kolstad, C.D., 2007. Prescriptive environmental regulations versus market-based incentives. In J. Freeman and Ch.D. Kolstad (eds) *Moving to Markets in Environmental Regulation: Lessons from twenty years of experience*. New York: Oxford University Press, 3-16.

Frey, B.S., 1992. *Umweltökonomie*. Göttingen: VandenHoeck & Ruprecht.

Frey, B.S., 1997. *Not Just for the Money: An economic theory of personal motivation*. Cheltenham, UK and Brookfield, USA: Edward Elgar.

Frey, B.S., 1999. Morality and rationality in environmental policy. *Journal of Consumer Policy*, 22: 395–417.

Frey, B.S., 2005. Beyond traditional borders: A new proposal for federalism. *The Economists' Voice*, 2(2), article 9. Available at: http://www.bepress.com/ev/vol2/iss2/ (accessed September 29, 2008).

Frey, B.S. and Eichenberger, R., 1996. FOCJ: Competitive governments for Europe. *International Review of Law and Economics*, 16(3): 315–28.

Frey, B.S. and Eichenberger, R. (eds), 1999. *The New Democratic Federalism for Europe. Functional, overlapping and competing Jurisdictions*. Cheltenham, UK: Edward Elgar.

Frey, B.S. and Eichenberger, R., 2001. Federalism with overlapping juridictions and variable levels of integration: The Concept FOCJ. In: *Regionalism in Europe, Geometries and Strategies after 2000*. Dordrecht: Kluwer Academic Publisher, 3–21.

Frey, B.S. and Jegen, R., 2001. Motivation crowding theory. *Journal of Economic Surveys*, 15(5); 589–611.

Frey, B.S. and Oberholzer-Gee, F., 1997. The cost of price incentives: An empirical analysis of motivation crowding-out. *American Economic Review*, 87(4): 746–55.

Frey, B.S. and Stutzer, A., 2006. Environmental morale and motivation. *Institute for Empirical Research in Economics*, University of Zurich, Working Paper Series ISSN 1424-0459. Working Paper No. 288.

Frey, B.S., Oberholzer-Gee, F., and Eichenberger, R., 1996. The old lady visits your backyard: A tale of morals and markets. *The Journal of Political Economy*, 104(6): 1297–313.

Friedheim, R. (ed.), 2001. *Toward a Sustainable Whaling Regime*. Seattle: University of Washington Press.

Fuller, M., Compagni Portis, S., and Kammen. D., 2009. Toward a low-carbon economy: Municipal financing for energy efficiency and solar power. *Environment*, 51(1): 22–32.

Gächter, S. and Fehr, E., 1999. Collective action as social change. *Journal of Economic Behavior and Organization*, 39: 341–69.

Gächter S. and Fischbacher, U. 2010. Social preferences, beliefs, and the dynamics of free riding in public good experiments. *American Economic Review*, 100(1): 541–56.

Gächter, S., Renner, E., and Sefton, M., 2008. The long-run benefits of punishment. *Science*, 322(5907): 1510.

Galaz, V., Olsson, P., Hahn, T., Folke, C., and Svedin, U. 2008. The problem of fit among biophysical systems, environmental and resource regimes, and broader governance systems: Insights and emerging challenges. In: O.R. Young, L.A. King, and H. Schroeder (eds) *Institutions and Environmental Change*. Cambridge, MA: MIT Press, 147–86.

Gale, F., 1998. Theorizing power in ecological economics. *Ecological Economics*, 27: 131–8.

Gatti, J.R., Goeschl, T., Groom, B., and Swanson, T., 2010. The biodiversity bargaining problem. *Environmental and Resources Economics*, 48(4): 609–28.

Gautam, U., Agarwal, N., and Subedi, S. (eds), 1992. Nepal: Managing large surface irrigation project: A participatory review. Kathmandu, Nepal: Department of Irrigation and Consolidated Management Services (Study Document NEP/89/006).

Gauthier, D., 1986. *Morals by Agreement*. Oxford: Oxford University Press.

Geertz, C., 1992. The Bazaar economy: Information and search in peasant marketing. In: M. Granovetter and R. Swedeberg (eds) *Sociology of Economic Life.* Boulder: Westview Press.

Gérard, A. and Holzweber, P., 2008. CWS 2.0: A 18-region integrated assessment model. CLIMNEG working paper #101, CORE, Université catholique de Louvain.

Germain, M., Toint, P., Tulkens, H., and de Zeeuw, A., 2003. Transfers to sustain dynamic core-theoretic cooperation in international stock pollutant control. *Journal of Economic Dynamics and Control*, 28: 79–99.

Ghate, R., 2000. The role of autonomy in self-organizing processes: A case study of local forest management in India. Paper presented at the Workshop in Political Theory and Policy Analysis mini-conference, Indiana University, Bloomington.

Gibson, C., McKean, M., and Ostrom, E. (eds), 2000. *People and Forests: Communities, institutions, and governance.* Cambridge, MA: MIT Press.

Gibson, C., Williams, J., and Ostrom, E., 2005. Local enforcement and better forests. *World Development*, 33(2): 273–384.

Gibson, J., Olivia, S., and Rozelle, S., 2006. How widespread are non-linear crowding out effects? The response of private transfers to income in four developing countries. Working Paper, University of Waikato, Department of Economics.

Giddens, A., 1984. *The Constitution of Society: Outline of the theory of structuration.* Berkeley: University of California Press.

Gimpel-Hinteregger, M., 1994. *Grundfragen der Umwelthaftung.* Wien: Manz, 19–58.

Gintis, H., 2000. Beyond "Homo Economicus:" evidence from experimental economics. *Ecological Economics*, 35: 311–22.

Gintis, H., Smith, E.A., and Bowles, S., 2001. Costly signaling and cooperation. *Journal of Theoretical Biology*, 213(1): 103–19.

Gintis, H., Bowles, S., Boyd, R., and Fehr, E., 2005. Moral sentiments and material interests: Origins, evidence, and consequences. In: H. Gintis, S. Bowles, R. Boyd, and E. Fehr (eds) *Moral Sentiments and Material Interests: The foundations of cooperation in economic life.* Cambridge, MA: MIT Press.

Gneezy, U. and Rustichini, A., 2000a. Pay enough or don't pay at all. *Quarterly Journal of Economics*, 115(3); 791–810.

Gneezy, U. and Rustichini, A., 2000b. A fine is a price. *The Journal of Legal Studies*, 29 (1); 1–17.

Goeree, J.K., Holt, C.A., and Laury, S.K., 2002. Private costs and public benefits: Unraveling the effects of altruism and noisy behavior. *Journal of Public Economics*, 83: 255–76.

Goeree, J., Holt, C., Palmer, K., Shobe, W., and Burtraw, D. 2009. An experimental study of auctions versus grandfathering to assign pollution permits. *Ressource for the Future*, discussion paper RFF DP 09-39, September 8, 2009.

Goeschl, T. and Swanson, T., 2003. On biology and technology: The economics of managing biotechnologies. *The Fondazione Eni Enrico Mattei* (FEEM) Note di Lavoro Series, 42.03.

Goeschl, T., Gatti, R., Groom, B., and Swanson, T., 2005. Incentivizing Ecological Destruction: The Joint International Regulation of the Conservation and Use of Biodiversity. *Indiana Law Review*, 38(3): 619–35.

Goldman, R.L., Thompson, B.H., and Daily, G.C., 2007. Institutional incentives for managing the landscape: Inducing cooperation for the production of ecosystem services. *Ecological Economics*, 64: 333–43.

Goodin, R., 1996. Enfranchising the Earth and its alternatives. *Political Studies*, 44(5): 835–49.

Gordon, H.S., 1954. The economic theory of a common property resource: The fishery. *Journal of Political Economy*, 62: 124–42.

Grafton, Q.R., Squires, D., and Fox, K.J., 2000. Private property and economic efficiency: A study of a common-pool resource. *Journal of Law and Economics*, 43(2): 679–713.

Granovetter, M., 1973. The strength of weak ties. *American Journal of Sociology*, 78(6): 1360–80.

Granovetter, M., 1985. Economic action and social structure: The problem of embeddedness. *American Journal of Sociology*, 91(3); 481–510.

Gravelle, H.S.E., 1987. Accidents, taxes, liability rules ind insurances. *Geneva Papers on Risk and Insurance*, 12: 115–31.

Greif, A., 2006. History lessons: The birth of impersonal exchange: The community responsibility system and impartial justice. *Journal of Economic Perspectives*, 20(2): 221–36.

Groosman, B., 2000. 2500 Pollution Tax. In: Boudewijn Bouckaert and Gerrit De Geest (eds), *Encyclopedia of Law and Economics, Common Property and Regulation of the Environment, Volume II. Civil Law and Economics*. Cheltenham, UK: Edward Elgar, 538–68.

Guan, Y., Zheng, B.J., He, Y.Q., Liu, X.L., Zhuang, Z.X., Cheung, C.L., Luo, S.W., Li, P.H., Zhang, L.J., Guan, Y.J., Butt, K.M., Wong, K.L., Chan, K.W., Lim, W., Shortridge, K.F., Yuen, K.Y., Peiris, J.S.M., and Poon, L.L.M., 2003. Isolation and characterization of viruses related to the SARS coronavirus from animals in Southern China. *Science*, 302(5643): 276–8.

Guiso, L., Sapenza, P., and Zingales L., 2007. Social capital and good culture. EUO Working papers ECO2007/57.

Gunderson, L. and Holling, C.S., 2002. *Panarchy: Understanding transformation in human and natural systems*. Washington, DC: Island Press.

Gunningham, M. and Grabosky, P., 1998. *Smart Regulation. Designing environmental policy*. Oxford: Clarendon Press.

Haas, P.M., 2004. Addressing the global governance deficit. *Global Environmental Politics*, 1(4); 1–15.

Haas, P.M., Keohane, R.O., and Levy, M.A., 1993. *Institutions for the Earth: Sources of effective international environmental protection*. Cambridge, MA: MIT Press.

Habermas, J., 1984. *The Theory of Communicative Action*. Boston, MA: Beacon Press.

Habermas, J., 1986. Hannah Arendt's communication concept of power. In: S. Lukes (ed.) *Power*. New York: New York University Press.

Habermas J., 1996 [1992]. *Between Facts and Norms: Contributions to a discourse theory of law and democracy*. Cambridge: MA: MIT Press.

Habermas J., 2001 [1998]. *The Postnational Constellation: Political essays*, trans Max Pensky. Cambridge: MA: MIT Press.

Hager, G., 1993. Umwelthaftungsgesetz: The new German environmental liability law. *Environmental Liability*, 41–4.

Hahn, R.W., 1989. A new approach to the design of regulation in the presence of multiple objectives. *Journal of Environmental Economics and Management*, 17: 195–211.

Hahn, R.W. and Hester, G.L., 1989. Where did all the markets go? An analysis of EPA's Emissions Trading Programme. *Yale Journal on Regulation*, 6; 109–53.

Hajar, M., 1995. *Politics of Environmental Discourse*. Oxford: Clarendon Press.

Hajer, M.A. and Wagenaar, H., 2003. *Deliberative Policy Analysis: Understanding governance in the network society*. Cambridge: Cambridge University Press.

Hampton, J., 1987. Free-rider problems in the productions of collective goods. *Economics and Philosophy*, 3: 245–73.

Hannesson, R. 2004. *The Privatization of the Oceans*, Cambridge, MA: MIT Press.

Hansson, I. and Skogh, G., 1987. Moral hazard and safety regulation. *The Geneva Papers on Risk and Insurance*, 12: 132–44.

Hanushek, E.A., 1986. The economics of schooling: Production and efficiency in public schools. *Journal of Economic Literature*, 24: 1141–77.

Hardin, G., 1968. The tragedy of the commons. *Science*, 162(3859): 243–8.

Harriss, J., 2001. *Depoliticizing Development: The World Bank and social capital*. London: Anthem.

Harriss, M. and Raviv, A. 1981. Allocation mechanisms and the design of auctions. *Econometrica*, 49: 1477–99.

Harrison, D.Jr, 2004. Ex post evaluation of the RECLAIM Emissions Trading Programmes for the Los Angeles Air Basin. In *Tradeable Permits: Policy evaluation, design and reform*. Paris OECD Publishing.

Harsanyi, J. 1955. Cardinal welfare, individualistic ethics, and interpersonal comparisons of utility. *Journal of Political Economy*, 63: 309–21.

Harsanyi, J.C. and Selten, R. 1988. *A General Theory of Equilibrium Selection in Games*. Cambridge, MA: MIT Press.

Harvell, D., Aronson, R., Baron, N., Connell, J., Dobson, A., Ellner, S., Gerber, L., Mccallum, H., Lafferty, K., Mckay, B., Porter, J., Pascual, M., Smith, G., Sutherland, K., and Ward, J. 2004. The rising tide of ocean diseases: Unsolved problems and research priorities. *Frontiers in Ecology and the Environment*, 2: 375–82.

Hatchard, J., 2005. Engaging stakeholder preferences through deliberative democracy in North Sea fisheries governance. In: T.S. Gray (ed.) *Participation in Fisheries Governance*. Dordrecht: Springer, 45–64.

Hatcher, A., Jaffry, H., Thébaud, O.B., and Bennett, E., 2000. Normative and social influences affecting compliance with fisheries regulations. *Land Economics*, 76(3): 448–61.

Hattori, K., 2003. Reconsideration of the *Crowding-out Effect with Non-linear Contribution Technology*. *Economics Bulletin*, 8(7): 1–10.

Hauck, M., 2008. Rethinking small-scale fisheries compliance. *Marine Policy*, 32(4): 635–42.

Hauert, C., Traulsen, A., Brandt, H., Nowak, M.A., and Sigmund, K., 2007. Via Freedom to coercion: The emergence of costly punishment. *Science*, 316(5833): 1905.

Hayek, F.A., 1931. *Prices and Production*. London: Routledge and Son.

Hayek, F.A., 1948. *Individualism and Economic Order.* London: University of Chicago Press.

Hayes, T. and Ostrom, E., 2005. Conserving the world's forests: Are protected areas the only way? *Indiana Law Review*, 38(3): 595–617.

Hess, C. and Ostrom, E. (eds) 2007. *Understanding Knowledge as a Commons: From theory to practice.* Cambridge, MA: MIT Press.

Hilborn, R., Orensanz, J.M., and Parma, A.M., 2005. Institutions, incentives and the future of fisheries. *Philosophical Transactions of the Royal Society of London, Series B*, 360: 47–57.

Hirschleifer, J., 1983. From weakest-link to best-shot: The voluntary provision of public goods. *Public Choice*, 41(3): 371–86.

Hodgson, G., 1997. The ubiquity of habits and rules. *Cambridge Journal of Economics*, 21(6): 663–84.

Hodgson, G., 1999. Structures and institutions: Reflection on Institutionalism, structurism theory and critical realism. Workshop on Realism and Economics, January 19, Kings College, Cambridge.

Hoel, M. and Schneider, K., 1997. Incentives to participate in an international environmental agreement. *Environmental and Resource Economics*, 9: 153–70.

Holland, A., 2002. Are choices tradeoffs? In: D.W. Bromley, and J. Paavola (eds) *Economics, Ethics and Environmental Policy. Contested Choices.* Oxford: Blackwell Publishing, 17–34.

Holmstrom, B., 1979. Moral hazard and observability. *Bell Journal of Economics*, 10(1): 74–91.

Homer-Dixon, T., 2006. *The Upside of Down: Catastrophe, creativity, and the renewal of civilization.* Washington, DC: Island Press.

Honoré, A.M., 1961. Ownership. In: A.G. Guest (ed.) *Oxford Essays in Jurisprudence.* Oxford: Clarendon Press, 107–47.

Howarth, R.B., 2007. Towards an operational sustainability criterion. *Ecological Economics*, 63: 656–63.

Hufnagel, L., Brockmann, D., and Geisel, T., 2004. Forecast and control of epidemics in a globalized world. *Proceedings of the National Academy of Sciences*, 101(42): 15124–9.

Hughes, T., Bellwood, D.R., Folke, C., Steneck, R.S., and Wilson J., 2005. New paradigms for supporting the resilience of marine ecosystems. *Trends in Ecology and Evolution*, 20(7): 380–6.

IHR (2005). *International Health Regulations.* Geneva: WHO Press.

Intergovernmental Panel on Climate Change (IPCC), 2007a. Climate Change 2007: Impacts, adaptation and vulnerability. Contribution of Working Group II to the Fourth Assessment Report. Cambridge: Cambridge University Press.

Intergovernmental Panel on Climate Change (IPCC), 2007b. *Fourth Assessment Report.* Geneva: IPCC.

Iritani J. and Yamamoto, Sh., 2004. The private provision of public goods: Neutrality, efficiency, equity and population. *Kobe University Discussion Paper Series*, n 31. Kobe University.

Iudicello, S., Weber, M., and Wieland, R., 1999. *Fish, Markets, and Fishermen: The economics of overfishing.* Washington, DC: Island Press.

Jackson, J.B.C., Kirby, M.X., Berger, W.H., Bjorndal, K.A., Botsford, L.W., Bourque, B. J., Bradbury, R.H., Cooke, R., Erlandson, J., Estes, J.A., Hughes, T.P., Kidwell, S., Lange, C.B., Lenihan, H.S., Pandolfi, J.M., Peterson, C.H., Steneck, R.S., Tegner, M. S., and Warner, R.R., 2001. Historical overfishing and the recent collapse of coastal ecosystems. *Science*, 293(5530): 629–38.

Jackson, R.B., Jobba'Gy, E.G., Avissar, R., Roy, S.B., Barrett, D.J., Cook, C.W., Farley, K.A., Le Maitre, D.C., Mccarl, B.A., and Murray, B.C. 2005. Trading water for carbon with biological carbon sequestration. *Science*, 310: 1944–7.

Jankowski, B., 2007. Poland. In: A.D. Ellerman, B. Buchner, and C. Carraro (eds) *Allocation in the European Emissions Trading Scheme: Rights, rents and fairness.* Cambridge and New York: Cambridge University Press.

Janssen, M.C.W. and Mendys-Kamphorst, E., 2004. The price of a price: on the crowding out and in of social norms. *Journal of Economic Behavior & Organization*, 55(3): 377–95.

Jentoft, S., McCay, B.J., and Wilson, D.C., 1998. Social theory and fisheries co-management. *Marine Policy*, 22(4–5); 423–36.

Johnson, R. and Libecap, G., 1982. Contracting problems and regulation: The case of the fishery. *American Economic Review*, 72(5): 1005–22.

Johnston, J.S. and Faure, M.G., 2009. Fashioning entitlements: A comparative law and economic analysis of the judicial role in environmental civilization in the United States and Europe. In A. Breton, G. Brosio, S. Dalmazzone, and G. Garrone (eds) *Governing the Environment.* Cheltenham, UK: Edward Elgar, 138–73.

Jones, B., 1999. Environmental law in the United Kingdom. In: N.S.J. Koemaned (ed.) *Environmental Law in Europe.* The Hague: Kluwer Law International.

Jones, K.E., Patel, N., Levy, M., Storeygard, N., Balk, D., Gittleman, J.T., and Daszak, P. 2008. Global trends in emerging infectious diseases. *Nature*, 451: 990–3.

Joshi, N., Ostrom, E., Shivakoti, G., and Lam, W.F., 2000. Institutional opportunities and constraints in the performance of farmer-managed irrigation systems in Nepal. *Asia-Pacific Journal of Rural Development*, 10(2): 67–92.

Joskow, P.L. and Schmalensee, R. 1998. The political economy of market-based environmental policy: The U.S. acid rain program. *Journal of Law and Economics*, 41(1): 37–83.

Kahneman, D. and Knetsch, J.L., 1992. Contingent valuation and the value of public goods: Reply. *Journal of Environmental Economics and Management*, 22: 90–4.

Kahneman, D. and Tversky, A., 2000. *Choices, Values, and Frames.* Cambridge: Cambridge University Press.

Kaiser, H.F. 1960. The application of electronic computers to factor analysis. *Educational and Psychological Measurement*, 20: 141–51.

Kapp, K.W., 1976. The nature and significance of institutional Eeconomics. *KYKLOS*, 29: 209–32.

Karalayali, N., 2004. Reading Bourdieu with Adorno: The limits of critical theory and reflexive sociology. *Sociology*, 38(2): 351–68.

Karesh, W.B., Cook, R.A., Bennett, E.L., and Newcomb, J., 2005. Wildlife trade and global disease emergence. *Emerging Infectious Diseases*, 11: 1000–2.

Karp, L., 1996. Monopoly power can be disadvantageous in the extraction of a durable nonrenewable resource. *International Economic Review*, 37(4): 825–49.

Kassar, I. and Lasserre, P., 2004. Species preservation and biodiversity value: A real options approach. *Journal of Environmental Economics and Management*, 48: 857–79.

Katz, E.G., 2000. Social capital and natural capital: A comparative analysis of land tenure and natural resource management in Guatemala. *Land Economics*, 76(1): 114–32.

Kaul, I., Conceiçao, P., LeGoulven, K., and Mendoza, R., 2003. *Providing Global Public Goods*. Oxford: Oxford University Press.

Kelly, M., 1994. *Critique and Power: Recasting the Foucault/Habermas debate*. Cambridge MA: MIT Press.

Keohane, R.O. and Ostrom, E. (eds) 1995. *Local Commons and Global Interdependence*. London: Sage Publications.

Keser, C. and van Winden, F., 2000. Conditional cooperation and voluntary contributions to public goods. *Scandinavian Journal of Economics*, 102(1): 23–9.

Khanna, M., 2001. Non mandatory approaches to environmental protection. *Journal of Economic Surveys*, 15(3): 291–324.

Kilpatrick, A.M., Chmura, A.A., Gibbons, D.W., Fleischer, R.C., Marra, P.P., and Daszak, P., 2006a. Predicting the global spread of H5N1 avian influenza. *Proceedings of the National Academy of Sciences*, 103: 19368–73.

Kilpatrick, A.M., Daszak, P., Goodman, S.J., Rogg, H., Kramer, L.D., Cedeno, V., and Cunningham, A.A., 2006b. Predicting pathogen introduction: West nile virus spread to Galapagos. *Conservation Biology*, 20: 1224–31.

King, K., 1994. *The Incremental Costs of Global Environmental Benefits*. Washington, DC: GEF.

Klaes, M., 2008. Transaction costs. In: S.N. Durlauf and L.E. Blume (eds) *The New Palgrave Dictionary of Economics*, 2nd edn. Basingstoke: Palgrave Macmillan.

Klemperer P., 2002. What really matters in auction design J. *Econom. Perspect. 16*, 169–90.

Kolstad, C.D. and Toman, M., 2005. The economics of climate policy. In: K.G. Mäler and J.R. Vincent (eds) *Handbook of Environmental Economics*, Amsterdam: Elsevier, vol. 3: 1561–618.

Kolstad, C.D., Ulen, T.S., and Johnson G.V., 1990. Ex post liability for harm vs. Ex ante safety regulation: Substitutes or compliments? *American Economic Review*, 80: 888–901.

Kooiman, J. (ed.), 1993. *Modern Governance: New government–society interactions*. London: Sage.

Kosfeld, M., Okada, A., and Riedl, A., 2009. Institution formation in public goods games. *American Economic Review*, 99(4): 1335–55.

Kosobud, R.F., Stokes, H.H., Tallarico, C.D., and Scott, B.L., 2006. *Cost Effective Control of Smog: The significance of the Chicago cap-and-trade approach*. London and New York: Routledge.

Kosoy, N., Martinez-Tuna, M., Muradian, R., and Martinez-Alier, J., 2007. Payments for environmental services in watersheds: Insights from a comparative study of three cases in Central America. *Ecological Economics*, 61: 446–55.

Kouchi, T., 1995. *Reading Reproduction Theory* (in Japanese). Tokyo: Toshindo.

Koziol, H., 1997. *Österreichisches Haftpflichtrecht*. Vienna: Manz.

Kreps, D.M., 1997. Intrinsic motivation and extrinsic incentives. *American Economic Review*, 87(2): 359–64.

Krier, J.E., 1994. The end of the world news. Symposium twenty-five years of environ-mental regulation. *Loyola Law Review*, 27(3): 851–66.

Krier, J.E. and Ursin, E., 1977. *Pollution and Policy: A case essay on California federal experience with motor vehicle air pollution, 1940–1975*. Berkeley: Univesity of California Press.

Kuhnert, S., 2001. An evolutionary theory of collective action: Schumpeterian entre-preneurship for the common good. *Constitutional Political Economy*, 12: 13–29.

Kunreuther, H. and Freeman, P., 2001. Insurability, environmental risks and the law. In: Heyes, A. (ed.) *The Law and Economics of the Environment*. Cheltenham, UK: Edward Elgar, 304–5.

Kvakkestad, V. and Vatn, A., 2008. Regulating the release of GMOs: Contrasts between the European Union and Norway. *Environment and Planning C: Government and Policy*, 26: 968–81.

Kvakkestad, V., Gillund, F., Kjølberg, K.A., and Vatn, A., 2007. Scientists' perspectives on the deliberate release of GM crops. *Environmental Values*, 16: 79–104.

Labatte, G., 2008. The incremental cost principle and the conservation of globally important habitats: A critical examination. *Ecological Economics*, 65: 216–24.

Laffont, J. and Tirole, J., 1993. *A Theory on Incentives and Procurement*. Cambridge, MA: MIT Press.

Lam, W.F., 1998. *Governing Irrigation Systems in Nepal: Institutions, infrastructure, and collective action*. Oakland, CA: ICS Press.

Lam, W.F., Lee, M., and Ostrom, E., 1994. An institutional analysis approach: Findings from the NIIS on irrigation performance. In: J. Sowerwine, G. Shivakoti, U. Pradhan, A. Shukla, and E. Ostrom (eds) *From Farmers' Fields to Data Fields and Back: A synthesis of participatory information systems for irrigation and other resources*. Colombo, Sri Lanka: IIMI, and Rampur, Nepal: IAAS, 69–93.

Lanciotti R.S., Roehrig, J.T., Deubel, V., Smith, J., Parker, M., Steele, K., Crise, B., Volpe, K.E., Crabtree, M.B., Scherret, J.H., Hall, R.A., MacKenzie, J.S., Cropp, C.B., Panigrahy, B., Ostlund, E., Schmitt, B., Malkinson, M., Banet, C., Weissman, J., Komar, N., Savage, H.M., Stone, W., McNamara, T., and Gubler, D.J., 1999. Origin of the west nile virus responsible for an outbreak of encephalitis in the northeastern United States. *Science*, 286(5448): 2333–7.

Landes, W. and Posner, R., 1981. The positive economic theory of tort law. *Georgia Law Review*, 15: 870.

Landes, W. and Posner, R., 1984. Tort law as a regulatory regime for catastrophic personal injuries. *The Journal of Legal Studies*, 13: 417–34.

Lange, O. and Taylor, F.M., 1938. *On the Economic Theory of Socialism*. Minneapolis: University of Minnesota.

Lavoie, D., 1985. *Rivalry and Central Planning. The socialist calculation debate recon-sidered*. Cambridge: Cambridge University Press.

Leach, M., Mearns, R., and Scoones, I., 1999. Environmental entitlements: Dynamics and institutions in community-based natural resource management. *World Devel-opment*, 27(2): 225–47.

Leakey, R. and Lewin, R., 1995. *The Sixth Extinction*. London: Weidenfeld and Nicolson.

Lee, D.R., 1985. Rent-seeking and its implications for pollution taxation. *Southern Economic Journal*, 51(3): 731–44.

Lee, K., 1992. *Compass and Gyroscope*. Washington, DC: Island Press.

Leggett, J., 2001. *The Carbon War: Global warming and the end of the oil era*. New York: Routledge.

Lehtonen, M., 2004. The environmental–social interface of sustainable development: Capabilities, social capital, institutions. *Ecological Economics*, 49: 199–214.

Lemos, M.C. and Agrawal, A., 2006. Environmental governance. *Annual Review of Environmental Resources*, 31: 297–325.

Lensink, R. and van Soest, D., 2000. Foreign transfers and tropical deforestation: What terms of conditionality? *American Journal of Agricultural Economics*, 82: 389–99.

Lessig, L., 2001. *The Future of Ideas*. London: Random House.

Levine, J.M. and D'Antonio, C.M., 2003. Forecasting biological invasions with increasing international trade. *Conservation Biology*, 17: 322–6.

Lewis, D., 1969. *Convention: A philosophical study*. Cambridge, MA: Harvard University Press.

Lewison, R.L., Crowder, L.B., Read, A.J, and Freeman, S.A., 2004. Understanding impacts of fisheries bycatch on marine megafauna. *Trends in Ecology and Evolution*, 19: 598–604.

Li, W.D., Shi, Z.L., Yu, M., Ren, W.Z., Smith, C., Epstein, J.H., Wang, H.Z., Crameri, G., Hu, Z.H., Zhang, H.J., Zhang, J.H., McEachern, J., Field, H., Daszak, P., Eaton, B. T., Zhang, S.Y., and Wang, L.F., 2005. Bats are natural reservoirs of SARS-like coronaviruses. *Science*, 310(5748): 676–9.

Libecap, G.D., 1989. *Contracting for Property Rights*. New York: Cambridge University Press.

Libecap, G.D., 1998. Unitization. In: P. Newman (ed.) *The New Palgrave Dictionary of Economics and the Law*. Basingstoke: Palgrave Macmillan, vol. 3: 641–4.

Libecap, G.D., 2007. The assignment of property rights on the western frontier: Lessons for contemporary environmental and resource policy. *Journal of Economic History*, 67(2): 257–91.

Libecap, G.D., 2008. Open-access losses and delay in the assignment of property rights. *Arizona Law Review*, 50(2): 379–408.

Libecap, G.D. and Smith, J.L. 1999. The self-enforcing provisions of oil and gas unit operating agreements: Theory and evidence. *Journal of Law, Economics and Organization*, 15(2): 526–48.

Libecap, G.D. and Smith, J.L. 2002. The economic evolution of petroleum property rights in the United States. *Journal of Legal Studies*, 31(2, Pt. 2): S589–S608.

Libecap, G.D. and Wiggins, S.N. 1985. The influence of private contractual failure on regulation: The case of oil field unitization. *Journal of Political Economy*, 93(4): 690–714.

Lin, N., 2001. *Social Capital: A theory of social structure and action*. Cambridge: Cambridge University Press.

Linden, E., 2006. *The Winds of Change: Climate, weather, and the destruction of civilizations*. New York: Simon and Schuster.

McCay, B. and Acheson, J., 1987. *The Question of the Commons: The culture and ecology of communal resources*. Tucson: University of Arizona Press.

McCay, B. and Jentoft, S., 1998. Market or community failure? Critical perspective on common property research. *Human Organization*, 57(1): .21–9.

McGinnis, M., (ed.), 1999a. *Polycentric Governance and Development: Readings from the Workshop in Political Theory and Policy Analysis.* Ann Arbor: University of Michigan Press.

McGinnis, M., (ed.), 1999b. *Polycentricity and Local Public Economies: Readings from the Workshop in Political Theory and Policy Analysis.* Ann Arbor: University of Michigan Press.

McGinnis, M., (ed.), 2000. *Polycentric Games and Institutions: Readings from the Workshop in Political Theory and Policy Analysis.* Ann Arbor: University of Michigan Press.

Mackaay, E., 1982. *Economics of Information and the Law.* Boston, MA: Kluwer Nijhoff Publishing.

McKean, M.A., 1992. Management of traditional common lands (Iriaichi) in Japan. In: Bromley, D. (ed.) *Making the Commons Work: Theory, practice, and policy.* San Francisco, CA: ICS Press.

McNiell, D., 2007. Social capital or sociality? Methodological contrast between economics and other social sciences. In: S. Ioannides and K. Nielsen (eds) *Economics and the Social Sciences: Boundaries, interaction and integration.* North Hampton, MA: Edward Elgar, 163–84.

McNutt, P. 2002. *The Economics of Public Choice II.* Cheltenham, UK: Edward Elgar Publishing.

Mansfield, C., Van Houtven, G.L., and Huber, J., 2002. Compensating for public harms: Why public goods are preferred to money. *Land Economics*, 78(3): 368.

Manski, C., 2000. Economic analysis of social interaction. *Journal of Economic Perspectives*, 14: 115–36.

March, J.G. and Olsen, J.P., 1995. *Democratic Governance.* New York: The Free Press.

Martinez-Alier, J., Munda, G., and O'Neill, J., 1998. Weak comparability of values as a foundation of ecological economics. *Ecological Economics*, 26(3): 277–86.

Maskin E. and Riley, J., 2003. Uniqueness of equilibrium in sealed high-bid auctions. *Games and Economic Behavior*, 45(2): 395–409.

Mason, R. and Swanson, T., 2003. A Kuznets curve analysis of ozone-depleting substances and the Montreal Protocol. *Oxford Economic Papers*, 55(1): 1–24.

Mayewski, P.A. and White, F., 2002. *The Ice Chronicles: The quest to understand global climate change.* Hanover, NH: University Press of New England.

Mayntz, R., 1993. Modernization and the logic of interorganizational networks. In: J. Child, M. Crozier, and R. Mayntz (eds) *Societal Change Between Markets and Organization.* Avebury: Aldershot, 3–18.

Meinzen-Dick, R., 2007. Beyond panaceas in water institutions. *Proceedings of the National Academy of Sciences*, 104(39): 15200–5.

Merrey, D.J., 1996. Institutional design principles for accountability on large irrigation systems. Research Report no. 8. Colombo, Sri Lanka: International Irrigation Management Institute.

Mikalsen, K.H. and Jentoft, S., 2008. Participatory practices in fisheries across Europe: Making stakeholders more responsible. *Marine Policy*, 32(2): 169–77.

Miles E.L., Underdal, A., Steinar, A., Wettestad, J., Skjaerseth, J.B., and Carlin, E.M., 2002. *Environmental Regime Effectiveness: Confronting theory with evidence.* Cambridge, MA: MIT Press.

Miles, L. and Kapos, V., 2008. Reducing greenhouse gas emissions from deforestation and forest degradation: Global land-use implications. *Science*, 320(5882): 1454.

Milgrom, P., 1993. Is sympathy an economic value? Philosophy, economics and the contingent valuation method. In: J. Hausman (ed.) *Contingent Valuation: A critical assessment*. New York: North-Holland.

Milinski, M., Semmann, D., Krambeck, H.J., and Marotzke, J., 2006. Stabilizing the Earth's climate is not a losing game: Supporting evidence from public goods experiments. *Proceedings of the National Academy of Sciences of the United States of America*, 103(11): 3994–8.

Milinski, M., Sommerfeld, R.D., Krambeck, H.J., Reed, F.A., and Marotzke, J., 2008. The collective-risk social dilemma and the prevention of simulated dangerous climate change. *Proceedings of the National Academy of Sciences*, 105(7): 2291–4.

Millennium Ecosystem Assessment (MEA), 2005. *Ecosystems and Human Well-being: Current state and trends: Findings of the Condition and Trends Working Group*. Washington, DC: Island Press.

Miller, K., Munro, G., McKelvey, R., and Tyedmers, P., 2000. Climate, uncertainty and the Pacific Salmon Treaty: Insights on the harvest management game. *Proceedings of the International Institute for Fisheries Economics and Trade* (IINET) annual conference.

Mintrom, M., 2000. *Policy Entrepreneurs and School Choice*. Washington, DC: Georgetown University Press.

Mitchell, R.B., Clark, W.C., Cash, D.W., and Dickson, N.M., 2006. *Global Environmental Assessment: Information and influence*. Cambridge, MA: MIT Press.

Mizumoto, K., 2003. *Medieval Japan Looked from Mountains* (in Japanese). Tokyo: Yamakawa Publishers.

Molina M.J. and Rowland, F.S. 1974. Stratospheric sink for chlorofluoromethanes: Chlorine atomiccatalyzed destruction of ozone. *Nature* 249: 810–12.

Montgomery, W.D., 1972. Markets in licenses and efficient pollution control programs. *Journal of Economic Theory*, 5: 395–418.

Monti, A., 2001. Environmental risk: A comparative law and economics approach to liability and insurance. *European Review of Private Law*, 9(1): 51–79.

Moran, E. and Ostrom, E. (eds), 2005. *Seeing the Forest and the Trees: Human-environment interactions in forest ecosystems*. Cambridge, MA: MIT Press.

Morotomi, T., 2003. *Environment* (in Japanese). Tokyo: Iwanami Shoten.

Mosse, D., 1997. The symbolic making of a common property resource: History, ecology and locality in the tank-irrigated landscape in South India. *Development and Change*, 28(3): 467–504.

Mosse, D., 2004. Is good policy unimplementable? Reflections on the ethnography of aid policy and practice. *Development and Change*, 35(4): 639–71.

Mosse, D., 2006. Collective action, common property, and social capital in South India: An anthropological commentary. *Economic Development and Cultural Change*, 54 (6): 698–724.

Munro, G.R. and Stokes, R.L., 1989. The Canada–United States Pacific Salmon Treaty. In: D. McRae and G.R. Munro (eds) *Canadian Oceans Policy: National strategies and the new law of the sea*. Vancouver: University of British Columbia Press.

Murdoch J.C., Sandler, T., and Sargent, K., 1997. A tale of two collectives: Sulphur versus nitrogen oxides emission reduction in Europe. *Economica*, 64(254): 281–301.

Murdock, K., 2002. Intrinsic motivation and optimal incentive contracts. *The RAND Journal of Economics*, 33(4): 650–71.

Myers, E.C., 2007. Policies to reduce emissions from deforestation and degradation (REDD) in tropical forests: An examination of the issues facing the incorporation of REDD into market-based climate policies. *Resources for the Future, Discussion Paper 07-50*, Washington, DC: Resources for the Future.

Myers, R.A. and Worm, B., 2003. Rapid worldwide depletion of predatory fish communities. *Nature*, 423: 280–3.

Myerson, R. 2008. Mechanism design. In: S.N. Durlauf and L.E. Blume (eds) *The New Palgrave Dictionary of Economics*. Basingstoke: Palgrave Macmillan.

Nadeau, L., 1997. EPA effectiveness at reducing the duration of plant-level noncompliance. *Journal Environmental Economics and Management*, 34: 54–78.

Nagel, T., 1970. *The Possibility of Altruism*. Oxford: Clarendon Press.

Narayan, D. and Pritchett, L., 1999. Cents and sociability: Household income and social capital in rural Tanzania. *Economic Development and Cultural Change*, 17(1): 871–97.

Nash, J., 1953. Two-person cooperative games. *Econometrica*, 21(1): 128–40.

Nash, J.R. and Revesz, R.L., 2001. The design of marketable permit schemes to control local and regional pollutants. *Ecology Law Quarterly*, 28: 559–661.

National Research Council, 1986. *Proceedings of the Conference on Common Property Resource Management*. Washington, DC: National Academies Press.

Netting, R.McC., 1981. *Balancing on an Alp: Change and continuity in a Swiss mountain community*. New York: Cambridge University Press.

Newell, S., Carole, T. and Huang, J., 2004. Social capital and knowledge integration in EPR project team: The importance of bridging and bonding. *British Journal of Management*, 15: S43–54.

Niezen, G.J., 2000. Aansprakelijkheid voor milieuschade in de Europese Unie. In: G.J. Niezen, M.J.G.C. Raaijmakers, and A.J.S.M. Tervoort (eds) *Ongebonden recht bedrijven*. Amsterdam: Kluwer.

Nikiforakis, N., 2008. Punishment and counter-punishment in public good games: Can we really govern ourselves?" *Journal of Public Economics*, 92(1–2); 91–112.

Niskanen, W., 1971. *Bureaucracy and Representative Government*. Chicago, IL: Aldine-Atherton.

Nordhaus, W., 2005. Paul Samuelson and global public goods. In: M. Szenberg, L. Ramrattan, and A. Gottesman (eds) *Samuelsonian Economics*. Oxford: Oxford University Press, 88–98.

Nordhaus, W., 2008. *A Question of Balance: Weighing the options in global warming policies*. New Haven, CT: Yale University Press.

Nordhaus, W.D. and Yang, Z., 1996. A regional dynamic general-equilibrium model of alternative climate-change strategies. *American Economic Review*, 86(4): 741–65.

North, D.C., 1990. *Institutions, Institutional Change and Economic Performance*. Cambridge: Cambridge University Press.

Nowak, M.A. and Sigmund, K., 1998. Evolution of indirect reciprocity by image scoring. *Nature*, 393: 573–7.

Nunes, P.A.L.D., 2002a. Measuring the economic benefits from protecting the parque natural do Sudoeste Alentejano e Costa Vicentina of commercial tourism development: Results from a contingent valuation Survey. *Portuguese Economics Journal*, 1: 71–87.

Nunes, P.A.L.D., 2002b. Using factor analysis to identify consumer preferences for the protection of a natural area in Portugal. *European Journal of Operational Research*, 140: 499–516.

Nunes, P.A.L.D. and Schokkaert, E., 2003. Identifying the warm glow effect in contingent valuation. *Journal of Environmental Economics and Management*, 45: 231–45.

Nyborg, K., 2000. Homo Economicus and Homo Politicus: Interpretation and aggregation of environmental values. *Journal of Economic Behavior & Organization*, 42 (3): 305–22.

Nyborg, K. and Rege, M., 2003. Does public policy crowd out private contributions to public goods? *Public Choice*, 115(3): 397–418.

O'Connor, D., 2008. Governing the global commons: Linking carbon sequestration and biodiversity conservation in tropical forests. *Global Environmental Change*, 18 (3): 368–74.

O'Neill, J., 1993. *Ecology, Policy and Politics. Human well-being and the natural world.* London: Routledge.

O'Neill, J., 1998. *The Market. Ethics, knowledge and politics.* London: Routledge.

Oakerson, R., 1999. *Governing Local Public Economies: Creating the civic metropolis.* Oakland, CA: ICS Press.

Oakerson, R. and Parks, R., 1989. Local government constitutions: A different view of metropolitan governance. *American Review of Public Administration*, 19(4): 279–84.

Oates, W.E., 1990. Economics, economists, and environmental policy. *Eastern Economic Journal*, 16(4): 289–96.

Oates, W.E., 1994. Environment and taxation: The case of the United States. OECD Documents, Environment and Taxation: The Cases of the Netherlands, Sweden and the United States, Paris: OECD Publications.

Oates, W.E., 1999. An essay on fiscal federalism. *Journal of Economic Literature*, 37(3): 1120–49.

Oates, W.E, 2002. A reconsideration of environmental federalism. In J. List and A. de Zeeuw (eds) *Recent Advances in Environmental Economics*. Cheltenham, UK: Edward Elgar, 1–32.

Oates, W.E., 2005. Toward a second-generation theory of fiscal federalism. *International Tax and Public Finance*, 12: 3349–73.

OECD, 2007. *Instrument Mixes for Environmental Policy.* Paris: OECD Publications.

Ogus, A., 1999. Nudging and rectifying: The use of fiscal instruments for regulatory purposes. *Legal Studies*, 19: 245–66.

Ohtsuki, H., Iwasa, Y., and Nowak, M.A., 2009. Indirect reciprocity provides only a narrow margin of efficiency for costly punishment. *Nature*, 457: 79–82.

Olson M., 1965. The logic of collective action: Public goods and the theory of groups. Cambridge, MA: Harvard University Press.

Ostrom, E., 1990. *Governing the Commons: The evolution of institutions for collective action.* Cambridge: Cambridge University Press.

Ostrom, E., 1998a. A behavioral approach to the rational choice theory of collective action. Presidential Address, American Political Science Association, 1997. *American Political Science Review*, 92(1): 1–22.

Ostrom, E. 1998b. Self governance of common-pool resources. In: P. Newman (ed.) *The New Palgrave Dictionary of Economics and the Law*, Basingstoke: Palgrave Macmillan, vol. 3: 424–32.

Ostrom, E., 2000a. Understanding social capital: Learning from the analysis and experience of participation. In: P. Dasgupta (ed.) *Social Capital: A multifaceted perspective*. Washington, DC: World Bank.

Ostrom, E., 2000b. Crowding out citizenship. *Scandinavian Political Studies*, 23: 3–16.

Ostrom E., 2001. Decentralisation and development: The new panacea. In: K. Dowding et al. (eds) *Challenges to Democracy: Ideas, involvement and institution*. New York: Palgrave Publishers, 237–56.

Ostrom, E., 2003. How types of goods and property rights jointly affect collective action. *Journal of Theoretical Politics*, 15: 239–70.

Ostrom, E., 2005a. Policies that crowd out reciprocity and collective action. In: H. Gintis, S. Bowles, R. Boyd, and E. Fehr (eds) *Moral Sentiments and Material Interests: The foundations of cooperation in economic life*. Cambridge, MA: MIT Press, 253–75.

Ostrom, E., 2005b. *Understanding Institutional Diversity*. Princeton, NJ: Princeton University Press.

Ostrom, E., 2007. A diagnostic approach for going beyond panaceas. *Proceedings of the National Academy of Sciences*, Going Beyond Panaceas, Special Feature, 104(39): 15181–7.

Ostrom, E., 2010. Beyond markets and states: Polycentric governance of complex economic systems. *American Economic Review*, 100(3): 641–72.

Ostrom, E. and Ahn, T.K., 2002. Introduction. In: E. Ostrom and T.K. Ahn *Foundations of Social Capital*. Northhampton, MA: Edward Elgar.

Ostrom, E. and Nagendra, H., 2006. Insights on linking forests, trees, and people from the air, on the ground, and in the laboratory. *Proceedings of the National Academy of Sciences*, 103(51): 19224–31.

Ostrom, E. and Walker, J. (eds), 2003. *Trust & Reciprocity. Interdisciplinary lessons from experimental research*. New York: Russell Sage Foundation.

Ostrom, E., Parks, R., and Whitaker, G., 1978. *Patterns of Metropolitan Policing*. Cambridge, MA: Ballinger.

Ostrom, E., Walker, J., and Gardner, R., 1992. Covenants with and without a sword—self-governance is possible. *American Political Science Review*, 86(2): 404–17.

Ostrom, E., Gardner, R., and Walker, J., 1994. *Rules, Games, and Common-Pool Resources*. Ann Arbor: University of Michigan Press.

Ostrom, E., Dietz, T., Dolsak, N., Stern, P.C., Stonich, S., and Weber, E.U., 2002. *The Drama of the Commons*. Washington, DC: National Academy Press.

Ostrom E., Gibson C., Andersson K., and Shivakumar S., 2005. *The Samaritan's Dilemma: The Political Economy of Development Aid*. Oxford: Oxford University Press.

Ostrom E., Poteete A., and Janssen M., 2010. *Working Together: Collective action, the commons, and multiple methods in practice.* Princeton, NJ: Princeton University Press.

Ostrom, E., Lam, W.F., Shivakoti, G. and Pradhan, P. 2011. *Improving Irrigation in Asia: Sustainable performance of an innovative intervention in Nepal.* Cheltenham, UK: Edward Elgar.

Ostrom, V., 1991. *The Meaning of American Federalism: Constituting a self-governing society.* Oakland, CA: ICS Press.

Ostrom, V., 1997. *The Meaning of Democracy and the Vulnerability of Democracies: A response to Tocqueville's challenge.* Ann Arbor: University of Michigan Press.

Ostrom, V., 1999. Polycentricity. In: M. McGinnis (ed.) *Polycentricity and Local Public Economies: Readings from the Workshop in Political Theory and Policy Analysis.* Ann Arbor: University of Michigan Press, 52–74.

Ostrom, V., 2008a. *The Intellectual Crisis in American Public Administration,* 3rd edn. Tuscaloosa: University of Alabama Press.

Ostrom, V., 2008b. *The Political Theory of a Compound Republic: Designing the American experiment,* 3rd edn. Lanham, MD: Lexington Books.

Ostrom, V., 2011. *The Quest to Understand Human Affairs: Natural resources policy and essays on community and collective choice.* Vol. 1., ed. Barbara Allen. Lanham, MD: Lexington Books.

Paavola, J., 2007. Institutions and environmental governance: A reconceptualization. *Ecological Economics,* 63: 93–103.

Paavola, J. and Adger, N., 2005. Institutional ecological economics. *Ecological Economics,* 53: 353–68.

Palfrey, T.R. and Prisbrey J. E., 1996. Altruism, reputation, and noise in linear public goods experiments. *Journal of Public Economics,* 61: 409–27.

Palfrey, T.R. and Prisbey, J.E., 1997. Anomalous behavior in public goods experiments: How much and why? *American Economic Review,* 87: 829–46.

Pandolfi, J.M., Bradbury, R.H., Sala, E., Hughes, T.P., Bjorndal, K.A., Cooke, R.G., McArdle, D., McClenachan, L., Newman, M.J.H., Paredes, G., Warner, R.R., and Jackson, J.B.C., 2003. Global trajectories of the long-term decline of coral reef ecosystems. *Science,* 301(5635): 955–8.

Parker, C. M. A., Trivedi, M., and Marda, N. 2008. *The Little REDD Book.* Oxford: Global Canopy Programme.

Parson, E., 2003. *Protecting the Ozone Layer: Science and strategy.* New York: Oxford University Press.

Patte, H.H., 1973. The physical basis and origin of hierarchical control. In: H.H. Patte (ed.) *Hierarchy Theory. The challenge of complex systems.* New York: George Braziller, 71–108.

Paulus, A., 1995. *The Feasibility of Ecological Taxation.* Antwerp, Maklu.

Pauly, D., Christensen, D.V., Guénette, S., Pitcher, T.J., Rashid Sumaila, U., Walters, C.J.,Watson, R., and Zeller, D., 2002. Towards sustainability in world fisheries. *Nature,* 418: 689–95.

Pauly, M.V. 1967. Clubs, commonality and the core: An integration of game theory and the theory of public goods. *Economica* 34(3): 314–24.

Peeters, M., 2003. Emissions trading as a new dimension to European environmental law: The political agreement of the European Council on greenhouse gas allowance trading. *European Environmental Law Review*, 12: 82–92.

Peltzman, S. 1976. Toward a more general theory of regulation. *Journal of Law and Economics*, 19(2): 211–40.

Perman, R., Common, M., Mcgilvray, J., and Ma, Y., 2003. *Natural Resources and Environmental Economics*. Essex: Longman.

Perrings, C., 1997. Ecological resilience in the sustainability of economic development. In: C. Perrings (ed.) *Economics of Ecological Resources. Selected essays.* Cheltenham, UK: Edward Elgar, 45–63.

Perrings, C., 2008. Biodiversity conservation in sea areas beyond national jurisdiction: The economic problem. In: K.N. Ninan (ed.) *Conserving and Valuing Ecosystem Services and Biodiversity: Economic, institutional and social challenges.* London: Earthscan, 59–83.

Perrings, C. and Gadgil, M., 2003. Conserving biodiversity: Reconciling local and global public benefits. In: I. Kaul, P. Conceicao, K. le Goulven, and R.L. Mendoza (eds) *Providing Global Public Goods: Managing globalization.* Oxford: Oxford University Press, 532–55.

Perrings, C., Williamson, M., Barbier, E.B., Delfino, D., Dalmazzone, S., Shogren, J., Simmons, P., and Watkinson, A., 2002. Biological invasion risks and the public good: An economic perspective. *Conservation Ecology*, 6(1): 1.

Perrings, C., Mooney, H., Lonsdale, M., and Burgeil, S., 2009a. Globalization and invasive species: Policy and management options. In: C. Perrings, H. Mooney, and M. Williamson (eds) *Bioinvasions and Globalization: Ecology, economics, management and policy.* Oxford: Oxford University Press.

Perrings, C., Fenichel, E., and Kinzig, A., 2009b. Externalities of globalization: Bioinvasions and trade. In: C. Perrings, H. Mooney, and M. Williamson (eds) *Bioinvasions and Globalization: Ecology, economics, management and policy.* Oxford: Oxford University Press.

Pindyck, R.S. and Rubenfield, D.L., 2001. *Microeconomics*. New Jersey: Prentice Hall.

Platteau, J.P., 2000. *Institutions, Social Norms and Economic Development.* London: Routledge

Platteau, J.P., 2003. Community-based development in the context of within group heterogeneity. Paper presented at the Annual Bank Conference on Development Economics, Bangalore, India.

Platteau, J.P., 2004. Monitoring elite capture in community-driven development. *Development and Change*, 35(2): 223–46.

Polanyi, K., 1944. *The Great Transformation. The political and economic origins of our time.* Boston, MA: Beacon Press.

Polinsky, A.M., 1979. Controlling externalities and protecting eentitlements: Property right, liability rule and the tax-subsidy approaches. *Journal of Legal Studies*, 8: 1–48.

Polinsky, A.M., 1983. *Introduction to Law and Economics.* Boston and Toronto: Little, Brown & Co.

Pope, C., Ezzati, M., and Dockery, D., 2009. Fine-particulate air pollution and life expectancy in the United States. *New England Journal of Medicine*, 360(4): 376–86.

Portes, A., 1998. Social capital: Its origins and application in modern sociology. *Annual Review of Sociology*, 24(1): 1–24.

Posner, E.A., 1996. Law, economics, and inefficient norms. *University of Pennsylvania Law Review*, 144(5s): 1697–744.

Posner, E.A., 1998. Symbols, signals, and social norms in politics and the law. *Journal of Legal Studies*, 27(s2): 765–97.

Posner, E.A., 2000a. *Law and Social Norms*. Cambridge, MA: Harvard University Press.

Posner, E.A., 2000b. Law and social norms: The case of tax compliance. *Virginia Law Review*, 86: 1781–819.

Posner, E.A., 2007. *Social Norms, Non-legal Sanctions, and the Law*. Cheltenham, UK and Northampton, MA: Edward Elgar.

Poteete, A., Janssen, M., and Ostrom, E., 2010. *Working Together: Collective action, the commons, and multiple methods in practice*. Princeton, NJ: Princeton University Press.

Pretty, J., 2003. Social capital and the collective management of resources. *Science*, 302: 1912–14.

Pretty, J. and Ward, H., 2001. Social capital and the environment. *World Development*, 29(2): 209–27.

Programmes for the Los Angeles Air Basin. 2004. In: *Tradeable permits: Policy evaluation, design, and reform*. Paris: OECD Publications.

Proudhon, P.J., 1840. *What is Property? or, An inquiry into the principle of right and of government*. trans. B.R. Tucker, 1876. New York: Humbold, 1890; New York: Dover, 1970; Cambridge: Cambridge University Press, 1994.

Putnam, R., 1993. *Making Democracy Work: Civic traditions in modern Italy*. Princeton, NJ: Princeton University Press.

Putnam, R., 2000. *Bowling Alone: The collapse and revival of American community*. New York: Simon & Schuster.

Pyke, C.R., 2004. Habitat loss confounds climate change impacts. *Frontiers in the Ecology and the Environment*, 2: 171–82.

Quine, W.O., 1967. Truth by convention. *Philosophica Essays for A.N. Whitehead*, Brasted, Kent: Russel and Russel Publishers.

Raakjær, N.J. and Mathiesen, C., 2003. Important factors influencing rule compliance in fisheries lessons from Denmark. *Marine Policy*, 27(5): 409–16.

Rabin, M. 1993. Incorporating fairness into game theory and economics. *American Economic Review*, 83: 1281–302.

Ray, D., 1998. *Development Economics*. Princeton, NJ: Princeton University Press.

Ray, D. and Vohra, R., 1999. A theory of endogenous coalition structures. *Games and Economic Behavior*, 26(2): 286–336.

Ray, I., 2008. Cooperative conversation: Outcomes and process in economics and anthropology. In: P. Bardhan, and I. Ray (eds) *Contested Commons: Conversation between economists and anthropologists*. Oxford: Blackwell Publishers.

Ray, S. and Bijarnia, M., 2007. Power relations and institutional outcomes: A case of pastureland development in Semi-arid Rajasthan. *Ecological Economics*, 62(2); 360–72.

Reeson, A.F. and Tisdell, J.G., 2008. Institutions, motivations and public goods: An experimental test of motivational crowding. *Journal of Economic Behavior & Organization*, 68(1): 273–81.

Reinicke W.H. and Deng, F., 2000. *Critical Choices: The United Nations, networks and the future of global governance*. Ottawa, International Development Research Council.

Roberts, C.M., 2002. Deep impact: The rising toll of fishing in the deep sea. *Trends in Ecology and Evolution*, 175: 242–5.

Roberts, C.M., Andelman, S., Branch, G., Bustamante, R.H., Castilla, J.C., Dugan, J., Halpern, B.S., Lafferty, K.D., Leslie, H., Lubchenko, J., McArdle, D., Possingham, G., Ruckelshaus, M., and Warner, R.R., 2003. Ecological criteria for evaluating candidate sites for marine reserves. *Ecological Applications*, 131: S199–214.

Roberts, M.J. and Spence, M., 1976. Effluent charges and licences under uncertainty. *Journal of Public Economics*, 5: 193–208.

Rockenbach, B. and Milinski, M., 2006. The efficient interaction of indirect reciprocity and costly punishment. *Nature*, 444: 718–23.

Rodrıguez, L.C. and Pascual, U., 2004. Land clearance and social capital in mountain agro-ecosystems: The case of Opuntia scrubland in Ayacucho, Peru. *Ecological Economics*, 49: 243–52.

Rodriguez-Sickert, C., Guzmán, R.A., and Cárdenas, J.C., 2008. Institutions influence preferences: Evidence from a common pool resource experiment. *Journal of Economic Behavior & Organization*, 67(1): 215–27.

Røpke, I., 2005. Trends in the development of ecological economics from the late 1980s to early 2000s. *Ecological Economics*, 55: 262–90.

Rose, C.M., 2002. Common property, regulatory property and environmental protection. Comparing community-based management to tradable environmental allowances. In: Ostrom, E. (ed.) *The Drama of the Commons*. Washington, DC: National Academic Press, 233–57.

Rose-Ackerman, S., 1992a. Environmental liability law. In: T.H. Tietenberg (ed.) *Innovation in Environmental Policy, Economic and Legal Aspects of Recent Developments in Environmental Enforcement and Liability*. Cheltenham, UK: Edward Elgar, 223–43.

Rose-Ackerman, S., 1992b. *Rethinking the Progressive Agenda. The reform of the American regulatory state*. New York: Free Press, 118–31.

Rose-Ackerman, S., 1996. Public law versus private law in environmental regulation: European Union proposals in the light of United States and german axperiences. In: E. Eide and R. Van den Bergh (eds) *Law and Economics of the Environment*. Oslo: Juridisk Forlag, 13–39.

Rosen, H.S., 1999. *Public Finance*. Chicago, IL: Irwin.

Rozell, S. and Swinnen, J.M.F., 2004. Success and failure of reform: Insights from the transition of agriculture. *Journal of Economic Literature*, 42(2): 404–56.

Rubinstein, A., 1982. Perfect Equilibrium in a Bargaining Model. *Econometrica*, 50(1): 97–109.

Runge, F.C., 1992. Common property and collective action in economic development. In: D. Bromley (ed.) *Making Commons Work: Theory, practice and policy*. San Francisco, CA: ICS Press, 17–40.

Rustagi, D., Engel, S., and Kosfeld, M., 2010. Conditional cooperation and costly monitoring explain success in forest commons management. *Science*, 330: 961–5.

Rweyemamu, M. M. and Astudillo, V. M. 2002. Global perspective for foot and mouth disease control. *Revue Scientifique Et Technique De L Office International Des Epizooties*, 21: 765–73.

Said, E., 1979. *Orientalism*. New York; Vintage Books.

Samuelson, P.A., 1993. Altruism as a Problem Involving Group versus Individual Selection in Economics and Biology. *American Economic Review*, 83: 143–8.

Sancton, A., 2000. *The Assault on Local Government*. Montreal: McGill-Queen's University Press.

Sandler, T., 1997. *Global Challenges*. Cambridge: Cambridge University Press.

Sandler, T., 2004. *Global Collective Action*. Cambridge: Cambridge University Press.

Sandler, T., 2005. Regional public goods and regional cooperation. Background working paper for the Task Force on Global Public Goods, Stockholm, Sweden.

Santore, R., Robinson, Y., and Klein, Y., 2001. Strategic state-level environmental policy with asymmetric pollution spillovers. *Journal of Public Economics*, 80(2): 199–224.

Sarr, M. and Swanson, T., 2009a. Economics of traditional knowledge as private information. Mimeo. Available at: http://graduateinstitute.ch/cies/home/programmes/biodiversity/page10136.html, accessed 6 March 2012.

Sarr, M. and Swanson, T., 2009b. IPR and north–south hold-up problem in sequential R&D. Mimeo. Available at: http://graduateinstitute.ch/cies/home/programmes/biodiversity/page10136.html, accessed 6 marach 2012.

Sarr, M., Goeschl, T., and Swanson, T., 2008. The value of conserving genetic resources for R&D: A survey. *Ecological Economics*, 67(2): 184–93.

Schelling, T.C., 1960. *The Strategy of Conflict*. Cambridge, MA: Harvard University Press.

Schellnhuber, H.J., Crutzen, P.J., Clark, W.C., Claussen, M., and Held, H. (eds), 2004. *Earth System Analysis for Sustainability*. Cambridge, MA: MIT Press.

Schmitz, P.W., 2000. On the joint use of liability and safety regulation. *International Review of Law and Economics*, 20(3): 371–82.

Schneider, M., 1986. Fragmentation and the growth of government. *Public Choice*, 48: 255–63.

Schotter, A., 1981. *The Economic Theory of Social Institutions*. New York: Cambridge University Press.

Schwartz, A. and Wilde, L., 1979. Intervening in markets on the basis of imperfect information: A legal and economic analysis. *University of Pennsylvania Law Review*, 127: 630–82.

Schwartz, G., 1997. Mixed theories of tort law: Affirming both deterrence and corrective justice. *Texas Law Review*, 75: 1801–34.

Schweik, C.M., 2000. Optimal foraging, institutions, and forest change: A case from Nepal. In: C. Gibson, M. McKean, and E. Ostrom (eds) *People and Forests: Communities, institutions, and governance*. Cambridge, MA: MIT Press, 57–85.

Scotchmer, Suzanne, 2002. Local public goods and clubs. In A. J. Auerbach and M. Feldstein (eds) *Handbook of Public Economics*. The Hague: Elsevier, vol. 4: 1997–2042.

Scott, A., 1955. The fishery: The objectives of sole ownership. *Journal of Political Economy*, 63: 116–24.

Scott, J.C., 1990. *Domination and the Arts of Resistance: Hidden transcripts*. New Haven, Yale University Press.

Scott, W.R., 1995. *Institutions and Organizations*. California: Sage Publications.

Sen, A.K. 1970. *Collective Choice and Social Welfare*. San Francisco, CA: Holden-Day.

Sen, A.K. 1979. Personal utilities and public judgements: or What's wrong with welfare economics? *The Economic Journal*, 89: 537–58.

Sewell, W.H., 1992. A theory of structure: Duality, agency and transformation. *American Journal of Sociology*, 98(1): 1–29.

Shannon C.E., 1948. A Mathematical Theory of Communication. *Bell System Technical Journal*, 27: 379–423 and 623–56.

Shavell, S., 1980. Strict liability versus negligence. *Journal of Legal Studies*, 9(1): 1–25.

Shavell, S., 1984a. Liability for harm versus regulation of safety. *Journal of Legal Studies*, 13(2): 357–74.

Shavell, S., 1984b. A model of the optimal use of liability and safety regulation. *Rand Journal of Economics*,15(2): 271–80.

Shavell, S., 1985. Criminal law and the optimal use of non-monetary sanctions as a deterrent. *Columbia Law Review*, 85: 1232–62.

Shavell, S., 1986. The judgement proof problem. *International Review of Law and Economics*, 6(1): 43–58.

Shavell, S., 1987. *Economic Analysis of Accident Law*. Cambridge, MA: Harvard University Press.

Shivakoti, G. and Ostrom, E., 2001. *Improving Irrigation Governance and Management in Nepal*. Oakland, CA: ICS Press.

Shivakoti, G., Vermillion, D., Lam, W-F., Ostrom, E., Pradhan, U., and Yoder, R. (eds), 2005. *Asian Irrigation in Transition: Responding to challenges*. New Delhi: Sage Publications.

Shotton, R. 2000. Current property rights systems in fisheries management. In: R. Shotton (ed.) *Use of Property Rights in Fisheries Management, Proceedings of the FishRights 99 Conference*, Fremantle Western Australia. Rome: FAO, Fisheries Technical Paper 404/1, 45–50.

Simon, H.A., 1973. The organization of complex systems. In: H.H. Patte (ed.) *Hierarchy Theory. The challenge of complex systems*. New York: George Braziller, 1–27.

Singh, E. and Saguirian, A., 1993. The svalbard archipelago: The role of surrogate negotiators. In: O.R. Young and G. Osherenko (eds) *Polar Politics: Creating international environmental regimes*. Ithaca: Cornell University Press, 22–55.

Sjåfjell, B., 2007. Rules, values and takeovers. Doctoral thesis, University of Oslo.

Skjaerseth, J.B. and Wettestad, J., 2008. *EU Emissions Trading: Initiation, decision-making and implementation*. Farnham, Surrey: Ashgate Publishing.

Skogh, G., 1982. Public insurance and accident prevention. *International Review of Law and Economics*, 2: 67–80.

Skogh, G., 1989. The combination of private and public regulation of safety. In: M. Faure, and R. Van den Bergh (eds) *Essays in Law and Economics. Corporations, accident prevention and compensation for losses*. Antwerp: Maklu, 87–101.

Slaughter, A.M., 2004. *A New World Order: Government networks and the disaggregated state*. Princeton, NJ: Princeton University Press.

Sliwka, D., 2007. Trust as a signal of a social norm and the hidden costs of incentive schemes. *American Economic Review*, 97(3): 999–1012.

Smith, A., 1759. *The Theory of Moral Sentiments*, ed. D.D. Raphael and A.L. Macfie, vol. I of the Glasgow Edition of the Works and Correspondence of Adam Smith. Indianapolis, IN: Liberty Fund.

Smith, E.A. and Bird, R.B., 2005. Costly signaling and cooperative behavior. In: H. Gintis, S. Bowles, R. Boyd, and E. Fehr (eds) *Moral Sentiments and Material Interests: The foundations of cooperation in economic life*. Cambridge, MA: MIT Press, 115–48.

Smith, J.L. 1987. The common pool, bargaining, and the rule of capture. *Economic Inquiry*, 25(4): 631–44.

Smith, K.F., Behrens, M.D., Max, L.M. and Daszak, P., 2008. U.S. drowning in unidentified fishes: Scope, implications and regulation of live fish import. *Conservation Letters* 1: 103–9.

Smith, V.L. 1969. On models of commercial fishing. *The Journal of Political Economy*, 77(2): 181–98.

Snidal, D., 1985. Coordination versus prisoners' dilemma: Implications for international cooperation and regimes. *American Political Science Review*, 79: 923–42.

Sobel, J., 2002. Can we trust social capital? *Journal of Economic Literature*, 15: 139–54.

Social Learning Group, 2001. *Learning to Manage Global Environmental Risks*, 2 vols. Cambridge, MA: MIT Press.

Söderbaum, P., 1992. Neoclassical and institutional approaches to development and the environment. *Ecological Economics*, 5: 127–44.

Solow, R.M., 1999. Notes on social capital and economic performance. In: P. Dasgupta, and I. Serageldin (eds) *Social Capital: A multifaceted perspective*. Washington, DC: World Bank, 6–12.

Somanathan, E., 1991. Deforestation, property rights and incentives in central Himalaya. *Economic and Political Weekly*, 26.

Sørensen, E. and Torfing, J. (eds), 2007. *Theories of Democratic Network Governance*. Basingstoke: Palgrave Macmillan.

Spash, C.L. and Villena, M.G., 1998. *Exploring the Approaches of Institutional Economics to Environment*. Cambridge: Cambridge University Press.

Spivak, G.C., 1988. Can the subaltern speak? Marxism and the interpretation of culture. In: C. Nelson, and Grossberg (eds) *Marxism and the Interpretation of Culture*. Urbana: University of Illinois Press.

Stavins, R.N., 2003. Experience with market-based environmental policy instruments. In: K.G. Mäler, and J.R. Vincent (eds) *Handbook of Environmental Economics, Volume I: Environmental degradation and institutional responses*. Amsterdam: Elsevier, 362–72.

Stavins, R.N., 2007a. A U.S. cap-and-trade system to address global climate change. Discussion Paper 2007-13 of the Hamilton Project. Washington, DC: The Brookings Institution.

Stavins, R.N., 2007b. Market-based environmental policies: What can we learn from U. S. experience (and related research)? In: J. Freeman and Ch.D. Kolstad (eds)

Moving to Markets in Environmental Regulation, New York: Oxford University Press, 19–47.

Steffen, W., Sanderson, A., Tyson, P., Jäger, J., Matson, P., Moore, B., Oldfield, F., Richardson, K., Schellnhuber, H.J., Turner, B.L., and Wasson, R.J., 2004. *Global Change and the Earth System: A planet under pressure.* Berlin: Springer Verlag.

Stephens, G.R. and Wikstrom, N., 2000. *Metropolitan Government and Governance: Theoretical perspectives, empirical analysis, and the future.* New York: Oxford University Press.

Stern, N., 2007. *The Economics of Climate Change: The Stern Review.* Cambridge: Cambridge University Press.

Stigler, G., 1961. The economics of information. *Journal of Political Economics*, 69: 213.

Stolarski R.S. and Cicerone, R.J. 1974. Stratospheric chlorine: A possible sink for ozone. *Canadian Journal of Chemistry*, 52: 1610.

Stoop, J., van Soest, D., and Vyrastekova, J., 2008. Two carrots and no stick: The effectiveness of second-order rewarding in social dilemma situations. Mimeo: Tilburg University.

Stranlund, J.K., Chavez, A.C., and Field, B.C., 2002. Enforcing emissions trading programs: Theory, practice and performance. *Policy Studies Journal*, 30(3): 343–61.

Sundberg, J., 1998. NGO landscapes in the Maya biosphere reserve, Guatemala. *Geographical Review*, 88(3): 388–412.

Sutinen, J.G. and Kuperan, K., 1999. A socio-economic theory of regulatory compliance. *International Journal of Social Economics*, 26(1/2/3): 174–93.

Sutter, M. and Weck-Hannemann, H., 2004. An experimental test of the public goods crowding out hypothesis when taxation is endogenous. *Finanz Archiv*, 60: 94–110.

Svendsen, G.T., 1998. *Public Choice and Environmental Regulation: Tradable permit systems in the United States and CO_2 taxation in Europe.* Cheltenham UK: Edward Elgar.

Swartz, D., 1997. *Culture & Power: The sociology of Pierre Bourdieu.* Chicago, IL: University of Chicago Press.

Swedeberg, R., 2001. Sociology and game theory: Contemporary and historical perspective. *Theory and Society*, 30(3): 301–35.

Swope, K. 2002. An experimental investigation of excludable public goods. *Experimental Economics*, 5(3): 209–22.

Tainter, J., 1988. *The Collapse of Complex Societies.* Cambridge: Cambridge University Press.

Takeuchi, T., 1990. Village society and communal customs (in Japanese). Tokyo: Meicho Shuppan.

Tanabe, H., 1995. Renewal of theory of behaviour: Structuralization, behaviour and reflexibity (in Japanese). In: T. Miyajima (ed.) *Sociology of Culture.* Tokyo: Yushindo.

Tang, S.Y., 1992. *Institutions and Collective Action: Self-governance in irrigation.* San Francisco, CA: ICS Press.

Tatem, A.J., Hay, S.S., and Rogers, D.J., 2006. Global traffic and disease vector dispersal. *Proceedings of the National Academy of Sciences*, 103(16): 6242–7.

Taylor, C., 1993. To follow a rule. In: C. Calhoun, E. LiPuma, and M. Postone (eds) *Bourdieu: Critical perspectives.* Chicago, IL: University of Chicago Press.

Teske, P., Schneider, M., Mintrom, M., and Best, S., 1993. Establishing the micro foundations of a macro theory: Information, movers, and the competitive local market for public goods. *American Political Science Review*, 87(3): 702–13.

Tiebout, C.M., 1956. A pure theory of local government expenditures. *Journal of Political Economy*, 64: 416–24. Reprinted in Cowen, T. (ed.), 1992. *Public Goods and Market Failures*. London: Transaction Publishers, ch. 9.

Tietenberg, T., 2000. *Environmental and National Resource Economics?* Reading: Addison-Wesley.

Tietenberg, T., 2002. The tradable permits approach to protecting the commons. What have we learned? In: E. Ostrom (ed.) *The Drama of the Commons*. Washington, DC: National Academic Press, 197–232.

Tietenberg T., 2003. The tradable-permits approach to protecting the commons: Lesson for climate change. *Oxford Review of Economic Policy*, 19: 400–19.

Tittensor, D.P., Worm, B., and Myers, R.A., 2006. Macroecological changes in exploited marine systems. In: J.D. Witman and K. Roy (eds) *Marine Macroecology*. Chicago, IL: University of Chicago Press.

Tol, R.S.J., 2008. The social cost of carbon: Trends, outliers and catastrophes. *Economics: The Open-Access, Open-Assessment E-Journal*, 2, 2008–25.

Toonen, T., 1996. On the administrative condition of politics: Administrative transformation in the Netherlands. *West European Politics,* 19(3): 609–32.

Toonen, T., 2010. Resilience in public administration: The work of Elinor and Vincent Ostrom from a public administration perspective. *Public Administration Review,* 70(2): 193–202.

Touza, J. and Perrings, C. 2011. Strategic behavior and the scope for unilateral provision of transboundary ecosystem services that are international environmental public goods. *Strategic Behavior and the Environment*, 1(2): 89–117.

Trotignon, R. and Ellerman, A.D. 2009. Cross-border trading and borrowing in the EU ETS. In: X. Labandeira, and J. M. Martin-Moreno (eds) *Climate Change Policies after 2012, Special Issue 2. The Energy Journal*, 30 (October).

Tuomela, R., 1995. *The Importance of Us: A philosophical study of basic social notions.* Stanford, CA: Stanford University Press.

Tuomela, R., 2007. *The Philosophy of Sociality: The shared point of view.* Oxford: Oxford University Press.

Turner B.J., Clark, W.C., Kates, R.W., Richards, J.F., Matthews, J.T., and Meyer, W.B. (eds), 1990. *The Earth as Transformed by Human Action: Global and regional changes in the biosphere over the last 300 years.* Cambridge: Cambridge University Press.

Turner, R.K., Pearce, D., and Bateman, I., 1994. *Environmental Economics: An elementary introduction.* New York: Harvester Wheatsheaf.

Tversky A. and Kahneman, D., 1974. Judgment under uncertainty: Heuristics and biases. *Science*, 185(4157): 1124–31.

Tversky, A. and Kahneman, D., 1981. The framing of decisions and the psychology of choice. *Science*, 211(4481): 453–8.

Tversky, A. and Kahneman, D., 1986. Rational choice and the framing of decisions. In: R.M. Hogarth and M.W. Reder (eds) *Rational Choice: The contrast between economics and psychology.* Chicago, IL: University of Chicago Press.

Tyler T.R., 1998. Trust and democratic governance. In: V. Braithwaite and M. Levi (eds) *Trust and Governance*. New York: Russell Sage Foundation, 269–94.

Tyran, J.R. and Feld, L.P., 2006. Achieving compliance when legal sanctions are non-deterrent. *The Scandinavian Journal of Economics*, 108(1): 135–56.

UN-Habitat. 2008. *Cities and Climate Change Adaptation*. Prepared for the UN-Habitat Donors Meeting, Seville, October 15–16, 2008.

United Nations Development Programme (UNDP), 2006. *Human Development Report 2006—beyond scarcity: power, poverty and the global water crisis*. New York: Palgrave Macmillan.

United Nations Development Programme (UNDP), 2007. *Human Development Report 2007–2008—fighting climate change: human solidarity in a divided world*. New York: Palgrave Macmillan.

United Nations Environment Programme (UNEP), 2008. Benefit sharing in ABS: options and elaborations. UNU–IAS Report. Available at http://www.cbd.int/doc/side-events/abs/abswg-07/unu-ias-2009-04-06-02-en.pdf (accessed 24 February 2012).

United Nations General Assembly, 2004. *Oceans and the Law of the Sea: Report of the Secretary-General*, Fifty-ninth session Item 51 (a) New York: United Nations.

United Nations General Assembly, 2010. *Oceans and the Law of the Sea: Report of the Secretary-General*, Sixty-fifth session, Item 75 (a). New York: United Nations.

Uttig P. and Clapp, J. (eds), 2008. *Corporate Accountability and Sustainable Development*. New Delhi: Oxford University Press.

Van Soest, D. and Vyrastekova, J., 2008. Higher fines, lower conviction probabilities, and the support for government regulation. Mimeo: Tilburg University.

Van Soest, D., de Zeeuw, A., and Bouma, J., 2010. Voluntary cooperation and local public goods provision: Coalition formation and the role of external labor markets. Mimeo: VU University Amsterdam.

Van Steveren, I., 2003. Beyond social capital and poverty research. *Journal of Economic Issues*, 37(2): 415–23.

Vanden Borre, T., 2007. Shifts in governance in compensation for nuclear damage, twenty years after chernobyl. In: M. Faure and A. Verhey (eds) *Shifts in Compensation for Environmental Damage*. Vienna: Springer, 261–311.

Vatn, A., 1998. Input vs. emission taxes. Environmental taxes in a mass balance and transactions cost perspective. *Land Economics*, 74(4): 514–25.

Vatn, A., 2001. Environmental resources, property regimes and efficiency. *Environment and Planning C: Government and Policy*, 19(5): 681–93.

Vatn, A., 2005. *Institutions and the Environment*. Cheltenham, UK: Edward Elgar.

Vatn, A., 2007. Resource regimes and cooperation. *Land Use Policy*, 24(4): 624–32.

Vatn, A., 2008a. Sustainability: The need for institutional change. In: P. Uttig and J. Clapp (eds) *Corporate Accountability and Sustainable Development*. New Delhi: Oxford University Press, 61–91.

Vatn, A., 2008b. Institutions and rationality. In: S. Batie, and N. Mercuro (eds) *Assessing the Evolution and Impact of Alternative Institutional Structures*. London: Routledge, 113–39.

Vatn, A., 2009. Cooperative behavior and institutions. *Journal of Socio-Economics*, 38 (1): 188–98.

Vatn, A., 2010. An institutional analysis of payments for environmental services. *Ecological Economics*, 69: 1245–52.

Vatn, A. and Bromley, D., 1994. Choices without prices without apologies. *Journal of Environmental Economics and Management*, 26: 129–48.

Veblen, T., 1904. *The Theory of Business Enterprise*. New York: The New American Library.

Veljanovski, C.G., 1981. The economic theory of tort liability. Toward a corrective justice approach. In: P. Burrows, and C.G. Veljanovski (eds) *The Economic Approach to Law*. London: Butterworths, 125–50.

Verhey, A., 2007. Shifts in governance: Oil pollution. In: M. Faure, and A. Verhey (eds) *Shifts in Compensation for Environmental Damage*. Vienna: Springer, 133–95.

Victor, D.G., 2001. *The Collapse of the Kyoto Protocol and the Struggle to Slow Global Warming*. Princeton, NJ: Princeton University Press.

Victor D.G., 2007. Fragmented carbon markets and reluctant nations: Implications for the design of effective architectures. In: J.E. Aldy and R.N. Stavins (eds) *Architectures for Agreement. Addressing global climate change in the post-Kyoto world*. Cambridge: Cambridge University Press, 133–60.

Vilà, M. and Pujadas, J., 2001. Land use and socio-economic correlates of plant invasions in European and North African countries. *Biological Conservation*, 100: 397–401.

Vitousek, P., Mooney, H., Lubchenko, J., and Melillo, J., 1997. Human domination of the Earth's ecosystems. *Science*, 277(5325): 494–9.

Vollan, B., 2008. Socio-ecological explanations for crowding-out effects from economic field experiments in southern Africa. *Ecological Economics*, 67(4): 560–73.

Vyrastekova, J. and van Soest, D., 2003. Centralized common-pool management and local community participation. *Land Economics*, 79(4): 500–14.

Vyrastekova, J. and van Soest, D., 2008. On the (in)effectiveness of rewards in sustaining cooperation. *Experimental Economics*, 11(1): 53–65.

Wagner, G., 1999. Haftung und Versicherung als Instrumente der Techniksteuerung. *Versicherungsrecht*, 1441–80.

Walker B. and Salt, D., 2006. *Resilience Thinking: Sustaining ecosystems and people in a changing World*. Washington, DC: Island Press.

Wang, H., 2007. Shifts in governance in the international regime of marine oil pollution compensation: Legal history perspective. In: M. Faure, and A. Verhey (eds) *Shifts in Compensation for Environmental Damage*. Vienna: Springer, 197–241.

Warr P.G., 1983. The private provision of a public good is independent of the distribution of income. *Economic Letters*, 13: 207–11.

Webb, E. and Shivakoti, G. (eds), 2008. *Decentralization, Forests and Rural Communities: Policy outcomes in South and Southeast Asia*. New Delhi: Sage Publications.

Weitzman, M.L., 1974. Prices vs. quantities. *Review of Economic Studies*, 41(4): 477–91.

Wendner, R. and Goulder, L.H., 2008. Status effects, public goods provision, and the excess burden. *Journal of Public Economics*, 92: 1968–85.

Whiteley, P.F., 2000. Economic growth and social capital. *Political Studies*, 48: 443–66.

Wiggins, S.N. and Libecap, G.D., 1985. Oil field unitization: Contractual failure in the presence of imperfect information. *American Economic Review*, 74(1): 368–85.

Williamson, O.E., 1975. *Market and hierarchies. Analysis and Antitrust Implications*. New York: Free Press.

Williamson, O.E., 1981. The economics of organization: The transaction cost approach. *American Journal of Sociology*, 87(3): 548–77.

Williamson, O.E., 1985. *The Economic Institutions of Capitalism*. New York: Free Press.

Willamson, O. 1996. *The Mechanisms of Governance*, Oxford: Oxford University Press.

Williamson, O.E., 1999. Public and private bureaucracies: A transaction cost economic perspective. *The Journal of Law, Economics & Organization*, 15(1): 306–42.

Williamson, O.E., 2005. The economics of governance. *American Economic Review*, 95 (2): 1–18.

Willis, P., 1977. *Learning to Labour: How working class kids get working class jobs*. Farnborough, UK: Saxon House.

Wilson, D., 2006. Predictions about European commons. *Common Property Resource Digest*, 77: 7–8.

Wilson, E.O., 2003. *The Future of Life*. New York: Vintage.

Wilson, J.A., 2006. Matching social and ecological systems in complex ocean fisheries. *Ecology and Society*, 11: 9.

Wilson, J., Acheson, J., Metcalfe, M., and Kleban, P., 1994. Chaos, complexity, and community management of fisheries. *Marine Policy*, 18: 291–305.

Wilson, J., Yan, L., and Wilson, C., 2007. The precursors of governance in the Maine lobster fishery. *Proceedings of the National Academy of Sciences*, 104(39): 15212–17.

Winter, S.C. and May, P.J., 2001. Motivation for compliance with environmental regulations. *Journal of Policy Analysis and Management*, 20(4): 675–98.

Wittman, D., 1980. First come, first served: An economic analysis of "coming to nuisance." *Journal of Legal Studies*, 9: 557–68.

World Bank (2003) Contracting for biodiversity conservation in agricultural landscapes. Environment Department Paper No. 96. Environmental Economics Series, World Bank.

Worm, B., Barbier, E.B., Beaumont, N., Duffy, J.E., Folke, C., Halpern, B.S., Jackson, J.B.C., Lotze, H.K., Micheli, F., Palumbi, S.R., Sala, E., Selkoe, K.A., Stachowicz, J.J., and Watson, R., 2006. Impacts of biodiversity loss on ocean ecosystem services. *Science*, 314(5800): 787–90.

Wunder, S., 2005. Payments for environmental services: Some nuts and bolts. Occasional Paper No. 42, Centre for International Forestry Research (CIFOR).

Yang, Z., 2008. *Strategic Bargaining and Cooperation in Greenhouse Gas Mitigations. An integrated assessment modeling approach*. Cambridge, MA: MIT Press.

Yew-Kwang, N., 1999. Utility, informed preference, or happiness: Following Harsanyi's argument to its logical conclusion. *Social Choice and Welfare*, 16(2): 197–216.

Yoder, R., 1994. *Locally Managed Irrigation Systems*. Colombo, Sri Lanka: International Irrigation Management Institute.

Yohe, G., 1976. Pollutors' profits and political response: Direct control versus taxes: comment. *American Economic Review*, 66: 981–2.

Young, O.R., 1989. *International Cooperation: Building regimes for natural resources and the environment*. Ithaca, NY: Cornell University Press.

Young, O.R., 1994. *International Governance: Protecting the environment in a stateless society*. Ithaca, NY: Cornell University Press.

Young, O.R., 1999. *Governance in World Affairs.* Ithaca, NY: Cornell University Press.

Young, O.R., 2002. *The Institutional Dimensions of Environmental Change: Fit, interplay, and scale.* Cambridge, MA: MIT Press.

Young, O.R. and Steffen, W., 2009. The Earth system: Sustaining planetary life-support systems. In: F. Stuart Chapin, G.P. Kofinas, and C.Folke (eds) *Principles of Ecosystem Stewardship: Resilience-based natural resource management in a changing world.* New York: Springer, 295–315.

Young, O.R., Berkhout, F., Gallopin, G.C., Janssen, M.A., Ostrom, E., and van der Leeuw, S., 2006. The globalization of socio-ecological systems: An agenda for scientific research. *Global Environmental Change,* 16(3): 304–16.

Zapfel, P., 2007. A brief but lively chapter in EU climate policy: The commission's perspective. In: A.D. Ellerman, B.K. Buchner, and C. Carraro (eds) *Allocation in the European Emissions Trading Scheme: Rights, rents, and fairness.* Cambridge and New York: Cambridge University Press.

Index